GLOBALIZATION

Sultan Nazrin Shah is the Ruler of Perak and the Deputy King of Malaysia. He is Chancellor of the University of Malaya, and an Honorary Fellow of Worcester College, Oxford, and Magdalene College and St Edmund's College, Cambridge. He holds degrees from Oxford and Harvard universities.

Sultan Nazrin Shah oversees and provides direction for the Economic History of Malaya project (www.ehm.my) and is the author of *Charting the Economy: Early 20th-Century Malaya and Contemporary Malaysian Contrasts* (2017) and *Striving for Inclusive Development: From Pangkor to a Modern Malaysian State* (2019).

GLOBALIZATION

Perak's Rise, Relative Decline, and Regeneration

SULTAN NAZRIN SHAH

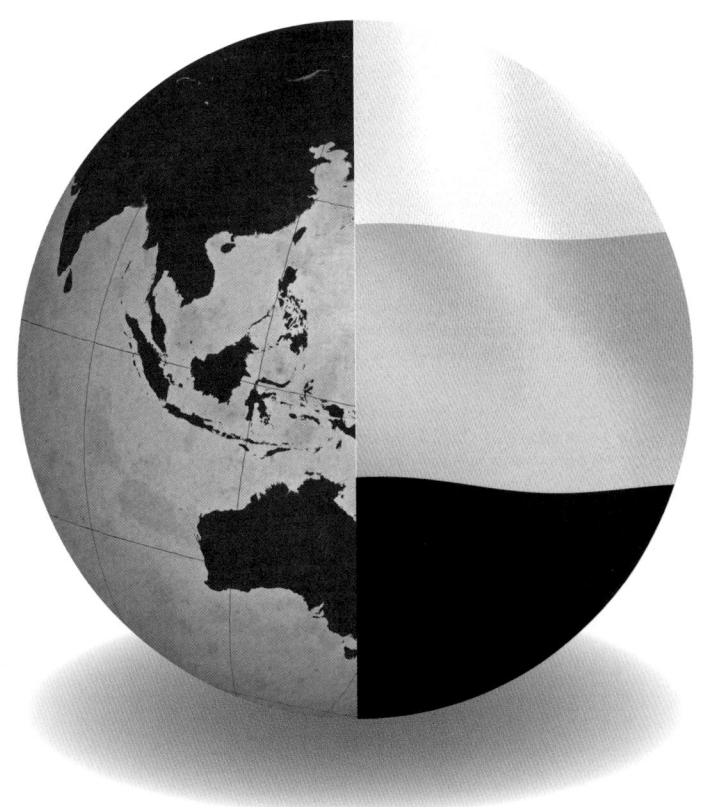

OXFORD
UNIVERSITY PRESS

Great Clarendon Street, Oxford, OX2 6DP,
United Kingdom

Oxford University Press is a department of the University of Oxford.
It furthers the University's objective of excellence in research, scholarship,
and education by publishing worldwide. Oxford is a registered trade mark of
Oxford University Press in the UK and in certain other countries

Published in the United States of America by Oxford University Press
198 Madison Avenue, New York, NY 10016, United States of America

British Library Cataloguing in Publication Data
Data available

Library of Congress Control Number: 2023941733

ISBN 9780198897774

DOI: 10.1093/oso/9780198897774.001.0001

Printed in the UK by
Bell & Bain Ltd., Glasgow

Cover image: A globe—one half of a monochrome world map highlighting Perak in its global
context; the other half overlaid with the white, yellow and black tricolour flag of Perak.
(Jacket images: mkdj/Shutterstock.com; adaptice photography/Shutterstock.com)

For
Perakians everywhere

Table of Contents

Figures, Tables, Maps, and Boxes

Figures

Box Figures

Tables

Box Tables

Maps

Boxes

List of Abbreviations

5G	Fifth-generation wireless technology
AFTA	ASEAN Free Trade Agreement
AMCJA	All-Malaya Council of Joint Action
ANRPC	Association of Natural Rubber Producing Countries
ASEAN	Association of Southeast Asian Nations
ASN	Amanah Saham Nasional Berhad
AVIA	Ministry of Aviation
BMA	British Military Administration
BNM	Bank Negara Malaysia (Central Bank of Malaysia)
BT	Board of Trade
CEIC	Census and Economic Information Centre
Covid-19	Coronavirus disease
CPM	Communist Party of Malaya
DO	Dominions Office
DRB–HICOM	Diversified Resources Berhad–HICOM
EEC	European Economic Community
EPU	Economic Planning Unit–Malaysia
EPZ	Export processing zone
EU	European Union
FAO	Food and Agriculture Organization of the United Nations
FDI	Foreign direct investment
FELCRA	Federal Land Consolidation and Rehabilitation Authority
FELDA	Federal Land Development Authority
FIDA	Federal Industrial Development Authority
FIMA	Food Industries of Malaysia
FTZ	Free trade zones
G7	Group of Seven
GATT	General Agreement on Tariffs and Trade
GDP	Gross domestic product
GDPpc	GDP per capita
GMT	Global minimum tax
HC	House of Commons
HICOM	Heavy Industries Corporation of Malaysia

HIS	Household income survey
HL	House of Lords
hp	Horsepower
IADP	Integrated Agricultural Development Project
IBRD	International Bank for Reconstruction and Development
ICA	International commodity agreement
IMF	International Monetary Fund
IMP3	Malaysia's Third Industrial Master Plan
INRA	International Natural Rubber Agreement
IT	Information technology
ITA	International Tin Agreement
ITC	International Tin Council
kg	Kilogramme(s)
km	Kilometre(s)
KMM	Kesatuan Melayu Muda (Union of Young Malays)
lbs	Imperial pounds
LME	London Metal Exchange
MARA	Majlis Amanah Rakyat (People's Trust Council)
MCA	Malayan Chinese Association
MERS	Middle East Respiratory Syndrome
MIC	Malayan Indian Congress
MIDA	Malaysian Industrial Development Authority
MIER	Malaysian Institute of Economic Research
MITI	Ministry of International Trade and Industry
MMC	Malaysia Mining Corporation
MNLA	Malayan National Liberation Army
MP	Malaysia Plan
MPAJA	Malayan Peoples' Anti-Japanese Army
NCER	Northern Corridor Economic Region
NCIA	Northern Corridor Implementation Authority
NEP	New Economic Policy
OECD	Organisation for Economic Co-operation and Development
OPEC	Organization of the Petroleum Exporting Countries
PERNAS	Perbadanan Nasional Berhad
PETRONAS	Petroliam Nasional Berhad
PKMM	Parti Kebangsaan Melayu Malaya (Malay Nationalist Party)
PMCJA	Pan-Malayan Council of Joint Action
PNB	Permodalan Nasional Berhad (National Equity Corporation)
PROTON	Perusahaan Otomobil Nasional Bhd

PSADC	Perak State Agricultural Development Corporation
PSDC	Perak State Development Corporation
PUTERA	Pusat Tenaga Rakyat (Centre of People's Power)
R&D	Research and development
RISDA	Rubber Industry Smallholders Development Authority
RM	Ringgit Malaysia
RSS	Ribbed Smoked Sheet
RUBpc	Malaya's per capita exports of rubber in Straits$
SARS	Severe acute respiratory syndrome
SEK	Société des Étains de Kinta
SME	Small and medium-sized enterprise
STC	Straits Trading Company
TINpc	Malaya's per capita exports of tin in Straits$
UiTM	Universiti Teknologi MARA
UK	United Kingdom
UKM	Universiti Kebangsaan Malaysia
UMNO	United Malays National Organisation
UNCTAD	United Nations Conference on Trade and Development
UNDESA	United Nations Department of Economic and Social Affairs
UNDP	United Nations Development Programme
UNESCO	United Nations Educational, Scientific and Cultural Organization
UNFPA	United Nations Population Fund
UNICEF	United Nations Children's Fund
UNWCED	United Nations World Commission on Environment and Development
UPEN	Unit Perancang Ekonomi Negeri
UPSI	Sultan Idris Education Universiti
US	United States
USAS	Universiti Sultan Azlan Shah
USM	Universiti Sains Malaysia
UTAR	Universiti Tunku Abdul Rahman
UTP	Universiti Teknologi Petronas
VOC	Vereenigde Oostindische Compagnie (Dutch East India Company)
WHO	World Health Organization
WMO	World Meteorological Organization
WTO	World Trade Organization

Introduction

Perak, the name of the state with which this book is concerned, as well as that state's main river, means 'silver' in the Malay language. Although the etymology is contested, it is plausible that the name refers to the silvery colour of the tin deposits formerly abundant in many of the state's rivers and streams (Map 1.0). For natural resources—first tin, later rubber, and still later oil palm—have indeed driven Perak's economic, institutional, and social development for most of the last three centuries.

This book analyses Perak's rise and subsequent decline relative to other Malaysian states, and suggests some possible steps which would help to regenerate its economy and bring benefits to its population, currently standing at 2.5 million. It begins with a brief historical introduction, covering the British colonial authorities' restoration of political order after the three tin wars in the 1860s and 1870s, and the seminal Pangkor Engagement of 1874, which consolidated British imperial power. It then reviews the impact of tin, and later rubber and oil palm, on the long-run economic and social development of Perak.

Tin was in high demand in Western industrializing countries from the mid-19th century onwards. By 1900, Perak accounted for 49 per cent of Malaya's tin output (a share that would increase to above 60 per cent over the next 60 years) and 25 per cent of world output. This brought the state prosperity, and boosted its population, such that Perak became the Malay peninsula's commercial capital. Likewise, during the global rubber boom, which began in the early 20th century with the advent of the mass production of cars, and continued until the late 1920s, Perak was a leading rubber-producing state in the Malay peninsula. British commercial interests dominated the state's tin and rubber industries.

Beyond the major theme of the shifting tides of economic globalization, this book brings together several interconnected sub-themes: economic geography, the institutional legacy of colonialism, the increasing centralization of federalism, and the forces of agglomeration and migration, all of which drove Perak's

Globalization: Perak's Rise, Relative Decline, and Regeneration. Sultan Nazrin Shah, Oxford University Press. © Sultan Nazrin Shah (2024).
DOI: 10.1093/oso/9780198897774.003.0001

| Map 1.0 | Perak and Malaysia in a globalized world |

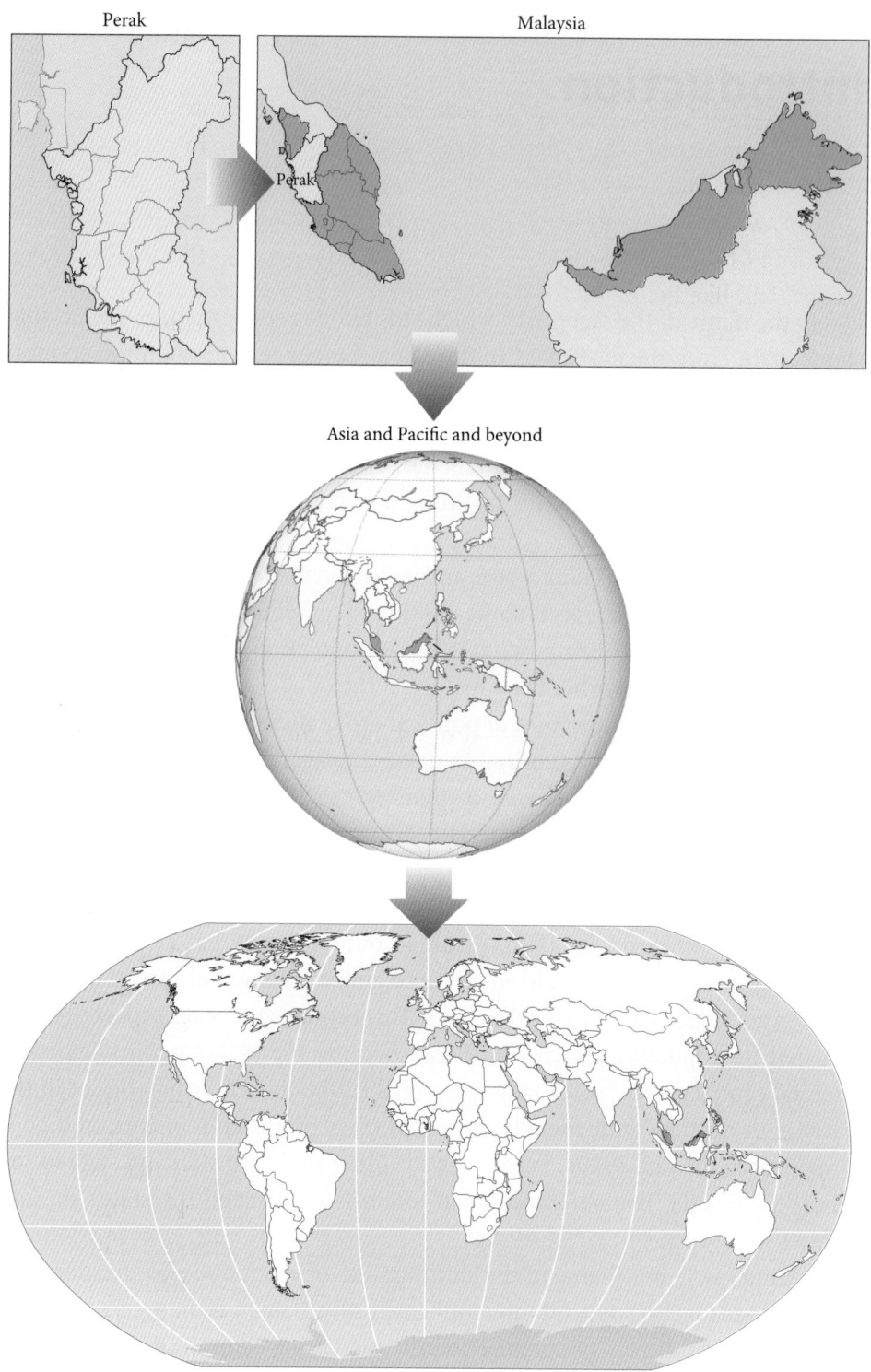

Sources of global maps: Wikimedia Commons (2021); UNDP (2015).

economic and social outcomes. These themes are woven through the analysis and assessed in more detail in text boxes.

Based on Perak's characteristics, and on lessons learned internationally from the experiences of regions and towns left behind by globalization, the book concludes with some ideas about how Perak could regenerate itself in the aftermath of the Covid-19 pandemic, and amid the economic impacts of the Russia–Ukraine war. It also includes short international case studies of the county of Cornwall and the city of Sheffield in the United Kingdom (UK), and the cities of Pittsburgh and Scranton in the United States (US). These are regions or cities that, like Perak, became industrial hotspots and grew extremely wealthy owing to their natural resource–based industries, but then suffered precipitous declines. Some parts of these places have since been successful in rebuilding their economies. Their experiences provide lessons that could help Perak's regeneration.

The Waves of Economic Globalization

Globalization is a process by which goods, labour, capital, and services, as well as technology and ideas, move and spread worldwide from their domestic environments. O'Rourke and Williamson (2000a) contend that the first wave of economic globalization began around the 1820s with increasing commodity-market integration, including a convergence of commodity prices worldwide.

Globalization invariably influences domestic economies. This influence begins to be felt when trade-creating forces come to affect domestic commodity prices and induce a restructuring of resources between primary and secondary economic activities—that is, between the extraction of raw materials, and manufacturing and industry—as well as between agricultural and non-agricultural activities. This, in turn, brings about a change in the scale of output, the distribution of income, and absolute living standards (O'Rourke and Williamson, 2000a).

As the four parts of this book demonstrate, globalization—the major driver of Perak's long-term rise, relative decline, and, it is hoped, subsequent regeneration—began to influence the economic performance of that state in the first half of the 19th century, when global trade networks broadened and deepened. Regional trade had begun much earlier, especially along the sea routes between India and China, but this was on a much smaller scale. By the second half of the 19th century, however, a new capitalist world order had emerged.

Propelling 19th-Century Globalization—The First Wave

Three major advances in the 19th century propelled the first wave of globalization, shaping the rise of tin-rich Perak and bringing great benefit to it, as it did to other Malay peninsula states and the British colony of the Straits Settlements of Penang, Singapore, and Melaka.

First, a *transport revolution* began from the fourth quarter of the 18th century, with the invention and steady advance of steam engines. Invented by James Watt, steam engines provided the momentum of the industrial era, and were increasingly used for mechanizing industrial and transport processes (Sachs, 2020). Steamships became important in the early 19th century, and a few decades later, in the 1840s, railways began to dominate land transport in some of the more advanced countries. These two applications of steam technology brought about a dramatic fall in the freight costs of moving bulk cargoes, which declined steadily for the next century or so. Freight rates along the Atlantic routes connecting the US and Europe, for example, fell by 55–75 per cent between the 1830s and 1850s, and trade costs showed a similar drop between 1870 and 1913 (Williamson, 2013).[1]

In the second half of the 19th century, technological advances in steamships, the 1869 opening of the Suez Canal—which greatly reduced the shipping distance between Britain and Asia—and advances in the use of refrigeration led to the further decline of freight rates, slashing the economic distance between the West and Asia. Exporters and importers benefited from better logistics and lower transport costs (Williamson, 2013). Moreover, from the 1850s the laying of undersea cables between the UK and the US for transmitting telegraphic signals helped to speed up communications on the prices of traded goods (and currencies), thereby improving information flows, reducing market inefficiencies, and lowering transaction costs.

Second, the British-led *industrial revolution* spawned both burgeoning demand for manufactured inputs and raw materials, and drove colonial expansion into territories distant from Britain that had major trading ports or were rich in natural resources. Rodrik (2011, p. 32) emphasizes that imperialism was a 'tremendously powerful force for economic globalization', and quotes Niall Ferguson: 'no organization in history has done more to promote the free movement of goods, capital and labour than the British Empire in the 19th and early

---

1 Trade costs refer to all costs associated with transacting goods across national borders. They include transport and time costs, tariffs and non-tariff barriers, distribution costs, communication, and information costs, as well as legal and financing costs. Freight and tariffs are quantifiable but many of the other trade costs are not easily measurable and are normally estimated using empirical and econometric models.

20th centuries'.[2] With the industrial revolution spreading to Continental Europe and North America, growth of world gross domestic product (GDP) accelerated, as did GDP per capita in the most industrially advanced countries in Europe and North America (as well as in a handful of South American countries). This led to increased demand for goods and services, and from around 1820 caused a boom in world trade that lasted for almost a century.

Third, reflecting the transport and industrial revolutions there was a *move to free trade*, which, at least between 1820 and 1870, was led by Britain. The end of the Napoleonic Wars following the 1815 battle of Waterloo paved the way for Britain to start relinquishing its protectionist stance and gradually lift trade barriers. During the 1820s and 1830s, the *ad valorem* tariff on British imports was cut by about half (Williamson, 2013). In 1846, under growing pressure from newly assertive industrial and urban business interests to maintain international competitiveness, the British government repealed the protectionist Corn Laws, sweeping away tariffs on food and raw materials. The upshot was free trade for most goods, prompting many European countries to follow suit.[3]

Free trade boosted Britain's manufacturing sector. Countries earned sterling—the de facto global currency which was pegged to the gold standard—through increased exports of food and primary commodities to Britain, enabling them to import British manufactures. For some, there was a non-economic motive for this, linked to British cultural norms and values: 'The spread of British trade and investment overseas was thus seen as good in its own right; it brought with it enterprise, progress, and civilization' (Lynn, 1999, p. 103).

With these three advances, linked also to the impact of the scientific revolution on transport technology and industrial engineering, and to rising urbanization and industrial development,[4] trade boomed. Traded commodity prices began to converge, and the world started to shrink in time and space.[5] Behind national borders, resources were increasingly drawn into activities that enjoyed comparative productive and specialization advantages, thereby lifting living standards

---

2 Studies have shown that countries trading within the same empire achieve lower transaction costs from the use of a common language and a common currency, and preferential trade agreements (Rodrik, 2011).

3 Trade was supported by many countries' use of the gold standard, which minimized transaction costs and encouraged free flows of capital by lowering the risks of variable exchange rates.

4 In the UK, for example, the focus of industry in urban areas shifted political power away from the land-owning classes, who had been the main beneficiaries of trade barriers.

5 For example, in 1870 Liverpool's wheat prices exceeded those in Chicago by 58 per cent, but the gap had fallen to 18 per cent by 1895 and to 16 per cent by 1912. The Anglo-American price gaps for non-agricultural commodities—such as the Boston–Manchester cotton textile price gap or the Philadelphia–London iron bar price gap—as well as international price spreads—such as the Liverpool–Bombay cotton price spread or the London–Rangoon rice price spread—also narrowed dramatically over the period, with some price gaps even falling to zero (O'Rourke and Williamson, 2000a).

and favouring the owners and workers of booming industries. Up to World War I, peace in Europe led to unprecedented international monetary cooperation, which supported the global trading system during this first wave (Eichengreen, 2019).

Impacts of 19th-Century Globalization on Economic Growth—How the West Won

Although globalization raised aggregate GDP and GDP per capita on average worldwide, it also led to the 'Great Divergence' between industrialized economies and the rest of the world: the industrialized world grew much faster and took a larger share of the increase in global wealth than countries and territories that were exporters of primary products, like those in the Malay peninsula. Williamson (2013, p. 5) estimates that GDP per capita in Western Europe grew at some 1.2 per cent a year between 1820 and 1913, while countries at the 'periphery' grew at only around 0.5 per cent, taking Western Europe's GDP per capita to 3.5 times the periphery's by 1913, compared to only double in 1820.[6]

There are several reasons for the divergence in income growth during this period. The first is that although initially the trade boom vastly improved the terms of trade for countries and territories at the periphery—or primary-product exporters—by raising export prices and lowering import prices, their terms of trade subsequently worsened. Peripheral countries found themselves specializing in the production of one or two primary products—often at the instruction of metropolitan powers or a leading foreign investor—with no ready pathway to industrialization. Meanwhile, those peripheral countries already engaged in industry, particularly in textiles, deindustrialized as cheaper imports of manufactured goods replaced output from local industry.[7]

Peripheral countries were also susceptible to export-price volatility. For example, Blattman et al. (2007) find that between the 1860s and the start of World War I, terms-of-trade volatility for 24 countries at the periphery with high export

---

6 In his study of economic divergence between Western Europe and the 'periphery', Williamson (2013) compares the GDP per capita of Western Europe with that of the unweighted average of the European periphery (Albania, Bulgaria, Czechoslovakia [now the Czech Republic and Slovakia], Greece, Hungary, Ireland, Poland, Portugal, Romania, Russia, Spain, and Yugoslavia); Latin America (Argentina, Brazil, Chile, Colombia, Mexico, Peru, Uruguay, and Venezuela); the Middle East (Western Asia, Egypt, Morocco, and Tunisia); South Asia (Burma [Myanmar], Ceylon [Sri Lanka], India, and Nepal); Southeast Asia (Hong Kong, the Dutch East Indies [Indonesia], Malaysia, Philippines, Siam [Thailand], and Singapore); and East Asia (China, Japan, Korea, and Taiwan).

7 At the onset of the industrial revolution, the level of industrial activity in Asia and Latin America—led by textiles—was comparable to that in Europe. The level of industrial activity went on to increase sixfold in Europe between 1750 and 1913 but fell by around 60 per cent in Asia and in Latin America (Rodrik, 2011).

concentration was larger than that of three European colonial powers—France, Germany, and the UK—by a factor of 2.7 (cited in Williamson, 2013, pp. 173–175).[8] This volatility in commodity prices impeded GDP growth and incomes at the periphery. Baldwin (2016), for example, finds that per capita income in the US was three times as high as in China in 1820, but was almost 10 times as high by 1914.

At the periphery, trade booms typically benefited landowners and investors much more than workers, and when trade and commodity prices sagged, workers' wages would bear a disproportionate share of the decrease. These adjustment patterns led to deepening inequality in Southeast Asia, Sub-Saharan Africa, the Middle East, and Latin America (Williamson, 2013). Colonization amplified these inequalities, with much of the colonies' profits from trade in their primary commodities being extracted and the money (or currency) repatriated to the metropolitan centres (Sultan Nazrin Shah, 2017).

Even at the centre, however, not all benefited equally. In the US and the UK, for example, the transfer of workers from rural to urban areas, or from the low-income, low-inequality agricultural sector to the higher-income, higher-inequality industrial sector, widened income inequality among workers (Milanovic, 2016). Only after World War I did inequality in industrializing, high-income countries start to decline (until around the 1980s), reflecting factors such as rising levels of education, social transfers, progressive taxation, and changing institutional attitudes towards the provision of public goods.

De-globalization and Inter-war Protectionism

Between the start of the First World War and the end of the Second—from 1914 to 1945—the volume of global trade fell and the world 'de-globalized'. The wars themselves, of course, made shipping risky and expensive, sharply increasing costs. Further, in the 1920s and 1930s, sparked by World War I, the industrialized economies—many of which had already been drifting towards protectionism since the 1870s[9]—embarked on a series of tariff increases. To

---

8 Blattman et al.'s (2007) classification of the periphery differs from Williamson's (2013): the European periphery (Italy, Portugal, Russia, and Spain); Latin America (Argentina, Brazil, Chile, Colombia, Cuba, Mexico, Peru, and Uruguay); the Middle East (Egypt, Greece, Serbia, and Turkey); South and Southeast Asia (Burma, Ceylon, India, Indonesia, Philippines, and Thailand); and East Asia (China and Japan).

9 In the European industrial core, a backlash against globalization was precipitated by the influx of cheap grain from Russia and the American Midwest, which posed a threat to rural agricultural incomes. The rise in protectionism was still modest, however, compared with the anti-trade sentiment in other parts of the world, with much higher tariffs between 1865 and 1900 in Latin America; in Australia, Canada, and New Zealand; and in the European periphery—Italy, Portugal, and Spain, as well as Scandinavian countries (O'Rourke and Williamson, 2000b).

protect American farmers and businesses, in 1930 the US passed the Smoot–Hawley Tariff Act, which imposed its highest-ever tariffs, raising them by about 20 per cent on foreign agricultural imports and thousands of other imported goods. In 1932, the UK imposed the Import Duties Act, which raised tariffs on all imports by 10 per cent, except food and raw materials (Capie, 1978).[10]

The Great Depression of the early 1930s, the harsh economic conditions that ensued with the collapse of global output and income, and painful banking crises encouraged the spread of trade protectionism to other European nations as well as to India and Latin America (Williamson, 2013). Between 1929 and 1937, world trade volume plunged by 50 per cent (Rodrik, 2011).

Post-World War II Globalization—The Second Wave

Only after World War II did countries begin to reduce tariffs and international trade start to revive, as world leaders sought to create a more prosperous global economy (Stiglitz, 2006). This was the second wave of globalization. One ambitious initiative was the attempt to create a new stable international economic order and monetary system through the establishment of the International Monetary Fund (IMF) and the World Bank under the Bretton Woods Agreement, signed in 1944 by 44 countries. Another important aspect was that countries would avoid competitive devaluation to prevent trade wars. The establishment of the General Agreement on Tariffs and Trade (GATT) in 1948, with a founding membership of 23 countries among which the industrialized world exerted leadership, helped to dismantle trade barriers and lower tariffs on manufactured goods. The GATT is credited with boosting global trade. Free trade was now seen as one mechanism for promoting harmonious international relations. Trade liberalization advanced most, however, in the sectors where the industrialized countries held a comparative advantage. This perpetuated an international division of labour between industrialized countries and commodity-producing countries.

Globalization's second wave was also fuelled by technological advances. The start of containerization in the 1960s and its exponential growth in the 1970s and 1980s greatly reduced loading and unloading times, making

---

10 Goods from within the empire, mainly comprising food and raw materials, were exempted.

shipping vastly cheaper and production and delivery times more predictable (Baldwin, 2016). So great were the efficiency gains from containerization that during the 1960s, and up to the 1970 London dock strike, tens of thousands of jobs had been lost, and the dockland waterfronts of wharves and warehouses were in a process of transformation.[11] Air courier services also began to accelerate with the beginnings of DHL and FedEx.

Beginning from the 1980s with the dawn of the Internet, and continuing through to the present, successive major advances in information and communications technology have led to much of the world becoming integrated and interconnected on a scale never before seen, in what Baldwin (2016) terms the 'Great Convergence'.[12] The virtually seamless sharing of knowledge, ideas, and information across borders enabled by the advent of the Internet meant that manufacturing activity no longer needed to be confined to a specific geographical location, making it possible for firms to shift some or all of their manufacturing and production to countries with lower labour costs and lower tax rates.

In 1970, the G7 countries—the US, Germany, Japan, France, the UK, Canada, and Italy—accounted for roughly two-thirds of the world's manufacturing activity, while China's share was a mere 1 per cent. In 2020, by contrast, China's share of world manufacturing output was almost 29 per cent (United Nations Statistics Division, 2020). This huge expansion was driven, in part, by the influx of foreign firms and factories to China after 1990 as the economy opened, as well as by the country's 2001 accession to the World Trade Organization, which had succeeded GATT in 1995. The equivalent shares of other developing countries with large populations and lower labour costs, including India, Indonesia, Thailand, and Viet Nam, also rose over the period 2000–2020, bringing about a narrowing in world GDP shares. Malaysia, which was deindustrializing over this period, experienced much less of an increase.

In this way, post-World War II globalization began to reduce inequality *between* countries in the late 20th century and into the 21st century, as many developing countries—especially those in Asia—rapidly industrialized and began to grow faster than the developed economies. Initially, in the first few decades after the war, inequality continued to widen, with the gap between incomes in the US and those in China and India reaching a high point in 1970

---

11 The strike lasted for three weeks and came shortly after the lifting of the ban on containers in the port of Tilbury. In July 1972, London's dock workers went on another strike to try to safeguard the remaining jobs (Turnbull, 2000). Both led to a state of emergency being declared.

12 The use of traditional airmail, international calls, telexes, facsimiles, and physical (hardcopy) data storage gave way to emails, instant chats, online collaborative group meetings, digitized data, and cloud storage.

(Milanovic, 2016). As GDP per capita growth rates in many low- and middle-income countries outpaced those of the developed world, relative and, eventually, absolute gaps in income, particularly between the West and Asia, began to close (Milanovic, 2016). This process accelerated after 2000.[13]

Just as the gains from globalization have not been evenly spread among nations, the benefits have also been unevenly distributed *within* national borders. The largest benefits have tended to accrue to areas that have diversified into manufacturing and tradeable services. Areas where economic activity has remained largely focused on the export of primary commodities have tended to lag. However, the impact of globalization is *not* predetermined by geography and resources. National and local policies—for example, in education, taxation, social transfers, land use, and public infrastructure provision—influence the ability of areas to discover, latch on to, and attract new economic activities, and to participate in globalization's rewards. The growing dichotomy between Perak's economic performance and that of the more dynamic states of Peninsular Malaysia since the country's independence in 1957 illustrates how the above forces filter and differentiate the spatial impact of globalization.

Impact on Perak—Shorter-term Gain, Longer-term Pain

External forces have played a decisive role in Perak's development. The first globalization wave greatly benefited the state, but the second bypassed it.

New industrial uses for tin in the 19th century, and the start of mass production of cars in the early 20th century, were the primary drivers of Perak's export-led economy. While a formidable export base generated wider benefits in the local economy, it also exposed the state to boom-and-bust cycles. The capital as well as the workers required by commodity export activity also came largely from outside Perak. Investment capital flowed into commodity production from Britain and other metropolitan centres, and overseas investors received annual dividends—sometimes extremely large—in return. Migrants from China mined for tin, and those from India cultivated rubber. The migratory flows were

---

13 A number of poor countries, however, have not reaped the benefits of globalization. Excluding the few Asian countries whose impressive growth has benefited their large populations—particularly China and Indonesia—the divide between rich and poor nations has substantially widened. According to Rodrik (2011), the gap between the richest and poorest regions of the world stood at 20:1.2 at the end of the first decade of the 21st century, compared with 2:1 at the start of the industrial revolution.

facilitated by the British colonial administration and augmented by inflows of Malays from the wider Malay archipelago to support food production, especially rice farming.

Malaya's prodigious commodity export activity did not occur in an institutional vacuum. From the late 19th century, new colonial arrangements secured property rights and the land needed for expanding commodity exports. Local rulers, who retained powers over traditional customary and religious matters, were co-opted and provided with incomes and other benefits. Crucial infrastructure that supported Perak's rising prosperity was funded largely by colonial levies on tin mining, and later on rubber cultivation. A dual colonial economic structure was intentionally created in which the bulk of the Malay population remained engaged in subsistence agriculture and fishing.

The eventual exhaustion of Perak's readily accessible tin deposits, waning global demand for natural rubber in the face of competition from synthetic substitutes, and the dawn of Malaysian independence spelled the beginning of a new, more difficult era for Perak. Rubber cultivation did provide a stepping-stone to more lucrative palm oil exports, but much of the income benefits from palm oil leaked from the state to federal investment entities. Economic diversification also proved difficult, with the state unable to capitalize on the global manufacturing boom that gained momentum in the 1970s and 1980s.

Perak's location, geographical conditions, and low economic density,[14] coupled with federal policies that siphoned financial resources out of the state, hobbled its industrialization efforts. By contrast, location, geographical conditions, and high economic density supported greater economic advances in Selangor and Penang. Although Perak saw incremental advances in incomes, the state steadily lost ground to other, more dynamic parts of the Malay peninsula. With job losses in its traditional industries—especially tin—in several localities the multiplier effect went into reverse, hurting communities and families. Once a magnet for young workers from abroad as well as closer to home, Perak now became a major exporter of talented and educated workers to the detriment of its own economic and social development.

---

14 Economic density refers to the geographical compactness of economic activity. It is highly correlated with both employment and population density, which are greater in towns and cities. It is measured as the value added, or gross domestic product (GDP) generated, per square kilometre of land (World Bank, 2009).

Colonialism in Perak and Malaya

The terms *imperialism* and *colonialism* are frequently used in historical explanations of British influence over the political, economic, and social evolution of the Malay states through to their independence in 1957. Beginning in 1786 with the acquisition of Penang by the British East India Company—a private company granted an international trading monopoly by the government—Britain extended its sphere of political and economic influence over the people and resources of Malaya. The Anglo-Dutch Treaty of 1824 later partitioned the world of the Malay archipelago into British and Dutch spheres (Stockwell, 1999a). However, the mechanisms through which Britain exercised its influence differed among the states of the Malay peninsula and did not always follow the modes of imperial rule and colonization adopted in some other parts of the British Empire. Two distinctions stand out.

First, in that colonization entails the settlement of a large permanent population that retains loyalty to its country of origin, Perak and the other Malay sultanates were never strictly colonies. The first population census to cover all the territories of the Malay peninsula, conducted in 1911, counted 2.34 million people, of whom fewer than 16,200—a mere 0.7 per cent—were of British or European origin. In Perak, the corresponding figures were just 0.5 million, 2,241, and 0.45 per cent. Instead, the presence of the British, and the economic development path that they pursued, led to large-scale migration of people from China, India, and parts of the Dutch East Indies (now Indonesia) to Malaya.

Second, the British never formally 'ruled' over Malaya. Only the Straits Settlements, whose people were designated as British subjects, were governed directly by London as a colony. Perak and the other states remained nominally independent under so-called indirect rule and the residential system. This was a system that entailed limited legal and financial responsibilities and was fortified through the agency of local sovereign rulers; so the British controlled all aspects of a state's administration, other than those relating to religion and Malay custom. The administrative methods of indirect rule, which limited local political opportunities, had been established by the British in India (Tharoor, 2017), and later applied in Fiji and in some African countries (Louis, 1999), before being implemented in Malaya.

Technically, under the Pangkor Agreement of 1874, Perak became a British 'protectorate', in which a British-appointed resident provided 'advice' to the sultan and his court. Through this mechanism, Perak's traditional rulers maintained their status and were given the appearance of authority: however, de facto executive power rested with the British resident, except on matters of Islam and

Malay custom, where the sultan held sway. Crucial policy matters were escalated to the governor of the Straits Settlements in Singapore, and through him to the Secretary of State for the Colonies in London. Residents were subsequently installed in three other Malay states—first in Selangor and Negeri Sembilan, and later in Pahang—and, in 1895, these three states were brought together with Perak as the Federated Malay States. Other states in the Malay peninsula, where British commercial interests were more limited, remained unfederated, and British advisors played a less intrusive role. In general, the British preferred to exercise influence through 'agents, advisers, and collaborating monarchs' rather than to annex territory (Stockwell, 1999a, p. 381).

British indirect rule over Malaya was therefore nuanced. It did not entail the forceful subjugation of indigenous rulers, the arrival of large numbers of loyal settlers, or, despite the presence of garrisons and gunships, the overt exercise of military might. However, the institutional arrangements crafted by the British authorities were nevertheless extractive—by design, they were intended to facilitate the unimpeded exploitation of Malaya's rich natural resources for Britain's benefit.[15] These arrangements created wide socio-economic inequalities in Perak and elsewhere in colonial Malaya. They led to imbalanced economic development between town and countryside as public and private infrastructure investments were channelled to the localities where the greatest profits could be earned from the extractive industries (Sultan Nazrin Shah, 2019).

In Perak, as elsewhere in the British Empire, the colonial administration tended to discourage the creation of local manufacturing industries, fearing that competition could undermine manufacturing interests at home. Perhaps the most egregious example of this form of protectionism took place in India, where the British authorities virtually destroyed the pre-colonial cotton industry, impoverishing large parts of the country (Beckert, 2014).

Migrant workers were fundamental to driving the economic growth that the British authorities sought. Perak's very small local population—just 81,000 in 1879—meant that expansion of its minerals- and plantation-based export-led economy was highly dependent on population inflows—especially of Chinese and, to a lesser extent, Indians. In boom times, many thousands were recruited, while in times of economic depression, thousands were repatriated. Many chose to settle permanently, which later gave rise to ethnic tensions and policy challenges.

---

15 They included political roles assigned to traditional leaders; the demarcation of economic functions among the population; labour, immigration, and trade policies; administrative, fiscal, and legal frameworks; and investments in local infrastructure (railways, seaports, paved roads, electricity supply, and irrigation) as well as in limited public services (policing, health, and education).

Federalism and a New In-country 'Periphery'? The Progressive Loss of States' Power

Faced with the complexity and costs of separate colonial administrative systems in different states, in 1896 the British created a single administrative unit, the Federated Malay States, through the Treaty of Federation. This combined the administration of Perak with Negeri Sembilan and Selangor, its two tin-rich west-coast neighbours, and with the east-coast state of Pahang. Such integration and centralization promoted administrative efficiency, created fiscal flexibility, and helped to resolve coordination issues on matters that crossed state boundaries.

Most powers were centralized and vested in a new resident-general who assumed de facto control through a centralized government and civil service based in Kuala Lumpur. In 1909, a Federal Council was established to administer the Federation. State residents responsible for implementing federal policy at state level were represented on the Federal Council, as were the four state rulers—the sultans—who still nominally 'ruled' each state. Each sultan was advised by a State Council, comprising a British resident, Malay chiefs, and representatives of the Chinese community.

The creation of the Federated Malay States marked the beginning of an era of increasing federalism and of the continued erosion of Perak's autonomy over its own finances and policy matters. The Malay population was especially affected because, although their participation in administration and *kampung* (village) agriculture was encouraged, they were 'neither expected nor educated to participate in the bustling "modern Malaya" being constructed around them' (Stockwell, 1999a, p. 386). The Malay elite were also largely marginalized by an increasingly centralized government controlled by British administrators in an economy controlled in turn by foreign (mainly British) interests and a small Chinese capitalist class.

After World War II and the defeat of the Japanese who had occupied the Malay peninsula, the British extended the federal administration, initially through the imposition of the Malayan Union (1946–1948), and then, after fierce opposition arose to the Union, through the Federation of Malaya (1948–1957). The federation now also included the previously Unfederated Malay States of Johor, Kedah, Kelantan, Perlis, and Terengganu as well as two of the Straits Settlements, Melaka and Penang. Britain's plans in instituting these arrangements were shaped by a desire to maintain its deep commercial interests, by the post-1948 communist insurgency, by emerging Malay nationalism, and by communal politics (Stockwell, 1999b). Then, with British interests in Malaya starting to wane, a newly independent Federation of Malaya was created in 1957, through a federal constitution that defined powers and relationships at federal and state levels. After a short period of laissez-faire policies between 1957 and 1970, much greater centralized government control of the economy was exercised in the five decades that followed.[16]

Federalism in Malaya and Malaysia—at first under British rule, and later under the federal constitution and its amendments—has been of an integrative nature, aggregating and centralizing powers rather than devolving them from the centre to the state level or lower. The functions that the federal constitution delegates to Perak and other states are highly circumscribed. Fiscal and taxable capacities are constrained as the states' ability to tax and levy fees is extremely restricted, and they cannot issue their own debt. Federal laws override state laws where there are inconsistencies. Later amendments to the federal constitution have further concentrated powers at federal level.

Perak and the other states have only ever had narrow scope and limited resources to craft and execute their own development policies, despite the State Development Corporation which leads and supports economic initiatives in Perak being under the direction of its Menteri Besar (Chief Minister). Even local responsibility for sewerage and solid waste management was appropriated by the federal government. Development planning for the states, including the creation of subnational 'spatial corridors', is firmly in the hands of the federal government. The upshot is that the conditions needed to foster the potential development benefits of decentralization have never been created, neither in colonial Malaya nor in independent Malaysia. In effect, the Malaysian states have now become clients of the federal government, often exchanging political support for development resources and favours.

Constitutionally guaranteed funding to the states through capitation and infrastructure grants is meagre. Along with some other states, Perak appears to have been less favoured by the federal government, even though for many decades it was a net contributor to federal funds. This may largely be a product of inertia: a continuation of past trends established when Perak was the richest state and was therefore not considered to require substantial federal support. In addition, federal financing for states has gradually shifted from grants to loans, ensuring

---

16 In colonial Malaya, the government played a key role in the maintenance of 'public safety and security, in ensuring property rights, in financing and operating infrastructure, and in the provision of public works and services' (Sultan Nazrin Shah, 2019, p. 206). In other areas, such as in trade and taxation, it generally adopted the principle of economic laissez-faire, with few interventions or restrictions on local and foreign ownership. There were, however, exceptions, such as its participation in various international trade agreements to support prices and to protect British companies' interests in the tin and rubber industries.

greater federal control. Owing to the states' limited revenue sources, however, state governments have struggled with repayments (Jomo and Wee, 2002).

After 1971, the imposition of a federally imposed affirmative action strategy replaced a laissez-faire policy as the main driver of Perak's economic fortunes. Malaysia's federal government had pursued a free-market strategy until the race riots of 1969. Subsequently, the predominance of ethnic Chinese in Perak's economy conflicted with the 1971 New Economic Policy (NEP) that sought a greater and more equitable role in the country's economy for the Malay majority population. Control over federal funding for state-specific projects, along with affirmative action programmes, had the effect of curtailing the economic prospects of ethnic Chinese, ultimately prompting large numbers to emigrate to other states and abroad, seriously eroding Perak's skill base.

The Federation Falters with Increasing Centralization

Malaysia overcame the setbacks of the 1997 Asian Financial Crisis and the 2008 Global Financial Crisis. The country has become vastly more affluent over the past half century. It has built a resilient economy and joined the ranks of upper-middle-income countries; and it has reaped dividends from greater agricultural productivity and from the movement of resources out of agriculture into more productive industry and services. Yet, in the first quarter of the 21st century, Malaysia has been caught in a 'middle-income trap', with slowing economic growth, wide income disparities, and, once again, a reliance on low-skilled and low-wage foreign labour, coupled with outmigration of skilled human capital. Poor educational outcomes, stagnant productivity growth, depressed levels of investment, and the crowding out of the private sector through excessive state involvement in the economy are other factors.

While affirmative action has enabled more equitable sharing in the country's prosperity, there have also been notable shortcomings due in part to poorly designed programmes, and in part to weaknesses in implementation. Funds have sometimes been diverted to pursue political ends and to enrich those with connected interests. The negative impacts of this corruption, and of the increasingly unhealthy relationship between the state and business, have been far-reaching (Sultan Nazrin Shah, 2019).

A strong unitary state has emerged in Malaysia, despite what is on paper a highly decentralized structure. There are many reasons for this, including: a legacy of top-heavy colonial institutions; an overarching concern with national security and unity in the face of the 1948 Emergency; a focus on highly centralized and interventionist national development plans; preoccupations over ethnicity; and political forces that have concentrated powers within the prime minister's department as a way of exerting control over disparate and opposing groups below. For example, many politically connected federal-level officials are typically seconded to senior positions at the state level (Ostwald, 2017).

Without appropriately delegated powers and funding, Perak will remain unable to identify its own major development priorities and to execute its plans accordingly. Existing arrangements that locate fiscal, administrative, and decision-making powers at federal level entail the sacrifice of Perak's potential development gains, of improvements in local governance, and of its citizens' empowerment.

Perak's Rise

From Chaos to a New Political Order

Part 1 of this book begins by setting the scene for Perak's incorporation into the rapidly globalizing world of the 19th century. The invention of the tin can in the early part of that century had transformed the packaging and preservation of food, and from its initial use by the British navy and, later, in the American Civil War, canned food became common in many industrialized countries. This led to increased demand for tinplate. As international shipping costs fell, costly deep-lode Cornish deposits—which had been the mainstay of the British tin industry—came under pressure in British and international markets from easily accessible sources in Australia, the island of Banka in the Dutch East Indies, and later Perak. As the sun began to set on the Cornish tin industry in the late 19th century, Perak and other parts of Malaya tapped Cornish mining expertise and capital, helping to propel the fortunes of the state's fledgling mining industry.

Part 1 also outlines Perak's unique geographical features, its 19th-century settlement patterns, and the diversity and growth of its population, fed by high rates of inward migration. Perak's rich endowment of mineral and other natural resources, especially tin, has always attracted foreign interests, often unwelcome—in earlier centuries, Acehnese, Siamese, and Dutch. Rival groups from outside Perak, allied to competing local royal interest groups within, fought bitterly for control of Perak's lucrative tin resources in the three Larut 'tin wars'. The ensuing chaos and instability, which disrupted mining activities, eventually led to British colonial intervention, the signing of the Pangkor Engagement in 1874, and Britain's subduing of initial resistance to its indirect rule.

Perak's traditional Malay system of governance was unable to withstand the competitive strains that came with the modern capitalist mode of production and the vastly increased trading networks that resulted from the rapid expansion of the mining industry to meet international demand. The British administration increasingly tightened and extended its political control, and shaped institutional arrangements to promote its strategic and economic objectives in Perak, as well as in the other main tin-producing Malay states of the peninsula that it had federalized.

Natural Resource Prosperity

Part 2 documents the rise in Perak's prosperity, which was driven by its abundant natural resources. With political stability and new state institutions imposed by the British colonial administration, Perak's economy became more integrated into the global economy. Colonial policies, helped by favourable economic geography including ready access to rivers and ports, as well as by a tropical climate that supported commercial agriculture, created a dynamic, export-led, natural-resource-based enclave that soon overshadowed Perak's traditional agricultural sector. Thriving new towns and businesses began to emerge around the tin-mining centres, with the population enjoying a new-found prosperity. In the years leading up to the Great Depression, Perak's estimated per capita GDP was over three times what it had been at the start of the 20th century.

British capital dominated the growth of Perak's commodity industries in the first half of the 20th century. Foreign investors derived huge profits from Perak's industries, which were largely repatriated. British commercial interests had little or no incentive to reinvest in new and more diversified economic activities. Moreover, the British authorities made few efforts to address the economic dualism that had been created between the export-oriented side of Perak's economy and the traditional low-income and low-productivity sectors such as small-scale agriculture.

Until the Great Depression, the growth of Perak's economy was also propelled by international labour mobility, another major dimension of globalization. Huge migrant inflows from the late 19th century onwards fundamentally changed the state's demographic composition, giving Perak a distinctive multicultural identity. In 1947, Chinese and Indians exceeded the number of Malays, who accounted for just 37.8 per cent of the state's population. This would come to pose political, social, and economic challenges to the state that would continue in the post-independence era.

During the post-World War II period of decolonization, the British administration sought to protect British investments in Perak and elsewhere in Malaya, and to ensure a politically compliant new order. Yet economically viable tin deposits were already gradually being depleted, and synthetic rubber had begun to challenge natural rubber, even though both commodities would remain important to Perak's economy in the early decades after independence.

Perak's Relative Decline

The Collapse of Tin

Part 3 analyses Perak's relative decline—and identifies the seeds of its regeneration. Post-independence, Perak's tin and rubber industries—which had largely defined its economy, population, and social organization—steadily waned, and by the early 1990s had faded into insignificance.

After World War II, a coalition of tin-producing and tin-consuming nations, convened by the United Nations, negotiated a sequence of six International Tin Agreements (ITA1–6) to regulate supply and support tin prices, with the International Tin Council (ITC) as the operating arm. The last of these, ITA6, dramatically unravelled in October 1985, beset by collapsing tin prices and chaos on the international tin market.

In a depressed global economy, a tin glut persisted in the early 1980s, and the agreed floor price advocated by producing countries in the ITC was out of line with fundamentals. Persistently weak demand and strong supply—especially with the entry of new tin producers—along with a grossly inflated 'floor price', left the ITC with an impossible task. Given ineffective export quotas, the ITC was obliged to defend the floor price by purchasing tin, but price support only elicited further supply as non-member producers ramped up production. ITA6 membership did not include a number of important producing nations—notably Bolivia, Brazil, and China—which meant only half the world's production was under ITC control. And, of course, higher prices also squeezed demand. To close the widening gap between production and consumption, the ITC was compelled to absorb the surplus tin that its support operations had helped to create. But it did not have adequate cash to support purchases to defend the floor price, and instead resorted to unsustainable borrowing.

The tin crisis and the demise of the ITC were consequences of the irreconcilable objectives of producer and consumer members. The fallout from the collapse of ITA6 and the ITC's failure was felt globally. In Bolivia, a high-cost producer, where tin accounted for about a third of export earnings, the crisis led to major governance challenges. In the UK, the remaining high-cost Cornish mines closed. In Perak, as elsewhere in Malaysia, tin-mining companies struggled to survive, unable to cover even their direct operating costs. The state's tin towns were economically and socially shattered, causing widespread suffering, with the loss of jobs and incomes among mine workers, their families, and their communities. The devastating impact of the 1985 tin crisis hastened the demise of an industry that was already in secular retreat. Perak was on the front line of these painful adjustments.

Absolute Growth but Still Relative Decline

After ethnic riots in May 1969, laissez-faire economic policy gave way to heavily interventionist central government management. Through measures outlined in Malaysia's NEP, the government sought to rectify imbalances in corporate equity ownership. For the most part, this meant moving ownership away from British and Malaysian-Chinese interests. The NEP marked a turning point for the British-owned companies and British agency houses that had dominated the tin, rubber, and oil palm industries. The NEP led to a dramatic shift towards Malay ownership in the 1970s through the Malayanization of some of the largest publicly listed, foreign-owned resource-based companies.

Diversification was a policy imperative, first within agriculture—with that sector diversifying into oil palm, a commodity of growing importance—and later into manufacturing and services. Perak's scattered townships did not, however, offer the scale, density, and international connections needed to attract new manufacturing industries. Even by 2010 roughly half of manufacturing activity in Perak was resource-based and served domestic markets—food, rubber processing, metallurgy, iron and steel, and non-metallurgical minerals (Athukorala and Narayanan, 2017). Nevertheless, by 2020, Perak's socio-economic profile had changed, with manufacturing and services dominating the state's economy and employing nearly four-fifths of its labour force.

In *absolute terms*, Perak's economy has become gradually much more prosperous, productive, and diversified. All communities are now more urbanized, have far higher real (inflation-adjusted) incomes, and are living much longer lives than their parents' generation. Incomes are distributed more evenly, and the absolute poverty rate has tumbled. Yet, as a 'late-mover' to Malaysia's manufacturing sector, Perak remains at a disadvantage from which it is struggling to recover.

In *relative terms*, Perak has undergone a much slower structural transformation than the neighbouring states of Selangor and Penang—the latter having had its free-port status revoked in 1969. Perak's GDP per capita growth has persistently lagged behind those of leading states over the last five decades. Forces of agglomeration have favoured locations which—with the aid of federal policies—moved first on industrial development, had greater economic density, and possessed better air transport links to the outside world. As gaps in incomes and job opportunities with neighbouring states widened, Perak began to lose population. This brain drain has been particularly pronounced among the young, skilled, and educated, and in the Malaysian-Chinese community. A negative feedback loop has been created in which a shrinking base of human capital has narrowed economic opportunities in Perak, resulting in further out-migration of the talent that the state so badly needs.

The Covid-19 pandemic came as a devastating blow and was a major setback to Perak's incipient economic regeneration. With many economic sectors unable to function, especially services linked to travel and tourism, business output and household incomes were battered, and unemployment and poverty rates rocketed.

Perak's Regeneration—and a *New Vision*

Part 4 presents an outline of a *New Vision* for Perak based on the state's comparative advantages and on lessons learned from the international experiences of regions and towns left behind by globalization—Cornwall and Sheffield in the UK, and Pittsburgh and Scranton in the US. Perak's economy will require conditions that encourage local talent to stay while also attracting new talent into the state. People with relevant capabilities are needed to invigorate the private sector and to stimulate innovation and creativity. Providing high-quality education and training on a large scale is part of the solution to building a deep pool of local talent and increasing social mobility. This requires the state's education and training institutions to adapt and evolve. Perak must also create an institutional climate for nurturing SMEs and other private businesses that will incubate entrepreneurship and stimulate capital investment, while at the same time drawing foreign investment into new industries that will retain and attract skilled workers.

With its *New Vision*, Perak can look forward to a period of renewed prosperity that will put the state at least on a par with the leading Malaysian states. Promoting a fair distribution of income must remain a key objective, however, including providing all communities with equitable access to opportunities and social protection (Sultan Nazrin Shah, 2019). Arresting the secular outflow of Perak's people, and working towards creating decent, skill-intensive, and higher-value-adding jobs within the state must also be aims. In addition, the effective management of Perak's bountiful and beautiful environment must be at the forefront of the *New Vision*.

The *New Vision* should anchor the plans and decisions of Perak's diverse stakeholders, and reset its citizens' expectations towards a more hopeful future. It should be a lodestar to help redirect the state's trajectory, especially since political and institutional leadership will be vital in championing and pushing forward this 'change agenda'. The agenda also requires greater decentralization of revenue collection and decision-making powers to cultivate increased local ownership and to pursue Perak's own development goals. Improved administrative efficiency, especially avoiding duplication of efforts, will be essential.

Perak's *New Vision* will also have to be ready to adapt to the increasing possibility of a *second wave of de-globalization*. As with the Covid-19 pandemic, Russia's war in Ukraine has seriously disrupted trade and supply chains, causing a big setback for the global economy. Countries across the world are now facing higher prices for commodities—especially for energy and food, of which Russia and Ukraine are major suppliers respectively. This has led to sharply rising global inflation, which, in turn, is eroding the value of incomes and weakening demand. Lower business confidence and higher investor uncertainty could potentially spur capital outflows from, and reduce investment in, countries like Malaysia. These shifts would likely have the deepest impact on the country's economically lagging states, including Perak—underlining the rationale for the state to have greater control over its own economic future.

People, Protection, and a Base for Prosperity

Kuala Kangsar, late 19th century, royal capital and location of the British residency

A Globalizing World

Malaysia has strongly benefited from the processes of globalization, through which borders and distances have become less of an impediment to the movement of goods, capital, people, and ideas.[1] Not all states in the country, however, have benefited equally. Globalization has amplified the initial advantages of locations which already had comparatively high population density, and which, typically, were situated near the established trading hubs of the Strait of Melaka. Other locations, such as the state of Perak, where geography and a rich endowment of natural resources had in earlier times bestowed advantages, have subsequently lagged, struggling to diversify their economic bases and to participate in the new, dynamic sectors of the economy that are unrelated to resource extraction. Over time, these places have fallen behind in terms of income growth, new business and employment opportunities, educational attainment, the general well-being of the local communities, and the vitality of their towns.

In the 18th century, trade networks were already beginning to develop into a loosely integrated international market for goods and services. By the second half of the 19th century, they had begun to take the form of a new capitalist world order—a system of economic organization driven by profit and supported by state governments. An international division of labour thus evolved: on one side was a handful of countries—principally Britain, Germany, the Netherlands, France, and the US—that were already engaged in manufacturing products due to their earlier industrial revolutions, which by the mid-19th century were well advanced; and on the other side were the many less developed places, such as in the Malay archipelago, that had now become suppliers of raw materials, with tin in high demand. More comprehensive networks of Western public and private institutions were being established—for instance, between state diplomatic representatives, agency houses, and Western commercial banks.

---

1 The first use of the term 'globalization' is usually attributed to Theodore Levitt (1983), whose article *The Globalization of Markets* described an emerging world in which global corporations vied to satisfy the tastes of globally scattered consumers—tastes that were rapidly becoming homogenized.

Globalization: Perak's Rise, Relative Decline, and Regeneration. Sultan Nazrin Shah, Oxford University Press. © Sultan Nazrin Shah (2024).
DOI: 10.1093/oso/9780198897774.003.0002

European-led Economic Globalization

Beginning in the second half of the 19th century and continuing into the early decades of the 20th, the states of the Malay peninsula became progressively integrated into a colonial-centric model of globalization. The benefits these states experienced as a result were largely the unplanned by-product of Britain's pursuit of its own interests in the region. By the end of the 19th century, Britain, with its massively superior naval strength, ruled the seas and was the dominant military and economic imperial power globally. It was, however, only the last of the European powers to exploit Malaya. The imprint of Portuguese and Dutch influence can be traced to the 16th and 17th centuries.

The Portuguese first established a stronghold in Melaka—situated at a strategic position at the narrowest point on the Strait—in 1511. The Portuguese had been lured to the East by the lucrative trade in spices that had, until that time, been the preserve of Arab traders. The arrival of the Portuguese was made possible by advances in navigational and shipping technology which enabled traders and settlers from Europe to sail longer distances in faster and bigger boats. Their superior fighting technology meant that the new arrivals met little resistance as they extended their empire. In the 17th century the Dutch asserted their military superiority, and ousted the Portuguese from Melaka after more than 120 years of rule. The Dutch East India Company or VOC (Vereenigde Oostindische Compagnie), perhaps the first multinational conglomerate, acted as the agent of the Dutch state: it raised capital in Europe, regulated and operated trade through treaty arrangements, exercised military control, and administered legal, monetary, and other matters in Dutch trading outposts in Asia and elsewhere.

The balance of colonial power in the Malay peninsula shifted again in the late 18th and early 19th century. In 1786, the British East India Company took advantage of Kedah's vulnerability in the recurrent Burma–Siamese wars and established a naval presence in Penang, in return for providing military protection. At the beginning of the 19th century, the Company also did the same in Singapore. Crucially, the emergence of Penang and Singapore as major entrepôt centres led to these locations overshadowing Melaka as the main ports in the Malay peninsula. Penang had the advantage of being the first port at which cargoes coming from Europe could be discharged, and Singapore had a similar advantage with cargoes from China, Japan, and other parts of East and Southeast Asia. From around the mid-19th century, Penang became the main port from which tin from

> **Map 1.1** — **Perak at centre of Southeast Asia's tin trade, circa late 19th century**

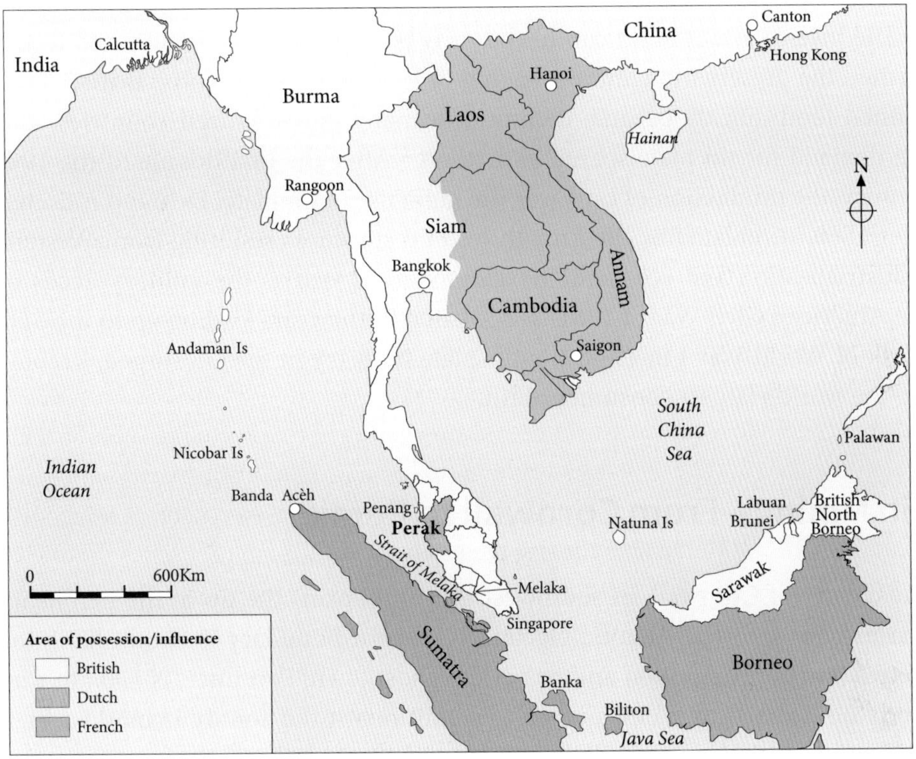

Source: Adapted from O'Brien (2007).
Note: Boundaries are approximate and illustrative only.

Perak—and to a lesser extent Kedah—was traded, and the Company managed it so that all international traders could operate freely (Map 1.1).

The Pangkor Engagement of 1874 gave Britain a firmer foothold on the Malay peninsula, and, starting from Perak, the colonial power progressively expanded its direct, and indirect, rule. Britain's interests in Perak were both strategic and commercial: Perak served as a bulwark against potential hostile foreign intervention, and also helped to shield Britain's commercial interests in the Straits Settlements (Penang, Melaka, and Singapore, and after Pangkor, the Dindings territory; see Map 1.5) from the violence that had erupted as rival Chinese clans aligned with different Malay royal factions fought to control the state's tin resources and Perak's throne. It would transpire that the solution to this problem—the assertion of Crown rights over subsoil minerals and the granting by the colonial administration of long leases and mining rights on clearly demarcated parcels of land—would later open the door for British involvement in the mining industry in Perak and elsewhere in Malaya.

The invention of the tin can in the early part of the 19th century had transformed the preservation and packaging of food. First used by the British navy, canned food quickly became common in many industrialized countries, and the demand for tin plate soared as a result.[2] After the first decade of the 19th century, the production of cans was the main use of tin plate. Demand rocketed after 1860, stimulated by the growth in food surpluses resulting from Western industrialization and economic development, as well as the military needs of the American Civil War of 1861–1865. Later, in the years leading up to the outbreak of World War I in 1914, the tin-plate industry in the US surged, becoming the world's largest consumer of tin.

Tin Mining—From Cornwall to Perak

The county of Cornwall, in southwest England, forms the tip of the peninsula that extends into the Atlantic Ocean. Its eastern boundary is about 320 kilometres (km) from London and its westernmost town, Penzance, is 130 km further still. Formed by a collision of two continents, the county is marked by a series of granitic intrusions that made it rich in tin and other mineral deposits—quite distinct from the landscape and geology of most other parts of the British Isles.

Cornwall was once the centre of the global tin-mining industry, with hundreds of mines. It produced almost the entire global supply of tin until the mid-1850s, and remained one of the largest tin producers until the early 1870s. Spurred by technological innovations, Cornish mines were highly efficient. The county's mining industry helped to propel Britain's industrial revolution. In the early 19th century, the Cornish Beam Engine—an advance on James Watt's transformational steam engine—was used to pump water out of deep underground mines and to lift workers and materials in and out of the mines. Cornwall's mining industry spawned economic and population growth, created new towns, farmsteads and smallholdings, seaports and harbours, and a rail network, and generated positive economic spillovers for the manufacturing and service industries (Sharpe, 2005).

---

2 Tin was also increasingly being used for containers that held oil and chemicals, for the manufacture of industrial alloys such as those used in bearings, for solder, and for antifriction metals used in axles. In all these applications, only small quantities of tin were required. Earlier uses of tin—for example in the manufacture of household pewter artefacts—became less common as industrial demand boomed.

Cornwall's tin-mining industry boomed during the early 19th century, though its scale, in terms of production and employment, never reached that of the copper-mining industry a century earlier (Barton, 1989). The boom was driven by the growth of the British tin-plate industry, which from 1805 to 1851 was the largest consumer of tin, accounting for between a third and a half of Britain's total tin consumption. However, Cornish tin increasingly came under pressure from cheaper sources outside the UK. Cornish tin mining was burdened by the heavy capital costs of extracting deep depth lode deposits. The elimination in 1853 of all import tariffs on tin entering the UK, at the urging of British tin-plate producers, removed a layer of protection for the cost-laden Cornish industry. Cheaper tin, initially from Australia and the island of Banka off Sumatra (see Map 1.1), which was part of the Dutch East Indies, and later from Malaya, began to push Cornish tin out of both the British and international markets that it had previously supplied. In this, the first wave of globalization, Cornwall was losing its competitive edge.

Changes in Global Tin Supply

The expansion of Britain's tin-plate industry in the 19th century coincided with several inter-related factors that affected the global tin supply and proved highly unfavourable for the Cornish tin industry. First, Cornish tin mines were unable to meet the growing demand of the tin-plate industry. Alluvial tin, which was the most suitable for the production of tin plate because of its superior purity and fluidity (in molten state), was becoming increasingly scarce as deposits from Cornish alluvial ores became exhausted (Wong, 1965).

Second, Britain's prime minister, Robert Peel (1841–1846), began to take measures to encourage free trade. In 1842, he lowered import tariffs on tin and granted preferential rates for imports from British overseas possessions that had previously been subject to the same tariffs as imports from non-British territories (Rowe, 1953). A year later, Peel abolished duties on tin ore, despite protectionist lobbying by Cornwall's mine-owning interests, and in 1853 all import tariffs on foreign tin were ended. The repeal of duties boosted tin imports: in 1880, around 63.5 per cent of the total tin consumed by Britain was imported, compared with just 8 per cent in 1850 (Wong, 1965).

Third, by the start of the 19th century, Dutch explorers had discovered a new source of alluvial tin on Banka. In 1813, Britain's East India Company, which had a monopoly to ship Cornish tin to Canton, China, transported some 1,700 Chinese labourers to Banka to help mine the deposits. Banka soon became an important source of Canton's tin imports, and by the 1830s Banka's tin—sold in

Amsterdam for far less than Cornish tin—had almost entirely driven Cornish tin out of the Chinese market (Barton, 1989).

Fourth, due to greatly increased demand, global tin exploration, mining, and production were growing rapidly. Cornish tin ore production peaked in 1871, with less consumed locally than elsewhere in Britain. Much of the tin ore imported into Britain came from Banka and Malaya, which, along with Cornwall, were the world's main producing regions between 1851 and 1870 (Figure 1.1).

Fifth, in 1871, rich alluvial tin deposits were discovered in Tasmania, Queensland, and other parts of Australia, and mining started there on a large scale using both Cornish emigrants and Chinese labourers. These mines were so productive that between 1875 and 1882 Australia overtook Cornwall to become the world's largest tin producer. Much of Australia's ore was exported to Cornwall for smelting, causing many of the less productive Cornish mines to close.

Tin ore production in Malaya—mainly from mines in Larut, Perak—grew rapidly from the mid-1870s. By 1883, with the addition of production from the deposits of Perak's Kinta Valley, Malaya had become the world's largest tin-producing country, a position it would occupy for many decades. Abundant deposits were later discovered in Bolivia, where mines transitioned from silver

Figure 1.1 Cornwall's share of the world's increasing tin ore output shrank as deposits were discovered and mined in other territories

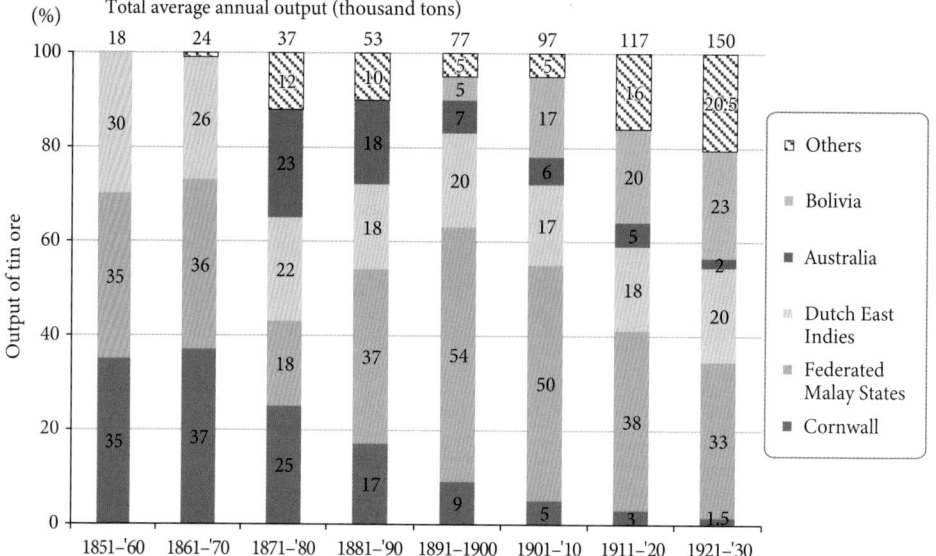

Source of data: Barton (1989).

Note: Within the category 'Others' Siam and Nigeria were the two biggest producers.

to tin after the global silver market slumped in the 1880s and early 1890s, and this heralded the arrival of another of the world's major tin-mining sources.

Cornwall's Struggle to Compete

A key factor in Perak's growth was the relatively low cost of mining its shallow alluvial deposits. This form of mining required limited equipment and, therefore, little fixed capital, and the high labour requirements were met through the influx of cheap, indentured migrant workers from China. In contrast, tin mining in Cornwall, which was predominantly deep-lode mining, was much more capital intensive and costly, and was only sustainable for as long as tin prices stayed high. By the 1880s, Malaya could make a profit from tin at a price lower than the cost of production in Cornwall, even with an export duty at that time of around 15 per cent.

Moreover, following the establishment of the Straits Trading Company (STC) in 1886, Malaya's smelted tin was becoming renowned for its quality. The only British company operating in what was, at that time, an almost entirely Chinese-owned industry, the STC capitalized on the main drawback of the Chinese approach—the inefficiency of charcoal-fuelled methods of smelting, which yielded only 60 per cent of tin in the ore (Tregonning, 1962). Its coal-operated smelting facility in Pulau Brani, British Straits Settlement of Singapore, produced high-quality tin that was much sought after in Europe (Wong, 1965).

Cornwall's Long-term Decline

With the huge growth in the world's tin supply, and in the face of increasing global competition, Cornish mines went into a long period of decline from the early 1870s, and many were abandoned. Tin production from Malaya, the Dutch East Indies, and Bolivia suddenly surged between 1885 and 1895, flooding global markets and causing tin prices to tumble by nearly a third between 1890 and 1896. Many Cornish mining companies were caught unprepared, and by 1897 more than half of Cornwall's mines had ceased operations (Barton, 1989). Although prices had recovered by 1900, tin production in Cornwall never did. Cornish investors were withdrawing their financial support away from Cornish mines and redirecting it towards foreign and colonial mining ventures. The late 19th-century tin crisis had the unfortunate effect of making the supply of tin from the Cornish mines even more price inelastic—that is, unable to respond to tin price changes (Burt and Kudo, 2015).

Cornwall's half-century of tin mining decline caused extreme hardship in local mining communities. Often poorly paid, the miners were also subjected to dangers, diseases, and other risks that led to high mortality rates (Hamilton Jenkin, 1927). The decline prompted further substantial emigration of Cornish miners to other mining areas worldwide, especially Australia, California, and South Africa. Between 1861 and 1901, about a fifth of the Cornish male population—mostly miners—emigrated, around three times the average for England and Wales in that period (Cornwall Heritage Trust, 2022).[3] Miners' remittances helped, to some degree, to alleviate destitution among the families that they often left behind.

Some of Cornwall's mining expertise and capital flowed into Perak and other parts of Malaya, which helped to propel the fortunes of the territories' mining industry. In 1891 for example, Francis Douglas Osborne, in partnership with Edward Rochfort Pike—the Inspector of Mines in Kinta, who had built his expertise in Cornwall—and James Wickett—a share broker in Cornwall—established the Gopeng Tin Mining Company in Perak, the first in Malaya to introduce hydraulic sluicing. Its success drew large British investments, with Cornish interests dominating the growing number of European companies operating in Kinta. These investments led to further technological progress in Perak's mining industry, with the introduction of the gravel pump in 1906 and the bucket dredge in 1913, both of which, though capital intensive, were highly productive (Yip, 1969). Gravel pumps had been used earlier for mining China clay in Cornwall, and dredges for mining precious metals in Australia and New Zealand (Allen and Donnithorne, 2003).

The Cornish mining legacy was responsible for helping to transform what had been a predominantly Straits-funded Malayan–Chinese industry into a largely Western enterprise, with tin output from European-owned mines rising to 70 per cent of the total in 1940, from just 10 per cent in 1900. By the early 20th century, the tin industry in Cornwall—once the world's pre-eminent tin region—had become a shadow of its former glory. Malaya and other low-cost tin-producing regions had surged ahead. However, by this time, the Cornish and Malayan tin-mining industries had become closely linked. Many of Perak's mining companies had come under the control of the Redruth Mining Exchange (formed in Cornwall in 1880) and its associates in Malaya (Khoo and Abdur-Razzaq Lubis, 2005).

---

3 Cornwall's out-migration continued until the 1960s. Among the 2,000 people on board the ill-fated *Titanic* in April 1912, there was a group of Cornish miners hoping to build a new life in America (French, 2012).

Perak in the International Tin Market

The development of the tin-mining industry in the states of Malaya—and pre-eminently in Perak—illustrates how processes of globalization worked in the latter half of the 19th and the early 20th century. Voracious industrial demand for tin in the West after the start of the industrial revolution, and the discovery of rich alluvial tin deposits in Larut, Perak, in the 1840s, changed the entire complexion of the industry. During this period, the speed of moving goods and people increased with advances in steamship technology: shipping costs declined, ideas spread faster, and long distances mattered less for the growth of trade (Baldwin, 2016).[4]

An international tin market was forming in which prices were becoming globally linked and determined by market forces that favoured the cheapest source of supply. Market integration deepened further with the rapid extension of telegraphic communications in the 1870s, which facilitated the centralized negotiation of contracts for future deliveries of tin on the London Metal Exchange. Established in 1877, the Exchange set benchmark prices globally for tins of different grades (Hillman, 2010).[5] Trade in tin, and in other goods, was supported by the gold standard and a system of fixed exchange rates that enabled capital to flow easily between countries. By this time, the commercial interests and international trading activities in Penang had become tightly linked to Perak's tin economy. As Perak lacked a large seaport, its tin was shipped first to Penang, or sometimes to Singapore, and from there transhipped to China, the UK, and India (Doyle, 1879).

Chinese capital, innovation, and technology from the Straits Settlements, and workers 'imported' from China, were what initially brought tin mined in Perak and other Malayan states to world markets. The Chinese dominance of the industry would, however, eventually weaken. By the late 19th century, British capital had built what would subsequently be known as a 'vertically integrated value chain' that delivered high-quality tin mined in Perak to industrial customers in Britain, the US, and other Western nations. Perak, along with

---

4 Baldwin (2016) argues that this phase of globalization stretched from around 1820 to 1990 and was triggered both by steam and the industrial revolution.

5 In 1870, submarine cables were laid from India to Penang and to Singapore—London having been linked to India some time earlier. Telegraphic services connecting the UK to the Straits Settlements began operating soon after. Before this, a letter from the UK to the Straits Settlements would have taken about two months. In 1876, inland telegraphic services were established in Perak, and by 1884 the first post office had been opened in its capital, Taiping.

other states of Malaya, had been inexorably drawn into the global markets for commodities, finance, and industrial goods.

Global demand for tin significantly affected Perak's trade, investment, demographics, settlement patterns, and infrastructure (with the development of paved roads, railways, power, and water). In addition, British institutional arrangements, as well as legal, financial, and administrative systems, were imported, displacing most traditional systems. Later, towards the end of the 19th century, the introduction of the Torrens system of land registration for demarcating property rights—which the British had previously introduced in Australia—facilitated the opening of the hinterland for large investments in rubber estate plantations. Although most arrangements—contractual, monetary, fiscal, and administrative—were fashioned to serve the goals of colonial Britain, they also provided a solid foundation for developing a market economy that would outlive tin.

*   *   *

This book will return to the phenomenon of economic globalization and its dynamic impact on the trajectory of Perak's past, present, and future development in Parts 2–4. The remainder of Part 1 is divided into seven sections that describe and assess key aspects of Perak's social, economic, and political history in the 18th and 19th centuries. Many of these continued to affect the people and prosperity of the state into the 20th century, and some even have a lasting impact to this day.

The first of these sections focuses on Perak's important enabling geographical features, its early patterns of settlement in villages and later small towns, and the diversity and growth of its people through high rates of inward migration. The second outlines how Perak's rich endowment of minerals, especially tin, and other natural resources, has always attracted foreign interests, and often unwelcome intrusions. The third describes the state's traditional Malay system of governance and how it was unable to withstand the competitive strains that came with the introduction of a modern capitalist mode of production when the mining industry rapidly expanded.

The next two sections describe how rival groups from outside Perak, allied to competing royal interest groups within, fought bitterly for control of Perak's tin resources, and how the ensuing chaos eventually led to British colonial intervention, the signing of the Pangkor Engagement, and the suppression of resistance to Britain's indirect rule. The penultimate section describes how, after Pangkor, the local British authorities were quick to reclaim territory that would be advantageous to their interests. Part 1 concludes by observing how the British administration increasingly tightened and extended its political control and institutional arrangements to consolidate and entrench its strategic and economic gains in Perak, and in the peninsula's other main tin-producing Malay states.

Perak's Lifeblood—Its Rivers, Settlements, and People

There are differing views on how Perak got its name. Some say that the name was taken in honour of Tun Perak (later made the bendahara) for leading Melaka's forces in defeating a Siamese invasion in 1445–1446. Others say that it comes from the 'flash caused by a fish in the water', which shone like silver. Yet it seems likely that the name comes from the Malay word for silver, *perak*, describing the tin which once gleamed in the states' waterways, but does so no longer (Map 1.2).

Perak covers an area of some 8,000 square miles, or 21,000 square kilometres, being about the size of Slovenia in Europe or the US state of New Jersey. Perak's coastal west side faces the Strait of Melaka, with its back towards a great range—the Titiwangsa Range—which rises to a peak of over 2,000 metres and runs down the centre of the peninsula. At its northwestern boundary, the Kerian River (formerly the Krian River) separates Perak from Seberang Perai (formerly Province Wellesley) and Kedah, while along the southern border the Bernam River divides Perak from Selangor. Along its eastern boundary are the states of Kelantan and Pahang. In the northeast is the boundary with southern Thailand (formerly Siam). Along its coast is Pangkor, Perak's main island.

A striking feature of Perak's geography is the multitude of rivers that flow from the mountains westward into the Strait of Melaka. Before the 20th century, the rivers were the lifeblood of Perak. They are inextricably intertwined with other aspects of its history—the movement of people and commodities, the location of chiefdoms, and patterns of human settlement. They engendered complex networks of kinship and power, and multifaceted relations between factions competing for control of Perak's rich tin resources (Husni Abu Bakar, 2015). For most of the state's people, 'the river was the high-road, the water supply, the bath and the drain' (Gullick, 1958, p. 28).

Globalization: Perak's Rise, Relative Decline, and Regeneration. Sultan Nazrin Shah, Oxford University Press. © Sultan Nazrin Shah (2024).
DOI: 10.1093/oso/9780198897774.003.0003

Map 1.2   **Perak's rivers and topography, circa 1900**

Sources: Adapted from Swettenham (1906) and ©Maphill/CC BY-ND (2020).

Journeying along Perak's Rivers in the 19th Century

The Perak River flows from north to south, from the mountains between Patani in southern Siam and Kedah, down to the sea opposite Pulau Sembilan (Map 1.2). The main branches and longest navigable tributaries of the Perak River are the Bidor and Kinta Rivers. James Wheeler Woodford Birch, the first British resident (1874–1875), who spent much time journeying up and down the river, described it as follows:

> The river is a very magnificent one. At least 150 miles [240 km] from the mouth, it is over 400 feet [122 metres] wide, and, as the tidal influence extends a very short distance from its mouth, it may be well imagined what rich and fertile lands are to be found along its valley. The greatest resources of this fine district lie in its soil. (cited in D'Almeida, 1876, p. 363)

Perak's rivers formed natural highways. Before roads were built, they served as the only channel of communication between the interior and the sea for transporting the state's exports of tin, timber, and other commercial products as well as for receiving imports. The Perak River was navigable by steamers for up to 50 km inland, and for smaller boats for about 300 km.[6] At its mouth, south of the Dindings territory, were Chinese fishing villages, the land flat and swampy with mangroves on either side. As one moved up the river, the water became crystal clear and mostly shallow. Malay *kampung*s (villages), generally controlled by the head, or *ketua kampung*, and separated by dense forest, lay along the banks,

> and consequently they for the most part build their villages on the river-banks; ... where it has been found convenient to carry tin to the nearest market, obtaining in return rice, salt, and salt-fish, which form the staple food ... (McNair, 1878, p. 5 and p. 16)

The port of Teluk Anson[7] (now Teluk Intan) was located on the Perak River some distance from the tin mines in Taiping (formerly Klian Pauh) and Kamunting (formerly Klian Bahru). Several small steamers plied between Larut and Penang with their cargoes of tin. Once a fortnight a steamer travelling from Singapore to Penang called at Teluk Anson, and another stopped at the Dindings and the Bernam River (Bird, 1883).

---

6 For example, Leech (1879) noted that in the 1870s a coasting steamer, the *Pyah Pekhet*, called weekly at Durian Sebatang, about 40 miles (64 km) up the Perak River, on its way to and from Singapore and Penang.

7 *Teluk* means bay in the Malay language.

In Perak during the 19th century, a man's wealth and importance were established by the number of his elephants, which were a vital means of transport until the 1920s. Elephants, being swimmers, could ford the rivers:

> we went down a steep bank into the broad, bright, river, ... shortly the elephant gently dropped down and was entirely submerged, moving majestically along, with not a bit of his huge bulk visible, the end of his proboscis far ahead ... and so we went for some distance up the clear, shining river, with the tropic sun blazing down upon it, with everything that could rejoice the eye upon its shores, with little beaches of golden sands, and above the forest the mountains with varying shades of indigo coloring. (Bird, 1883, pp. 404–5)

To the north of the Perak River valley is Larut, drained by the Larut River—some 25.7 km from the nearest point of the Perak River. Larut is located outside the valley of the Perak River, and is bounded by the Kurau River to the north, the Strait of Melaka to the west, and the Bruas River to the south (Map 1.2). Until around the third quarter of the 19th century, there was only one road in Perak that connected the two mines and villages of two rival Chinese communities—the Ghee Hin and the Hai San—to the landing at the Larut River estuary. Around the midpoint of this road, there was a connection to the village of the Malay chief, the menteri, one of Perak's four highest chiefs after the sultan (see Box 1.1 in 'Traditional Governance Destabilized', below). North of Larut is Kerian (formerly Krian), sparsely populated, where peasant farmers and coastal fishermen lived.

On the southeastern side of the Perak Valley is the Kinta Valley, which had been populated largely by Malays until a few rich tin mines opened. Below the mouth of the Kinta River is Batang Padang, where Chinese miners exported tin to the seaboard and brought up supplies and provisions (Daly, 1882). It had just a few thousand inhabitants. The Bernam River area comprised a huge stretch of virgin forest, with even fewer inhabitants.

The Rivers' Economic Vitality

The rivers and water supply were indispensable to successful mining, and miners from rival groups fought over the control of the rivers. For this reason:

> The most important and valuable rule laid down in the Malay States in connexion with land ... was that every stream and water-course in the country should remain under the absolute control of the Government. (Swettenham, 1906, p. 235)

This regulation was introduced by the British resident at the beginning of indirect rule, following the Larut 'tin wars', which broke out intermittently between 1861 and 1873. Most mines in the valleys were drained by one or two streams. After the agreement at Pangkor in 1874, mine inspectors prevented disputes, and ensured that water was fairly apportioned and that mines at the head did not shut off the water supply to those further down the valley. The British also recognized the need to try to prevent silt from mining activity from flowing out of smaller rivers and polluting the Perak River, the state's main highway, but ultimately did little to prevent this from happening (Birch, 1910).

Jacques de Morgan, a French mining engineer and geologist, was commissioned in 1884 by Hugh Low, Resident of Perak (1877–1889), to produce the first geological and mining map of the district of Kinta in exchange for a tin concession near Gopeng. He described the use of water in tin mining:

> The Chinese are extremely skilled in all hydraulic work; they build their machines with great care. … In early tin mining, extraction was achieved using a noria—an inclined chain of buckets driven by a hydraulic wheel. … Since Europeans settled, norias were replaced with rotating steam pumps powered by small locomotives which … allows for the removal of all water from the mines to just a few hours whereas norias would require nearly an entire day. (cited in Jaunay, 2020, p. 153)

Traditional subsistence cultivation of *padi* (unmilled rice) was concentrated in the river valleys with alluvial soils, mainly Kerian, Kinta, and Batang Padang. In the 1890s, to generate income for the peasants, save foreign exchange, and increase production to feed the growing number of Chinese migrants, the British authorities constructed the Kerian Irrigation System, which improved the quantity and quality of *padi* yields. The government partially funded and provided administrative services to support smaller land settlement and irrigation projects carried out by Malay entrepreneurs (Hill, 1973).

Early Village Settlements

Perak's early settlement patterns were mainly governed by geographical and geological factors: proximity to the coast or rivers, and the availability of mineral resources. In the early decades of the 19th century, Perak was land-abundant and sparsely populated. Most of its fewer than 50,000 inhabitants were Malays, who were spatially dispersed and culturally diverse, with relatively small numbers of *Orang Asli* (aborigines of the interior), Chinese, and others.

Malays had initially settled along the coast of the Strait of Melaka and were mainly maritime traders. This pattern of settlement changed with the 16th-century arrival of European traders, who sought Perak's tin and other produce. After this point, Malays began settling close to rivers, forming riverine agricultural and fishing communities organized in small chiefdoms. As Wilkinson (1957, p. 66) observed:

> Agriculture is the soul of Malay life. … He is essentially a planter; his festivals are seasonal; his joys and sorrows depend on the crops; and his whole life is regulated by the great rice-planting industry.

Land along the rivers was fertile and well adapted for agriculture, with pure water flowing in abundance for irrigation. Malays cultivated corn, tea, coffee, and pepper, as well as fruit, rice, and vegetables. By the early 19th century, the estuaries of the rivers had become Malay population centres.

> The people … live on the very edge of the river, some of them in houses supported by four poles stuck into the bed of the river, and others on its banks in houses concealed in a forest of fruit and jungle trees. The houses are built of wood and are thatched with the dried leaf of the nipa, known as *attap* by the natives. (D'Almeida, 1876, p. 363)

The nucleus of a Malay settlement was the village, commonly founded by the head of a family and his kindred by blood and affinity. Settlements varied significantly in size. Some comprised only half a dozen mainly bamboo and palm houses and were home to around 20 inhabitants. There were also well-established villages of 200 or 300 houses, with up to 1,000 inhabitants or even more; a village of this size would have formed the centre of a district and been home to the district chief (Sadka, 1960). Houses were almost always built in lines close to the banks of navigable rivers, where the availability of arable land for rice cultivation often determined the size of village settlements. All villages had a mosque.

The lives of Perak's Malays were governed both by *adat* (custom and traditions), and by the Muslim religion; the latter being a consequence of the Islamization of the peninsula that had begun in the 13th century. The Five Pillars of Islam were of paramount importance and were obligatory, although not always enforced. Many Malays still believed in 'petty superstition' and turned to the 'cult of older divinities' in times of stress or danger (Wilkinson, 1957, p. 1).

Society was stratified into two main classes—the ruling elites and the *rakyat* (subject class). The division was sharp and marked by birthright (Jomo, 1986). There was rarely any transition from the *rakyat* to the ruling class. The life of the *rakyat* in the *kampungs* was harsh. They were often called upon by the *penghulu* (generally the headman of a cluster of *kampungs* or sub-districts) to work in the fields during peak harvesting times, collect forest produce, and build mosques, with their labour compensated only by food, according to the *kerah* system (often called the corvée in Europe). The *rakyat* 'were there to do what their chiefs told them—no more, no less' (Swettenham, 1906, p. 141). The *kerah* labour system was often exploited by the elites for their own personal benefit. The royals and others privileged by birth kept slaves (often *Orang Asli*), or debt slaves who were paid nothing for their labour, 'a custom loathed by those who had to bear the burden of this iniquitous bondage, but upheld as a cherished privilege by the class which was benefited' (Swettenham, 1906, p. 141). Once people became slaves, moreover, their descendants also became and remained slaves (Maxwell, 1890).

Population movements were extremely sensitive to political events; people moved from their villages in response to oppression, invasion, and civil war. The district chief was in absolute control; there were practically no sanctions the *rakyat* could use against him, except their fleeing. Oppressed groups could undermine a chief's power by leaving the district, as land was abundant and free, and so settlements were often temporary. A village could be dismantled and packed into boats in a matter of days.

Perak was culturally and linguistically diverse even before the inflows of large numbers of migrant Chinese (and later Indians) in the latter half of the 19th century (see 'Surging Migration Flows', below). Many of the Malays living in upper Perak had migrated from Patani and Kelantan, and therefore spoke with the same dialect as inhabitants of these southern Siamese territories. Malays in north Perak spoke with a Kedah dialect, having been displaced from Kedah during the Siamese invasion of 1821 (Khoo, 2017) (see 'Resisting Siam—Holding Back the Traditional Tributary Offering', below). The western part of Perak saw several migration waves from Sumatra in the Dutch East Indies, comprising Batta Batak, Korinchi, Mandailing, Rawa, and other smaller groups, who tended to settle in lower Perak. The Korinchis held themselves to be purer adherents of Islam, and the men always dressed in white (McNair, 1878). There were also settlements of Bugis, mainly traders, who came from the southern part of the island of Sulawesi (formerly Celebes) (Sadka, 1960). In describing the Bugis, McNair (1878, pp. 130–131) observed:

> The Malays fear and respect them above all other races of the archipelago; and among them are to be found the principal native traders and merchants …

In the mid-19th century, new districts opened in northern Perak, in lower Kerian, and Kurau, which later became rich rice-producing areas cultivated by Malays who arrived from the already settled areas of Province Wellesley, Kedah, and the Siamese province of Patani (Sadka, 1960). Later, when Siam returned territory south of Patani to Perak in the first decade of the 20th century, more than 10 per cent of the population who were Siamese remained in the district (Birch, 1910).

The *Orang Asli* in Perak were distinguished generically into two main tribes—the *Senoi* and the *Semang*—with divisions within each. These tribes inhabited the interior, and were nomadic to differing degrees (Daly, 1882; Harrison, 1923).[8] The two largest subgroups of the *Senoi* were the *Temiar* and the *Semai*, who spoke distinct dialects of the *Senoi* language that were not mutually comprehensible. The *Temiar* were highly concentrated around the mountain range of Gunung Korbu in the Kuala Kangsar district, north of Kinta, while the Semai were found south of Sungai Raya (Map 1.2). The *Senoi*, particularly the *Temiar*, could speak Malay, bartering with Malays for wood-cutting tools, sarongs, cooking utensils, and weapons (Khoo and Abdur-Razzaq Lubis, 2005). With the abolition of slavery in all forms in 1883, the *Senoi* were employed to clear jungles, gather rattan, and collect gutta-percha—a tough plastic substance from the latex of trees used to make moulded and functional products such as containers and knife handles (Maxwell, 1879).

The *Semang* mainly inhabited upper Perak, in the areas of the Perak–Kedah border as well as northeast and north-central Perak (Dodge, 1981). A Negroid people, they bore less similarity in appearance to the Malays than the *Senoi* did, being of darker complexion (McNair, 1878), and adopted the Aslian family of the Mon-Khmer languages (Hood Salleh, 2006). They were nomads, and their lifestyle was one of hunting and foraging (Andaya, 2002).

Emergence of Towns in the Late 19th Century

From the last quarter of the 18th century and into the 19th, small groups of Chinese labourers were procured to work in Perak's mines. Beginning in 1776, Sultan Alauddin Mansur Shah (1773–1786) allowed Chinese indentured labourers to mine for tin along the rivers at Kinta and at Sungkai, on the recommendation of the Dutch East India Company which had employed Chinese miners in Banka (Andaya, 1979). The earliest Chinese settlement in Perak was at Sungkai. Migration of non-Malay groups to Perak began on a larger scale with the

---

8 McNair (1878) and Harrison (1923) refer to the *Sekai* and not the *Senoi*. It is probable that these earlier references to the *Sekai* relate to both the *Senoi* and the *Proto-Malays*, as these two groups more closely resembled the Malays than the *Semang*.

expanding production of tin from around the late 1840s, when a new type of settlement—the mining camp—emerged. Some camps were short-lived, but others gained permanence as collection and distribution centres for tin exports. These settlements grew with the addition of shops and other trading facilities.

The boom in Perak's tin industry from the less volatile period of the mid-1870s brought with it the arrival of large numbers of migrant Chinese workers, and changed the state's economic and human geography. New township settlements, with public infrastructure and amenities, began to form in areas close to tin ore deposits. Tin mining helped to create a hierarchy of settlements. For example, the towns closest to ore deposits functioned as service centres for tin-mining and ancillary activities, and a variety of activities and services appeared to support their expanding populations. Larut, and later Kinta, became important centres of settlement. Inflows of capital came from the merchants in the Straits Settlement of Penang, as did large influxes of migrant workers. Typically, the larger settlements performed more diverse and specialized economic functions. The construction of transport networks followed, connecting the new mining towns to each other, and the mines to smelting centres and ports.

After Resident Birch's assassination (see 'Resistance, Retaliation, and Reflection', below), the British moved the administrative centre away from the Malay heartland to Taiping, where there was a more even mix between Malays and Chinese (Khoo, 2017). Much later, as Kinta became the state's mining centre, the capital was moved to Ipoh along the Kinta River.[9] Between 1876 and 1885, Taiping, built on the strength of Larut's mining income, became the premier town not only of Perak but of the entire Malay peninsula. In 1877, the British administration also permanently fixed the location of the royal residence in Kuala Kangsar, on a hillside on the right bank of the Perak River where the Kangsar River debouches (Map 1.2).

Many of the new riverside towns were flooded during the annual monsoon season. Ipoh, for example, suffered severe flooding as the Kinta River became increasingly silted from mining upstream. In December 1898, following heavy rainfalls, Ipoh was inundated by almost one metre of water, and, around two decades later, even heavier flooding was recorded during the Great Flood of 1926,[10] which suspended train services between Ipoh and Kuala Lumpur, and brought the Kinta Valley's tin-mining industry to a standstill (Abdur-Razzaq Lubis et al., 2010).

---

9 Ipoh was founded on Malay village land controlled by the territorial chief, Panglima Kinta Seri Amar Bangsa Diraja. The enterprising panglima laid out the early town and sold building lots to local Chinese. In 1894, he became one of the unofficial members of the newly established Ipoh Sanitary Board.

10 The Great Flood of 1926 was also significant in motivating the British administration to improve land and river management (Williamson, 2016).

The port at Kuala Bidor, situated at the confluence of the Perak and Bidor Rivers, had become the most important trading centre in Perak, and was also a royal weighing station for tin exported from Perak where taxes were collected. The Laksamana Raja Mahkota established his residence there, from where he was able to monitor the flow of Perak's trade (see Box 1.1). When Teluk Anson was founded nearby in 1882, the Kuala Bidor port became known as the port of Teluk Anson. Lower Perak, however, had benefited little from the growth of Larut's tin-mining industry, but when Kinta became the state's leading tin producer towards the end of the century, Teluk Anson increased in importance, becoming the major gateway to and from the Kinta district via the Kinta and Perak Rivers, until the arrival of rail transport connecting Ipoh to Port Weld (now Kuala Sepetang) in 1894.[11]

In contrast to the tin industry, rubber cultivation—which grew exponentially in the first two decades of the 20th century, eventually eclipsing tin as the major source of Perak's export earnings—had a less direct impact on settlement patterns. This was because, unlike tin mining, around which towns were formed, rubber cultivation was an inherently dispersed rural activity that required access to large tracts of suitable land. Migrant Indian labourers who worked on the plantations were generally accommodated on the estates.

Surging Migration Flows

With Perak's stability largely restored from the mid-1870s following the tin wars of the previous two decades, there was a substantial influx of migrants to the state, attracted by its booming tin-based economy. These were mainly tin miners, traders, construction workers, rice planters and other agriculturalists, drawn from southern China, India, Ceylon (now Sri Lanka), and elsewhere in the Malay archipelago. With the large inward flows, Perak's population surged and became even more culturally diverse.

Previously, estimates of Perak's population and its composition had been, at best, rough approximations. However, the British administration started to conduct regular population censuses, and these made available reasonably reliable estimates of Perak's population size and composition. The first census was taken in 1879 and provides a baseline for assessing the state's demographic profile. When combined with later censuses, it offers an insight into how this profile has changed.

---

11 Malaya's first railway line, running from Port Weld to Taiping over a distance of 12.8 km, began service in 1885, having been approved by the Perak State Council in 1880. It was extended to Ipoh in 1894.

In 1879, Perak's population was just over 81,000, of whom 74 per cent were Malays and other culturally diverse indigenous groups of the Malay archipelago, and a further 25 per cent were Chinese.[12] Over the next 12 years, Perak's population grew spectacularly to 214,000 (Figure 1.2, upper panel), reflecting huge migration inflows of all manner of peoples, most notably of Chinese males, but also drawing people from communities located throughout the Malay archipelago. There were also inflows of Tamils and others from India, mainly to work on government infrastructure projects and on coffee, sugar, and tea plantations, even before the rubber boom that began at the start of the 20th century. Their numbers were negligible in 1879, but by 1891 they totalled almost 15,000.

Out of Perak's eight districts in 1879, almost one-third of the population lived in the district of Larut, reflecting the extent to which this area dominated the state's mining industry. Over the course of the next 12 years, as Kinta's mining industry took off, its population grew significantly, at almost 16 per cent a year, so that by 1891 it rivalled Larut in its share of the state's total population of 214,000 (Figure 1.2, lower panel). By 1891, these two districts accounted for 55 per cent of Perak's population. Also notable during this period was the large inflow of Malays from elsewhere in the archipelago, annually averaging almost 10 per cent. They typically migrated to cultivate land in the rich rice-growing district of Kerian.

By the turn of the century, Perak's rapidly growing population was benefiting from the state's abundant natural resources and from the systems put in place by the colonial administration. Slavery having been abolished, the *rakyat* were enjoying more freedoms: their services could no longer be demanded without wages, and they now cultivated land that they owned. As Swettenham[13] observed:

> The wealthiest Malays in the Peninsula are the Perak Malays. It is for them that the richest silks of Trengganu and Batu Bara are woven, it is they who vie with each other in the building of expensive houses and the possession of horses and carriages ... (Swettenham, 1906, p. 294)

---

12 Although there is no reliable information on the size of Perak's Chinese population until 1879, numbers increased as the 19th century progressed, especially with the significant development of mining in southern Perak, and later in Larut. By the 1830s, a 'Capitan China' had already been appointed by Perak's sultan to manage the affairs of the Chinese community, suggesting a fair number.

13 Frank Athelstane Swettenham, whose illustrious career included positions as the Resident of Selangor (1882), Resident of Perak (1889), Resident-General of the Federated Malay States (1896), and Governor of the Straits Settlements (1901), started his overseas career in Singapore at the youthful age of 20 as a cadet in the Straits Settlements civil service in January 1871. Within his first 18 months of service, he learned to speak fluent Malay and to read and write Malay Jawi script. He was posted to Penang and Province Wellesley in 1872–1873. His seminal work on the progress of British influence in Malaya was first published in 1906 as *British Malaya*.

Figure 1.2	How Perak's population size and composition changed in the late 19th century

The population[a] surged between 1879 and 1891, especially of males

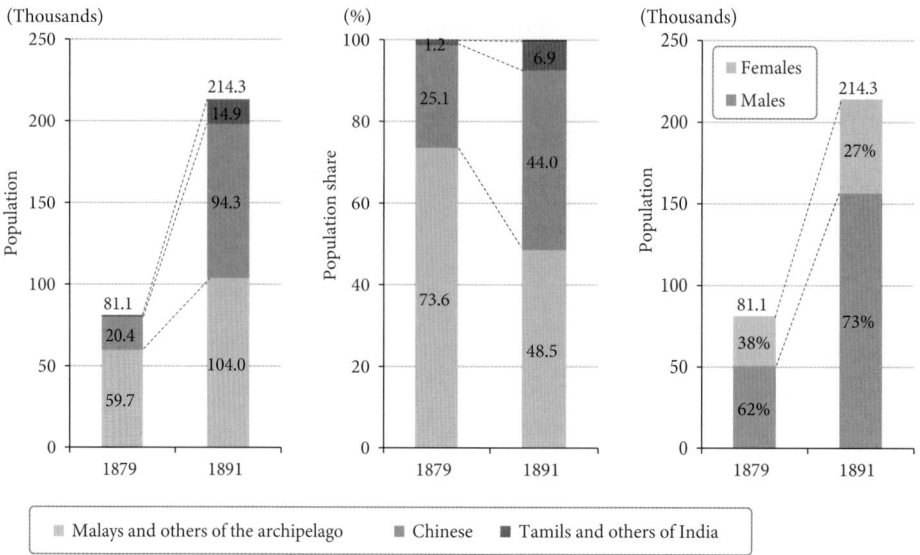

Malays and others of the archipelago   Chinese   Tamils and others of India

The most populated district was Larut, with Kinta fast catching up by 1891

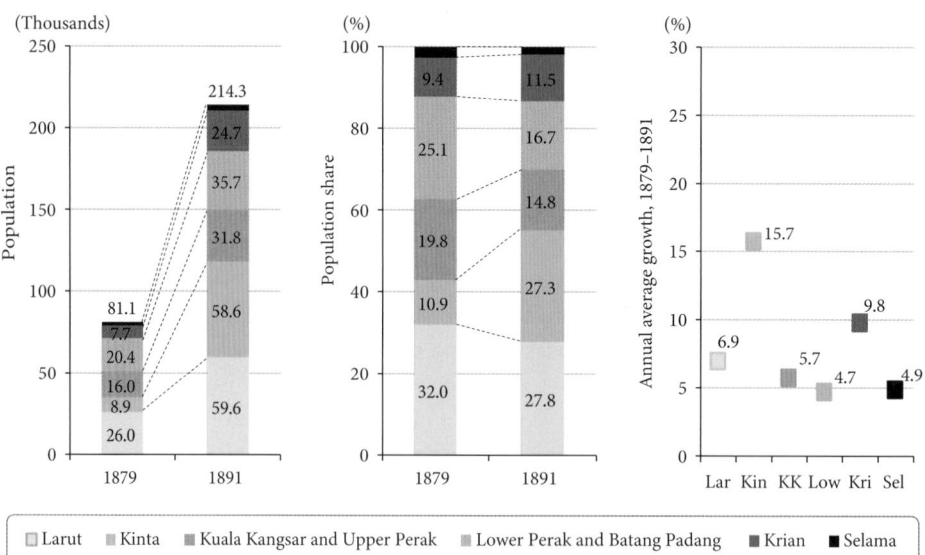

Larut   Kinta   Kuala Kangsar and Upper Perak   Lower Perak and Batang Padang   Krian   Selama

Note: [a] The number of people of other ethnic groups was 92 in 1879 and 1,032 in 1891.
Source of data: Merewether (1892).

While many of the traditional chiefs of the ruling class had lost their former powers, the status and prestige of Perak's ruler had been enhanced, as the ordinary people joined the new global capitalist mode of production under the British colonial administration.

Invading Traders and Powerful Neighbours

For centuries, Perak's rich mineral deposits had been bitterly fought over by rapacious neighbours and foreign invaders. The Acehnese, Bugis, Siamese, Portuguese, the Dutch East India Company, and the British East India Company—the last two with vast naval, military, and economic resources at their disposal—were Perak's most prominent foes, and also sometimes friends, from the 17th to the 19th centuries. Granted trade monopolies in the East Indies by their respective governments, the two Companies competed bitterly for international trade and territories, displacing earlier colonizers. Both were pioneers of globalization, with other state-supported European conglomerates entering later.

In the late 16th century and for much of the 17th century, Perak was a vassal state of the politically powerful Aceh, which was a major international trading port town and a meeting point for Arab, Chinese, and Dutch merchants as well as those from Bengal, Gujarat, and Patani (Reid, 2006). Through various treaties, the Acehnese monopolized Perak's tin trade, and for short periods shared this monopoly with the VOC to the exclusion of all other traders (Winstedt, 1935).

Era of VOC's Trading Dominance

In 1641, the VOC captured the port of Melaka, and gradually drove out the Portuguese—who had held it since 1511—using their naval superiority and better weapons (Winstedt, 1935). Perak's trade accelerated when the VOC signed treaties with Sultan Muzaffar Riayat Shah II (1636–1653) in 1650 and with Sultan Mahmud Iskandar Shah (1653–1720) in 1659, giving the VOC a monopoly over the state's tin at a fixed, low price in return for protection against the Siamese and other invaders (de Witt, 2007). By 1663, Perak supplied around 277,000 lbs (about 28 per cent of all the tin the VOC acquired in Asia), and five years later this had risen to 450,000 lbs, a significant share of which was sold through auction in

Globalization: Perak's Rise, Relative Decline, and Regeneration. Sultan Nazrin Shah, Oxford University Press. © Sultan Nazrin Shah (2024).
DOI: 10.1093/oso/9780198897774.003.0004

Amsterdam (Glamann, 1958, cited in Lewis, 1969, p. 57).[14] While the Dutch had control of Melaka, no ships could pass through the Strait without calling at its port and getting a pass. Sometimes ships bound for Perak were refused passes so that they could not defy the VOC's monopolies over tin and pepper (Winstedt, 1948).

The VOC's monopoly fuelled animosity among Perak's chiefs. The bendahara and court officials destroyed the first Dutch fort at Teluk Gedung on Pangkor Island, which was built to safeguard against English traders and to check the influence of the Bugis (Andaya, 1979). After 1690, having lost its monopoly, the VOC's supply of tin from Perak was severely curtailed. The state's Malay chiefs, who had long been involved in regional trading (Ramli Ngah Talib, 2022), began selling tin directly to British and other foreign merchants from Penang and elsewhere, where they could secure much higher prices than those offered by the Dutch.

Diplomatic relations between the VOC and Perak were not re-established until around 1746, when the Treaty of Peace and Alliance was signed with Sultan Mudzaffar Shah III (1728–1752), the agreement being modified two years later. Like the treaties of the previous century, this treaty gave the Dutch a trading monopoly, with the price of tin fixed and with duty on it payable to the sultan on every *bahar* sold (Maxwell, 1882a).[15] The agreement brought a period of wealth and stability to Perak and bolstered the influence of its sultan, as documented in *Hikayat Misa Melayu* (Raja Chulan, 2015). The Dutch strengthened their presence by building a fort at Pangkalan Halban on Tanjong Putus, at the mouth of the Perak River, and established a garrison to protect the sultan's and the VOC's interests. By the mid-18th century Perak had become so important to the VOC that Willem Albinus, Governor of Melaka (1741–1748), declared that Melaka's tin trade was solely dependent on Perak, with roughly equal amounts exported to China, India, and the Netherlands. He noted:

> As a result of these arrangements I had the satisfaction last year of not only completely fulfilling the requirements of the home country and the Indies to the amount of 420,250 lb. (that is, 200,250 lb. for the Netherlands, 200,000 lb. for China, and 200,000 lb. for Surat), but also of being able to send 100,125 lb. in the ship 'Ida' to Batavia, thus making a total of 520,375 lb. (cited in Harrison, 1954, p. 26)

In the 18th century there was high demand for tin in prosperous Canton, China. It was used for lining tea chests to keep the packaging airtight so as to preserve the taste (Yong, 2007). Circumventing the VOC's monopoly to exploit this

---

14 These figures were collated by Winstedt and Wilkinson (1934) from the historical records of the Dagh-Register held in Batavia castle in Jakarta and the VOC's headquarters in Asia; and by Lewis (1969) from the reports of the Dutch Governor of Melaka.

15 According to the 1746 agreement, tin was sold at 30 rials a *bahar* (1 *bahar* = 450 lbs), increasing to 34 rials a *bahar* in 1747.

high demand, other traders, including Bugis, Chinese, and British, who entered ports in the Strait of Melaka, continued to buy tin and ship it directly to Canton. For example, tin from Larut and Klian Intan in Hulu Perak was transported to Kedah and Penang, where it could be sold and shipped at a higher price.[16] Realizing that the VOC's tin monopoly was being undermined by leakages of tin from northwestern Perak and by smuggling, Pieter van Heemskerk, the Dutch Governor of Melaka (1748–1753), wrote in 1752:

> In spite of the careful watch kept at our Perak fort, the cunning natives leave no way unexplored in order to deceive our guards. They bring their tin down in two or three slabs in fishing perahu. Concealing them under nets and, under pretext of fishing, go past our fort to the mouth of the river. Here the tin is buried until the amount reaches a few Bahar. (cited in Andaya, 1979, p. 122)

In an attempt to thwart such 'cunning' moves, the VOC signed another contract, this time with Sultan Mahmud Shah II (1765–1773) in October 1765, through which the state's tin would continue to be sold exclusively to Dutch interests. Now, however, the sultan was expected to take harsh measures against smugglers, including confiscating their vessels and cargo, which would then be shared between the two parties (Maxwell, 1882a).

VOC's Decline and the Start of British Influence

By the late 18th century, the British East India Company was emerging as the VOC's most powerful regional trading rival, and in 1795 the Dutch temporarily gave up custody of Melaka. In the same year, the British sailed up the Perak River with a small force and forced the Dutch to surrender the Tanjong Putus fort. The VOC's influence declined further during the Napoleonic Wars (1803–1815). Despite the British returning Melaka to the Dutch in 1818 through the Treaty of Vienna, and although the Sultan of Perak signed a new contract with the VOC, Dutch traders were never able to regain a monopoly of Perak's tin (Maxwell, 1882a).

By the early 19th century, the port of Melaka had been eclipsed by the better-located commercial ports of Penang and Singapore, situated on the west and south coasts of the Malay peninsula. These two ports emerged as the pre-eminent trading centres of the Strait of Melaka. After the Anglo-Dutch Treaty of 1824, Dutch influence in the Malay peninsula ended, with the British giving up Bencoolen in Sumatra in exchange for Melaka. In 1825, the trading port-towns of Melaka, Penang, and Singapore were grouped together as the Straits Settlements under the

---

16 The *perahu* (a small sampan or wooden boat) operated by Malay traders sailed between Kedah and Penang, and brought back various goods to Perak, including cloth, salt, gambier, chinaware, tools such as *parang* and *keris*, and gold threads, all of which could be exchanged for tin.

authority of the East India Company, and were ruled by British India as a single administrative entity. Each of the Settlements had free-port status, with shipping and cargo entering and leaving without taxes imposed. International trade with Europe and the rest of Asia—particularly India and China—prospered.

British influence over the region began to be felt more strongly after its industrial revolution in the late 18th and early 19th centuries, which brought innovations in the large-scale factory production of manufactured goods. With the patenting of tin canning for preserving food in 1810, international demand for tin greatly increased. In Britain, canned foods were initially used by the British Army and Royal Navy, and were later commercialized and mass-produced for the public.[17] Tin had now become an indispensable commodity.

Perak's trade with its British, European, and other international partners was significantly boosted from around 1830, when Britain introduced more technologically advanced ships, boasting steam power and iron hulls, thus reducing transport time and freight rates. Moreover, the opening of the Suez Canal in 1869 shortened the vital sea route between Europe and the East by 4,000 miles, and the journey between Britain and the Straits Settlements now took weeks rather than months (Stopford, 2009).[18] The extension of the undersea cable network from Europe to Singapore in 1870 provided more timely information to agency houses about shipping and cargoes. During this period, Perak's trade became increasingly centred on the ports of Penang and Singapore, while the commercial importance of Melaka faded. In 1867, these three trading ports of the Straits Settlements came under the ambit of the British Colonial Office in London; at this time, Perak's tin trade was again starting to increase, with small steamers making daily trips conveying tin between Port Weld on the Larut River and Penang.[19]

Resisting Siam—Holding Back the Traditional Tributary Offering

At a time when international trade was starting to grow and there were prospects of a British trade monopoly, the British East India Company was keen to establish a base on the island of Penang. Captain Francis Light, a shipmaster of the Company,

---

17 Sardines were first canned in 1834, green peas in 1837, condensed milk in 1856, pineapples in 1882, and soup in 1897 (Reilly, 2002).

18 In the year following the opening of the Suez canal, 486 vessels passed through, with an aggregate of 435,911 tons. Five years later, this had increased to 1,494 vessels annually, with an aggregate of nearly 3 million tons (Bogaars, 1955).

19 In 1876, Perak's tin, valued at over Straits$147,000, accounted for more than 92 per cent of total exports. Rice was the main import, at Straits$50,000; it made up about 26 per cent of total imports, with opium the next biggest at 13 per cent (Straits Settlements, 1882).

landed in Penang in 1786 and took possession of the island. An agreement was reached between Light and the Sultan of Kedah, Abdullah Mukarram Shah (1778–1797), to cede Penang, based mainly on a promise to protect Kedah from enemy attacks (Anderson, 1856). However, the Company's leadership declined this condition, and the sultan disputed the occupation, which led Light to attack and defeat his forces in April 1791.[20] In May of that year, Penang was ceded to the Company by the sultan through a peace and friendship treaty. The signing of the treaty, and a subsequent treaty in 1800 which also ceded Province Wellesley, were, however, viewed by Siam as acts of defiance by Kedah, which was under Siamese influence during this period.

Siam sought to maintain its hold on the strategically important northern and east-coast states of the Malay peninsula. From the beginning of the 19th century, it was also trying to extend its sphere of influence further down the west coast and to incorporate Perak as a tributary state. As a sign of vassalage, the Malay rulers of Kedah, Kelantan, and Terengganu sent a tributary offering of the *Bunga Mas* (a golden flower) to the King of Siam in Bangkok every three years in return for peace. As long as Malay vassals recognized Siamese suzerainty and submitted their tribute, there was little interference in their internal affairs (Andaya and Andaya, 2017).

In 1816, Siam reasserted its influence and ordered the Sultan of Kedah to attack Perak, which was independent of Siamese control. The attack was repelled, however (Winstedt and Wilkinson, 1934). In 1818, after the British East India Company refused a request by Abdul Malik Mansur Shah, the Sultan of Perak (1806–1825), for support against the Siamese, Kedah mounted a second attack and reduced Perak to vassal status. At first the sultan refused to dispatch the *Bunga Mas* to Bangkok, but later succumbed to Siamese pressures (Bonney, 1974).

In 1821, Siamese troops overran Kedah. The Sultan of Kedah fled to Penang, as the troops once again pushed to expand Siam's control over Perak. However, they were defeated by Perak's Malays, and by 1822 the state's Siamese conquerors had been expelled with the help of Sultan Ibrahim Shah (1778–1826) of Selangor.[21]

---

20 The British East India Company's royal charter allowed it to wage war and to use military force to protect itself and fight rival traders. It seized control of states, appointed governors, and collected taxes and customs that were used to purchase local goods for export to the UK.

21 Perak was to pay tribute to Sultan Ibrahim for assisting it during this war. As early as 1819, Sultan Ibrahim's two sons were levying tolls on Perak's tin exports along the Perak River. In 1824, Selangor attacked and captured boats from Perak carrying tin for Ligor, and stationed a representative at Kuala Bidor to collect taxes on goods along the Perak River. In 1825, Perak asked for Siamese aid against the exactions of Selangor and to expel the Selangor forces. Because of Perak's own weakness, its strategy was to pit Siam against Selangor; the British refrained from armed intervention in the Malay states (Winstedt and Wilkinson, 1934).

The British East India Company adopted a favourable policy stance towards Siam because of its trade links with Bangkok, and because of their mutual hostility towards Burma.[22] British relations with Burma had deteriorated, and the British government did not want Siam to form an alliance with that country. Captain Henry Burney, a British envoy to the court of Siam, was assigned by the East India Company to negotiate with the Siamese. In June 1826, the Company signed a secret treaty, known as the Burney Treaty, with the Kingdom of Siam. Through the treaty, the Company acknowledged Siamese suzerainty over Kedah, Terengganu, and Kelantan—although the rulers of these states were not signatories—and Siam accepted British ownership of Penang and Province Wellesley, and agreed not to attack either Perak or Selangor. In Article XIV of the treaty, both the British East India Company and Siam recognized Perak's independence consistent with the Company's trading interest in the state.

In August 1826, however, Siam violated the Burney Treaty. Raja Ligor, Governor of the southern Siamese city of Ligor (now Nakhon Sri Thammarat), tried to force Sultan Abdullah Mu'azzam Shah of Perak (1825–1830) to send the *Bunga Mas* to Bangkok, and stationed Siamese troops in Perak.[23] The sultan requested British assistance, and Robert Fullerton—the first governor of the Straits Settlements (1826–1830) appointed by the East India Company, who was stationed in Penang—dispatched a warship and sepoys led by Captain James Low—a Malay- and Thai-speaking officer of the Company responsible for settling disputes with local leaders—to protect the sultan.

As Perak's sultan and chiefs considered the state to be independent under the Burney Treaty, they sided with the British instead of Siam. The Siamese troops withdrew, and on 18 October 1826, Low signed the Anglo-Perak Treaty with the sultan, with Articles I and II stipulating that Perak would not communicate or engage diplomatically with the King of Siam and his vassals, or 'give or present the *Bunga Mas* or any other tribute to Siam' or receive embassies, armaments, or the smallest parties of men other than non-political traders' (Hertslet, 1856, pp. 909–910). Based on these conditions, the British East India Company promised to assist the sultan if the Siamese attacked. The sultan publicly declared that he would not send the *Bunga Mas* to Bangkok. Given that the second 1826 treaty granted Perak British protection, Captain Low had violated British non-intervention policy taking these actions. In practice, however, the treaty was never formally ratified and eventually lapsed.

---

22 The pro-Siamese policy continued after the transfer of rule from the British East India Company to the Colonial Office in 1867.

23 Raja Ligor was responsible for ensuring that the Malay vassals submitted the *Bunga Mas*.

Traditional Governance Destabilized

Perak inherited its traditional political governance structure from the 16th-century Melaka royal court.[24] From as early as the 18th century, and even before, the state of Perak (*negeri Perak*) was a defined political territory within the Malay archipelago under an independent sovereign ruler—the sultan. Its capital was at Bandar Bahru, in the south of the state, where the Perak River runs into the Strait of Melaka. From these locations, the ruler could defend the state from external attack, control the movement of those who wished to enter or leave, and levy taxes on trade.

Perak was divided into districts (*daerah*), which were the main political units—territories shaped by the use of the Perak River and its tributaries as the dominant means of transport and communication. Each district was ruled by a chief whose lineage reflected long-established ties with the area. The *kampung* was the smallest political unit, one of common residence and, to some extent, of kinship and economic cooperation. The head of the *kampung*, the *ketua kampung*, was the bridge between the villagers and the *penghulu*, the sub-district chief (Gullick, 1958).

In 1746, a century after ties were first established, the Treaty of Peace and Alliance between Sultan Mudzaffar Shah III and the VOC marked the start of Perak's political autonomy; with reconfirmations, this treaty lasted for almost half a century until 1795.[25] As a written contract, the treaty provided Perak with Dutch protection, both against the increasing threat of the Bugis in the Strait of Melaka, and from invasion by the Siamese.[26] It also facilitated the Company's

---

24 The first Sultan of Perak, Mudzaffar Shah I (1528–1549), was the son of Sultan Mahmud Shah, the ruler of Melaka who survived the Portuguese attack of 1511.

25 The Dutch East India Company was temporarily expelled from Melaka by the British. On its return, the Company signed a new treaty that resumed its monopoly of the tin trade. However, this lasted just six years, after which Melaka became a British possession through the Anglo-Dutch Treaty of 1824.

26 Perak's diplomatic treaty with the Dutch East India Company marked the start of the use of written documents and letters within the Perak Court (Andaya, 1979).

Globalization: Perak's Rise, Relative Decline, and Regeneration. Sultan Nazrin Shah, Oxford University Press. © Sultan Nazrin Shah (2024). DOI: 10.1093/oso/9780198897774.003.0005

role in the small but profitable tin trade, over which it exercised a near monopoly, fixing the price of tin at a level which was advantageous to the Dutch while securing a small tax for the sultan. A Dutch resident was appointed by the Company as an intermediary between Melaka and the Perak Court. He was responsible for commanding a detachment of soldiers maintained at the Tanjong Putus fort, acted as the 'eyes and ears' of the Dutch Governor, and kept the Melaka Council well informed about events in Perak and the surrounding areas (Andaya, 1979, p. 89; Koster, 2005).

The Symbol of Perak's Unity—The Sultanate

The sultan was drawn from a royal patrilineage. By Malay tradition and custom, he was invested with the attributes of supernatural power and dignity. His main role was to symbolize and preserve Perak's unity through his government (*kerajaan*) (Gullick, 1958). Having a sultan or raja was, according to Milner (1982), the axis of Malay political culture from the 16th to the 19th century. The sultan was vested with royal majesty (*daulat*) at his installation. This made the sultan sovereign. Any Malay subject who undermined or threatened the sovereignty of the sultan would suffer retribution from the impersonal force of outraged royal dignity. Opposition was considered treason (*derhaka*), which brought severe punishment of death and dishonour. The formal submission of the chiefs to the sultan was symbolized and expressed in the obeisance (*menghadap*) ceremony; this had to be made by all chiefs at the installation of a sultan, and by an individual chief on first appointment. The chiefs, similarly, derived the title of their authority from the sultan under the 'constitutional theory of the Malay state' (Gullick, 1958, p. 48). A chief's power was derivative, and in important acts he sought the sultan's approval first.[27]

As the leader of a coalition of chiefs, the sultan led in matters of foreign affairs and defence. A treaty with a foreign power required the signature of the sultan. In translating his decisions into actions, the sultan made use of secretaries (kerani) for the drafting of written documents. There was no automatic right of succession; the succession was generally determined on a rotational basis among the leading royal families. The choice of a successor from among the royal lineage rested with the chiefs.[28]

---

27 For example, the maharaja lela and other chiefs who planned the assassination of the first British Resident of Perak in 1875 obtained a letter of authority to do so from Sultan Abdullah (Burns and Cowan, 1975).

28 Frequently, a sultan would advance the ablest of his sons so that he would stand a good chance in succeeding to the throne. The personality of the candidate greatly affected his prospects, as did the status of his mother. A man whose mother was of royal descent, especially if a daughter of a sultan, was preferred (Khoo, 1986).

In this traditional political system, religion helped to symbolize the unity of the state. While the Malays identified strongly with their state, which was symbolized more by their sultan than by their religion, the Islamic concepts of *dar al-Islam* (the abode of Islam) and *dar al-harb* (the abode of war) helped to define those who were legitimately excluded from the political system (Means, 1969). From 1874, post-Pangkor, when Malay rulers were given autonomy over matters of religion and *adat*, religion helped to support the ruler's legitimacy.

The Centrality of the Royal Court

Perak's Royal Court—the inner circle (*waris negeri*)—comprised (in descending order of authority) the raja muda, the raja bendahara, and members closely related to the ruler and in direct line to the throne (Khoo, 1986). Royals inherited their positions and status through birth. The raja muda was designated the future ruler of the Royal Court; he was a deputy of the sultan and acted as head of the members of the royal lineage (Gullick, 1958; Andaya, 1979).

No decision could remain secret from the Royal Court, and anything that affected the state had to be discussed in the Assembly, which included the raja muda, four chiefs of the first rank who formed the permanent core, and eight chiefs of the second rank. The roles of the first and second rank chiefs as they stood in the early 1870s are set out in Box 1.1.[29] Within the Assembly, the ministers of the state (*wazir negeri*) were the most influential, and a coalition of senior chiefs could in fact undermine the ruler's authority. The common man took no part in decision making, but could bring his grievances to the Assembly. The chiefs maintained the political and administrative power of the state.

Being the local focus of authority, the district chiefs formed the key institution in Perak's political system. As the administrator of justice, leader in war, collector of taxes, and provider of funds, a Malay chief exercised political power to preserve the basis of that authority. Traditional Malay political organization was incapable of operating as a centralized unitary system of control over the entire state, and power was dispersed among the district chiefs (Gullick, 1958). The

---

29 After the assassination of J. W. W. Birch in 1875, the royal positions of Orang Kaya-Kaya Seri Agar Diraja (Dato' Sagor) and Orang Kaya-Kaya Maharaja Lela were left vacant. Both titles were replaced with Orang Kaya-Kaya Setia Bijaya Diraja (in 1898) and Orang Kaya-Kaya Mahakurnia Indera Diraja (in 1933) respectively. In June 1987, Sultan Azlan Muhibbuddin Shah (1984–2014) reinstated the title of Orang Kaya-Kaya Seri Agar Diraja (Dato' Sagor) to replace that of Orang Kaya-Kaya Mahakurnia Indera Diraja. And in June 2023, Sultan Nazrin Muizzuddin Shah reinstated the title of Orang Kaya-Kaya Maharaja Lela to replace that of Orang Kaya-Kaya Setia Bijaya Diraja. The structure of the Royal Court as described in Box 1.1 remains much the same to the present, except that in 1958 the position of Raja Bendahara was abolished and replaced with Orang Kaya Bendahara Seri Maharaja by Sultan Yussuff Izzuddin Shah (1948–1963).

rights and privileges of district chiefs were usually left to be implied by custom and precedent. The actual political power of a chief depended on the size of his following in terms of kinsmen, aristocratic aides, and villagers—mainly farmers and fishermen—bound to him by ties of compulsion and of reciprocal self-interest. A Malay chief sought to promote the development of his district and to increase its productive population, so as to maximize the surplus which could be diverted for his own use and for the enhancement of his power (Gullick, 1958).

The chiefs imposed taxes on almost all varieties of traded goods, of which tin was by far the most valuable and in demand. As migrant Chinese mining communities began to settle in the state, some of the chiefs also benefited from taxes on opium, alcohol, and gambling through revenue farms. While the sultan was in theory entitled to collect certain taxes throughout the state, in practice it was not feasible to maintain tax collectors in every district without a centralized administration in the state capital. It appears that the sultan rarely received all the taxes that were due to him from outlying districts, and so was forced to rely on what he could collect at the royal capital, given that fiscal capacity was constrained. For the chiefs, tax revenues provided the means to achieve and maintain their hold on political power, especially through payments to their armed followers, which in turn preserved order (Gullick, 1958).[30]

Box 1.1   **The Malay chiefs of Perak, circa early 1870s**

The institution of the Malay chiefs was central to Perak's traditional political system. Beneath the sultan was the raja muda, and then the hierarchy centred on two divisions.

The Four Chiefs (Orang Kaya Empat)—First Division

1 **The Raja Bendahara** was the prime minister and commander-in-chief. On the death of a sultan, it was his duty to take possession of the royal regalia (the symbols of greatness that the sultan wears at his installation such as ceremonial swords—see appendix g in Winstedt and Wilkinson, 1934), and to act as regent. His income came mainly from tolls on the Kinta River.
2 **The Orang Kaya Besar Maharaja Diraja** was the sultan's treasurer, secretary, and chamberlain. This position was vacant in the 1870s. His income came largely from tolls at the mouth of the Perak River.

---

30 By contrast, Milner (1982, p. 163) contends that on the eve of colonial rule the relationship between the rulers and the ruled was motivated by the rulers' desire to retain their subjects, and was not simply about the rulers' exercise of power over the ruled. Services to the rulers offered 'social and spiritual possibilities inherent in the Malay system'.

3 **The Orang Kaya Temenggong Paduka Raja** was the chief of Kota Lama with responsibility for police and security matters. His income came predominantly from a monopoly on the sale of salt and thatched palm roofing (*atap*).

4 **The Orang Kaya Menteri Paduka Tuan** (the menteri) was assigned to the *de facto* ruler of Larut, Ngah Ibrahim, in 1858. He held wide powers, with the authority to make laws and deal directly with the British administration in Penang. In 1862, the sultan gave him full powers over tin-rich Larut.

The Eight Chiefs (Orang Besar Delapan)—Second Division

1 **The Orang Kaya-Kaya Maharaja Lela Tanjana Putra** (the maharaja lela) was the law enforcer, and stood at court ceremonies with naked sword, ready to behead anyone guilty of disloyalty. The last to hold the position of maharaja lela was Pandak Lam, the territorial chief of Pasir Salak. His income came chiefly from his district and from customs and tolls on the Dedap River.

2 **The Orang Kaya-Kaya Laksamana Raja Mahkota**, or Admiral, was the office held by the chief of Durian Sabatang. The laksamana had charge of the seacoast and the tidal reaches of the Perak River, and guarded against attack by sea. His income came primarily from fines in lower Perak and from tolls on the Batang Padang River.

3 **The Orang Kaya-Kaya Seri Adika Raja Shahbandar Muda** held a position in the upper Perak River similar to that held by the laksamana in its tidal reaches. His revenue came principally from duties on tin collected in upper Perak.

4 **The Orang Kaya-Kaya Shahbandar Paduka Indra** was a chief from Bandar Bahru, lower Perak, who acted as harbour master, chief customs officer, and controller of trade. His income came mainly from commissions on customs.

5 **The Orang Kaya-Kaya Panglima Kinta Seri Amar Bangsa Diraja** was the chief who oversaw the Kinta Valley, in east central Perak, and guarded Perak's eastern frontier with Pahang and Kelantan. His income came largely from a 10 per cent royalty on all tin mined in the Kinta area.

6 **The Orang Kaya-Kaya Panglima Bukit Gantang Seri Amar Diraja** guarded Perak's northern frontier. Initially, his income came primarily from Larut, but in the mid-19th century the menteri—a first-division chief—secured all the revenues of the Larut area.

7 **The Orang Kaya-Kaya Seri Agar Diraja** (the dato' sagor), Ngah Kamaddin, oversaw the banks of the Perak River from Kampung Gajah and Pulau Tiga. His income came principally from his district.

8 **The Orang Kaya-Kaya Imam Paduka Tuan** was the precursor of the modern-day Mufti who also served as the chief *kathi*. His income came from his congregation.

Sources: Winstedt and Wilkinson (1934); Cowan (1952); Gullick (1958).

Rising Tensions

As the 19th century progressed, tin became ever more important both in Perak and internationally. New tin fields were discovered, scattered throughout the state, and these were exploited using migrant Chinese communities that had largely replaced Malay miners. The richest early discoveries were in Larut. From here, tin could be exported to Penang without being transported down the Perak River. The inability of Perak's sultan to obtain more than a small proportion of the total tax revenues on tin, and the increased power of the chiefs in tin-rich districts, were the main factors that caused a dispersal of power from the central government to districts.

Perak's decentralized political system, regulated by *adat*, was thus ultimately highly vulnerable to the disruptive pressures and destabilizing forces that emerged as the tin industry grew. The presence of tin-mining centres greatly enhanced the value of some districts at the expense of others. The new pressures not only intensified struggles between the chiefs for control of the tin-rich districts but also heightened the complications of choosing a sultan. As the next section discusses, tin was to become the curse of Perak's traditional political system, which was ultimately to give way to a new colonial order.

From the Curse of Conflict to Colonialism, 1860–1874

Discovering valuable mineral resources should enable a state to strengthen its institutions and improve the well-being of its people. The more the market price of the mineral exceeds the costs of extraction, the higher the yield or economic rent; in boom times the windfalls are large and, with the right policies, can be converted into physical and human capital (Collier and Venables, 2011). But for the people of Perak, over the two decades between 1860 and 1880, there was little, if any, trickle-down benefit from the state's rich tin-mining fields. Instead, there was a 'curse' of civil wars, similar to the situation that prevails today in some mineral-resource-rich countries, especially in Africa.

The district of Larut, in the northwest of Perak, saw dramatic growth in its tin-mining industry from the 1840s. It remained the state's mining hub until its output was overtaken by Kinta's in the late 1880s. Yet, in the absence of a strong Perak-wide authority, Larut suffered from an early version of the 'resource curse', in the shape of three 'tin wars' between 1861 and 1873.[31] The intermittent violence claimed thousands of lives at a time when the international demand for tin ore for England's growing tin-plate manufacturing industry was rapidly increasing.

Disputes stemmed from bitter conflicts between rival secret societies—the Ghee Hin (predominantly Cantonese) and Hai San (predominantly Hakka and Hokkien)—for control of the increasingly lucrative mines.[32] Each side, mainly formed around dialect groups and clan membership, had supporters among the capitalist Chinese merchants based in the Straits Settlement of Penang, where the international port served Larut's tin exports. Aligned to the rival Chinese clans, and patronized by the Malay territorial chiefs, were two Penang-based

---

31 For discussion of the resource curse theory, whereby resource endowments can constrain growth, feed corruption, and spark conflict, see Collier (2007), Sachs and Warner (2001), and Stevens et al. (2015).

32 The Ghee Hin were known in Penang and Larut as the *Si Kwans* (four districts) and the Hai San as the *Go Kwans* (five districts) according to their district of origin in China.

Globalization: Perak's Rise, Relative Decline, and Regeneration. Sultan Nazrin Shah, Oxford University Press. © Sultan Nazrin Shah (2024). DOI: 10.1093/oso/9780198897774.003.0006

Malay groups: the *Bendera Putih* (White Flag), allies of the Ghee Hin and supported by Raja Abdullah; and the *Bendera Merah* (Red Flag), allies of the Hai San and supported by the menteri, Ngah Ibrahim, and by Raja Ismail (Purcell, 1967).[33]

Later, the conflicts became further complicated by brutal quarrels among the Malay rajas and their chiefs over succession to the throne, and the associated commanding share of the tin revenues. The rajas were allied to one or other of the secret societies' leaders, their allegiances shifting as they fought for dominance of the revenues from the tin trade. The chiefs, some of whom were much richer even than the sultan, regarded the mining revenues as their personal estates (Sadka, 1971).

Larut's mines were initially established on land owned by Long Ja'afar, a local Malay territorial chief.[34] At first, he directly engaged migrant Chinese mine workers, but later granted concessions to Chinese financiers from Penang who recruited and paid for their own workers.[35] The mining financiers paid a tax on the concessions. The sultan and his chiefs controlled the Perak River—the state's main highway at the heart of the traditional political order—and its network of tributaries (Map 1.3). Rivers were the main means of communication at that time: there were no tarred roads, and inland travel through the dense jungle took place mainly along pathways as well as bullock-cart and elephant tracks. The chiefs built stockades along the rivers, and every boat going up or down was obliged to stop and pay a toll. The chiefs fought—literally—for the right to collect these tolls. The Chinese readily paid, except when rival chiefs each placed stockades on the same river demanding double or even triple tolls. To protect themselves against extortion, the Chinese sometimes supported one of the contending parties and assisted in

---

33 The Red and White Flag secret societies gained prominence during the 1867 Penang riots (Mahani Musa, 1999), and became increasingly involved with opposing sides in the Larut tin wars (Wynne, 1941).

34 During the late 1840s, Long Ja'afar, the son of one of Perak's minor chiefs, was employed by the Panglima Bukit Gantang Seri Amar Diraja, a second-ranking chief, to collect taxes at Kerian and Kurau, with Larut also included in his territory. Before Long Ja'afar's arrival in Larut, only the panglima had any hold over the district. Even so, he was, as Wilkinson describes, 'simply a sort of warden of the marches guarding the pass that gave access to a large and isolated district' (Winstedt, 1935, p. 78).

35 Long Ja'afar granted the concession of the Larut mines to Chang Ah Kwee, a leader of the Hai San society, who subsequently parcelled out the land to miners originating from different districts in China for them to manage (Khoo, 1991). On Long Ja'afar's death in 1857, his son Ngah Ibrahim was granted the administration of Larut. The following year Sultan Ja'afar Mua'azzam Shah (1857–1865) granted him greater powers as the Orang Kaya Menteri Paduka Tuan—one of the four highest-ranking chiefs of Perak—including the power to make laws and deal directly with the British administration in Penang (Cowan, 1952).

Map 1.3   Perak, circa 1877

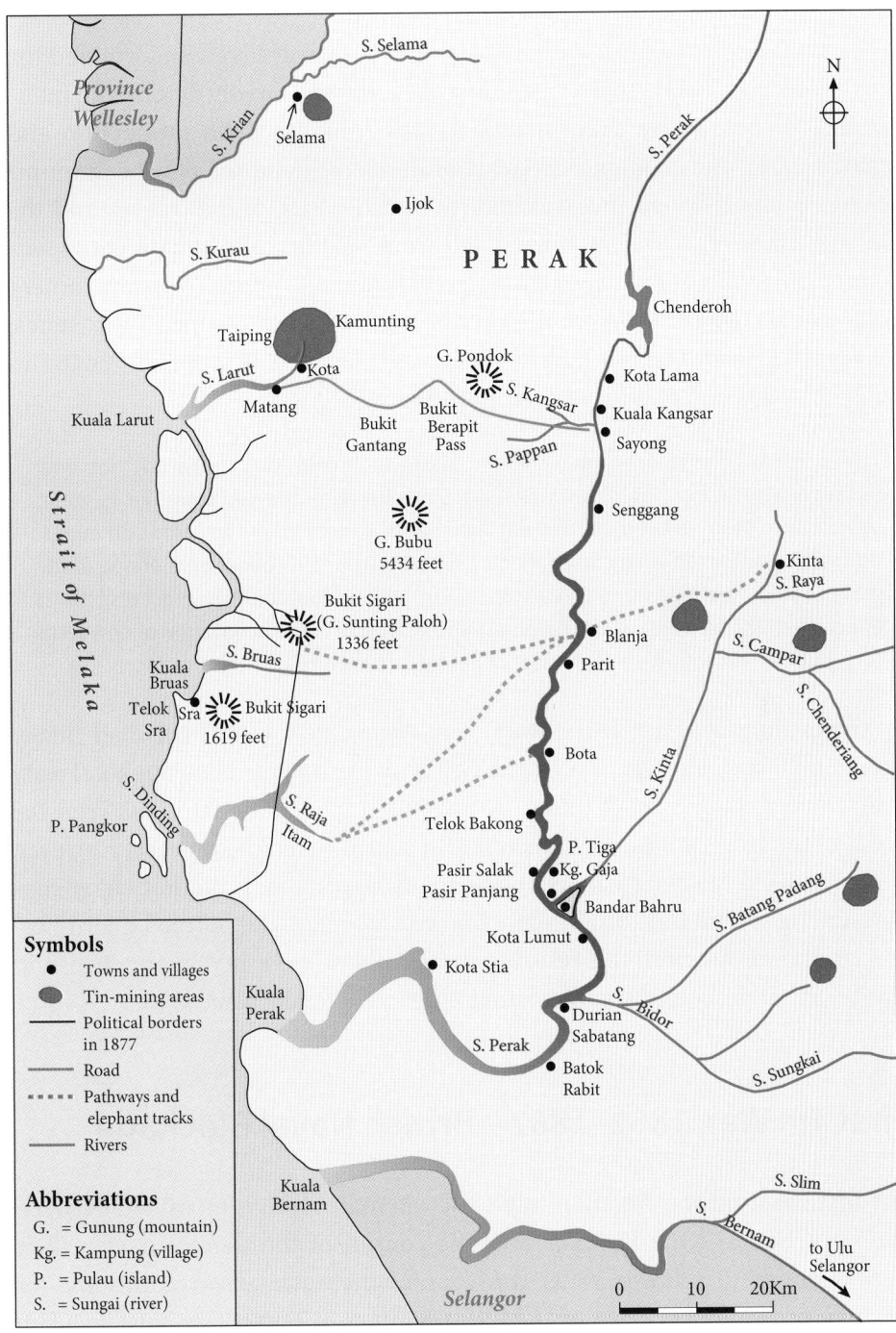

Province
Wellesley

S. Selama

Selama

S. Krian

Ijok

S. Kurau

P E R A K

S. Perak

Chenderoh

Taiping   Kamunting

Kota

G. Pondok

S. Kangsar

Kota Lama

S. Larut

Matang

Bukit
Berapit
Pass

Kuala Kangsar

Kuala Larut

Bukit
Gantang

S. Pappan

Sayong

Senggang

G. Bubu
5434 feet

Kinta
S. Raya

Bukit Sigari
(G. Sunting Paloh)
1336 feet

Blanja

S. Campar

Kuala
Bruas

S. Bruas

Parit

Telok
Sra

Sra

Bukit Sigari
1619 feet

S. Chenderiang

Bota

S. Kinta

S t r a i t   o f   M e l a k a

P. Pangkor

S. Dinding

S. Raja
Itam

Telok Bakong

P. Tiga

Pasir Salak
Pasir Panjang

Kg. Gaja

Bandar Bahru

S. Batang Padang

Kota Lumut

Symbols

- Towns and villages
- Tin-mining areas
— Political borders
  in 1877
— Road
▪▪▪▪ Pathways and
  elephant tracks
— Rivers

Kuala
Perak

Kota Stia

Durian
Sabatang

S. Bidor

S. Perak

Batok
Rabit

S. Sungkai

Abbreviations

G. = Gunung (mountain)
Kg. = Kampung (village)
P. = Pulau (island)
S. = Sungai (river)

Kuala
Bernam

Kuala
Bernam

S. Slim

S.

Bernam

to Ulu
Selangor

Selangor

0   10   20Km

N

Source: Adapted from Cowan (1952).

driving the others away, resulting in violent disturbances along the rivers (Archive document, CO 882/2, 1872–1874).

The chaos in Larut, including piracy along the Larut River, undermined the political stability and security necessary to exploit the rapidly developing international tin trade. The disturbances seriously disrupted tin production and began to affect the economic interests of the British and the other communities in Penang that had invested heavily in the mines. These factors, and the fear of Chinese civil war in Penang, led to increasing calls by influential sections of the Straits Settlements' trading community for the British government to change its long-standing policy of 'non-interference' in the Malay states. George William Robert Campbell, acting Lieutenant-Governor of Penang in 1872, observed (Command Papers [C.] 465, 1874, p. 10):

> This Settlement is deeply interested in whatever befalls Laroot [Larut], not only because, lying at our doors as it does, the trade between the two countries is great, but because much of the wealth of our merchants is invested in the Laroot tin mines. But the consideration which most affects us, perhaps, is that sooner or later one of the great Chinese fights is sure to spread to Penang, with undoubtedly the most disastrous effect. I believe the policy of the Colonial Office is averse to the acquisition of new territory, but if an exception is ever to be made it might well be made this instance.

By the beginning of 1874, the wars over control of the tin fields had finally ended, following intervention by the British government. The Pangkor Treaty was signed, bringing Perak under British protection, and a bond between the heads of the rival Chinese factions was also signed to maintain peace. However, fierce localized Malay resistance to the treaty continued. It did not enjoy support among several territorial chiefs, who considered that it harmed their interests, and it was not until this resistance was ruthlessly crushed by the British in late 1876 that peace and a new colonial order were finally achieved.

First Tin War, 1861–1862—British Naval Blockade

The first Larut tin war began in July 1861 when the rivalry intensified between the Ghee Hin and the Hai San over the control of the watercourse to their mines—access to a flow of water was vital for the water-wheel pumps and for washing tin ore. The Hai San worked the tin mines in Taiping and the Ghee Hin the mines in Kamunting (Map 1.3). The Chinese clan system meant that any quarrel between the men of the two rival villages could quickly develop into a serious clan fight, riot, or even civil war (Wilkinson, 1923). In what started as a conflict between rival miners, the Hai San took advantage of their numerical strength and attacked the Ghee Hin. The Ghee Hin were driven out of their mines with considerable loss of life and retreated to Penang, having first sought refuge in Larut's neighbouring district of Matang.

When news reached financiers and the Ghee Hin's leaders in Penang—many of whom were British subjects—appeals were made to William Orfeur Cavenagh, Governor of the Straits Settlements (1859–1867), for assistance in compelling Sultan Ja'afar, Perak's ruler, to secure compensation for the financial losses incurred in Larut. Sultan Ja'afar and his representative, Laksamana Mohamed Amin, failed to respond. As a result, two British gunboats, the *Mohr* and the *Tonze*, and a screw steamer, the *Hooghly*, were sent to blockade the Larut River. The blockade was effective. After coming to an agreement with Sultan Ja'afar, Ngah Ibrahim (the son of Long Ja'afar), who had grown extremely wealthy and influential from Larut's tin trade, agreed to pay the compensation, and was consequently rewarded by the sultan, who gave him full powers over Larut.

On 11 May 1862, Sultan Ja'afar wrote to Governor William Cavenagh:

I explained to Menteri Ngah Ibrahim what had been arranged by my representative, the laksamana, and my friend's representative regarding the sum of $174,474 to be paid as compensation to the Ghee Hin Chinese. Ngah Ibrahim accepted the arrangement and undertook to settle the claims to my friend's satisfaction and I also confirmed the administration of Larut in the hands of Ngah Ibrahim who will have full authority to deal with all matters with the concurrence of the laksamana. It is hoped that my friend will give assistance and consideration to Ngah Ibrahim to help relieve him of the burden imposed by the blockade of the steam ships and also my friend will arrange so that the laksamana may bring Ngah Ibrahim to meet the Resident Councillor of Penang so that the compensation may be paid. (cited in Khoo, 1972, p. 129)[36]

An uneasy peace settled in Larut; but further disturbances lay ahead, with Menteri Ngah Ibrahim at the forefront.

Second Tin War, 1865—Escalating Chinese Clan Rivalry

On 16 June 1865, after three years that had witnessed first a lull and then an increase in demand for tin, Larut's mining production was again disrupted when the second tin war broke out following a quarrel between a Hai San and

---

36 The Mexican/Spanish silver dollar was widely used in the Malay peninsula until the Straits$ was introduced in 1903 (see Box 1.6). Any reference made here to the dollar before 1903 is to the silver dollar.

a Ghee Hin at a gambling parlour. In the words of eye-witness Loh Chong, a Hokkien merchant from Penang:

> Soon afterwards about 20 Hai San men attacked the shop … the tin tongs began to beat from house to house and after them the drums' signals to call all the Hai San men together. They assembled quickly in great numbers. I think seven or eight hundred, and in my presence, seized and bound three or four Ghee Hin men whom they found in the bazar. About ten others were also taken and bound … and many of the Ghee Hin men there and in the neighbouring mines took the alarm and fled to Kamunting. On the morning of 17 June, about 1,000 Hai San men armed with muskets, knives, spears, shields and clubs attacked all the Ghee Hin shops and mines in Kamunting. (cited in Khoo, 1972, p. 136)

Fearing that the situation would worsen, Loh Chong mediated the conflict before Abdul Jabbar, a judge and magistrate of Larut. To resolve the quarrel, about 20 to 30 Malay armed guards were sent to Kamunting, and a few Hokkiens to Taiping. They returned at night, and implied that the Ghee Hin were willing to settle the matter and that an agreement would be drawn up the following morning. However, at midnight, the Hai San took 14 of their Ghee Hin prisoners and killed all except one, who managed to escape to Kamunting. At daybreak, 300 to 400 armed Ghee Hin retaliated and attacked the Hai San in Taiping.

Again, the Hokkiens mediated. On 19 June, they proposed that the Ghee Hin pay a fine of Silver$1,000 to the Hai San for their attack. But the Ghee Hin were indignant as so many of their number had been killed. Another fight broke out between the two parties and between their White and Red Flag allies. Some 200 armed Malays were sent to disperse the parties, but fighting continued until the Malays discharged a gun at the Ghee Hin, who then retired to Kamunting (Khoo, 1972).

The Hai San sought the aid of Ngah Lamat and Kulop Mat Ali, brothers-in-law of Menteri Ngah Ibrahim. They agreed that the spoils would be equally divided between the two of them, and made an oath to the Hai San leaders to assist them with an attack on the Ghee Hin, with approval from the menteri, who returned to Matang. Some 400 of their Malay Red Flag followers joined the Hai San in the attack and, by 20 June, the Ghee Hin had been decisively defeated. Their houses were destroyed. The victors plundered large quantities of tin and other valuables. The Ghee Hin, about 2,000 in number, were driven out of Kamunting and made their way through the jungle to Province Wellesley.

Third Tin War, 1872–1873—Battle for Perak's Throne

At the start of 1872, after a fragile seven years' peace, fighting broke out among Larut's Chinese miners, once again seriously damaging tin production. The Ghee Hin, forced out of Larut in 1865, were replaced by the Ho Hup Seah secret society from Penang. The Ho Hup Seah had only about 2,000 men, compared to the Hai San's approximately 10,000. The Ho Hup Seah eventually teamed up with the Ghee Hin to fight the Hai San, who continued to enjoy the support of Menteri Ngah Ibrahim (Khoo, 1972). Captain Tristram Charles Sawyer Speedy, the British Superintendent of Police in Penang, wrote this account:

> The jealousy of the headman of these societies culminated in an appeal to arms. After some serious fighting (in which it is stated that 3,000 Chinese lost their lives) the Hai San faction were expelled from Laroot [Larut], and the tin mines given over to the conquering party. During that disturbance the menteri of Laroot appears to have discountenanced the Hai San faction ... (C. 465, 1874, p. 14)

The fighting began in Larut and spread across other mining areas of Perak with raids and counter-raids, as each side attempted to oust the other. The Ho Hup Seah and Ghee Hin then drove the Hai San to Ngah Ibrahim's fort at Matang and finally out of Larut. Ngah Ibrahim, whose primary interest was the income from the mines, had no choice but to cooperate with the Ho Hup Seah. In October 1872, the Hai San counter-attacked from Penang and drove the Ho Hup Seah and Ghee Hin out of Larut. But in December 1872, the Ghee Hin from Penang raided the Larut coast and captured Matang. For several months after that, the belligerents saw near-stalemate, with the Ghee Hin and Ho Hup Seah controlling Kuala Larut up to Simpang, and the Hai San entrenched in the interior.

At this stage, another secret society entered the war; the Hokkien-based Toa Peh Kong. Traders belonging to different factions that had settled in villages in Perak—Kurau, Gula, Kalumpang, Selinseng, and Sapetang—began to suffer from depredations committed by the rival camps' ravaging parties. In early 1873, the Ghee Hin were reported to be in combat with the Toa Peh Kong at Gula. In retaliation, 'the Toa Peh Kong and Hai San went to Gula in five junks and six or seven boats and ... beat and plundered property and afterwards burnt houses of Ghee Hin traders' (Khoo, 1972, p. 172). The Hai San subsequently regained Larut, supported by Raja Muda Abdullah, and Ngah Ibrahim's properties in Matang were destroyed. The fighting later spread to other parts of Perak, including Kerian, Pangkor, and the Dindings.

The power struggle between the rival Chinese factions in Perak became increasingly linked to local Malay politics and a battle for the state's throne. Following the death of Sultan Ali Al-Mukammal Inayat Shah (1865–1871), Perak was no longer united by the authority of its ruler.[37] The throne had three competing claimants—Rajas Yusof, Ismail, and Abdullah. Raja Yusof, who controlled Senggang (Map 1.3), was the son of the previous sultan, Sultan Ja'afar, and had the most direct lineage claim, but he was disliked by many of the chiefs; he was overlooked, just as he had been previously, following the death of his father (Cowan, 1952). Raja Ismail, who controlled Sayong in upper Perak and had strong mining interests in Kinta, was supported by the powerful and wealthy menteri and his Hai San and Red Flag Malay allies. Raja Muda Abdullah controlled lower Perak from Batok Rabit, and tried to secure the support of the Ghee Hin in return for the promise of mining concessions, but he, too, was passed over. Abdullah could legitimately claim succession to the throne as the raja muda. However, he failed to attend Sultan Ali's funeral out of fear of being attacked by Raja Yusof at Senggang on his way upriver; and attendance at the former sultan's funeral was deemed essential to succeed to the throne. This is what led several of the chiefs to choose Raja Ismail as the new sultan in an election that was to be long and bitterly contested.

Raja Muda Abdullah, meanwhile, was also acknowledged as sultan by other chiefs, and he appointed Raja Yusof as the raja muda to gain his support.[38] In September 1872, Abdullah intervened in Larut's affairs by aligning himself with the opponents of the menteri—the Ghee Hin and the White Flag Malays—and started collecting tin revenues along the river. This Malay struggle for control of the river outlets was complicated by the far more bitter and violent struggle between the Chinese factions for control of Larut's tin mines. Until 1872, the menteri enjoyed all the district's royalties and other revenues, which surged with the growth of the Chinese mining population, roughly estimated at around 40,000 by end-1871. The value of tin imported by Penang that year, the greater part of which came from Larut, was stated in official returns at Silver$1,276,518. In early 1873, however, because of the menteri's vacillating conduct in dealing with the rival factions—he was indifferent to both sides so long as he received the revenues from Larut—the Ghee Hin and Hai San jointly drove the menteri and his Malay followers out of Larut and into Penang (CO 882/2, 1876), thereby ending the third war.

---

37 Sultan Ali had succeeded Sultan Ja'afar upon his death in 1865.

38 Raja Muda Abdullah wrote to the governor of the Straits Settlements, stating what had happened and asking that he should be recognized by the British as Perak's rightful sultan. Raja Ismail had earlier done the same.

From February of that year, the rival Chinese clans in Larut extended their war from land to sea. Serious disturbances in the form of river piracy and raids off the coast of Larut flared between rival fleets of boats, with the loss of many lives. In September 1873, two Ghee Hin war boats plundered Malay vessels that were proceeding up the Larut River and killed their sailors. Around this time, Raja Muda Abdullah, who wanted a share of Larut's tin revenues, saw an opportunity to obliterate the menteri. He and his Ghee Hin allies—to whom Abdullah had promised sole possession of the mines on the condition that they pay taxes to him—destroyed the menteri's private residence in Penang, wounding five of his men and killing a policeman who had sided with the opposition (Winstedt and Wilkinson, 1934).

The Chinese merchants in Penang appealed to the Chinese in Singapore and even as far as China for assistance, arms, and boats. In February 1873, the Executive Council of the government of the Straits Settlements issued a proclamation under the 1867 Arms Exportation Act to prohibit the export of arms, ammunition, and warlike stores to any part of the country between the Kerian boundary and the rivers that provided access to the Perak River. The menteri employed Captain Speedy—who, in July 1873, resigned from his position as a British police officer in Penang—to recruit Indian troops from the Punjab for service in Larut.[39] Speedy enlisted more than 100 men and, with a flotilla of two steamers and 15 small sailing-craft, conveyed arms, munitions, and stores to the Hai San miners in Larut. In September 1873, the menteri, who still enjoyed moral support from the Penang government, was exempted from the arms embargo (CO 882/2, 1876). The Ghee Hin were in a terrible position—blockaded and starved, with British gunboats surrounding them from the sea, and Captain Speedy and his troops surrounding them on land (Wilkinson, 1923). Yet, despite the huge advantages possessed by the Hai San, the Ghee Hin held their own.

The *rakyat* were also badly hit, because traders feared pirates who often attacked them along the coast; nor would traders bring rice up the river, wary of punitive and arbitrary tolls. Consequently, Kuala Kangsar experienced famine in 1874 (Gullick, 2010). All the while, the ordinary people had to provide both the manpower and the supplies to sustain the ongoing disputes over the succession to the throne. Ultimately, the three tin wars were highly consequential because they caused local Malay leaders to press British authorities in the Straits Settlements to intervene in Perak.

---

39 Captain Speedy had been a police officer in India before heading the force in Penang in 1872. There, his services were highly praised by Penang's Chinese community for his handling of the repercussions of the Larut disturbances (Gullick, 1953).

The Pangkor Engagement, 1874—From War to Uneasy Peace

Alarmed by the high costs of war, loss of life, lawlessness, and destruction of the Larut mines, some Malay chiefs, Chinese clan leaders, and merchants in the Straits Settlements sought British intervention. Penang's colonial government was concerned about the serious fighting, both because of the huge fall in trade with Larut—much of the wealth of Penang's merchants was invested in the now idle mines—and because of the possibility that the disturbances might spread to Penang.

In March 1873, some 248 merchants of the Straits Settlements signed a petition to Harry Ord, the first Governor of the Straits Settlements (1867–1873) appointed by the Colonial Office, requesting that he intervene in the Larut war and establish British authority in the Malay states. By this time, disorder had spread beyond Perak to Langkat, Rembau, and Sungai Ujong (now Negeri Sembilan), and both Perak's and Selangor's trade had virtually ceased (CO 882/2, 1876). Faced with these dire circumstances, the Straits Settlements' government appealed to the British Colonial Office—which had been averse to the acquisition of new territory because of the potential costs of defending it—to make an exception. Ord later reported in 1874:

> I was well aware that if the natives could be brought to feel that the Government was prepared to interfere, by force if necessary, for the protection of life and property within their territories, their security would be easily maintained, and it was notorious that such a policy was in entire accord with the views and wishes of the Straits community. But this course, as I have shown, was not open to me, and the measures that were at my disposal, though freely made use of, proved insufficient to attain the desired end. (CO 882/2)

At the end of 1873, seizing an opportunity to strengthen his claim to the throne, Raja Muda Abdullah requested that Andrew Clarke, the new Governor of the Straits Settlements (1873–1875), prepare a mutually beneficial treaty with the British government.[40] His letter inviting the colonial administration to 'pacify' Perak and appoint a resident provided the basis for the British to intervene more formally in protecting and expanding their economic interests (Parkinson, 1964).

The rival Chinese clans also appealed to the British government to arbitrate their disputes, particularly on the distribution of Larut's mines and in relation

---

40 As Andrew Clarke was contemplating intervention, he was forced to choose between two 'sultans', and to decide how to handle the menteri who had been recognized by his predecessor Ord. He chose to deal with Raja Muda Abdullah.

to the watercourses. They also requested that a British officer govern the people based on principles of justice. At a meeting between Andrew Clarke and the Chinese headmen, Singapore's Attorney-General Thomas Braddell (1867–1882) recorded:

> They said they were tired of fighting, their losses were enormous, thousands of their men had been killed, and their property destroyed; that, if left to themselves in this, as in other cases of quarrel, … they would have settled; but they had got mixed up with Malay politics and found it now impossible to do anything without the assistance of government … (cited in Jackson, 1965, pp. 23–24)

A Straits Settlements Association was established in London to pressure the Colonial Office into extending British influence over the Malay states. Instructions from John Wodehouse, the Earl of Kimberley, Secretary of State for the Colonies (1870–1874), to Andrew Clarke to restore peace and order are generally understood to have provided the basis for British intervention. These instructions were seen as both highly beneficial to British economic interests and closely aligned with those of the mercantile community in the Straits Settlements (Khoo, 1966). They helped to protect existing British investments while also creating an enabling environment for future ones. As Kimberley noted in his instructions to Governor Clarke:

> The anarchy which prevails and appears to be increasing in parts of the Peninsula, and the consequent injury to trade and British interests generally, render it necessary to consider seriously whether any steps can be taken to improve their condition. (C. 465, 1874, p. 39)

In 1874, Clarke stated that the disruption to trade along the northern coast of the peninsula made it imperative for the British 'to end this condition of anarchy and confusion' (C. 465, 1874, p. 70). The governor was determined to take up the matter himself. There were four key issues to be dealt with: the disputed succession to the Perak throne, the position of the menteri, the disputes among Chinese over the Larut mines, and the actions of the combatants at sea, which had degenerated into piracy (CO 882/2, 1872–1874). Reinforcing the belief in the economic benefits of having a British resident in Perak, and reflecting the views of the Penang Chamber of Commerce, Clarke wrote in his response to Kimberley:

> I find, on every side, the most unhesitating and unvarying expression of opinion, both European and native, that nothing but the residence of a British officer can bring about in any of these States [Perak, Selangor, and Negeri Sembilan] that pacification which

is so greatly needed, and from the absence of which trade and commerce have at last become completely paralyzed. (C. 465, 1874, p. 109)

At Pangkor, Raja Muda Abdullah, whom Clarke had favoured over Ismail, was unanimously chosen by the Malay chiefs to be the Sultan of Perak.[41] A treaty was signed—the Pangkor Engagement of 1874—with the British authorities administering his state. The menteri was confirmed as the chief of Larut, but was no longer its independent ruler. Captain Speedy, who had ended his employment with the menteri, was appointed Assistant Resident (1874–1877), and was immediately stationed at Larut. Speedy quickly set about administering Larut—which had a predominantly Chinese population at that time—establishing several government departments, including for revenue collection and public works, and a network of police stations and a magistrate's court (Sadka, 1954).

> The Governor's action was received with high approval by all classes and nationalities in the colony. ... This new departure was not to be plain sailing; indeed, the real difficulties had not even begun. They were to last for years, and only after the loss of many valuable lives, the expense of infinite persistence and resources, did this novel experiment end in complete success. (Swettenham, 1906, pp. 177–178)

The treaty provided for the appointment of a British resident to 'advise' the Sultan of Perak in all matters affecting the general administration of the state, except those relating to Malay custom and religion. The resident's advice was to be sought and acted upon, including in the areas of maintaining peace and security, and overseeing the collection of tax revenues, out of which the costs of British administration would be met. The treaty strengthened the sultan's sovereignty and his power over the chiefs, and by this means also provided the British government with the agency of the sultan to bolster its governance. It also provided the basis for establishing and developing the institutions, systems, and infrastructure that would support the exploitation of Perak's natural resources. It marked an important first step towards integrating the Straits Settlements' economies with those of the peninsula's west-coast Malay states.

One key objective of British government policy was to restart Larut's tin production, but this could only happen after the mining disputes among the Chinese factions were settled. With the fighting ongoing, the Larut mines were at

---

41 Besides Raja Muda Abdullah, the Pangkor Treaty was signed by all of the first-ranking chiefs who were in office, the bendahara, the temenggong, and the menteri; three of the second-ranking chiefs, the shahbandar, the laksamana, and the dato' sagor; and one of the third-ranking chiefs, the raja mahkota (Allen et al., 1981). The proceedings of the Pangkor meeting as written by Thomas Braddell are given in CO 809/1, with extracts in Cowan (1952).

a standstill. Only about 10 per cent of the population remained, mainly fighting men of both sides—the Hai San and Ghee Hin (Khoo, 1991). Clarke sent William Alexander Pickering to negotiate with the Chinese factions. Pickering was the officer in charge of Chinese affairs in Singapore, being the only European officer who spoke fluent Chinese, and in 1877 was appointed Protector of Chinese for the Straits Settlements. His objective in Penang was to persuade both sides to accept the Governor's arbitration of their differences, and to meet Clarke at Pangkor. Pickering achieved this outcome (Gullick, 1953).

The leaders of the rival Chinese factions also signed an agreement at Pangkor, stating that all contending parties should be disarmed and stockades destroyed and that all miners should return to work. A Commission of Settlement was established at the arbitration meeting to ensure that the agreement was followed and to adjudicate on the disputed claims to Larut's tin-mining areas. After a month's work, the Commission agreed to divide the mining areas into two halves, allocating one group to each side, and decreed that all future arrangements for the supply of water to the mines would be regulated by the British assistant resident stationed in Larut (Gullick, 1953).[42] Although both the Taiping and Kamunting mines were reopened in March 1874, it took some months to repair the damage inflicted during the wars, and no significant tin ore shipments were sent out before the end of July 1874. Output for the rest of the year, however, was 11,000 piculs, with the number of mining workers also rising rapidly, and the number of mines increasing from 30 to 120 (Gullick, 1953).

---

42 The Commission of Settlement—comprising William Pickering, Frank A. Swettenham, Colonel Dunlop, Chang Ah Kwee (leader of the Hai San), and Chan Ah Yam (leader of the Ghee Hin)—visited Larut and neighbouring districts for a month in February 1874. The Commission rescued several women and children who had been held captive during the fighting (Swettenham, 1906).

Pangkor—Resistance, Retaliation, and Reflection, 1874–1877

The Pangkor Treaty was signed on 20 January 1874 by the British government and many, but not all, of Perak's hereditary Malay leaders (Sultan Nazrin Shah, 2019). Crucially, both Raja Yusof and Maharaja Lela Pandak Lam—an important chief of Pasir Salak—were not invited to the meeting. In addition, Raja Ismail, although invited, neither attended the meeting nor acknowledged his invitation.[43] The 'failure of the Straits government to consider Yusof's claims or invite him to the Pangkor meeting' were serious oversights on Clarke's part (Cowan, 1952, p. 57). The treaty guaranteed British protection of Perak and began a period of indirect rule, which was soon extended to two other west-coast states of the Malay peninsula—Selangor and Sungai Ujong (later to the whole of Negeri Sembilan)—and to Pahang in 1888.

Although the treaty led to a resolution of the disputes in the mines and to the appointment of Raja Muda Abdullah as the Sultan of Perak, it was met with immediate resistance from some of the competing sections of Perak's royalty, their chiefs, and their followers—especially from Raja Ismail, whom Menteri Ngah Ibrahim now strongly supported despite having signed the treaty. This was in part because the Engagement, while securing the position of the sultan, undermined traditional Malay institutions as well as existing administrative and financial systems.

Foremost among the grievances about the Engagement was the fact that local chiefs were disempowered and could no longer collect and spend revenue as they pleased and according to custom. The sudden transition towards a centralized system of revenue collection also severely curtailed the existing modes of wealth acquisition used by other members of Malay royalty. Although Article IX of the treaty provided for a civil list that sought to compensate the local chiefs for their loss of revenue and power by offering generous pensions and

---

43 Ismail was, however, allowed to retain the title of Sultan Muda with a pension, and a small territory was assigned to him through one of the provisions of the treaty (Allen et al., 1981).

Globalization: Perak's Rise, Relative Decline, and Regeneration. Sultan Nazrin Shah, Oxford University Press. © Sultan Nazrin Shah (2024).
DOI: 10.1093/oso/9780198897774.003.0007

allowances, as well as appointments to offices in the administration, it was only implemented after the arrival of Hugh Low, Resident of Perak, in 1887 (Sadka, 1954).

In April 1874, Andrew Clarke sent James W. W. Birch,[44] accompanied by Frank A. Swettenham,[45] on a month's visit to Perak to observe and report on progress since the signing of the treaty. On their journey inland down the Perak River they separately interviewed Sultan Abdullah, Raja Muda Yusof, and Raja Ismail, and tried unsuccessfully to persuade Ismail to relinquish the royal regalia. Ismail—who was still strongly supported by the menteri whose power had been confirmed in the treaty—refused to pass on the royal regalia to Sultan Abdullah, thereby delaying the final ceremonial installation. This was despite threats by Birch and Swettenham that if he did not give up the regalia, it would be taken by force by the governor and his troops (Cowan, 1952).

In June, Clarke, recognizing that Ismail and Yusof were two of the most important opponents of the treaty, sent Swettenham to try to persuade them to meet him in Penang. Yusof agreed and, after meeting Clark, he and his son-in-law Raja Idris were alone among the royalty in supporting British policy. Ismail declined to attend, however, and remained implacably opposed to the treaty and other political proposals made by the British.

Resistance, Assassination, and Uprising

Political resistance to the Engagement among some of Perak's Malay royalty, chiefs, and their followers was eventually brutally crushed, but not before it had led to the killing, on 2 November 1875, of the state's first British Resident, J. W. W. Birch.

In early November 1874, London's formal approval for the Pangkor Treaty had finally arrived in Singapore, and the appointment of Birch as the Resident of Perak was confirmed after a 10-month delay. At Andrew Clarke's direction, a proclamation was published stating that the British Secretary of State for the Colonies had approved all of the arrangements made at Pangkor, and warning that these arrangements must be strictly observed. Even though the disputes of

---

44 Before his appointment as Perak's resident, Birch served as Colonial Secretary of the Straits Settlements (1870–1874), reporting directly to the governor in Singapore. Before that he served in Ceylon for 24 years, culturally a world away from the Malay states.

45 In 1874 and 1875, Swettenham went on several special missions to Perak, aged just 24 on the first, where he also helped as an interpreter (including during the meeting of the Pangkor Engagement) and served in the Perak War, which he chronicled in five journals that were first edited and published in 1952 (Cowan, 1952).

the Chinese had been settled, and Larut's tin mines were now increasing output, engendering a prosperity 'exceeding anything ever known before' (Swettenham, 1906, p. 194), it was an uneasy calm that reigned in Perak.

Since the Pangkor signing, Sultan Abdullah had used his increased status and power to grant a licence to mine for tin on land in the district of Selama. This upset the menteri, who considered this his territory (Gullick, 1953). The menteri was also dissatisfied because, instead of holding an almost independent position, as he had done previously, he was now subordinate to Sultan Abdullah, whom he disliked. Sultan Abdullah was not acknowledged by Perak's up-country people, and with Raja Ismail, Raja Muda Yusof, and their chiefs also quarrelling among themselves over revenues, Resident Birch was quickly drawn into the dispute.[46] The drafters of the treaty had seriously miscalculated the challenges of establishing a uniform state-wide taxation system. Tensions heightened further when Birch gave shelter and assistance to runaway slaves, threatening the Malay elite custom of slave-keeping.[47] Both these matters challenged traditional customs.

By mid-1875, 18 months after the signing of the treaty, implementation progress was slow. Persistent and assertive attempts by Resident Birch to get Raja Ismail and the maharaja lela to sign up to the terms of the treaty had failed. Birch and Sultan Abdullah disagreed about many matters. Sultan Abdullah delayed accepting Birch's advice on reforms, especially on stopping the chiefs from collecting taxes, and Birch could not force the other's hand. Abdullah and Ismail and their respective chiefs were still grappling over who was the rightful sultan, which in effect meant that two sultans were ruling over different parts of Perak—an untenable state of affairs.

At the end of May 1875, William Francis Drummond Jervois succeeded Andrew Clarke as the new Governor of the Straits Settlements (1875–1877). In September 1875, Jervois visited Perak accompanied by Birch, Swettenham, and other officials. Journeying from Larut down the Perak River, Jervois met first with Raja Ismail, then with Raja Muda Yusof, and finally with Sultan Abdullah at Pasir Panjang, where Birch was temporarily stationed. The meetings ended without a satisfactory conclusion, with Raja Ismail, at the menteri's instigation, distancing himself from the Pangkor Treaty and Jervois's new policy proposals.

---

46 At a meeting with Swettenham in June 1874, Sultan Abdullah had requested approval to manage Larut's mining revenues, which under the rule of the menteri had gone to him. His request, however, was refused. Now a portion of the revenues would be retained for the British administration, and the remainder would be used for the development of Perak (Cowan, 1952).

47 Purcell (1965, p. 287) estimated that at least one-eighth of Perak's population in 1875 were slaves.

Having taken stock of his briefs, Jervois was frustrated by the lack of reforms since the Pangkor Treaty had been signed, and unconvinced of the efficacy of the residential system. Without seeking London's prior approval, he decided unilaterally that he would appoint a Queen's Commissioner with the assistance of a Malay Council to run Perak's administration, instead of the resident—thus adopting direct rather than indirect rule.[48] He may have felt emboldened by the fact that, a year earlier, the Conservative Benjamin Disraeli had taken over as British prime minister from the enlightened Liberal William Ewart Gladstone, with a new and much more forceful imperial policy.

After his return to Singapore on 27 September 1875, Jervois wrote to Sultan Abdullah expressing his disappointment with matters in Perak, noting that the agreed tax arrangements were not being implemented, and that the administrative progress envisaged at Pangkor had not been achieved. In his letter, Jervois set out a new arrangement whereby the British would govern Perak in the sultan's name; Sultan Abdullah was offered a large allowance if he agreed. In the same letter, Jervois presented Sultan Abdullah with an ultimatum, threatening that if he did not agree to the proposed new arrangements, he would no longer be sultan. With this dire warning, and knowing that Yusof had already agreed to the proposed arrangement 'to declare Perak British territory, and govern it accordingly', Sultan Abdullah reluctantly accepted, signing the relevant documents, which he gave to Birch (C. 1505, 1876, No. 49, p. 36).

There were two proclamations, one about the collection of taxes and spending of revenues, including for the payment of allowances to Perak's chiefs, and the other about maintaining justice through the appointment of judges (of which Birch was to be one) who would also have the power to appoint magistrates. With Sultan Abdullah's signature now secured, on 3 October 1875 Swettenham left Birch and briefly returned to Singapore to meet Jervois to obtain the official proclamation necessary to give effect to the new arrangements—which was issued on 15 October. It was now the declared intention of the British government seemingly 'in compliance with the request of the sultan and the chiefs of Perak' to rule in the sultan's name (Cowan, 1952, p. 28).

On 16 October 1875, Jervois reported to Henry Herbert, the Earl of Carnarvon, Secretary of State for the Colonies (1874–1878), that while Larut had prospered since the Pangkor Treaty, the area was an exception, and that in all the districts where 'Abdullah, Ismail, and other chiefs have had their sway, there are

---

48 On his visit to Perak, Jervois had also remarked that 'the conditions of the slaves in Perak must in time form the subject of investigation by the British officers and the *Waris*' (Cheah, 1998, p. 95).

but few signs of improvement' (C. 1505, 1876, No. 49, p. 33). At the same time, Perak's treasury had no money available for payment of the fixed allowances for Sultan Abdullah, Raja Muda Yusof, and other chiefs as set out in the treaty (C. 1709, 1877, No. 12). Jervois then requested approval for his new political proposals for governing Perak by direct rule.

Meanwhile, marking the start of Perak's war of resistance, Sultan Abdullah had summoned the chiefs—though not those aligned with Raja Yusof. At the first meeting, on 21 July 1875, there was an agreement to kill Birch, and Abdullah then proceeded to procure weapons and ammunition from Penang with the aim of driving the British out. At a second meeting, in early October, Sultan Abdullah informed the chiefs that under British instructions he had reluctantly handed over the government of Perak. The maharaja lela, critical of Abdullah for signing away his authority to the British but friendly with Ismail and the menteri, said that he 'would not accept any orders from the Resident, and if Mr Birch came to his village he would kill him' (Swettenham, 1906, p. 201), and the dato' sagor concurred.

The chiefs, so disunited on many matters—indeed, so accustomed to double-crossing one another—put up a united front and, at the menteri's insistence, Abdullah instructed his clerk to write a letter, also sent to Ismail, authorizing the maharaja lela to kill Birch, and sent him arms and ammunition, and later a valuable *keris* (dagger), which was a symbolic command to proceed with the killing of the sultan's enemy (Winstedt and Wilkinson, 1934).[49]

From his residency in Bandar Bahru, Birch instructed Swettenham to travel up the Perak River to Ismail and the up-country chiefs, and there distribute the two proclamations signed by Sultan Abdullah, Jervois's proclamation, and several notices relating to the new governance and taxation arrangements. Swettenham was then to return to meet Birch around 3 November at Pasir Salak, the home village of the maharaja lela.

On 28 October, Swettenham set out along the Perak River to post the proclamations at strategic villages, passing through Kuala Kangsar—where he had a cordial meeting with Raja Muda Yusof, who was supportive of the proclamations—and on to Kota Lama (Map 1.3). The further upriver he went, the more hostile his reception, but he managed to complete his mission, surviving failed attempts on his life as he returned (Swettenham, 1903).

Departing on the same day, Birch went downriver to distribute the proclamations. On 1 November he arrived at Pasir Salak, accompanied by Lieutenant

---

49 According to Cheah (1998), the maharaja lela distrusted Abdullah and considered Ismail to be Perak's real ruler.

Thomas Francis Abbott,[50] his Malay interpreter Mat Arshad, sepoy guards, and several boatmen. They moored on the right bank of the Perak River, close to the maharaja lela's house. The sepoys and boatmen went ashore, but Birch remained aboard. He sought an interview with the maharaja lela but was refused.

Before Birch's arrival, the maharaja lela had met the villagers of Pasir Salak and informed them that Sultan Abdullah and the downriver chiefs had ordered the killing of Birch. He produced the sultan's letter, giving it to his brother-in-law, Pandak Indut, who was one of Raja Ismail's chiefs, to read out, and requested that the villagers follow his brother-in-law's orders (Swettenham, 1906; Gullick, 1958). The maharaja lela declared that he would not submit to anyone but the sultan, and waited to hear if the resident would post the proclamations, which he saw as presaging the end of Malay traditional rights and rule. He ordered his men, who numbered about 70, to tear down the proclamations and, if they were reposted, to run amok and kill.

The next morning, Birch directed Mat Arshad to attach the proclamations to the shutters of a Chinese goldsmith's shop, and he himself entered a floating bathhouse to take a bath on the riverbank. Pandak Indut tore down the proclamations and took them to the maharaja lela. Birch asked Mat Arshad to post them again.[51] As he set about doing so, he was speared by Pandak Indut who cried out 'Amok! Amok!' (Swettenham, 1906, p. 206). The crowd of villagers, armed with spears and daggers, rushed the bathhouse, where they speared the resident and hacked him with a sword. His body fell into the river (Winstedt and Wilkinson, 1934).[52]

After Birch's murder, the maharaja lela came from his house and gave the order to burn Birch's boat and kill the sepoys and boatmen. But they managed to escape, and only two others died. The maharaja lela then sent a message to the laksamana for Sultan Abdullah, and wrote to Raja Ismail, informing him of what he had done, sending the shell of Birch's burned-out boat along with the letter. The maharaja lela was 'above the law [in Perak], … ready to behead anyone for disloyalty. It was his privilege to execute for such crimes without awaiting the Sultan's permission' (Box 1.1 and Swettenham, 1952, p. 138).

---

50 On arrival at Pasir Salak, Lieutenant Abbott left Birch and went across the river to Kampung Gajah, the dato' sagor's village, to shoot snipe. On hearing about what had happened to Birch, he escaped downstream in a canoe (Swettenham, 1903).

51 P. B. Maxwell, based on a report in *The Times* (1875), stated that their fellow Malay countryman Mat Arshad had antagonized the perpetrators in Pasir Salak by striking Pandak Indut, and that this had resulted in Birch's murder (Maxwell, 1878).

52 Birch's body was recovered and buried on 6 November 1875 on the right bank of the Perak River facing upstream at Bandar Bahru in lower Perak, where he had established the residency. Captain William Innes, and other soldiers who lost their lives, were buried in the same place a few days later.

The proclamations that had led to so much bloodshed constituted a symbolic taking of possession of Perak by the British government. Peter Benson Maxwell—father of William Edward Maxwell, who later became Governor of the Straits Settlements—noted that this was an act of hostility which the actual rulers had a right to repel, and that the maharaja lela did his duty by his sovereign of an independent state in resisting an attack on his sovereign's rights (Maxwell, 1878, p. 56). Governor Jervois had had no authority to try to enter into these new political arrangements and was later reprimanded by the Colonial Office in London. When censured, Jervois said that he had taken the initiative because it was imperative to restore order (C. 1505, 1876).

Retaliation

On 5 November 1875, Swettenham and Lieutenant Abbott returned to the residency at Bandar Bahru with its garrison of Indian Sikhs, and summoned support from Penang to put down the perpetrators of Birch's murder. Sultan Abdullah also offered to send support, but Swettenham diplomatically declined the offer. The next day, Captain William Innes, acting Resident of Perak, who was from Her Majesty's 10th Regiment, arrived from Penang with two officers and some 60 men. Joined by the Superintendent of Penang's police and around 20 local constables, he took steps to take charge of the residency. On 7 November, this combined force, along with Lieutenant Abbott and his four naval men, as well as a group of Mandailing volunteers (Box 1.2), attacked Pasir Salak (some five miles of jungle terrain from Bandar Bahru). This hasty attack failed, however, as they came under unexpected fire from the maharaja lela's strategically positioned and well-fortified stockade, and Captain Innes was among several killed.

After the initial British defeat, a further attempt was made a week later, with reinforcements of 150 soldiers from Singapore and Perak and a naval brigade summoned by Jervois, this time armed with guns and rockets. This second attack destroyed the villages of the maharaja lela (Pasir Salak) and the dato' sagor (Kampung Gajah). However, the maharaja lela and the dato' sagor managed to retreat upriver to Blanja and, joined by Ismail, settled in Pengkalan Pegoh on the Kinta River, 15 miles inland from the bank of the Perak River.

With the possibility of further serious disturbances in Perak, as well as elsewhere in the Malay states, British reinforcements with naval support were brought in from Calcutta under the command of Brigadier-General John Ross, and from Hong Kong under the command of Major General Francis Colborne and Captain Alexander Buller. The combined military and naval expedition that set out in pursuit of the maharaja lela and the other perpetrators, possessed overwhelming firepower, consisting of:

… 200 infantry of the 10th and 80th Regiments, 40 artillery men with two steel guns, and a rocket tube, and a naval brigade consisting of about 70 officers and men of H. M. ships Modeste and Ringdove, with two steel guns on boats' slides, and three rocket tubes. (*The Illustrated London News*, 1876, p. 204)

Box 1.2 **The Mandailing connection**

The Mandailings were Malays, an ethnic cultural group from south Sumatra who fled Selangor after the Civil War (1867–1873) there and changed sides to become British allies. During the Perak War, a group of some 14 Mandailings, led by Nakhoda Orlong, served as guides and bounty hunters in the searches for the Perak chiefs who had murdered Birch. Nakhoda Orlong, a friend of Frank A. Swettenham, was killed in an ambush while walking alongside him during the first British-led attack on Pasir Salak.

Among the chiefs being sought was Raja Ngah, a close ally of Raja Ismail, whom Birch had earlier asked Raja Asal, leader of the Mandailings, to keep under surveillance. In February 1876, Raja Asal reported having sighted him, and Swettenham sent a letter and arms asking Raja Asal to apprehend Raja Ngah, which he did after a battle at Perlak in Sungkai.

Swettenham, with the approval of the governor of the Straits Settlements, rewarded Raja Asal for his support in the Perak War with the Papan tin mines at the mouth of the Kinta River, which had been abandoned by the opposition to the British administration. On the death of Raja Asal, his nephew Raja Bilah took over the leadership of the Mandailings and operated one of the biggest, richest, and most productive Malay mines in the state, with hundreds of Malay labourers. Bilah was appointed revenue-collector of Papan and, in 1882, became the first *penghulu* of Papan. He mechanized his mines, but the venture was ultimately unsuccessful and he ceased mining operations in 1890 (Abdur-Razzaq Lubis and Khoo, 2003; Ho, 2005).

The expedition, comprising just a fraction of the military resources available, led an attack on Pengkalan Pegoh. After a three-day march through jungle, taking out several stockades on the way and suffering some losses, Colborne's forces occupied Pengkalan Pegoh and then Kinta by 17 December. With most of Ismail's supporters located in upper Perak, Malay resistance was largely confined to the village of Kota Lama, which was taken by British troops in January 1876.

The British forces were engaged in several other localized skirmishes with the Malays, burning and destroying villages that they felt could serve as centres of resistance. But the expected widespread uprising, for which the British had assembled a huge military force, did not materialize. Nor did the conflict turn into a wider religious war, as was speculated in London news reports.[53] Nevertheless, the military operations came with human costs on both sides.

After hostilities ended in early 1876, garrisons of British troops remained quartered in strategic locations in upper and lower Perak for the next 18 months. When they withdrew, security was maintained by armed police. Amid the disorder and bloodshed in Perak, British troops, with overwhelming military power, had forced the dissident Perak chiefs into submission with little resistance.

Raja Ismail and several of his followers fled north to Kedah, eventually giving themselves up to the Sultan of Kedah, who surrendered Raja Ismail to Penang's governor on 20 March 1876.

The maharaja lela and Pandak Indut surrendered in July 1876 to emissaries for the Maharaja of Johor on condition that they should receive a fair trial. The dato' sagor had been apprehended earlier (Swettenham, 1906). The trial took place at Matang over seven days before two Malay judges, Raja Yusof and Raja Hussein,[54] and with two British assessors, James Guthrie Davidson and W. E. Maxwell. Swettenham and Colonel Samuel Dunlop were prosecuting, and Jonas Daniel Vaughan was defending. Both the defence counsel and the prosecutors were proficient in the Malay language (Hashim Sam, 2002). During the trial, the maharaja lela unsuccessfully sought through his lawyer to exonerate himself by blaming Sultan Abdullah (Cheah, 1998). Maharaja Lela Pandak Lam, Pandak Indut, and Dato' Sagor Ngah Kamaddin were found guilty of murder and treason. They were sentenced to death and hanged at Matang in January 1877.

Sultan Abdullah was persuaded by the British authorities to resign as ruler of Perak for his complicity in the murder, and was banished to the Seychelles, along with the menteri (Box 1.3), the laksamana, and the shahbandar. They were accompanied by their families and provided with allowances by the Perak government. Later, they were allowed to return and live in Singapore. As the state sovereign, Sultan Abdullah could not be tried by his own courts, or by those of the Straits Settlements, which had no jurisdiction outside the Straits Settlements' boundaries. Ismail was banished to Johor, where he died in 1889. Perak was placed under the Regency of Raja Muda Yusof, who was later appointed sultan. Perak's royal regalia, which Ismail had long refused to pass over to Abdullah, were sent to Singapore, and later transferred to Sultan Yusof—by this time most of Perak's first- and second-division chieftain positions were vacant because of the banishments and earlier hangings.

---

53 For first-hand British accounts of the Perak War, see Swettenham (1906) and McNair (1878); for British newspaper coverage, see also *The Daily Telegraph* (1875) and *The Graphic* (1875).

54 Raja Hussein was the son of Sultan Abdullah.

| Box 1.3 | **The role of the menteri in Larut's tin wars and Resident Birch's murder** |

The Menteri of Larut, Ngah Ibrahim, was rich and powerful through his ownership and control of the district's lucrative tin mines. Governor Jervois's report to the Earl of Carnarvon in December 1876 included a memorandum about charges against the menteri, who was described 'as a clever scheming man and Abdullah himself has stated that the menteri and his father-in-law, the laksamana, were the two principal originators of the [Larut] disturbances' (C. 1709, 1877). During the Larut wars, Ngah Ibrahim used his wealth and title to gain the favour and support of British government officers in the Straits Settlements.

The Chinese accused the menteri of issuing double mining rights, which were the root of all the troubles between the rival Chinese clans (CO 882/3, 1875). In 1873, Ngah Ibrahim hired four junks from China with ammunition and arms, and later employed Captain Speedy—who by that time had resigned from British government service in Penang—and Indian mercenaries to attack the Ghee Hin. At the menteri's request, Governor Ord rescinded the Order in Council 1873 to allow the export of arms from Penang to Larut. Later, in 1874, Governor Clarke reported that this had made matters worse: the Chinese felt that the government had interfered and allied itself to one faction, showing partisanship towards the menteri, who they saw as the cause of the problems (C. 1320, 1875).

During the Larut wars, the menteri incurred considerable personal loss to his property in Matang, the destruction of his residence in Penang (see 'Third Tin War, 1872–1873', above), and huge expense on behalf of the Perak state, estimated at some $75,000. In 1875, Clarke arranged an agreement between the menteri and his creditors for the payment of the debt, with a plan to issue scripts and dividends to be paid by the Perak government (C. 1505, 1876).

In dealing with the two sultans aspiring for the throne, Jervois reported that Ngah Ibrahim had incited the minor chiefs to make Raja Ismail the Perak sultan, despite his having no claim to the throne, with a view to paving the way for his own eventual succession. In a letter sent to Jervois by Ismail, the menteri persuaded Ismail not to recognize the Pangkor Engagement. Jervois reported to the Earl of Carnarvon that Ismail was 'completely in the hands of the menteri and other minor chiefs' (C. 1505, 1876, p. 27). Indeed, he believed that the menteri wrote letters on behalf of Ismail as Ismail could neither read nor write.

The menteri openly expressed dissatisfaction with the Pangkor Treaty, even though he had signed it. Clarke withdrew the recognition Ord had made of the

(Continued)

independence of the menteri (C. 1320, 1875), and Ngah Ibrahim's income and power were greatly reduced when Captain Speedy was appointed in Larut in 1874.

Worse still, the menteri conspired with both Abdullah and Ismail to break the treaty, inciting Abdullah to claim the royal regalia, and inducing Ismail not to give up the regalia to Abdullah. He encouraged Ismail to authorize the maharaja lela to kill Birch. He also instigated the murder of *kerani* (secretary) Yusof for revealing secrets to Birch, and provided arms, ammunition, and instructions to Mat Ali, *penghulu* of Kuala Kurau, to attack Kota Stia after the murder of Birch. He made further arrangements with the laksamana to send assistance to the maharaja lela and to attack Kuala Kangsar, while the laksamana was to attack Bandar Bahru (C. 1709, 1877). For his role in the conspiracy, Ngah Ibrahim was exiled to the Seychelles in July 1877, never to return to Perak. He died in Singapore in 1895.

Reflection

Views on Birch's legacy are mixed. Birch was brave and reform-minded, championing the causes of the poor and oppressed, and challenging the institution of debt-slavery, throughout his extensive travels around the state.[55] Swettenham (1906, p. 215) concluded that Birch's death was not in vain, writing that

> His death freed the country from abominable thraldom, and was indirectly the means of bringing independence, justice, and comfort to tens of thousands of sorely oppressed people.

However, lacking an appreciation of Perak's constitution regulated by traditional Malay customs and cultural practices, and not adopting a more inclusive approach to governance, Birch was disadvantaged when negotiating with the sultan and chiefs. The disputes among the royals were seemingly intractable, and the policy reforms necessary for developing Perak economically could not,

---

[55] This is well recognized in the publications of two of his contemporaries, Swettenham (1906) and McNair (1878), as well as more recently by Cheah (1998). Conversely, Khoo Kay Kim (undated) questioned Birch's fiduciary standards, noting that the Colonial Office had had misgivings about his financial dealings when he served as Colonial Secretary. However, Clarke held an enquiry before Singapore's Executive Council which exonerated him of alleged abuses.

at the time, be implemented through mere 'advice', as had been stipulated in the Pangkor Treaty.

Birch has also been accused of being harsh, disrespectful of the hereditary chiefs, and threatening their livelihoods. Perak's Malays were governed by two customary codes largely influenced by the Islamic religion (C. 3429, 1882). Centralized administration was a foreign idea to a state where territorial powers were devolved to hereditary chiefs. In early 1875 Sultan Abdullah had sent a deputation to Singapore, consisting of the Malay chief Orang Kaya Mat Arshad, Raja Idris—who later became Sultan Idris Murshidul Azzam (1887–1916)—and the laksamana, to request Clarke to direct Resident Birch not to interfere in questions of Malay custom; to give up slaves who ran away; not to abolish taxes that the chiefs were accustomed to collecting; and not to act without consulting the sultan. But it was to no avail. Clarke's parting response before he left Singapore for his new appointment in India, sent in a letter of 13 May 1875 to Sultan Abdullah, was:

> All our friend's troubles arise from a want of confidence, and a want of thought, which is most unreasonable. (C. 1709, 1877, No. XXI, p. 102)

The new governor, Jervois, was given and maintained the impression that the sultan was heedless of advice, growing in duplicity, and eager to break all the pledges contained in the Pangkor Treaty.

In messages to Clarke, Birch is said to have disparaged Sultan Abdullah in undiplomatic words (though his sentiments were echoed by others, including governors of the Straits Settlements):

> Firmness will, I trust, do it all: and with him [Abdullah] one must be firm and even peremptory. God help a country left to a man like that, unadvised by sound counsellors! I very often despair when I think of him. (cited in Wilkinson, 1923, p. 124)

Birch is likewise said to have slighted the maharaja lela upon the latter's refusal to acknowledge the Pangkor Treaty, after having initially agreed to do so:

> I told him unless he signed before twelve o'clock tomorrow, he would never see the treaty again. He would get no allowance, and, if he ever did anything, such as I heard he had said he would collect taxes, it would be put a stop to by force. (cited in Cheah, 1998, pp. 89–90)

Given his influential position and military strength, it was said that the maharaja lela was a man who could hardly bear such an insult from Birch. This led to his personal animosity towards the resident. The maharaja lela had, indeed, frequently volunteered to kill him (Cheah, 1998).

Birch was the victim of the seriously flawed and ambiguous treaty arrangements of Pangkor. The Pangkor Treaty undermined Perak's existing political governance—which relied on Malay traditions and custom—and also denied the chiefs what they felt were their rightful privileges (Gullick, 1953). The Colonial Office had long held the position that placing a British resident in Perak should be with the full consent of its government. That necessary condition for transformative political change and rapid economic development was not in place. Birch's repeated attempts to prevent the chiefs from collecting taxes, and his opposition to royalty keeping slaves, in effect, constituted his signature on his own death warrant. His vulnerability was magnified in the absence of British military protection to counter any local defiance and resistance.

By May 1875, both the Malay and British sides were frustrated by the slow pace of progress since the Pangkor Treaty. In 1876, after his return to London, former Governor Ord wrote to the Secretary of State for the Colonies that Clarke had not had an intimate acquaintance with Malay character or custom when framing the terms of the treaty. The Malay chiefs who attended Pangkor were quick to agree to the treaty's terms but slow to understand British expectations. Clarke had failed to explain governance based on British laws, or to make the chiefs aware that it would take time before they would eventually benefit. This led to Jervois assuming a responsibility beyond what London had originally agreed, and ultimately cost Birch and others their lives (C. 1505, 1876, 98, p. 168).

By 1877, peace and order had been established under the new government, albeit through force of arms, which the British administrators felt was justified even at the cost of violating Colonial Office policy of non-intervention in the Malay states. As Gordon (2021, p. 81) observes:

> The events in Perak demonstrate the imbalance in relations between the colonizer and the colonized in the British Empire because of the significant amount of resources and the number of troops that Britain had at its disposal. This imbalance was underpinned by imperial ideology, which presented the indigenous population as … inherently incapable of ruling themselves.

But, above all, it was the economic imperative of exploiting Perak's rich and abundant natural resources, especially tin, and creating the right conditions for investment, that drove Jervois's actions. As he observed in his proclamation of 15 October 1875:

> The continued instability in the state has hitherto deterred foreigners from investing capital in Perak to any considerable extent, and the resources of the country are still undeveloped. (C. 1505, 1876, pp. 50–51)

P. B. Maxwell (Box 1.4) was critical of the British colonial administration, and sympathetic towards Malay society. In his book *Our Malay Conquests* (1878), penned after his return to England, he said he was writing:

> On behalf of a weak race, whose voice cannot be heard in this country, to obtain redress for some of the injustice done, and to prevent similar injustice in future; but partly also on behalf of the public that they may consider whether it is wise to extend the Empire, with the accompanying burdens and responsibilities. (Maxwell, 1878, p. 2)[56]

His views echoed William Gladstone's observations that expansions of the British empire are rarely achieved except by means that are questionable, risky, and that tend to compromise the national character. He warned against the arrogance of good intentions which end up dissipating 'blood and treasure' in foreign wars (HC. 234, 1877, p. 32).

Box 1.4   **A distinguished judge's perspective on events after the Pangkor Treaty**

Reflecting on events in Perak before and after the Pangkor Treaty, P. B. Maxwell asks rhetorically:

> How did it happen, it was natural to ask, that acts which are unheard and even undreamed of in this country, and which would excite universal reprobation here if done by any other nation, could yet be committed on natives of the East by English officers, and be sanctioned by an English Minister? (Maxwell, 1878, pp. 1–2)

When he was the Secretary of State for the Colonies (1870–1874), the Earl of Kimberley's stated intention was for British residents to give advice, and advice alone—yet in practice Sultan Abdullah signed the territory away to foreign rule, albeit 'indirect'. He seemed unaware that there would be restraints put on his powers. Andrew Clarke brought the treaty into operation and undermined traditional Malay structures and systems in order to impose a colonial order, which eventually

(Continued)

---

56 P. B. Maxwell had been appointed a supreme court judge in Penang in 1856 and was the first Chief Justice of the Straits Settlements (1867–1871). His ability to understand Malay and to read Malay Jawi script enabled him to write about British intervention in the Malay states based on his interpretation of official records. Maxwell's book was written at the suggestion of the Committee of the Aborigines' Protection Society—an international human rights organization founded in 1837 to ensure the health, well-being, and the sovereign, legal, and religious rights of indigenous peoples who were subject to colonial power.

evolved into a British system of justice and a civil service. In executing their instructions from London, or in taking policy decisions without Colonial Office approval, Governors Clarke and Jervois, Resident James Birch, and Assistant Resident Speedy imposed British will with little respect for either English law or Malay custom, or the rights of the local peoples.

Property seizure

The British delineation of the Kerian boundary was not what the treaty had stipulated (see 'Claiming Strategic Territory', below). The laksamana, acting on behalf of Sultan Abdullah, took exception to the watershed delineation; the menteri remarked on the violation of good faith; and the chiefs objected to the seizure of valuable property. In July 1875, Jervois recognized that the delineation was 'a breach of faith towards the State of Perak' (C. 1505, 1876, p. 3). However, not wanting to reverse the decision, which could be interpreted as a sign of weakness, Jervois instead proposed for the revenue collected, after deducting administration costs, to be paid into a separate account in the Treasury of Penang, and to be credited to Perak once the boundary issue was resolved (C. 1505, 1876, p. 3). He believed that this would redress the unjust acquisition of territory and revenue. Jervois's representation to London elicited no response from the Earl of Carnarvon until a year later, when he incidentally remarked that it was a 'delicate matter' (Maxwell, 1878, p. 19).

Proprietary rights and customary law

Sultan Abdullah, who was without a resident advisor for 10 months after signing the Pangkor Treaty, decided to farm out the collection of tolls at the mouth of the Perak River to a Chinese businessman for $26,000, without asking Governor Clarke who regarded this act as 'disobedient and contrary to the terms of the treaty' (Maxwell, 1878, p. 31). When, after receiving official approval from London for his appointment, Resident Birch arrived in Perak on 4 November 1874, he informed the businessman that his contract was not sanctioned under the treaty, and forbade him to receive any dues. He then reprimanded Abdullah. Maxwell, however, argued that the contract between the sultan and the Chinese businessman was valid because, when it was given, the sultan had had no resident to consult. He viewed the resident's behaviour as 'unjust' to both parties. Maxwell also contended that the resident's proposal to abolish the Malay chiefs' rights to tolls was a violation of the rights of property, especially as they were not being given any compensation for their loss. The collection of revenue had long been an established practice under customary law and within their lawful rights; moreover, it was the chiefs' principal source of income.

Imposition of English law or of government by English officers in a native ruler's name?

After Birch's death, the colonial government and British public objected to the annexation of Perak. The London press questioned how, without Parliament's knowledge, colonial officers had been allowed to increase the burden of responsibility and territory of the empire. In December 1875, the Earl of Carnarvon explained that the residential system had been provisionally sanctioned as an experiment in government by English officers in a native ruler's name. P. B. Maxwell concluded that British rule in the Malay territories should have been governed under English law, including a proper judicial system, and control of public revenue and land, which would have been more costly than the residential system (Maxwell, 1878, p. 78).

A political decision or British justice?

The Commission of Enquiry into the Perak Outrages and its report on the Enquiry into the Complicity of Chiefs in the Murder of Birch resulted in the deportation and exile of Abdullah, the menteri, the laksamana, and the shahbandar—without trial. In examining the evidence, Maxwell judged that there were no reasonable grounds for believing that the men had conspired to murder Birch. More than a century later, Cheah (1991) argued that this was the start of political detention without trial in Malaya, which would continue long thereafter.

After Pangkor—Claiming Strategic Territory

From the early 19th century, treaties between states increasingly became part of international relations. States with greater bargaining power benefited most, exploiting weaker states and territories. And so, with its vastly superior naval power and dominance of the seas, Britain maximized its gains at the expense of less powerful states. The treaty arrangements that Britain signed, usually with territorial cessions, furthered its imperial ambitions, including commercial and revenue interests. As with certain articles that formed part of the 1874 Pangkor Treaty and the 1909 Anglo-Siamese Treaty, Britain ensured that it gained influence over strategic land along porous and shifting borders so as to bolster these ambitions, sometimes securing the support of local chiefs.

In framing the Pangkor Engagement, Governor Andrew Clarke acted beyond explicit instructions from London by incorporating articles into the treaty to obtain possession of such strategic land: namely, the Dindings, which commanded the entrance to Perak, and land along the Kerian boundary with Province Wellesley, ostensibly to improve management from a police and revenue point of view (CO 882/3, 1875). Clarke's predecessor, Ord, who had made London aware of the commercial and strategic interests of these territories, had been repeatedly refused permission by London to take 'any measure entailing addition of territory, nor any step that is likely to bring us into collision with the natives' (C. 1111, 1875, No. 1, p. 3).

The Dindings

The sparsely populated Dindings territory (Map 1.4)—now the Manjung District in Perak, comprising Pangkor island, Lumut, and Sitiawan—strategically located facing the Strait of Melaka and not far from the mouth of the Perak

Globalization: Perak's Rise, Relative Decline, and Regeneration. Sultan Nazrin Shah, Oxford University Press. © Sultan Nazrin Shah (2024). DOI: 10.1093/oso/9780198897774.003.0008

| Map 1.4 | Land acquired by Britain from Perak, Kedah, and Siam after two treaties in the late 19th and early 20th centuries |

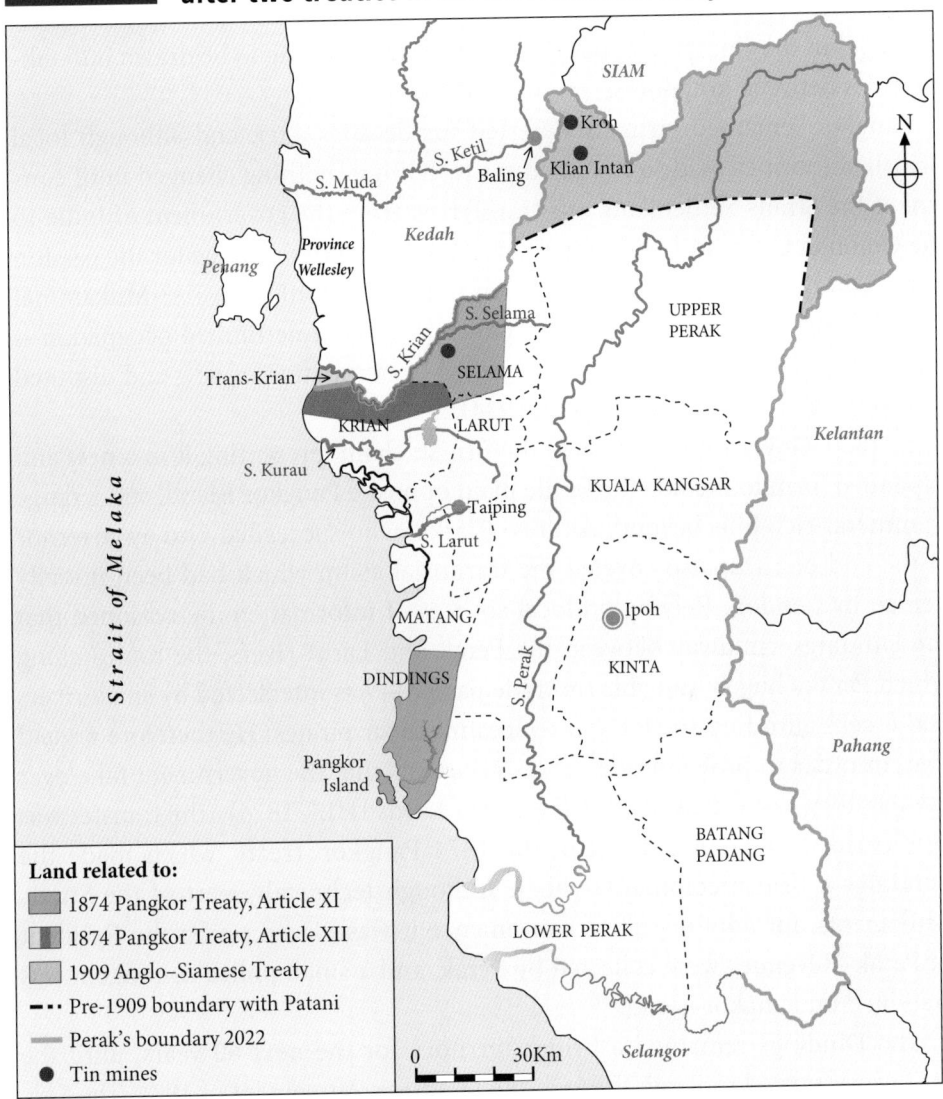

Sources: Adapted from C. 1505–I (1876) and Foreign Office–Great Britain (1909).
Notes: S. denotes Sungai. State and district boundaries are approximate and illustrative only.

River, became a contested area. In 1826, it was ceded to the British East India Company by Perak's Sultan Abdullah Mu'azzam Shah, as Perak did not have the force to drive out pirates from Pangkor island.[57] According to Captain Low, the sultan was keen to see the English flag hoisted in Perak, as the British had

---

57 Pirates were attracted to Pangkor island by the growing sea trade along the Strait of Melaka and used it to store their booty and captives. They were driven out by the British navy in 1836.

helped it maintain its independence in the 1826 Burney Treaty with Siam. An instrument of cession was drafted and sent to the British port settlement of Penang, but the Company refused to ratify it, not wanting to be drawn into taking sides between kingdoms.

Pangkor remained virtually deserted for decades after, and although local British authorities made a few attempts to claim it, nothing changed until control of the Straits Settlements was transferred from the government of India to the Colonial Office in London in 1867.[58] An attempt to arrange for the cession of the Dindings that year was rejected by both Perak's sultan, Ali Al-Mukammal Inayat Shah—who wanted a one-off payment and a time-limited occupation— and by the Colonial Office, which objected to occupation of new and disputed territory (Winstedt and Wilkinson, 1934).

In 1870, Governor Ord revived the British claim, presenting it in a new and expanded form to include the fertile plain opposite Pangkor island, and a range of mineral-rich hills beyond. Andrew Clarke, who succeeded Ord as governor at the end of 1873, also coveted the territorial claim which had been initially denied by London. Relying on local sources of information, he reasoned that the Dindings—midway between the Perak and Larut rivers, the routes along which Perak's hugely valuable tin trade passed—was intersected by small rivers and creeks affording shelter and concealment for pirates. He therefore argued that, in order to protect trade, it was necessary that the government take over the territory first ceded in 1826 (House of Lords [HL], 1874). The transfer was confirmed through Article XI of the 1874 Pangkor Treaty, which made the Dindings a British colonial territory. Although technically part of the Straits Settlements, for administrative convenience it was placed under the Resident of Perak. Revenues were collected by Perak, and a small police contingent was stationed on Pangkor island.

The Dindings remained a British territory for the next 60 years, until the area was returned to Perak through the Dindings Agreement of 1934. The Secretary of State for the Colonies, Philip Cunliffe-Lister (1931–1935), explained to parliament that it was inconvenient for the Dindings to be administered by the Straits Settlements, owing to differences in tariffs and duties between Perak and the colony, which encouraged smuggling (House of Commons [HC], 1933–1934).

---

58 Between 1825 and 1867, the Straits Settlements of Penang, Melaka, and Singapore were ruled from British India.

Kerian and Selama

In 1848, Penang's British authorities invoked Captain Low's 1826 engagement with Perak and tried to force Sultan Zainal Rashid Mu'adzam Shah I (1845–1854) of Kedah to cede Trans-Kerian to Perak, this being the disputed border with Kerian (formerly Krian) adjoining Province Wellesley (Map 1.4). The territory was a potentially valuable water resource, which Penang would then claim from Perak. Kedah's sultan refused to transfer the area, conscious that he was subordinate to both the British and the Siamese (Andaya and Andaya, 2017). The boundary remained contested for the next quarter of a century.

Under Article XII of the 1874 Pangkor Treaty, Clarke sought the rectification of Perak's boundary with Province Wellesley based on the southern watershed of the Krian River. The British authorities in Province Wellesley experienced difficulties in stopping opium smuggling across the Krian River, and in preventing crime by people coming over from Perak (C. 1505, 1876). These difficulties were attributed to the Krian River forming the boundary between Perak and the Province, and it was proposed that the frontier should be set back to a line running eastward from a point halfway between the Krian River and the Kurau River. When agreeing to the delineation of the watershed, the Perak royal chiefs were informed by the British negotiators that they did not want to take land higher up the river than the line of boundary on the Kedah side, and that the width would not be more than three or four miles, to make the boundary match with the Larut district at the Kurau River. The exact boundaries were to be settled by commissioners, according to the British side (HL, 1874).

Subsequently, Clarke issued two proclamations, dated July 1874 and May 1875, to implement Article XII of the Pangkor Treaty (C. 1505, 1876). The first declared that the watershed south of the Krian River, just south of the confluence of the Krian and Selama rivers, was British territory; the second annexed that territory to Province Wellesley, part of the Settlement of Penang—a reinterpretation of Article XII by Clarke more favourable to British interests (Map 1.4).

The initial proposal in the Pangkor Treaty had been that the rectification should cover 30 square miles. However, this second delineation, made at the direction of British commissioners, now covered 200 square miles, to incorporate the rich tin-mining district of Selama in northern Perak (C. 1505, 1876). It even encroached on the territory of the Raja of Kedah, who was urged to build a road on his land so British commercial interests could have ready access to the Selama mines. A police force was established, and the British administration exercised rights of proprietorship on the territory—even before the boundary dispute was fully settled—receiving revenues from passes for timber cutting and charcoal burning, and licences for opium and spirit farms.

This new delineation was a serious point of dispute between the British administration and the Perak chiefs (Box 1.4). Clarke had pushed the 'watershed' line to its easternmost limits, and Perak's Malay chiefs greatly objected to this interpretation. A couple of years later, as British rule of Perak was consolidated, it became immaterial whether the Selama mines fell north or south of the line—that is, beyond or under imperial authority. By 1877, Governor Jervois had restored Selama to Perak, and the remaining part of Kerian formed the Trans-Kerian district in Penang. The Selama mines remained a source of dispute with the Raja of Kedah, who sought to claim customary royalties (Wilkinson, 1907). Abdul Karim (the menteri's agent), who had discovered the mining prospects in Selama and claimed sole rights to them, was determined to protect the mines from these claims and invoked the protection of the Straits Settlements' governor (Maxwell, 1882b). Discrete tracts of land in Kerian were requisitioned by the British administration for sugar planting in the south and for rice growing in the north.

Perak's Northeastern Border with Siam

In April 1874, soon after the Pangkor Treaty had been signed and Perak had come under British protection, a request was made by the state's chiefs to J. W. W. Birch—at that time, Perak's resident designate—for British government help in recovering long-claimed territory at the northern boundary with Patani in southern Siam (Map 1.4). This territory comprised a large area of land, including the rich Klian Intan and Kroh tin mines that had passed into Siamese hands after the 1817–1818 war with Kedah, and was incorporated into the neighbouring state of Raman, one of seven small states in Patani under Siamese rule (see 'Resisting Siam—Holding Back the Traditional Tributary Offering', above).[59] The disputed territory also encompassed the upper Perak River basin, a primary source of water for the tin-mining industry.

Before the 1817–1818 war, tin was transported from these mines on elephants and then sent down the Perak River, with royalties paid to Perak's sultan. After the war, however, when the area passed to Patani, the Raja of Raman

---

[59] This territory was later fought over in three Perak–Raman wars between the Malays in Hulu Perak and those in Patani. The first of these wars was in 1826, the second in 1852, and the third in 1856 (Mohd Zamberi A. Malek, 2017).

granted mining concessions and collected taxes on the ore mined in these areas. When it was transported to the British commercial interests in Penang, via Baling in Kedah and down the Ketil and Muda rivers to Kuala Muda, it was also taxed by the Raja of Kedah (Birch, 1910).

In an account of his expedition to the Patani frontier in early 1876, William E. Maxwell (1882b, p. 59) observed about the Klian Intan and Kroh mines that '[t]here can be little doubt that, under proper management, and a government which would give some security for life and property, these mines might be rendered very productive and remunerative'.[60] Perak's Sultan Abdullah offered the tract of land to the British, on payment of $6 per *bahar* on tin exports, if they were able to secure it from Siam (Swettenham, 1952, p. 50). In reporting to London, Swettenham argued that it was in Britain's commercial interests to recover the territory from Patani and return it to Perak. As Perak's revenue and population had rapidly expanded under British protection, this view was also later relayed to London by other British administrators.

In 1882, Raja Yusof raised the boundary dispute with Hugh Low, who took up the matter with the governor of the Straits Settlements, Frederick Weld (1880–1887). In June 1883, William Henry Newman, the British Consul-General in Bangkok, wrote to Lord Granville George Leveson-Gower, Secretary of State for the Colonies (1868–70), that the Straits government considered Perak's claim to the whole basin to be entirely just (FO, 422/8, 1882–1884). In advancing Perak's territorial claim to London through the Straits Settlements' governor in March 1884, Low argued that the delineation of the Perak River's 'watershed', now in Raman, was inconsistent with that of watersheds in Borneo's kingdoms and provinces, all of which were bounded by their watersheds. He also alluded to the territorial encroachments as an infraction of the 1826 Burney Treaty.

In 1885, Weld wrote to Frederick Stanley, the Earl of Derby, the new Secretary of State for the Colonies (1885–1886), requesting that representations be made to the government of Siam:

> The territory in question was occupied by the Raja of Raman, a Malay, and our excuse for not then interfering was that he was a Malay, and that it was a domestic quarrel between Malays. But the Raja of Raman is subject to Siam, and, however unwillingly, submits to their yoke, though no Siamese official resides, or perhaps could safely reside, in his country. The Siamese consequently claim the upper Province of Perak as

---

60 W. E. Maxwell, who later became Selangor's British resident (1889–1892), was at this time attached as a political officer to the Larut Field Force on an expedition to capture the maharaja lela, who was wanted for Birch's murder.

part of Raman. This consequently violates the treaty, which we are bound to respect, and to make Siam respect, and Perak, through her Regent and State Council, calls upon us to maintain and uphold her rights. (FO 422/107, 1882–1887)

The Colonial Office did not take up the case until much later, however, because the political boundaries of some other states on the Malay peninsula were not fixed either. Finally, after more than two decades of discussions, and initial resistance to direct negotiations, Siam brought the dispute to the British government. A settlement was eventually reached through the March 1909 Anglo-Siamese Treaty.[61] Siam ceded the tin-rich land it had encroached on almost a century earlier, significantly enlarging Perak, such that the entire 260-mile length of the Perak River, from its source to its mouth, was returned to Perak's territory (Map 1.4).[62] In 1909, the annual tin ore output from the Klian Intan and Kroh mines was estimated at 14,000 piculs (Birch, 1910; Kiernan, 1956)—a substantial amount for the time.

Despite misgivings at the Colonial Office, these treaties and land cessions show that the governors of the Straits Settlements were a powerful force in overcoming local pressures. After falling under British protection, these three strategic and commercially valuable areas—the Dindings; Trans-Kerian and Selama; and parts of northeastern Perak—were used to further colonial interests. Revenue from Perak's tin trade, which Britain eventually came to dominate, proved especially important in this.

---

61 For an account of the official territorial handover on 16 July 1909, including the handover of its 3,000-plus people, and further detail on the long borders, see Birch et al. (1910).

62 At the source of the Perak River, the mountain Gunung Jambul Merak forms the division and the watershed between Perak and Patani. An ancient Malay boundary mark exists between Raman and Perak, said to be drawn from Lobang Gandang to Padang Limau Nipis, and from there to Gunung Jambul Merak (Maxwell, 1882b).

British Governance and Federalism Fortified, 1870s–1920s

The prolonged wars had seriously hit Perak's economy. James Guthrie Davidson, appointed acting resident in June 1876, found the state bankrupt, and he resigned in January 1877 due to the heavy responsibilities of the job and ill health.[63] He was succeeded by Hugh Low, who was fluent in Malay and knowledgeable about Malay custom, thanks to his 24 years of administrative experience working in Labuan, which had also involved extensive travels in Sarawak on the island of Borneo. Low's immediate challenges were to reassure Perak's people and gain their confidence, and to create the institutions and enabling conditions that would support economic development after many years of wars and crises. He recognized that attempts to govern a discontented people were most likely to succeed through a conciliatory partnership approach.

A New Beginning

Low relocated the residency to Kuala Kangsar to be close to Raja Muda Yusof, who had been recognized by the British as Perak's regent in March 1877 when military operations in the state concluded.[64] Low strove hard to encourage the Malay chiefs and aristocracy to work with him and to share responsibility for administrative policy reforms. After consultation with the many royals and chiefs, Low abolished debt-slavery at the end of 1883,[65] which had been so denounced by Birch (Box 1.5). He settled the issue of revenue for the chiefs

---

63 Captain Speedy, Perak's assistant resident, also resigned at the same time and was succeeded by W. E. Maxwell. William Jervois left the Straits governorship in early 1877.

64 On the appointment of Yusof as the regent, Raja Idris, a cousin of Sultan Abdullah, became the raja bendahara and in 1886 the raja muda. On the death of Sultan Yusof, he became the new Sultan of Perak (1887–1916).

65 The institution of debt-slavery had earlier been abolished in Selangor and Negeri Sembilan.

Globalization: Perak's Rise, Relative Decline, and Regeneration. Sultan Nazrin Shah, Oxford University Press. © Sultan Nazrin Shah (2024). DOI: 10.1093/oso/9780198897774.003.0009

by implementing the civil list and giving them a share of the government dues collected by them in their districts. At the grassroots level, he adapted the traditional political institution of the village *penghulu*, forging a more productive working relationship by listening to their concerns. He paid the *penghulus* wages and vested them with local-government-type responsibilities, and the role of implementing British policies. The *penghulus* were paid, for example, to collect tin duties and land rents, and were given local policing responsibilities through the removal of the village police stations, which had previously been operated by Sikhs and Pathans recruited from northern India.

Under the far-from-perfect treaty arrangements of Pangkor, the sultan's sovereignty over his subjects was maintained, and he retained control over Malay custom and religion. Perak's regent, later the sultan, supported the necessary adjustments to the state's traditional political system. The sultan was allowed a great deal of latitude, and, as Perak prospered, he became wealthy on the revenues derived from tin (and later rubber). The sultan never initiated radical change, however, nor opposed British policy as a whole. Indeed, the British residential system was itself bolstered by the agency of the sultan.

Box 1.5   Abolition of slavery in Perak: British persuasion

Soon after the British began to rule Perak, parliament pressured the colonial administrators to adopt a social system consistent with the UK's principles and policies (C. 3285, 1882). In 1833, some 40 years earlier, the Abolition of Slavery Act had sought to end slavery in all British colonies. In 1875, however, Perak's Assistant Resident Speedy reported to Governor Clarke that slavery still existed in Larut. Soon after, the Earl of Carnarvon instructed Governor Jervois to end slavery in Perak (C. 1320, 1875).

Without understanding Malay custom, the British intruded on the Malay elite's prestige, social stature, and accustomed way of life, to the protest of Sultan Abdullah, who stated that the abolition of slavery was not one of the articles of the Pangkor Treaty (C. 1709, 1877). P. B. Maxwell (1878) conjectured that it would probably not have been difficult to persuade the Perak chiefs to put an end to debt slavery. Instead, however, the resident and assistant resident took the more incendiary course of action of freeing and harbouring runaway slaves, in breach of the treaty. A customary code regulated slavery—the *Undang-undang Kerajaan*, or 'Laws of the

Monarchy'. This was translated by W. E. Maxwell, Perak's assistant resident (C. 3429, 1882). Two forms of slavery existed:

- *Abdi*: captives taken in war (mainly Battacks, Sakais, and Habshi) or 'infidels' captured by force; criminals who surrendered themselves and their families; offspring of female slaves; and *hulur/hamba raja*, or royal slaves, Malays who had subjected themselves to the protection of the raja, who was privileged by custom to retain them.
- *Orang berutang*: debt slaves, formerly free men, whose wives and children were also liable to serve their creditors in menial employment until their debts were fully paid. As the number of slaves owned enhanced prestige, the *rakyat* was often exploited by the aristocracy, with imaginary offences arbitrarily added, making it impossible for them to gain their freedom (Sadka, 1954).

When Hugh Low arrived to take up the position of British Resident of Perak (1877–1889), he found that 'one of the greatest causes of complaint against the then existing state of things arose from the natural reluctance of the European officers employed in the country to assist attempts of the creditors of slave debtors and owners of runaway slaves to obtain possession of what they considered their property' (C. 3285, 1882). Before 1874, slaves were considered property of high value, but soon after British rule began, slaves came to be considered worthless, as owners could legally neither compel them to work nor punish them for disobedience.

Low explained to the sultan and chiefs how abhorrent it was to subject a person to servitude. Through consultation, they agreed to his proposal for the gradual phasing out of slavery. The key terms of Low's proposals were that slaves would be allowed to redeem themselves for a fair price; no new slaves would be permitted; existing slaves would be treated well; and, at a date specified, the state would redeem the debts and set free the remaining slaves. The policy was implemented by district officers without formal proclamation (C. 3285, 1882). Low's December 1878 report to the Secretary of State for the Colonies estimated that $60,000 to $80,000 would be enough to compensate slave owners. Raja Idris reported that most masters would liberate their slaves voluntarily without payment, following his example.

Perak's 1879 census reported that there were 47,359 free native Malays and 3,050 slaves—1,670 *Abdi* (775 males and 895 females) and 1,380 *Orang berutang* (728 males and 652 females), *excluding* the sultan's and regent's claims, which were not declared (C. 3285, 1882).

In October 1882 the State Council finally approved the abolition of all forms of slavery in Perak. By the end of 1883, all claims would lapse and be irrecoverable. The government allowed debtors to apply to district courts for loans to redeem themselves. By January 1884, all slaves had been set free and slavery was illegal (C. 4192, 1884).

By the early 1880s, was Perak well on the way to transforming its tin resources—a curse during the extensive Larut wars—into a blessing? Or had the conditions merely been created for the systematic commercial exploitation of tin and the state's other natural resources by the British? Had Perak simply exchanged the old curse of war for a new one: foreign political and economic dominance under colonial capitalist structures?

Moving from Traditional Power Structures—Perak State Council, 1877

After establishing the residency system in Perak through the Pangkor Engagement, the British colonial administration introduced three main bodies that imposed increasingly firm control—often under the guise of 'protection'—over the state. The first was the Perak State Council, founded in 1877. The authority of this first administrative body was undermined, however, once Perak joined the centralized administration of the second—the newly constituted Federated Malay States—in 1896. The Perak State Council was further weakened by the creation of the Federal Council—the third administrative body—in 1909. The Federal Council deepened British jurisdiction over financial and legislative matters, and further undercut the sultans' political authority and prestige.

By 1887, the British Resident Hugh Low exercised control over Perak's administrative and political affairs. He established a state secretariat in Taiping to handle all matters related to administration and finance.[66] The Perak chiefs were paid an allowance as part of the civil list established through the Pangkor Treaty, and a few of the more influential became members of the Perak State Council, not long after military operations in Perak had ended. Regent Yusof was made president of the newly formed State Council, and in May 1886 became the Sultan of Perak. Key members of the former ruling class were thereby integrated into the new system of state governance.

The State Council—a new executive and legislative body—was an extension of Jervois's idea of a Malay Council to provide an opportunity for the principal chiefs to take part in Perak's administration. It was responsible for issuing resolutions and orders in Council that set out policies and provided guiding principles for state governance. These were disseminated through

---

66 For details of Perak's administrative divisions and how they evolved, see Raja Kamarulzaman bin Raja Mansur (Malaysia Archive Documents, 1942).

proclamations.[67] In practice, the Council also served to limit the regent's powers and legitimize British control; although the regent served as the president of the Council, it was the resident's decision that counted most on important matters. Apart from the regent, the resident, and his deputy, the Council's membership consisted of Malays from the ruling class and Chinese mining leaders.[68] Malay members were chosen for their political reliability and not their rank.

The first State Council meeting, conducted in Malay, was held at Kuala Kangsar on 10–11 September 1877. Among the topics discussed were proposals for increasing tax revenue, terms for granting agricultural and mining leases, changes to the position and conditions of appointment of *penghulus*, and other tax-related matters (Wilkinson, 1907).[69] Revenue and tax matters were the highest priority, as Perak needed to repay the heavy 1875–1876 war debts to the British administration. This would require financial reforms and the centralized management of the collection of tax revenues. In a subsequent meeting of the Council, however, the resident's proposals for collecting land rent and introducing a poll tax to help pay off the state's debts were not supported by the Malays on the Council. These proposals were eventually dropped (Wilkinson, 1909), in part because state revenues were greatly boosted by the booming tin trade which obviated the need for a local tax system.

With Perak's economy growing quickly in the late 1880s, driven by surging tin production in Larut and Kinta, and with prosperity spreading, more Malay chiefs, British officials, and Chinese entrepreneurs were added to the State Council. By 1895, the Council consisted of 12 members—seven Malays, three Chinese, and two British officers. Malay members tended to speak most often on routine questions, such as the appointment of *penghulus*, farming matters, and queries on local administration, while Chinese members tended to focus on regulations governing the tin industry, such as the granting of long leases for mining land, which they argued would enable them to raise capital more easily for plant and machinery (Wilkinson, 1909).

The chiefs and *penghulus* contributed information and ideas, supported the implementation of new policies, and acted as key influencers to help unify the

---

67 The minutes of the State Council meetings are available at the Perak Museum in Taiping.

68 The first eight members of the Council were the resident, his assistant, Raja Yusof, Raja Idris, the temenggong, Abdul Karim, and the heads of the two rival Chinese communities, the Hai San and Ghee Hin—Chang Ah Kwee and Chan Ah Yam. These were the same individuals who had signed the Chinese peace agreement in 1874 at Pangkor. The resident lived close to the senior Malay Council members, and the meetings, which were invested with much ceremony, were held at Kuala Kangsar.

69 The Council also approved an end to import duties (except on alcohol, opium, and tobacco), and export duties (except on tin, gutta-percha, and jungle produce), thereby abolishing the traditional custom of levying duties on all imports and exports.

state. The Council served as a forum where these influencers within the state were represented. It gave the semblance of people's participation in local affairs, even though their powers were, in reality, limited. Low targeted and achieved an active administrative partnership to build state-wide consensus among key stakeholders over economic and social policy down to the village level. He was also notable for introducing systems for handling water rights, land policy, and revenue farms, as well as for encouraging investment in railways and roads—all of which propelled the state's economic development (Winstedt and Wilkinson, 1934).

The State Council was Perak's dominant institution of governance, replacing traditional systems. It helped to strengthen the resident's influence well beyond mere 'advice'. It gave him firm control over policymaking and, more widely, reinforced Britain's capacity to promote its political and economic interests. For example, the minutes of the Council's meetings show that it regularly supported the granting of long leases on large plots of agricultural land to British business ventures in coffee, sugar, and tea plantations. Among other early successful impacts of the Council were the introduction of compulsory vaccination against smallpox in 1880; the abolition of slavery in 1883 (despite initial opposition from some of the chiefs); and the setting out of regulations to govern registration of land ownership, including that of Malay land entitlements to be issued with titles and 999-year leases, through district land offices. In time, the State Council became a model for the British administration in other Malay states.

Emerging Centralization—Federated Malay States, 1896

During the 1880s and early 1890s, capital and labour came to Perak mainly through the Straits Settlements, whose prosperity was also closely linked to Perak's tin industry. To differing degrees, the same was also true of Selangor and Negeri Sembilan, which also received capital and labour via the Straits Settlements. In each state, the British administration strongly supported the tin-mining sector—which was its dominant source of revenue—through the provision of infrastructure, such as roads and railway networks, and through enabling policies.[70] A common currency, the Straits dollar (Straits$), was introduced in 1903, heavily influenced by British colonial legislation designed to facilitate the growth of trade (Box 1.6)

---

70 The bulk of the population were not miners, however, and the administration of Malays was handled mainly by Malay-speaking British district officers.

Box 1.6   **Adopting a common currency to facilitate trade**

The currencies in use as units of money in Perak and Malaya evolved through four stages over the century from the mid-1850s.

'Casual money', 1850–1867. In the mid-19th century, the currencies in circulation in Perak were mixed, comprising those earned from international trading trans-actions—notably the Indian rupee, the Spanish dollar, and the Mexican peso. The Indian rupee became prominent in the region through the activity of the East India Trading Company, when the British colony of the Straits Settlements was governed from India. Formal approval as legal tender was not required for the use of these currencies, and any currency could be used if taken to be an acceptable means of exchange. As Drake (1969, p. 14) observes: 'Mexican and other silver dollars circu-lated freely in the Straits not because of any privileged status as legal tender but because they were useful in the China trade.'

Legal tender, 1867–1903. The Straits Settlements Legal Tender Act of 1867 bestowed legal tender status on silver dollars issued from Her Majesty's Mint in Hong Kong, and on the silver dollars of Spain, Mexico, Peru, and Bolivia (Lee, 1990). The legisla-tion also ended the Indian rupee's status as legal tender, as the governance of the Straits Settlements came under direct British control in that year. The Hong Kong Mint was legislated in 1864, and established in 1866, but closed in 1868. In 1874, the Japanese yen and the American trade dollar were also admitted as legal tender by the colonial authorities. All coins suitable for local commerce were entirely of foreign origin. Although not legal tender, banknotes issued by exchange banks were much in demand towards the end of this period. In 1897, the Board of Commission-ers of Currency was established by the British administration of the Straits Settle-ments, with powers to issue government currency notes, subject to a legal tender, silver-coin reserve of two-thirds of the value of the notes issued (Drake, 1969).

Sterling fixed exchange rate, 1903–1939. As trade with the gold-standard countries of Europe increased, and as silver continued to depreciate relative to gold, Straits money was changed from a silver standard to a gold standard (Chiang, 1966). In 1903, the Straits Settlement Currency Board introduced the Straits dollar (Straits$), which was exchangeable with the British pound at a fixed rate set in 1906 at 2 shil-lings and 4 pence (2s 4d)—a parity that lasted until 1967. When Britain went off the gold standard in 1931, the Straits$ (and later the Malayan dollar) was kept on a sterling exchange standard, still at the 2s 4d rate.

Malayan dollar, post-1939. The Straits$ was replaced at par by the Malayan dollar in 1939. The newly established Board of Commissioners of Currency, Malaya, began

(*Continued*)

minting the first coins bearing the name 'Malaya' in 1939. However, the official notification of issue and declaration of this new Malayan currency as legal tender took place only on 24 January 1940. Use of the Malayan dollar was temporarily interrupted during the Japanese occupation when, in early 1942, the new military administration issued what became known as 'banana' money (because the $10 note carried a picture of a banana plant). The Malayan dollar resumed circulation in 1945 when the occupation ended (Kratoska, 2018).

From the perspective of the British Straits administration, however, weaknesses in governance were reflected in inconsistent policies between states, including on labour, land, and taxes. The states had separate administrations that all looked remarkably similar; each had its own British resident, and its own departments with similar functions, such as audit, police, and public works. The railway lines of Perak, Selangor, and Negeri Sembilan were connected to their respective ports only and not linked together, which added to the costs of trading (Map 1.5). The British authorities regarded separate state administrations as a severe impediment to Malaya's economic—not political—integration and, more importantly, to the economies of scale that would generate greater revenues. But long-standing state rivalries worked against the colonial idea of 'rationalizing' their administrations, and the rulers and chiefs of neither Perak nor Selangor wanted to share their states' prosperity with the poorer states of Negeri Sembilan and Pahang.

By the early 1880s, Malaya had become the world's largest producer of tin, accounting for 30 per cent of global output in 1883, with around 17,000 tons. Perak and Selangor accounted for 90 per cent of Malaya's output. Investment, however, suffered in 1889–1891 when global tin prices began to fall. To relieve the strain on finances from large public works projects, the British government began raising tin and opium duties so that, by 1892, the tax take of *each* of the two states individually exceeded that of the Straits Settlements *combined*.[71]

The downturn in global tin prices was felt beyond these two states: it also hit the Straits Settlements' budget, which was coming under stress because of its contribution to proposed increases to UK defence expenditure. Paid to Britain in sterling, this spending rose further in local terms as the value of the dollar declined after 1890. Other demands were made on the Straits Settlements'

---

71 In 1888, opium duty was raised from $240 to $280 per chest. Tin duty varied between $10 and $11 per *bahar* of tin in 1889–1991, and was increased to $12.50 in 1892.

| Map 1.5 | The Federated Malay States, 1898 |

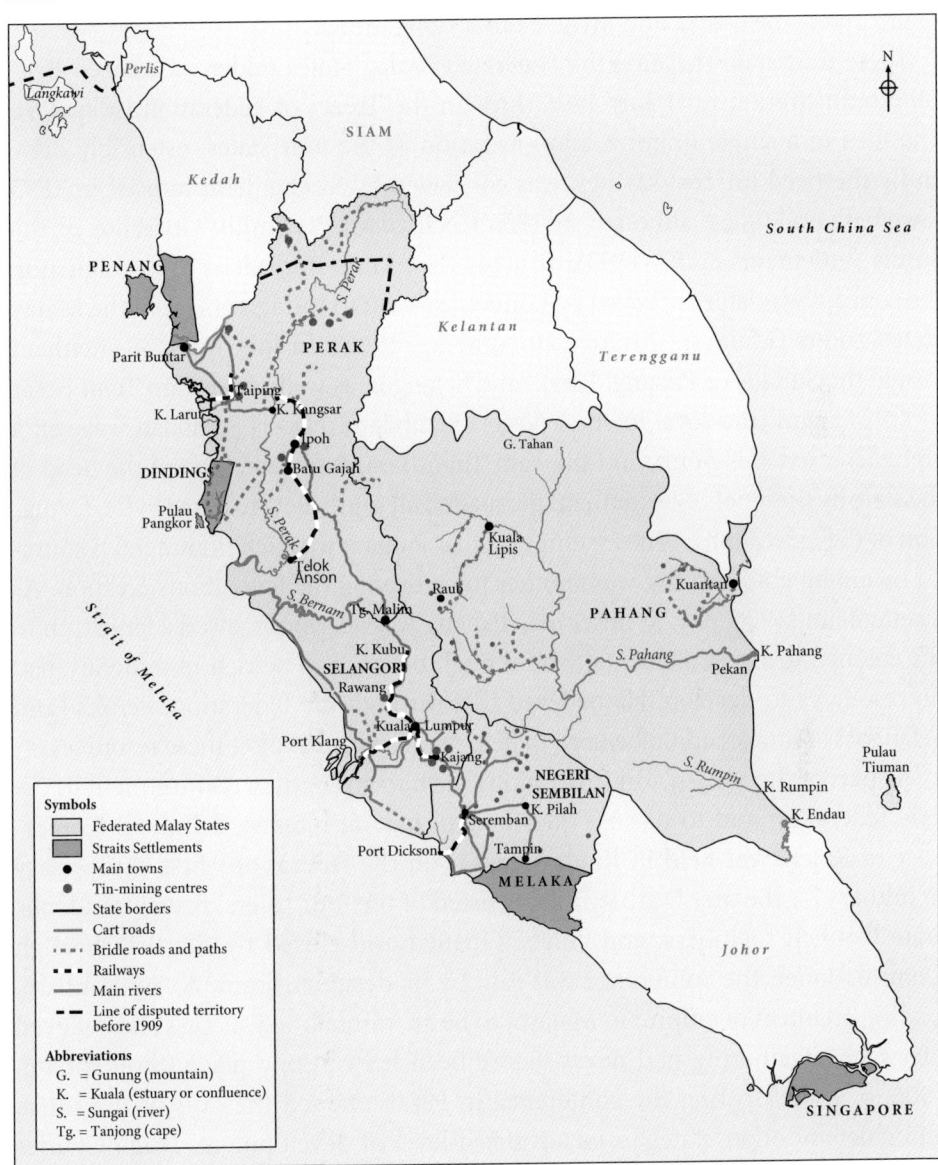

Source: Royal Asiatic Society of Great Britain and Ireland (1898).

finances, particularly loans to Pahang (whose natural resources were as yet unexploited). Pahang's insolvency was to become a critical factor in the relationship between the Straits Settlements and the peninsula's Malay states. In March 1892, when the Straits Legislative Council granted an additional $100,000 to Pahang after substantial earlier grants, the question of the future administration in the four Malay states with British residents—Negeri Sembilan, Pahang, Perak, and Selangor—reached a tipping point, as the Straits government demanded action to reduce its financial burden. While British annexation of these states was considered, Swettenham (1893) argued that this would break faith with the Malay rulers, be costly, and involve other obligations.

These four states became the Federated Malay States under centralized British administration on 1 July 1896 through the Treaty of Federation (Map 1.5). The idea of a single uniform administration of the four states, ostensibly driven by the need for cost savings, was conceived by Swettenham himself in 1893 (Swettenham, 1906), although in 1906 Cecil Clementi Smith, Governor of the Straits Settlements (1887–1893), disputed this claim. Regardless of its originator, the concept was later approved by London, subject to the agreement of the Malay states' rulers (Malaysia Archive Documents, 1926). In July 1895, Swettenham visited the Sultans of Pahang, Perak, and Selangor, as well as the Yam Tuan Besar of Sri Menanti (the royal town of Negeri Sembilan). Negeri Sembilan was still a confederacy at this point, and the Yam Tuan Besar had been elected the head of the state by the chiefs. Swettenham persuaded all four rulers to agree to the formation of the federation.[72] The assumption that Pahang was rich in mineral resources, including gold and tin, was another force driving the federation's creation. As Swettenham (1906, p. 273) observed, 'Pahang was very poor, owed a large sum to the colony [Straits Settlements], and though believed to be rich in minerals, had no resources to develop'. He believed that through the federation, Perak's (and Selangor's) tin taxes could be used to help open up and exploit these resources.

As part of the British administration's push to strengthen commitment to the new federation and to discuss questions of federal interest, a Federal Conference of Rulers was held in Kuala Kangsar on the federation's first anniversary in July 1897—the first Durbar.[73] It consisted of the four rulers, British residents, State Council members, and chiefs. Opened and closed by the British High Commissioner, the conference was said by its designer Frank A. Swettenham, leading architect of empire in Malaya, to be an 'unqualified success'; he believed that such a gathering had never before been held in one place (Swettenham, 1906, p. 288). Hosting the conference in Perak opened the eyes of the rulers and chiefs of other states to its advanced level of development. Hugh Charles Clifford quoted (1898, p. 22) a remark of one of Pahang's rulers who observed, 'until we visited Perak we were like unto the frog beneath the coconut shell, not dreaming that there were other worlds than ours!' The Federal Conference of Rulers, however, had no legislative powers and was merely ceremonial.

---

72 As there were some limitations on the Yam Tuan Besar's (lord of the state's) powers, the agreement was also signed by some of the other Negeri Sembilan chiefs (Allen et al., 1981). The Yam Tuan Besar became the Yang di-Pertuan Besar (ruler of the state) of Negeri Sembilan in 1898.

73 Royalty arrived in sailing boats and chieftains on elephants. The subjects camped along the riverbank, at the foot of the British High Commissioner's residence, for days of festivities (Gullick, 1993). The sultans decided to repeat the prestigious event from time to time, and a second Rulers' Conference was held in Selangor in July 1903.

The Treaty of Federation contained six articles through which the four rulers and the chiefs agreed to place their states under the protection of the British government, and to be administered under its advice (Belfield, 1902). At the first conference, Perak's Sultan Idris Murshidul Azzam Shah astutely described British protection as a form of control. The treaty provided for the appointment of a Resident-General as the 'agent and representative of the British government' who was to be directly responsible to the Straits Settlements' governor. The treaty's final article stated that:

> Nothing in this Agreement is intended to curtail any of the powers or authority now held by any of the above-named Rulers in their respective States, nor does it alter the relations now existing between any of the States named and the British Empire. (Belfield, 1902, p. 2)

The articles of the treaty neither altered the formal powers of the residents vis-à-vis the sultans nor gave the Resident-General executive control over the individual states. Moreover, while it proclaimed the formation of a 'federation', it did not create a federal system of government (Burns, 1965). The four states were united in a federation, but the state governments' authority over local matters was preserved. The aims were to maintain the positions of the sultanates and to provide the basis for central and uniform state administrations. Yet, in strengthening and streamlining British political and legislative control, the federation 'also undoubtedly helped to coordinate and promote colonial economic objectives' (Sultan Nazrin Shah, 2019, p. 12).

The headquarters of the Resident-General was based in the rich mining town of Kuala Lumpur in Selangor—its capital since 1880—as were the heads of the federal departments. The Resident-General was head of the administration of the four states, and was supported by a federal secretariat. The British administration had selected Kuala Lumpur as the federal capital because of its central location, good communications, and growing commercial importance.[74] The Resident-General was now the 'channel of communication' between the residents and British High Commissioner, who also served as the Governor of the Straits Settlements. He could issue instructions to federal or state officers as well as to the residents, and any appeals arising from his decisions had to go through his office to the High Commissioner. In financial matters, his authority was considerable. The independence of the individual state administrations was now heavily curtailed.

---

74 Sultan Idris would have much preferred the headquarters of the Resident-General and federal officers to be in Perak (Swettenham, 1897, p. 19).

Up to 1902, the Resident-General was able to issue orders on any aspect of the state governments; after 1902, the existing state departments—such as post and telegraph, printing, and medical—along with new ones—such as labour and agriculture—became federal departments under the direct control of federal officers located in Kuala Lumpur. State governments were powerless to check centralization and to escape from the expanding activities of the federal departments. At the meeting of the rulers of the Federated Malay States in 1903, the Sultan of Perak, Idris Murshidul Azzam Shah, unsuccessfully pleaded for the maintenance of state rights (Cmd. 4276, 1933, p. 7). According to Burns (1965), this shift towards federal government led to the over-centralization of administration in the hands of the Resident-General who, as executive head of the larger Federated Malay States, tended in practice to supersede the authority of the Malay rulers. The four centralized Federated Malay States were increasingly falling under the influence of the governor of the Straits Settlements.

In summary, the reforms under the Treaty of Federation and the appointment of a Resident-General consolidated British administrative and economic control, with federal-level policies taking effect at state level for the first time. The federation eroded the authority of Perak's sultan and its resident, in a trend that became further pronounced after the Federal Council was established.

Strengthening Colonial Control—Federal Council, 1909

The Federal Council was established as an extension of British political and legislative authority. It would meet annually, presided over by the British High Commissioner.[75] As the Federated Malay States had no single head, with sovereignty vested in four different rulers, the Resident-General became the rulers' representative. The Federal Council was inaugurated on 11 December 1909 and convened for a few days each year (until it was reconstituted in 1927). It conducted its business in a manner similar to the Straits Settlements' Legislative Council. The first meeting was held at Kuala Kangsar, with later sittings at Kuala Lumpur. The inclusion of the sultans as 'ordinary' members of the Federal Council underlined the erosion of their powers and the diminution of their

---

75 The Federal Council comprised the British High Commissioner, the Resident-General (renamed the Chief Secretary to the Government of the Federated Malay States after 1910), the Sultans of Perak and Selangor, the Yang di-Pertuan Besar of Negeri Sembilan, the Regent of Pahang, the four residents, and five unofficial members.

royal status. The Council increasingly included leading trade representatives from all communities, who also influenced policy.

The Federal Council simplified legislative procedures, especially where an enactment was applicable to more than one state. It shifted responsibility for public finances from the executive—previously concentrated in the office of the Resident-General—to the legislature (Burns, 1965). It also strengthened federal oversight of infrastructure such as roads, railways, and other services essential for promoting the mining and rubber industries. The maintenance of the federal structure had become vital for supporting British economic interests, including ensuring that these interests were aligned with those of the Straits Settlements' merchant community and other business lobbying groups (Shennan, 2015).

Just as the Federal Council strengthened British political control over the Federated Malay States, so it correspondingly weakened the power of the State Councils—so much so that, in 1924, Iskandar Shah, the Sultan of Perak (1918–1938), went to London to present a list of grievances to the Colonial Office.[76] Among these grievances was the fact that, although Perak was the richest state in Malaya, it could not use its revenues without the authority of the Chief Secretary or a Federal Department Head; the extent to which the Perak State Council had become a body 'with practically no work to do, and no powers to exercise'; and the issue that, by contrast, the State Councils of the unfederated states of Johor and Kedah retained their functions as 'the paramount authority in the State' (Loh, 1972, p. 45). He pleaded for the Perak State Council to be restored to the position it had held prior to the federation, when it had been able to enact state laws and approve state policy. The colonial authorities took Sultan Iskandar's concerns seriously and, in 1927, agreed to a policy of gradual decentralization, giving some measures of financial control to the states. That year, the four rulers withdrew from membership of the Federal Council by agreement, and by the early 1930s control of some departments had been transferred back to the states (German, 1937).

Still, over time, Perak's State Council had diminished in importance as the centralized Federal Council usurped its powers and purpose, strengthening British colonial control. Centralized control was exercised at the lowest level of administration, with even district officers now appointed by the federal authorities. By contrast, in two of the unfederated states—Johor and Kedah, where the residential system had always remained at arm's length—the sultans retained

---

76 Sultan Iskandar attended Balliol College, Oxford. On returning to Perak in 1902, his first civil service posting was to the Perak secretariat. Later, he joined the Federated Malay States police force in Kuala Lumpur and became the first Malay assistant commissioner. In 1916, on his return to Perak, he became raja bendahara and was proclaimed sultan in 1918.

far more power over the state's administration and finances. Concerns about over-centralization lingered, especially in relation to the weakened voice of the sultans in state administration and legislation. Dissatisfaction was also growing with the influence exerted by the Governor of the Straits Settlements, who concurrently served as Malaya's High Commissioner, because he appeared to favour the Settlements, especially Singapore, in major infrastructure decisions (Khoo, 2002).[77] These issues continued to dominate political discourse in the 1920s and 1930s.

---

77 For example, in the 1920s, engineers studying the Dindings estuary in Lumut reported that it was potentially the best harbour east of Suez, even better than Singapore's Tanjong Pagar, but the British administration decided not to proceed as it feared it would outdo Tanjong Pagar (Khoo, 2002).

PART

2

Perak's Prosperity—Propelled by Natural Resources

An open-cast tin mine in Kampar,
early 20th century

Globalization of Perak's Tin and Rubber Industries

The Tin Industry

By the second half of the 19th century, a new capitalist world order had begun to take hold which was increasingly embracing the states of Malaya as suppliers of tin to the geographically distant industrialized West (see 'A Globalizing World', above). Rich in mineral resources, the county of Cornwall in the UK had been the epicentre of the global tin-mining industry. But the expansion of Britain's tin-plate industry in the 19th century gave momentum to substantial increases in the global tin supply that eventually proved to be highly unfavourable for Cornish tin mining. By the late 19th century, production in Cornwall, once the tin capital of the world, was in serious decline—an early casualty of economic globalization. Malaya and other low-cost tin-producing frontier regions, including Australia and the Dutch East Indies, were surging by exploiting their rich, shallow alluvial ore deposits. With the progressive integration of Malaya into the global economy, its fortunes became inseparably tied to the vagaries of commodity price markets. As Malaya's dominant tin-producing region, the state of Perak was at the forefront of this global integration, at first through Larut and later through Kinta.

Until the mid-1870s direct British interests in Perak's tin industry were limited. After the signing of the Pangkor Treaty in 1874, and as the world's demand for tin continued to surge, the levies and duties on tin production and exports accrued to the British colonial authorities, eventually helping to make Malaya Britain's strongest dollar-earning colony (Curtis, 2003). Unlike the approach adopted by the metropolitan administrations of many Dutch, French, and Portuguese colonies, the British colonial government used at least some of these huge revenues to finance early investments in institutions and infrastructure in Perak as well as in other Malayan states. This helped to provide a foundation for

Globalization: Perak's Rise, Relative Decline, and Regeneration. Sultan Nazrin Shah, Oxford University Press. © Sultan Nazrin Shah (2024).
DOI: 10.1093/oso/9780198897774.003.0010

the development of a market economy that would later broaden to include the state's other natural resources.

With Cornish tin production in its twilight years, British commercial interests saw an opportunity to enter Perak's tin-mining industry. Chinese-owned mines had enjoyed great success in the state with their labour-intensive mining of shallow alluvial deposits. But these deposits were now near exhaustion, and Chinese ventures typically lacked access to the capital required to open deposits that were unworkable and too poor to exploit without substantial mechanization. Nevertheless, many Chinese-owned mines did survive, prospering through the use of steam-driven gravel pumps to exploit smaller deposits at greater depths. By 1900, Perak contributed 49 per cent of Malaya's tin output (a share that would increase over the next 60 years) and 25 per cent of the world's output.

British Private Company Interests

In 1888, even before the colonial government began supporting the entry of British companies into Perak's tin-mining industry, the STC—a joint-stock enterprise owned by British and Continental European interests—obtained the rights to export ore from Perak for the lucrative tin-smelting industry. Until then, ore had mainly been smelted in small Chinese workshops close to mines, partly because of the costs of transport, but also because mine owners could then more closely monitor the metallic value extracted from their ore. But the STC had developed superior smelting technology that used coal rather than charcoal and extracted higher metallic content of better quality. The STC had also developed a novel business model that incentivized small mining operations by providing them with 'cash for ore', based on assays that gave miners full value for the metallic content of the ore.

At its centralized smelting facilities on Pulau Brani in the Straits Settlement of Singapore, the STC produced higher-quality tin at lower prices, benefiting from superior technology, economies of scale, and colonial policy support. In 1901, and after a blanket ban by the colonial administration on all charcoal smelters in Perak, the STC opened a second furnace in Province Wellesley in Penang, where all Perak's ore was eventually smelted. Through an associate company—the Straits Steamship Company—the STC transported the refined tin ingots to export markets in Asia and Europe. By 1912, the STC had become a company of global standing, smelting and shipping about two-thirds of the tin produced and refined on the Malayan peninsula, roughly equivalent to one-third of global supply.

As the end of the 19th century approached, Perak's tin mining was becoming more mechanized, thanks to the adoption of imported technologies. The Gopeng Tin Mining Company—financed with investment from the Redruth Mining Exchange in Cornwall—introduced hydraulic sluicing mining methods to Perak, a technology developed in California's gold fields a few decades earlier. After some experimentation, this technology—combined with traditional *dulang* washing in open ditches—proved highly profitable, capable of exploiting deposits that would otherwise have been uneconomical. Gravel pumps, which had been invented in France in the late 18th century, were in wide use by 1905. Hydraulic elevators entered Perak's mines five years later, these having been developed in Tasmania, one of Australia's leading mining locations. More important, however, were the bucket dredging machines, which transformed the ownership and production of Perak's tin mining. First successfully operated in 1913 by the Malayan Tin Dredging Company, a London-based joint-stock company, bucket dredges remained in use until the eventual exhaustion of most viable deposits towards the end of the 20th century.

Perak's integration into the globalized world generated winners and losers. While the economy benefited from price booms in tin (and later, rubber), it also suffered from sharp cyclical commodity price falls, which damaged the employment prospects and welfare of the population that was dependent on these commodities for a living. There were wide fluctuations in the earnings of workers, and therefore in their standards of living.

The Winners

The spectacular emergence of Perak's tin-mining industry in the mid-19th and early 20th century benefited many individuals and organizations, both locally and internationally. Tin mining generated local jobs and income, as did the money spent on materials, equipment, and power—although much of the gain went to the mine *towkay*s (owners), and later to British and Continental European investors. Many of the workers were indentured and were often caught in a vicious circle of debt. Yet, despite the hardship faced by mine workers, tin attracted hundreds of thousands of migrants from poorer countries, especially China. Tin mining gave birth to new townships, and the duties and taxes levied on mining helped pay for substantial investments in local rail and road networks to support and expand the colonial economy. Tin revenues also supported the delivery of health and education services, which especially benefited those living in or near the flourishing new towns.

Internationally, investors from London, Cornwall, the Straits Settlements, and other locations received handsome dividends from their holdings in Perak's tin-mining and smelting firms, and in shipping and distribution companies more widely. In Britain and elsewhere, the manufacture of tin plate and other industrial products that used tin as an essential input created jobs and generated income. Tin contributed to the pool of sterling reserves both through direct exports of ingots from Malaya to the US, and through the export of tin plate and other industrial products from Britain. Consulting engineers and dredging-equipment manufacturers in Britain built a lucrative business designing and selling their equipment to mining companies operating in Malaya.

The Losers and Missed Opportunities

By their very nature, industrial capitalism and the global tin industry created losers as well. Given the low tin content (in terms of both value and weight) in most industrial uses of tin, there was little incentive for organizational integration between tin producers and end-using industries, or for end-using industries to locate themselves close to the sources of ore.

Almost all the demand for the final product of tin mining—for instance, in food canning—was in Western countries. One consequence of this was that Perak had little opportunity to develop the manufacturing industries that could have leveraged its ore wealth. As there were no vertically integrated downstream tin businesses, tin was traded on an international market. Competitive pressures began to drive Cornish mines out of business in the second half of the 19th century, since they could no longer compete with better-quality, lower-cost tin from Australia, the Dutch East Indies, the Federated Malay States, and elsewhere. In turn, in the early part of the 20th century, Chinese ventures in British Malaya that had displaced Cornish tin production using labour-intensive methods lost ground to British companies which deployed highly mechanized methods.

Crucially, the tin industry was never completely free from government intervention. The colonial authorities exercised their power to protect British capitalist interests and to neutralize competition through various regulatory mechanisms. The imposition of heavy export duties on ore concentrates from Malaya—with exemptions for those bound for Britain and Australia—was intended to hinder the development of a smelting industry in the US. Likewise, in the allocation of mining leases on land, the colonial authorities favoured British over Chinese merchant investors. Globalization was occurring in imperial 'silos'. Malaya, like other colonies, had become a captive market for British exports of textiles, manufactured goods, iron and steel, and other industrial products, and the colonial authorities had little interest in encouraging the development of industry there.

World War I marked the end of the wave of European-led globalization that had begun in the 19th century. Trade volume fell and countries started to implement protectionist policies, with many European countries and the US embarking on tariff hikes by the 1920s (Baldwin, 2016). Until this point, the gold standard had greatly facilitated trade and commerce, and had anchored the system of international capital flows and payments, but it collapsed as countries started to use monetary policy and capital controls to support their own domestic goals. As the 20th century progressed, global free trade gave way to patterns of trade and investment that were increasingly configured by international trading laws and political alliances. Malaya's tin exports had become ever more reliant on the US market. Revenues and economic growth were closely correlated with the volume and prices of exports, which were determined by global demand.

But it was price volatility—caused mainly by large swings in the US economy—that eventually ended the largely unregulated global tin market. A combination of strong competitive pressures from new sources of supply, and the Great Depression of the early 1930s, drove the price of tin down to such low levels that international intervention was required. In 1931, the International Tin Restriction Scheme—agreed on by the governments of the major tin producers, namely Bolivia, British Malaya, the Dutch East Indies, and Nigeria—set output and export quotas. The goal was to support tin prices and protect the industry's investors. A cartel had now supplanted free trade and market competition in determining the global allocation of tin production and exports.

The Rubber Industry

A similar story can be told about the emergence of the rubber industry in colonial Malaya. Alongside Johor and Selangor, Perak was one of the largest rubber-producing states in the Malay peninsula. In the rubber sector, smallholders and peasants tried to eke out a living from the fortunes of rubber when prices were high, growing it alongside other farm crops. The coexistence of Malay smallholder producers with the dominant colonial-supported plantation companies meant that more people benefited from expanding global demand for rubber than for tin.

It was soaring industrial demand, mainly from the US automotive industry for rubber car tyres, that drove investment and activity in Malaya. Just as
tin mines in Perak and other parts of Malaya had relied on large numbers of
migrant workers from China for their operation in the 19th and early 20th century, so the rubber plantations owned and operated by the British relied to a
great extent on migrant workers from India as the rubber industry took off.

The spoils from rubber, as from tin, were widely dispersed, with the colonial authorities, the UK government (through the sterling reserve balances),
plantation investors, and local smallholders all benefiting. Once again, as with
tin, there was very little downstream development of industry based on rubber. Part of the reason for this was that rubber products such as tyres gain
in bulk and weight during manufacturing, limiting the geographical extent
of potential finished-product markets. Even as late as 1967, 98 per cent of
Malaysia's rubber was exported (Thoburn, 1977).[1] In the 20th century, by contrast, when rubber production was declining due to the shift to more profitable palm oil production, Malaysia started to import natural rubber to meet
the demand of its growing downstream activities, such as the manufacture of
tyres and rubber gloves.

Rubber prices, like tin prices, were highly volatile, and the Stevenson
Restriction Scheme of 1922–1928 (also known as the Stevenson Plan) was the
first of numerous attempts to regulate production and exports. But rubber,
along with tin, had brought Perak, and colonial Malaya more widely, into the
orbit of the global economy, and these commodities were to feel the chill of the
Great Depression. On the eve of World War II, rubber and tin prices had yet
to recover, and the world economy was sinking further into 'beggar-thy-neigh-
bour' protectionism. World War II stimulated an acceleration in the commercial production of synthetic rubber, at first by Germany and later by the US
(Barlow et al., 1994); production of tin substitutes also increased. When the
price of Malaya's natural rubber was high, therefore, users in industrialized
countries could replace it with synthetic rubber substitutes. As with tin, there
was little the colonial government could do to increase demand; rubber, too,
was a price taker.

*   *   *

---

1 The Federation of Malaysia was formed on 16 September 1963, with Sabah, Sarawak, and Singapore as the
three new components joining the Federation of Malaya. Singapore separated and became an independent
nation on 9 August 1965.

Part 2 analyses how Perak's natural-resource-based economy was increasingly exploited through the processes of European-led economic globalization. It describes how the state's primary commodity-based economy prospered as a result of huge inflows of foreign investment and migrant labour, which occurred against a background of British institutions, enabling policies, and an infrastructure designed to buttress the extractive economy.

The first two sections describe how tin became the driver of Perak's early prosperity, with the industry's commanding heights dominated by Chinese capital and labour as its epicentre shifted from Larut to Kinta. They go on to describe how, in the early 20th century, British mining interests came to dominate the industry, thanks to their greater capital and more advanced technology, bolstered by strong policy support from the colonial authorities.

The next section describes the boom in Perak's natural rubber industry, a sector controlled largely by British and Continental European interests, but in which Malay and non-Malay smallholders came to play an increasingly significant role. Both tin and rubber were subject to wildly fluctuating global demand and high price volatility, which adversely impacted incomes. Export restriction schemes in both industries, introduced to stabilize prices, worked against the interests of Chinese-owned mines and greatly disadvantaged rubber smallholders.

The fourth section shows that Perak's per capita income was well above the Malayan average, and, at its peak on the eve of the Great Depression, was over three times larger than it had been 25 years earlier. The colonial economy boomed and living standards surged, especially for those in the burgeoning towns. Taxes on tin and rubber financed rudimentary education, health, and other basic services.

The penultimate section describes the period after the Japanese occupation, including the communist insurgency. It examines the British administration's efforts to protect its massive investments in the tin and rubber industries during decolonization, and describes how the formation of the highly centralized Federation of Malay States in 1948 further diminished Perak's control over decisions related to its local development. The final section reflects on the implications of Perak's remarkable natural-resource-based prosperity. Owing to colonial policies that encouraged huge capital and migrant inflows, Perak's natural resources were in fact a mixed blessing.

Inevitably, the model of economic development implemented in Perak in the colonial era was most beneficial for colonial investors, who derived huge profits from tin and rubber production and related commercial activities. It generated great wealth in booming tin-towns but had only limited 'trickle-down' benefits for most workers in these industries, and even fewer for subsistence farmers. It also had only minimal spillover impact on the creation of new industries. Trade and commerce were largely in the hands of British, Straits Settlements, and other foreign interests. In addition, Perak's economic model was hampered by its dependency on natural resources, which degraded the state's rivers and forests. It created a social and economic divide within and between the state's multicultural communities, and between town and countryside. Significantly, this colonial model of economic development also sowed the seeds of ethnic tension—even conflict—that was to affect the state and country beyond independence.

Tin's Shift from Larut to Kinta, 1850–1900

Perak's association with tin stretches back to before the 17th century, and hence even before the Dutch and Acehnese fought to gain a monopoly over its output, a monopoly which they then shared to the exclusion of other foreign traders (see Part 1).[2] Tin production at that time was simple, manual, and informal—far from the organized and mechanized industry it would later become. Tin was typically washed out of sand in river beds or dug out of earth at the edges of mountains, mainly by Malay miners (Hale, 1885). It was, however, the discovery of rich alluvial tin fields, first in the district of Larut in northwestern Perak in the late 1840s, and later in the central district of Kinta in the 1880s, that dramatically increased the scale of the industry and its value to the state's economy.

The discovery of these tin fields eventually led to Perak's tin-mining booms generating great wealth, causing the state to emerge as a leading global tin producer and exporter with important links to the international economy. In the second half of the 19th century, Perak exploited its resource blessing, leading to the emergence and growth of its tin and port towns, largely on the back of Chinese capital and Chinese labour, while the British colonial administration provided the enabling security for economic take-off following the signing of the Pangkor Treaty in 1874.

The discovery of rich tin deposits in Larut coincided with global developments that contributed to growing interest in the tin industry among a small group of investors in the Straits Settlement of Penang. Tin consumption was on the rise thanks to the significant expansion of the tin-plate industry in Britain, the rest of Europe, and the US. Britain's supply of tin until the mid-1850s had largely been

---

2 Tin was a valuable metal even in the Bronze Age, for it was the hardening agent for copper and, alloyed with copper, formed bronze. A bronze coin of the Catholic Monarchs of Spain, Ferdinand and Isabella, who ruled jointly from their marriage in 1469 until her death in 1504—he died in 1516—was found buried 13 feet below the surface at Klian Kalong, in Kinta, and likely belonged to a miner. This suggests that tin was already being mined here in the late 15th century (Wray, 1894).

Globalization: Perak's Rise, Relative Decline, and Regeneration. Sultan Nazrin Shah, Oxford University Press. © Sultan Nazrin Shah (2024). DOI: 10.1093/oso/9780198897774.003.0011

met through its mines in Cornwall, which was the world's leading commercial tin-mining centre at the time. However, the supply of tin from Cornwall's deep underground mines was no longer sufficient to meet the surging demand associated with the industrialization of food production and the use of tin cans for food preservation. With a tariff reduction on foreign tin in 1843, and preferential duties for tin produced in British territories, Britain took a step towards free trade, beginning to source more tin, at newly competitive prices, from overseas via Penang and Singapore. Britain's demand for 'Straits tin' increased even faster after all import tariffs on foreign tin were ended in 1853.

The growth of Larut's tin-mining industry, however, suffered serious setbacks as a result of brutal wars that raged between 1861 and 1873 among rival Chinese groups who, in the absence of clearly defined property and mining rights, sought control of the highly lucrative mines and their waterways. British protection, the end of the disputes between the Malay chiefs and between the rival Chinese clans,[3] and a return of confidence among Penang's investors, heralded an era of soaring prosperity for Larut as its tin production surged. Larut's prosperity was, however, an exception, as there was not much improvement in other parts of Perak, especially in areas where there was short-lived resistance to British colonial rule. In 1872, William Henry Read, Chairman of the Singapore Chamber of Commerce and a member of the Singapore Legislative Council, wrote in a letter to J. W. W. Birch, the Colonial Secretary of the Straits Settlements:

> I would urge upon Government the absolute necessity of adopting some straightforward and well-defined policy in dealing with the rulers of the various States of the Malay Peninsula, for the purpose of promoting and protecting commercial relations with their respective provinces … the trade … with Perak, Laroot and other places in the neighbourhood is well known to be of great value. (Board of Trade [BT], 1880–1932, 34/2489/14056, p. 14)

Emergence and Then Relative Decline of Larut

When tin was discovered in Larut, the district was very sparsely populated, with just a few thousand people. In order to exploit the mining opportunities, it was necessary to recruit migrant labour. Workers recruited from China to mine in the island of Banka's tin fields in the early part of the 19th century

---

3 Captain Speedy, Assistant Resident of Perak, reported several outbreaks of violence between the 'fighting men' who had been brought from China in the wars of 1871–1873. Periodic riots of secret society members also erupted in the Straits Settlement of Penang, which had direct repercussions on the Larut miners, and attempts to establish new district lodges of these societies had to be curtailed (Gullick, 1953, p. 42).

had already established an excellent reputation as miners. Long Ja'afar, a local Malay territorial chief and administrator of Larut, recruited a small group of indentured Chinese migrants to mine at Taiping, about 16 km from the mouth of the Larut River and a short voyage from Penang (Map 2.1, upper panel). When tin was later discovered in Kamunting, just north of the mines in Taiping, Chinese workers were brought in to open mines there as well. At first, Long Ja'afar engaged workers directly using capital advanced to him by Penang's Chinese merchant investors; later, he granted mining concessions to these financiers to recruit and pay for their own workers, and they paid him a tax for these rights.

Up to the last years of the 19th century, Perak's tin industry was highly labour intensive and made minimal use of machinery. In Larut, the Chinese method of mining was simple and incurred low capital expenditure: it involved digging a ditch from a nearby stream and using a chain-pump, or *chin-chia*, which was worked by a simple overshot wheel, to drain the ditch and to channel water from the hills towards the washing of tin ore in wooden sluice boxes or *lanchut* (Singh, 1960). Smelting was typically carried out on site at the mines, and the tin was shipped to Penang to be further refined and exported (Hampton, 1886). From Penang, Larut's tin was transhipped to Singapore and from there to its export destinations, mainly in Britain, China, and India.

Before the 1860s, tin was generally mined on a small scale, with labour estimated to account for around 80 per cent of a mine's production costs (Yip, 1969). Legislation by the Chinese government in 1860 allowing trade in workers precipitated an increase in Chinese migrants entering Perak, which propelled the growth of the mining industry. In 1862, there were 19 mines and an estimated 25,000 Chinese miners in Taiping and Kamunting (Jackson, 1963). Around this time, Taiping had around 100 shophouses and Kamunting some 40 to 50.

The Larut River was the main link between the mines and the depot at its estuary. Alternative routes from the mines were more circuitous; a path to Kuala Kangsar, for instance, took two days to traverse by elephant. Soon after Ngah Ibrahim succeeded his father Long Ja'afar as administrator of Larut in 1858, a new bullock-cart road connecting the mines with the Larut River was built at a point about 16 km from the open sea at Port Weld, which had a small *godown* (warehouse) facility with provision for storage, weighing, and stamping of ore. Because Larut is located outside the Perak River valley, its tin was liable to be smuggled so as to avoid the toll stations on that river (Andaya, 1979).

Chinese Tin Miners

In Larut, migrant labourers were almost all indentured; most had been brought as *sinkhehs* (new recruits) by brokers or agents who advanced a sum of money for their passage from China. They were then sold to a mining *towkay*, who belonged to a secret society, and were made to labour at the mines in order to work their way out of their debt. They worked in the open around eight hours a day and were employed on the 'truck' system, in which their food and daily supplies, such as rice, opium, tobacco, and alcoholic spirits, were provided in advance by the *towkays* at up to double the market rate. They received the surplus of their wages over their consumption only once each year, usually at Chinese New Year. Often, they received 'very little, if anything, at the final settlement' (Doyle, 1879, p. 10) and were instead locked in a cycle of perpetual debt, having to work year after year to pay off what was owed to the *towkays*. By the mid-1870s, free migrants—those who had paid for their own passage from China to Malaya—began to form the larger proportion of labourers. They were, nonetheless, still employed under the truck system and were tied to their employers until they paid off their debts (Wong, 1965).

The Kinta tin rushes of the 1880s and early 1890s precipitated the rise of *tribute* workers who were in a cooperative relationship with the mine owners and shared the risks and profits of the mining venture—a system that had also been adopted by the Chinese in the Dutch East Indies. If the venture produced large quantities of ore, the workers shared the profits; but if the venture failed, the workers would lose their wages, although they would have been fed, clothed, and housed. This risk-sharing system positively incentivized mining and prospecting even when tin prices were low. Many mine owners preferred to let their mines out to *tributers* even though it meant that their share of the output, at around 8 per cent or less, would be lower than the 10 per cent they would have been able to obtain in Larut (Wong, 1965).

While a few miners who worked under the truck and tribute systems went on to start up mines on their own, becoming rich tin-mining *towkays* themselves, in general the working and living conditions of miners in Perak, and elsewhere, in the 19th and early 20th century, were particularly harsh (Box 2.1).

Despite conflicts between rival clans and an uneasy peace, and despite high death rates among miners, the number of Chinese working in the Larut mines rose during the late 1860s. With the growth in labour, tin production rocketed between 1868 and 1871. Based on data on exports of tin from Larut to Penang, and on imports of tin into Penang in 1879, most of the tin imported into Penang

Box 2.1   Harsh conditions, disease, and death among Perak's miners

Chinese tin miners worked and lived in dangerous, harsh, and disease-prone conditions. Those who were indentured were threatened with flogging if they attempted to abscond (Jackson, 1963). Fatal accidents in the open-cast, *lombong*, mines—where the soil or rock above the tin deposit was removed—were numerous, especially when these mines reached greater depths, or where the grounds were unstable after having been worked.

Medical treatment was rarely provided if miners fell ill, and many were left to die by the roadside or in 'a little hut on the outskirts of the mine' (Selangor Government Minute paper 1894, cited in Wong, 1965, p. 74). State hospitals were essentially 'reception houses for the dying' where friends made 'a convenience of the hospitals and send in the men to die', either to save the expense of a funeral, or because a death in a *kongsi* or clan house was considered unlucky (Birch, 1896, p. 13).

Mine owners housed workers in insanitary lines of huts. Their water supply was often contaminated, leading to water-borne diseases. Ernest Woodford Birch, Perak's eighth British Resident, (1904–1910) observed:

> There are about 75,000 miners in Kinta: from them most of our hospitals in Kinta obtain their inmates, while many die without even seeing a hospital. While care is taken to make towns sanitary, while the labourers on agricultural estates are hemmed round with rules of health, nothing whatever of any description is done for the miners. Thousands of [labourers] live in a manner that courts disease. (Birch, 1907, p. 15)

Cases of beriberi, a non-infectious disease, filled hospitals and headed the list of the main causes of death among miners. Arsenic, a chemical found in the rock in the mines, was initially said to cause neuritis in beriberi cases.

> When we know that arsenic in combination with other metals is common in the soil, where these Chinese have to stand for hours while searching for tin, we may regard the possibility of arsenic as a cause for beriberi as being something more than problematic. (Walker, 1901, p. 15)

Later, beriberi was discovered to be caused by a deficiency of Vitamin B1, associated with the mine workers' dominant diet of polished white rice. At the turn of the century, some 95 per cent of Perak's beriberi cases treated were Chinese, and 90 per cent were miners.

(Continued)

Together with beriberi, the infectious diseases of malaria, dysentery, cholera, and pulmonary tuberculosis caused the greatest number of deaths. As the mining industry grew and dense jungles were cleared for its expansion, Chinese workers came into direct contact with malaria-carrying mosquitoes, which multiplied very rapidly in the new open environment. Death rates were very high as a result (Winstedt and Wilkinson, 1934; Lim, 1967).

Opium smoking was common among Chinese mine workers as it helped to relieve their hardship. Consumption was encouraged by mine-owning *towkays* who profited financially from its sale; in addition, some believed that opium gave workers the strength to toil under the arduous and hazardous conditions of open-cast mining. The colonial government also encouraged the habit, as taxes on opium were an important source of state revenue. Opium addiction became a major health challenge, but opium smokers were reluctant to enter hospital, dreading being deprived of the drug. Many who entered the Chinese Hospital at Taiping and were unable to obtain opium either discharged themselves or absconded (Treacher, 1892).

As the 20th century progressed, the working conditions and health of Chinese miners gradually improved. This was the result of increased regulatory oversight; the implementation of preventive health measures; advances in medical knowledge; and improved hospital facilities, protocols, and standards.

originated from Larut (Doyle, 1879).[4] In 1872, annual tin exports were valued at an impressive $1 million, compared with only some $220,000 in 1868 and 1869 (Straits Settlements Blue Book, 1868–1871).

Tin Duties and Tax Farming

Tin taxes and duties were a lucrative source of income for some of Perak's Malay chiefs and a vital source of revenue that enabled Larut's prosperity. In Long Ja'afar's era, only a quit rent (land tax) of $100 a year was payable to the Sultan of Perak, while the revenue Long Ja'afar received from Larut alone was around $60,000 to $70,000 annually (Wee, 1952). Under his son Ngah Ibrahim, the duty on tin was as high as $22 per *bahar*;[5] this had been reduced to $19 per *bahar* by 1872, but still yielded Ngah Ibrahim a massive revenue of about

---

4 Penang also imported tin from Siam and Kedah.

5 One *bahar* is equivalent to around 450 lbs (imperial pounds).

$200,000 a year. Of this, $6 per *bahar* was owed to the sultan, though the actual amount received by the sultan is uncertain (Gullick, 1953).[6] Nonetheless, this method of revenue collection—tax farming—adopted from the Straits Settlements and employed by Long Ja'afar, was particularly successful, circumventing the obstacles inherent in collecting tax from the mine owners directly, such as dishonesty or tax evasion.

Under the tax farming system, one of Perak's chiefs 'farmed out' the privilege of collecting taxes for a given period in return for a contracted sum of money. During the era of Long Ja'afar and Ngah Ibrahim, the tax was collected and kept by the tax farmer. Any increase in tin production and profits during the contract year went to the tax farmers, while the chief was able to claim higher fixed monthly amounts in the next contracting period based on the higher volume of production (Gullick, 1953). In mining districts, the tax farmers were typically Chinese *towkays* who provided the capital and other inputs for the mines.

The British colonial administration initially abolished Perak's lucrative tax farms a few years after the Pangkor Treaty in favour of direct tax collection. But it quickly realized that the farms were crucial for the sustainability and profitability of the entire mining industry. The reintroduction of tax farms in 1880 spurred tin production between 1881 and 1883. They were a vital factor in the survival of the Chinese-owned mines, enabling them to dominate the tin fields in the first 25 years of British colonial rule. The British broadened tax farming and applied it to the imports of opium, spirits, and tobacco, to pawnbroking, and to the profits of organized gambling. Because mine owners generally controlled the supply of all these goods and services—on which the mine workers became dependent—taxes could be collected without much difficulty.

This system of tax farming was modelled on the *chandu* (cooked opium) farms which had operated in the Straits Settlements since the first half of the 19th century. There, the right to import raw opium, prepare it for smoking by boiling and converting it into *chandu*, and then sell it to customers, was farmed out to the highest bidder (Sultan Nazrin Shah, 2017). In Larut, however, the opium farmers only had the right to collect duty on opium and not to manufacture or retail *chandu*, unlike in the Straits Settlements. As a result, prices of *chandu* in Larut were lower than in the Straits Settlements.[7]

---

6 Tin duties represented nearly 30 per cent of the market price in 1874.

7 In 1875, the British administrators tried to introduce a *chandu* farm in place of the existing opium farm in Larut. But the Chinese were against the proposal, and riots ensued with some 4,000 Chinese miners leaving the district for Klang in Selangor, where the tax on opium was lower. The proposal was quickly abandoned (Wong, 1965).

The combination of farming and truck systems enabled Chinese capitalists to run occasional production losses, particularly during periods of declining tin prices, as long as they were able to profit from the truck system. Competition for control of the farms often led to clashes between *towkays* from rival clans.

Stability and Wealth of Larut

By April 1874, with Perak now under British administration, Taiping contained about 250 shophouses—described by Frank A. Swettenham (1952, p. 44) as being 'very nice looking'—established in well-formed streets, as well as around 200 to 300 ordinary houses. By end-1874, both Taiping and Kamunting had populations of around 5,000, with 1,000 shopkeepers in Taiping and 300 shops in Kamunting, mainly run by Chinese traders (Gullick, 1953). New infrastructure and public works were put in place, including a 6 km bullock-cart road joining Taiping and Kamunting, a 35 km road between Bukit Gantang and Kuala Kangsar, and another road from Kamunting to the Kurau River.

By 1875, the colonial administration had established Judicial, Mining, Road, and Revenue Departments in Larut, with an administrative unit operating in Matang to the west of Taiping and near the mouth of the Larut River (Khoo, 1991). Government buildings and other infrastructure, especially roads, were built throughout the district, with about $100,000 spent in 1874 and $226,000 in 1875, mainly from the district's own revenues.[8] After the 1875 Perak War (see Part 1: 'Resistance, Retaliation, and Reflection', above), the reconstruction of Larut and other areas in Perak depended heavily on revenue from the tin industry (Gullick, 1953).

The British brought stability through policing and institutional reforms that demarcated property rights. In 1879, within 18 months of its formation, the Perak State Council passed landmark legislation that divided state land into four classes (the first three on 999-year leases): agriculture; native land under Malay tenure; building allotments; and mining reserves.[9] The new system of land tenure was based on the Torrens land registration system introduced in southern Australia in 1858, and a register containing details of the landholder's rights was established in the district Land Offices. For mining land, the legislation allowed the government to grant an applicant a licence to remove tin

---

8 There was probably an initial subsidy from the Penang treasury in the first year after Pangkor (Sadka, 1968).

9 Less than three months later, on the advice of Governor Jervois, the Council reduced leases for agricultural land to 99 years (Harrison, 1907). But under pressure from potential plantation investors, however, the Council reinstated the lease length of 999 years in 1880 (Wilkinson, 1909).

on payment of a fee of $2 and an annual royalty on renewal of $2 per *bahar* (Harrison, 1907). The institutionalization of property rights encouraged investment and gave momentum to economic growth in Larut.

Despite the conflict over opium, the Perak uprising of 1875, and the fall in the price of tin between 1874 and 1878, the revenues from Larut's mines were sustained due to increased production; these made up three-quarters of Perak's total revenues. The reduction of duties on tin from $19 to $15 per *bahar* in 1875, and to $10 per *bahar* in 1877, helped to mitigate the impact of the depression in tin prices, as did the decline in the gold value of silver. During this period, when most countries in Europe were converting from the silver to the gold standard, Straits tin was sold in currencies using the gold standard in Europe and the US, but labour and other production costs in the Malayan mines were based on silver.

Lower Perak had been the main focus of Perak's political economy up to 1877, with the rulers and first-ranking chiefs reigning from this part of the state. Apart from the tin produced at Larut, all other tin produced in Perak had to be exported out of the state along the Perak River. The toll stations of the chiefs were traditionally concentrated in Lower Perak, where the mouth of the Perak River is located, and where J. W. W. Birch had established the British headquarters in 1874. In 1877, however, Kuala Kangsar was made the new royal capital. Kuala Kangsar was the heart of Perak and was where the British Resident Hugh Low had based his administration; it had previously been the capital between 1742 and 1743 (Khoo, 1991). By this time Larut had far surpassed Lower Perak in economic importance, and in 1884 Taiping was made Perak's new administrative capital.

Given its immense mineral wealth and the huge revenue that this generated, Taiping developed faster than all other towns in the Malay states, with new concrete buildings, shophouses, workshops, and brick houses already being built at a time when Kuala Lumpur—chosen in 1896 to be the capital of the Federated Malay States—was full of old houses and sheds (Mohd Zamberi A. Malek, 2001). In 1879, the 19th-century British explorer and writer Isabella Lucy Bird described Taiping as:

> a thriving, increasing place … this important Chinese town, with a street about a mile long, with large bazaars and shops making a fine appearance, being much decorated in the Chinese style, halls of meeting for the different tribes, gambling houses, workshops, the Treasury, a substantial dark wood building, large detached barracks for the Sikh Police, a hospital, a powder magazine, a parade ground, a Government storehouse, a large new jail, neat bungalows for the minor English officers, and on the top of a steep isolated, terraced hill, the British Residency. (Bird, 2010, p. 259)

Government buildings in Taiping, such as the mining board, treasury, court-house, and museum, were said to be better than any others elsewhere in Perak or in Selangor—the next most developed state (Gullick, 1953).

With its mining industry booming, this was a period of great prosperity for Larut. Larut's tin production soared between 1875 and 1884, with its exports surging from 31,000 piculs to 127,000 piculs (Table 2.1).[10] In 1875, Larut's tin accounted for 30 per cent of the volume of tin exported from Singapore; by 1885 this had risen to 82 per cent (Chiang, 1978), with the bulk now coming from Kamunting. With the gradual reduction in easily accessible surface tin deposits in Taiping towards the end of the 1870s, new capital and labour were increasingly being concentrated in Kamunting, where mining was more diffi-cult and expensive, requiring the use of steam pumps to cope with flooding in the mines. Of the 13 steam pumps operating in Larut in 1880—which contrib-uted to the sharp increase in tin production—11 were in Kamunting.

Table 2.1	Larut's tin exports surged until 1884 before falling (thousands of piculs)							
1874	1876	1878	1880	1882	1884	1886	1888	1890
11.0[a]	30.6	46.2	69.9	95.4	127.0	94.0	102.3	95.3

Sources of data: Annual Report of Perak (various years).
Note: [a] Exports between August and December only.

Larut's Many 'Firsts'

The construction of rail infrastructure was a high priority for Perak's British administration. One of the earliest decisions taken by the State Council in 1880 was to establish a railway network to improve the efficiency of the growing export-based mining economy. This railway was to be paid for out of govern-ment revenues from tin duties. The development of transport infrastructure to support the export-based mining industry mirrored what had happened in Cornwall in England, where mules and horses were initially used to transport coal, tin, and copper from mines until the adoption of steam engines in the early 19th century. Transporting ore by rail brought enormous efficiency gains over the alternatives of rivers and bullock-cart roads: ore tailings were starting

---

10 During this time, the weight of tin was measured in piculs, a traditional Asian unit of weight, with 1 picul equivalent to 133 lbs, and 16.8 piculs equivalent to one imperial ton.

to silt up sections of Larut's rivers and the use of metalled roads began only towards the end of the 19th century (Annual Report of Perak, 1896).

The initial aim of the railway construction project was to link the main tin-mining areas to Perak's leading port in the Strait of Melaka, so as to facilitate both the export of ore and the import of goods required by the industry (Malayan Railway Economics Commission, 1961). Perak's—and Malaya's—first railway line was built at a cost of $400,000. It connected the mining centre of Taiping to Port Weld, covering a distance of 12.8 km, and came into operation in June 1885.[11] Port Weld served as a port of call for local steamers, and was also a supply centre for the mangrove firewood used in mines for smelting. By 1890 the Taiping to Port Weld line had been extended to Kamunting. A few years later, it was extended further to Perak's northern towns of Ulu Sapetang and Pondok Tanjong. Similar railway links from mining towns to ports, such as from Kuala Lumpur to Port Swettenham (now Port Klang) in Selangor and from Seremban to Port Dickson in Negeri Sembilan, came into operation in 1886 and 1891, respectively.

The towns of Taiping and Kamunting, which were populated mainly by Chinese, continued to prosper in the 1880s. Significantly, these towns recorded many 'firsts' for the states of the Malay peninsula, including the first English-medium school (1878), hospital (1880), police station (1881), public library (1882), museum (1883), post and telegraph office (1884), golfing club (1885), along with many others (Teoh, 2004). These institutions improved the built and natural environment of the two towns. They blended with the mine owners' houses, tin mines, smelting houses, and *kongsi* houses, as well as with the bazaar, liquor shops, licensed gambling houses, licensed pawnbroker's shop, Chinese theatre, the Canton Club, and prison (Hall, 1888). The mushrooming prosperity of Larut's mining towns and villages acted as a magnet for international migrant workers of all communities, especially Chinese, with the growth rate of its population far exceeding that of Perak's other districts. Population census data show that, over the 12 years between 1879 and 1891, Larut's population more than doubled, from 26,000 to almost 60,000.

Demand for English-medium education grew with Larut's rising prosperity and the steady inflow of British and Continental European families. The first English-medium school was opened in Kamunting in 1878, with children from the families of railway engineers, government officials, and prominent miners among

11 The Port Weld line was opened by Cecil Clementi Smith, Acting Governor of the Straits Settlements, and Frank A. Swettenham, Acting Resident of Perak (Federated Malay States Railways, 1935).

its intake.[12] By 1883 a second school had opened, the Central School in Taiping, which later became the King Edward VII School in honour of the monarch who succeeded Queen Victoria to the throne of England in 1901. As school enrolment began to grow rapidly among children of the leading families and urban elite, the importance of English-medium education was also acknowledged by the Malay rulers. In 1887, Sultan Yusof Mudzaffar Shah (1886–1887) submitted a request to the Perak State Council for English classes to be conducted in an existing Malay boys' school in Kuala Kangsar, which subsequently became the Government English School. Girls were admitted in 1907, making the institution the first coeducational school not only in Perak but also in the Federation (Hicks, 1958). In 1927, this school moved to a new building and became known as the Clifford School.

English-medium schools were supported by the British administration for the leading families of Perak's urban communities: despite different cultural identities, they shared the same business and social interests. For the sons of the rajas and chiefs, meanwhile, the British authorities established the Malay College, which was managed as an exclusive English public school.[13] The founding of the College was a response to a statement by Sultan Idris Murshidul Azzam Shah at the second Durbar in Kuala Lumpur in 1903, where 'he protested, behind the veil of Malay courtesy, at the inadequate Malay role in the new federal structure' (cited in Raja Nazrin Shah, 2006, p. 18). The College, proposed by John Pickersgill Rodger, Resident of Perak (1901–1904), opened in 1905 in Kuala Kangsar as a federal institution—Sultan Idris having donated 30 acres of land for its grounds (Khasnor Johan, 1984).

Although the College's emphasis was on English, the Malay language was made compulsory in order to allay fears that students would be distanced from their mother tongue and cultural identity. Graduates from this elite college were groomed for admission to the higher levels of colonial government service (Khasnor Johan, 1984). They were expected to bridge the gap between the government and the *rakyat*. By this means, the British solidified the trust and confidence of the royal class, whose agency they used to help legitimize their control.

---

12 The educational heritage of French missionaries in Perak also dates to the 1880s. The first schools were established by parish priests from the Paris Foreign Mission Society. Other French organizations—the Infant Jesus Sisters and the La Salle Brothers—later grew the schools into larger institutions, such as St Michael's Institution in Ipoh which supported the education of all communities (Laplanche, 2020).

13 Built in a distinctive architectural style characterized by imposing columns, with boarding accommodation, dining halls with high tables, and spacious playing fields, the school attracted students from aristocratic families from across the peninsula. Later on, it also began admitting talented Malay students from a broader spectrum of families.

The location of Perak's centre of commercial and social development was soon to shift, however, with the discovery of even richer surface tin deposits in Kinta district and the gradual depletion of Larut's readily accessible deposits. By 1889 Kinta had become the main mining hub of Perak and of the peninsula with its tin production increasingly exceeding that of Larut.

Emergence of Kinta

The Kinta Valley at the heart of Kinta district, about 50 km south of Taiping, was described by British geologist Richard Alexander Fullerton Penrose Jr as an enclosed area

> about 40 miles in length in a north-and-south direction, about 30 miles in width at its south end, and about 5 miles at its north end. To the east is the high granitic range, forming the backbone of the peninsula and rising in some places about 8,000 feet above the sea; to the west is a lower granitic range, rising some 3,000 feet and separating the valley from the Strait of Malacca. Between these ranges are lower mountains and areas of limestone, surrounded and partly covered with great tracts of alluvium. (Penrose Jr, 1903, p. 140)

Kinta's previous near-inaccessibility had held back the development of its tin-mining potential. Before the fourth quarter of the 19th century, mining in Kinta mostly took place on a very small scale and was carried out by Malays, especially Mandailings.[14] According to Burns (1976), J. W. W. Birch, who visited Kinta several times in 1875, reported seeing five large mines in Gopeng with up to 1,000 miners working them, and four years later the colonial State Commissioner of Lands, Hunt Walsh Chambré Leech (1879), also observed that 700 to 800 miners were working in the area. Partners Eu Kong (a Chinese medicine-shop owner) and Imam Prang Ja Barumun (a trader from Sumatra and respected leader of the Rawa and Mandailing community) contributed to the early development of mining activities in Gopeng.

By 1881, when French civil engineer John Errington de la Croix went to Kinta (he later opened mines there), tin mining had expanded into six main mining subdistricts named after the streams that drained them (de la Croix, 1881).[15] Mining settlements in Gopeng, Lahat, Papan, Blanja, Batu Gajah, Tronoh, Kampar, and

---

14 In 1885, Abraham Hale, Kinta's Inspector of Mines, observed that traces of abandoned mines—*Lombong Siam*, or Siamese mines—had been discovered that appeared to have employed different mining methods from Malay mines (Hale, 1885). About 50 such wells, roughly 20 feet deep and 8 feet wide, were said to have existed on the Lahat hill; it was estimated that these mines could have been left undisturbed for at least 100 years.

15 The six subdistricts were Ulu Kinta, Sungai Terap, Sungai Raya, Sungai Tejah, Sungai Kampar, and Sungai Chenderiang.

Chemor developed alongside the mines and later became vibrant towns. Alluvial tin ore was in abundance in these areas, especially in the Gopeng valley, exceeding the quantity and quality of the best mines in Larut.[16] In Kinta's subdistricts, both Chinese and Mandailings were engaged as mine workers.[17]

Three main factors had helped to keep the Chinese capitalists' primary focus on Larut; access, cost, and land ownership. Kinta's tin fields were further inland from the Strait of Melaka and were therefore harder to reach. The costs of transporting tin from Kinta's interior to Penang were far higher: it cost as much as five times more to transport a picul of tin from Gopeng to Penang than from Taiping to Penang. In addition, all of Kinta's mines were claimed as private or ancestral Malay mines, which meant that prospective Chinese investors would have to pay additional charges to mine them. Around the mid-1870s, the total duty on tin was $21 per *bahar*, which included $10 per *bahar* payable to the Malay mine owners, or $6 per *bahar* more than the prevailing duty in Larut (Wong, 1965).

Kinta's First Tin Rush, 1884–1888

With many of Larut's rich surface deposits showing signs of depletion, tin-mining activities in Kinta began to take off, leading to the district's first tin rush between 1884 and 1888. Global trends also contributed to this, particularly the continued rapid growth of Britain's tin-plate industry, the ongoing decline in Cornwall's tin deposits, and the decrease in tin production in Australia after 1882.

To attract investment from Penang's Chinese merchants for Kinta's mining industry, the colonial government set out a plan to improve land and river transport and to reduce land taxes. In 1877, the first year after its formation, Perak's State Council passed a law requiring Malays to register their claims on ancestral mines and allowing for their development at a royalty of only $2 per *bahar*, reduced from $10 per *bahar*. This law narrowed production cost differentials between Kinta and Larut, and gave momentum to increased tin exploration and mining. Some 70 per cent of the 500 mines claimed to be ancestral mines in 1874 were still recognized as such in 1885 (Wong, 1965).[18] Between 1884 and

---

16 The Sungai Terap subdistrict was on the right bank of the Kinta River and in 1881 had 13 mines in the Papan Valley.

17 Another large group of Mandailings, experienced in gold mining in Sumatra, in the Dutch East Indies, came to Kinta in around 1875 (Khoo and Abdur-Razzaq Lubis, 2005).

18 Later the Council also gave Penang's opium farmers rights over Perak's revenue farms for the period 1881–1883.

1888, the total acreage of mines in Kinta jumped fourfold. This acreage was made up of numerous, generally small, mines.

Kinta's mining industry grew spectacularly, supported by a surge in migrant labour. Some miners came from Larut to work the newly discovered richer fields, but most were recruited directly from China through Penang. Unlike in Larut, where the population of Chinese migrants comprised a mix of Hokkiens, Cantonese, and to a lesser extent Hakkas (Khehs), in Kinta Chinese migrants were overwhelmingly Cantonese and Hakkas. Despite being exploited under the truck system, Chinese labourers preferred to work in Chinese-owned rather than foreign-owned mines, largely because of the availability of non-monetary provisions such as food. For a Chinese miner to be enticed to work in a foreign mine, he was said to require at least double or treble the wages offered in a Chinese mine (Yip, 1969). Reflecting the pre-dominance of Chinese-owned mines, and despite British government efforts to attract British investments, there was only one foreign company operating in Kinta during this period, at the largest mine in Kampar. This was a French company, the Société des Étains de Kinta (SEK), which was started by John Errington de la Croix and Jacques de Morgan in 1886 (Khor et al., 2017).[19] It was the first European company to start industrial mining in the Kinta Valley.

The SEK exploited mining concessions in Lahat and Klian Lalang, developed the town of Kampar, and built a hydroelectric power plant as early as 1906 (Laplanche, 2020). In 1887, the company produced around 5,000 piculs (about 300 tons) of tin. Larut had three foreign companies—the Melbourne Tin Mining Company, the Sandhurst Mining Company, and the Larut Tin Mining Company—which together produced around 14,000 piculs (830 tons) of tin. The combined production of all foreign mines was about 20,000 piculs (1,200 tons) or 8 per cent of Perak's total tin output. In comparison, the largest Chinese mine was producing 29,000 piculs (1,700 tons), nearly 50 per cent more than the total output of foreign mines (Yip, 1969).

With Kinta's new-found tin-based prosperity, small towns began to develop quickly, including Batu Gajah, Gopeng, Papan, and Ipoh—which later became Perak's commercial capital. Until the early 1880s, Gopeng had been Kinta's largest and most important mining town, with mining activities concentrated in the Gopeng Valley where there were around 1,500 Chinese miners (Ho, 2005).

---

19 Three other French mining companies were later present in Perak: the Société Française des Mines d'Étain de Tekkah, which began operations in 1909; the Société Civile Minière de Changkat Papan, which was present from 1912, and the Société des Étains de Baya Tudjuh, which started work in Perak in 1924 (Laplanche, 2020).

Despite Gopeng's pre-eminence, in 1884 Batu Gajah was made the Kinta district's administrative capital; this was the river port for the mines in the Papan Valley. Batu Gajah was the collection centre for tin mined by the Mandailings and Chinese in Papan (Box 2.2), the oldest tin-mining village in the Kinta Valley. Tin was shipped from Batu Gajah on the Kinta River to the port of Teluk Anson, at the mouth of the Perak River (Khor et al., 2017). With the relocation of government offices to Batu Gajah, the town began to adopt the architectural style and character of Taiping, with similar infrastructure, state institutions, and social attractions, including a railway station and racecourse. In 1892, during his visit to the district headquarters, the British Resident Frank A. Swettenham referred to

the nearly completed Government offices, an ambitious brick structure with accommodation for the offices of the Collector, the Land Department, Chinese Protectorate and Court; also the Treasury … the new post and telegraph buildings, commodious and suitable; the gaol, and the excellently kept hospital under the charge of Dr Wright, Senior District Surgeon. A new road leading from the hill, on which the Government buildings and officers' quarters are situated, to the proposed station on Kinta Valley was also visited. (cited in Khoo and Abdur-Razzaq Lubis, 2005, p. 115)

Box 2.2   **The rise and fall of Papan's tin-mining industry**

The British administration awarded Papan's rich alluvial tin fields to Raja Asal, leader of the Mandailings, for his support in the Perak War (see Part 1, Box 1.2). On his death in 1877, his nephew Raja Bilah succeeded him as head of Kinta's Mandailing community, with the support of Hugh Low, who appointed him to administer Raja Asal's estate. Having settled debts inherited from his uncle, Raja Bilah took over the mines and became Kinta's largest Malay mine owner, employing hundreds of Malay workers (Abdur-Razzaq Lubis and Khoo, 2003).

As Papan began to prosper, more Mandailing migrants were attracted to the small town, as well as to Kinta's other emerging mining towns such as nearby Gopeng. By 1880, Papan was one of Kinta's most important mining settlements, with good drainage and sanitation. The British administration constructed schools, houses of worship, and metalled roads, and established public horse-cart transport between Gopeng, Batu Gajah, and Papan. The mines were worked mainly by Mandailings, but there were also small groups of Chinese miners in Chinese-owned mines, on whom the Mandailings sometimes called to help them overcome technical issues, such as flooding.

The Mandailings chose to run the mines themselves, from the excavation of tin ore to smelting and marketing. Raja Bilah tried to mechanize his mines by using steam engines to solve the problem of flooding, but his mining operations were ultimately unprofitable. He was unable to compete with the Chinese mine owners on technology, labour productivity, and marketing networks (Gullick, 2010). Raja Bilah had to sell his mines in 1890, and many of the Mandailing mine workers migrated elsewhere and turned to agricultural cultivation to earn their livelihood. In contrast, the Chinese mines continued to operate and were quick to adopt more advanced technologies. By 1901, Papan, which had grown quickly, had a predominantly Chinese population.

About 10 years after Raja Bilah's mines closed, most of Perak's tin mines were in the hands of Chinese and Europeans. The story is similar for Kinta's other Malay-operated mines: Chinese operators were simply much quicker to adopt more efficient mining methods. Many Malay mines were later leased to Chinese miners, enabling Malay landowners to earn royalties.

However, Papan started to decline after 1921, especially following the drastic fall in tin prices. People dependent on the tin industry left; the Mandailing community moved to Chemor and Batu Gajah. The Chinese theatre and shop houses were abandoned, the prison closed, and the railway service between Ipoh and Tronoh no longer stopped in Papan.

Kinta's Second Tin Rush, 1889–1895

The building of new roads and railway lines in the Kinta Valley paved the way for Kinta's second tin rush, between 1889 and 1895. By 1889 there was a direct road from the Kinta district to Taiping, which had a rail connection to Port Weld. A line was built linking Ipoh to the port of Teluk Anson, covering a distance of some 62 km. This line became operational in 1895, and in the following year was extended to Tanjong Rambutan and Chemor. This Ipoh–Teluk Anson line was considered so important that E. W. Birch, Perak's acting British resident, wrote:

> I was able to arrange with the shippers of tin ore for a special rate for the carriage of their stuff which is easy to pack and to handle and have secured for the railway the entire carriage of that article of export. (cited in Annual Report of Perak, 1895, p. 11)

With the opening of the Kinta Valley railway, Ipoh became an interchange for goods shipped by rail, river, and road, and continued to grow and prosper as the business and social capital of Perak. Although the British made Batu Gajah the capital of Kinta,

> the business people, especially the Chinese, preferred Ipoh as their commercial cen-
> tre. This was because Ipoh was in the middle of all the tin ore producing places such
> as Gopeng, Kampong Kepayang, Lahat, Penjeh, Chemor, Tanjong Rambutan, Tambun,
> Pulai, and others. (Abdul Talib Ahmad, 1959, p. 80)

As tin mining expanded, Malay participation in commerce remained significant until the arrival of railways, when river transport became less important. As most of Perak's rivers were not navigable for larger boats, *perahu* were used by Malays to transport goods and equipment to the mines, as well as tin ore for loading on to larger boats at the ports. They also carried goods to be sold to villagers and food to mining workers.

Kinta's tin rushes opened up vast opportunities. Many miners made fortunes, some even becoming millionaires, including some who did not own mining land and were simply tribute workers who struck lucky (Ho, 2009). Kinta's min-ing prosperity thus led to the rapid growth of Ipoh, which also became a transit centre for miners travelling from Larut. A short distance from the mining vil-lages with their lines of *kongsi* houses, Ipoh developed rapidly after the 18 km road connecting it to Batu Gajah was metalled and a bullock-cart road was built to Gopeng. Ipoh's population surged, especially once it had its own railway sta-tion, from just 3,200 in 1891 to 12,800 in 1901 (Hare, 1902).

As with Larut, tin-mining affluence also generated social prosperity, with a network of government-supported English-medium schools opening in Kinta's main mining and port towns. Among the most prominent were the Methodist Anglo-Chinese schools with intakes of students from families of all communities.[20] Perak's first Anglo-Chinese School was established by Methodist missionaries in the town of Parit Buntar, northwest Perak, in 1892, and a few years later one was built in Ipoh (Hicks, 1958). When it opened in the mid-1890s, it had only two Chi-nese and two Malay students, but the school's enrolment grew rapidly such that by 1901 it had some 200 students, with numbers surging even further in the early dec-ades of the 20th century (Hicks, 1958). Overcoming the prevailing apathy towards girls' education, parents' advocacy led to the establishment of Ipoh's Anglo-Chi-nese Girls' School in 1897. Anglo-Chinese schools quickly spread to other major towns around Ipoh, as well as Teluk Anson in 1899, and Kampar and Sitiawan in 1903. A second English-medium girls' school was founded in 1907 —the Convent of the Holy Infant Jesus in the compound of St Michael's Church, Ipoh.

---

20 Reflecting the growing prosperity, a new mosque was also built, the Panglima Kinta Mosque founded in 1898, with a madrasah attached—the first Arabic and Islamic school in Ipoh.

Perak's prosperity also created plenty of employment opportunities for English-educated persons, especially from neighbouring Penang, who were recruited to teach in English-medium schools, as well as for the administrative services, to work as clerks on European estates, and to assist the state's growing Chinese business community who had to deal with the new British administration. Chinese, Indians, and Jaffnese also entered the medical and legal professions.

In 1889, a liberalized land policy was introduced which allowed anyone to work a 25-acre block of land if they paid $100 for survey fees and rent. This greatly increased the rate of prospecting and fossicking (searching for tin in abandoned workings). From 1889 onwards, the STC began establishing ore-purchasing centres throughout Kinta, with its first branch at Gopeng. Through the 'cash-for-ore' scheme of the STC, small capitalists obtained greater liquidity. These factors helped to propel Kinta's second tin rush, even though global tin prices were actually on a downtrend, with Straits tin falling from £93 per ton in 1889 to £64 per ton in 1895.

Two major developments helped to spur tin production. The first was the continued decline in the gold value of silver, which greatly moderated the impact on Malaya's tin producers of falling tin prices in sterling. When the sterling price of tin dropped by 19.5 per cent between 1893 and 1894, the price of silver against sterling fell by 18 per cent, leaving the dollar price of tin almost unchanged (Chiang, 1966). The second major development was the emergence of the tribute system.

During Kinta's second tin rush, Kampar, at the southeastern border of the district, began to emerge as a major new tin-rush town, eclipsing even Gopeng, thanks to the prospectors and fossickers who went in search of new tin fields, as well as the employment of the portable wooden sluice box (*lanchut kechil*). By 1891 the town was thriving, and its population had trebled; yet only a decade earlier it had been inaccessible, and was one of Kinta's least developed areas. John Bourke Massey Leech, Kinta's first District Magistrate, brother of H. W. C. Leech, who visited Kampar in 1891, said of the town:

> I visited the village of Mambang di Awan, in Kampar, on the Dipang-Tapah road, which has during the last two months grown from a little cluster of huts into a large and flourishing mining village with 154 shops in it. It has been laid out by the Assistant Penghulu Iman Prang Jeberemum in 60ft streets with the usual blocks of ten 20ft building lots and is now one of the most thriving places in Kinta. There has been a regular rush into this part of Kampar and over 1000 acres of mining land have been taken up in the neighbourhood of the new village. (Leech, 1891, p. 1,048)

By this time, the surface deposits of the mines in Gopeng—among the earliest to be mined—were approaching exhaustion and required more capital-intensive methods. British- and European-owned mining companies began operations and would eventually come to dominate the business—for instance, the Gopeng Tin Mining Company with money raised from a small group of Cornish investors, and later the French Tekka Mines.[21] These companies started to shift mining production away from the traditional labour-intensive methods and towards more technologically advanced methods, such as hydraulic sluicing where high-pressure hydraulic jets were used to break up the ore-bearing ground and dislodge the ores.

By the end of Kinta's first tin rush in 1888, the district's tin production had grown to 100,000 piculs (6,000 tons)—nearly equalling Larut's 102,000 piculs (6,100 tons)—compared to only 34,000 piculs (2,000 tons) in 1884 (Figure 2.1). By the end of the first year of Kinta's second tin rush in 1889, its tin production had risen to 119,000 piculs (7,100 tons)—exceeding that of Larut for the first time. And by the end of Kinta's second tin rush in 1895, its production had soared to 319,200 piculs (19,000 tons), a volume that would not be seen again until the early 20th century. By contrast, Larut's production had fallen to 70,000 piculs (4,200 tons) from its 1884 peak of 127,000 piculs (7,700 tons).

Figure 2.1   **Kinta increasingly dominated Perak's tin mining after 1889[a]**

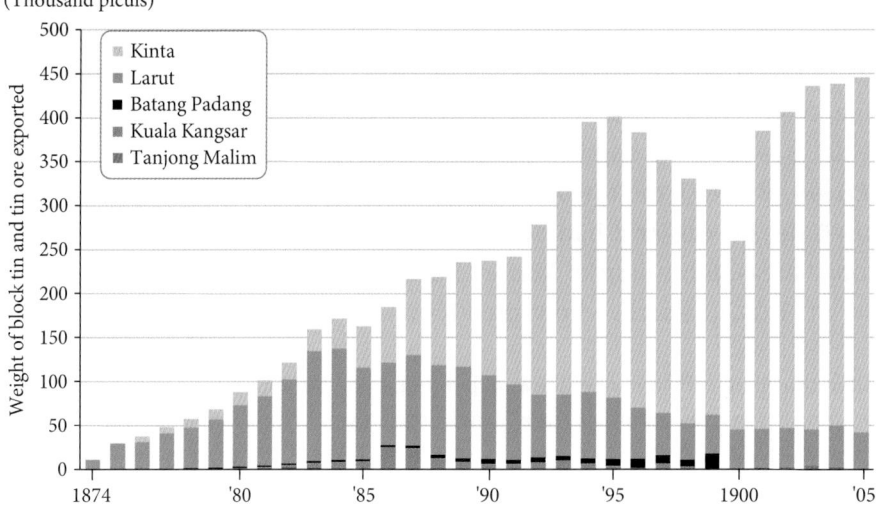

(Thousand piculs)

Sources of data: Annual Report of Perak (various years).
Note: [a] Upper Perak, Matang, Lower Perak, and New Territory are not shown as they produced only small quantities of tin.

---

21 In 1912, Gopeng Tin Mining Company merged with New Gopeng and Ulu Gopeng to form Gopeng Consolidated.

Recession, Recovery, and Impacts, 1870–1900

Recession

International commodity prices suffered a sustained decline during the period of the Long Depression, which was triggered by a global financial crisis in 1873 and lasted until the late 1890s (Fels, 1949). The price of Straits tin tumbled after 1888. Although prices slowly began to recover in 1897, it was only in 1899 that they exceeded the levels of the previous decade (Lim, 1967). Kinta's tin production fell steadily from a peak of 319,200 piculs (19,000 tons) in 1895 to 256,000 piculs (15,240 tons) in 1899. Output began to pick up in 1900, but rising costs from acute labour shortages had forced some mines to shut. Most of the Malay mines had been sold, and many Mandailings had withdrawn from mining in the face of Chinese competition. By 1901 the share of Perak's 78,000 miners who were Malays had fallen to less than 2 per cent, compared with almost 5 per cent of the 50,000 miners a decade earlier.

Several legislative measures passed by Perak's colonial government led to increased labour demand and rising wages for mine workers between 1896 and 1899. The Mining Code of 1895, passed by the Perak State Council, imposed minimum labour requirements for the resumption of unworked tin land in an attempt to prevent the land from being idle, thereby intensifying labour demand.[22] However, increased demand for agricultural labour in China around this period had led to a slowdown in the inflow of Chinese migrant workers to Perak, which experienced a tight labour market as a result. In addition, the Labour Code of Perak—also passed in 1895—had, in securing greater protection for workers, loosened the employers' grip on labour and strengthened labourers' bargaining power. Thus, with demand for labour exceeding supply amid a huge international tin boom, mining wages shot up from around 33 cents per day in 1896 to between 70 and 80 cents in 1899 (Wong, 1965). By this time, around two-thirds of mining workers were tribute workers, who were already on higher wages and potentially stood to gain from a share of profits.

The Mining Code of 1895 also contained a measure that halted applications for new land leases. This meant that existing mines had to be worked deeper (rather than laterally), which was more costly. Moreover, the abolition of the opium revenue-farm in favour of direct collection, along with an increase in

---

22 The Mining Code of 1895 stipulated that a lessee of a parcel of mining land had to begin mining works within two years of leasing the land, and that during these two years the land could be retained by employing a labour force of two labourers per acre. The lessee also had to increase his labour force if required to do so by the Warden of Mines.

duties on opium, reduced the profits from the sales of opium for the mine capitalists and other advancers, which in the past had supported them during difficult times.

Yet another contribution to increased tin production costs came in 1897
when the British administration introduced a sliding scale of tin duties in the
four politically unified Federated Malay States. With the rates of duty tied to
the price of tin on this graduated scale, the *ad valorem* duties ended up higher
when tin prices were high and lower when tin prices were low, thereby increasing the absolute tax charges on mine owners (Wong, 1965). The practice in the
past had been the opposite.

Recovery—With Malaya Becoming the World's Largest Tin Producer

Towards the end of the 1890s, several Chinese mining companies turned to
foreign management with the aim of modernizing their operations. In 1897,
for instance, the operation of the Tronoh mines, owned by Foo Choo Choon
(a member of the Perak State Council), was taken over by an Australian engineer, Captain John Addis. The Tronoh mines became the largest in Blanja
and the 'most Westernized Chinese mining operation of its time' (Khoo and
Abdur-Razzaq Lubis, 2005, p. 79). In 1901, the Tronoh mines were floated on
the London Stock Exchange under the registered name of Tronoh Mines Ltd,
and were taken over by a British company from Cornwall. A decade later they
had become the world's largest producer of tin with an annual output of nearly
3,860 tons of ore (Wong, 1965). As the Tronoh mines grew, the town that shared
their name developed rapidly, attracting migrant miners and allied workers.

Although labour scarcity and rising labour costs continued to affect the
mining sector, the surge in tin prices in 1899 on the back of rising global demand, particularly from the US, saw production recover to almost
pre-recession levels. By 1900, with the recession now over, Perak—Malaya's
pre-eminent tin-producing region—now contributed 49 per cent of the peninsula's output (a share that would increase over the next 60 years) and 25
per cent of the world's output (Figure 2.2). Malaya was now the world's largest tin producer, accounting for over half of global output at nearly 44,000
metric tons in 1900. Duty on tin exports had become a vital source of revenue for Perak's government. Perak's mines were still predominantly owned by
Straits Chinese interests, whose use of open-cast mining methods, as well as
the labour-intensive traditional *chin-chia* and steam pump, was effective in
increasing output, and by the end of the century Kinta had overtaken Larut as
Perak's largest tin-producing district.

Figure 2.2

At its peak in the mid-1890s, Malaya accounted for more than half of the world's tin production, and almost half of Malaya's output was mined in Perak

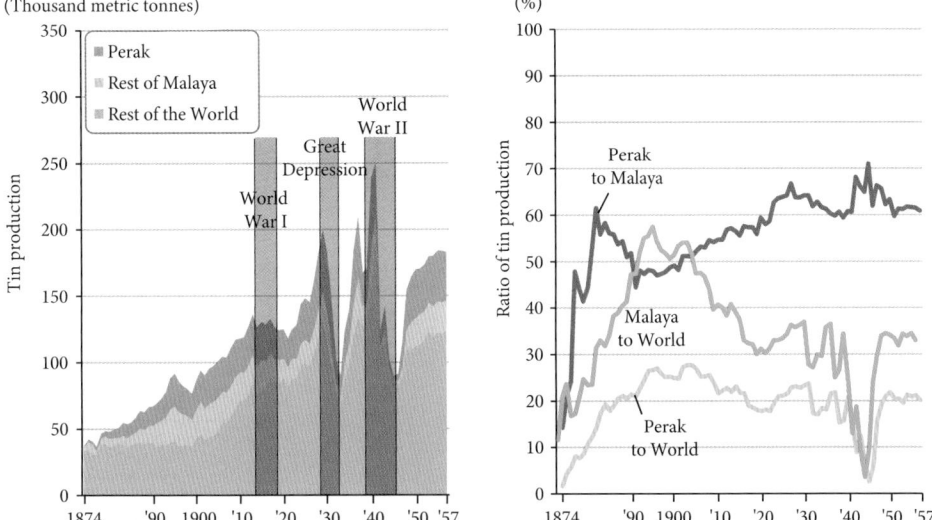

Sources of data: For 1874–1899 and 1940–1957: (Lim, 1967); for 1900–1939: Sultan Nazrin Shah, (2022). https://www.ehm.my/data/historical-gdp-accounts

A Huge Impact on Perak's Government Revenue

Perak's colonial government maintained tight discipline over its fiscal affairs and generated substantial surpluses to support its administrative machinery, to maintain security, and to provide capital investment in railways (one-third of total government revenue was used to build Perak's railway system between 1894 and 1902), roads, utilities, and other infrastructure as well as in rudimentary health services and education. The British administration justified its model of economic development as a 'virtuous circle', investing particularly in the building of roads and railways to encourage more mining and thus generate greater revenues from tin duties.

In 1876, Perak's government revenue stood at $273,000, 80 per cent of which was derived from Larut's tin industry. By 1888, at the end of Kinta's first tin boom, when Kinta and Larut accounted for almost all of Perak's tin production, the state's revenue had surged to $2 million (Figure 2.3, left panel). This was more than half of the total revenue accrued by the peninsula's three main tin-producing states of Perak, Selangor, and Negeri Sembilan. Between 1891 and 1901, tin duties still contributed an average of about 40 per cent of government revenue; this changed when the rubber boom began (Figure 2.3, right

| Figure 2.3 | Duty on tin exports was a vital source of Perak government revenue |

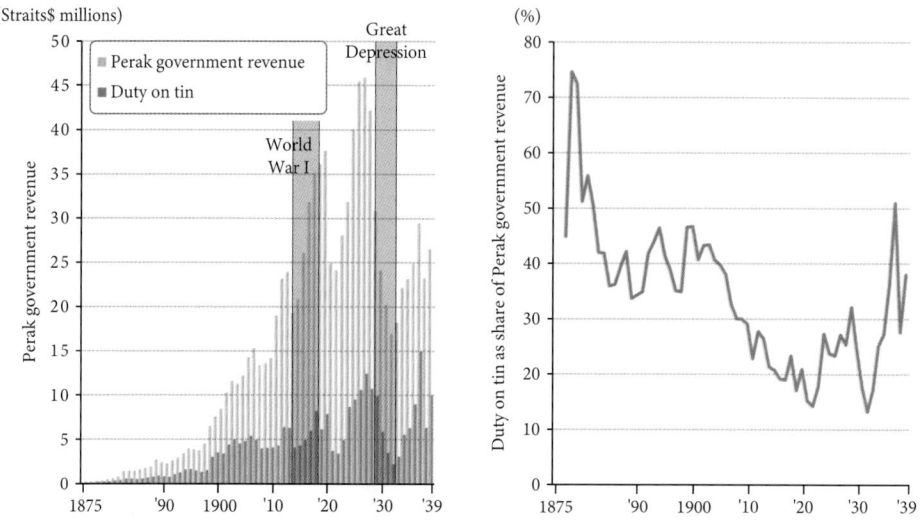

Sources of data: Annual Report of Perak (various years); Report of Federated Malay States (various years).

panel). Especially when taking into account the revenues from opium and the railways—two industries that thrived only because of tin—the importance of tin, through its direct and indirect contribution to Perak's government revenue, cannot be overstated (Drake, 1979).

... And on Its Demography

In the last quarter of the 19th century, Perak's demographic characteristics—the size of its population, its composition in terms of age, sex, and ethnicity, as well as its distribution within the state—were conspicuously shaped by the inflows of migrant labour. Migration, which trended according to the needs of the economy, was pivotal in the growth of Perak's tin industry and related service activities, as well as in the growth of agriculture and the development of the state's infrastructure and towns. As the state's economy prospered and demand for labour soared, its population grew spectacularly, from only 81,000 in 1879 to 214,000 in 1891, and to 330,000 by 1901—a figure four times larger than it had been just 22 years earlier (Figure 2.4, upper panel). Almost three-quarters of the inhabitants of Perak in 1901 were males, reflecting the population's migrant-worker character. Perak's European population was very small and predominantly British, numbering just 661 people in 1901, up from 364 a decade earlier. Most of these were government administrators, managers, engineers, and other professionals.

The largest influx of migrants in this period came from southern China. The number of Chinese rose by 129,000 over these 22 years, making this Perak's largest population group, at 45 per cent (Figure 2.4). Perak's Chinese population exceeded that in every other state of Malaya, and continued to do so for the next six decades. From 1879 to 1901 the inflow of Malays from elsewhere in the Malay archipelago amounted to 82,000, while that of Tamils and others from India—brought in mainly to work on plantations, as bullock-cart drivers, in railway and road construction, and in other public works—was about 35,000 (Hare, 1902). Despite this sizeable inflow of Malays, their share of Perak's population declined from 73.6 per cent to 43.0 per cent between 1879 and 1901.

All of Perak's seven administrative districts grew rapidly with the inflows of migrant workers. Kinta's population surged from just 8,900 in 1879 to 58,600 in 1891, and then more than doubled over the next decade to 122,700 (Figure 2.4, lower panel). By 1901, Kinta's share of Perak's population had grown to 37 per cent, double that of Larut. Another area that grew very rapidly was the district of Kerian, which was the centre both of Perak's rice-growing region and of many new sugar plantations;[23] sugar was the most rewarding of all Perak's cash crops in the late 19th century. These three districts accounted for almost 70 per cent of Perak's population. However, whereas more than half of the population in Kinta and Larut were Chinese, in the rice and agricultural district of Kerian some 60 per cent were Malays, with Chinese and Indians accounting for about 20 per cent each.

The Chinese, who made up the early sugar plantation labour force, expanded cultivation from Province Wellesley to Kerian. The British administration provided grants of land to incentivize Chinese *towkays* who provided the capital, labour, and imported machinery for sugar mills, while their estates were run by European managers. By 1900 the Chinese controlled 25 of Kerian's sugar estates covering some 10,500 hectares (Tate, 1996, p. 123).

Of Perak's total population in 1901, 75 per cent could be classified into four broad categories of work: agriculture, industry, professional, and commercial (Table 2.2). The largest share, at 58 per cent, was in industrial activities (mainly mining), with just 31 per cent in agriculture. Chinese held the dominant share

---

23 Leech (1894, p. 60) observed that Kerian had a large proportion of non-resident *padi* planters who 'lived on the island of Penang, and along the coast of Province Wellesley, as far as the north of Kedah, and go to Kerian to plant their *padi* and when that is done return to their homes till the crop is ready to be cut'. This would likely have led to inefficiencies and low production yields.

in industry, at 76 per cent; they were mainly miners, but significant numbers also worked in artisan and service jobs, as carpenters, fishermen, pawnbrokers, rickshaw-pullers, shoemakers, shop assistants, weavers, and wood-cutters.

Figure 2.4 **Migration dramatically changed Perak's population characteristics in the last two decades of the 19th century**

The population surged over 1879–1901, and Chinese formed the largest community[a]

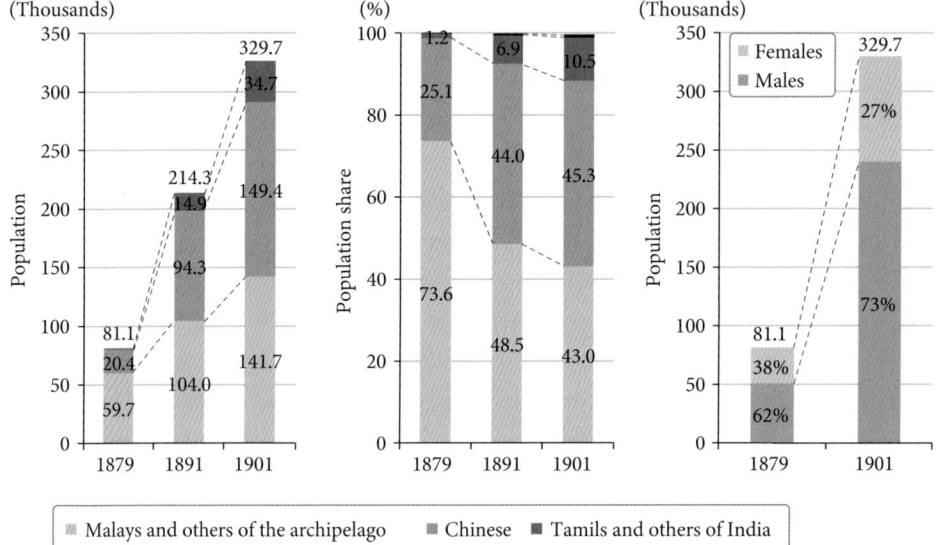

Kinta overtook Larut as the most populous district after 1891, and Kerian increased its share

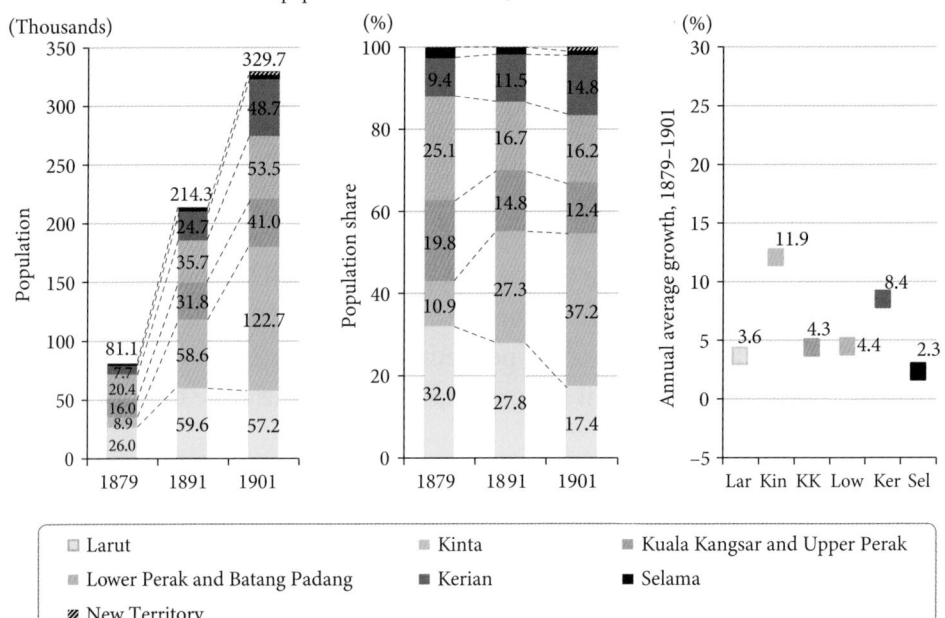

Sources of data: Merewether (1892); Hare (1902).

Note: [a] The population of other communities was 92 in 1879, 1,032 in 1891, and 2,487 in 1901.

Meanwhile, Indians made up 16 per cent and Malays just 8 per cent of the industrial labour force. Conversely, Malays accounted for 86 per cent of those engaged in agriculture, and within this sector were mainly *padi* planters, while Chinese accounted for just 13 per cent, and were mainly vegetable gardeners and sugar-cane planters.

Table 2.2	Perak's labour force was heavily concentrated in industry (mainly Chinese) and agriculture (mainly Malays) in 1901				
Occupational category	**Malays**	**Chinese**	**Indians**	**Others**	*Total*
	Share by ethnic group (%)				*(Numbers)*
Agriculture	86.1	12.8	0.9	0.2	*75,777*
Industry	8.1	75.7	16.1	0.2	*143,744*
Miners[a]	1.8	97.6	0.6	0.1	*77,868*
Professional	21.1	37.9	32.5	8.6	*7,103*
Commercial	10.5	81.7	7.5	0.3	*12,279*
All sectors	33.2	54.9	11.4	0.6	*248,515*[b]

Source of data: Hare (1902).

Notes: [a] Includes tin miners and a small number of gold miners.
[b] Includes 3,666 domestic servants, and 5,946 people whose jobs were unclassified.

… And on Its Forests

Concerned about deforestation, in 1897 the British administration passed legislation that banned the use of charcoals made from trees deemed to be economically valuable. Even stricter legislation was passed by the Federated Malay States legislature through the Mineral Ores Enactment of 1904, which prohibited smelting-houses from using furnaces that could not be fuelled from a small number of woods, and gave the authorities power to refuse licences to smelting-houses not adhering to these rules. Again, this seriously disadvantaged many Chinese smelters, while European smelters were significantly less affected.

Tin-smelting furnaces destroyed valuable forest resources. With some 10,000 Chinese engaged in cutting timber for mines, in 1893 alone an estimated 280,000 cubic metres of wood was converted to charcoal for the Federated Malay States' tin-smelting industry (Kathirithamby-Wells, 2005). Hugh Low had emphasized the value of forests beyond their immediate economic uses, and recognized the environmental implications of forest depletion. Low encouraged the preservation of upland forest in the Larut Hills, which was gazetted a forest reserve in 1891, and observed:

> The preservation of the timber on all mountains in the neighbourhood of valuable deposits of tin is of such obvious necessity, unless cheap and efficient means other than water power of draining the mines be introduced, that it requires no comment. (cited in Burns, 1971, p. 208)

Towns like Taiping, exposed to above average annual rainfall and already prone to flooding, were at high risk if the steep hills were cleared without adequate provision for floods.

Consolidation of British Control of the Smelting Industry

Against the backdrop of the rapid growth of Perak's tin ore production and exports after the mid-1870s, the smelting industry saw a major change in 1886 when Herman Muhlinghaus and James Sword established the STC. Supported by colonial policies, the STC was destined to become a leading global player in the buying and smelting of tin ore. The STC worked closely with the Straits Steamship Company, a joint European and Chinese venture formed in Singapore in 1890 which became heavily involved in shipping tin ores to the STC and in transporting migrant Chinese workers (Tregonning, 1965).

Before tin ore is marketed to the tin-plate industry, it is smelted to convert the ore concentrates into metal of high tin content (Ingulstad et al., 2015). Until the STC was founded, Perak's tin smelting was decentralized: large and medium-sized Chinese-owned mines generally smelted the ore on site at the mines, while smaller mines transported their ores either to the nearest smelter in the larger mines or to smelting operators in town centres. Chinese smelters were more cost-effective at producing tin concentrates than the few Malay smelters still in business. The STC, however, saw an opportunity to use its superior smelting technology, as employed in Australia and California during their gold rushes. Chinese smelting relied on charcoal. Clean tin ore, further refined in Penang before being shipped to England, yielded 75–82 per cent of the metal (Doyle, 1879), compared with 60 per cent using the Chinese method. But even this would be far surpassed by the STC whose smelting methods produced tin of up to 99.9 per cent purity (Greig, 1924).

The STC established its first coal-fired smelter at Teluk Anson to circumvent the restrictions on exporting tin ores from Perak that had been imposed by the State Council in 1880 (Wilkinson, 1909). But the relative locational disadvantages of the smelting site at Teluk Anson—the lack of nearby infrastructure and the limited communication channels—prevented the smelter from being cost-effective. In 1887, the company purchased a more strategic and cost-effective smelting site on Pulau Brani, Singapore (Tregonning, 1962). The coal stores of the Tanjong Pagar Dock Company were nearby, and the newly built Keppel Harbour was just across the island. The STC installed large modern smelting furnaces greatly superior to those used in Chinese mines. After securing the right to export ore from Perak in 1888, the STC relocated its smelting works entirely to Pulau Brani in 1890, and ceased its operations at Teluk Anson.

In the late 1880s, Perak's colonial authorities had banned the *relau semut*—a traditional and widely used furnace that burned local hardwoods for charcoal—because of concerns about the loss of commercially valuable hard timber resources and related problems of deforestation. By procuring ore from Chinese mines that no longer had access to these furnaces, the STC expanded its ore exports from Perak. The Chinese smelters were forced to switch to the *relau tongkah*, which could function using hard or soft charcoal but was more expensive to operate, requiring more labour and yet producing lower-quality tin than the *relau semut*. With competition from the *relau semut* smelters eliminated, the STC gained a stronger foothold in the international smelting business. By 1895 the STC was smelting 30 per cent of Perak's tin exports (Wong, 1965).

The STC continued to enjoy the protection of colonial government policy. In 1903, in order to stave off competition, the British authorities imposed very high export duties on tin ores—except on ore to be smelted in the Straits Settlements—to prevent companies in the US from developing a domestic smelting industry (CO 852/33/11, 1936). The tax amounted to 33 per cent on ore exports to countries other than Australia and Britain (Tregonning, 1962). The STC also benefited from the lower duties on ore exports—higher duties would have increased demand for smelting *in situ*—as well as from freight concessions from the state-owned railways.

By the early 20th century, only a few large Chinese smelters remained. One of them, the Seng Kee Tin-Smelting Works, started smelting tin ore in Penang in 1898, obtaining ores from Perak, Phuket, and elsewhere. Seng Kee became the STC's biggest competitor. The shorter distance to Penang from both Perak and Siam was a key locational advantage for Seng Kee. Aware of this competition, and conscious that the available volume of tin ore that could be smelted at Pulau Brani was greater than capacity—the smelting works here also obtained ores from mines in the Dutch East Indies, Australia, and South Africa—the STC established another smelting site along the coastline of Butterworth (now Seberang Prai), which had excellent transport links and was close to George Town, Penang's capital. The STC began smelting at Butterworth in 1902, and until 1932 all of the tin ore the STC procured in Perak was refined there.

The STC grew hugely and made enormous profits. Its original capital of $150,000 was increased to $500,000 in 1890, and this had more than doubled by 1893. Supported by British policy, the STC's dividends kept rising, while the reserve fund of retained profits grew to $1.1 million by 1907 (Tregonning, 1964).

E. W. Birch encouraged Chinese mining interests to enlarge the Seng Kee smelter, which they did in 1907, forming the Eastern Smelting Company. 'The Eastern', as it was generally known, was owned entirely by Chinese investors of whom the most prominent was the Khaw family of Siam and Penang. The Eastern increased its share of total shipments from Penang to 29 per cent in 1910, up from 18 per cent in 1908 (Cushman, 1986). Like the STC, the Khaw family had interests in an international shipping company, which had established links with Chinese mining firms in the Straits Settlements and Perak. The Eastern did not remain in Chinese hands for long, however: in 1911, after raising capital on the London exchange, it was reorganized. Birch—now conveniently retired from the British colonial service—was appointed the chairman of what became a British company with a minority Chinese interest (Hillman, 2010). In 1911, the Eastern smelted about 30 per cent of the total tin output of the Federated Malay States, while the STC remained the largest player with a 70 per cent share.

From Chinese to British Tin-mining Dominance, 1900–1940

Fifty years after the dramatic rise of Perak's tin-mining industry under a near production monopoly—over both capital and workers—by ethnic Chinese, a far-reaching transition began that would eventually lead to British dominance of the industry. In the last quarter of the 19th century, several British and European companies had attempted to enter Perak's mining sector, but they were generally unsuccessful due to their higher-cost production methods and operations, as well as because of a preference among Chinese miners to work in Chinese-owned mines. With the dawn of the new century the tide began to turn, reflecting the increasingly supportive policy and regulatory environment aided by the formation of the federation of Perak, Selangor, Negeri Sembilan, and Pahang in 1896. British interests in the industry were also bolstered by massive inflows of European (mainly British) capital and of advanced technology, feeding into infrastructure building, particularly of railways.

The progressive exhaustion of surface alluvial tin deposits and the need to extract tin at greater depths meant that British and other European companies, with their more capital-intensive and large-scale methods of mining—such as hydraulicking, gravel pumping, and dredging—now had an advantage over the smaller labour-intensive and shallow-mining methods of Chinese-owned companies. Chinese-owned open-cast mines, which were abandoned once the richest portions had been exhausted, were now seen as wasteful.[24] Crucially, dredging technology was potentially available to the Chinese operating in Perak and elsewhere in Malaya, but they were hesitant to make long-term investments for fear of discrimination by the British authorities. By contrast, in southern Siam the Chinese mining *towkays* introduced a tin-mining dredge in 1907 (Hennart, 1986).

---

24 The Tambun mine near Ipoh, for example, provided evidence that there was value in working the mines at greater depths; it was a highly profitable mine in the early 20th century when it was first worked by shafting before it later became an open-cast mine (Osborne, 1911).

Globalization: Perak's Rise, Relative Decline, and Regeneration. Sultan Nazrin Shah, Oxford University Press. © Sultan Nazrin Shah (2024). DOI: 10.1093/oso/9780198897774.003.0012

British joint-stock companies using more modern mining technologies began to show signs of success. By the mid-1890s, for example, the Gopeng Tin Mining Company, with deep Cornish interests, had already succeeded in its attempts at hydraulicking. The company reported profits in 1896, having managed to achieve a lower cost of treating a cubic yard of *karang* (tin-bearing earth) than had previously been possible with open-cast mining.[25] Noting the success of hydraulic mining at Gopeng, in 1896 the *Mining Journal* sought to publicize the vast opportunities offered by Malaya's tin fields to British interests:

> We did not undertake the task of keeping order in this Peninsula from purely philan-thropic motives. We went there, as becomes 'a nation of shopkeepers', because there was something to be made by it—and that something is dependent on the mineral wealth of the country. (cited in Wong, 1965, p. 215)

Over the next three decades, British mining companies came to dominate the numerous mining centres of Larut and Kinta (Map 2.1). They were supported by specialized engineering, management, and agency services (Palmer and Joll, 2011).

A More Supportive Policy and Regulatory Environment for British Investors

The formation of the centralized Federated Malay States on 1 July 1896, through the Treaty of Federation, marked a consolidation and strengthening of British political dominance in the peninsula via the newly established office of the Resident-General (see Part 1: 'British Governance and Federalism Fortified, 1870s–1920s'). The federation weakened the decentralized powers of the state residents and sultans, including over revenues and expenditures. Crucially, it also became a vehicle for further promoting British economic objectives in the four states.[26] The Federated Malay States government, heavily influenced by capitalist commercial interests, provided a policy and regulatory environment that strongly favoured British and Continental European

---

25 Based on 1912 estimates, the working cost of treating *karang* with a hydraulic pump was Straits$0.13 per cubic yard, compared to Straits$0.57 per cubic yard with the gravel pump and Straits$0.61–0.94 with the open-cast method (Yip, 1969).

26 British companies had also begun to show an interest in Siam as a source of tin, but Siam was an independent country and cautious about potential British intervention (Thoburn, 1994a).

Map 2.1 Towns and tin-mining centres in Larut and Kinta, circa 1920

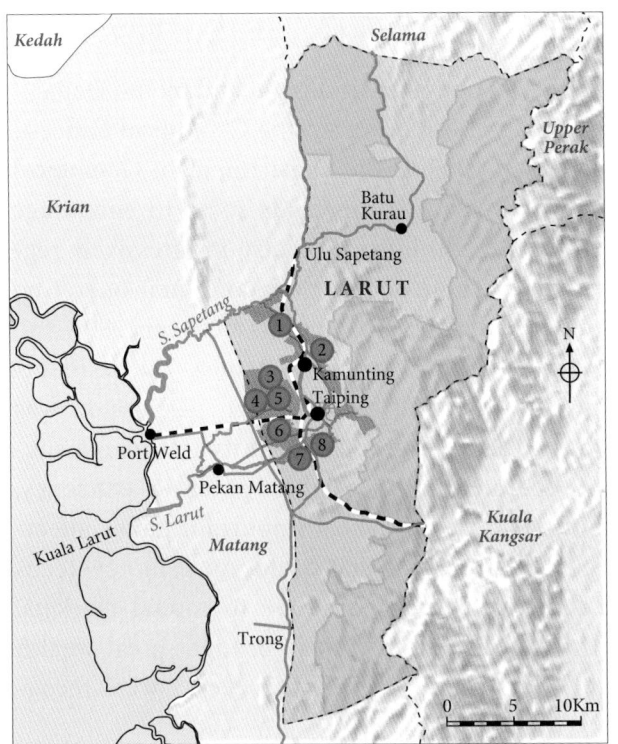

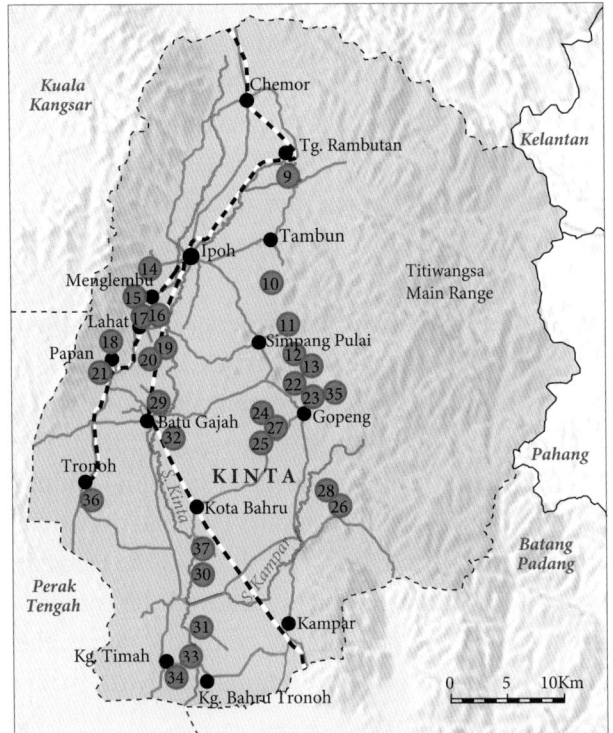

Symbols

⬤ Tin-mining centres
▮ Mining land
▮ Forest reserve
● Towns and villages
── State borders
---- District borders
── Roads metalled
▬ ▬ Railways
── Rivers

Abbreviations

Kg. = Kampung (village)
S. = Sungai (river)
Tg. = Tanjong (cape)

Tin-mining centres

Larut
1. Kamunting Dredging
2. Kg. Kamunting Dredging
3. North Taiping Dredging
4. Tekka Taiping Dredging
5. Asam Kumbang Dredging
6. Taiping Dredging
7. Larut Dredging
8. Tupai Dredging

Kinta
9. Rambutan
10. Ampang
11. Kramat Pulai
12. Tekkah
13. Eu Tong Sen
14. Kledang
15. Chendai
16. Pengkalan
17. Lahat
18. Johan
19. Ipoh
20. Pegang
21. Papan
22. Tekkah
23. Ulu Gopeng
24. Kinta Dredging
25. Eu Tong Sen
26. Sultan Idris Murshidul
    Azzam Shah
27. Gopeng
28. Cholit
29. Southern Malayan Dredging
30. Tanjong
31. Kuala Kampar
32. Southern Kinta
33. Tronoh Dredging
34. Changkat
35. Jelantoh
36. Tronoh
37. Southern Malayan Dredging

Sources: Adapted from various archive maps, NAS (2020a).

companies. It framed the conditions for the systematic commercial exploitation of tin at greater depths that would erode the dominance of less well-resourced Chinese competitors.

The tin-mining industry had been supported and regulated by the Department of Mines from 1874. After federation, however, the Geological Office—established in 1903 and upgraded in 1927 to the Department of Geological Survey—helped to locate and demarcate new tin fields so as to encourage British investment. The British federal administration also progressively regulated both the granting of licences to mine on state land and their operating principles, through a series of Mineral Ores Enactments between 1899 and 1928, which were enforced by the colonial Warden of Mines. The residents had to be informed of any mineral discovery and written permission was needed to work it. When mining leases were granted, priority was increasingly given to mines which would operate with the highest potential efficiency, and the total capital of a mining firm was the most important factor affecting the decision. This obviously favoured firms that could invest in new technologies, and disadvantaged those which lacked access to capital markets. Labour-intensive mining methods that had previously brought great wealth to Perak were discouraged and ancestral mining rights in Perak were recognized for alluvial tin only.

The government had discretion to cancel any mining licence without giving a reason, and to take possession of all mining land held by Malay and Chinese owners who had left it unworked, or had failed to maintain the number of labourers required to continue operations. These measures led to many forfeiture orders being issued to Chinese miners (Tai, 2013). To encourage capital-intensive and technology-based companies, the new laws also gave dredging companies the ability to buy lands that fell between two plots that they already owned.

The truck system, which had allowed Chinese mine owners to operate their mines on credit, was now rendered illegal through the Truck Enactments of 1908 and 1909. This meant workers could no longer be employed on the truck system and be supplied with opium or liquor in lieu of wages (Loh, 1988). The abolition of revenue farms, beginning with the opium farms in 1910 and ending with the gambling farms in 1912, further reduced the profits that had previously enabled mine owners to mine at a loss during tin-price slumps. The reforms to mining labour regulations and administrative policies removed the comparative advantage that Chinese-owned mines had previously enjoyed—that is, the ability to open and operate mines profitably with little capital, and with maximum control of their labourers.

Construction of Enabling Infrastructure

When the Federated Malay States was formed, the British administration regarded it as an economic imperative to improve inter-state transport links by connecting the rail, road, and coastal port networks of the peninsula's three main tin-mining states—Perak, Selangor, and Negeri Sembilan (Box 2.3). Links to the international ports of Penang and Singapore were also critical for developing Perak's tin and rubber industries. Without them, the flow of labour, capital, and external trade would not have progressed. As Frank A. Swettenham observed when reflecting on the economic justification of rail links, '[i]t is doubtful whether anything can confer such benefits on this country and its people …' (cited in Federated Malay States Annual Report, 1897, p. 7).

In addition to the new railway lines, the tin-mining towns and new rubber plantations in the Federated Malay States were also being connected via metalled roads to encourage investment. By 1895 Perak was already linked by road at its southern border with Selangor. By 1911 it was also linked at its northern border with Province Wellesley, and to the east with Kuantan. In 1923, the road link from Ipoh to Singapore was completed via a causeway to the island from Johor Bahru, nine years earlier than a railway connection was established; motor cars were becoming much more common from the 1920s onwards. Migrant Tamils from southern India replaced Chinese as the largest group of construction workers on railways and roads.

Box 2.3 **Extending Perak's rail and road networks after federation**

Soon after the formation of the Federated Malay States, the Perak and Selangor Railways merged to form the Federated Malay States Railways, headquartered in Kuala Lumpur. This now-merged entity later purchased the railways of Negeri Sembilan, which had been built by a private syndicate. By 1903, the state railway lines which had previously been unconnected (Map 2.2, top panel), were connected longitudinally from Prai, Penang, via Perak to Seremban in Negeri Sembilan. This line was officially opened in July 1903 when the Sultan of Perak travelled in a special train from Kuala Kangsar to Kuala Lumpur for the second Durbar (Chai, 1964). In 1909, the west-coast line was extended to Johor Bahru (Map 2.2, bottom panel). Latitudinal links were also built to connect

(Continued)

Kinta's main tin-mining centres—for instance a 15-mile branch line from Ipoh to Tronoh (Federated Malay States Railways Report, 1909). The east-coast railway link was completed just over two decades later, and in 1932 the west-coast line was extended to Singapore.

As Perak's rail network grew, bridges across rivers became vital. The construction of the 1,000-foot Victoria Bridge across the Perak River at Enggor, close to Kuala Kangsar, was perhaps the greatest feat of forward-looking engineering of the time. Opening in 1900 after three years of construction work, the bridge enabled a rail connection between Ipoh and Taiping (Federated Malay States Railways, 1935).

Although the early phase of rail and road infrastructure was mainly intended to serve the needs of the tin industry, from the early 20th century these transport networks also became essential for meeting the commercial needs of Perak's rubber industry (Map 2.3). A location close to existing railways and roads was a key determinant when it came to identifying suitable land to be alienated for estate rubber planting. This is one reason why Malaya's plantations were heavily concentrated in the peninsula's west-coast states where transport links and other infrastructure were more advanced.

Railways and roads boosted Malaya's export-led economy. They also helped stimulate the growth of new centres of population, tin towns, and local enterprises. While the primary aim of the rail and road infrastructure was to transport commercial and agricultural goods, the number of passengers also increased steadily. However, because railway construction depended almost entirely on imports of physical and human capital—materials, engineers, and workers—it did little to spur local industrial development. Britain's iron, steel, and engineering industries were major gainers (Kaur, 1980).

The railways made profits throughout the colonial period until the start of the Great Depression, when the Federated Malay States Railways ran a deficit for a few years until recording a surplus again in 1934 (Tate, 1979). As noted by William Hood Treacher, Perak's sixth British Resident (1896–1902), however, '[t]he object of the state railway is not to show large profit but to develop the economy', consistent with colonial economic objectives (cited in Annual Report of Perak, 1898, p. 8).

Map 2.2 **Perak's railways increasingly connected to other Malayan states after 1900**

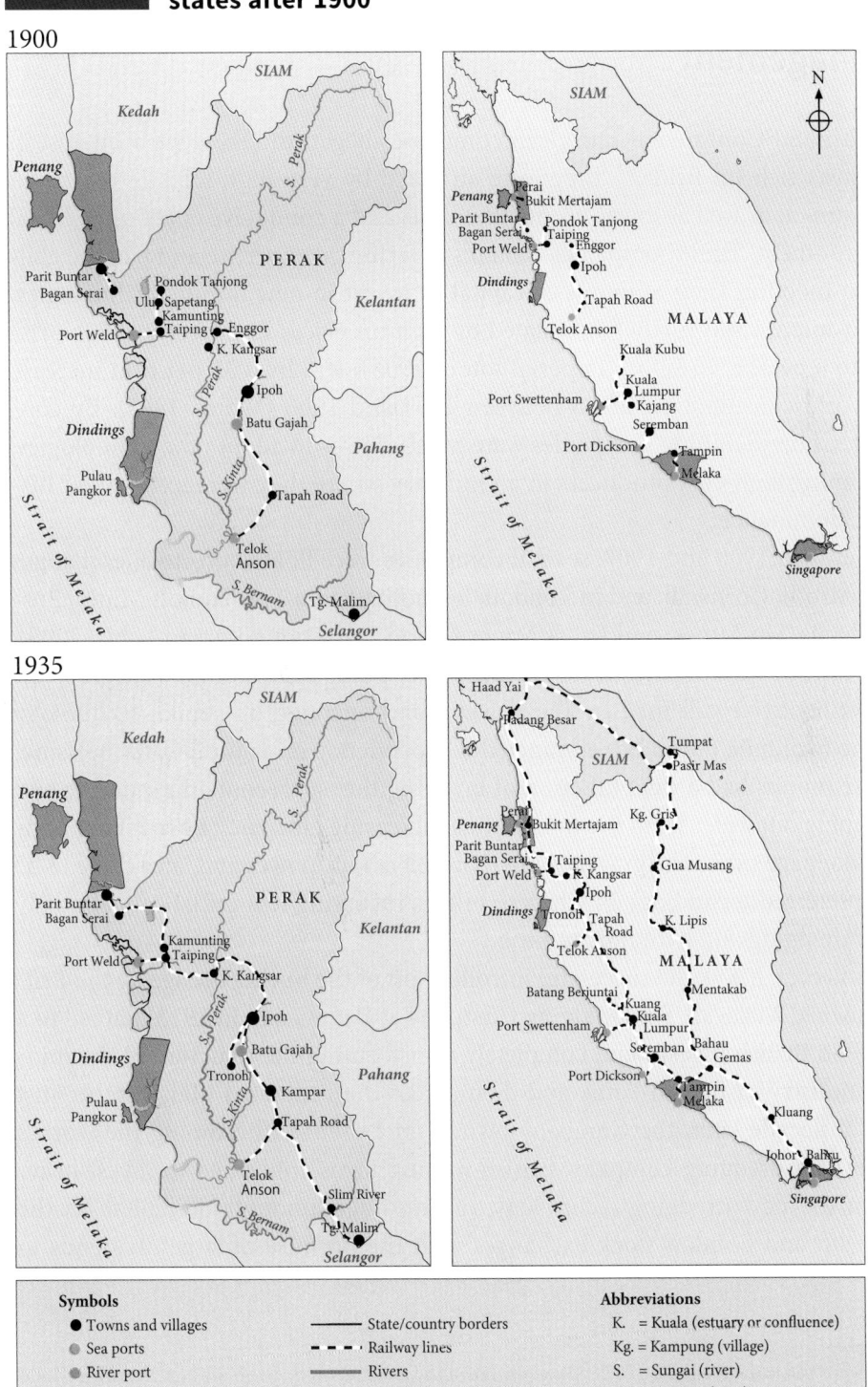

Symbols

● Towns and villages   ——— State/country borders

● Sea ports   ----- Railway lines

● River port   ——— Rivers

Abbreviations

K. = Kuala (estuary or confluence)

Kg. = Kampung (village)

S. = Sungai (river)

Tg. = Tanjong (cape)

Sources: Adapted from various archive maps, NAS (2020b); Federated Malay States Railways Report (1906 and 1935).

Inflows of Technology, Investment, and Western Management

British and Continental European companies began to take a keen interest in Malaya's rich tin fields.[27] They were attracted by very high rates of return on investment as well as lower production costs and a conducive enabling political environment. These companies brought in technical expertise and had the ability to mobilize large amounts of capital to invest in new mining technologies. Their interest was further stimulated by high tin prices in the early 1900s—rising to a peak of £180 per imperial ton in 1906—and by a 35 per cent increase in world consumption of tin between 1899 and 1906 (Wong, 1965). By contrast, Chinese mining companies were much slower to adopt new technologies, becoming high-cost producers in an industry where they were losing their historic dominance.

Between 1900 and 1907, several companies were floated on stock exchanges in Redruth, Cornwall, and in London, including Kinta Tin, Tronoh Mines, Pusing Lama Tin Mines, and Lahat Mines (Khoo and Abdur-Razzaq Lubis, 2005). The introduction of the steam-driven gravel pump and monitors in 1906 saw investment rise still further. The gravel pump operated on similar technology to the hydraulic pump but eliminated a dependency on natural water pressure. These pumps had a dual function of breaking the earth containing tin ore and pumping out water from the mines, thus increasing efficiency by reducing mining stoppage time. The gravel pump replaced labour power and later came to be the preferred technology in Chinese mines, incurring less initial capital outlay than dredging and hydraulic mining.

However, it was the successful introduction of the bucket dredge by the British-owned Malayan Tin Dredging Company at Batu Gajah in 1913 that led to a surge in British investment, completely transforming the structure of the mining industry, at first in Perak and then across the Federated Malay States. Just over a decade later, the Company owned four dredges, becoming the world's largest tin-dredging company. British mining firms continued to invest heavily in the new dredging technology, raising huge amounts of capital on the Redruth and London stock exchanges with the promise of large dividends to

---

27 By contrast, in the Dutch East Indies the government had a monopoly on tin mining on Banka Island and the Dutch Billiton company controlled mining elsewhere (Thoburn, 1994b).

shareholders. Some mining companies registered in the UK while others were locally incorporated. By 1920, out of the cumulative foreign capital raised for Malayan mining companies of £5.3 million, 96 per cent was British; cumulative capital had doubled by 1927, with 90 per cent remaining British (Yip, 1969).

Replacing Labour with Capital

The advantages of dredging were that it enabled tin mining in swampy grounds, such as in the centre of the Kinta Valley, and at greater depths, including on abandoned mining lands where the surface alluvial ores had been depleted. With higher productivity came greater profits. Moreover, the Chinese open-cast mining system, which was irregular and non-systematic, had left large tracts of tailings and unmined land in Larut, which the British and Continental European dredging companies sought to exploit.[28] Dredges made these grounds economical once again, and in 1914, shortly after the introduction of the first dredge in Kinta, the Kamunting Tin Dredging Company (which also expanded its operations into tin mining in Siam) and Tekka Taiping Tin Dredging began using dredges in Larut's mines as well (see Map 2.1).

A decade later, the 1923 Report of the Mines Department (p. 18) observed:

> This form of mining [dredging] continues steadily to increase in popularity and is supplanting the wasteful methods of mining employed by the Chinese in former years. It is due to this form of mining that the rapid decrease in output which has been noticeable since 1914 has been arrested.

The Kinta Valley, however, remained the main beneficiary of huge investment flows from London-based dredging companies, such as Southern Malayan Tin Dredging, Tanjong Tin Dredging, Kampong Lanjut Tin Dredging, Kramat Tin Dredging, Southern Tronoh Tin Dredging, and Lower Perak Tin Dredging (Khoo and Abdur-Razzaq Lubis, 2005). The opening up of large dredging areas in the region of the Kinta River and elsewhere compensated for the decreased output from gravel-pump mines (Report of the Mines Department, 1925).

With the introduction of the first dredge and the increasing adoption of other machinery in the mines, the mechanical capacity of Perak's mines is estimated to have surged from 3,500 horsepower (hp) in 1904 to around 18,000 hp in 1913

---

28 The tailings and iron ores could yield 0.5–1 *kati* per cubic yard, which made dredging profitable. In 1925, the average yield for all dredging in Perak was around 0.6 *kati* per cubic yard (Yip, 1969). By that year dredges could dig to a depth of 85 feet (Report of the Mines Department, 1925). A *kati* was equivalent to 600 grams or 1.3 lb.

(Figure 2.5), equivalent to almost 150,000 labourers (Loh, 1988).[29] In 1920, close to 20 dredges were operating in Perak's mines and mechanical capacity had more than doubled, reaching almost 41,000 hp—equivalent to around 330,000 labourers. By 1929 this had trebled to 125,000 hp. Conversely, labour employment had almost halved, with the number of miners declining from 126,000 in 1913 to 65,000 in 1929. Between 1913 and 1929, Perak's total output of ore rose by more than 40 per cent to 700,000 piculs (46,700 imperial tons).

By 1929, dredging, gravel pumping, hydraulicking, and open-cast mining were the four main methods of mining ore in Perak. However, it was the dredging and gravel-pumping mines that increasingly came to dominate tin-mining output, accounting for four-fifths of Perak's total by 1930, and even more in later years. About 2 per cent of Perak's mining output came from traditional *dulang* washing, a method of recovering ore from the tailings washed away into rivers.

Figure 2.5   **Perak's mines became less labour intensive as production became more machine dependent**

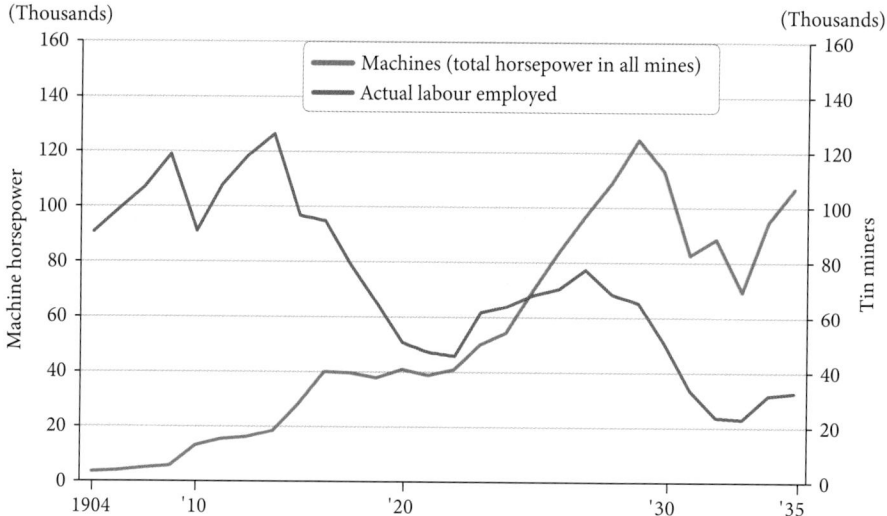

Sources of data: Federated Malay States (various years), Report on Administration of the Mines Department and of the Mining Industry; Loh (1988).

Note: According to section 16 (b) of the Mining Enactment 1911, labour-saving apparatus is calculated by a factor of eight workers per hp. For example, in 1915, the total hp used by all apparatus was 39,927, and the labour equivalent was therefore 4,991 workers (39,927/8).

---

29 The Malayan Tin Dredging Company dredged and treated 579,014 cubic yards for a return of 3,780 piculs of ore, with labour of 54 men and a 300 hp plant (Annual Report of Perak, 1913). A dredge with a 12-foot bucket of about 300 hp with 90 workers under European supervision could perform digging equivalent to 2,000 workers in the Chinese mines (Yip, 1969).

A *dulang*—a large shallow pan which was swirled in a stream—was used to separate sand and gravel from tin ore.

The trends in Perak were replicated across the Federated Malay States. Between 1900 and 1920, production of tin in mines owned by British and Continental European interests rose from 4,300 tons to 12,600 tons—that is, from 10 per cent to 36 per cent of total production. Over these two decades, consumption of tin grew much faster in the US than in Britain, and after the 1920s the US became the largest and most important export market for Malayan tin.

In 1919, a new generation of dredges was introduced in Perak. These dredges represented a substantial improvement on their predecessors in terms of cost, excavating capacity, and ore saving (Report of the Mines Department, 1919). This led to an increased use of dredges in Perak and their adoption elsewhere in the Federated Malay States. With the doubling of (mostly British) foreign investment between 1920 and 1927, and with much of that investment channelled into dredging, the number of dredges in the Federated Malay States surged from 38 in 1925 to 107 in 1930 (Table 2.3). This brought about a near doubling of tin production in the Federated Malay States, from 34,000 tons in 1921 to 67,000 tons in 1929; the output from dredging contributed 80 per cent of the increase (Yip, 1969). Many of the dredging companies employed Malays and Indians as technicians.

Table 2.3	Perak was the first state to employ tin dredges and was the biggest user					
	1913	1915	1920	1925	1930	1935
	Number of dredges					
Perak	1	10	18	30	66	70
Federated Malay States	1	10	22	38	107	119

Sources of data: Federated Malay States (various years), Report of the Administration of the Mines Department and the Mining Industries.

British mining companies had a near monopoly over the use of high-productivity dredges. Chinese mine owners were unable to adapt and use dredges in their mining fields, partly because they had no access to the necessary long-term capital, and partly because they mainly operated on relatively small parcels of mining land unsuitable for dredges. In the 1920s, Perak's banks were providing only short-term trade-financing credit, and most Chinese mine owners were hesitant to shift to joint-stock forms of organization (Hennart, 1986). The outcome was that by 1930, British-owned tin mines accounted for around 60 per cent of total output in the Federated Malay States, up from just 10 per cent in 1900.

Adopting British Mining Management

Following common UK business practice, Perak's British tin-mining companies saw an increasing separation between management and ownership, which was much less common among Chinese-owned mining companies. Such separation led to improved efficiency and governance. Anglo-Oriental (Malaya) Limited, Osborne and Chappel, and the Tronoh Group, which between them had control over many of the British mining companies, were Perak's leading tin-mining management companies. They maintained local and international networks, provided technical mining expertise, and had a very important lobbying influence with the colonial administration that ensured that their commercial interests remained a priority. Further, the large mining corporations, such as Anglo-Oriental, heavily influenced the decisions of the Ipoh-based Federated Malay States Chamber of Mines, which was established to represent mining companies' interests and was incorporated on 10 December 1914 (White, 2014).

British agency houses, by contrast, had relatively little investment in mining. This was possibly due to their lack of technical expertise in mining, and also because they were highly involved in the management of the plantation sector, which was less technologically demanding, required less capital investment, and was generating attractive profits during the early 1900s as a result of the rubber boom (Jones, 2000). Among the large agency houses, Guthrie, Sime Darby, and Harrisons & Crosfield did serve as managing agents in the tin industry but they played a far more important role in the plantation industry (Allen and Donnithorne, 2003).

Tin-price Volatility

During World War I, 1914–1918, disruption to shipping and export controls led to shortages in tin-consuming countries and stockpiling in tin-producing locations (Box 2.4). In 1918, the authorities in London indicated that tin was needed for war purposes, and in April of that year Arthur Henderson Young, British High Commissioner (1911–1920), visited Ipoh and met mine owners to explore ways to increase production and to listen to their grievances (Annual Report of Perak, 1918).[30] The meeting led to a new enactment allowing mining on

---

30 Among the grievances expressed by Perak's mine owners were difficulties in obtaining firewood, the prohibition of mining in certain areas, and insufficient labour supply.

agricultural land and forest reserves. Some mining regulations and orders were relaxed, and certain areas previously closed to mining were opened (Report of the Mines Department, 1918). Yet, despite these measures, production failed to increase even after the war, as financing was unavailable and physical equipment and machinery were hard to obtain.

Although global tin prices climbed steeply during World War I, they tumbled during the economic depression of 1920–1921, reflecting the imbalance in supply and demand (Figure 2.6). However, the price slump was successfully moderated through a voluntary joint-stock pool called the Bandoeng Pool, which functioned from 1921–1923. This was initiated by the STC and served, primarily, to protect the interests of British mining investors. It was the first in a series of cartel-like arrangements that continued for over half a century, which included pools, buffer stocks, and private and inter-governmental agreements, all designed to stabilize tin prices and protect the interests of tin producers.

Through the Bandoeng scheme, when tin prices were depressed the governments of the Federated Malay States and the Dutch East Indies purchased and stockpiled tin at a given price and withheld it from the market. As tin prices rose from 1922, the stock acquired during the depression was gradually released until in 1925 it was exhausted (Sultan Nazrin Shah, 2019). The rise in the price of tin gave fresh impetus to the tin industry, and many new mines were opened (Report of the Mines Department, 1922).

Investment in the mining industry boomed after prices recovered from the 1920–1921 depression, peaking in 1927. But high tin prices were short-lived. From the point at which the operation of a new dredge began, it took about two years for it to reach peak production. Production surged between 1927 and 1929, with tin output in the Federated Malay States reaching 70,000 tons in 1929, equivalent to 36 per cent of world output, and up from 47,800 tons (33.4 per cent) in 1926. With excess global tin production capacity, there was oversupply worldwide, leading to a gradual decline in prices from 1927. Tin's low demand and its supply price inelasticity, which was due to the inflexibility of dredges in reducing production when prices decline, generated large price fluctuations whenever supply and demand conditions changed (Yip, 1969). Most tin mines, including those operated by dredging companies, were hit very hard by the low prices, and many reported losses, or only marginal profits (Annual Report of Perak, 1929). Many Chinese mine owners survived by using high-power oil engines and other labour-saving machinery, and many Chinese miners worked for food alone (Report of the Mines Department, 1930).

> **Box 2.4   Perak during World War I**
>
> World War I was a global conflict fought mainly between the leading European powers, but its effects rippled throughout social and economic life in their distant colonies. The war involved the mass mobilization of military forces, and many young British professionals in Malaya felt a patriotic duty to return to the UK to join the war effort. In the first six months of the war, about 1,000 British nationals working in Malaya enlisted—mainly government officers, planters, miners, and merchants, some of whom were part of the Malay States Volunteer Rifles. Many would not return (Shennan, 2015). In Teluk Intan, a World War I memorial bears the well-known words '*At the going down of the sun and in the morning, We will remember them, 1914–1918*'. In the square in front of the Ipoh Railway Station stands a cenotaph erected in memory of the men from Perak who were killed (Raja Nazrin Shah, 2006, p. 164).
>
> The Malay States Guides, a predominantly Indian force based in Taiping, were sent to join the British garrison in Singapore. The Guides offered to serve on the front line, but the British War Office felt that they were better deployed in Singapore owing to perceived threats from a German cruiser in the Indian Ocean. Nevertheless, in September 1915, about 700 Guides were sent to the strategic port of Aden to engage the Ottomans (Abdul Karim Bagoo, 1962).
>
> Government revenues of the Straits Settlements and Federated Malay States were used to support the war effort, building a battleship, HMS *Malaya*, for the Royal Navy based on a proposal by the Sultan of Perak. The Sultan of Johor, meanwhile, invested £1 million in government bonds. While wealthy Chinese residents, businesses, and professional groups also contributed funds, reactions to the war among the various communities differed: some saw it as distant and unlikely to affect their interests, while a religious minority opposed the Allies.
>
> There was an official concern that peninsular Malay Muslims would side with Germany and the Ottomans, after the Sunni Muslim Ottoman Caliph issued a ruling against the Allies. Malay-language newspapers were censored. But in November 1914, the Sultans of Perak and Selangor, and the Yang di-Pertuan Besar of Negeri Sembilan, signed a joint statement that banned their states' citizens from rendering any assistance to the Ottomans, and from raising funds for the war effort against the Allies (Abdul Karim Bagoo, 1962). Despite this, there was a short-lived mutiny by an Indian Muslim Regiment in Singapore in early 1915, joined by a small group of Malay States Guides; they were apparently influenced by anti-British propaganda from the nationalist movement in India, and possibly by the statement of the Caliph (Ooi, 2014). After the mutiny, an Ordinance was issued in 1915 to strengthen internal security. All male British nationals aged under 40 were conscripted into a Reserve Force, and those aged 40 to 55 into the Civil Guard (CO 574/14, 1915).

Perak's economy was affected in different ways by the war. Although some plantations were left without managers and technical experts, rubber production boomed
to meet surging demand from the US automobile industry, with the bulk of this
increased production shipped across the Pacific (Sultan Nazrin Shah, 2017). However,
trade with Europe was disrupted by shipping difficulties, which delayed exports and
imports, including the delivery of essential equipment for the mining industry (Palmer and Joll, 2011). The wider deployment of tin dredges was therefore delayed, as the
materials needed to build them were required for the war effort. However, after an initial price shock when tin prices fell from £202 per ton in 1913 to £151 per ton in 1914,
they had recovered to £330 per ton by 1918.

Figure 2.6   **International tin prices were often highly volatile**

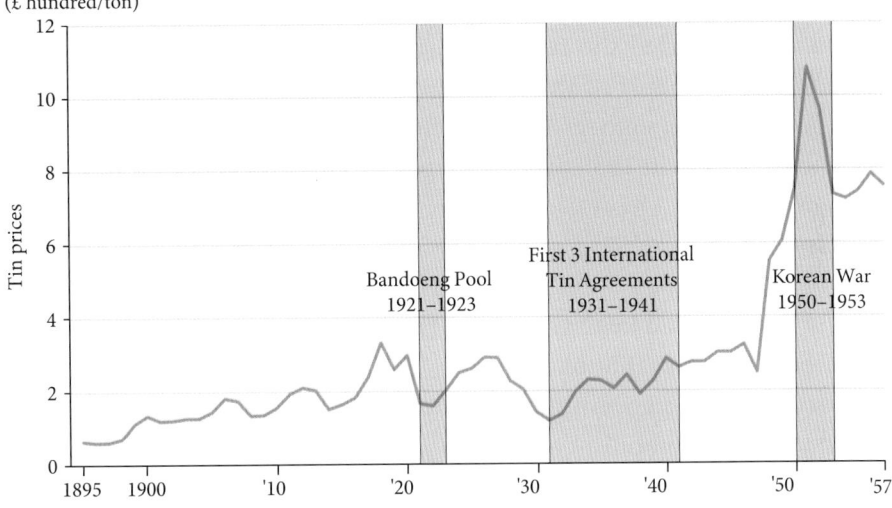

(£ hundred/ton)

Source of data: Lim (1969).

An International Tin Cartel

In an attempt to limit the damage caused by falling prices at the start of the
Great Depression, a large international meeting of directors of tin-mining companies was convened in London in June 1929. The meeting was initiated by
Malayan British mining interests—in particular Anglo-Oriental, which was the
largest managing agent of tin producers in the Federated Malay States—as well
as by British interests in Siam and Burma. It resulted in the formation of the Tin

Producers' Association, consisting of British tin-mining companies, incorporated under the auspices of Anglo-Oriental and sanctioned by the British Board of Trade. On the Malayan side, the Executive Committee of the Tin Producers' Association initially had representatives from long-established firms, now known as the Tronoh-Malayan Group, the Gopeng Group, the Taiping Group, and Anglo-Oriental Corporation. The last of these entered Malaya's tin industry only after 1925, but also had substantial tin interests in Bolivia, Nigeria, Siam, and Burma (Yip, 1969).

The Association attempted to restrict tin production among its members through a voluntary international arrangement so as to raise prices to a breakeven point of £240 to £250 per ton—a price that would protect the industry's high-cost producers. In Bolivia, the Aramayo and Patino groups agreed, as did Nigerian companies (Hillman, 2010). Two large Dutch companies, Billiton and Banka, also agreed, but only on the condition that other major producers would do so as well. However, not all the major tin-producing companies supported the restriction. In Malaya, for example, the Association lacked the support of the Gopeng Group as well as of Chinese mine owners who were not members.[31] Although global production did fall sharply in 1929, the reduction in 1930 was only modest. Tin prices crashed soon after the onset of the Great Depression, due in part to the failure of the Tin Producers' Association to achieve a voluntary consensus on tin quotas. By 1930, the price of tin had fallen by 51 per cent from its 1926 level, and at £142 per ton was the lowest it had been since 1909 (Figure 2.6).

At the request of the Billiton Company and the Patino Group, a proposal was put forward by the governments of the Dutch East Indies and Bolivia for the introduction of compulsory restrictions, which was eventually accepted by the governments of Malaya and Nigeria, largely through the support of the Anglo-Oriental Group.[32] With the massive investments of British companies at risk, the governments agreed on a compromise proposal and formed a cartel with the objectives of controlling production, based on 1929 output levels, and stabilizing prices.

---

31 The Gopeng and Tronoh groups were among the lowest-cost producers; they had thrived in a laissez-faire economy and could survive on tin prices as low as £150 per ton. The Anglo-Oriental group was a relatively higher-cost producer and needed higher tin prices (Hillman, 1988).

32 Simón Iturri Patiño, who controlled the majority of the Bolivian tin-mining industry, and John Howeson, who created the Anglo-Oriental Corporation, were allied through their substantial holdings in Consolidated Tin Smelters, the world's largest tin-smelting organization, of which the Eastern Smelting Company in Penang and the Billiton smelter in Arnhem, the Netherlands, were subsidiaries.

First International Tin Agreement: Strengths and Limitations

The First International Tin Agreement was in effect between 1931 and 1933. It involved the Dutch East Indies, Bolivia, Malaya, and Nigeria, who agreed in 1931 to reduce their output by about 22 per cent; collectively, these four countries accounted for about 87 per cent of world tin production in 1929. The Federated Malay States Tin and Tin-Ore Restriction Enactment of 1931 enforced the restrictions for all Malayan producers, whether or not they supported them. Firms' production quotas were allocated to each producer based on assessments made on the production of mines by a Central Standing Committee, with British mining company interests well represented.[33] The two domestic tin smelters, the STC and the Eastern Smelting Company, were also required to comply with export restrictions and were to hold in trust for the government the ore already purchased but not yet exported (Yip, 1969). In 1932, when quota restrictions were tightened, the STC's Butterworth smelter was mothballed.[34]

Owing to the ramped-up production of parties not included in the Agreement—in particular, tin producers in Siam—tin exports had to be reduced even more after 1932. Although Siam had joined the Agreement in September 1931, restrictions were tightened further for the four original signatories between 1932 and 1933, with the export quota set at just one-third of 1929's output level. By 1933, world production had fallen to 88,000 tons, a decline of 12,000 tons from the previous year. Tin prices rose to £230 per ton in 1934, up from £204 per ton in 1929. The output restriction was supplemented by an unofficial international tin pool—a private pool that was not part of the Agreement. By April 1934 the pool had sold its entire stock at around £226 per ton; the stock had been acquired when the price was below £140 per ton (Ali Liaqat, 1966).

At the end of the First Tin Agreement in December 1933, tin prices had recovered to around £230 per ton, providing a basis for support for subsequent agreements.[35] The exceptions, in Malaya, were Chinese mining interests, represented by the Perak Chinese Mining Association and the Selangor Miners' Association. They had been concerned from the start that foreign dredging mines would receive a

---

33 The Standing Committee consisted of three members of the Federated Malay States Chamber of Mines, two unofficial members of the Federal Legislative Council, the Senior Warden of Mines, and the Acting Chief Secretary to the Government.

34 It was revived in 1941, though only briefly, when demand for tin increased after the Soviet Union, Japan, and the US entered World War II, and restrictions on tin production were eased.

35 The Second International Tin Agreement ran from 1 January 1934 to 31 December 1936, and the Third from 1 January 1937 to 31 December 1941. The Fourth Agreement, scheduled for 1942–1946, was stalled by the war. International tin controls resumed in 1956.

higher production quota than Chinese mines, and they were not represented in the local Standing Committee that signed the Second International Tin Agreement (1934–1936) on behalf of Malaya (Yip, 1969). While the Continental Europeans and the Anglo-Oriental Group were consistently in favour of output restrictions, the Cornish interests and the Gopeng Group were consistently opposed to them.

The restrictions had their most severe impact on production at gravel-pump mines. Mainly owned by Chinese interests, gravel-pump mines saw output slump by about 70 per cent, from 29,030 tons in 1929 to 8,710 tons in 1933. By comparison, there was only a 39 per cent fall in production at dredging mines, from 27,210 tons to 10,760 tons over the same period (Yip, 1969). This was largely due to the higher quota allowance given to the mines that had already installed labour-saving mining equipment but had not yet begun mining in 1929–1930—mainly dredging mines owned by the Anglo-Oriental Group. The sale of domestic quotas by the Chinese to the British and Continental European mines contributed further to the sharper contraction of output from gravel-pump mines. By 1938, Anglo-Oriental's share of tin output in the Federated Malay States had risen to 12 per cent, from only 6 per cent in 1929; its share of dredging mines over the same period rose to 27 per cent, from 16 per cent (Hillman, 1988).

Between 1929 and 1933, Malaya's tin production fell from 70,000 tons to 24,000 tons, and the number of mines operating declined by 25 per cent to 944. The export value of tin plunged by 74 per cent from Straits$117.5 million in 1929 to a nadir of Straits$30.7 million in 1932, before recovering slightly to Straits$37.7 million in 1933 (Figure 2.7). Of the four Federated Malay States, Perak's tin industry was the hardest hit in terms of both the volume and the value of exports.

By late 1933, demand for Perak's exports had begun to recover. The number of workers employed in the tin and rubber industries picked up, although emigration and repatriation that had occurred during the Great Depression now ensured a tight labour market.

The Second Agreement was signed against a backdrop of rising consumption and relatively high tin prices. Export quotas continued to be enforced, with an official buffer stock mechanism in place to try to stabilize high prices at £225 to £230 per ton between 1934 and 1935. When stocks fell, export quotas were raised to the extent that Malaya's output nearly doubled, from 36,000 tons in 1934 to almost 65,000 tons in 1937 (Yip, 1969). In the second half of 1937, the global economy went through a short recession, prompting a reduction of export quotas and the adoption of a new buffer stock under the Third Agreement, 1936–1941. Much of this buffer stock was released at the outbreak of World War II. Malaya's production declined from 75,000 tons in 1937 to 43,000 tons on average between 1938 and 1939 before rising again to 81,000 tons in 1940.

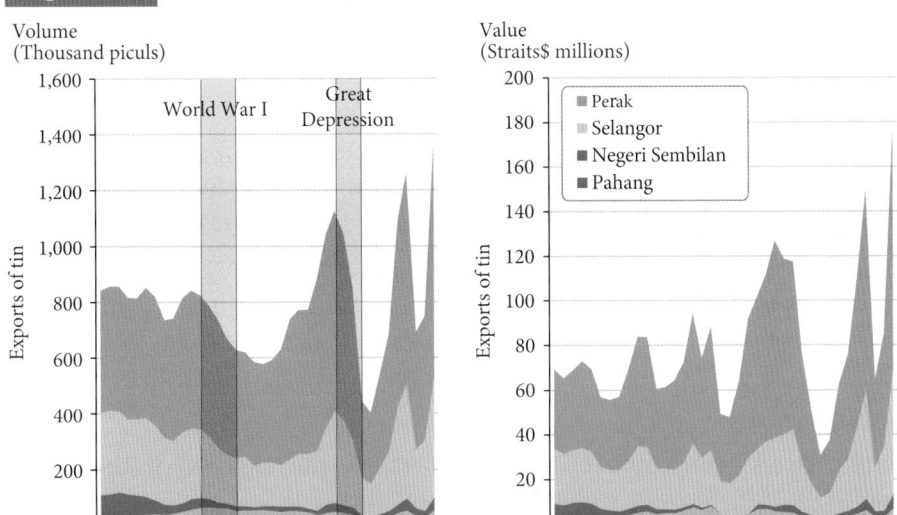

Figure 2.7   **Perak's tin exports were hit hard in the Great Depression**

Sources of data: Federated Malay States (various years), Report of the Administration of the Mines Department and of the Mining Industries.

Economic Gains, Ecological Losses

Rising Prosperity

Over the period 1900 to 1930, Kinta—in particular its epicentre, Ipoh—continued to grow and modernize. A new railway station was built in 1915, said to be one of the largest in Malaya, with three platforms and an adjoining hotel (Federated Malay States Railways, 1935). This was followed by the construction of the town hall and post office in 1916. Houses with *attap* roofs (similar to thatched roofs) gave way to brick buildings. Ipoh's development was so well planned that Richard Curle, a distinguished author and traveller, noted:

> of all the towns of this country it is the neatest and most modern in the trim American plans of its outlay. The streets run parallel with one another and cross at right angles, the roads have a brushed appearance, and the growing town is carefully patched on to the chess-board of the built. A model place, but without that destroying blight of the 'model village'. It is not artificial. … Altogether, Ipoh is rather an attractive spot, though I daresay it is also rather tame. There it lies in its metalliferous valley, watched by untrodden hills, and year by year it swells in size as its tin-concentrates go rumbling into the sea. (Curle, 1923, p. 203)

By 1923, Ipoh had begun to be powered by electricity supplied by Peng-kalen Mines Limited, a company operated by Osborne and Chappel (Gough, 2013). After an agreement in December 1925 between Armstrong, Whitworth and Company, and the Sultan of Perak, Iskandar Shah, the Perak River Hydro-Electric Power Company Limited was capitalized on the London Stock Exchange to invest in building power stations. In 1928 and 1929 the company's Malim Nawar and Chenderoh power stations were put into commission to supply electricity to the Kinta Valley's tin mines (Lim, 1967). The former was an 18-megawatt coal-fired plant and the latter a 27-megawatt hydroelectric station on the Perak River. Both were extraordinary feats of engineering (Kinloch, 1966). A second thermal power station was built in Batu Gajah in 1933.

Perak's rivers were thus critical 'enablers' in the success of the state's tin-mining industry, from the early days of mining in Larut through to the era of technological advancement in the first decades of the 20th century. Flowing water was crucial to a range of mining technologies: the Chinese *chin-chias* (waterwheel and chain pump) depended on water from streams, the hydraulic monitors depended on high-pressure water collected at altitude, and the dredges depended on electricity generated by dams.

With the influx of foreign investment in Kinta, Ipoh became the headquarters for many branches of foreign banks and firms. Whereas banking and financial services had previously been provided by the Kinta Treasury, the STC, and *chettiers* (Indian money lenders), foreign bank branches now began proliferating in the town, beginning with the Chartered Bank of India, Australia and China in 1902, followed by the Hongkong and Shanghai Banking Corporation in 1910, and the Mercantile Bank of India in 1928 (Khoo and Abdur-Razzaq Lubis, 2005). The Perak Chamber of Commerce, founded in 1911 and chaired by Walter Richard Haighton Chappel, had representatives from 21 British and Continental European Ipoh-based businesses at its establishment, ranging from accountants, auditors, and estate agents to dispensaries and businesses involved in consumer goods, engineering, and the production of mining equipment. The flourishing town of Ipoh was eventually made the capital of Perak in 1945.[36]

---

36 Discussions started about transferring the Perak state capital from Taiping to Ipoh in 1927, as it had already become the administrative headquarters, but the proposal was not implemented. It was the Japanese who confirmed Ipoh's status as the premier town of Perak and established it as their administrative capital in early 1942 and, after liberation in 1945, Ipoh remained the capital.

Environmental Costs

The prosperity that tin mining brought to Perak and to the Federated Malay States more widely came at an ecological cost which had lasting impacts. The Chinese open-cast mines—abandoned once the most accessible alluvial deposits had been exhausted—had left behind severely eroded hillsides, abandoned wastelands, and silt-laden rivers. Their smelting furnaces relied heavily on valuable wood, which led to the destruction of forests. Hydraulic mining and gravel pumping denuded entire hillsides of vegetation, sluiced by high-pressure hydraulic monitors. The tailings that ran into the rivers raised the riverbeds by several feet and increased flooding (Box 2.5). Tin mining polluted and silted up Perak's rivers. Although British and Continental European dredging was less damaging to rivers than other mining methods, the mixing of fertile topsoil with infertile soil dug from great depths 'left behind a landscape of sterile sand hummocks and miniature dunes that contemporaries regarded as permanently damaged' (Ross, 2014, p. 468).

Box 2.5   **Deforestation and the impact of the Great Flood of 1926**

Human activities—intensive tin mining, deforestation, and commercial agriculture—harmed Perak's landscape, polluted rivers, and led to serious flooding. When these environmental impacts began to threaten economic prosperity, the colonial government implemented some measures to control deforestation.

The colonial authorities' aim of managing forest resources for efficient wood production aligned with the aim of the Royal Botanic Gardens in Kew, near London, of protecting forests for the preservation of economically valuable species. By 1901 this synergy had resulted in the establishment of professional forestry practices through forest reservations. The Federated Malay States Forestry Department implemented silviculture—the practice of controlling the growth, composition, and quality of forests; this included planting heavy hardwoods, afforesting mining land, reforesting forest lands, and administering forest resource extraction of timber, *nibung* (palm), *nipah* (palm thatch), and *bakau* (mangroves) (Kathirithamby-Wells, 2005). Several enactments were passed to control the cutting of valuable trees—for instance, for use in smelting.

(Continued)

Enforcement of hill protection and a ban on logging were often maintained where the extension of mining and agricultural settlements put catchments at risk, despite objections by those who proposed controlled logging as a means of promoting development. Some 95,000 hectares of hill country north of Gopeng were declared Protected Forest in 1927 in order to forestall impending damage to the Perak River and its tributaries. In Perak, the highest share of reservation was secured in 1932; by this year, over 700,200 hectares or 34.7 per cent of its land had been designated Reserved Forest, compared with only 19.9 per cent designated alienated land (Kathirithamby-Wells, 2005).

The devastating consequences of deforestation were made evident by the Great Flood of December 1926. In Parit, the Perak River rose by more than 25 feet above normal levels. Malay peasants, in particular, suffered great hardship when their *padi* crops were ruined, and their houses, cattle, and other possessions were washed away. Roads and railway lines were inundated, and telegraphic communication cut. The destruction was so bad that a Perak Relief Fund was established, raising over Straits$107,000 from private and public donations for the emergency provision of food, grants to help people rebuild houses, and flood-prevention measures (Williamson, 2016).

The Great Flood also had longer-term effects. Its devastation of virgin forests increased the intensity and frequency of future inundations. Trees were replaced by quick-growing plants—creepers, vines, and rattans—but these did not perform the vital role of protecting riverbanks and flood plains, thereby intensifying the process of erosion and silting. The flood served, however, as a catalyst for improving flood prevention and river management. By 1933 a dedicated Drainage and Irrigation Department had been established in Perak, with a mandate for river restoration, the removal of sediment, and the building of embankments, canals, and dams.

The Natural Rubber Boom, 1900–1940

Unlike tin, natural rubber was not a resource indigenous to Perak and other Malayan states, having originated in the Brazilian Amazon jungles. It was brought over to Malaya by British officials in the late 19th century, nurtured, and subsequently fully developed into a major export industry. Whereas the 19th-century tin industry's prosperity had been driven mainly by Chinese initiatives, Perak's spectacular rubber industry boom in the early 20th century was driven by British enterprise. The growth of both industries was triggered by the industrial revolution in the West, which led to vastly increased demand for resources and an associated international trade boom. Demand for tin came from the UK's tin-plate industry, and for rubber from the burgeoning US automobile industry. For both of these natural-resource industries, the Federated Malay States—led by Perak—were prime movers.

There were key differences between the institutions of governance that supported the early growth of these two primary-commodity industries. When tin mining took off, Perak was governed through an indigenous traditional political system, and later as an independent state under British colonial rule with decentralized decision-making. The initial rubber take-off, meanwhile, occurred when Perak was already on a path towards increasingly centralized colonial governance as part of the Federated Malay States. This was a period when individual state control over political decision-making and finances weakened while colonial control became stronger, with economic policies formulated at the federal rather than state level.

The government of the Federated Malay States played a crucial role in the growth and strategic direction of Perak's rubber industry, both because of rubber's central role in the economies of these states and because the commodity was such an important US dollar earner for the UK. Seeking to attract

Globalization: Perak's Rise, Relative Decline, and Regeneration. Sultan Nazrin Shah, Oxford University Press. © Sultan Nazrin Shah (2024). DOI: 10.1093/oso/9780198897774.003.0013

international investment, and under pressure from powerful private-sector lobbying groups—notably the Rubber Growers' Association and the Planters' Association of Malaya[37]—the government enacted multiple supportive policies explicitly favouring British and Continental European estate interests. These included investment support (with no taxes on profits), arrangements for land alienation (the disposal of state land) and tenure—both of which were unknown under Malay customary rights—assistance for research and development (R&D), labour and migration policies, and, most significantly, output restrictions during periods of rubber price slumps.

Lacking a political voice to counter the powerful estate interests, the interests of rubber smallholders—predominantly Malay and Chinese—were disadvantaged by government policies. Concerned also about the potential of Malays to switch from *padi* farming to rubber cultivation, the colonial authorities enacted legislation to ensure that Malays continued as rice farmers. This was to reduce dependency on imports with its associated foreign exchange loss—rice imports had been rising with Perak's fast-growing migrant population.

Take-off in Rubber Cultivation

To broaden Perak's economic base away from reliance on the tin industry alone, in the final decades of the 19th century the British authorities began to encourage commercial agriculture. They sought greater British and Continental European engagement in plantation agriculture—at first in coffee, sugar, tea, and coconut—by offering long land leases at minimal cost. However, capital and labour were scarce, and these crops were soon to become less attractive to investors than rubber. Coffee, which initially achieved high prices, faced fierce competition, particularly from Brazil, and was subject to severe price swings— coffee prices tumbled after 1895 to just one-third of their earlier levels, ending colonial interest in this crop (Tate, 1996). Substantial investments were made in Perak's sugar plantations by Penang-based Chinese and British interests, and the expansion of sugar cultivation continued into the early 20th century. Sugar was seemingly set to become a highly successful export industry.

But sugar production began to fall sharply and, by 1914, exports had virtually ceased as Perak's estate owners switched en masse to more profitable rubber

---

37 The Rubber Growers' Association was formed in June 1907, headquartered in London, and most of its members were British. The Planters' Association of Malaya was formed later the same year and organized from among planters' associations in the Federated Malay States and Johor.

planting. This shift away from sugar was prompted partly by a rising number of complaints over water supplies from *padi* farmers. While sugar and rice need the same type of land, sugar is a dry crop whereas rice requires a constant supply of water. As sugar cultivation expanded, *padi* farmers began to complain that the irrigation canals of the sugar fields were depriving them of water. Meanwhile, emerging signs of potential profitability persuaded some British and Chinese estate holders to start investing in natural rubber. Large-scale investment in rubber plantations did not begin until the start of the 20th century (Barlow et al., 1994). When it did, most sugar and coffee plantations were converted entirely to rubber.

From Brazilian Beginnings

Natural rubber was established as a cultivatable crop in Malaya as part of a plan by British officials and scientists to break Brazil's monopoly and begin commercial production in Britain's colonies. In around 1875, the British government began funding research into rubber planting, centred at the Royal Botanic Gardens in Kew, London. They commissioned Henry Wickham, an explorer, to go to Brazil to obtain seeds of the three main varieties of rubber plants—*hevea*, *ceara*, and *castilloa*—so that an assessment could be made of their suitability for planting in the soil and climatic conditions of the British colonies of Ceylon, India, and Malaya as well as in Java in the Dutch East Indies (Loadman, 2005). In June 1876, Wickham shipped a consignment of Para (*hevea brasiliensis*) tree seedlings to Kew gardens. More than 2,000 germinated, and most were sent to Ceylon in 1877 (Wray, 1893).[38] Twenty-two of these seedlings were forwarded to the Botanic Gardens in Singapore, and of these 10 were brought to Perak by Hugh Low, the British Resident, and planted in the grounds of the residency at Kuala Kangsar on the bank of the Perak River in 1877.[39]

About a decade later, some seeds were obtained from the Kuala Kangsar trees and planted in the grounds of the Taiping Museum, situated on former mining ground, where the soil was considered infertile. Finding that rubber grew well there despite the apparently poor soil, the colonial authorities decided to

---

38 Clements Robert Markham, Director of the Royal Botanic Gardens, also sent Robert Cross to the Amazon later in 1876 to provide backup in case Wickham was not successful. Cross also collected some 1,000 *hevea* seedlings.

39 Low was a keen naturalist and farmer interested in the improvement of strains and in farming methods. Under his administration, a museum of Malay flora, fauna, and minerals was established in Kuala Kangsar and placed under the direction of Leonard Wray, its first curator.

spread its growth to wasteland in Kuala Kangsar; to land occasionally flood-ed in Parit Buntar, near the sea; to Tapah and Batu Gajah in Kinta; to Matang in northwestern Perak; and to other locations in the state (Wray, 1894). It was found that rubber trees thrived in 'any locality, from the bakau swamps to the foot-hills, and on any soil, from rich alluvial to old mine heaps' (Wray, 1894, p. 94), and that a six-year-old tree could produce viable yields.

Over time, the trees planted in Perak provided seeds for distribution to other Malayan states. At first, there was little private interest in large-scale planting of a crop that would take around six years to mature. By 1897, however, Henry Ridley—an English botanist and director of the Botanic Gardens in Singapore—had developed a new tapping method that confirmed that the latex yields would be sufficient to make rubber production profitable, and that there would be a ready global market for Malayan plantation rubber because it was of higher quality than the wild rubber produced in Brazil from uncultivated trees.

Soaring Investment

With the US automobile industry rapidly expanding from the end of the 19th century and especially during the first decade of the 20th, and as bicycles also grew in popularity, the demand for rubber for making tyres rocketed, and pric-es surged to previously undreamed-of heights. This, in turn, stimulated a huge appetite for investing in rubber plantations. Owners of land that had previous-ly been used to plant other crops—in Perak and elsewhere in Malaya—were incentivized to shift to rubber cultivation, and large tracts of virgin forest land were cleared for new plantations.

With the colonial government offering land on long leases and supporting experimental planting, and as rubber prices surged, Perak's total land acreage planted to rubber rose spectacularly. It soared from just 9,500 acres in 1905 to 122,000 acres in 1910, and further to 425,000 acres in 1920, after which the rise became less steep (Figure 2.8, left panel). Perak's rubber acreage increased by more than 56 times between 1905 and 1930. In 1910, Perak accounted for 39 per cent of land planted to rubber in the Federated Malay States, and 26 per cent of land planted to rubber in Malaya as a whole. As other Malayan states followed Perak's lead in cultivating rubber, the corresponding shares declined to 35 per cent and 18 per cent by 1930 (Figure 2.8, right panel). Although initially a source of great profit, this stunning surge in rubber planting would even-tually lead to overproduction, causing widespread hardship and laying the ground for the growth of some anti-British sentiment.

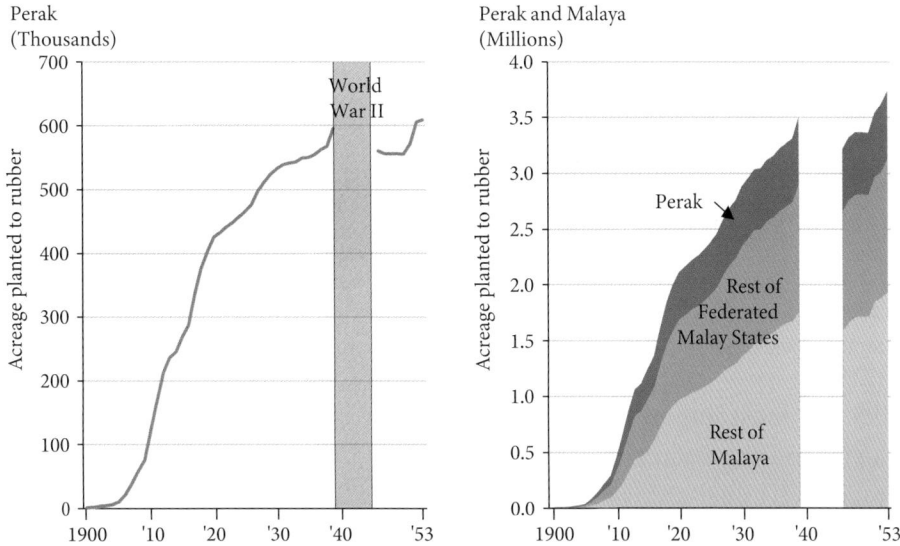

Figure 2.8 **Perak's total land acreage planted to rubber rose spectacularly up to 1920, before moderating**

Sources of data: For 1900–1939: Sultan Nazrin Shah (2022), https://www.ehm.my/data/historical-gdp-accounts; for 1946–1953: Department of Statistics–Federation of Malaya (various years), Malaya Rubber Statistics Handbook.

Note: Data for Perak include the Dindings after its retrocession in 1935.

With the meteoric rise in acreage under rubber cultivation, combined with high prices—the price of rubber nearly trebled from £331 per metric ton in 1905 to £965 per metric ton in 1910—Perak enjoyed an economic boom, which spread prosperity to 'shopkeepers, cart and elephant owners' and well beyond (Annual Report of Perak, 1906). As Resident E. W. Birch stated:

> Numerous companies had been floated. Most of the Government loans have been repaid. All nationalities are acquiring land in various quantities to plant it with rubber by varied methods. (cited in Annual Report of Perak, 1909, p. 11)

The rubber boom attracted many Javanese and Sumatran Malays who worked on cultivating thousands of acres of rubber. R. O. Winstedt, British administrator of Matang, observed:

> The example of one Malay here (Matang), who sold twelve acres of clean rubber for $8,000, has brought home the importance of diligent supervision to his whole mukim [a sub-division of a district] with most salutary results. Another Malay, the headman of some 50 partners, got an offer, on almost the same scale, for 100 acres but he refused it, and is spending the hundreds of dollars a month he wins from his old trees on white-ant killer, fungus cures and clean weeding, and looks forward to making soon his thousands of dollars a month. (cited in Annual Report of Perak, 1909, p. 11)

Perak's tax revenues were expanded to include duties of 2.5 per cent *ad valorem* imposed on rubber exports, and its economic base broadened, with the economy no longer founded upon tin alone. In addition, the benefits from the rubber industry were more widely distributed. In 1911, Oliver Marks, Acting British Resident of Perak (1911–1912), vividly described how the state's landscape was being transformed:

> Estates have been opened in every district in the State, and the year was characterised by steady development and maintenance of opened areas after the rush for new land and the promotion of companies prevailing during 1910. The whole face of the country, as seen from our main roads, has been transformed from virgin forest to the monotony of miles of rubber trees, and a patch of jungle along the cart-roads will soon be the exception rather than the rule of less than ten-years ago. (cited in Annual Report of Perak, 1911, p. 11)

Perak's two most important districts for rubber cultivation were Lower Perak and neighbouring Batang Padang, which together accounted for 45 per cent of the total area under cultivation by 1920 (Figure 2.9). However, rubber estates were found in every district (Map 2.3), and Kuala Kangsar saw such a surge in planting that, by the end of the 1930s, it had 28 per cent of the state's total. In 1931, Lower Perak had the largest number of rubber estates, at 74, while Kuala Kangsar and Kinta also had more than 50 each. Rubber was generally planted

Figure 2.9   **In 1920, Lower Perak, Batang Padang, and Kinta were the main centres of rubber cultivation, but by 1939 Kuala Kangsar had overtaken them**

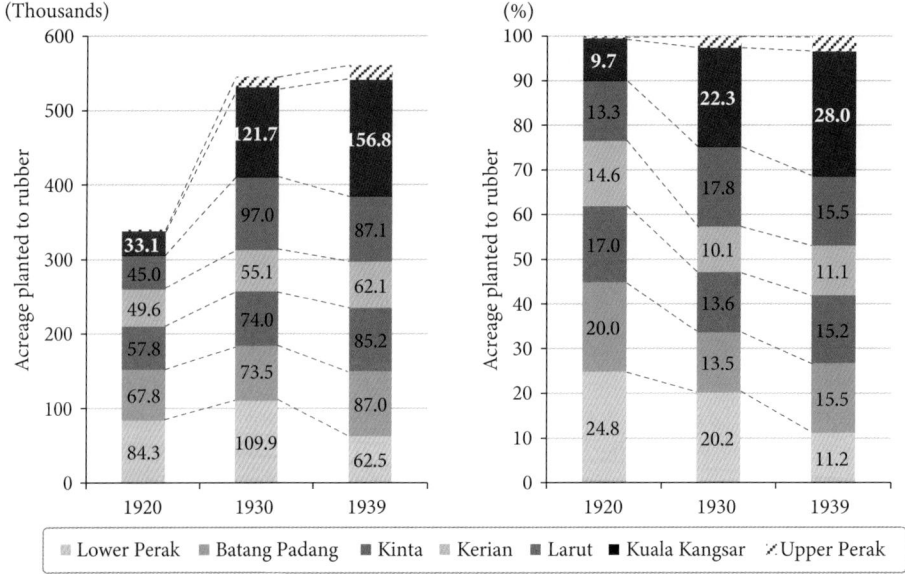

Sources of data: Annual Report of Perak (1920, 1930, and 1939).

close to roads and railway lines to exploit the investments in transport infra-structure, which by this time was expanding throughout the peninsula's west-coast states. As rubber estates mushroomed beyond existing transport links, feeder roads were built to link them to the main roads and railway lines.

Map 2.3   **Perak's rubber plantations, circa 1920**

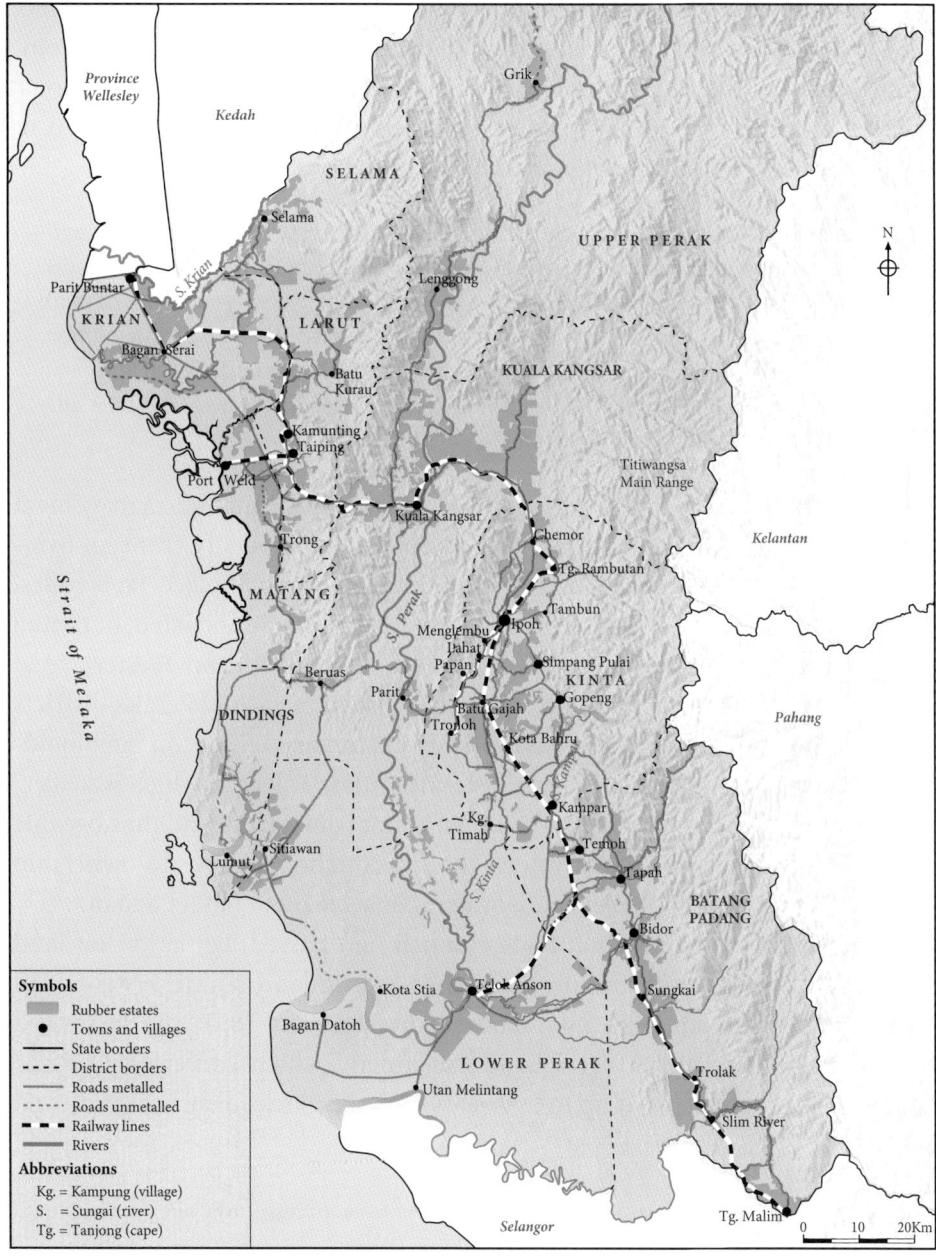

Sources: Adapted from various archive maps, NAS (2020c).

Colonial Policies on Land Alienation

At the start of colonial rule in 1874, much of Perak was covered by dense forest land that had very little if any market value. Only land in the small towns, and in the valleys where tin ore deposits had been discovered, was of commercial worth. Land was used communally by the Malay peasantry and, once the soil had been exhausted, cultivation shifted to another location. This approach changed radically with the growth of mining towns, port towns, and villages, the construction of roads and railways, and the expansion of commercial agriculture. British administrators adopted liberal landholding policies that mainly favoured international capitalist investors who were provided with the best land situated near roads or railway lines. As Frank A. Swettenham, Resident of Perak, wrote:

> The present object of the Government is to give the greatest encouragement to agriculturists and miners of all nationalities. The unoccupied lands (especially those distant from lines of communication) are really of very little actual value, and it is of more importance to get in capital and labour, especially a fixed agricultural population, than to worry people who are easily frightened away and do not understand European methods, by a quantity of regulations that under other conditions would be not only excellent but necessary. (cited in Annual Report of Perak, 1890, p. 21)

Keen to attract British and Continental European investors and management to develop the commercial agricultural sector and to diversify from an over-dependence on tin, the British administration quickly put in place 'land codes'. These set out the terms on which government land could be alienated, outlining the forms of land tenure and private property rights, based on Western legal principles.[40] Land and survey offices were established in each of Perak's districts to demarcate and survey claims, and Malay customary tenure on smallholdings was converted into individual transferable titles, or leases, which were certified and registered in return for a nominal annual quit rent. Land thus became a tradeable commodity with a value. The introduction of private ownership meant Malay farmers could sell land, or use it as security to obtain a loan.

Twenty years after the Perak State Council had passed legislation on land rights, the British administration made the existing land tenure system even more attractive to potential international investors. In 1897, the Federated Malay States passed the Federal Land Enactment, which conferred freehold ownership through leases of up to 999 years on large blocks of agricultural land

---

40 In the 1880s and 1890s, Perak's government granted generous terms to prospective coffee planters, including government loans.

of over 100 acres, without the need for a special instrument of title or a prior survey. The annual quit rent payable to the government was initially fixed at 10 Straits cents an acre, rising after 10 years to 50 Straits cents; these low rates were justified on the grounds that cheap land and security of tenure were necessary to attract international investors. However, the administration hiked the quit rent sharply following the land rush in the first year of the 20th century, to Straits$1 an acre, rising to Straits$5 after five years (Tate, 1996). On these terms, the colonial state alienated hundreds of thousands of acres for rubber land at low prices and with few restrictions.[41] The cumulative amount of land alienated for agriculture by Perak's government rose from 294,000 acres in 1906 to 815,000 acres by 1 January 1920 (Annual Report of Perak, 1906, p. xiii and 1920, p. 2). Land sales and fees became another important source of state revenue.

Shortages of suitable plantation land emerged, however, as the rubber industry came to dominate commercial agricultural activity in the state, as British and Continental European companies sought estates, and as the numbers of smallholders of all communities rose. Land values in many areas climbed sharply as use increased, leading to huge speculation in land. This had potential long-term negative impacts for Malays themselves as well as for colonial rice policy. As Drabble observes:

> Malays, locally-born and immigrant, speculated in selling rubber land to such an extent that officials feared major losses of 'ancestral' land, integral to village life, to non-Malay interests. (Drabble, 2000, p. 64)

As many Malays shifted from rice growing to the more remunerative rubber industry—becoming smallholders or wage-earning labourers on estates—British administrators became concerned that the industry's rapid development could lead to the permanent abandonment of *padi* land. The colonial authorities preferred Malays to grow rice to meet local food demand and to reduce the import bill for rice.[42] After much reflection, including discussions with the British residents and Malay rulers, the government of the Federated Malay States introduced the Malay Land Reservations Enactment of 1913 to prevent Malays from selling land to non-Malays. Land could only be alienated to Malays, though the enactment did allow leases of three years to non-Malays (Lim, 1971). In the

---

41 Two restrictions were imposed: cultivation had to be started in the first year, and one-quarter of the total area had to be under cultivation at the end of the fifth year.

42 According to Rudner (2018), the Malay aristocratic elite considered *padi* growing more in keeping with traditional village culture, and exclusive Malay involvement in *padi* a defence against the perceived threat of Chinese economic domination.

year after the enactment, each of Perak's seven districts established Malay land reservations.

With the British administration's concerns about the loss of foreign exchange due to the growing dependence on rice imports, and as a step towards increasing food self-sufficiency, the Malay Land Reservations Enactment was coupled with the Rice Lands Enactment of 1917 (Box 2.6). The effect of these two laws was to keep much of the Malay population in rural subsistence production and out of the towns. Thus, non-Malays could not hold land in Malay Reservations, while Malays could not plant rubber on land granted for rice planting. As Rudner (2018) notes:

> Malayan rubber policies stifled peasant innovation, aiming primarily to support the estate pattern of plantation agriculture on the one hand and upholding the traditional pattern of kampong life on the other. (Rudner, 2018, p. 1)

Concerned by the prospect of competition from powerful US corporate interests, as well as by potential overproduction, the Rubber Growers' Association strongly opposed attempts by US tyre manufacturers to acquire land for rubber planting. Towards the end of World War I, Firestone Tire and Rubber Company had negotiated a large land concession in Perak, which had been approved by the government of Perak, while Goodyear Tire and Rubber Company had shown a similar interest in Johor (Tate, 1996). In response, the Federal Council passed the Rubber Lands (Restriction) Enactment in 1917, which prevented the alienation of areas of land of over 50 acres to foreign interests.[43] Protective regulatory restrictions were enacted, similar to those which prevented the US from establishing a foothold in the tin-smelting industry (see 'Consolidation of British Control of the Smelting Industry', above).

Box 2.6 **Stimulating rice cultivation: Programmes in Kerian and Lower Perak**

For Malay peasant farmers, rice growing was a way of life, not a purely economic undertaking. Methods of rice cultivation evolved with buffalo-drawn ploughs and traditional hand tillage giving way to the more scientific methods for efficient planting and harvesting introduced by the British administration.

---

43 The restriction applied to all except British subjects, subjects of the Malay rulers, UK-registered corporations, and persons resident in Malaya for at least seven years. However, after objections by potential Japanese investors who were trying to secure Malayan land for rubber planting, the legislation was amended and the ban was temporarily extended to all for one year in 1918.

Perak was heavily reliant on rice imported from Siam and Burma to feed its fast-growing population, and with ever larger tracts of land coming under rubber cultivation, the British administrators perceived a danger that *padi* acreage would increasingly be taken up by estates. Perak's rice imports as a share of its total imports had grown during the period of the first rubber boom, from 24 per cent in 1900 to 27 per cent in 1915 (Table 2a).

Table 2a	Perak's rice imports as a share of the value of all imports rose and then declined over the period 1900–1920		
	Rice imports		Total imports (Straits$ thousands)
	(Straits$ thousands)	Share (%)	
1900	3,499.2	24	14,741.1
1905	4,567.4	23	20,153.3
1910	5,220.3	24	21,784.4
1915	6,544.8	27	24,011.2
1920	11,571.2	21	54,364.4

Sources of data: Annual Report of Perak (various years).

To reduce dependence on rice imports, the colonial government waived initial land assessment fees for *padi* cultivators and approved the construction of the Kerian Irrigation Scheme—a costly mega-project that opened in 1906 after almost a decade of planning and construction. The scheme greatly increased *padi* production and, by around 1910, Kerian accounted for more than half of the Federated Malay States' wet *padi*—the rice grown in flooded fields (Short and Jackson, 1971). Wet *padi* was favoured as it minimized soil erosion. Rice production in Kerian was commercially oriented and the government maintained two rice mills at Bagan Serai and Parit Buntar (King, 1939).

Between 1909 and 1911, some 300 loans were given by Perak's Agricultural Loan Fund to help Kerian's *padi* cultivators, who needed seasonal credit while their fields were prepared or after a crop failure (Lim, 1977). The colonial authorities increasingly came to see Malays as the food producers for the commercial rubber estate and tin-mining sectors, even though rice trading was almost entirely the remit of the Chinese. During World War I the British administration instituted measures to increase food output, including the Rice Lands Enactment of 1917, which stipulated that land granted to smallholders for rice planting could only be used

(Continued)

for producing food, and the Food Production Enactment of 1918, which required estates to devote 10 per cent of allotted land to that purpose.

Around 1930, the administration also designated Lower Perak as an area in which to expand rice cultivation and establish new Malay settlements. Newly developed *padi* areas were reserved for Malays with allocated holdings (*bendangs*) of six acres each (King, 1939). The importance of water control in *padi* cultivation was recognized: the Drainage and Irrigation Department opened the Sungai Manik Scheme in Lower Perak, increasing the irrigated cultivated area by 7,000 acres with a settlement of 6,000 people by 1939 (Lim, 1977). Later that year, in a move to further encourage rice cultivation, the government established a rice mill at Teluk Anson, which was important to Malay cultivators as Chinese-owned private mills preferred to buy imported rice at lower prices.

British Agency Houses on the Commanding Heights

British agency houses, which provided the financial, commercial, and shipping services essential for the state's export-based economy, also played a pivotal role in the growth of Malaya's rubber industry. They mobilized resources from international investors and provided management support for the estates. At the beginning of the 20th century, the five largest British agency houses—Guthrie Corporation, Harrisons & Crosfield, Barlows, Boustead, and Sime Darby—were already familiar with Malaya's import and export trade, having worked with pioneering coffee and sugar planters (Drabble and Drake, 1974). By 1917, over 40 per cent of all Malaya's estate lands were managed by these five agency houses, directed from London boardrooms—with the exception of Guthrie, which operated in Singapore (Tate, 1996).

Typically, representatives of these agency houses would approach landowners or planters of other crops with proposals to plant rubber. Once terms were agreed between the parties, an estate company was formed, and the agency house would arrange for it to be floated on the London Stock Exchange to raise the huge investment capital required to bring the estate to maturity over the next six years. As investors frequently recovered their capital in two or three years after maturity, the floats were usually oversubscribed (Barlow et al., 1994).[44]

---

44 The very high rates of return on investment also attracted Shanghai capitalists, who launched their own companies on the local market. The first to do so was the Kalumpong Rubber Company, registered in 1909, which established a successful rubber estate in Bagan Serai in Kerian district (Thomas, 1998).

The main costs incurred in converting Perak's virgin jungle land into estates included paying for tree felling, burning, weeding, soil conservation, and drainage, as well as management fees. After listing, landowners were paid by stock options. The agency houses hired experienced staff to manage the estate and provide auxiliary services, such as accounting, legal support, and export logistics. In Perak, some of the first estates to come under agency house management were Sungei Krian Rubber Estates (1904), Krian Rubber Estate (1904), Sungkhai Chumor (1906), Chersonese Estates (1909), and Kinta Kellas (1910) (Purdie, 2018).[45]

Agency houses were themselves also investors in rubber estates, accumulating significant rights through minority shareholdings, although they seldom made outright acquisitions. Normally, a member of the agency house board would sit on the board of the new company (Stillson, 1971). The agency houses worked closely with major British banks operating in Malaya, such as the Chartered Bank, and Hongkong and Shanghai Banking Corporation, to arrange financing, investment advice, short-term credit lines, and foreign exchange. Between 1904 and 1922, the estimated average investment in rubber estates via agency houses in Malaya amounted to 39 per cent of the total, and in some years was as high as 75–85 per cent (Stillson, 1971). By contrast, while considerable Chinese capital was also invested in the rubber planting industry, it was not of a volume comparable to British capital (Tai, 2013). Chinese-owned rubber estates—either incorporated locally or run as family partnerships—remained small as they had less access to capital to expand operations (Barlow, 2018).

Agency houses made huge untaxed profits as global rubber demand boomed: in 1919 Guthrie's overall profit was £265,000, and Harrisons & Crosfield's was £116,000 (Purdie, 2018). Through their political and trading networks as well as their business strength, agency houses could ensure that their interests were at the forefront of colonial Malaya's economic policy (Sultan Nazrin Shah, 2017). As Puthucheary (1960, p. xiv) observes, the agency houses came to 'control not only the commanding heights of the Malayan economy but also much of the plains'. They established local networks and made large profits by purchasing much of the rubber harvested by smallholders, who cultivated a substantial part of Perak's total acreage under rubber. During the initial rubber boom of 1909 to 1911, annual dividends averaging 30 to 40 per cent were paid to investors (Mako, 2008).

---

45 Agency houses worked with local entrepreneurs, and several had representative offices in Ipoh. Guthrie, for example, partnered with Loke Yew, a prominent *towkay*, and with Alagappa Chettiar, a leading businessman, in buying a large rubber estate in Kamunting.

Divide between Estate and Smallholding Rubber

Perak's rubber plantation sector comprised estates and smallholdings—the latter defined as an area of rubber land of less than 100 acres, with anything between 25 and 100 acres considered a medium-sized smallholding.[46] Estates were highly capital intensive, requiring huge investment. Establishing and running an estate involved not only the steep initial capital investments but also high running costs to pay for a large labour force. This made estates much less flexible than smallholdings, which had much lower overheads and capital needs (Lim, 1974). Nonetheless, colonial policies strongly encouraged and nurtured the estates, which were concentrated in prime locations along roads and railways for ready access to ports, as shown in Map 2.3 above. By contrast, rubber smallholdings were mainly Asian-owned and received far less support from the authorities—and at times they were even discouraged. They were often located on the fringes of large estates and relied on networks of intermediaries to bring their rubber to export. The estate and smallholding subsectors coexisted, but tensions between them increased at times when global rubber prices were falling, and especially when export quotas were imposed.

In 1910, Perak's rubber estate acreage was virtually double its smallholdings acreage, at 80,000 acres compared to 41,600 acres (Figure 2.10, left panel). However, due to the prosperity that rubber brought to many smallholders, by the 1920s smallholdings had expanded to cover almost the same acreage as estates. Meanwhile, as rubber planting spread rapidly to other states in the peninsula, Perak's share of Malaya's total acreage of both estates and smallholdings fell sharply: in 1910, rubber estates in Perak accounted for 25 per cent of all Malaya's estates and 29 per cent of all Malaya's smallholdings but, by 1922 these shares had fallen to only 17 per cent and 23 per cent, respectively (Figure 2.10, right panel). Productivity on estates and smallholdings, measured by rubber production per acre, varied widely depending on factors including how the trees were cared for, planting density, and the trees' maturity. Despite their often minimal capital investment, smallholdings could sometimes be even more productive than estates because their trees were planted more densely and tapped more often than those on estates.

---

46 The distinction between estates and smallholdings is not as sharp as these acreage figures may suggest. As Drabble (1991, p. 2) observes, 'the evidence reveals a continuum from the very smallest holdings up through the medium holdings with inputs of capital and wage-labour etc. increasing steadily, accompanied by a shift in methods of finance, management and production towards the estate style'.

Figure 2.10

In some periods, Perak's estates and smallholdings had roughly similar shares of rubber acreage, but their combined share declined in Malaya's total

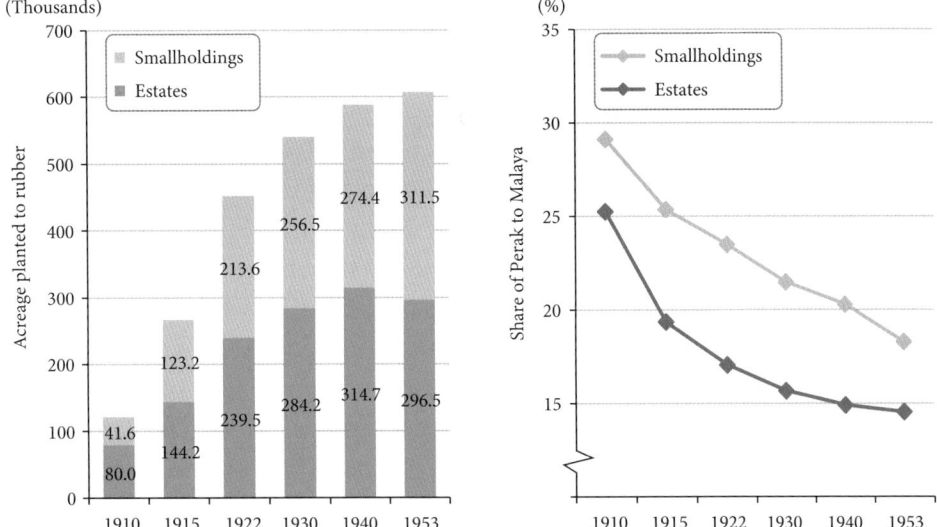

Sources of data: For 1910 and 1915: Sultan Nazrin Shah (2022), https://www.ehm.my/data/historical-gdp-accounts; for other years: Lim (1967).

Rubber Estates—A Key Beneficiary of Government Policy but Little Malay Involvement

Estates typically had a hierarchical structure organized according to ethnicity, which mirrored the glaring social and economic inequalities of the time. A European manager and his European assistants were at the apex, responsible for day-to-day management.[47] Eurasians handled much of the clerical work. Beneath them were Indian foremen or *kanganis*, who oversaw a large male and female labour force. The larger estates had factories to manufacture smoked rubber sheets in smoke houses with wood-burning furnaces, or to make pale crêpe rubber—crinkled yellow sheets prepared by pressing bleached coagulated latex through corrugated rollers (German, 1937, p. 108). On an average estate, a

---

47 A typical day on an estate began with tapping the rubber trees in the early morning. Latex from the individual trees was collected and weighed in a central weighing station, then taken by tankers to a factory for processing. The latex was mixed with acid to begin coagulation, and the coagulum milled into sheets that were then hung over bamboo poles to dry. The process was completed after the rubber sheets were dried and smoked in a kipper kiln, graded, and packed into bales to be sold (Arabis, 2018).

little over half of those employed were tappers, while most of the rest were field workers and weeders; about 2 per cent of those employed were factory workers. They received cash wages, rudimentary housing, and medical care, and their children received a basic vernacular education (Bauer, 1947).

Almost all of Perak's larger estates were owned by British and Continental European companies, with the largest plantations of over 1,000 acres accounting for more than half of the total estate acreage planted to rubber (Figure 2.11). By contrast, the ownership of estates of between 100 and 500 acres was fairly evenly split, with British and Continental Europeans owning 35 per cent, Chinese 32 per cent, and Indians 28 per cent.[48] Many of the Chinese estate owners were either *towkays*, who reinvested the money they had made from tin mining, or planters of other crops, such as sugar and coffee, who had switched to rubber during the boom (Tai, 2013). Indian estate owners were often financed by *chettiers* (Lim, 1967). However, the overwhelming majority of Malays, having little or no access to capital, were unable to venture into estate plantations.

Estates benefited considerably from R&D sponsored by the colonial government. This was initially carried out by the Department of Agriculture of the Federated Malay States, and later by the Rubber Research Institute of Malaya, which was established in 1926 with headquarters in Kuala Lumpur, and funded through a small cess (tax) imposed on rubber exports.[49] The Institute's work included soil investigations; improvements in planting material, tapping, and disease and pest control; and the trial production of various types of rubber suitable for manufacture. While its research was mainly for the large estates' benefit, in 1934 it appointed a smallholders' advisory service and began providing guidance at district level. The benefits of agricultural R&D endured beyond the colonial period. This marked a sharp contrast with the experiences of much of Sub-Saharan Africa, where agricultural production regressed.

---

48 These shares relate to Perak in 1935, but largely reflect the pattern of estate ownership throughout the colonial period.

49 The Institute worked closely with the laboratories of the London Advisory Committee for Rubber Research (Ceylon and Malaya) and with the botanical gardens in Buitenzorg (Bogor), Dutch East Indies, for example, on bud grafting, which was carried out from around the mid-1920s (German, 1937). This process involved developing clones from parent trees and produced much higher-yielding rubber plants than natural seedlings did.

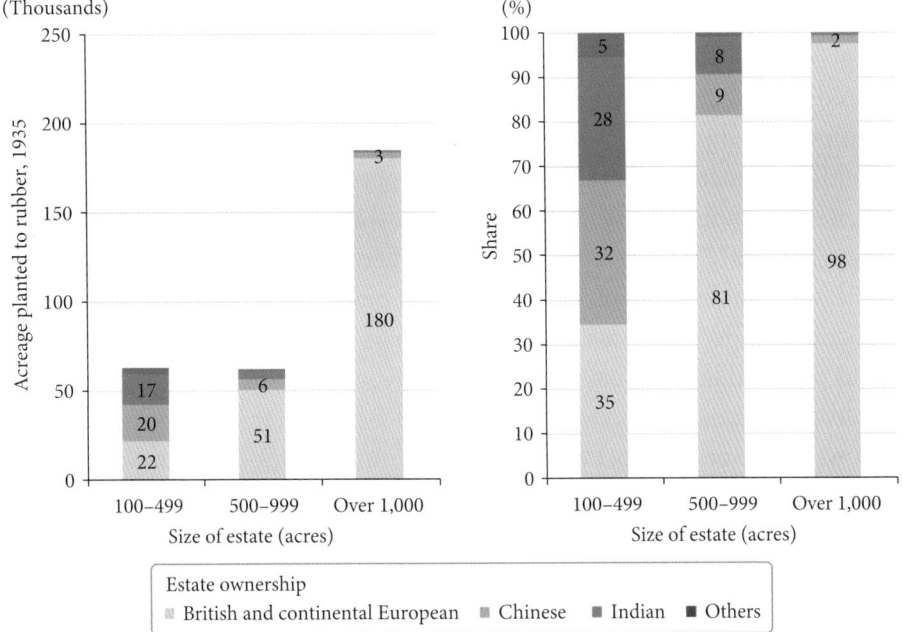

Figure 2.11   **British and Continental Europeans dominated ownership of Perak's largest estates**

Sources of data: Department of Statistics–Federation of Malaya (various years), Malaya Rubber Statistics Handbook.

Rubber Smallholdings—Another Key Driver of Migration

Soaring rubber prices at the start of the 20th century encouraged many of Perak's Malay *padi* farmers to switch to rubber planting, or to add rubber trees to the fields that they were cultivating. Land and household labour were the main inputs required; seedlings were free or bought at minimal cost. Rubber cultivation not only provided such farmers with higher incomes but also had the great advantage of delivering continuous cash returns throughout the year. This was in stark contrast to rice cultivation, which yielded income only once a year at harvest time, leading to high levels of indebtedness as farmers were often forced to borrow in the lean months just before the harvest. The prosperity that rubber generated also encouraged heavy migration from areas outside Malaya, with individuals coming to work on smallholdings as well as estates.

Rubber smallholdings, scattered throughout Perak, constituted a significant part of the state's commercial agricultural economy, and provided employment for many Malays—both locally born and migrants—who were increasingly drawn to the state and into its monetary economy. Chinese[50] and, to a substantially smaller extent, Indians, were also prominent in the smallholding sector, growing rubber either as a main or as a supplementary economic activity.[51] Smallholdings were normally run by the owner and his relatives, and they sometimes also employed a few paid helpers to tap rubber and to weed. Malay smallholdings generally averaged about four acres, while holdings by Chinese were generally about four times larger, with some considered medium-sized holdings (Lim, 1977). Some smallholders worked multiple plots of land.

While smallholders' aggregate share of rubber acreage was high, their capital expenditure per acre was much lower than that of larger estates because they had minimal labour costs and little, if any, management costs. Smallholders could use family labour to cut down and burn a few acres of jungle, and plant it with free or low-cost seed from adjoining estates. After an 'immature' period during which rubber trees grew, smallholders could start tapping their trees and secure regular daily incomes (Barlow et al., 1994). Malay smallholders relied on Chinese traders who supported the collection, processing, and marketing of their rubber to international buyers through agency houses. While the returns to smallholders were relatively low due to the inferior quality of the latex, the industry was still much more attractive than subsistence farming (Barlow et al., 1994). Smallholders benefited especially when rubber prices were high, and when the prices were low some could go back to rice cultivation or other agricultural work.

By 1921, the total area alienated for smallholdings in Perak was 242,000 acres, accounting for 48 per cent of its total rubber cultivated area. Between 1926 and 1930, 23,000 applications were received by district offices for rubber land totalling 90,000 acres, of which 5,000 were approved, for a total of 17,000 acres (Lim, 1971, p. 185). Of those approved, Malays accounted for about 50 per cent of smallholding acreage and Chinese about 46 per cent. Crucially, the well-being of Perak's Malays no longer depended primarily on traditional rice cultivation. Their involvement in the rubber industry, however, also meant that they were exposed to international market forces. In

---

50 All Chinese dialect groups took part in the rubber industry. In this way, the industry differed from tin mining, which mainly involved Cantonese and Hakkas (Tai, 2013).

51 A Foochow Chinese rubber smallholding settlement was established in Sitiawan in the 1900s under a missionary initiative supported by Perak's government. The original purpose was to increase agricultural production, but rubber planting proved more profitable and became a magnet for further migration from China's Fujian province (Tai, 2013).

boom times they prospered, while during recessions and rubber-price drops many fell into debt.

Meeting Rubber Estates' Labour Needs

Perak's Malay working-age population was too small to meet the very high demand for labourers to facilitate the rapid expansion of rubber plantations, with their highly labour-intensive processes of planting, tapping, and weeding. As early as the late 19th century, W. E. Maxwell realized that:

> If the Malay peninsula is to be a great rubber growing and exporting country, the importation of labourers from India is a necessity … and the government should do what is possible to facilitate and cheapen immigration. (Annual Report of the Protected Malay States, 1892, p. 38)

Colonial labour policies became critical 'enablers' of the rubber industry—Perak's largest employer in the first half of the 20th century—just as they had earlier been for the tin-mining industry. Supportive recruitment policies incentivized migration, especially from southern India, which had abundant surplus labour. There was, however, also competition for southern Indian migrant workers from Burma and Ceylon; these countries are geographically closer to India and so had lower costs of sea passage, and they also offered more attractive terms of employment (Sandhu, 1969). Although workers from southern India were preferred to Javanese and Chinese for Perak's rubber estates, these labourers were also recruited, with those from China often employed on estates owned and controlled by Chinese businesses. Indian labourers came at a lower cost and were easier to recruit given that India was part of the British Empire, and they had proved to be compliant, disciplined, and adaptable to agricultural work (Ramachandran, 1994).[52]

Until the early 20th century, recruitment mainly happened through an indentured labour system, which was highly prevalent on plantations. Agents in India recruited workers for a particular estate through a legally binding contract, generally for three years with a fixed wage, but with part of that wage deducted to repay advances and recruitment expenses (Kaur, 2004). Only after

---

52 Some British officials also saw immigration of Indians as a balance to counter the influence of heavy Chinese migration (Sandhu, 1969).

the contract had been served and the debts repaid did workers become free to work with another employer. If they absconded before their debt was recovered to work on estates paying higher wages, they were subject to criminal charges, although in practice many who did so were not apprehended. This exploitative system gradually came under an increasingly critical international spotlight, ceasing in 1910, and finally outlawed in 1914.

The *kangani* system, which was gaining popularity in the 20th century, had been introduced by estate managers to bypass recruitment agents in India. A *kangani* served as both a labour recruiter and estate foreman, managing the people he recruited. A *kangani* would go to India, sponsored by his estate manager, to recruit workers from his own and surrounding villages, for which work he was paid a commission. The *kangani* paid the workers' fares on behalf of the estate managers, and later collected refunds. The workers would be free to leave and work for a different employer once the money advanced for their passage had been repaid. In a later iteration of the *kangani* system, workers could leave with one month's notice, and any debts unpaid had to be recovered in civil courts (Ramachandran, 1994). The *kangani* wielded considerable control and discipline over the workers he brought in and supervised, such that the system suffered serious inherent abuses (Sandhu, 1969).

At the start of the rubber rush in 1905, given the very tight labour market and rapidly growing demand for workers, the colonial government provided free tickets for the sea passage of some labourers to ensure a large supply of low-cost labour (Tate, 1996). A centralized assisted immigration scheme became the main mechanism for recruiting Indian plantation labourers, adopted after much discussion between the British administration, the Rubber Growers' Association, and the Planters' Association of Malaya. This scheme was spurred by legislation establishing a Tamil Immigration Fund in 1907—renamed the Indian Immigration Fund in 1910—through which recruitment policy and costs were centralized (Sultan Nazrin Shah, 2019). The costs of recruiting Tamil labourers were now funded by an annual levy on employers of plantation labour, based on the number of labourers they engaged; this was supplemented by a government subsidy through its contribution to the fund.

The Fund became operational in 1908. In its first year, it covered only the cost of the sea passage from Madras or Negapatam in India to Penang. However, from 1909 onwards it also defrayed travelling expenses inside India as well as paying a recruiting allowance to employers for each new migrant recruited through a *kangani*. By 1913, all recruiting costs, including the *kangani's* commission, were covered by the Fund, and labourers could keep all their meagre monthly wages (Tate, 1996). The *kangani*, now working under federal licence, still played a critical role in recruitment. The large numbers of Indians brought to Perak depressed plantation wages, while the social ties and obligations established by the *kangani* system helped to keep the plantation workers on the same estates for long periods.

Labour migration thus enabled Tamils from southern India—where jobs were scarce and living standards very low—to seek better economic outcomes on the Malay peninsula. Yet estates kept the wages of Indian workers very low, despite labour regulations. As Lees observes, planters defined a fair wage as merely

> one that allowed Tamils to maintain an 'accustomed' style of living, which they defined as a primarily rice and salt fish diet, a few bits of cotton clothing, one mat, one pillow and a monthly visit to the barber. (Lees, 2017, p. 187)

Workers were obliged to remain on the estates to which they were recruited, and little investment was made in labour-saving machinery, either in the field or factory (Hagan and Wells, 2005). While the conditions under which international recruitment took place improved, working and living conditions on rubber estates were generally harsh, and the risks of disease and death were never far away (Box 2.7). The rapid inflows of migrant workers further exacerbated the spread of infectious diseases. Many had escaped from India's local famines,

---

Box 2.7   Harsh conditions, disease, and death on Perak's rubber estates

Infectious diseases were highly prevalent in the early decades of the 20th century, leading to very high rates of morbidity and mortality. The rapid development of Perak's export-oriented economy, and of its infrastructure, unsettled the ecological balance, generating even higher mortality rates (Lim, 1967).

Large swathes of Perak's virgin jungle were cleared to open estate lands and new mines, as well as for road, railway, and irrigation construction. This work, often undertaken by migrant Malay workers, was extremely hazardous because it left large pools of stagnant water that bred mosquitoes—vectors for malaria (Manderson, 1987). It also meant the destruction of natural habitats and the presence of native wildlife, such as tigers, elephants, wild boars, and snakes, in close proximity to humans. This posed a danger to local Malay *kampungs* and to isolated estate 'lines' (Kaur, 2012)—rows of overcrowded open-barrack structures with temporary *attap*, where

(Continued)

estate workers were housed (Jain, 1993, p. 2,367). At the height of the first rubber land rush, Perak's Chief Medical Officer, Stephen Charles Fox, observed:

> During the past year new estates and fresh clearings, probably fifty, have been opened and I regret ... the primitive points of hygiene have not been observed ... the refuse from the [...] lines and washings from storm water have been able to pollute the supply, no latrine accommodation has been provided, everything has been left to happy chance ... The present apathy of the owners or directors will have to be met. (cited in Annual Report of Perak, 1906, p. 11)

Workers were poorly fed and there was high turnover. Water was often bacteria-infested. Perak's Annual Reports lamented the severe and prolonged outbreaks of cholera and smallpox. Malaria was also rampant, especially in the lower hill estates, and recurrent attacks of fever weakened workers' capacity to resist other diseases. In a containment effort, a Malaria Advisory Board was formed in 1911 to direct anti-malaria campaigns, but it had limited impact. High mortality continued due to difficulties in carrying out drainage works and in supplying potable water to Perak's more distant affected areas.

Hookworm was another serious disease spread through unhygienic conditions and open defecation on estate grounds, given that most Indian workers walked barefoot. In Perak in 1919, an estimated 70 per cent of people dying from malaria also had hookworm (Parmer, 1990). Tuberculosis, dysentery, and diarrhoea were similarly rife.

Various enactments began to make it compulsory for estates to provide basic health facilities for their workers, especially in areas without government hospitals, and stipulated that they had to provide clean water and safe sanitation. Compliance was weak, however. Health facilities were often makeshift and staffed by dressers with only rudimentary training in medical care. While district health officers endeavoured to improve labourers' dire housing, surrounding sanitation, and water supplies as the 20th century progressed, conditions overall remained harsh (Liew, 2010).

arriving in emaciated condition and carrying infections; some did not even survive the journey to Penang (Annual Report of Perak, 1900 and 1907).

By 1921, the number of people employed in Perak's rubber cultivation exceeded the number employed in other agricultural work; this was in contrast to the situation a decade earlier (Figure 2.12, left panel). Those engaged in other agricultural activities were predominantly *padi* farmers,[53] but this group also

---

53 The share of Perak's workers employed in rice cultivation declined from 15 per cent in 1921 to 11 per cent in 1931.

included relatively large numbers working as fruit and vegetable growers, and foresters and woodsmen. By 1921, Indians (generally Tamils) accounted for 85 per cent of Perak's estate population, Chinese 7 per cent, and Malays 6 per cent; the figures a decade earlier were 53 per cent, 26 per cent, and 20 per cent respectively (Figure 2.12, right panel).

During booms, the demand for plantation labour surged and thousands were recruited; however, low rubber prices during recessions—especially the Great Depression—led to large-scale retrenchment and repatriation. Labour, as a major cost in estate production, was the first casualty. The number of people employed in Perak's rubber sector—estates and smallholdings combined—declined by 17 per cent between 1921 and 1931, from 128,000 to 107,000 (Table 2.4).

In 1921, Indians made up slightly more than half of the rubber workers in Perak on estates and smallholdings together, but their share declined to just 45 per cent in 1931. Malays, who constituted the largest group working on smallholdings, also declined as a share of total rubber workers, from 29 per cent in 1921 to 26 per cent a decade later. By contrast, the share of Chinese rubber workers increased from 21 per cent to 29 per cent over this period,

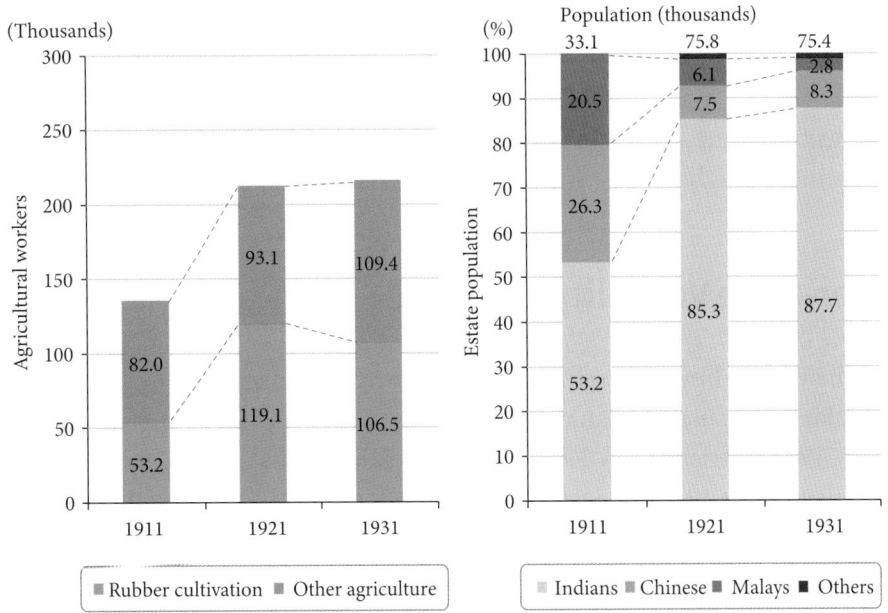

Figure 2.12   **A large share of Perak's agricultural workers cultivated rubber, and most of these were Indians working on estates**

Sources of data: Pountney (1911); Nathan (1922); Vlieland (1932).

| Table 2.4 | In 1921, Indians made up half of Perak's rubber workers, but after lay-offs in the late 1920s their share had fallen to 45 per cent by 1931 |

Sector	Malays	Chinese	Indians	All groups[a]	All groups[a] (numbers)
	1921 share among ethnic groups (%)				
Agriculture	45.6	22.7	31.2	100	212,241
Rubber subsector	28.8	21.0	50.1	100	127,906
1921 share among sectors (%)					
Agriculture	88.3	31.6	67.1	58.4	
Rubber subsector	33.6	17.6	64.9	35.2	
All sectors (numbers)	109,754	152,536	98,713	363,555	
1931 share among ethnic groups (%)					
Agriculture	40.7	30.4	28.5	100	215,924
Rubber subsector	25.5	28.6	45.3	100	106,514
1931 share among sectors (%)					
Agriculture	79.1	34.8	59.0	52.9	
Rubber subsector	24.5	16.2	46.3	26.1	
All sectors (numbers)	111,133	188,251	104,204	407,882	

Sources of data: Nathan (1922); Vlieland (1932).

Note: [a] Includes a small number of people of other communities.

likely reflecting some drift from the mining sector, which also shed workers as it became increasingly capital intensive.

Rubber-price Volatility

During the rubber boom, Perak was one of the largest rubber-producing states in the Malay peninsula. Its annual production shot up from 2,500 metric tons in 1911 to 53,000 metric tons in 1922 (Figure 2.13, left panel). By the early 1920s, when Malaya accounted for just over half of global rubber production, Perak accounted for about 25 per cent of Malayan production and 13 per cent of the world's (Figure 2.13, right panel). Production surged again in the late 1920s but was hit badly by the Great Depression. Until this point, the state had been

Figure 2.13 By the early 1920s, Perak accounted for about 25 per cent of Malayan and 13 per cent of global rubber production

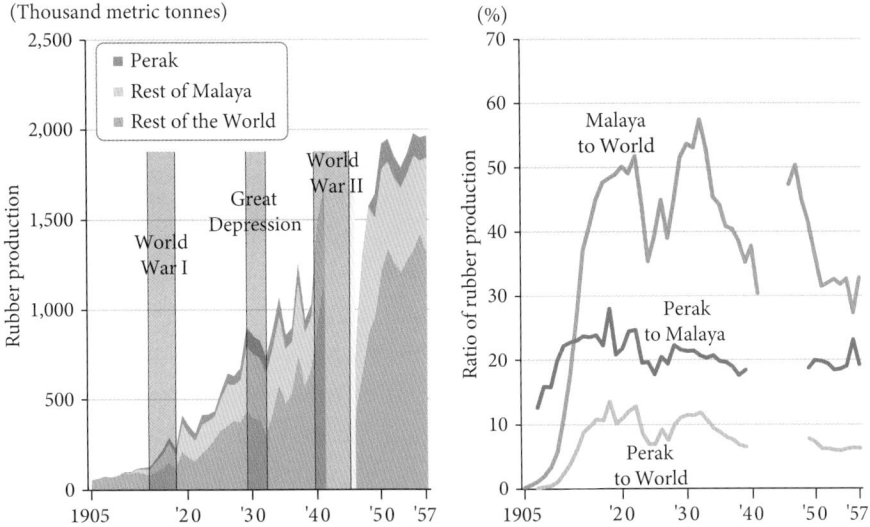

Sources of data: Annual Report of Perak (various years); Department of Statistics–Malaysia (2015), Malaysia Economics Statistics–Time Series; Department of Statistics–Federation of Malaya (various years), Malaya Rubber Statistics Handbook.

Note: The data for Perak assume that all production before 1940 was exported.

making rapid development progress, boosted by rubber exports. Perak's income over the following decades was limited, however, by overproduction. The state's economy thus became more and more trade-dependent as it was increasingly integrated into the global economy.

An important characteristic of the rubber industry—even more so than of the tin industry—was huge price volatility (Figure 2.14). This volatility severely battered Perak's local economy, hitting export earnings, investors' profits, small-holders' incomes, jobs in the rubber industry, and businesses dependent on it (Sultan Nazrin Shah, 2017).

Structural features of the rubber market—such as price-inelastic supply and demand—are the main reasons for the large price swings (Sultan Nazrin Shah, 2019, Box 5.4)[54]. On the supply side, as described above, a rubber tree yields latex around six years after it has been planted, so even if prices increase, planting will have little short-term impact on supply. On the demand side, and in the case of a finished product such as a car where the cost of the rubber input is only a fraction of the total price, any change in the price of rubber has only a marginal effect on

---

54 Without structural changes in rubber supply and demand, small changes in the quantity supplied or demanded will not significantly affect prices.

the final cost of producing a car or even on its sales price. Given these character-istics, any factor that leads to a shift in market demand or supply for rubber will have little impact on volume but a large effect on price.

The outbreak of World War I in 1914 temporarily disrupted the rubber mar-ket, but prices remained steady (Figure 2.14). Freight restrictions, particularly to Europe, increased the importance of the Singapore market in meeting US demand, and prices there were not affected. However, the post–World War I deflationary economic recession in the US, which lasted for about 18 months from January 1920, had a major impact on rubber prices. Malaya's rubber exports were highly dependent on US rubber consumption, which was closely linked to US car sales. Malaya's rubber industry faced a serious crisis when in the autumn of 1920 prices dropped to a level at which many estates could not produce at a profit. By April 1921, the output of rubber on estates was being voluntarily restricted, and in many cases tapping had been entirely discon-tinued. Development work was curtailed, the number of European staff working on estates was drastically reduced, and estate labour was kept to a minimum. Many estate workers of all communities were retrenched, with a preference among estate managers for retaining lower-cost Tamils (Nathan, 1922). Smallholdings, too, were hit, though less severely than estates as their production costs were lower and more flexible.

Figure 2.14 **International rubber prices were plagued by volatility, especially in the first three decades of the 20th century[a]**

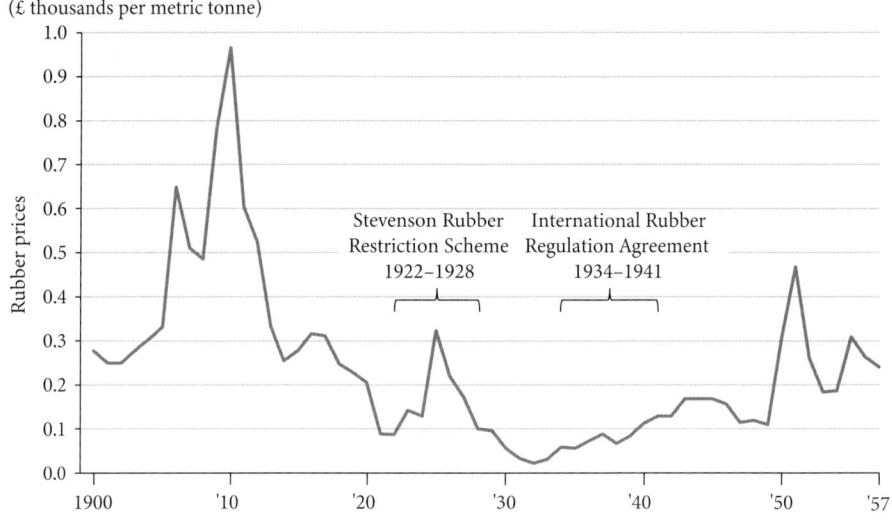

Source of data: Budiman (2003).

Note: [a] Refers to ribbed smoked sheets grade 1 prices.

Malaya's rubber export prices fell by some 57 per cent in 1921, one of the steepest declines in the pre-independence era (Figure 2.14). In 1925, with renewed growth in the US economy and the automobile industry, prices then rebounded by 153 per cent. Rising expectations of profitability stimulated another heavy wave of new planting. This continued until the onset of the Great Depression, which again saw sharp declines in demand for rubber. As rubber production greatly outstripped demand, prices tumbled by an annual average of 39 per cent between 1929 and 1932, and new planting once again halted. As in 1921, some estates stopped tapping their trees and many suffered financial losses. In Perak in 1933, only 2,069 acres were newly planted, just 4 per cent of the 1917 peak.

International Production Restrictions—Another Gain for Estates, Another Loss for Smallholders

As British commercial interests had a huge stake in Perak's and Malaya's rubber industry, the colonial administration attempted to stabilize rubber prices by compulsorily restricting production through the Stevenson Rubber Restriction Scheme of 1922–1928.[55] This market regulation scheme was proposed and strongly supported by the Rubber Growers' Association after attempts at voluntary restrictions on estate output in 1921 foundered. Smallholders, who had much lower production costs and were less concerned about price, were opposed to the scheme but lacked formal representation to advocate for their collective interests. In the event, Ceylon—another of the world's major producers—joined with Malaya and signed up to the scheme. Crucially, the Dutch East Indies—also a major producer—did not sign, which weakened the scheme's chances of success from the outset.

Under this scheme, the basic principle of restricting production was to estimate aggregate rubber output in open market conditions, and then distribute this among individual producers according to an official formula (Drabble, 2000). Prices and export quotas were determined quarterly. Rubber producers in Malaya and Ceylon were given quotas assessed on previous levels of production, and within a country the sale of rubber was carried out through coupons distributed by land and district offices (Lee, 1978). The output of estates was limited to a given percentage based on their production on 31 October 1920. Smallholdings

---

55 The enabling legislation for the Stevenson Restriction Scheme in the Federated Malay States was the Export of Rubber (Restriction) Enactment, 1922.

fared worse in their allocated quotas. They were automatically put on an annual scale of 320 lbs per acre of mature trees; this was later revised to 426 lbs, but was still much lower than both their actual production and the assessment of estates (Lim, 1974). In Perak, the output quotas for large estates led to retrenchments of workers, especially in Larut and Kuala Kangsar, with many repatriated to India. Among smallholders, the quotas led to some opposition, including petitioning of the government to end the restrictions.

During the scheme's first two years, the international price of rubber remained low. Prices then rose between 1924 and 1926, as global demand increased. While British producers enjoyed some profits from this, those in the Dutch East Indies profited even more significantly, as their costs per unit were not being increased by the restriction (Whittlesey, 1931). One of the scheme's unintended effects was that because of high prices and unrestricted rubber production in the Dutch East Indies, its rubber acreage grew substantially, so that by 1928 it was almost the world's largest producer (Lim, 1974).

Rubber prices tumbled again during the Great Depression, from 1929 through to 1932 (Figure 2.14). Once again there were thousands of retrenchments among Perak's estate workers, and many Tamils were repatriated. In January 1934, after more than four years of negotiations and much lobbying for government intervention, nine of the world's largest rubber producers—which collectively controlled over 99 per cent of global natural rubber exports—formed a cartel under the International Rubber Regulation Agreement of 1934–1941. This was administered in London by the International Rubber Regulation Committee, with Colonial Office secretariat support (Tate, 1996).[56]

Annual output quotas that favoured estate interests were again introduced: in 1938, these were set at 450 lbs per assessed mature acre for estates, compared to only 400 lbs per assessed mature acre for smallholders. New planting of rubber was forbidden, and replanting limited to 5 per cent a year on any estate or smallholding. Quotas were determined with coupons. Tapping by smallholders decreased—much more so than under the Stevenson Restriction Scheme—and as with that earlier scheme there was a serious under-assessment of smallholders' output (Bauer, 1944).

The scheme succeeded in restoring price stability in the international rubber market. Moreover, because of cost-saving adjustments made during the

---

56 The International Rubber Regulation Committee comprised Malaya and the Dutch East Indies with four representatives each; Ceylon and French Indochina with two representatives each; and British North Borneo, Burma, India, Sarawak, and Siam with one representative each. The interests of the rubber manufacturing industry in the main consumer countries—especially the US—in ensuring an adequate supply of rubber at a fair price were recognized through an Advisory Panel (Tate, 1996). The scheme was extended up to the time of the Japanese occupation of Malaya.

depression years, estates could now be profitably operated at costs far below those formerly considered necessary (Tempany, 1935). With the improvement in the price of rubber, estates were once again able to make a profit and pay dividends to shareholders. The regulations succeeded in controlling surplus output capacity and thus supported rubber prices, which rose slowly up to 1937, dipped in 1938, and then climbed again (Figure 2.14). However, as with the Stevenson Restriction Scheme, new sources of rubber supply and synthetics eventually undercut the agreement (Barlow et al., 1994).

In most areas of Perak the number of smallholdings fell; many owners of more than one holding closed some of their properties, finding that they could provide enough rubber from one property to fill the restriction quota. In addition, many smallholders sold their coupons to the owners of larger holdings. Many of the estates in the districts of Lower Perak and Batang Padang were also affected. The estates in these areas were worked by Malays and Javanese; indeed, half of the Malays working on rubber estates in Perak were based in Lower Perak. In an attempt to support those Malays affected by the price restriction schemes, the government created relief jobs and opened land for dry *padi* cultivation.

Both the Stevenson Scheme and the International Rubber Regulation Agreement hurt rubber smallholders and undermined their potential to promote rural development (Kinney, 1975). They perpetuated uneven development between communities and engendered a system of 'economic dualism', with a dynamic export sector existing alongside a farming sector that was little changed. Faced with relatively low prices, and pressured by powerful estate interests, the colonial government chose to protect the rubber industry so that prices could rise even with stunted demand. The restrictions ensured that less efficient producers, whose production costs exceeded the market price, continued to profit.

Without the restrictions, it is probable that many of Perak's relatively high-cost British and Continental European estate producers would have made huge losses and been forced out of the industry, while most of the lower-cost Malay and Chinese smallholders would probably have survived. This was a period in which, as Odin Tom Faulkner, Director of Agriculture, noted, 'considerably more attention was being paid to tapping methods and quality of tapping on smallholdings', with this improvement particularly noticeable on the medium-sized Chinese-owned holdings, where the tapping was 'often equal to the standard of estate practice' (Faulkner, 1938, p. 8). Smallholders were thus severely disadvantaged by the restrictions. Their incomes suffered as they were prevented from producing at a level commensurate with their competitive advantage.

Yet despite the severe recessions and price swings, the benefits of Perak's rubber industry were distributed much more widely than those of the tin industry, precisely because many low-income Malays and Chinese were smallholders. A far higher proportion of the labour force was employed in rubber—about 35 per cent in 1921, falling to 26 per cent by 1931, compared with around 12 per cent in the tin industry in both years. This more widespread employment would have lifted the local economy through increased levels of consumption, with profits from smallholdings probably reinvested, helping to spread prosperity and raise living standards.

Population Impacts from Migrant Workers, 1901–1931

Attracted by the continued prosperity of Perak's economy, migrant workers of all communities surged into the state in most years in the first three decades of the 20th century. The state's population more than doubled, from 330,000 in 1901 to 766,000 in 1931, despite the large-scale repatriation of Chinese and Indian migrant workers at times of recession. The annual population growth rate of Indian migrants—the mainstay of the rubber estates—was the highest of all the population groups over these three decades (Figure 2.15, upper panel).

The net effect of the huge waves of migration in this period was that Malays came to account for a smaller and smaller share of Perak's population. In 1901, they accounted for 43 per cent, whereas by 1931 they made up just 35.6 per cent. Over the same period, the Chinese share fell slightly from 45.3 per cent to 42.5 per cent. The Indian share had doubled to 21.8 per cent by 1921, and remained around that level in 1931. Indian migrants, like Chinese, tended not to bring their wives with them, and the imbalance in the population's sex ratio continued, although it was less marked in 1931 than in 1901 as the migrant communities tended more towards permanent settlement (Figure 2.15, upper panel).

Each of Perak's communities was heterogeneous in terms of tribal membership, dialect, and customs, reflecting their different migratory areas of origin. In 1931, the three main Chinese subgroups were Cantonese (37 per cent), Hakka (27 per cent), and Hokkien (16 per cent). The Indian population was mainly Tamil (79 per cent), Telegu (9 per cent), and Punjabis (6 per cent). Persons classified as Malays mainly comprised local Malays (76 per cent), Banjarese (8 per cent), and Javanese (6 per cent) (Vlieland, 1932).

At the district level, while the two large mining districts of Kinta and Larut remained the largest in terms of population size and share, annual population growth was generally higher in Perak's other districts between 1901 and 1931 (Figure 2.15, lower panel). In this period, large numbers of Malays came to Perak

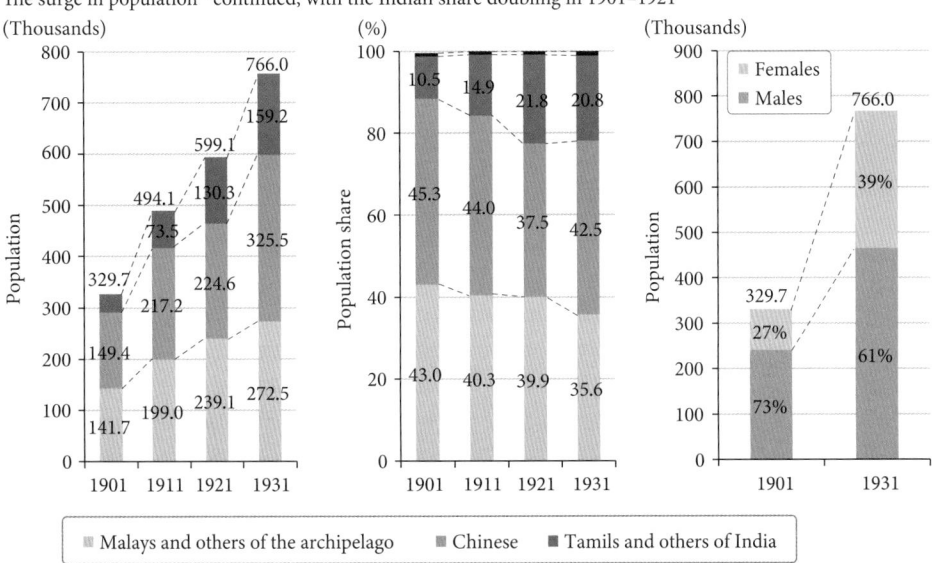

| Figure 2.15 | Migration continued to change Perak's population characteristics in the first three decades of the 20th century |

The surge in population [a] continued, with the Indian share doubling in 1901–1921

Kinta remained the most populous district, but its share declined as both Upper and Lower Perak saw steep growth

■ Malays and others of the archipelago   ■ Chinese   ■ Tamils and others of India

□ Larut   ■ Kinta   ■ Kuala Kangsar   ■ Upper Perak
■ Lower Perak   ■ Batang Padang   ■ Kerian   ⁒ New Territory

Sources of data: Hare (1902); Pountney (1911); Nathan (1922); Vlieland (1932).

Note: [a] The population of other communities was 2,487 in 1901, 4,278 in 1911, 5,017 in 1921, and 8,764 in 1931.

from Java, Sumatra, and elsewhere in the archipelago, with Banjarese the dominant group. They were attracted by better jobs as rice cultivators, rubber smallholders, and wage labourers on estates. Migrant inflows into Batang Padang and Lower

Perak—especially into the coconut plantations—saw the populations of these areas growing rapidly, at 4.8 per cent and 3.9 per cent annually. Coconut plantations were important to Perak's economy, and coconut products—mainly copra and coconut oil extracted from copra for use in cooking and margarine—ranked second in value to rubber among its agricultural exports (Box 2.8).

Box 2.8   **Malay migration into Lower Perak increases coconut cultivation**

Lower Perak, one of Perak's principal rubber-producing districts, had the largest area under coconut cultivation of all the districts in the Federated Malay States, at 27 per cent of its total acreage in 1911 (Federated Malay States, 1912, p. 11). Most of its coconut plantations were situated on the soils of the alluvial coastal plains of the west coast.

Coconut palms yield fruits after around five years and continue to do so for decades. They were the main cash crop in the Bagan Datuk *mukim* (a subdivision of a district) where the colonial authorities alienated thousands of acres of land for planting, as they did in the *mukim*s of Hutan Melintang and Sungai Rungkup. Coconut palms require relatively little attention other than to protect the palms from diseases. At first, the cultivation of this crop was almost entirely confined to Malay smallholdings. Later, British and Continental Europeans came to Bagan Datuk and built a large coconut oil factory.

The British administration encouraged Malay migration from the rest of the archipelago by offering cheap land, teaching smallholders how to manufacture copra, and building kilns. Bagan Datuk had over 300 kilns by the start of the 1930s. However, these kilns did not satisfy the Federated Malay States Agricultural Department's standard for high-grade copra, and so a local Malay officer was trained to supervise the construction of kilns and to give advice on copra preparation. By the late 1930s, there had 'been a very marked improvement in the general standard of copra produced by estates and they are now producing copra for export which is above the best standard grade' (Faulkner, 1938, p. 11).

An Agricultural Loan Fund provided loans for Malays to purchase land and build houses, as well as for coconut development. However, because of stringent conditions, difficulties in administration, and competition from *chettiers* and others, the loans were not well taken up. *Chettiers*, well-off Malays, and Chinese middlemen provided cash loans to market the crops. There was little indebtedness when copra prices were high and fairly stable, but this changed during the Great

Depression when exports to the US fell after it imposed a very high processing tax. Coconut cultivators and proprietors who depended on the returns for their livelihoods suffered considerable indebtedness and hardship. This was especially the case in Bagan Datuk, where the village head estimated average debt at Straits$300 and reported that nearly all Malay cultivators owed money (Lim, 1977, p. 87).

Rising Living Standards, 1900–1940

How did the substantial changes in Perak's economic activities affect the living standards of the state's residents, and how did these living standards compare with those in Malaya as a whole? For much of this period, Perak played a pre-eminent role in Malaya's economy: it was the single largest producer and exporter of tin, and a prominent producer and exporter of rubber—the twin engines that propelled Malaya's economy. Perak also became the most populous of all the states in Malaya, with job opportunities attracting large inflows of migrants from China, India, the Dutch East Indies, and other parts of the Malay peninsula, as discussed above. Its towns, big and small, prospered.

An understanding of the role that Perak played in the larger economy of Malaya can be gained by identifying the broad contours of its contribution to Malaya's GDP and estimating its export-based income multipliers. Drawing on multiple and disparate sources of statistical data and applying modern economic accounting methods, Sultan Nazrin Shah (2017) produced estimates of Malaya's GDP for 1900–1939. These provide an important reference that helps to clarify questions about Malaya's socio-economic development, which had previously been examined in largely qualitative terms.

Angus Maddison, the distinguished British economist, pioneered methods of estimating the historical size and profile of an economy (Lo Cascio and Malanima, 2009; University of Groningen, 2018a). His approach, which is also used by others, involves estimating the separate components of consumption, investment, and government expenditure, adding them, and then cross-referencing these data with information about wages and the size of the working population. While Sultan Nazrin Shah (2017) adopted a bottom-up approach very similar to this for colonial Malaya, the use of such methods is not feasible for Perak because of the large information gaps about crucial expenditure components, including the flows of exports to and imports from the other parts of Malaya. A simplified indirect method is therefore used here to estimate Perak's GDP per capita between 1900 and 1939.

Globalization: Perak's Rise, Relative Decline, and Regeneration. Sultan Nazrin Shah, Oxford University Press. © Sultan Nazrin Shah (2024).
DOI: 10.1093/oso/9780198897774.003.0014

Economic Dualism and Perak's Specialization

Perak's economy in the first half of the 20th century was dualistic. A dominant extractive commodity export sector of tin and rubber coexisted with a still largely low-productivity agricultural subsector centred on *padi* production, on other crops such as coconut and gambier, and on fishing. In 1931, this subsector accounted for 27 per cent of Perak's working population, of whom 61,000 were Malays and 35,000 were Chinese. Of the Malay working population, 55 per cent were engaged in these agricultural activities, compared with 19 per cent for the Chinese. With the exception of foodstuffs, local materials such as timber and stone, and non-tradeable services, many of Perak's needs were met by imports, although Perak's export-oriented economy consistently registered a large trade surplus (Figure 2.16).

Figure 2.16   **Perak had a trade surplus throughout 1900–1939**

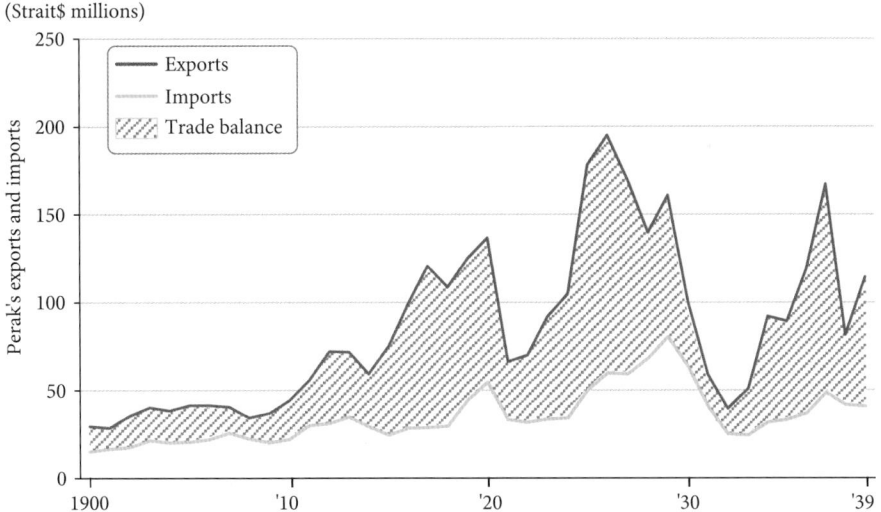

Sources of data: Annual Report of Perak (various years); Perak Administration Report (various years); Annual Report on the Social and Economic Progress of the People of Perak (various years).

Figure 2.17 shows the degree to which Perak specialized in tin and rubber production compared with Malaya as a whole.[57] Perak specialized heavily in tin-mining exports, with the volume of its exports per capita often three times as large as the Malayan average. By contrast, the volume of rubber exports per capita was not dissimilar to that for Malaya as a whole, with the ratio of exports

57 Specialization is measured as the ratio, at constant prices (that is, the volume), of exports per capita in Perak divided by the volume of exports per capita in Malaya, including Perak. A value of one would indicate identical levels of the volume of exports per capita for Perak and Malaya.

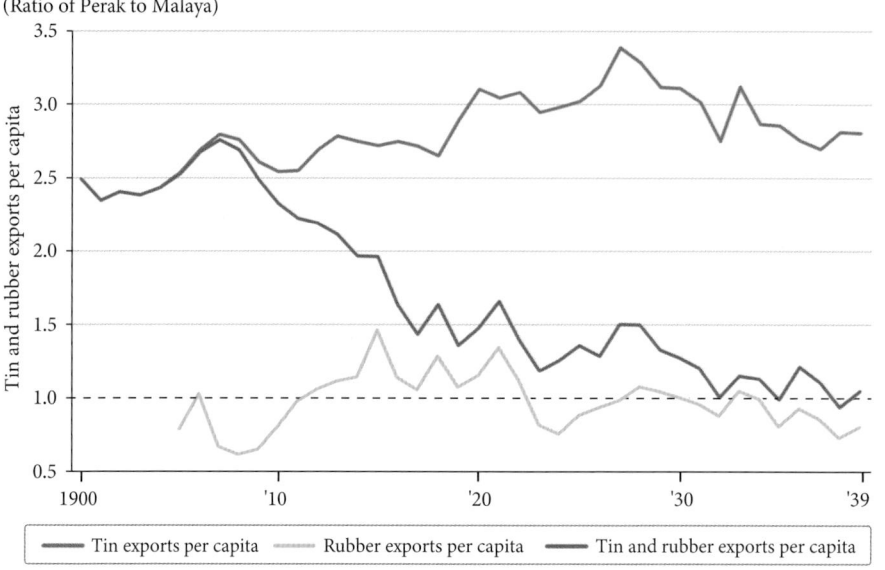

Figure 2.17   Perak's tin exports per capita greatly exceeded those of Malaya as a whole

(Ratio of Perak to Malaya)

Source of data: Sultan Nazrin Shah (2022), https://www.ehm.my/data/historical-gdp-accounts

per capita hovering around one—in some periods it was larger, and in others it was smaller. Measured from a base around 1914, Perak's share of Malaya's total rubber exports steadily tapered.

Perak's volume of tin exports, measured in constant prices, was larger than rubber exports through to the later years of World War I. From then on, and even with the state's comparative specialization in tin, the volume of Perak's rubber exports came to overshadow the volume of its tin exports. From 1917 through to 1939, rubber exports from Perak were roughly twice the volume of tin exports measured in constant prices.

As rubber emerged as a principal export commodity, the volume of Perak's combined rubber and tin exports per capita started to converge with the Malayan average. Still, Perak remained comparatively specialized in primary commodity exports through to the 1930s. Thereafter, Perak's shares of Malaya's tin and rubber exports retreated sharply, suggesting that the state may have been harder hit than other Malayan states by the ruptures of the Great Depression and its aftermath.

Other inferences can be drawn from these data. At an aggregate level, Perak's economy was more capital intensive than the broader Malayan economy. Perak was at the forefront of pioneering new and productivity-boosting technologies, especially in tin production. Tin mining became increasingly mechanized with the early adoption of dredges and other technologies. Electrification came early to Perak, and the state was better served than most of Malaya by rail and road infrastructure. Mining activity was also closely associated with the formation and growth of urbanized populations. The upshot was that Perak was more urbanized than other parts of Malaya (with the exception of Penang and Selangor) and reaped the economic benefits that greater population density creates.

Nonetheless, agriculture remained a prominent activity throughout the period. By 1931, over half of Perak's working population was employed in agriculture, with about half of those employed in rubber, on smallholdings and estates (Table 2.5). By ethnic group, most Malays worked in traditional agricultural activities, but many Malays were also engaged as rubber smallholders, with some on estates. In 1931, 79 per cent of Perak's Malay workers were engaged in agriculture and fishing occupations. Few Malays worked in industry or in commercial services. Nearly as many ethnic Chinese worked in agriculture as in industry, with an even agricultural split between rubber cultivation and market gardening. The commercial and personal services sectors were dominated

Table 2.5	Perak's Malays were heavily concentrated in agricultural jobs in 1931				
Sector	Malays	Chinese	Indians	Others	All groups
	Share of employment by sector (%)				
Agriculture and fisheries	79.1	34.8	59.0	23.0	52.9
Rubber workers	24.5	16.2	46.3	13.6	26.1
Industry	4.8	38.1	11.7	23.9	22.2
Miners	0.6	24.7	3.6	5.9	12.6
Professional	2.8	1.3	2.5	20.1	2.2
Commercial	1.0	13.0	5.6	7.4	7.8
Personal services	2.4	6.1	5.9	5.2	5.0
Others	2.8	6.4	15.0	19.7	7.8
Unknown	7.0	0.3	0.3	0.6	2.2
All sectors	100	100	100	100	100
All sectors (numbers)	111,133	188,251	104,204	4,294	407,882

Source of data: Vlieland (1932).
Note: Rubber workers include estate owners, managers and assistants, rubber tappers, and other estate workers.

by Chinese and to a lesser extent Indians. Indian workers were largely concentrated in the rubber sector, but they also had a presence in the commercial and personal services sectors.

Although some investments were made in non-rubber agricultural activities, particularly in *padi* irrigation schemes and coconut cultivation, agricultural productivity advances were modest. Throughout the four decades, Perak continued to be a net importer of *padi*, partly because its population was growing very rapidly, and partly because of the sequestration of agricultural land for mining and rubber estates. In addition, reflecting a colonial policy that sought to ensure the preservation of a settled, *padi*-cultivating Malay peasantry, Perak's traditional agricultural sector released few workers into the non-agricultural economy.[58] Indeed, Malay families from other parts of the Malay archipelago migrated to Perak, suggesting that its rural economy offered better living standards and opportunities than other locations.

Of the minority of Malays employed in non-agricultural activities—about one-fifth in 1931—many became drivers, technicians, electricians, and mechanics. A small number of these were vocationally trained for three years in mechanical trades and automobile repair at the Ipoh Trade School. Established in 1930, this industrial school began with an annual intake of just 25 trainees, of whom almost all were Malay. After three years, it had 75 students enrolled. Trainees at the school also undertook mechanical tasks for government departments, including the Medical Department of Perak, which commissioned the school to repair all its ambulances, from Parit Buntar in the north to Tanjong Malim in the south (Hicks, 1958).

Perak's Economic Growth above the Malayan Average

The Estimation Process

There are only limited time-series data available that can be usefully linked to the size and profile of Perak's GDP between 1900 and 1939. Census and administrative data suggest that Perak's education and health levels—especially in and near the towns—were more advanced than those in most other Malayan states. However, there are no wider data on household welfare or consumption.

---

58 The Sultan Idris Training College, established in 1922 in Tanjong Malim, Lower Perak, had a strong focus on agriculture. A primary purpose of teacher training at this college was to retain Malay peasantry in the rural economy (see Box 2.13).

Although there are data on capital investments made by estates and small-holdings in cultivated assets—rubber, coconut, coffee, tea, gambier, pineapple, and areca nut—these constitute only part of Perak's capital investment and there would have been variable lags between capital outlays and crop production, and therefore between outlays and income. While annual estimates exist of total government expenditure for Perak dating back to 1875, this cannot be readily translated into an estimate of final government consumption expenditure, which is needed to construct an estimate of GDP. The government expenditure estimates, which were compiled primarily for administrative purposes, include income transfers made to recipients outside the state, government capital spending, and government payments for services. Unfortunately, these elements of the expenditure data for Perak cannot be identified separately.

As it is not possible to identify and combine the components of GDP for Perak from either the expenditure or income side, an indirect approach is employed (Box 2.9), based on the close relationship between Malaya's GDP per capita and its per capita exports of tin and rubber (Sultan Nazrin Shah, 2017). Tin and rubber exports were also the main drivers of Perak's economy in the first four decades of the 20th century and their effects on the state's macro-economy are likely to be similar to those at the national level.

Box 2.9   **Estimating Perak's GDP per capita, 1900–1939**

Statistical information on Perak's exports of tin and rubber are among the few economic data series that exist for the first four decades of the 20th century. A number of specifications were tried to 'fit' Malaya's GDP per capita to contemporaneous figures for tin and rubber exports per capita, with additional dummy variables capturing periodic 'intercept shifts'. Dummy variables are included in the preferred model to identify the pre–World War I period and the roaring twenties, the effects of which were transmitted to Malaya though channels additional to those of its exports of tin and rubber. The pre–World War I dummy had a negative and statistically significant effect on Malaya's GDP per capita and the roaring twenties dummy had a significantly positive effect. A dummy variable for the years of the Great Depression, 1929–1934, was not statistically significant, indicating that the Depression's effect was transmitted only through the impact that it had on Malaya's exports of tin and rubber.

(Continued)

Expressing variables in per capita terms removes scale effects and allows comparisons between Perak and Malaya as a whole. Although Perak's tin and rubber export data include exports to other parts of Malaya, virtually all of Perak's exports were ultimately destined for markets overseas, eliminating a potential difficulty created by interregional trade within Malaya.

A log-linear model proved statistically preferable—the linear specification showing signs of first-order serial correlation of the errors. In the logarithmic specification, the estimation period is 1905–1939 as the logarithms of zero values (for rubber exports before 1905) are not defined. The estimated equation for Malaya over the period 1905–1939 is:

$$\ln (GDPpc) = constant + 0.109 \ln (RUBpc) + 0.410 \ln (TINpc) + dummies,$$
$$\qquad\qquad\qquad\quad (0.016) \qquad\qquad\qquad (0.048)$$

where *GDPpc* is Malaya's GDP per capita, *RUBpc* and *TINpc* are respectively Malaya's per capita exports of rubber and tin in Straits$. The numbers in parentheses below the estimated coefficients are their standard errors. They indicate that the coefficients are statistically significant at a 1 per cent confidence level. The statistic indicates that 92 per cent of the variation in Malaya's GDP per capita is explained by the model. Thus, in Figure 2.18, the model's estimated (or predicted) values for Malaya's GDP per capita align very closely with its actual values.

An estimate of Perak's GDP per capita is obtained by replacing Malaya's per capita tin and rubber exports in the above equation with those of Perak. As the dummy variables are exogenous and common to both Malaya and Perak, all estimated differences between GDP per capita in Malaya and Perak are, in this approach, solely attributable to differences in their tin and rubber exports per capita.

Economic Growth and Living Standards

Irrespective of the precise model specification used, all indirect estimates peg Perak's GDP per capita at levels significantly higher than the all-Malaya average. In the logarithmic formulation, Perak's estimated GDP per capita is well above Malaya's in every year (Figure 2.18, left panel) and on average 58 per cent higher than Malaya's over the period 1905–1939. Only in 1905, 1919, and 1938 was Perak's income advantage over all-Malaya below 40 per cent. In 1920, 1928, and 1934, meanwhile, it exceeded 80 per cent (Figure 2.18, right panel).

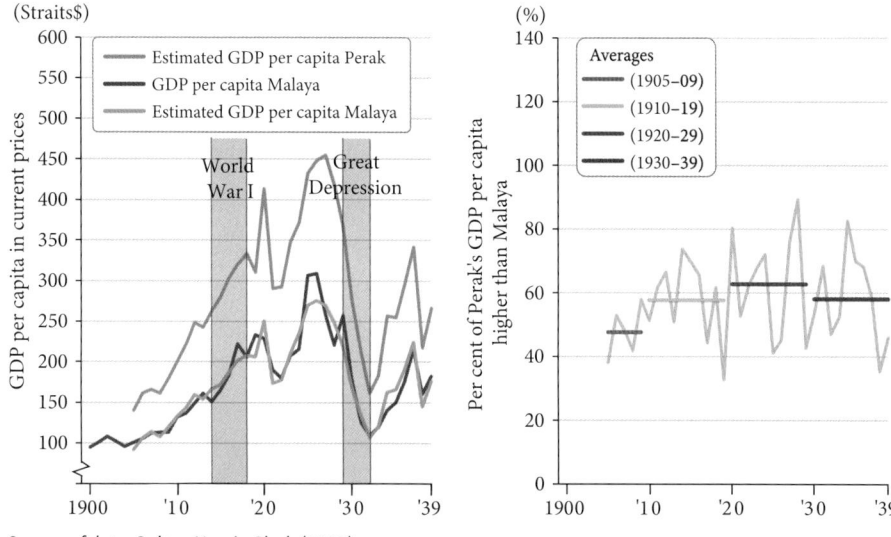

Figure 2.18 **Perak's GDP per capita was consistently much higher than that of Malaya as a whole, although the gap narrowed during the Great Depression**

Source of data: Sultan Nazrin Shah (2017).

It would be imprudent, however, to place too much weight on any single year's estimate. Decadal averages help remove measurement and other errors, and these suggest that the 'premium' on Perak's GDP per capita climbed during the roaring twenties, from an average of 58 per cent over the previous decade to 63 per cent in this one (Figure 2.18, right panel). Despite the onset of the Great Depression, the estimates suggest that Perak maintained its income advantage over Malaya throughout the 1930s, with the premium falling back to 58 per cent. As Perak's exports were hit harder by the Great Depression than those of the wider Malayan economy, it is probable that the premium would have fallen sharply during the 1930s.

In qualitative terms, the results showing a substantial income gap between Perak and all-Malaya are plausible. Similar or even larger regional income gaps can be observed in contemporary Malaysian data. For example, in 2020 the GDP per capita of the federal capital, Kuala Lumpur (plus Putrajaya), was 7.3 times as large as that of Kelantan, Malaysia's least prosperous state (Department of Statistics–Malaysia, 2022). That year, Kelantan's GDP per capita was just 34.2 per cent of the national average.

At its peak, Perak's estimated per capita GDP in the years leading up to the Great Depression was over three times higher than it had been in

1905. In this period of booming export-led economic growth, the people of Perak enjoyed fast-rising standards of living, and the state was a magnet for migrants. However, the estimates suggest that more than half of the gains in GDP per capita were lost during the Great Depression and by the eve of World War II had not been regained.

Impact of the Great Depression

Neither Malaya as a whole nor Perak were spared the devastating effects of the unprecedented collapse in global trade during the Great Depression. Indeed, Perak was hit especially hard. Real GDP recorded large contractions between 1931 and 1932 (Sultan Nazrin Shah, 2017). With tin and rubber exports now heavily dependent on demand from the US market, any downturn in that economy inevitably affected Malaya, and Perak in particular, which was the world's leading tin producer and a major rubber exporter.

By the time of the Great Depression, Perak had become locked into an interconnected globalized capitalist order. As the state progressed from subsistence agriculture to become a natural-resource-based export-led economy, influenced by Western ideas and technology, it became increasingly reliant on the health of the US economy. Table 2.6 shows just how tightly linked the two economies were, with positive correlation coefficients of 0.93 and 0.81 between US GDP and Perak's tin and rubber exports respectively. Both primary commodities, which had become essential inputs for industrialization processes, were affected by the US economic downturn. With the collapse in US demand, prices tumbled; this had a devastating effect on the economy of the Federated Malay States (Bauer, 1944), and especially on Perak.

In the domestic sector, the Great Depression hit Perak's government revenue and expenditure hard—both were highly positively correlated with tin and rubber exports (Table 2.6). The adverse trend in these two industries reverberated across the whole of Perak's economy. With the closing of many mines and rubber estates, there was a sharp drop in nominal wages at those which did remain open. Although prices declined, nominal wages fell even further, indicating a fall in purchasing power. Workers were laid off and many thousands were repatriated to China and India. Those who remained were subject to prolonged hardship and destitution, as unemployment and hunger returned. The consequences of the economic crisis pervaded the state.

Table 2.6	How the Great Depression hit Perak's economy					
	1929[a]	1930	1931	1932	1933	1934
US GDP	1.00	0.88	0.74	0.57	0.54	0.64
Perak's tin exports	1.00	0.65	0.43	0.25	0.32	0.52
Perak's rubber exports	1.00	0.55	0.27	0.18	0.29	0.59
Perak's imports	1.00	0.79	0.50	0.31	0.30	0.39
Perak's government revenue	1.00	0.78	0.66	0.55	0.59	0.72
Perak's government expenditure	1.00	0.99	0.77	0.66	0.61	0.55
Nominal wages[b]	1.00	0.79	0.67	0.61	0.60	0.83
Nominal wages[c]	1.00	0.82	0.59	0.54	0.57	0.53
Real wages[c]	1.00	0.86	0.77	0.82	0.95	0.85

Sources of data: Annual Report of Perak (various years); Kaur (2004); Sultan Nazrin Shah (2017); University of Groningen (2018b).

Notes: [a] 1929 = 1.00. [b] Indian males in the Federated Malay States. [c] Relates to Malaya.

The declines in the purchasing power of households and in business activities, together with a drastic cut in government expenditure—sustained at first to pay for the repatriation of migrant workers—inevitably led to lower household consumption. Perak's imports, a reliable consumption indicator, tumbled by 70 per cent between 1929 and 1933 (Table 2.6). Conversely, as the US economy began to recover in 1934, Perak's key economic indicators also started to improve. This symmetric relationship affirmed Perak's dependency on the boom-and-bust cycles of the US-led global economy.

Business and Human Costs

In terms of *finances*, the Great Depression caused great hardship for both businesses and people (Box 2.10). Perak's businesses across all sectors were seriously affected and bankruptcies multiplied. Banks and finance companies, for example, were hit badly owing to the low commodity prices that prevented debtors from repaying loans. They were also hit by the decline in trade with China and the remittance business, and they suffered losses when the British pound left the gold standard in 1931, as many were involved in hedging against the fluctuating exchange rate (Cheong et al., 2013). The Bank of Malaya Ltd, a Chinese bank incorporated in Ipoh in 1920, was one of the casualties. It ceased operations in April 1932.

Box 2.10   Human suffering during the Great Depression

The years of the Great Depression had a devastating effect on the lives of Perak's miners, planters, and their families, as well as on the businesses that depended on the consumption spending of such workers. Severe suffering was experienced across all classes of society.

Local newspapers were filled with reports of stranded European planters who had been given three months' notice on their jobs. The majority were unmarried and below the age of 30, with little money to survive. Many tried in vain to sell their household goods and other possessions. Their assistants, even the most experienced and able, were paid off and sent home.

> A neglected allure hung over everything that once reflected the lavish lifestyle of wealthy European miners and planters—empty clubs, silent roads, abandoned bungalows with weed-grown paths and broken shutters. (Shennan, 2015, p. 240)

As Chinese tin mines were abandoned and labour forces on rubber plantations minimized, emergency meetings were convened to petition the government to assist retrenched workers. While some moved to Ipoh and to other towns in search of work and odd jobs, many turned to hawking to earn a living. Illegal hawking activities surged: for many, they were a 'last resort and only outlet for the local unemployed' (Loh, 1990, p. 86). In Ipoh, itinerant Chinese and Indian hawkers would often go on house-to-house rounds, although many pitched their stalls outside the popular Sun Cinema or the Olympia Amusement Park (Ho, 2009). Crime rates shot up. Out of desperation, some resorted to looting shops, house-breaking, theft, and the use of counterfeit coins to put food on the table (Loh, 1990). In 1930, criminal cases reported to the police in Perak—such as serious thefts, robberies, and housebreakings—more than doubled from the previous five years' average (Lee, 1978). Tin ore thefts were common (Abdul Azmi Abdul Khalid, 1992).

Kinta's once-bustling tin towns were brought to a standstill, and even the schools saw reduced numbers of students, as parents could not afford the modest fees. Unemployed workers flooded the Chinese Protectorate seeking repatriation to China for a fresh start. Successful petitioners gathered in relief camps, and were provided with free food, usually congee or porridge, by the Perak Chinese Chamber of Commerce. Many unemployed who remained in Perak were saved from hunger and destitution by private charitable organizations and welfare funds.

In the Kinta Valley, distress in the Malay community was also inevitable because the fall in rubber prices deprived smallholders of an income, and some Malays who had worked on estates were retrenched. Malay civil servants were also affected by administrative cuts resulting from the fall in government revenue. Although government policy was that Malay civil servants would be the last to be laid off, this was not strictly adhered to by the Retrenchment Commission, which was established in March 1932 by Cecil Clementi, Governor of the Straits Settlements and the British High Commissioner (1930–1934), to review administrative costs and staffing. By the end of 1932, many Malays working in Perak's district and land offices had in fact been retrenched (Nadaraja, 2016). Indebtedness became a serious problem, with many forced to borrow money from Chinese shopkeepers, Indian chettiers, and others to support their daily needs. In the district of Batang Padang, the hardship of the Depression meant that some people

> had to eat rice boiled with tapioca, or could have only one meal a day. Others were unable to pay their land rents and had to lose the land, and many became heavily indebted. (Badriyah Haji Salleh, 1985, p. 209)

Malay reserve land was often used as a form of security in obtaining the loans, despite the legal prohibition of its transfer to non-Malays. Many unemployed Malays living in towns such as Gopeng, Tapah, and Kampar migrated as labourers to work on tea farms in the Cameron Highlands (Rashid Maidin, 2009).

In terms of *labour conditions*, miners who continued to work suffered huge wage cuts and experienced a serious deterioration in their terms of employment. Some ended up working for food alone. About 60,000 mining labourers in Malaya were retrenched, with the highest number of retrenchments in Perak's gravel-pump mines. The government repatriated many thousands of unemployed mine and estate workers to China and India to reduce the potential for social unrest, while many thousands emigrated of their own accord. Unrestricted entry into Malaya was curtailed, with quotas imposed on Chinese male immigrants.

In Perak alone, almost two-thirds of mine workers were retrenched between 1929 and 1932, the majority of whom were Chinese (Table 2.7). The number of workers employed in gravel-pump mines fell by over 70 per cent, from 43,000 in 1929—when they accounted for two-thirds of the state's total mining labour force—to 14,000 in 1933. By January 1930, 50 gravel pump mines in Perak had closed (New Straits Times, 1930). The severity of the unemployment situation caused the State Council in June 1930 to set up the Kinta Unemployment Committee, which sought to provide some relief in the face of destitution among

Table 2.7	Job losses among Perak's miners during the Great Depression hit the Chinese community particularly hard				
	Chinese	**Malays**	**Indians**	**Europeans**	**Total[a]**
			Number of miners		
1929	55,568	7,328	2,079	390	65,411
1930	44,021	4,887	1,539	351	50,876
1931	28,487	3,331	1,373	230	33,486
1932	20,338	2,247	965	154	23,736
1933	20,518	2,276	1,057	151	24,043
1934	25,503	4,292	1,466	199	31,550

Sources of data: Report of the Mines Department (various years).

Note: [a] Includes a small number of 'others'.

mine workers and those whose businesses depended on the prosperity of the tin industry. However, the majority of laid-off labourers still had to fend for themselves.

In terms of *living standards*, by 1931 wages had been depressed to bare subsistence levels and homelessness was rife. Ipoh was inundated with hundreds of unemployed tin miners experiencing extreme hardship. They settled on riverbanks and slept under bridges. Many were forced to turn to growing their own food and cultivating groundnuts, tapioca, tobacco, and other cash crops, as well as tending livestock. This led to the emergence of agricultural squatter communities, although, according to Loh (1990), Chinese agricultural squatting had begun during the tin-price slump at the start of the 1920s.

Some vegetable growers also occupied their land legally through Temporary Occupation Licences issued by the colonial authorities during the depression years, but it was extremely difficult for non-Malays to acquire agricultural land and become legal occupants (Loh, 1988). With the gradual recovery of the tin industry from 1933, much of the land cultivated under Temporary Occupation Licences was required by the mining industry. At first it was difficult to evict the land occupiers because of a lack of enabling legislation, but in 1938 an amendment was made to the Mining Code so that the authorities could evict them without compensation (Lim, 1977). Malays working on rubber estates in Lower Perak and Batang Padang were also hit hard by the depression. To counter this, the state government opened up land in Bidor on which unemployed Malays could grow *padi* (Lee, 1978). In 1931, a fund was set up by Sultan Iskandar Shah to help Malays affected by the depression.

Despite being small players in tin production, *dulang* washers—mostly either squatters or farmers around the mining areas—were one group of workers who appeared to 'thrive', relatively speaking, during the crisis (Box 2.11). In 1929, they constituted less than 9 per cent of tin mine workers, but in the desperate times at the depth of the depression in 1932, their share grew to 22 per cent, despite restrictions imposed on the issuance of *dulang* passes to regulate tin output. Neither did their annual income decline as quickly as tin prices, because they managed to increase production from 1929 to 1931 (Nim, 1953). The Kinta mining zone also saw more applications from Malay and Indian women during this period. In 1931, the Warden of Mines issued some 30 passes to Malay women in Kinta, where there was a limit of 100 passes (Abdul Azmi Abdul Khalid, 1992, p. 96).

Box 2.11   *Dulang* **washers and illicit tin-ore dealing**

Dulang washing was a marginal economic activity in the tin-mining industry, performed predominantly by Chinese women—mostly of the Hakka clan—and also by a few Malays and Indians. The work was tedious, requiring these workers to stand up to their waists in a stream to wash for ore. They lived in shacks near the mines and sold the recovered ore to local buyers.

From the early 20th century, *dulang* 'washing passes' were issued by Perak's Mines Department for an annual fee to regulate *dulang* workers in an attempt to stop illicit ore dealing and safeguard the interests of mine owners (Federated Malay States Annual Report, 1904). *Dulang* workers were permitted to recover a fixed quota of tin concentrates per month from the streams and discarded tailings, and to sell the recovered ore to a licensed ore dealer (Nim, 1953 and 1961). But these quotas were difficult to impose in practice and *dulang* workers often sold more than the permitted legal limit. Buyers who traded with *dulang* washers could be prosecuted for illicit ore dealings.

Local dealers were charged a fee for an annual licence to purchase, store, smelt, and treat mineral ore, and a security deposit was required to try to ensure control and curtail illicit mining (Federated Malay States Annual Report, 1908).

In periods of high unemployment and economic hardship, *dulang* washing and illicit mining increased. Landowners sometimes issued false certificates for ore mined illegally on agricultural or forest reserve lands and sold it through *dulang* washers. In Batu Gajah, numerous cases of ore theft and criminal intimidation were reported; there was also an incident in which one hundred labourers forcefully occupied and mined illegally on land belonging to Kay Yew Tin Mines (Abdul Azmi Abdul Khalid, 1992). When caught, illicit dealers and miners generally claimed that, without the proceeds, they would starve.

(Continued)

Consequently, arrest and imprisonment, with good food and not too much work, have little deterrent effect, and it is extremely difficult to ascertain how they dispose of the tin. (Abdul Azmi Abdul Khalid, 1992, p. 97)

Despite various legislative measures, including arrangements to track stolen ore—whereby district police officers were instructed to inform the Mines Department once a report of tin ore theft had been made (Report of the Mines Department, 1925)—ore stealing remained rampant. After minor ore thefts from the mines in Tronoh, Papan, and Pusing, with the ore sold by *dulang* women under the authority of their passes, new regulations required the buyer to record the date, weight, and value of all ore sold by the pass-holder (Federated Malay States Annual Report, 1927). Even with tighter regulations, including penalties of fines and imprisonment, however, ore thefts persisted, continuing throughout the Japanese occupation between 1941 and 1945, during the Emergency between 1948 and 1960, and even after independence.

Labour Unrest and the Emergence of Communism

The extremely harsh economic conditions during the Great Depression, especially in the Malay peninsula's tin and rubber belt, coupled with the British policy of deporting unemployed migrant workers, gave birth in April 1930 to the Malayan Communist Party (MCP)—later known as the Communist Party of Malaya (CPM)—with Perak-born Lee Chay Heng one of its founders (Yong, 1997). Its membership was predominantly Chinese, although even before its founding there was a small group of Malay communists.[59]

At first, during the early 1930s, the British succeeded in suppressing the growth of communism through legislative measures, such as controls on trade unions and printed publications, and using the police Special Branch to curb political activism. However, emboldened by the outbreak of the Sino–Japanese war in 1937, the CPM grew in strength and influence through a network of workers' associations with campaigns to improve the working conditions of labourers (see 'Rise of the Communist Party of Malaya, Post-1945', below).

---

[59] Six Malay leaders were arrested in 1929 because of their association with communist activities just before the official formation of the MCP in Singapore, creating a vacuum for the nomination of Malays to key party positions (Belogurova, 2019, p. 63).

Perak's Kinta Mining Workers' Association, which had members in many tin-dredging mining areas, such as Malim Nawar and Tajong Tualang, was one of Malaya's largest workers' associations with some 20,000 labourers from all ethnic communities (Rashid Maidin, 2009).

Reasons for Perak's Greater Prosperity

Indirect estimation shows that Perak's GDP per capita was significantly higher than the average for Malaya as a whole (including Perak) between 1900 and 1939. Several factors support this finding and help to explain it. Most immediately, Perak's dominant position as a global tin producer throughout the period probably conferred an income advantage. Although rubber cultivation and exports accounted for much of the growth and volatility in Malaya's economy, tin exports still contributed greatly to income levels. Even though tin's share of total Malayan exports was on a downward trend during these decades, exports of the commodity still accounted for an average of 30 per cent of that total and, on average, Perak contributed 61 per cent of Malaya's total tin exports during the period. At the same time, Perak was an important player in and beneficiary of the rubber boom, with its contribution to rubber exports more or less matching the all-Malaya trajectory.

It is not possible to establish with any certainty how much of the income generated from tin production in Perak stayed in the state. However, trickle-down effects in the local economy seem highly likely through the hiring of workers, the purchasing of materials, the operation and maintenance of plant and equipment, and the payment of taxes and levies (Box 2.12). Thoburn (1977) estimates that for tin dredging in the 1930s—which was highly mechanized and largely British controlled—up to 50 per cent of income was remitted overseas from Malaya's mining enterprises. For gravel-pump mines, which were mostly owned locally by Chinese entities and were less mechanized, he conjectures that perhaps 15 per cent of income was remitted overseas.

However, as Thoburn's (1977) estimates for the Malay peninsula do not account for 'leakages' across state boundaries, they could be interpreted as lower bounds on the overseas remittances of income from Perak's tin mining. Still, a substantial portion of tin earnings would no doubt have remained in

Box 2.12   **Export-based income multipliers**

From the mid-19th century and into the 20th century, tin and rubber export activities generated substantial trickle-down income effects for Perak's local economy as well as shaping the state's settlement patterns, built environment, and demographics. Perak's local economy during the colonial era was closely linked to its tin and rubber exporting activity. These industries propelled the economy's growth but also exposed it to external volatility.

Export-based frameworks assign a central role to activities that generate external income in explaining a territory's wider economic performance. The impulse from export earnings stimulates demand for local material and service inputs and adds to the wages of export workers and to the profits of local owners of export firms. Inter-industry linkages and spending on locally produced goods and services elicit additional rounds of income creation. Through these channels a booming export sector can energize a local economy. Equally, if export fortunes reverse, these same mechanisms will cause income to pull back. The extent of the dependence of the local economy on its export base depends on the scale of export income and the share of export income that is retained locally. If there are no other independent sources of income, the local economy becomes subordinate to its export sector.

Thoburn (1973) collated detailed data on the structure of tin mining and rubber cultivation expenditures for Peninsular Malaysia, and showed that the linkages between these industries and the domestic economy were robust, debunking the idea that tin and rubber were enclave export sectors. For tin dredging, Thoburn estimates that, in 1967, as much as 75 per cent of export earnings were retained in the form of purchases of materials, wages, dividends, and taxes, in addition to a still substantial share of local ownership in dredging (around 30 per cent). For the pre–World War II payment structure, when state taxes were lower and a smaller proportion of mining was locally owned, retention would have been smaller.

Unfortunately, comparable data for Perak do not exist. Procurement of materials outside the state, as well as wage and profit remittances to other parts of the peninsula, mean that retention of export earnings in Perak would have been smaller than Thoburn's (1973) estimates for Peninsular Malaysia. Yet, even if only 40 per cent of dredging income had been retained in Perak, each additional dollar of exported tin would have added 67 cents of income to the local economy—based on a simple income multiplier calculation where the increment to income is equal to the reciprocal of one minus the export income retention rate. Larger earnings retention for locally owned gravel-pump tin mining, for labour-intensive rubber estates, and especially for rubber smallholders, would have generated larger income spillovers in Perak's local economy.

More subtle impacts worked through other channels. For example, taxes and duties from tin and rubber exports funded Perak's infrastructure investments in railways, roads, ports, irrigation, and electrification. Likewise, tin and rubber exports also acted as a catalyst for investment in new activities such as tool-making and chemical fertilizer production. In important ways, rubber cultivation and its associated organizational structure enabled the eventual diversification into palm oil (Giacomin, 2018). The supply-side dynamics of these long-term investments and the discovery of new activities are not readily captured by simple export-based models and companion multiplier calculations.

Perak, bolstering average standards of living. Additionally, the taxes and levies on tin, which were used to finance the costs of locally provided social and economic services, would have contributed to the welfare of Perak's population.

Relative to all-Malaya, Perak's specialization in tin mining conferred an additional benefit that is not captured by the method used to estimate its GDP per capita. In 1914, Perak's tin exports in value terms were approximately 1.8 times the size of its rubber exports. By 1939, the value of Perak's tin exports had fallen to just 1.3 times the value of its rubber exports, although Perak's tin–export ratio remained higher than that for all-Malaya. However, over this same period, tin prices fared considerably better than rubber prices and, although they were volatile, they were much less so than rubber prices.

Exports of rubber had begun to surge after 1905, becoming a major component of Perak's and Malaya's economy. By 1910, Perak's rubber exports constituted 17.5 per cent of the total value of its exports, soaring to a peak of 59 per cent in 1917 (Figure 2.19, upper panel); the corresponding values for tin were 74 per cent and 37 per cent respectively. However, whereas for Malaya the value of rubber exports greatly exceeded the value of tin exports and dominated the value of total exports between 1910 and 1939 (Figure 2.19, lower panel), Perak's tin and rubber exports were of a similar value to each other throughout much of this period.

The prices for Perak's tin and rubber exports in nominal terms confirm that favourable tin prices compensated for declining volumes of tin exports, relative to rubber exports, with the value of Perak's tin exports remaining at par with the value of its rubber exports in many years, and even exceeding it in some. The evidence suggests that, for given import prices, and in view of its specialization in tin, Perak's terms of trade would generally have fared better than that of all-Malaya. To the extent that this was the case, the premium on Perak's gross domestic income would have been even higher than that imputed for GDP.[60]

The demographics of pre–World War II Perak also indicate that its GDP per capita would have been higher than Malaya's in general. There was a high representation of ethnic Chinese in the state's total population, who typically had higher than average consumption spending and incomes, and a relatively small share of Malays. In each of the population census years—1901, 1911, 1921, and 1931—more Chinese were recorded living in Perak than in any other state of Malaya and, other than in 1921, their share consistently exceeded 40 per cent. As a share of the total population, only Selangor had larger Chinese representation. Between 1900 and 1939, Chinese labour had higher per capita consumption levels than either Malay or Indian labour (Sultan Nazrin Shah, 2019).

In addition, Chinese were strongly represented in Malaya's town-based merchant and commercial class, for whom standards of living were undoubtedly much higher than average, particularly compared with the rural areas where most Malays lived. In the 1930s, Perak had more average-sized towns than any other state in Malaya.

For those Chinese engaged in agriculture, their smallholdings were often larger (and possibly more productive) than those of other communities, and most Chinese agriculturalists were producing mainly for the cash economy rather than for subsistence. In Perak, Chinese also dominated the lucrative fishing industry based around Pangkor (Lee, 1978).

In summary there is ample reason to believe that the population of Perak, on average, enjoyed a better standard of living than the populations of other parts of Malaya over 1900–1940. However, Perak's dependence on tin and rubber meant that it was the hardest-hit state during the Great Depression, according to output, export, and employment data. The price of tin collapsed and the drastic restrictions on tin output were shouldered disproportionately by Chinese-owned mines. Savage job losses followed, with negative impacts on Perak's businesses and communities reliant on the tin industry.

During rubber price crashes, similarly, smallholders experienced particular hardship as they carried a disproportionate share of the burden of the

---

60 Gross domestic income is equal to GDP plus an adjustment for trading gains or losses (Sultan Nazrin Shah, 2017). With tin export prices more favourable than rubber export prices, and Perak's comparative specialization in tin, Perak was more likely to benefit from trading gains, or to experience smaller trading losses, than all-Malaya.

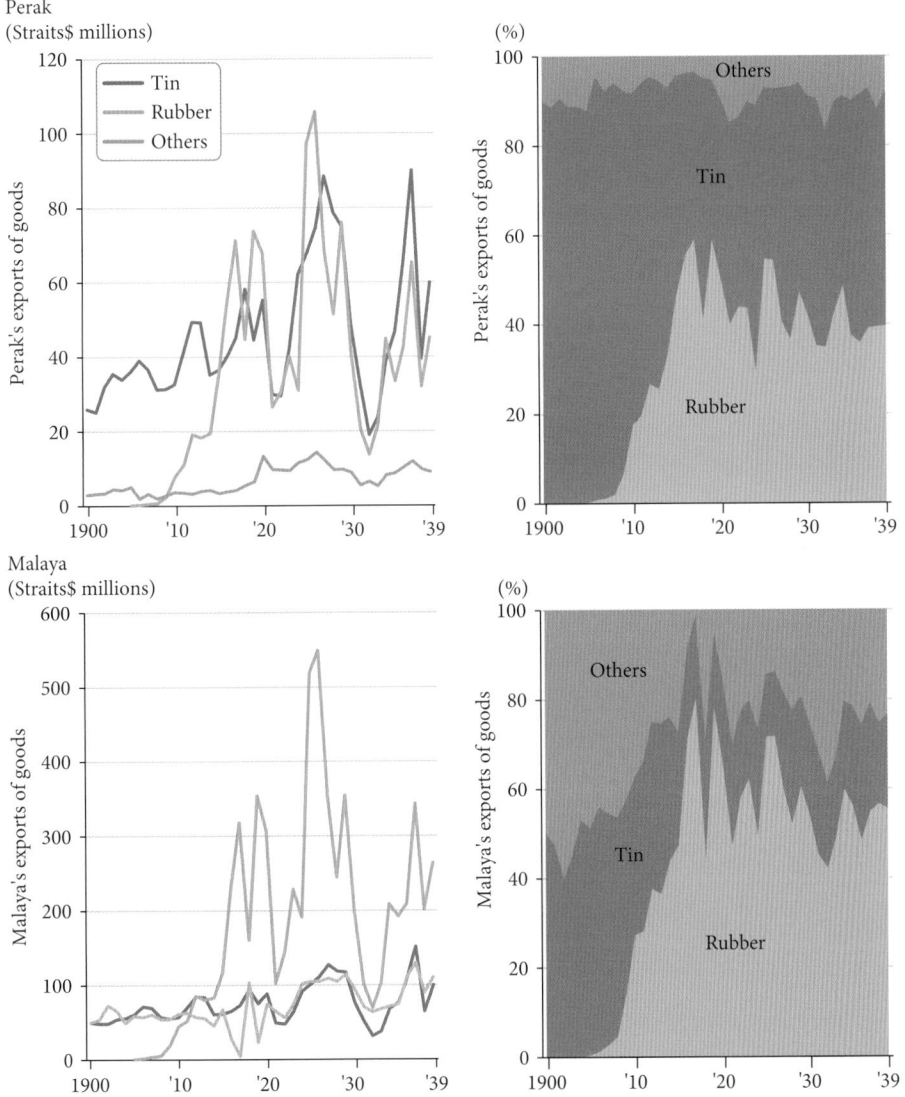

Figure 2.19 From around 1914, the values of Perak's tin and rubber exports generally moved in tandem, while the value of Malaya's rubber exports eclipsed that of tin

Sources of data: Annual Report of Perak (various years); Federated Malay States (various years), *Report of the Administration of the Mines Department and the Mining Industries.*

output restrictions. Smallholders accounted for about half of Perak's rubber acreage. This helped to distribute income gains from booming rubber exports in times of prosperity, but left smallholders vulnerable to episodic downturns. Those fortunate enough to retain their jobs endured steep wage cuts, while tens of thousands of migrant Chinese and Indian workers were repatriated from Perak. Both of these outcomes lowered private consumption and the income multiplier.

In harsh economic circumstances, and despite some efforts to provide relief to the destitute, most smallholders were left to fend for themselves, often resorting to marginal agricultural activity, with serious longer-term political consequences (see 'The Emergency, 1948–1960', below). Between 1929 and 1933, the area under dry *padi* cultivation on Perak's infertile soils and hills more than trebled. Social indicators, too, suggest increased stresses. Homelessness and its deprivations stalked major urban areas.

Japanese Occupation, Insurgency, and Decolonization, 1941–1957

Despite international restrictions on production, at the beginning of World War II in late 1939, Malaya was unrivalled as the world's largest producer and exporter both of tin—a position it had held since the end of the 19th century—and of natural rubber. Malaya's tin production accounted for around one-third of the world's tin output, with 70 per cent of the country's exports destined for the US—the UK, with a share of 10 per cent, was a distant second place. In 1940, Malaya's tin production rose further to a peak of 80,700 tons on the back of increased demand in the first full year of the war. Perak was still at the forefront of Malaya's tin industry, contributing some 60.7 per cent of production, and was a major player in its rubber industry, contributing 18.5 per cent.

However, with the start of the Japanese occupation of Malaya in December 1941, the great natural resource boom ended. Tin and rubber production fell dramatically to only a fraction of pre-war levels. Perak's economy suffered greatly. Incomes from tin and rubber output and exports dipped sharply, unemployment rocketed, and people experienced severe hardship, including malnutrition. With war imposing constraints on the imports of rice, the Japanese administration prioritized food production, especially rice cultivation, and some farmlands were converted into *padi* fields. The number of workers engaged in agriculture (excluding rubber) rose, while the number employed in the rubber and tin industries declined, with many mines and estates left unattended. Some smallholders even cut their rubber trees and turned to cultivating food crops.

Japanese Occupation, 1941–1945

Japan planned to exploit Malaya's strategic natural resources to support its war efforts: tin and rubber were among its priorities, as were bauxite and iron ore. In addition to Malaya, Japan designated several other territories it occupied in

Globalization: Perak's Rise, Relative Decline, and Regeneration. Sultan Nazrin Shah, Oxford University Press. © Sultan Nazrin Shah (2024). DOI: 10.1093/oso/9780198897774.003.0015

Southeast Asia as parts of its 'Greater East Asia Co-Prosperity Sphere'. A key economic objective was to gain control of these territories' natural resources, including petroleum in the Dutch East Indies, rice in Thailand and French Indochina, and minerals and rice in Burma (Mako, 2008).

The British adopted a scorched-earth policy to prevent the Japanese from accessing Malaya's natural resources. Under direct orders from the UK Mines Department, the retreating forces flooded British-owned mines, overturned and sank dredges, and dismantled and hid vital machine parts. They also burned rubber stocks. They put the Perak Hydro-Electric Company's power stations at Chenderoh out of action, as well as the two subsidiary stations at Batu Gajah and Malim Nawar, by removing essential machinery and blowing up part of the Perak River dam. This put the tin mines dependent on electricity out of action (Maxwell, 1944).

Despite these efforts, the Japanese army appropriated mines and rubber estates, and resumed some production under the supervision of private companies. The British and Continental European tin mines in Perak were initially put under the management of the Japanese administration and later, in 1943, were transferred to government-supported firms: Mitsui Kosan Kabushiki Kaisha, Toyo Kosan Kabushiki Kaisha, and Jun-An Kogyo Kabushiki Kaisha (Nim, 1953). These companies also operated the Eastern Smelting Company's smelters in Penang and the STC's smelters in Singapore. The management of rubber plantations was given to Japanese companies that had been operating in Malaya before the occupation. For example, the Showa Gomu Company, with a main office in Ipoh, was allotted a quarter of a million acres of rubber estates in Perak, with Nomura Tohindo Shokusan and Senda as exporting companies (Mako, 2008). By March 1943, the Japanese regime was claiming the satisfactory rehabilitation of 'numerous rich tin mines, rubber estates, coconut and tea plantations in the state' (*Perak Government Gazette*, 30 March 1943, p. 1).[61]

A small proportion of Malaya's Chinese mines resumed production immediately after the Japanese occupation, and some others did so after minor repairs. By the end of 1942, however, just 20 per cent of Malaya's Chinese gravel-pump and hydraulic mines were in operation. The British-owned dredging mines took longer to fix without foreign engineering expertise and replacement parts, although some were revived through the help of local mining technicians. Malaya's tin production rose in 1943, but machinery began to

---

61 At the end of the occupation, privately owned Japanese rubber estates and companies were requisitioned and auctioned by the British administration, with the proceeds used mainly to compensate for war damage to British-owned assets.

break down and there was a shortage of spare parts for repairs. Unsurprisingly, by the end of 1945 there were no dredges working and only 45 of Malaya's Chinese tin mines were still in operation. The result was that output collapsed (Yip, 1969). In 1942, Perak's tin production was only 10,700 tons, but by 1945 it had tumbled even further to just 2,200 tons. Perak's cumulative output over the four years from 1942 to 1945 was about 36,000 tons—less than half of what it had been in the single year of 1940 (Report of the Mines Department, 1949, cited in Nim, 1953, p. 9).

As it did elsewhere in the region, rubber production in Malaya came to a virtual standstill, as the rubber market was seriously disrupted during the war. The value of rubber exports collapsed to a minimal amount during the Japanese occupation (Lim, 1967).

Evacuation

A Japanese invasion of Malaya had been expected by the British from as early as 1937. They had long been aware of Japanese spies operating under the guise of photographers and barbers in the region. Nonetheless they were caught unprepared when Japanese troops landed in Kota Bahru, Kelantan, on 8 December 1941 (Tregonning, 1964).

The first Japanese bombs fell on Ipoh on 15 December 1941, damaging the Hugh Low Street Bridge, railway yards, some shop houses, and the Gunung Rapat aerodrome (Anderson, 2011).

> Aircraft strafed Ipoh town with machine-gun fire. It was pure hysteria, even civilians became targets … many were killed. Thousands ran along the banks of the Kinta River, confused and frightened … the innocent people who knew nothing about war. (Abdul Talib Ahmad cited in Mustapha Hussain, 2005, p. 157)

On 16 December, all European women and children were evacuated from Perak and headed south. On 17 December, central Ipoh was bombed again, and the next day Taiping was hit, with heavy casualties (Shennan, 2015). Many people moved out of the towns to mines, rural villages, and limestone caves around Ipoh for safety as the bombing continued in the following days. By the end of the first week of 1942, the combined battles of Kampar and Slim River—critical lines of British defence—had sealed the fate of central and eastern Malaya. By the end of January, the entire Malay peninsula was in the hands of the Japanese (Tregonning, 1964). As the Japanese made rapid advances, retreating British troops destroyed roads and railway bridges.

Life in Perak during the Japanese Occupation

By late December 1941, Japanese troops had assumed control of Perak. Men were assembled and made to stand all night in the town squares, and then given instructions on what the new administration expected of them. The new Japanese Governor of Perak, Taosa Kubota, endeavoured to establish good relations with Sultan Abdul Aziz (1938–1948) and the Malay aristocracy (Cheah, 1987). Malays were the new government's preferred vigilantes, and became favoured members of the auxiliary Japanese police force (Andaya and Andaya, 2015). Some of those with experience in the civil service were promoted to positions formerly held by the British, such as district officer.

The Japanese administration made use of the Kesatuan Melayu Muda (KMM—Union of Young Malays) as the 'fifth column' of their army (Andaya and Andaya, 2017) (Box 2.13). The KMM was a radical anti-colonial political organization founded in 1938 with socialist ideals—its leaders were imprisoned by the British, released by the Japanese, but later also banned by them (Syed Husin Ali, 2019). In Ipoh, Malay youths were given brief military training and instructions on the use of small arms and explosives for sabotage work behind British lines. Some youths were excited, but others felt that

> the war we were facing was not our fight; it was a war between two colonisers. From Ipoh, KMM and other youth moved [to the warfront] as saviours of the people, and not as traitors. Although the KMM had fought on the side of Japan, it was under duress. KMM was still anti-colonial, British or Japanese. ... The occupation played a catalytic role in the emergence and development of Malay nationalism. (Mustapha Hussain, 2005, p. 178)

The banning of the KMM by both the British and Japanese led to the formation of the Parti Kebangsaan Melayu Malaya (PKMM—Malay Nationalist Party) in October 1945, with many of its leaders and members coming from the KMM.

Chinese and Indians experienced the harshest treatment by the Japanese during the occupation, as they did throughout Southeast Asia. The Japanese forced Chinese mining *towkays* to donate large sums of money to support the war effort. Lee Meng Hin, one of Perak's many prominent mine owners, had to sell properties to raise money demanded by the Japanese, while others took loans from the Sumitomo Bank using land titles, leases, and other assets as collateral (Salt Media Group, 2021). The Japanese occupiers sent 19,000 Perak labourers, predominantly Indians, to work on the Siam–Burma and Kra railways: only 3,300 returned (Kratoska, 2018).

Box 2.13	Seeds of Malay nationalism sown at the Sultan Idris Training College (SITC)

The SITC was conceived by R. O. Winstedt, Director of Education of the Federated Malay States and named after Sultan Idris Murshidul Azzam Shah. Its policy of teaching in *Bahasa Melayu*—adopted by its first principal, Oman Theodore Dussek—instilled a deep sense of pride in Malay culture and identity among its students (Koay, 2018). Established for the purpose of training Malay students to become schoolteachers in rural Malay-vernacular schools, which had a strong agricultural orientation, the SITC became a hotbed for Malay-educated left-leaning nationalists.

After the Malay Translation Bureau was transferred from Kuala Lumpur to the SITC in 1924 and the renowned Malay linguist Zainal Abidin bin Ahmad—popularly known as Za'ba—was appointed to lead the Bureau in writing, translating, and overseeing educational publications, numerous Malay documents, including banned revolutionary literature from the Middle East and Indonesia, were disseminated among students (Syed Muhd Khairudin Aljunied, 2015). A new strand of Malay nationalism emerged that contrasted sharply with that of the conservative-leaning ruling class, who were educated in English at the exclusive Malay College in Kuala Kangsar. This new nationalist faction comprised a small group of SITC graduates, who were mainly from the working class and were advocating for a Greater Indonesia, uniting Malays of Indonesia, Borneo, and the Malay peninsula (Roff, 1967).

Nationalist ideas engendered a sense of political awakening among young Malays, causing the SITC to become known as the 'cradle of Malay resurgence and centre of Malay intellectual and literary life' (Abdullah Firdaus Haji, 1985, p. 8). Exposure to radical teachings broadened the students' horizons and led to the rise of the Malay left, with two of SITC's graduates, Ibrahim Yaacob and Ishak Muhammad, forming the KMM—the first Malay political party to lead the anti-British colonial struggle during World War II. As well as being anti-colonialist, the KMM 'had an almost equal contempt for the "lick-spittle" traditional elite who profited from colonial rule and maintained their own positions at the expense of the peasantry and the urban proletariat' (Roff, 1967, p. 233).

Perak's Malay-language newspapers also helped build momentum for nationalism. They contained hard-hitting articles, many written by teachers and religious scholars, against British colonialism. These newspapers raised political awareness, arguing for people's social and economic rights. Before the Japanese occupation, Perak's most popular newspaper was *Warta Kinta* which included radical articles by Ahmad Boestamam and Ahmad Noor Abdul Shukor—members of the KMM who were arrested by the British authorities in 1941 for their anti-colonialist writings.

In enforcing order, the Japanese went to extreme lengths to brutally intimidate the Chinese, with the Kempeitai—the Japanese military police—summarily executing those suspected of disloyalty, opposition, or support for the underground resistance, and displaying their severed heads to strike terror into the population (Kratoska, 2018). Despite the terror it engendered, this brutality increased Chinese support for the Malayan Peoples' Anti-Japanese Army (MPAJA), a paramilitary resistance group of the CPM formed in December 1941 and inspired by communist ideals. The MPAJA expanded rapidly into a force of several thousand fighters.

Food shortages and malnutrition remained a pervasive problem in Malaya throughout the occupation; the situation was similar in other parts of Southeast Asia, and especially in densely populated Java (van der Eng, 1994). In April 1942, rationing was in effect, and by 1943 the Japanese had increased food cultivation by drawing up a farm-based resettlement scheme, moving people from towns to rural areas where they could grow their own staple foods. Tapioca and sweet potatoes were the main crops, along with sugar cane and other fruit.

Anti-Japanese Resistance

Perak was an important centre of anti-Japanese resistance. The MPAJA was at its strongest and most organized in the state (Loh, 1988). And as Harper observed, the MPAJA 'conducted a relentless harassment of the Japanese and their Malay and Chinese "collaborators" and spread a terror that would cast a long shadow over the post-war years' (Harper, 1999, p. 48). From the MPAJA perspective, killing those who passed intelligence to the Kempeitai was in line with the military campaign being waged by the British against a common enemy. With strong anti-Japanese sentiment among Chinese, many gave support such as food, clothing, funds, information, and even recruits, to the MPAJA. As Frederick Spencer Chapman, a British officer turned guerrilla fighter, noted: 'many former tappers, tin mining [labourers], woodcutters and squatters joined the ranks of the MPAJA' (Chapman, 1949, p. 136).

The MPAJA's Fifth Independent Regiment of Perak was formed in 1942 and headquartered in the Bidor Hills in south Kinta. Led by Liao Wei Chung, it included many prominent leaders of the CPM, including Lau Yew, a reputable CPM guerrilla commander, and the Sitiawan-born and -raised Ong Boon Hua, better known through his *nom de guerre* Chin Peng, who was the regiment's liaison officer with the British military authorities and who in 1947 at the age of 22 became the CPM's Secretary-General.[62]

Some members of the MPAJA had been trained and armed by the British in Singapore and Malaya shortly before the occupation and during the early months. Force 136, a clandestine Special Operations Executive of the British forces, established to collaborate with underground resistance groups, contacted the MPAJA, and they worked together to compile intelligence information ready for the day when the Allies returned. Perak served as the central location for the intended counter-offensive. It was close to neither Kuala Lumpur nor Singapore, which made intelligence work safer and facilitated the transmission of information to the Supreme Allied Headquarters in India (Foong, 1997).

The first few agents of Force 136, led by intelligence officer John Lewis Haycraft Davis, a fluent Cantonese speaker who had earlier been a police officer with the Federated Malay States, arrived on the coast off Pangkor, Perak in May 1943, via submarine from Ceylon, for an intelligence gathering mission. Having established that there was a Malayan-wide anti-Japanese communist guerrilla network, Davis, with the help of Chin Peng, later organized a secret meeting with the leadership of the CPM. In late December 1943, an agreement was signed in a camp on Blantan Hill, just north of Bidor town. Through the agreement, which provided for military cooperation and mutual support in constructing intelligence networks, the MPAJA was provided with weapons, ammunition, and funds to support its guerrilla army (Chin Peng, 2013). However, a large-scale anticipated counter-offensive never materialized before the Japanese surrender in August 1945, although many heroic individuals, military and civilian, formed part of the resistance to the Japanese (Box 2.14).

Following the Japanese surrender, the MPAJA forces emerged from the jungles as heroes and were well received in Perak's cities and towns as well as

---

62 During the Japanese occupation, the CPM was led by the double agent Lai Teck. For over a decade he did extraordinary damage to the CPM's cause, orchestrating the deportation and killing of many of its leaders, as well as misguiding its top-down policy directions (Hack, 2022). He had been recruited by the British Special Branch in 1934 to infiltrate and sabotage the CPM. In 1942, after being captured by the Kempeitai, he changed sides and masterminded the Batu Caves massacre of many of the CPM's leaders by the Japanese (Yong, 1997). At the end of the Japanese occupation, he once again continued to support the British until he was uncovered, apprehended, and assassinated in Bangkok in 1947.

> ### Box 2.14   A courageous female nurse
>
> Sybil Medan Kathigasu was a Eurasian Catholic nurse and wife of an Ipoh doctor who assisted the MPAJA. With their medical practice at 74, Main Street, Papan, in Kinta district, the Kathigasus provided free treatment to the poor, including the MPAJA. Being a committee member of a Japanese-controlled support group, Mrs Kathigasu also secretly passed on information to the resistance forces (Foong, 1997). The Kathigasus were subsequently arrested, separated, interrogated, and tortured by the Kempeitai between July 1943 and September 1945.
>
> When the Japanese surrender came, the paralysed Mrs Kathigasu was released from Batu Gajah prison and sent to the Batu Gajah Hospital for recuperation, while her husband was released from Taiping prison. On 14 October 1947, she was awarded the George Medal by King George VI, the highest British civilian award for services to the forces during military operations. She died in Britain in June 1948.

in other west-coast states (Hack, 2022).[63] According to Huff (2023, p. 1), the MPAJA 'took control of some 70 per cent of the smaller towns and villages as well as large parts of the peninsula'. However, the show trials conducted by the MPAJA and the summary executions of perceived Kempeitai collaborators, including many Malay police officers, led to serious inter-ethnic tensions, conflicts, and prolonged communal ill-will (Harper, 1999). Ethnic tensions had emerged during the occupation, with the Chinese supporting the British counter-offensive while many Malays sided with the Japanese. In Perak, communal fighting resulted in dozens of Chinese and Malay casualties. The racial violence engendered Malay hostility towards communism and many Malays 'became suspicious if not hostile to communism' and began to see the Chinese as 'synonymous' with it (Cheah, 1981, p. 117).

---

63 In January 1946, Chin Peng was awarded two medals, the Burma Star and the 1939–1945 Star, by Lord Louis Mountbatten, the Supreme Allied Commander South East Asia Command, in recognition of his contribution to the war effort, and a year later he was awarded the Order of the British Empire (OBE). The OBE was later revoked, and in September 1951 the British authorities put a Straits$80,000 bounty on his head, increased to Straits$250,000 in May 1952, when he was declared public enemy no. 1.

Rise of the Communist Party of Malaya, Post-1945

The Japanese surrender did not mark a return to the status quo antebellum. During the British Military Administration (BMA) from 5 September 1945 to 31 March 1946,[64] many very serious political and socio-economic problems remained. Beyond the ill-conceived attempt to force a new constitution on Malaya without proper consultations in anticipation of the Malayan Union (see 'Decolonization, 1945–1957', below), these problems included rising ethnic tensions, violent crime, food shortages, high inflation, widespread unemployment, and low wages and poor conditions for those in work. This climate of discontent led to a turbulent period of protests.

On 30 September 1945, within a month of the British return to Malaya, Ipoh saw a major demonstration involving 3,000 people, with workers demanding more food, jobs, higher wages, and better working conditions (Gamba, 1962). Large demonstrations spread to Perak's other mining towns and plantation areas, including Sungai Siput and Batu Gajah where BMA troops were called on to quell the crowds, opening fire and killing several demonstrators (Hack, 2022). The CPM capitalized on people's grievances and championed their causes through the Perak Federation of Trade Unions, the Perak General Labour Union, and other trade unions.

To begin with, the CPM had mainly comprised disaffected Hainanese communist activists who had come to Malaya after the breakdown of the alliance between the Kuomintang (National Party of China) and the Chinese Communist Party in 1927. During the Great Depression, the colonial administration had become concerned that there could be political agitation in Perak's Chinese community, especially in the aftermath of this breakdown. In Malaya, supporters of the Kuomintang were generally from the wealthier and middle-class segment of the Chinese community, whereas most of the communists were from the lower-middle and working classes (Abraham, 2006). Political activity among Perak's Chinese had increased in the wake of the split, as had competition for support by the leaders of the Chinese community on each side (Lee, 1978). The CPM had gained a stronger footing after

---

64 The allied forces arrived in Penang on 3 September 1945, and two days later Malaya was administered by the BMA, headed by Brigadier Harold Curwen Willan. The BMA was a transitional arrangement to restore civilian rule before the proposed Malayan Union. The BMA assumed the functions and powers of government, with full judicial, legislative, executive, and administrative powers and responsibilities (Rudner, 1968).

the outbreak of the Sino–Japanese war in 1937 through the National Salvation Movement. This movement rallied support from Malaya's Chinese—especially students and workers—who were spurred into action upon learning about the atrocities committed in Nanjing, China, by Japanese forces (Heng, 1988).

The rising tide of nationalism driven by Indian nationalist Subhas Chandra Bose had inspired many Indian labourers to serve in the Indian National Army to overcome British imperialism with Japanese support, but many then found themselves exploited by the Japanese. Disillusioned, some gave their support to the MPAJA. Although the MPAJA was disbanded by the CPM in December 1946, the CPM—as a former wartime ally of the British—was allowed to operate legally as a political party for a short time after the war under the BMA (Harper, 1999). Branches of the CPM's Ex-Comrades Associations operated legally throughout Malaya, and the CPM had representatives in both Federal and State Advisory Councils.

Perak had emerged as a CPM stronghold during the Japanese occupation, and the state's mountainous terrain also became the main sanctuary of the MPAJA, heavily supported by Chinese agricultural squatters, who comprised a sizeable proportion of the state's population. The squatters and their families included those displaced during and after the Great Depression, and those who had fled the towns during the Japanese occupation. Because of this, Perak became a battleground in events leading up to the Emergency. Its business elite and industries were prime targets for attacks as the communists sought to disrupt the economy and ultimately drive out the British from the peninsula. In early 1948, the CPM, now led by Chin Peng, stepped up its agitation, instigating many strikes, and intimidating owners of mines and plantations as well as those working in government buildings (Loh, 1988; Tan, 2020).[65]

However, due to Malaya's strategic and financial importance to the British Empire, and against a wider backdrop of fears about the spread of communism in Southeast Asia, the UK government was determined to defend Malaya from communism by military means, and steer the country to eventual independence.

---

65 Apart from Chin Peng, Perak was home to several prominent CPM leaders including Che Dat Abdullah, Chen Tien, Musa Ahmad, and Rashid Maidin.

The Emergency, 1948–1960

By 1948 Malaya was the 'biggest single repository of British overseas investment' (Nyce, 1973, p. xxxiii) and its 'rubber and tin mining industries were the biggest dollar earners in the British Commonwealth' (Curtis, 2003, p. 335). The British administration was determined to protect the country's key industries at almost any cost.

Gerard Edward James Gent, British High Commissioner to Malaya (February–July 1948),[66] at first declared a State of Emergency for Perak on 16 June 1948, immediately after the murder of three British planters by CPM members in Sungai Siput, in the district of Kuala Kangsar about 20 miles north of Ipoh.[67] In the weeks leading up to the killings, the rubber estates in Sungai Siput had become a target for CPM-led strikes for higher wages. With tension mounting, the Emergency was progressively extended, covering the entire Federation of Malaya and Singapore by 24 June. Malaya's business community had urged Gent to make such a declaration for some time, worried about industrial unrest, the increasing level of violence, and the loss of their income due to depleted dollar earnings to the UK (Curtis, 2022). Dissatisfaction with Gent's slow response led to his replacement by Henry Lovell Goldsworthy Gurney as Malaya's British High Commissioner (1948–1951), a month after the declaration of the State of Emergency.[68]

The declaration banned the CPM; led swiftly to the arrest of hundreds of insurgents and sympathizers, including left-wing Malays; and placed the country under severe civil rights restrictions, enforced through an increasingly heavy military and police presence. The British were concerned that a broader non-racial alliance between the CPM and left-wing Malays would harm their substantial economic interests (Abraham, 2006). Emergency regulations gave the government powers to search and arrest CPM sympathizers without a warrant, to detain suspects without trial for up to a year, to administer heavy penalties for assisting communist party members, to impose curfews, and to apply the death penalty for possession of firearms. With these measures having only limited success in reducing the number of incidents, Gurney introduced even tougher regulations, which gave the authorities even greater powers, similar to those employed in Palestine and other colonies. These included powers to 'detain and deport'; use of lethal weapons by the authorities to prevent suspected communists or their

---

66 Gent previously served as the Governor of the Malayan Union between April 1946 and January 1948.

67 The murdered planters were Arthur Walker from the Elphil rubber estate, and John Allison and Ian Christian from the Phin Soon estate. They were the first of many planters to be killed by communists (Ho, 2006).

68 Gurney had a military and civil background, and came to Malaya after serving as Chief Secretary of Palestine.

sympathisers from escaping arrest—as contentiously applied in Batang Kali in northern Selangor; the infamous Emergency Regulation 17D that permitted 'collective punishment'; and powers to compulsorily 'evict and resettle' both individuals and whole villages (Tan, 2020, p. 47). The squatter resettlement programme became a government priority, although progress was initially slow because of difficulties in obtaining suitable land from state governments.

Following the declaration of the Emergency and waves of arrests, the CPM responded by reviving and rebranding the disbanded MPAJA as the Malayan National Liberation Army (MNLA) in early 1949.[69] The CPM then took its fight into the Malayan jungle and reorganized itself into an armed rebellion against the colonial government (Jomo and Todd, 1994). Most of its sympathizers were Chinese from the Min Yuen (People's Movement), which was the civilian branch of the MNLA, who supplied food and medicine and were a source of intelligence and recruitment. By contrast, most English-speaking Chinese engaged in business and the professions were still willing to accept a British-ruled Malaya. And although many ethnic Chinese did support the CPM and Mao's revolution in China, and others were content with the status quo, a large group remained as neutral 'fence sitters'.

The first phase of the Emergency came to a head in October 1951, following the assassination of Gurney in an MNLA ambush. The resettlement programme had been proceeding apace, but the new settlements created were of variable quality. A shortage of doctors and nurses limited the improvements to healthcare, while insurgency incidents remained high, and police training was an urgent concern (Hack, 2022). Gerald Walter Robert Templer, who served concurrently as the new British High Commissioner and Director of Operations (1952–1954)—that is, civil and military roles respectively—was tasked with changing this situation.[70] He was directed to prioritize the Emergency, and instructed by the Colonial Office to adhere to the preamble to the Federation of Malaya Agreement and achieve a 'United Malayan Nation', with a 'common form of citizenship' for those loyal to Malaya, and with each community's traditions, culture, and customs maintained (Cloake, 1985, p. 457).

One of Templer's first initiatives, in March 1952, was to rebrand the resettlements as 'New Villages' (Box 2.15). At first under his direction, harsh

---

69 The MNLA was largely Chinese, although its 10th Regiment based in Pahang was Malay. It also had a few Indian members.

70 Gerald Templer, a highly distinguished and ruthless military officer who had served in Palestine during the Arab Rebellion that broke out in 1936, was appointed by Britain's prime minister Winston Churchill. He later became a Field Marshal. He served in Malaya for 28 months, making a crucial contribution to the resolution of the Emergency and to eventual decolonization.

collective punishments were meted out for non-cooperation by resettled communities. But he eventually abolished the use of Emergency Regulation 17D. His approach instead placed great emphasis on winning the 'hearts and minds' of the Malayan people, both by enhancing the quality of life in the New Villages, and through massive media campaigns, which used radio broadcasts and films, as well as leaflets dropped from the air. He also passed legislation to grant automatic citizenship to Chinese born in the Straits Settlements, as well as to those of immigrant origin who had been born in Malaya and had at least one parent also born in Malaya. Other reforms included recruiting more Chinese into the police and armed forces, and persuading Malaya's rulers to open the higher ranks of the Malayan Civil Service to the federation's Chinese citizens.

Box 2.15   **Perak in the Emergency: Internment in New Villages**

The 1948–1960 Emergency was a period of guerrilla warfare between the British Commonwealth's armed forces and the MNLA, the military arm of the CPM. The CPM was fighting to achieve an independent and communist Malayan People's Democratic Republic. Chinese squatter communities were its main backers, having earlier supplied many of the needs of the MPAJA during the Japanese occupation, but now seen as a major security problem by the British authorities.

In Perak, about half of Kinta's scattered rural population were squatters. In March 1950, with insurgency incidents climbing, Lieutenant-General Harold Rawdon Briggs was appointed as Malaya's first military Director of Operations (1950–1951), at the request of Henry Gurney, British High Commissioner. Briggs, who retired in 1948 after serving as Commander-in-Chief of the Burma Command, had a successful military background and was recalled for duty in Malaya. He argued that combating MNLA forces without eliminating their grass-roots rural support was ineffective. And so, in mid-1950, the government launched a new harsh, but ultimately effective, strategy: the Briggs Plan—the Federation Plan for the Elimination of the Communist Organisation and Armed Forces in Malaya—involving the military, police, and civil authorities. Its aim was to establish control of populated areas with security maintained by the police.

Its core and most damaging component was the mass displacement of Chinese squatters from the jungle fringes and foothills, and their internment in 'New Villages', which deprived the MNLA of their main source of rice, herbal medicines, and other supplies, as well as intelligence, from a network of Min Yuen cells. Squatters were given no warning of resettlement and had to move on the same day that their former homes and crops were razed. By June 1952, Perak had the greatest

(Continued)

concentration of New Villages in Malaya: 129 New Villages with 206,900 inhabitants (Loh, 1988). Its largest resettlement area was Sungei Durian, at Tanjong Tualang (Department of Information–Federation of Malaya, 1950). The New Villages were heavily fenced and subjected to differing degrees of security restrictions and curfews depending on perceived risks.

In March 1952, shortly after his arrival in Malaya, Templer ordered residents of Tanjong Malim, a town of some 20,000 people in southern Perak, to be subjected to a 22-hour curfew and to further reductions in their rice rations as a collective punishment for their 'crime of silence' after several deadly ambushes, including on staff at the Public Works Department (Tan, 2020). Present in Tanjong Malim, Templer demanded that information be given anonymously, or punishment would continue. The curfew was lifted only after the arrest of 40 communists (CO 1022/54, 1952). Some time after this incident, a detachment of the Chinese Home Guard was sent to Tanjong Malim, and 'the town was surrounded with a double barbed wire fence interspersed with fifteen look-out towers' (Tan, 2020, p. 20).

Simultaneously with his tough military measures, Templer initiated huge propaganda campaigns, which ran in parallel to development measures in an attempt to win the 'hearts and minds' of local populations. These included promises of future independence, citizenship rights, provision of lawful land tenure in the New Villages, and grants to build new homes on plots of land allotted to squatters. The New Villages were gradually provided with piped water, electricity, community halls, and schools, with some social services offered by the government and various missionary and non-governmental organizations like the Red Cross (CO 1022/29, 1951–1953). The government had learned from the experience of the earliest settlement in Sungai Siput, where the land was not adequately prepared for agriculture, causing hardship to the settlers (Purcell, 1955). The pioneering Development Plan of the Federation of Malaya, 1950–1955, formulated by the British administration, included large allocations for the resettlement programme (Federation of Malaya, 1950 and 1953).

Political reforms were also initiated. For example, branches of the Malayan Chinese Association (MCA) were set up, and a Local Councils Ordinance was passed in 1952 to provide New Villages with elected local councils as a step towards democracy (Tan, 2020). By 1958, Perak had 81 elected local councils with some devolved powers (Malaysia Federation, 1970). However, while some of the MCA representatives assisted Chinese squatters in settling in the New Villages through social and welfare support, the local councils were dominated by MCA-connected affluent elites, many of whom were seemingly preoccupied with enhancing their own wealth, and did little to improve the lives of ordinary villagers (Loh, 1988).

The powerful Pan-Malayan Federation of Trade Unions—the CPM's main vehicle on the labour front—was outlawed along with its affiliates, including its Perak branch. Detention camps were set up in Ipoh, Klang, and elsewhere to house agitators and communist sympathizers, who then faced repatriation if they were not born in Malaya. Strikes ceased after some 6,000 people—mainly Chinese as well as a few hundred Indians—were deported in 1949 (Tan, 2020). Because of the impracticability of mass deportation, and after the communist victory and the declaration of the People's Republic of China by Mao Zedong on 1 October 1949,[71] when Chinese ports were temporarily closed to British ships, the repatriation programme tapered off later that year.

With increased insurgency incidents continuing to threaten Malaya's economic and political future, Britain quickly reinforced its military and police forces at great financial cost.[72] By the early 1950s, it had brought in many battalions and air force squadrons from Commonwealth countries, primarily Australia and New Zealand, as well as a Gurkha Rifles Regiment. Direct reinforcements came from those called up for National Service in the UK and Hong Kong. The Malay Regiment and Dayaks from Sarawak were also heavily involved in counter-insurgency operations.[73] British military forces, including the Royal Air Force, mounted a massive bombing campaign against the insurgents' hideouts, which proved effective at first, until the insurgents retreated deep into the jungle to conduct guerrilla warfare (Department of Information–Federation of Malaya, 1951).

The security situation remained serious, with the communists continuing their attacks from their jungle bases in all of Perak's districts, and elsewhere in Malaya, peaking in 1951. Chinese- and British-owned tin mines in the Kinta Valley and in other locations were frequently sabotaged, suffering huge damage, as the small security units employed to guard them were overrun. Some mining companies issued arms and ammunition to their staff so they could better protect themselves from insurgents. A scheme was proposed by members of the Perak Chinese Tin Mining Association to protect the mines using a mobile armed force of Chinese, funded by a levy of Straits$8 per picul on tin ore

---

71 The communist victory in China boosted the morale of the CPM, which 'began to believe that it was only a matter of time before Chinese troops would be on the way to help them' (Cloake, 1985, p. 195). A further boost came in 1950 when the British government recognized the new communist government in China.

72 Under Gurney's command, the police force expanded rapidly, led by British officers and sergeants, many of whom had previously served in Palestine until the British government withdrew its mandate. Templer later greatly strengthened police training and funding as well as the force's coordination with the military (Hack, 2022).

73 The *Orang Asli* on the peninsula were initially used by the CPM as couriers, sources of intelligence, and food suppliers, but from around 1952 were progressively won over by the British through the provision of medical and other basic services. The Department of Aborigines, previously managed at state level, was reorganized under federal authorities to improve coordination and service delivery (Short, 1975).

produced by mines seeking protection. In early 1952, Templer formed a large armed Chinese Home Guard in the Kinta Valley, incorporating Kuomintang sympathizers in Ipoh, Batu Gajah, and Kampar, to help defend the mines and root out the Min Yuen sympathizers (Cloake, 1985). This paid volunteer force prevented the MNLA from 'dominating the Kinta Valley area until the Emergency ended' (Comber, 2012, p. 57).

On rubber estates, thousands of trees were destroyed, and labour 'lines', smoke houses, and other buildings were burned. The cost to the estates of the damage inflicted by the insurgents between July and December 1951 is estimated at Straits$8.1 million, up from Straits$6.3 million in the same period of 1950 (Ho, 2006, p. 3). Communists attacked police stations and Chinese schools, destroyed railway stations, and burned down a village in the Sitiawan area, making 1,000 villagers homeless. The colonial administration imposed local curfews in response.

In October 1951, having suffered serious losses and with relatively limited resources to draw on because of the severe impact of the Briggs plan which weakened its links with the Min Yuen—the MNLA was vastly outnumbered militarily—the Central Committee of the CPM issued 'New Directives' to radically change strategy. It placed key assets deeper in the jungle, and although military action continued, the MNLA took a less violent approach. This included an end to the sabotaging of tin mines and plantations that had harmed the interests of workers and smallholders (Purcell, 1955). The CPM increased its own efforts to win 'hearts and minds', and its members endeavoured to embed themselves in the new settlements, the Chinese Home Guard, the civil service, and political parties. Yet, despite this change of approach, the government had seized the upper hand, and the number of violent incidents in Malaya declined from a peak of 6,082 in 1951 to 3,727 in 1952, and to only 1,170 in 1953 (Hack, 2022, p. 457).[74]

In 1953, Chin Peng and other members of the CPM Politburo sought and were granted refuge in southern Thailand, where new recruits were trained and from where food was smuggled across the border. At that time the CPM was unable to get direct material support from China (unlike the situation in Viet Nam, which shares a long land border with China). Although the CPM had its Min Yuen organization, trade union agents, and propaganda machine, it never fully succeeded in becoming a nationalist movement (Cloake, 1985).

In June 1955, Chin Peng requested a meeting with the Malayan authorities to negotiate an honourable settlement, and following the September 1955 general elections of the Federation of Malaya, an amnesty was declared by the newly

---

74 Reported incidents declined rapidly thereafter to only 190 in 1957 (Hack, 2022, p. 457). In 1958, a large group of CPM members surrendered in Teluk Anson.

elected Chief Minister Tunku Abdul Rahman, to try to end the conflict. Ahead of constitutional talks in London scheduled for January 1956, the British authorities agreed that Tunku could proceed, and peace negotiations were then held in Baling, Kedah, on 28–29 December 1955. At the Baling talks, the CPM demanded political recognition, freedom of movement, and an undertaking that any member who surrendered would not be detained.[75] In exchange it would lay down its arms and disband its forces once the federation secured control of its internal security from the British. Tunku Abdul Rahman rejected the CPM's proposals, insisting that all those who surrendered must be investigated, and the talks broke down (Tunku Abdul Rahman Putra, 1977).

On 31 July 1960, just under three years after Malaya's independence, and with the rate of serious violent incidents greatly reduced, the Emergency was officially ended by the Malayan government. Independence had undermined the CPM's anti-colonial rationale and weakened their cause. The CPM had ultimately been defeated by the vastly superior military strength of the British, coupled with their intelligence gathering, propaganda and public relations abilities and by the provision of services to the New Villages. The British had succeeded in protecting its huge business interests—the primary concern—and preventing communism from taking root in Malaya, but at enormous financial and human costs, with both sides having committed appalling atrocities. Normal life in Perak and much of Malaya had been seriously disrupted for several years, and the scars of the New Villages remained. The insurgency had sharpened community divides.[76]

Consequences of Resettlement

The most evident of the far-reaching consequences of resettlement during the Emergency was that it altered Malaya's human geographical landscape, especially in Perak, which had the largest squatter population. In 1950 alone, the state saw

---

75 Chin Peng, Chen Tien, and Rashid Maidin, senior members of the CPM's Central Committee, participated in the Baling peace negotiations held with Tunku Abdul Rahman, Tan Cheng Lock, President of MCA, and David Marshall, Singapore's Chief Minister. John Davis, who had entered Malaya during the Japanese occupation and worked closely with the MPAJA as part of Force 136, had joined the Malayan Civil Service and had served in many strategic positions, including as Butterworth's Senior District Officer. He welcomed the CPM delegation to the Baling talks, and after their failure he negotiated privately with Chin Peng but without success (Shennan, 2014).

76 With the end of the Emergency, the CPM regrouped and, in 1968, inspired by communist movements in China, Viet Nam, and elsewhere, continued its armed struggle against the Malaysian government from its base in southern Thailand. The CPM was still led by Chin Peng, exiled in Beijing since 1960, and received substantial financial support from China. After 21 years, and a second Emergency declared in 1968, a formal peace treaty between the CPM, Malaysia, and Thailand was signed in Hat Yai in 1989. By then the CPM had lost its support from China. A total of 1,188 armed CPM members surrendered, of whom 402 were ethnic Chinese and 77 were Malays from Malaysia, with the rest from Singapore and Thailand (Chin Peng, 2013, p. 491).

the resettlement of more than 95,000 squatters in 49 areas throughout Kinta, with many settlements added to existing small towns and villages. Most settlements were predominantly Chinese, though a handful in Batu Gajah and Malim Nawar were made up exclusively of Indian workers (Dobby, 1952). Relocation also gave rise to a degree of multiculturalism as villagers met individuals of different ethnic origins. Chinese villagers now had frequent contact with Malays and Indians who lived in adjacent villages. It seems that, though most interactions were occasional and casual, they were generally friendly (Nyce, 1973). However, the resettlement programme, which mainly targeted Chinese communities, led to some criticism by the Malays that Templer was pro-Chinese because of the high costs involved. Conversely, Purcell (1955) argued that as Chinese were the object of the campaigns, they were unfairly seen by other communities as the enemy of the state.

The New Villages were generally situated along main roads so that military and police forces could easily control them. It may have been some consolation to those living in the Villages that these locations provided better access to markets, and even to credit facilities, than the areas in which they had previously been squatting. Similarly, amenities that the squatters had not had access to before were available in most of the New Villages. And for the first time, some squatters also enjoyed title to the land on which they lived. The organization of squatters into responsible social entities allowed the growth of political sophistication within a framework determined by the British government, leading to a massive increase in Malayan citizenship and integration into the 'new Malaya' as London had also envisaged (Coates, 1992).

Recovery of Tin and Rubber, 1945–1950s

The cost to Britain of its support for supressing the insurgency was estimated at £56m per annum, with still other charges met by the Malayan government (Stockwell, 1984, p. 82). To fund counter-insurgency operations, the government imposed a corporation tax in Malaya of 20 per cent in 1947, raising it to 30 per cent in 1951.[77] The government also increased Malayan export duties, although to avoid damaging Anglo-American relations it found it necessary to forewarn the US of proposed tax increases (Treasury [T], 220/186, 1950–1951). Between 1951 and 1955, some Malayan mining firms were reportedly paying

---

77 This and similar fiscal impositions can be understood in the context of Britain having to shore up its financial reserves after the massive drain of the war, and restoring sterling to international convertibility (Hinds, 1999). Sterling had left the gold standard in 1931 and was no longer the leading currency of international trade. Ironically, however, with many Chinese businesses evading taxation, the burden of defence fell disproportionately on British corporations (White, 1998).

more in export duties and income tax than they were in dividends to share-holders (White, 1997), although there was no limitation on dividend pay-outs for profitable tin-mining and rubber companies. British shareholders were once again enjoying high dividends.

Tin's Tentative Recovery

Rehabilitation was much slower for the tin than the rubber industry after World War II (Lim, 1967), partly because of the scorched-earth policy, and partly because vital machine parts had been taken by the Japanese when they left.[78] Many claims were made by mining companies to the Colonial Office for war damage (Ministry of Aviation [AVIA], 55/218, 1947–1948).[79] Colonial policy once again supported British and Continental European mines, with priority for post-war financial aid given to those with greater capital spending and high-er expected profitability, rather than to those with a larger workforce. Close to 80 per cent of the financial aid given through low-interest loans was awarded to British and Continental European mining companies.

A report by Arthur Ditchfield Storke[80] estimated the cost of rehabilitating the dredging industry at around £3 to £4 million (T. 220/134, 1950–1951). Just after the war, the dredging mines had been forecast by the colonial administration to achieve much higher production than the other mines by 1949 (Krug, 1945). In practice, however, the dredging mines did not reach even 70 per cent of tar-geted production, whereas the Chinese-owned gravel-pump mines exceeded the targets by 1949. This was because, being less technologically advanced and much less affected by the British scorched-earth policy, the gravel-pump mines were quicker to get back into production. British-owned mines needed first to repair their dredges.

Malaya's tin production rose during the post-war global economic recov-ery, from just 8,000 tons in 1946 to a high of 58,000 tons in 1950. Its share of the world's tin production rose over the same period from less than 10 per cent to

---

78 The STC's smelter at Butterworth was rehabilitated and modernized only in 1955, and began operations with a production capacity of 55,000 tons. By then the smelter at Pulau Brani had become obsolete, while the Eastern Smelting Company's smelter in Penang had a production capacity of 65,000 tons.

79 In April 1948, the British government proposed that the total war damage claims should be to a maximum of £55 million, of which £35 million should be provided by Malaya, £10 million by the United Kingdom, and £10 million in reparations by Japan. After the Legislative Council and tin-mining companies expressed unhappiness over Britain's share, and in view of the increased burdens that Malaya had to bear after the Emergency was declared, its share was doubled to £20 million in May 1949 (T. 220/134, 1950/1951).

80 Storke was advisor to the Secretary of State for the Colonies on matters of rehabilitation, and was commis-sioned to survey the mining industry at the end of the Japanese occupation.

35 per cent—recovering to the 1940 figure. During the early post-occupation years, a significant proportion of the ore produced by Perak's mines came from women *dulang* washers, as it became easier to wash for tin illegally (Box 2.11, above). The number of *dulang* washers had increased after the Great Depression, and grew even more after the Japanese occupation. They formed an important component of Perak's mining labour, estimated at 14,000 between 1946 and 1950, when they produced an annual average of 2,000 tons of ore (Nim, 1953).

The Korean War, 1950–1953, increased tin demand, causing tin prices to skyrocket to over £1,000 per ton in 1951 on the back of the associated US stock-piling programme. This supported production at 56,000 to 57,000 tons a year until 1953. Cumulative export duties collected on tin rose to around Straits\$250 million between 1950 and 1953, up from Straits\$85.6 million between 1946 and 1949 (IBRD, 1955). Until 1938, duty collected on tin in the Federated Malay States was, on average, about 3.6 times higher than that collected on rubber, which was first subject to export duties in 1906. However, this trend reversed between 1947 and 1957. During this period, export duties collected on rubber were twice those collected on tin.

The tin boom ended after the Korean War, tarnishing the metal's prospects. By the second half of 1953, the price had fallen back to around 1949–1950 levels of £600 per ton. With excess production of over 40,000 tons in 1953, and as the US reached its stockpiling limit, it was necessary to re-establish a buffer stock and export controls to prevent a fall in tin prices below a minimum of £640 per ton (IBRD, 1955). The 1953 International Tin Agreement that ensued, which brought about the formation of the International Tin Council, was only enforced in 1956. It had the effect of reducing Malaya's average production to 50,000 tons a year between 1956 and 1960.

Beyond the International Tin Agreements, several other factors clouded the outlook for Malaya's tin industry. No new major tin fields had been discovered since 1930. This lent support to the view of the US International Materials Policy Commission of 1951, which estimated that tin production in Malaya would only be sustained for another 20 years before deposits grew close to exhaustion (International Tin Study Group, 1952). Further, secondary tin production[81] in the US climbed after World War II, and the supply of tin from China rose after 1955, meaning that Malaya's tin industry faced much stronger competition. Meanwhile, the Emergency still cast a lingering shadow. Tin production in the Federated Malay States never quite regained its 1940 peak.

---

81 Secondary tin is a substitute for primary tin obtained either from detinning plants through the treatment of tin-plate scrap or by re-using the tin content of bronze, solder, babbitt, and other alloys.

Rubber's Rebound

Rubber production throughout Malaya recovered quickly after the Japanese occupation. As with tin, prices also rose to record levels owing to the Korean War and the US stockpiling programme. However, the 1950s also saw the emergence and then prolific use of synthetic rubber. By 1955, synthetic rubber made up 59 per cent of the US's total rubber consumption (Lim, 1967). With generous government grants given to British and Continental European estates, high-yielding clones were replanted at record levels. But many smallholders refrained from replanting because of the high costs involved. While estates' productivity improved, moreover, this did not greatly benefit estate workers, and neither did the establishment of the National Union of Plantation Workers in 1954 (Jomo, 1990). Though it sought to encourage diversification within agriculture, the British government still saw rubber as a large export earner.

Decolonization, 1945–1957

World War II and the Japanese occupation marked the beginning of the end of British colonialism in Southeast Asia, heralding a more-than-decade-long march towards the full transfer of political power in Malaya. The war had caused Britain to lose its legitimacy as the country's 'protector'. Britain was also heavily indebted in the aftermath of war, and its policymakers were extremely aware of the country's very heavy financial investments in, and huge returns from, Malaya. British businesses and capital were behind most of Malaya's plantations and larger mining enterprises, and investment returns from the country helped to support general living standards in post-war Britain (Curtis, 2003).[82]

Planning for Malaya's eventual self-rule—though not, at this stage, its full political independence—had been under way in London in the twilight years of the war. But the heavy financial toll of the communist insurgency on Britain's and Malaya's economies, coupled with international pressures for decolonization, especially from the US, brought forward the envisaged date. To a degree, therefore, the insurgency achieved one of its aims of driving out the British after all.

While the seeds of Malay nationalism had surfaced in the 1920s and 1930s (Box 2.13, above), Malaya's anti-colonialist left-wing political parties—PKMM,

---

82 In 1957, the British government passed the United Kingdom Finance Act, 1957, which allowed companies designated as Overseas Trade Corporations to be exempt from UK company tax. This would provide a stimulus for UK investment in Malaya and similar territories (Cmnd. 451, 1957–1958).

led by Burhanuddin al-Helmy and Ishak Muhammad, with the radical Angkatan Pemuda Insaf (Awakened Youth Movement), led by Ahmad Boestamam—were the first to call for Malaya's independence after the end of the Japanese occupation (Abraham, 2006; Rashid Maidin, 2009). In December 1946, PKMM, alongside other parties and trade organizations, formed the Pan-Malayan Council of Joint Action (PMCJA) whose aims included self-government and citizenship for all in Malaya (Stockwell, 1979).

In February 1947, PKMM left PMCJA (later renamed the All-Malaya Council of Joint Action (AMCJA)) and together with other Malay political groups formed PUTERA (Pusat Tenaga Rakyat—Centre of People's Power) as a separate Malay front. In mid-1947, PUTERA and AMCJA—Malaya's first multi-ethnic coalition—argued that the draft 1948 constitution had been imposed without the people's full representation and presented as an alternative the *People's Constitutional Proposals*, which also gained the support of the CPM. The alternative proposals were rejected by the government as too radical.[83]

However, the nationalist cause was boosted under the leadership of Onn Jaafar, who founded the United Malays National Organisation (UMNO) in 1946 and became its first president. He championed Malay rights and led the fight against the Malayan Union, rallying opposition across the country with the aim of eventually achieving self-government. Partly because of the groundswell of support among the Malays, and partly because of it being anathema to parties of the left, UMNO became acceptable to the British in the drive towards independence.

Nationalism was slower to take hold in Malaya than in some Asian colonies, such as India, Indonesia, and Viet Nam. It was held back by a mix of social, economic, and political factors. These included the disparate histories of the constituent parts of Malaya, each of which had its own system of governance; greater loyalty among inhabitants to their individual states and rulers than to the wider country; preoccupation with containing the communist insurgents; the migrant character of some ethnic communities, with many having split national loyalties; differences in economic and social development, language, and religion across communities; antipathy between some communities; and the divide between the elite of all the communities and the rest of the population. The populations of the Malay and non-Malay communities were finely balanced in terms of size and, as Myrdal (1968, p. 158) observes, 'the Malays did not want British rule to end until they were in a better position, socially, economically, and politically, to hold their own against the Chinese'.

---

83 With the declaration of Emergency in 1948, many PUTERA-AMCJA leaders were arrested and either deported or jailed, and its affiliated organizations were banned (Syed Husin Ali, 2019).

One strand of the planning for self-rule was the decision for the colonial authorities and the Malayan elite to be more active in developing the emerging nation socio-economically by creating 'enabling' national institutions. Another was a belated recognition of the importance of fostering a spirit of national unity and common identity among the country's ethnic communities. Yet another strand was the granting of Malayan citizenship to members of all ethnic groups who met certain residential criteria. British policymakers saw these thrusts as aligned with the United Nations Charter of 1945, which the UK had been instrumental in drafting with the US, and which advocated 'respect for the principle of equal rights and self-determination of peoples' (United Nations, 2015, p. 37).

Malaya's First Elections

At the beginning of the 1950s, Gurney proposed, and Templer later endorsed, a timeline for elections, beginning with towns and municipalities, and progressing to the state and federal level. The Malay elite was hesitant about giving political rights to the migrant population, as it could undermine their community's special constitutional rights. Nevertheless, in September 1952, after much persuasion by the British administration, citizenship was granted to most non-Malays by the Legislative Council and endorsed by the Council of Rulers.

The 1951–1952 town and municipal council elections started this electoral process, beginning in George Town, Penang, a predominantly Chinese area. For the Kuala Lumpur municipal elections, UMNO formed a cross-communal alliance with the MCA, a Chinese party which was in the ascendancy, to win nine out of 12 seats, and this alliance was continued thereafter.[84] The alliance was created because of UMNO's fear of losing urban seats in Kuala Lumpur's election to the multiracial Independence of Malaya Party. This party was headed by Onn Jaafar, who had left UMNO when his proposal to make it a multiracial party was rejected by Tunku Abdul Rahman. The mutually beneficial alliance of UMNO and the MCA held together, and going beyond the level of towns and municipalities, they went on to contest and win state and federal elections, held over the period 1954–1955.

Federal elections, as championed by Tunku Abdul Rahman, now UMNO's president, were held in 1955. The Alliance, also now including the Malayan Indian

---

84 The MCA was formed in 1949, at the urging of Gurney, to represent non-communist Chinese interests and cooperate with the government. It was dominated by wealthy Straits Chinese and by leaders of Malaya's Kuomintang supporters.

Congress (MIC),[85] won 51 out of 52 seats, giving further momentum to the drive for independence.[86] An alliance of individual communal parties was not the preference of the British administration, who favoured a multiracial, non-communal, political grouping. The Alliance was, however, considered a moderate nationalist movement, and one that campaigned for independence within the framework of the constitution (Fernando, 2003). With assurance from the Alliance leaders that British economic interests in Malaya would be safeguarded, the British agreed to grant independence, which was declared on 31 August 1957. Compared with neighbouring Indonesia, Malaya's road to independence was relatively smooth.

Federation of Malaya: Consolidation of Centralized Powers

Discussions about the merits of devolving powers to the states versus increasing centralization, long a matter for debate between the colonial authorities and the state rulers, continued after the Japanese occupation. The maintenance of the authority and prestige of the Malay rulers had been a fundamental principle of British colonial policy. However, ideas for a political union of the Malay states conflicted with this principle. Samuel Herbert Wilson, Permanent Under-Secretary of State for the Colonies (1925–1933), had earlier argued that the maintenance of 'indirect rule will probably prove the greatest safeguard against the political submersion of the Malays which would result from the development of popular government on western lines' (Cmd. 4276, 1933, p. 34). Sultan Abdul Aziz Shah of Perak expressed his concern that the rulers and their council would lose all real power under the new constitutional proposals (Smith, 1995). Although the idea of a Malayan Union with stronger centralization created fears among the state rulers—especially those from the Unfederated Malay States—the colonialists still tried to impose this political arrangement as a first step towards self-government (Purcell, 1955).

The Federation of Malaya was formed in 1948, less than two years after the hurried and failed attempt by the British administration to impose a strong centralized government in the form of the Malayan Union. It comprised the nine peninsular Malay states and two of the former Straits Settlements—Penang and Malacca. Singapore was excluded from the federation because its population was predominantly Chinese and because of its strategic importance to the

---

85 Unlike UMNO and the MCA, the MIC—formed in 1946 by John Aloysius Thivy—comprised mainly the Indian working class.

86 The Federal Legislative Council had 98 seats altogether, of which 52 were elected, and the others appointed by the British High Commissioner. Only a small proportion of non-Malays—11 per cent of Chinese and less than 5 per cent of Indians—registered to vote in the 1955 federal election (Cheah, 2002, p. 30).

British administration. While some limited powers were devolved to the constituent states under the new federal constitution, in practice the creation of the Federation of Malaya represented the beginning of a new, highly centralized system of democratic governance and planning (Box 2.16).[87] Perak—until then the prosperous commercial centre of the four Federated Malay States, and having retained some significant devolved powers—was to become politically and economically sidelined as a decision-making state in the federation.

Decolonization thus gave birth to the modern state, and 'the Emergency made it bigger, more centralized and powerful than it would otherwise have been' (Harper, 1999, p. 359). Government development spending became increasingly tilted in favour of national political priorities—but Perak was not a priority.

Box 2.16   **Emergence of highly centralized planning**

The period of decolonization also saw the emergence of British-led centralized economic and social development planning for the new Federation of Malaya, with the first Draft Development Plan, 1950–1955, presented to the Legislative Council in July 1950 (Federation of Malaya, 1950). The plan had three main themes: trade and industry, national resources and utilities, and social services. It emphasized the need to diversify economic activities in agriculture towards palm oil—some estates in Perak had already started to transition from rubber to oil palm cultivation. At that time, oil palm cultivation was estate-focused, and smallholders were unable to convert readily to it because of the large start-up costs.

The economy—especially in Perak and in Malaya's other west-coast states—had reached a fairly advanced stage compared with nearly all other countries in Asia in terms of both per capita income and structure. Power, transport, and communications were reasonably well developed, a foundation for industry had been established, and there was a wide pool of skills and enterprise to hand. Standards of public administration were high and institutional patterns of commerce and finance were well advanced. By 1955, however, with the end of the post-war economic boom after the Korean War, the federation's financial position had deteriorated owing to declining export revenues, the heavy financial burden of containing the communist insurgency, and rising spending, especially for social services.

(Continued)

---

87 See The Federation of Malaya Agreement, 1948, signed by Gerald Gent, the British High Commissioner, and the nine rulers of the Malay states (Malayan Government, 1948).

A major international study was conducted in 1954 by the International Bank for Reconstruction and Development (IBRD) at the request of the Federation of Malaya, the Crown Colony of Singapore, and the UK government. The study argued that successful formulation and execution of development policy must be planned and implemented by a centralized institution (IBRD, 1955). These findings formed the basis for the First Malaya Plan, 1956–1960 (see Part 3).

The plan still regarded rubber and tin—which together accounted for 98 per cent of export duties—as the pillars of the Malayan economy (Federation of Malaya, 1956). The plan's emphasis was on how to develop Malaya using federal revenue to finance development programmes. Once the plan was approved at the federal level, federal ministries would implement the programmes within budget allocations. States would only be informed of the federal decision. Although Perak would benefit from the plan's programmes—through irrigation and drainage projects in Lower Perak and Kerian, and substantial allocations for its education and healthcare systems, which were still the most advanced in Malaya—the state government was now distant from centralized decision-making and less in control of its own development path.

Population Changes and Onset of Outward Migration, 1931–1957

Migration into Perak had slowed dramatically during and after the Great Depression. Large numbers of Chinese and Indians had been repatriated between 1930 and 1932, and the imposition of immigration controls had sharply slowed the rate of population growth (Figure 2.20, upper panel). The Immigration Restriction Ordinance, 1930, allowed the colonial authorities to regulate the inflow of lower-skilled immigrants at times of emergency. In August of that year, monthly quotas were set on the numbers of Chinese males permitted to enter; Indians were still free to enter because they were British subjects. This ordinance was superseded by the Aliens Ordinance, 1933, which imposed even stricter regulations, and established a new Department of Immigration to regulate and register foreign migrants. Chinese women, Chinese children under 12 years of age, and British subjects were exempt.

Figure 2.20 How Perak's population changed between the Great Depression and independence

The growth in population[a] slowed, and while Chinese still formed the largest ethnic group, the Malay share began to increase

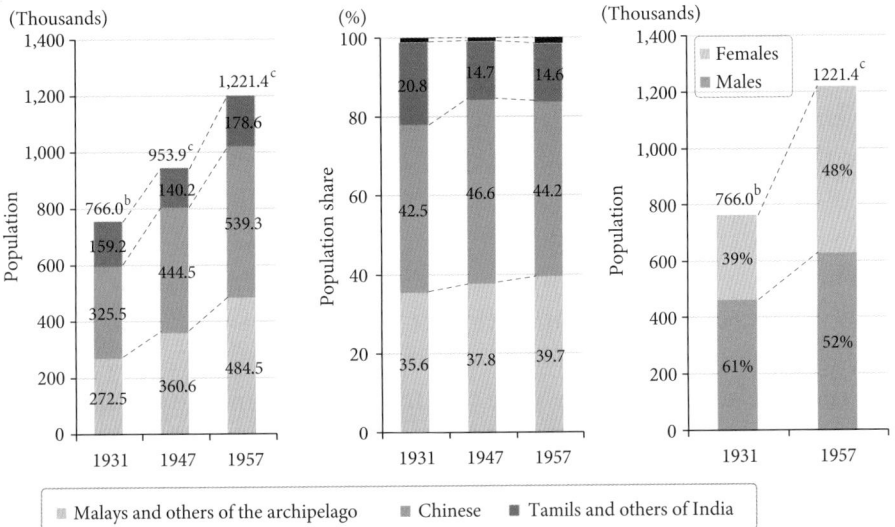

District shares of population changed little, with just under one-third in Kinta

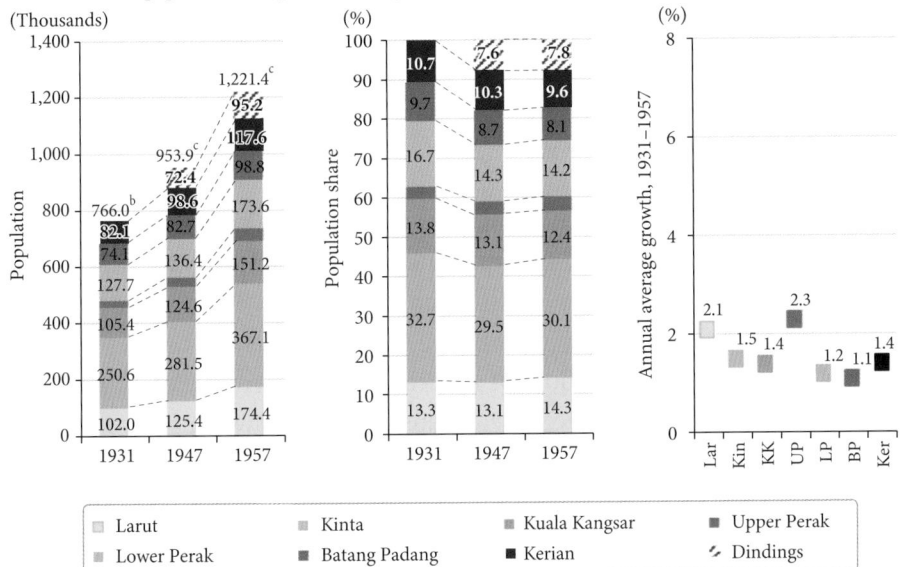

Sources of data: Vlieland (1932); Del Tufo (1949); Fell (1960).

Notes: [a] The population of other communities was 8,764 in 1931, 8,622 in 1947, and 18,959 in 1957.

[b] Excludes the Dindings, which was part of the Straits Settlements until 1935.

[c] Includes the Dindings.

Perak's population grew from 766,000 to 1.2 million between 1931 and 1957. During this period, and especially in the 1930s, many overseas Chinese women entered the state. Government policy sought to improve the sex ratio of the Chinese population, and Chinese women faced no entry restrictions. By 1957 the sex ratio was much more balanced than in 1931 (Figure 2.20, upper panel) and, through marriage, this more balanced sex ratio helped to increase the number of families among this community.[88] Perak's population was now starting to grow through natural increase—that is, through births exceeding deaths—precipitated by steadily declining mortality rates, especially between 1947 and 1957. The population of every district in Perak grew between 1931 and 1957, though not nearly as spectacularly as they did during the commodity boom of the early decades of the 20th century (Figure 2.20, lower panel).

Multiple factors had affected the ethnic composition of Perak's population. Crucially, ethnic Chinese were the dominant community at the dawn of Malaya's independence. In 1957, the Chinese share was 44 per cent, down slightly from its peak of 47 per cent in 1947, due to the strict entry quotas for males and some net outmigration during the Japanese occupation and the Emergency. The Indian population's share fell more sharply, from 21 per cent in 1931 to just 15 per cent in 1947, reflecting the high level of repatriation that occurred during the Great Depression, as well as the impact of forced migration to work on the Siam–Burma railway during the Japanese occupation. Consequently, the Malay share of the state's population rose from 36 per cent in 1931 to 40 per cent in 1957 (Figure 2.20, upper panel).

Although Perak experienced massive inflows of migrants in the 50 years leading up to the Japanese occupation, including some net inflows from other states in the peninsula, the situation began to change with the post–World War II political and economic crises. The 1947 population census showed that there was a small net outflow of lifetime migrants from Perak, and this had increased by the time of the 1957 census. This outflow mainly comprised people moving to the neighbouring state of Selangor as well as to Singapore (Figure 2.21), and foreshadowed a trend that set in at much higher rates after independence.

---

88 After the decline of China's silk industry during the years of the Great Depression, nearly 200,000 Chinese women, mostly peasants and factory workers, migrated to work in Malaya between 1933 and 1938 to try to help support their families in China. Many were recruited as *dulang* washers (Nim, 1953).

Figure 2.21 **By 1957, Perak had a net outflow of lifetime migrants**

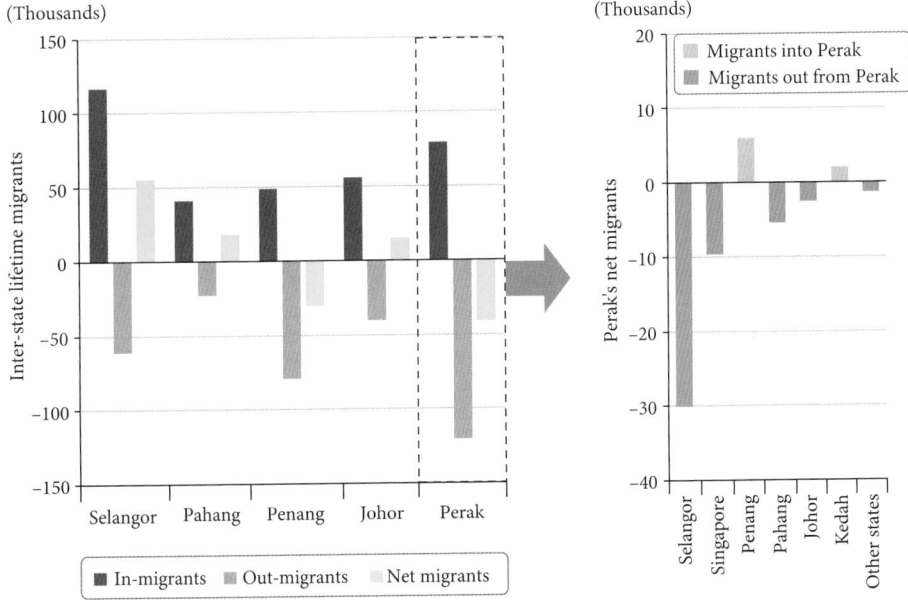

Source of data: Fell (1960).

Looking Back—and Forward

Perak's incipient prosperity in the mid-19th century was curtailed by brutal conflicts between rival Chinese clans and feuding local aristocratic Malay chiefs. But with political stability and the new state institutions put in place by the British colonial administration, Perak's economy was progressively integrated into the global economy during some 80 years of tightening colonial rule. Perak benefited from favourable economic geography—ready access by river to natural, expandable ports, and a tropical climate that supported commercial agriculture. Colonial policies capitalized on those conditions, helping transform Perak's economy from one dependent on subsistence agriculture to one that was dynamic, export-led, and natural-resource-based.

Tin, and later rubber, formed the bedrock of Perak's prosperity. The pursuit of these industries led the colonial authorities to open up and develop territory in the state that had, until this point, been almost entirely covered by lush virgin forest, much of which had hardly been touched by human activity. Perak's successful, world-leading natural resource industries developed following a comprehensive package of initiatives in land registration, capital and labour mobilization, and investments in public goods, especially for security. Policies that favoured British and Continental European private interests were reinforced by the change in governance structure when Perak became part of the Federated Malay States in 1896. This strengthened the executive power of the federal government to carry out reforms supportive of colonial interests, while inexorably weakening the powers of Perak's sultan and resident.

Only limited efforts were made to address the economic dualism that existed between the export-oriented side of Perak's economy and the traditional low-income and low-productivity sectors. Such dualism was strengthened by legislation enacted by the British that sought to entrench Malays in *padi* farming to feed the state's growing population. There was little attempt to diversify the economy to include more processing activities based on natural resources, to move towards downstream development, or even to progress towards light manufacturing, leveraging the state's natural-resource wealth. Such path dependency—the natural resource curse—would prove difficult to overcome.

Globalization: Perak's Rise, Relative Decline, and Regeneration. Sultan Nazrin Shah, Oxford University Press. © Sultan Nazrin Shah (2024). DOI: 10.1093/oso/9780198897774.003.0016

Sustainability of Economic Development

Perak's economic development—and by extension that of Malaya—was the result of its integration into global trade and investment networks. The production and export of tin, and later natural rubber, which served the needs of the Western manufacturing industries, provided the catalyst for Perak's substantial GDP growth and the emergence of its market economy. But overdependence on a narrow primary-commodity base, operating within a globalized trading environment, created economic vulnerability and instability, with tin and rubber subject to wildly fluctuating demand and high price volatility. Such volatility hurt incomes and hence human well-being, despite the imposition of restriction schemes for rubber and tin to stabilize prices. Since the rubber industry employed many more workers than the tin industry, volatility in rubber prices had far greater impact.

British capital dominated the growth of Perak's commodity industries in the first half of the 20th century. Innovative, world-class, capital-intensive technology modernized production and transformed the ownership structure of the state's tin-mining industry. To encourage capital-intensive and technology-focused companies, new mining land leases were granted only where advanced technology and equipment would be used. The reforms to mining labour regulations and colonial policy biases largely removed the advantage that Chinese-owned mines had previously enjoyed. Similarly, the rubber restriction schemes were skewed to benefit large British and Continental European estates at the expense of Malay and Chinese smallholdings.

The exploitation of Perak's natural resources also came with ecological and economic costs, with lasting environmental impacts on the state's landscape. While private—and often foreign—companies reaped tremendous financial benefits, Perak suffered huge social costs from deforestation, contamination of fertile topsoil, siltation of rivers, and floods. Local populations suffered great hardship when their livelihoods, homes, and meagre infrastructure were destroyed or greatly damaged. Although some enlightened British administrators emphasized the value of preserving natural resources beyond their immediate economic use, passing enabling laws and developing institutions to support professional forestry, drainage, and flood management, most of these efforts were ineffective. Foreign investors, meanwhile, derived huge profits from Perak's industries, largely repatriating the windfall from exploiting the state's natural resources and failing to reinvest in new and more diversified economic activities.

After three and a half years of Japanese occupation and more than a decade of communist-led internal conflict, it was perhaps inevitable that business and job opportunities should have diminished, while capital and labour outflows began to gather pace. During the post-war period of decolonization, the British administration sought to protect Britain's substantial investments in Perak and elsewhere in Malaya, and to ensure a politically compliant new order that would enable British businesses to continue to exploit Malayan economic resources. Yet, already, economically viable tin deposits had been heavily depleted and synthetic rubber had begun to challenge natural rubber, though these commodities would remain important to Perak's economy after independence.

Migration and Human Settlements

Perak's economy was also enmeshed in another major dimension of globalization—international labour mobility. Migrant workers were crucial in driving growth as envisaged by the British authorities. The state's mineral- and plantation-based export-led economy was highly dependent on inflows of migrant labour—Chinese, Indians, and Malays—until the 1930s, owing largely to its very small local population. In boom times many thousands were recruited, while in times of economic depression thousands were repatriated.

Differing patterns of settlement, determined largely along ethnic and occupational lines, were established as part of Perak's pathway to economic modernization, reflecting divergencies in labour productivity. The growth of small mining and port towns, which mushroomed throughout Larut and Kinta, attracted a predominantly Chinese population. The dwellings of tin miners and Indian estate workers and their families were spartan and offered access to only basic services and facilities. Malay subsistence farmers and smallholders, as well as non-Malay smallholders, lived in rural villages with minimal social infrastructure. By contrast, the elite British and Continental Europeans, *towkays*, local government officers, financiers, and professionals lived mainly in the prosperous and vibrant metropolitan towns of Ipoh, Taiping, and Kuala Kangsar, where the level of economic and social development was a world away from that in rural villages.

Almost a century of huge migrant inflows fundamentally changed Perak's demographic composition, giving the state a distinctive multicultural identity, with the Malay population at less than 40 per cent on the eve of independence. This was the lowest of any of the peninsula's 11 states, except Selangor and Penang, and would pose political, social, and economic challenges to the state post-independence. Similarly, the varying patterns of settlement were associated with vastly different levels of education, healthcare systems, and infrastructure (including transport), which entrenched inequalities between Perak's communities, slowing post-independence efforts to create a unified state.

In short, natural resources were a mixed blessing for Perak. They generated great prosperity in booming tin-towns, which generally saw all-round welfare gains in living standards, especially during commodity price booms. Indeed, Perak's GDP per capita was some 60 per cent higher than Malaya's during the 1920s and 1930s. The British and Chinese investor class benefited most.

Yet, on the eve of independence, large inequalities in living standards were common within and among communities, including access to education, healthcare, clean water, and safe sanitation. Perak—now part of the Federation of Malaya, and increasingly distant from the centralized processes determining planning, decision-making, and government expenditure—was destined to face formidable hurdles in tackling these challenges in the post-independence era.

PART 3A

The Decline of Tin and Rubber—Continued British Economic Dominance

Ipoh, Perak's
emerging commercial capital,
early 20th century

Globalization and Perak's Changing Fortunes

For much of the 20th century, tin and rubber were the drivers of Perak's export-led economy. Among the states on the Malay peninsula, Perak was by far the largest producer of tin, and one of the leaders in rubber exports, two primary commodities for which Western industrialization had created massive demand. Both industries were heavily supported by British finance and were steered by British-dominated multinational trading companies, or agency houses. These institutions epitomized early globalization, providing services in management, investment, finance, shipping, and other business and intermediary areas. These well-networked trading companies helped to spread ideas, institutions, and technological innovations that exerted a powerful influence on local and international policy, and indeed set the terms on which international commerce was conducted.

At independence in 1957, Perak was still the country's commercial capital despite growing economic rivalry from neighbouring Selangor. It was perhaps Malaya's largest economy measured in GDP, and by the metric of GDP per capita was one of the richest states. Revenues from tin and rubber had allowed the state government to invest in and build some of the most advanced economic and social infrastructure of the newly formed nation. Perak's historical budget surpluses had also supported fiscal transfers to other less developed states.

Malaysia's post-independence rise towards upper-middle-income status was closely tied to its deeper integration with global markets. The country has made remarkable strides in terms of job creation, real income growth, and reduction in extreme poverty. However, deeper integration with international markets has benefited some Malaysian states much more than others.

Perak—the first state to be drawn into the globalized trading world—has fared less favourably since independence than its peers, despite being one of the wealthiest and most urbanized states in the country at the moment it entered

Globalization: Perak's Rise, Relative Decline, and Regeneration. Sultan Nazrin Shah, Oxford University Press. © Sultan Nazrin Shah (2024). DOI: 10.1093/oso/9780198897774.003.0017

nationhood. In the first few decades after 1957, Perak's continuing reliance on exports of natural resources, as well as its exposure to swings in global demand and its vulnerability to competition from other sources of supply of tin and rubber—the collapse of tin itself having been partly the result of globalization—left it trailing some of the peninsula's other states that had benefited more from globalization in the manufacturing sector (Box 3.1).

Economic growth is strongly influenced by the interaction between physical geography, technological innovation, and the policies of international, national, and state institutions (Sachs, 2020). These factors, along with Perak's initial conditions, were critical in determining the trajectory of the state's economic development after independence.

Box 3.1   Perak gets left behind

Historically, economic activity has often developed in circular patterns around urban centres—the so-called von Thunen rings (Hall, 1966). These rings, however, tend to be characterized by markedly different levels of economic development. Productivity tends to be higher in densely populated areas than in peripheral ones, as do real incomes. Productivity typically declines with increased distance from urban centres and markets, a pattern repeated globally (World Bank, 2009). As countries urbanize and density increases, spatial inequalities widen.

Malaysia's spatial development reflects some of these general observations about how the forces of *concentration* and *dispersion* evolve as nations develop. Physical geography played an important role in defining the spatial structure of the peninsula up until industrialization took off. Thereafter, as the country industrialized, and as service activity mushroomed, *agglomeration externalities* conferred advantages on selected localities, reconfiguring opportunities and widening spatial inequalities.

In the 1970s, as Malaysia's export-oriented industrialization progressed and the service sector grew, the influence of geography on the shape of the spatial economy began to wane. Industries were now required to be close to trained and skilled workers and to suppliers, and import-substituting industries also needed to be near local markets. Agglomeration and density took on added significance, and urbanization accelerated. New industrial activities—particularly those tied to fast-growing global markets—were increasingly attracted to Penang, to Selangor, and to Johor and its environs. The creation of tax-free zones and other inducements to locate in these centres helped to accelerate the spatial concentration of economic activity, while putting other areas at further disadvantage.

The once-vibrant tin towns of Perak faltered in the 1970s and 1980s, with Batu Gajah, Gopeng, Kampar, and Tapah in the Kinta Valley being particularly affected, reflecting the fortunes of the mining industry. Economically, some areas stagnated, and others went into decline, shedding population. Perak's scattered townships simply did not offer the scale, diversity, and connectivity needed to attract new industries. Even as recently as 2010, roughly half of the state's manufacturing activity remained resource-based and served domestic markets—including food production, rubber processing, and the processing of metallurgical and non-metallurgical minerals, and of iron and steel (Athukorala and Narayanan, 2017). While some international electronic manufacturers found the state's fiscal and other inducements attractive, these activities focused largely on standardized, low-value-added assembly, with many firms based near the state's northern border with Penang.

As Malaysia grew, economic activity became further concentrated in the sprawling conurbations of Selangor and Kuala Lumpur. In the process, Perak became a victim of locational disadvantage, losing out to Selangor and Johor to the south and Penang to the north.

*   *   *

Part 3A analyses how Perak responded to the manifold challenges of globalization after independence: tin and rubber no longer formed the bedrock of Perak's prosperity, palm oil displaced rubber, and laissez-faire policies steered the economy in the decade-plus period after independence in 1957.

The first section recalls that tin remained important for Perak's economy after independence, but began to decline from the 1970s despite the initial success of the International Tin Agreements (ITAs) in minimizing price instability. Underlying tensions between rich consumer countries and lower-income producers began to surface after the US joined the fifth ITA, 1976–1982, and prevented the net transfer of resources to producer countries. Multiple factors conspired to hasten tin's decline. The aftermath of the 1985 tin crash devastated Perak's tin towns, causing great suffering among mining workers, their families, and the communities that depended on their earnings.

The second section looks at the boom in Perak's rubber industry after independence and explores the circumstances of its decline towards the end of the 1980s. Slower industrialization in Perak meant that rubber remained more important in this state than in other parts of the peninsula, so that when rubber went into decline, the impacts of this were also more pronounced. Similar in intent to the ITAs, the International Natural Rubber Agreements (INRAs), while preventing a freefall in prices, mainly benefited the interests of rubber consumers rather than producers. Estate rubber led the decline in Perak, with smallholders exiting the sector more slowly. The spectacular rise of palm oil in the 1980s, with the acreage of oil palm overtaking that of rubber and palm oil production doubling, sealed rubber's decline.

The third section assesses how the laissez-faire approach to economic management, adopted by the British administration during colonial rule, broadly continued up to 1970, but with the development goals of Perak's state government now driven by federal Malayan/Malaysian five-year plans. In this period, the economic interests of a political alliance between the upper-class elites of the three main ethnic groups were closely tied to those of British and locally owned mining and rubber-plantation companies. These dynamics served to limit government ambitions in national economic planning. Despite real progress towards building a stronger and more diversified economy, there were persisting issues of high unemployment, absolute poverty, and uneven quality of life, both in Perak and elsewhere in Malaysia. The ethnic riots that broke out after the May 1969 general election radically changed the country's political, economic, and social direction.

Tin—Slump, Recovery, and Ultimate Collapse, 1957–1990

Perak's tin industry, which had been so crucial for the state's and the country's prosperity during the British colonial era, never regained its former pre-eminence as a source of income and export earnings after national independence, and by the late 1990s had faded into insignificance. Reserves in Perak's traditional tin-mining areas had been seriously depleted, and with land-use restrictions placing tight limits on prospecting, there were few major new discoveries. Tin substitutes also became available globally at comparable and even lower prices.

In this 'long decade' after independence, Perak still accounted for almost 60 per cent of Malaysia's and around 15 to 25 per cent of the world's tin output. The sector remained dependent on volatile global demand, and its fate was tied to the policies of the six post–World War II ITAs negotiated by major tin producer and consumer countries operating under the ITC. Unlike the pre-war ITAs which, although heavily influenced by the UK, were established between producer countries alone, the new structures brought tin-producing developing countries together with tin-consuming developed countries (initially, 6 of the former and 14 of the latter), thus giving the consumer countries a powerful voice.[1] At first, from around 1956, the ITAs sought to ensure that there were no excessive fluctuations in the tin price; this was to be done by guaranteeing the limits within which prices could move, while also seeking to ensure adequate tin supplies and to secure a price consistent with maintaining mining employment in producer countries, so as to support their development. From the third ITA, 1966–1971, however, the emphasis was firmly on price stabilization.

---

[1] The ITC was established by the ITA of 1954 that came into force in July 1956. The 6 producer countries were the Belgian Congo (now the Democratic Republic of the Congo), Bolivia, Indonesia, Malaysia, Nigeria, and Thailand; and of the 14 consumer countries the UK (also still a small tin producer) was the leading player. A two-thirds majority was required to pass motions on important policy matters.

Globalization: Perak's Rise, Relative Decline, and Regeneration. Sultan Nazrin Shah, Oxford University Press. © Sultan Nazrin Shah (2024). DOI: 10.1093/oso/9780198897774.003.0018

Demand for tin, as for any other commodity, is subject to global economic conditions. The ITC sought to maintain price stability by controlling global supply using export quotas, and by maintaining buffer stocks. The latter was controlled by a buffer-stock manager at the ITC, headquartered at the centre of the international tin market in London (Box 3.2). Export quotas were used to manage large price fluctuations—with quantities determined by the ITC and distributed across the six producing member-countries according to a set formula—while buffer stocks were used to manage smaller ones. The price range maintained by the cartel comprised the ceiling price (with its own price range), the floor price (with its own price range), and the range between the ceiling and floor prices.

Box 3.2 **International commodity agreements: How they regulated the international terms of trade**

Frequent changes in world demand for primary products led to disruptive fluctuations in their prices. To regulate prices and the terms on which commodities were traded internationally, governments of producing and consuming countries drew up international commodity agreements (ICAs). Apart from the ITAs and the INRAs, in which Malaysia was a prominent participant, there were also agreements covering cocoa, coffee, sugar, and wheat. Additionally, there were several less ambitious agreements, generally limited to information collection and dissemination, market promotion, and research.

The declared objective of most ICAs was to stabilize prices and thereby reduce volatility in producer incomes. When the United Nations Conference on Trade and Development (UNCTAD, 1976, p. 1) was formed in 1964, ICAs came under its auspices. They were part of the Integrated Programme for Commodities, a key component of the 'New International Economic Order', which sought to transfer resources from the developed to the developing world. ICAs were seen as an important vehicle for achieving this objective. UNCTAD Resolution 93(IV) aimed to stabilize commodity prices around levels that would be 'remunerative and just to producers and equitable to consumers' (UNCTAD, 1976, p. 3). The remit of ICAs thus went further than commodity price *stabilization*—the *level* of prices also had to be 'just' and 'equitable'.

Buffer-stock intervention
The International Natural Rubber Organization only used buffer stock adjustments to stabilize prices; the ITC, established in 1956, also used export controls, although it increasingly favoured buffer stocks. During the first three post–World War II ITAs

(1956–1971), the buffer-stock manager could only buy when the tin market price was below the prescribed floor price range, but in later agreements the manager could also sell tin when the price rose as high as or higher than the ceiling price (World Bank, 1981).

For both commodities, floor and ceiling prices were set either side of a 'long-run equilibrium' price. If the price fell below the floor, the buffer-stock manager would add to the buffer, thus reducing supply to the market to prevent prices from falling further. If the price exceeded the ceiling, the buffer-stock manager would run down the buffer, increasing the supply to moderate further price increases. In this way, supply to the market could be adjusted to help mute the effects on prices of production shocks and changes to global demand, thus stabilizing the incomes of producers. For rubber, the buffer-stock manager was obliged to act by reducing/increasing the buffer stock if the market price was more than 20 per cent above/below the estimated long-run equilibrium price. The price range for tin was narrower, at 15 per cent (Gilbert, 1995).

The case for a 'public' buffer stock managed by an ICA buffer-stock manager was that 'private' stocks managed separately in each country would not be enough to stabilize prices. If the future price of stocks carried forward was uncertain, risk aversion might lead individual countries to underinvest in buffer stocks. There would then be a strong case for the ICA to set up an additional, collective buffer stock anyway, and so it made sense to establish public buffer stocks from the outset. When there are forward markets—as for rubber and tin—this uncertainty over the price of stocks carried forward is removed. Buffer-stock management is difficult, however. It entails:

- *Updating the stabilization range as the long-run stabilization price level changes over time.* With tin, the ITA had no effective mechanism for revising the price support range and, over time, the range became out of touch with market prices—a key factor in the collapse of the sixth ITA in 1985. Although still not without its challenges, rubber price stabilization was managed more effectively. The INRA stabilization band was updated if the average Daily Market Indicator Price of the Kuala Lumpur, London, New York, and Singapore cash prices was above the upper or below the lower intervention price over a six-month period, or if buffer stock sales or purchases exceeded a specified amount over a six-month period (Gilbert, 1995).
- *Limiting price rises once the buffer stock is exhausted.* Buffer-stock management is more effective in limiting price falls by adding to the buffer than in curtailing price spikes by reducing it.
- *Maintaining enough capital to finance the buffer stock, especially during lengthy periods of low prices.* Funding came mainly from compulsory contributions by ICA members, but the buffer-stock manager could also borrow funds when required. The unsustainable cost of funding its tin buffer stock was a major factor in the collapse of the ITA.

(Continued)

Export controls

The mechanism adopted to stabilize prices through direct controls on member producers' exports—adopted by the ITAs but not the INRAs—faced several challenges:

- *Gaining the support of major consuming countries to control exports.* The 1973 success of the oil producers' cartel—the Organization of the Petroleum Exporting Countries (OPEC)—encouraged tin and rubber producers to organize themselves independently of consuming nations, although there is little evidence that these organizations raised prices in the way that OPEC did.
- *Controlling either production or exports.* This presupposes that governments can do so. Because they are likely to find it easier to control exports, production will simply add to stocks held by producers. The difference between export controls and buffer-stock mechanisms lies in *who* holds the stocks and at *whose* cost.
- *Ensuring compliance by individual producers.* Individual producers are tempted to maintain or increase output when prices increase as a result of other producers cutting their output. There is also a temptation to use smuggling to bypass export controls, an issue which at times was rampant.

Limits of ICA effectiveness

In addition to the structural flaws outlined above, the lack of participation by other major consuming countries—notably the US and the Soviet Union—and producer countries—Bolivia, Brazil, Canada, China, and Peru—severely weakened the ITA's effectiveness. Without more complete coverage, the ITA 'was essentially subsidizing the production of non-members' by guaranteeing and maintaining prices above the floor as non-members added to supply (McFadden, 1986, p. 825). For the ITA, Hillman (2010) noted that the only consuming countries that maintained long-term membership were those in Western Europe along with Canada, India, and Japan. The dramatic collapse of the sixth ITA in 1985 persuaded the developed world that international commodity price stabilization was unfeasible. As Gilbert (1995, p. 2) asserts, 'commodity market control sits uneasily in a world in which all markets (primary, manufacturing, labour) are becoming increasingly competitive'. At best, the promise of ICAs was only partially fulfilled and price levels were often far from 'just' for producer countries.

Until the tin-market collapse of 1985 (discussed below), the ITAs were fairly successful in keeping prices within prescribed ranges (Thoburn, 1994a). However, producer country members were forced to cut production in line with export quotas, and at times mines had to close temporarily, or were even driven to bankruptcy, leading to local unemployment and hardship. As the world's largest tin producer, Malaysia—and particularly Perak—was hit hard by the ITC's export restrictions. There were also challenges when prices rose and/or export quotas were lifted, with many mining operators struggling to resume or increase their production in the short run (Geer, 1970). The counterfactual of what would have happened had tin prices and supply been freely determined by market conditions is, of course, unknown, but maintaining tin prices within their target range undoubtedly came at a cost to producer country members.

The price-management operations of the ITC were complicated by two issues (Raffaelli, 2009). First was the growing volume of tin being sold in European markets by non-member producing countries—primarily the Soviet Union, Brazil, and China. Second was the large episodic sales of tin by the US, from the stockpile of critical and strategic materials it had established during the Korean War. Because it did not want to be constrained in managing this stockpile, the US was unwilling to join the ITAs. It did become a one-time member of the fifth agreement, 1976–1981, when it sought to limit any increase in the price range.[2] Despite its agreement with the ITC not to engage in disruptive stockpile sales, the periodic large sales by the US did conflict with the objectives of the ITA, causing discontent among members.

These two issues, alongside weaknesses in the ITC's price mechanism and tin smuggling, were the main factors that led to the failure of the sixth and final ITA, 1982–1989.[3] The collapse of the tin market in 1985, coupled with the depletion of Perak's economically accessible deposits, led to the eventual demise of the state's tin industry.

Between 1957 and 1990, Perak's tin production went through three broad and volatile phases, with ITAs playing a major role in determining production levels (Figure 3.1):

Slump, recovery, and growth, 1957–1971. Following a severe global recession in 1957, Perak's tin production expanded to reach a peak in 1971, amid steadily increasing tin prices. Malaysia remained the world's largest tin producer, with Perak producing about 61 per cent of national output, and about a fifth of global supply.

Gradual decline, 1972–1981. Production began to contract, despite fast-rising tin prices, as Perak's readily accessible tin deposits were gradually exhausted and mining costs increased. Tin production rebounded only marginally

---

2 As a member, the US felt that it was unable to sufficiently influence changes to the ITC. Bolivia also left after the fifth ITA, but Australia joined the sixth ITA as a tin-producing country member.

3 Although the ITA collapsed in 1985, it struggled on until 1989. The ITC ended export controls in March 1986, after which the international tin market was managed by UNCTAD and the Association of Tin Producing Countries. The ITC grappled with lawsuits by creditors until the ITA expired on 30 June 1989. Creditors managed to recoup about 40 per cent of their claims (Mallory, 1990).

in the late 1970s, again despite high prices. Nevertheless, by 1981 Perak still accounted for 57 per cent of national production, but its contribution to global output had fallen to 17 per cent, from a peak of 24 per cent in 1971.

Steep output decline and tin-market collapse, 1981–1990. In a turbulent market, production tumbled to its lowest level since independence. In 1985, with the sector hit once again by a global recession while constrained by export quotas, the ITC collapsed. Although Perak still dominated Malaysia's greatly diminished national production, it was no longer one of the main global producers, accounting for 11 per cent of the world's output in 1990, and a mere 1.7 per cent by 2000.

Slump, Recovery, and Growth, 1957–1971

Slump and Recovery

During the Korean War, the US began to create strategic stockpiles of tin and other minerals, as well as natural resources, to ensure their availability in case of a prolonged conflict. This helped to generate a moderate tin boom, and by 1955 the country had acquired a stockpile of 350,000 tons of tin, equivalent to two years' global consumption (Mallory, 1990). In August 1957, however, there was a severe global recession, and the US ended its stockpiling programme. Global tin consumption fell sharply, and tin production, though also declining, remained at a higher level than was warranted by the reduced demand.

The buffer-stock purchase mechanism established during the first ITA, 1956–1961, initially failed to stabilize prices, and so the ITC imposed nine quarterly tranches of export quotas from January 1958 through to end March 1960. These restrictions harmed Malaya's tin-mining industry, and Perak's tin production slumped, falling from 36,100 tons in 1957 to just 21,700 tons in 1958, remaining at that level in 1959 (Figure 3.1). The number of active tin mines—both dredging and gravel-pump—fell by almost half, with most of the closures in the Kinta Valley. Employment in the sector was badly affected. Although no longer as labour intensive as in colonial times, Perak's tin-mining sector still employed over 21,400 people in 1957. Just two years later, this figure had fallen to only 14,000.[4] State-wise, however, this had only a small impact on employment, as tin mining accounted for just 7 per cent of employment in 1957 despite its much larger contribution to the state's economy.

---

4 As long as tin mines could cover production costs, their mining operations and layoffs would be less affected than under a cartel arrangement in which the ceiling price is artificially set and production is restricted by export quotas. Thus, in effect, tin-mining workers were hurt by the very mechanism—the cartel—that was intended to protect them (Lim, 1960).

Figure 3.1   **Three phases of changing tin production and tin prices**

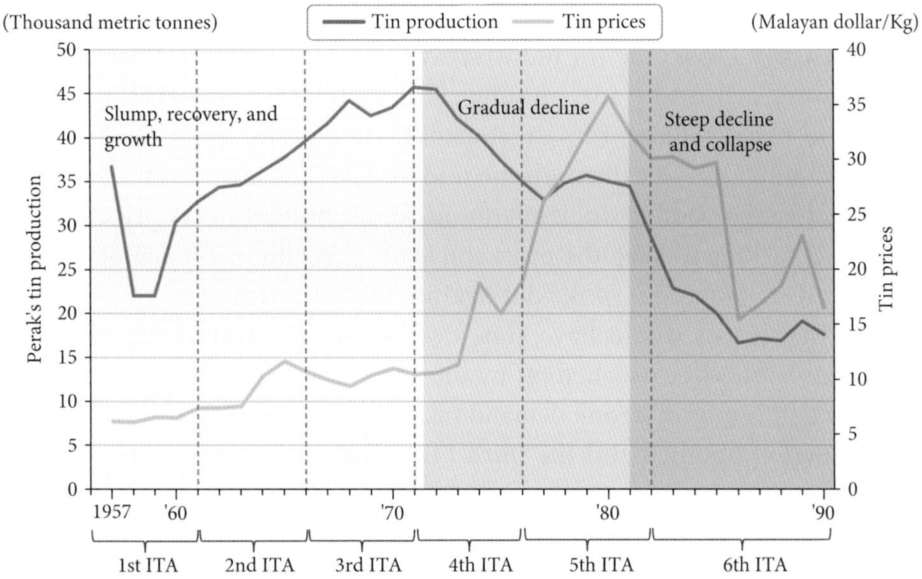

Sources of data: For 1961 and 1970: Department of Mines–West Malaysia, Ministry of Primary Industries–Malaysia (various years); for 1971–1990: Department of Mines, Ministry of Primary Industries–Malaysia (various years).

In 1958, tin prices were undermined by massive inflows of tin to European markets from the Soviet Union, which re-exported it from China, another non-member against which the ITC was powerless to act. These inflows only diminished after the UK and other European countries imposed severe restrictions on tin imports from the Soviet Union. In the first quarter of 1960, the export quota for Malaya was set at 91.7 per cent of its quarterly output in 1957, which meant that all existing mines in operation between January 1953 and December 1957 could resume production (ITC, 1960). But it took Perak until 1965 to reach the production level it had achieved in 1957, the year before export quotas were initially imposed. Lam (1978) has argued that the slow recovery was partly due to the high export duties imposed on tin, as well as the introduction of steep corporate taxes in the late 1950s.

Growth

Following the slump of 1957–1958, Perak's tin production rose sharply between 1959 and 1971, driven by global demand amid steadily increasing prices (Figure 3.1). The number of mine workers rose to the pre-slump level of 29,000. Tin demand and supply were volatile, however, and in the second and third

ITAs covering 1961–1971, the ITC had to deal with issues of undersupply by increasing the ceiling price and on several occasions by selling buffer stocks.

By the early 1960s, the tin industry was benefiting greatly from the general recovery in world trade, although this was offset somewhat by the US starting to release some of its tin stockpile—beginning in September 1962, and continuing periodically until the mid-1980s.[5] These disposals forced the ITC to activate its buffer-stock operation, and it bought tin as prices started to decline, seeking to keep the price above the ITA's floor. The major tin producers, led by Malaysia, spoke out against the sales from the US stockpile, arguing that prices would have gone even higher without them. However, their complaints were brushed off by the US government (Raffaelli, 2009).

Under conditions of strong demand from the mid-1960s to the early 1970s, tin production boomed and the third ITA, 1966–1971, ran its course without any need for intervention, except for the imposition of an export quota from September 1968 to December 1969. This had minimal impact on Perak's tin output, however. Booming global demand for tin was met by increased production in Bolivia, China, and Thailand, as well as in Malaysia (Hillman, 2010). Perak's tin production grew by an average of 3.3 per cent a year from 1965 to reach a post-independence peak of 45,000 tons in 1971 (Figure 3.1).

As a share of the global total, Perak's production rose from 20.1 per cent in 1957 to a peak of 23.9 per cent in 1971, when it accounted for 60.6 per cent of Malaysia's output (Figure 3.2). By 1970, tin mining—still Perak's second-largest economic sector—contributed about 18.9 per cent of its total GDP (EPU, 1976).[6] Tin brought large revenues for the federal government, contributing 50.2 per cent of its total export duties—equivalent to about 10.7 per cent of total government receipts (BNM, 1972). However, hardly any of these revenues were ploughed back into Perak's development. For Perak, this was a major—and continuing—drawback.

Resurgence of Gravel-pump Mining

After independence, there was a resurgence in the use of the more labour-intensive gravel pumps for mining ores as opposed to the bucket dredge, in a reversal of the trend seen in the first half of the 20th century (Figure 3.3). Political and

---

5 The US released over 20,000 tonnes of tin each year in 1964, 1965, 1973, and 1974 (Raffaelli, 2009). Putting this figure into perspective, Perak's production in those years was 34,000, 37,000, 41,500, and 39,600 tons, respectively.

6 The agricultural sector contributed 30.4 per cent of Perak's GDP.

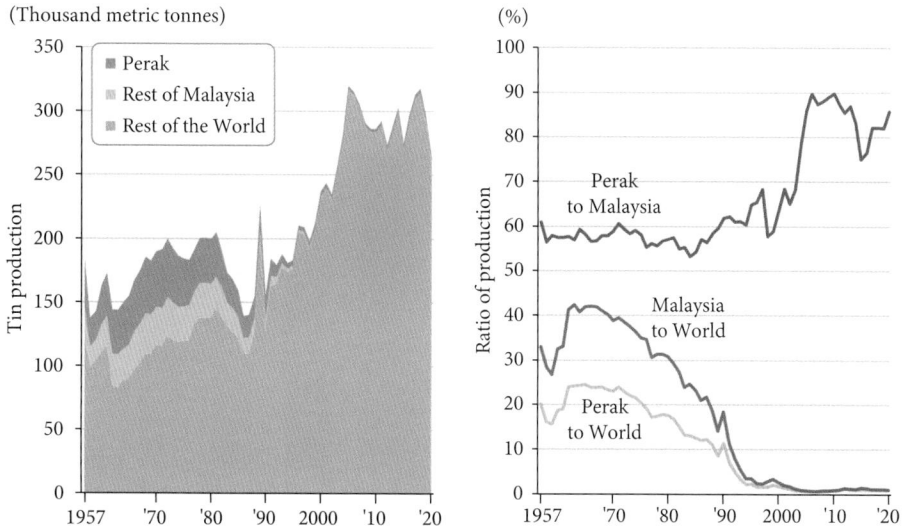

Figure 3.2 **Perak remained the world's leading tin producer until 1981, though its share of global output declined steeply after 1971**

Sources of data: For 1957–1999: International Tin Council (various years); for Perak and Malaysia: Department of Mines, Ministry of Primary Industries–Malaysia (various years); Minerals and Geoscience Department–Malaysia (various years); for World data, United States Geological Survey (various years).

social turmoil during the communist insurgency, 1948–1960, and the national and regional upheavals of the 1960s, had led to a climate of uncertainty for investors, and there was hardly any new investment in dredges. Further, the ore in many dredged riverbeds had been exhausted.

The popularity of gravel-pump mining, dominated by Malaysian Chinese interests, reflected its much lower capital costs and greater efficiency compared to dredges in working different kinds of low-grade tin deposits, such as those between limestone pinnacles (Yap, 2006). Moreover, dredges could not be easily dismantled and moved from one location to another, whereas gravel pumps were more portable. By 1970, 62 per cent of Perak's production was mined using gravel pumps, up from 42 per cent in 1961. Dredges contributed just 29 per cent, down from 49 per cent in 1961—a trend also observed to a lesser extent elsewhere in Malaysia (Figure 3.3). As Perak's high-quality tin deposits in its traditional large mining areas were depleted, low-grade tin mined using gravel pumps steadily came to account for a larger share of production.

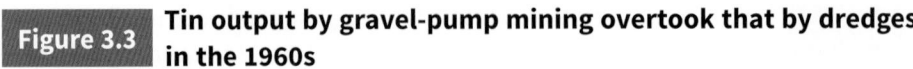

Figure 3.3   **Tin output by gravel-pump mining overtook that by dredges in the 1960s**

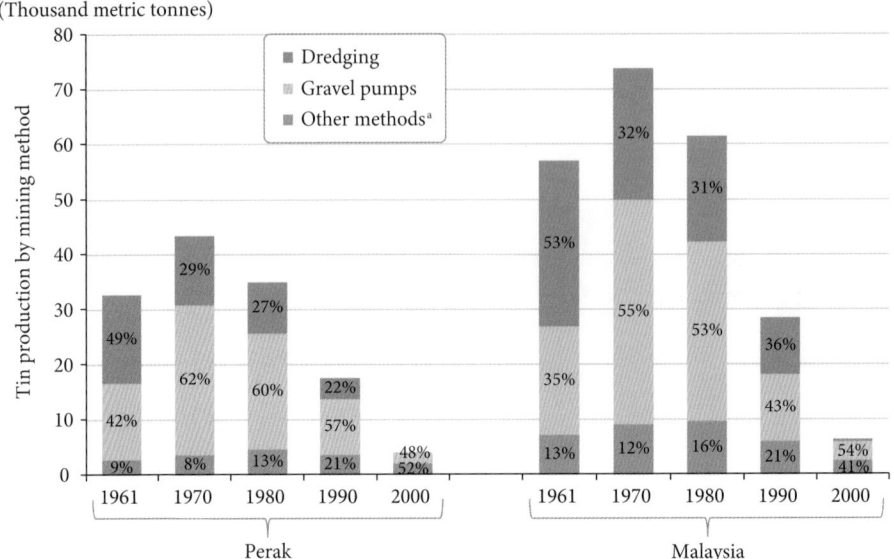

(Thousand metric tonnes)

Sources of data: For 1961 and 1970: Department of Mines–West Malaysia, Ministry of Primary Industries–Malaysia (various years); for 1980–2000: Department of Mines, Ministry of Primary Industries–Malaysia (various years).

Note: [a] Other methods include open-cast and underground mining, retreatment, and panning.

Higher Taxes with Ownership Patterns Maintained

During all three periods—slump, recovery, and growth—the Malaysian government successively increased export duties on tin and corporate taxes, which reduced foreign investors' appetite for tin mining. From 1957 to 1973, the export duty was set at a fixed average rate of 15 to 16 per cent of the tin price, which producers had to pay regardless of that price. Corporate income tax was 40 per cent in 1961, but in 1964 this was increased to 50 per cent if the price of tin reached a certain level (White, 2004, p. 153). Mining companies considered these taxes excessive, especially compared to the low-tax regime before independence, and at first the taxes had a destabilizing effect on output and employment in marginal mines.

The upside of this policy was that most of the value of tin sales was retained in Malaysia (Thoburn, 1973). Using data for 1967, Thoburn estimated that for dredges, nearly three-quarters of the annual value of tin sales was retained. The government collected about one-third of total export income through taxes, and another one-third was paid in dividends to local shareholders. Most of the materials needed were also purchased locally. For gravel pumps, most after-tax profits were retained in Malaysia, with outflows limited to a small dividend of about 15 per cent of the export income. In addition, most of the materials and services consumed by gravel-pump mines were locally produced.

Over the period 1957 to 1971, spanning independence through to the New Economic Policy (NEP), the ownership and management of tin mines remained similar to the pre-war era. In 1954, three years before independence, about 78 per cent of locally incorporated tin-dredging companies were foreign-owned, mainly by British interests, while Malaysian Chinese interests controlled about 90 per cent of gravel-pump mines (Yip, 1969). In that same year, some 108 European-owned mines in Malaya, predominantly British, produced about 60 per cent of total output, while the more than 600 Chinese-owned mines accounted for the remaining 40 per cent (Puthucheary, 1960). In 1970, foreign investors, mainly British, still held about 72.4 per cent of the share capital in Malaysian tin-mining companies (Lim, 1981).[7]

On balance, in the post-independence era, tin mining continued to favour the interests of British capital, although the heavy tax burden on mining companies meant that they received a smaller share of the sales proceeds. As Perak produced an average of 58 per cent of all of Malaysia's tin in this period, British interests there were hurt by the high taxes, which also appeared to curtail new foreign investment in the industry. In the mid-1960s, however, there were new discoveries of tin on Malay reservation land, on which prospecting and extraction had been forbidden since World War II, and this did encourage some new investment (White, 2004).

Gradual Decline, 1972–1981

Higher Prices but Diminishing Deposits

Between 1972 and 1981, even though international tin prices were surging (Figure 3.1), Perak's tin production declined steadily from its 1971 peak, as tin deposits were gradually diminishing and production costs were rising. This was also a period of consolidation of mining companies as well as purchases of shares by the government, which was seeking to ensure local majority ownership of the largest British-owned tin mines as part of its 'Malayanization' policy.

In 1971, tin prices, being set in British pounds, were fairly high due to a substantial devaluation of the US dollar against sterling.[8] However, the oil embargo

---

7 In 1965, three mining agencies—Anglo-Oriental, Osborne and Chappel, and Associated Mines—managed 25 of Malaysia's 43 public-limited tin-mining companies (Saruwatari, 1991).

8 Tin prices were quoted in pounds on the LME where the ITC conducted its financial and market operations. But from 1972 the ITC reference price ranges for tin were expressed in ringgit and set in the Malaysia market. With the ringgit tied to the US dollar, an appreciation (depreciation) of the ringgit (US dollar) against sterling would raise (lower) sterling prices to ensure parity with ringgit prices in Kuala Lumpur. In effect, by targeting prices in ringgit and using the LME and sterling operations as the main platform to conduct its operations, the ITC had assumed unhedged exchange rate risks.

led by OPEC after the 1973 Arab–Israeli war led to a global recession between 1973 and 1975. Strict export quotas were imposed from January to September 1973 and from April 1975 to June 1976, as part of the fourth ITA, 1971–1976, to control tin supply and maintain prices.[9] Perak's tin production consequently fell by an average of 6.0 per cent a year in this period. These restrictions severely hurt Perak's marginal mines such that 'a hardship quota pool' was introduced in October 1975, which allowed those mines with insufficient export quotas to apply for additional quotas to meet their operating costs and prevent layoffs (Third Malaysia Plan, 1976, p. 325). After the export quota was lifted, Perak's production rebounded, growing by an annual average of 4.2 per cent between 1977 and 1979. This period also marked the unprecedented acceleration of tin prices after the recovery of the global economy at the end of the fourth ITA, 1971–1976.

Between 1980 and 1981, however, Perak's production reversed its temporary uptrend, even though tin prices reached a post-independence peak in 1980 (Figure 3.1), and although global production also declined, it fell by less than Perak's in relative terms. The state's tin mining industry was in secular decline, reflecting the depletion of existing deposits and a lack of major new discoveries—the Malaysian Geological Survey Department had already stopped tin exploration in 1979, foreshadowing the approaching precipitous decline of the industry's fortunes (Abdul Ghani, 1989). Many gravel pumps were working in low-quality fields previously mined by dredges (Thoburn, 1994b).

Overall, from 1972 to 1981, Perak's production declined by an annual average of 3 per cent. As a share of Malaysia's total, Perak's tin production still hovered between 55 and 58 per cent, but the status of Perak—and thus of Malaysia—as a global tin producer was greatly diminished at a time when other countries, such as Brazil and China, were starting to increase production (Hillman, 2010). Perak's tin production over this period slipped from 23 per cent to 17 per cent of global output (see Figure 3.2).[10]

End of British Mining Dominance: Malayanization

The British presence in Malaysia's tin industry, dominated by two large companies—London Tin and Charter Consolidated Ltd, both operating under British agency house management—was significantly reduced by the country's localization policy implemented as part of the NEP (see 'The New Economic Policy—A Fundamental

---

9 In 1975, supply was also affected by large exports of tin originating from sources not directly under the ITC's control, especially from China and Burma (HC. 305, 1986, p. 155).

10 In the mining sector, the share of export earnings from tin in Malaysia declined from 86.1 per cent in 1970 to 25.5 per cent in 1980, while that of petroleum increased from 13.9 per cent to 73.3 per cent.

Shift', below).[11] In July 1976, Perbadanan Nasional Berhad (PERNAS)[12] acquired London Tin Corporation, the holding company for London Tin, through its subsidiary New Trade Winds. PERNAS was the government's main vehicle for its 1970s Malayanization programme, which targeted some of the largest publicly listed companies, particularly those under foreign ownership (Gomez and Jomo, 1999).

After the acquisition, New Trade Winds was renamed Malaysia Mining Corporation Bhd, which then formed a global alliance with Charter Consolidated Ltd through an exchange of shares.[13] With this affiliation, by 1980 Malaysia Mining Corporation (MMC) had become the largest tin-mining company in the world by capitalization, with 71.3 per cent of its stock held by PERNAS through its subsidiary, and the remaining 28.7 per cent held by Charter Consolidated Ltd. In 1981, MMC was merged with Malayan Tin Dredging Berhad to become the world's largest integrated tin producer by capitalization, owning 38 of 55 dredges in the country (Saruwatari, 1991). The merger meant that MMC now owned 70 per cent of the country's dredges, equipment which had once been the pride of British ownership.

After these and other takeovers, the net profits of foreign-owned tin companies operating in Malaysia dropped by more than half, from 88 per cent of the total in 1972 to 34 per cent in 1978 (Khor, 2019). And with the tin-mining industry in decline, it is unlikely that the returns on equity after localization were high.

Continuing High Taxation

In 1974, amid falling tin output and dramatically rising prices, export taxes were revised and producers paid taxes only when the tin price rose above a given level. As the cost of production escalated, this level was revised upwards from RM19,842 per ton in 1974 to RM23,149 per ton in 1981 (Mohammed Yusoff, 1990). Between 1974 and 1981, the price of tin dropped below RM19,000 per ton only in 1974. The new tax structure did not, however, affect dredging mines and the more labour-intensive gravel-pump mines equally, given that the operating costs for dredging mines were much lower. Gravel-pump mines thus paid more

---

11 In 1972, London Tin Corporation produced a quarter of all tin output of Malaysia's listed companies (Tan, 1982).

12 PERNAS was established in 1969 with an initial paid-up capital of M$110 million under the control of Ministry of Finance Incorporated.

13 In partnership with Charted Consolidated Ltd, PERNAS also set up PERNAS Charter Management, a company with functions similar to a British agency house, to manage the MMC. In April 1982, MMC also took a 42 per cent share of the tin-ore buying and smelting of STC (Tantalum Producers International Study Centre, 1983). The STC weathered the 1985 tin crash until prices recovered in 2004, with rising global demand for tin from the technology boom for batteries in electric vehicles, solar panels, and tin chemicals.

export duties as a share of their net earnings. With corporate tax rates remaining high at 40 per cent throughout the 1970s, mining companies continued to express their dissatisfaction with the heavy tax burden from both export duties and corporate taxes (White, 2004).

As ore deposits became less accessible and more difficult to extract, the costs of mining rose steeply. Although in 1980 nominal tin prices peaked at more than three times their level in 1970 (Figure 3.1), gross profit margins narrowed. Tin mining continued to be heavily taxed, with the bulk of tax revenues accruing to the federal government and only 10 per cent of revenues flowing back to Perak's state treasury.

Steep Output Decline and Tin-market Collapse, 1981–1990

This decade was marked by the accelerating decline in tin output in Perak and Malaysia (Figures 3.1 and 3.2). Alluvial tin-bearing deposits were rapidly depleting at a time when no major discoveries were being made. Mining land leases were increasingly difficult to secure as many land parcels near working mining companies were in Malay reservations (Thoburn, 1994a). Further, the cost of operating marginal mines was rising and their operators struggled to make a profit. The decline in Perak's tin production coincided with two significant events on the international tin market: Malaysian speculation on the London Metal Exchange (LME) between 1981 and 1982, and the disastrous collapse of the tin market in 1985—and with it, the ITC.

Malaysian Speculation on the London Metal Exchange, 1981–1982

By 1981, a severe and prolonged decline in tin prices had begun, due to the deep global recession caused by the second oil shock following the 1978–1979 Iranian Revolution. The decline in global tin consumption opened a yawning gap between demand and supply, one not seen since 1939 (Hillman, 2010). The growing use of tin substitutes—aluminium and plastic—for food packaging also depressed demand for tin, and thus prices.[14] The international aluminium cartel provided fierce competition for tin by pursuing a strategy of lowering prices to spur demand

---

14 With substitutes available at comparable prices, the demand curve for tin became highly elastic, such that if tin prices increased, demand fell because consumers had lower-cost options.

(Lines, 2007). Advances in technology also enabled the tin-recycling industry to flourish, lowering demand for new tin ores (Bell, 2018).

The tin market was at crisis point, and the major producers that were party to the fifth ITA, 1976–1982, demanded that the ITC set a higher price in the face of falling tin prices and rising operating costs. In July 1981, the ITC proposed adjusting prices upwards, but this was rejected by consumer members. From this point until early 1982, the government-owned MMC, with Cabinet approval, decided to act anonymously and unilaterally to drive prices up by forward dealing on the LME. Working with a commodity-trading firm, Marc Rich & Co, and based on advice from Marc Rich, it established a subsidiary company, Maminco, to purchase tin on the LME.[15] Maminco moved aggressively to corner the market, first by buying for three-month forward delivery, and later by buying physical tin, in the hope of pushing tin prices even higher (Jomo, 1990). As a result, monthly spot tin prices were highly volatile, rocketing from a low of £5,000 per tonne in mid-1981 to a high of £9,000 per tonne in February 1982 (HC. 305, 1986, p. 137). The large spike in prices led to an increase in global tin production, and spurred the US to release tin from its huge stockpile. These developments prompted traders to sell tin short, three-month forward, on the presumption that the mystery buyer would not be able to sustain the increase in prices and that tin prices would collapse.

However, Maminco started to purchase excess physical tin for cash on the spot market, which initially succeeded in maintaining prices. Maminco assumed that short sellers would be forced to pay higher prices for physical tin to cover their contracts once they expired. However, it was caught by surprise when, to prevent a crisis, in February 1982 the LME suddenly changed its non-delivery rules to prevent short sellers from defaulting. The short sellers instead paid a fine, allowing them to avoid purchasing physical tin from Malaysia at a steep premium. The tin price immediately fell below the ITA ceiling price and within a month had fallen from £9,000 to £7,000 a ton (Jomo, 1990). Having already purchased tin worth some US$750 million (Singh Dhillon, 2009), Maminco suffered huge losses amounting to RM660 million, which were met by the Malaysian government out of public funds.[16]

---

15 Before coming to Malaysia, David Zaidner, an Egyptian metal trader representing Marc Rich & Co, had offered a similar speculative tin-buying scheme to Indonesia. He was, however, rebuffed by Indonesian officials who were familiar with past allegations that he may have bribed an ITC buffer-stock manager (Pura, 1986).

16 In 1982, the Chairman of the Board of the LME noted that there was an attempt by an unknown party, 'Mr M', to corner the tin market (HC. 305, 1986 p. 265). The UK's Trade and Industry Department was also aware of the Malaysian government's speculative operations on the LME (HC. 532, 1986, p. 1). Much later, after years of denial, the Malaysian government admitted to costly market manipulation (New York Times, 1986). Dr Mahathir insisted that it was the fault of Marc Rich who had sold him the idea, but then acted beyond his contractual obligations by buying excessive quantities of tin without Maminco's knowledge (Mahathir, 2011).

These costly misadventures at the LME had major knock-on effects. They created a massive surplus of tin which resulted in global production cuts and closures of mines, devastating Malaysia's tin-mining industry. The sharply lower tin prices resulted in layoffs of thousands of tin-mining workers as many mining operations became unprofitable. From 1981 to 1982, Perak's production shrank by 16.6 per cent and nearly one-quarter of its tin-mining labour force was laid off.

Collapse of the International Tin Market and the ITC, 1985

From the failed speculative episode of 1982 to the collapse of the international tin market in 1985, which occurred in the period of the sixth ITA, 1982–1989, the ITC kept tin prices from falling below the floor by strictly enforcing export controls and managing buffer stocks.[17] Production cuts of between 36 and 39 per cent were imposed on all member producing countries, but even these were not enough to prevent oversupply. At the same time, Brazil, China, and Indonesia—all lower-cost producers—ramped up production during the support effort, putting further downward pressure on tin prices (Figure 3.4).[18]

The production restrictions upset ITC producer members, who felt that they had made huge sacrifices that benefited non-member producers (HC. 176–iv, 1986). Moreover, the US continued to sell from its strategic stockpile, though this amounted to less than 3,000 tons a year from 1983 to 1985 (Raffaelli, 2009). Further, to circumvent the prolonged period of export controls as well as to avoid paying taxes, tin was still being smuggled to Singapore by some Malaysian, Indonesian, and Thai producers. In 1983, an estimated 16,550 tons of tin—nearly 10 per cent of world consumption—was smuggled into Singapore for re-export (McFadden, 1986).

From 1980 to 1984, the US dollar appreciated against sterling, providing support for the sterling price of tin. The appreciation initially arrested the fall in the sterling-denominated price, which then reversed and in 1983 started to rise sharply. This boosted the value of tin as collateral and thus boosted the resources of the ITC, as most of its financial arrangements were made in sterling.[19] Still, the price increases were insufficient for the ITC to cease buying tin, and its accumulating buffer stocks were becoming a financial burden. It had already

---

17 The Association of Tin Producing Countries consisting of Thailand, Indonesia, Australia, Bolivia, Nigeria, and Zaire (now the Democratic Republic of the Congo), was formed in 1983, led by Malaysia, with the aim of controlling market prices by means of export quotas. Its purpose was to exclude leading tin-consuming countries. However, without the membership of Brazil and China, which by then had become two of the main producer countries, it had little impact on the tin market and remained largely symbolic (McFadden, 1986).

18 By 1988, Brazil, China, and Indonesia had overtaken Malaysia in tin production.

19 The US implemented a series of tax cuts and increased government spending, driving up interest rates, attracting capital inflows, and leading to US dollar appreciation.

Figure 3.4 Brazil, China, and Indonesia raised their tin output from the second half of the 1980s, while Malaysia's, constrained by export quotas, stagnated

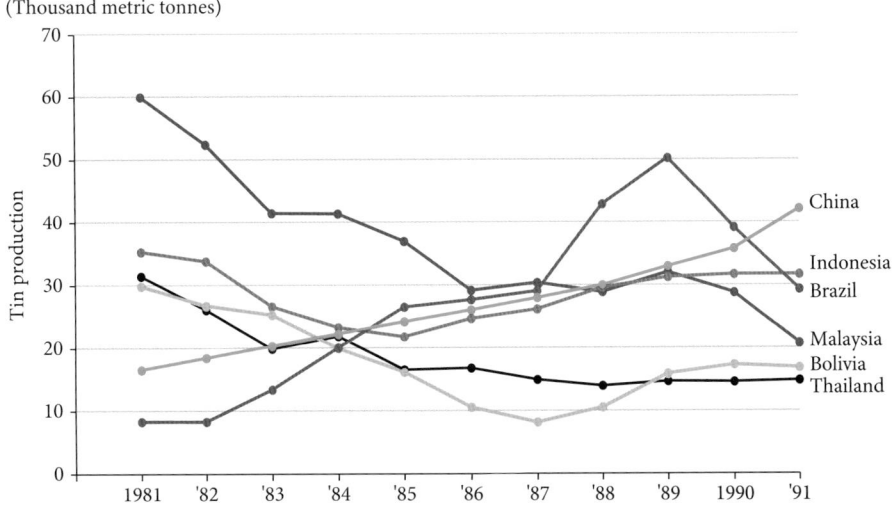

(Thousand metric tonnes)

Sources of data: Department of Mines, Ministry of Primary Industries–Malaysia (various years); United States Geological Survey (various years).

used most of its funds to buy tin during the 1981 recession, and its holding of tin had reached the legal limit (Gilbert, 1995). The non-participation of the US in the sixth ITA also reduced the funding available to manage buffer stocks. This compelled the buffer-stock manager to rely increasingly on bank loans to finance complicated forward-market positions, eventually leaving it seriously exposed.[20] As the ITC did not act to lower the floor price to reflect lower demand, instead keeping it unrealistically high in the interests of tin producers, the buffer-stock manager was forced to continue buying tin (McFadden, 1986). The ITC's actions to sustain and maintain tin prices, quoted in Malaysian ringgit, might still have been a success had it not been for sterling's reversal and sudden appreciation.[21]

In April 1985, the pound recovered sharply against the US dollar, causing the price of tin to fall in sterling terms and harming its value as security. By October 1985, sterling prices of tin had fallen by as much as 20 per cent from

---

20 The buffer-stock manager was given much discretion in the sixth ITA and could actively engage in contracts for both immediate and forward delivery on the LME, with no explicit limits on the type and volume of transactions. The buffer-stock manager made huge purchases of tin—51,665 tons in 1982, 2,415 tons in 1983, and 6,727 tons in 1984 (Mallory, 1990).

21 In September 1985, the US signed the Plaza Accord with France, West Germany, Japan, and the UK, under which the US agreed to allow the US dollar to depreciate.

their most recent peak. Banks started to demand more collateral and refused to advance further loans to the ITC. The buffer-stock manager made losses on forward trades, and the ITC—unable to secure additional loans from banks, given the manager's damaged creditworthiness—reached the limit of its resources to reverse the price slide. The buffer-stock manager attempted to squeeze short sellers by demanding delivery of physical tin, of which it was the only ready source of supply. Had the manager succeeded, this would have raised the spot price and limited losses. But the LME defended its members and brokers by arbitrarily restricting backwardation—when future prices exceptionally fall below the spot price. In 1982, the LME had similarly defended its members and brokers when faced with a squeeze in the market.

ITA members attempted to secure a £60 million loan, but were unsuccessful (Hillman, 2010). On 24 October 1985, with debts estimated at £900 million, the ITC was declared insolvent as it was unable to honour its contracts. The LME's tin brokers and financiers had assumed that it would be impossible for the ITC's 22 member countries not to fulfil the Council's obligations.[22] Lawsuits against the ITC were dismissed as it claimed diplomatic immunity (HC. 176–iv, 1986). The ITC argued that the debts should be shared among creditors, metal dealers, and the ITC member governments, but this proposal was rejected by the creditors and dealers (HC. 305, 1986).

The total accumulated stockpile of physical metal and forward contracts amounted to more than 100,000 tons, equivalent to over six months of global consumption (McFadden, 1986). To avoid a chain of bankruptcy and to protect its brokers—as each LME broker had unlimited liability and owed directly to one another—the LME suspended tin trading.[23] Overnight, on 25 October, the price of tin quoted on the exchange dropped from £8,900 to £5,500 a ton (Hillman, 2010). The collapse of the tin market heralded the end of the post–World War II ITAs and the ITC.[24]

The British House of Commons launched an official inquiry into the tin crisis, spurred by the reputational damage done to the LME, the adverse effect of the crisis on other international agreements, and the repercussions for Cornwall's tin-mining industry (HC. 305, 1986). The tin industry was still of great

---

22 Two Malaysian banks, Bank Bumiputra and Maybank, were among a group of 16 creditor financial institutions affected by the collapse (HC. 176–ii, 1986).

23 The much smaller Kuala Lumpur Tin Market, which did not trade in futures contracts, also suspended trading in October 1985, but resumed trading a year later.

24 In Malaysia, a direct corporate casualty of the tin collapse was MMC Metals, a subsidiary of the MMC. It went into liquidation, unable to recoup payment for a large sale of tin, and as a result defaulted on £13.9 million of its obligations to another broker (Wagstyl, 1986).

importance to Cornwall's economic life. The drop in tin prices and the collapse of the ITC had major implications for wages and the local economy. Some 4,000 people lost their jobs. Many of the larger remaining mines, such as the Geevor mines, closed permanently (HC. 176–i, 1986). Appeals for British government financial assistance to revive these mines were rejected because it was felt that any investments would be unprofitable in an environment of low prices (HC. 457, 1986).

Among the inquiry's conclusions were, first, that the ITC, with 22 members possessed of diverse opinions, was not a suitable body for day-to-day management in a rapidly changing global environment. Second, that the ITC did not provide adequate guidance on debt and risk management, in particular exchange rate risk hedging. Third, that the manipulation of international prices by cartel action, so that prices were substantially above both marginal and new-entrant production costs, had stimulated production by existing and new non-cartel producers, discouraged consumption, and promoted the use of synthetics.

Impact of Tin-market Collapse on Perak

The ramifications were felt sharply in Perak, causing tin output to fall by 17 per cent in 1986, and tin prices by nearly 50 per cent. Most of the state's tin-mining companies struggled to survive, unable to cover even their direct operating costs. By 1986 more than 100 of Malaysia's estimated 500 tin mines had closed, and another 100 had suspended operations or were operating part-time (Wagstyl, 1986). Malaysia's export earnings from tin fell sharply, from RM1.65 billion in 1985 to RM650 million in 1986, marking a huge drop in their contribution to total exports, from 4.3 per cent to 1.8 per cent (CEIC database, 2020).

With declining global demand for tin, most of Perak's mines were forced either to curtail their production or—for the less efficient—to close altogether. This had serious consequences for the livelihoods of those dependent on the mining industry. The income of those directly employed in tin mining tumbled. Employment in the tin industry in Perak was virtually eradicated, falling from about 24,000 jobs in 1980 to some 5,000 in 1990, and to around only 1,000 in 2000 (Table 3.1). These job losses, and the larger *indirect* ripple effect on other jobs that relied on the mining industry, devastated local communities:

> The repercussions on the whole of the Kinta Valley were horrendous. Men and women lost their jobs. They stood to lose everything else. Those who kept their jobs did not get paid. Tin mines had nothing to pay them with. Those who supplied the mines could not get any payment. Others who supplied the suppliers were, in turn, not paid. The ripple effect multiplied hardships and suffering. The school where I taught cut pay all around,

from the principal to the lowest office boy… Being Chinese, whose grandparents and parents had come from China to seek work, these people of Ipoh, Kampar, Tapah and all over the Kinta Valley, knew what to do… Like those before them, if they had to go where there was work, they would do so. (Thong, 2011, p. 1)

Many of those who lost their jobs had worked in relatively labour-intensive gravel-pump mines which, despite requiring little capital, had high operating costs (Thoburn, 1994a). The closure of mines, losses of livelihoods, and the spike in unemployment accelerated the outflow of migrants. Perak's tin towns lost the skills, ingenuity, hardiness, and resilience of the people who had been drawn there by the mines and their associated industries. With a lack of alternative employment opportunities, those who remained in the Kinta Valley's tin towns suffered severely. Some towns like Kampar declined and then began to regenerate, while others such as Gopeng suffered a secular decline (Box 3.3).

After the tin-market collapse, the large overhang of tin stocks kept prices depressed for the next few years until the final liquidation of the ITC's enormous stockpile. Between 1987 and 1990, Perak's tin production fluctuated between 16,900 and 19,100 metric tonnes. Some mines that had become uneconomic were reopened as prices gradually rose after 1986, but tin mining was already on a permanent declining trend. By 1990 Perak produced less than 40 per cent of its 1971 production peak, and by the end of the millennium output had dwindled to a negligible amount, with tin accounting for less than 1 per cent of the state's GDP.[25] With the collapse of the tin industry, the attention of policymakers shifted to other primary commodities, especially palm oil, and to other economic sectors such as manufacturing and services (as discussed in subsequent sections).

Table 3.1	The number of jobs in the tin industry in Perak and Malaysia fell dramatically after 1980				
	1957	1970	1980	1990	2000
Perak	21,400	28,500	23,800	5,400	1,000
Malaysia	36,600[a]	46,500	39,000	8,500	1,700

Sources of data: For 1957 and 1970, Department of Mines–West Malaysia, Ministry of Primary Industries–Malaysia (various years); for 1980–1990, Department of Mines, Ministry of Primary Industries–Malaysia (various years); for 2000, Minerals and Geoscience Department–Malaysia (2000).

Note: [a] Relates to Malaya.

---

25 Few of Perak's mines survived into the 21st century. A notable exception is the Rahman Hydraulics mine in Klian Intan, Pengkalan Hulu in northern Perak. Even by 2020, this mine was producing 2,300 tons of ore annually and employing close to 800 mine workers. Klian Intan is believed to be Perak's oldest tin-mining area, having existed for over 250 years (Roslelawati Abdullah, 2017).

Box 3.3   **Kampar and Gopeng: Memories**

Kampar: The tin crash in 1985 devastated local communities, and Kampar town's population fell over the following decades, from 24,600 in 1980 to 17,000 in 2000, and to only 15,100 in 2010, as young people were forced to seek work elsewhere. Small businesses, foundries, grocery shops, and cinemas along Jalan Idris closed. Jalan Gopeng, the commercial centre, is today almost deserted, with many dilapidated buildings—but quite a few of the people who remain, as well as some who have left, have fascinating stories to tell.

Hew See Tong, 90 years old, was born in China but moved at age five to Kampar where his father worked for a tin-ore dealer. Instead of going to high school, Hew worked in his father's mine, and then took on managerial roles. At the peak, Hew oversaw 24 mines, with two in Kampar that stayed open until 1992.

Clan associations opened the first schools in Kampar in the 1900s. Subsequently, mining tycoons contributed land and funds to expand them, including the Hokkien Chinese School (later named the Pei Yuan School), the Anglo-Chinese School (now SK Methodist, built in 1936), Chung Huah School, and SJK(C) Kampar Girls School. Today there is also a Westlake International School.

Hew, who became a generous philanthropist, was instrumental in opening Tunku Abdul Rahman College in Kampar in 1998. Housed initially in five shophouses rented for RM1 a year, the permanent campus opened in 2003, built on 20 hectares of land donated by Hew. He persuaded Universiti Tunku Abdul Rahman (UTAR) to start a campus in Kampar, and the state government granted UTAR 526 hectares of ex-mining land on a 99-year lease (see Box 3.16). Hew says:

> We Chinese, since our ancestors, believe in the teachings of Confucius. Education is the first priority, however poor we are. We work hard for our children's education. It is a shared responsibility provided by the clans and supported by business people. In the past, we opened mines; today we open minds.

On average, students spend RM1,000 a month on their accommodation and other living costs, bringing an estimated RM11 million in revenue each month to Kampar. The campus has created jobs and supporting businesses, including hotels, eateries, laundromats, serviced apartments, and blocks of flats.

Some foreign students complete their study years in Kampar and then move to larger cities. Many local students return home to Penang or Kuala Lumpur at weekends and public holidays. The electric train service that began operating in 2010 provides easy access to major cities—two and a half hours to Kuala Lumpur and three hours to Butterworth, Penang. After graduation, most UTAR students leave Kampar to find a job.

(*Continued*)

Jacky Chew, curator of the Kinta Tin Mining Museum, which opened in 2011, says that 'Kampar needs to diversify and not rely only on education. Tourism is an option. While unable to attract large numbers of tourists like Ipoh, Kampar attracts niche tourists interested in history and conservation'. Kampar has many old Chinese and Indian temples, Catholic churches, schools, and shophouses of character.

UTAR's success has made it a model for the revival of old mining towns—a mix of higher education and property development. There are plans to build a non-profit teaching hospital, owned by UTAR Education Foundation and funded by benefactors including the Perak Chinese Mining Association, established in 1935. The hospital will initially have 250 beds for Western medicine and 100 beds for traditional and complementary medicine. At the initial stage, it will create 485 healthcare jobs and 250 jobs for supporting staff. It will also provide clinical training for students from UTAR's Faculty of Medicine and Health Sciences, established in 2009. Students who study at UTAR will have an opportunity to work in the hospital and settle in Kampar, bringing much-needed young families to an ageing town.

Gopeng: *Ponchannanu* worked in Gopeng as a security guard for Osborne and Chappel for 15 years, watching over the mine's power station, generators, pipelines, and dam. He remembers how bustling Gopeng town was on pay day when workers went to the head office for their money. The cinemas showed Malay, Chinese, and Indian movies, and the shops stayed open till 11pm. *Orang Asli* would also be there to trade their goods.

Life was difficult for Ponchannanu after the tin crash, as he spent many years away from his wife and five daughters. He struggled at his studies and failed the Lower Certificate of Education twice. However, by reading the newspapers every day he improved his English, enabling him to work for an American manufacturing company in Singapore. He returned to Gopeng in 2011 and found work on a rubber plantation, also working at weekends at Gaharu Tea Valley as a driver. After retraining, he is now a full-time tour guide. He thinks that Gopeng's future lies in tourism.

Others, like *Chellaraju*, were lucky to find work elsewhere after being retrenched from Osborne and Chappel in 1982. His salary had been RM5.25 a day in 1974 as a labourer on a tin dredge, where he was part of an outside gang of 10 who helped control and stabilize the steel ropes of the dredger. When he lost his job, he went to Singapore to work in construction, but returned when his mother fell ill. He found a job in Gopeng's post office, where he worked until reaching retirement age.

Today, Gopeng town is eerily quiet after four in the afternoon and at weekends, when most shops are closed. Before the Covid-19 pandemic, Ulu Geruntum, just outside of Gopeng town, had started to attract adventure tourists for white-water rafting, hiking, all-terrain vehicle tours, and visits to the waterfall, prompting several small homestays to open there, and later some resorts. (Tourists would only stop in Gopeng town itself for a visit to the museum and the heritage house.)

Phang See Kong, the co-founder of the Gopeng Museum, housed in Eu Yang Sang's horse stable, was a school teacher and then headmaster in the days when Gopeng had more young people. After retirement, he made it his mission to preserve the history of Gopeng. Phang says: '[When] the tin crash [came] and rubber prices fell, about two-thirds of the businesses in town closed down and all the young people left. Now Gopeng is an old folks' town.'

Kampung Lawan Kuda was where the British used to play polo. The houses there on the edge of the mining ponds are somewhat newer. *Lee Chen Loong* worked for a few decades in construction before the tin crash. He then went to Singapore and found work as a labourer, but eventually returned to Gopeng. He rented a parcel of ex-mining land near Lawan Kuda, where he built a small house and started to breed ornamental fish, including koi, goldfish, and arowana, for export.

Before the tin crash in 1985, *David Ho* supplied heavy machinery to the mining industry. Surprisingly his business continued to do well for several years afterwards, as he bought and then sold abroad used machinery from mining enterprises that had closed.

Gnasergaram is an elderly barber in his 70s in Kampung Kepayang, which was surrounded by mines owned by Gopeng Consolidated. People from some 300 households worked in the mines, supporting many small businesses. After the crash, most people found work in the emerging marble and limestone industries on the outskirts of Gopeng, and at Simpang Pulai, north of Kampung Kepayang. Today fewer than 20 shophouses remain standing, and some of the roofs have caved in. Yet Gnasergaram stays because he owns a shophouse, which he bought for RM30,000 in the 1970s, and the traffic along the Gopeng–Ipoh road that runs through Kampung Kepayang brings business.

Source: Interviews conducted in Kampar and Gopeng in April 2021.

The pressing need to diversify was reinforced as deposits became less accessible and more costly to mine, and the operational costs of mining began to increase. This meant that the profitability of mining companies diminished, even as tin prices were softening. The global tin-market collapse of the mid-1980s devastated Perak's economy (Box 3.4). Although prices later recovered somewhat, they never regained their peak. With sagging prices and steeply rising costs, gross profit margins in the tin-mining industry tumbled. By 1991 tin accounted for just 0.8 per cent of Perak's employment, down from 4.6 per cent in 1980.

Box 3.4   **Impact of the collapse of tin mining on Perak's economy**

The sharp fall in global tin prices and in the volume of Perak's tin exports after 1980 had a devastating impact on the state's economy. The average price of tin, which had peaked at RM36 per kg in 1980, plummeted to RM15 per kg in 1986, hurting state revenues and employment, and affecting land-use patterns.

After tin prices cratered, the federal government's payment of tin export duties to the Perak government fell by half, from RM30.8 million in 1980 to RM15.8 million in 1981, before dropping to just RM2.0 million in 1985 (Ismail Bakar, 2004)—and the only reason Perak received even this amount is that the federal constitution entitles tin-producing states to 10 per cent of total tin taxes. No revenues were paid after 1986, as tin production had by then virtually ceased. The state's treasury also suffered through shrinking receipts due to the loss of licences and other revenues related to leases on land occupied by tin mining. The huge fall in state revenue had major impacts on its ability to fund development.

Although a large share of tin interests was owned outside the state—more so in dredging than gravel-pump production—the squeeze on profits and dividends would have hurt local incomes. The decline in tin production between 1980 and 1990 would also have had a substantial impact on the state's GDP. Impacts on the wider state economy would have been huge: tin mining was not an 'enclave' activity and was linked to the local economy through purchases of materials and equipment, and through the demand for goods and services made possible by the local incomes it generated.

The fading tin-mining industry left behind vast tracts of idle mining land; this included areas where mining operations had ceased because the ore had been depleted, as well as ones where operations had stopped temporarily. In 1987, Perak's government put this figure at around 7,190 hectares, of which 88 per cent was in the Kinta Valley (Perak State Development Office, 1987). Some of this land was later converted for agricultural uses and aquaculture farms.

Summary

In the first decade or so after independence, tin remained important for Perak's economy, with production reaching a peak in 1971. Output then declined, at first steadily despite fairly high prices, then more rapidly as the state's tin fields began to deplete. Perak's tin output eventually decoupled from prices.

Did the ITAs help Perak's tin-mining industry? The first four appear to have succeeded in minimizing price instability and in sustaining prices at a higher level than would have been seen had tin prices been left to market forces alone. However, this was principally because producer countries, including Malaysia, complied with export controls and cut back their production, which at times severely affected the livelihoods of their mining communities. The US—which was outside the ITC—arguably benefited the most as it was able to step into the market whenever it wanted to offload tin from its huge strategic stockpile, unconcerned about the impact on producer countries.

Underlying tensions between rich ITC consumer countries and lower-income producers began to spill over after the US joined the fifth ITA. During this ITA period, 1976–1982, the US argued against raising ceiling prices, called for producers to enlarge their buffer stocks, and increased its stockpile sales as prices rose (Burke, 1990). This was despite the ITA's emphasis on price stability and on maintaining export earnings to developing countries (EEC, 1976). Through its actions, the US reduced the net transfer of resources to producer countries.

The second half of the 1970s was a period when Perak's large mining companies consolidated and localized. Tin production in British-owned dredging mines became more challenging and was overtaken by the predominantly Chinese-owned gravel-pump mines. But production in these mines also sank from the mid-1980s, never recovering to earlier levels. Multiple factors conspired to hasten this decline, including rising production costs, the steady depletion of readily accessible deposits, and difficulties in securing suitable new land and obtaining mining licences.

There had also been a long-term lack of investment in downstream tin-based manufacturing industries, which could have incentivized production in marginal mines. Rising export duties and corporate taxes after independence appear to have discouraged foreign investment—and although these taxes provided a vital source of revenue for the federal government, they did not greatly benefit Perak.

The secular decline of the tin industry, and especially the impact of the 1985 crash and its aftermath, devastated Perak's tin towns, causing widespread suffering among mine workers, their families, and their communities. Tin, for many, had become a curse, and just as their forebears had done when they first came to Perak, they would be forced to migrate, this time to elsewhere in Malaysia or abroad. Yet, while tin mining's economic profile continued to recede into the 1990s, its imprint on the state's spatial and physical structure—its settlement patterns, towns, railways, and its environment, especially in the form of river pollution—endured.

Rubber and the Transition to Palm Oil, 1957–1991

In the mid-1950s, rubber cultivation was Malaya's most important economic activity, with Perak accounting for about 19 per cent of the country's production and 6.3 per cent of global output. Shifts in global production and consumption patterns, however, had greatly reduced the returns on natural rubber compared with the 1930s, and at independence, with the miniboom from the Korean War having just ended, the industry was heading for tough times.[26]

The synthetic rubber industry had made rapid advances such that, by 1945, the US—previously Malaya's largest market for natural rubber—had become the world's largest producer of synthetic rubber (Tate, 1996).[27] This intense competition weighed heavily on the price of natural rubber, as synthetic rubber could substitute for natural rubber in about a third of the rubber market (White, 2004).[28] This pressure, coupled with rising costs of production, led to narrower margins for rubber producers, and many sought out alternative crops, including oil palm.

European planters had already begun to diversify into oil palm cultivation in the 1920s and 1930s as part of efforts to maximize their profits. The first commercial planting in Malaya was in Selangor in 1917, initiated by French ex-schoolteacher Henri Fauconnier to replace failing coffee crops. The British-owned Guthrie and Company planted an oil palm estate in Kluang, Johor, under the newly formed Elaeis Oil Palm Company in 1924. By 1930, the Franco-Belgian group Hallet had become Malaya's largest producer of palm oil.

---

26 In the early 1950s, rubber production on estates and smallholdings was on an uptrend, spurred by higher demand and prices during the Korean War, 1951–1953, and by US stockpiling.

27 Between 1950 and 1955, US consumption of synthetic rubber as a share of total rubber consumption jumped from 43 per cent to 59 per cent, while world consumption also grew rapidly, from 25 per cent to 36 per cent (Fong, 1989).

28 Subsidies on synthetic rubber and mandatory usage requirements imposed in the US also ensured a market for synthetic rubber at the expense of natural rubber (Rudner, 1976).

Globalization: Perak's Rise, Relative Decline, and Regeneration. Sultan Nazrin Shah, Oxford University Press. © Sultan Nazrin Shah (2024). DOI: 10.1093/oso/9780198897774.003.0019

The first planting in Perak was undertaken in 1918 by United Plantations Ltd—a Danish company that had started in 1906 as the Jendarata Rubber Company—on its Sungai Bernam estate. One of the earliest oil palm enterprises, United Plantations became a market leader known for its above-average productivity and best practices. At their peak, estates under United Plantations and its sister company Bernam Oil Palms, located north of the Bernam river, accounted for 27 per cent of Malaya's palm oil output (Martin, 2003). By the mid-1950s United Plantations and Guthrie were the largest producers of palm oil in Malaya (Tate, 1996).

At independence, rubber was still Perak's—and Malaya's—most important crop, with palm oil yet to take off as a major export commodity. With manufacturing still in its infancy, these two primary resources, together with tin, were Malaya's main link to the global economy. However, the country was still a price-taker in international commodity markets with little real influence on global production and export patterns. Its openness to and dependence on international trade in these natural resources left it exposed to the vicissitudes of the global economy. Between 1957 and 1991, Perak's rubber production went through three broad phases:

> *Growth of rubber, 1957–1973.* Propelled by aggressive replanting programmes and higher-yielding trees, Perak's rubber production grew steadily to reach over 180,000 metric tonnes by 1971, or 6 per cent of global output. However, its performance paled against that of oil palm, which registered spectacular growth during this period, with Perak becoming the third-largest palm-oil-producing state in Malaysia.
>
> *Rubber's stagnation, 1974–1987.* The first decade of the NEP brought about major changes to estate ownership patterns and marked the end of British and European control of the rubber industry. While rubber prices were falling, exacerbated by two oil price shocks in the 1970s, oil palm planting continued unabated. Perak's rubber production stagnated at just under 228,000 metric tonnes a year, while its palm oil output was more than double that of rubber by 1981.
>
> *Rubber's decline, 1988 onwards.* This period of the INRAs cushioned the fall in rubber prices and brought about a degree of stability. The price and buffer stock mechanisms implemented to maintain higher prices did not significantly benefit Malaysia, however, as its wage costs were higher than those of most other rubber producers. After peaking in 1983, Perak's rubber production began to falter and by 1989 was on a path of permanent decline. By 1991 its share of global natural rubber output had fallen to 3.3 per cent, although its share of Malaysia's output held steady at 13.5 per cent.

Rubber was no longer the critical economic pillar it had been in the first half of the 20th century, and the face of the industry had changed completely. By 1991, the NEP had brought the entire rubber industry—once dominated by foreign-owned estates—under local control through state-owned agencies. The government's moves to prioritize rubber smallholdings, owned mainly by Malays, helped smallholders to overtake estates and become the backbone of the industry. By 1991 smallholdings accounted for 71 per cent of Malaysia's rubber production, compared to less than 50 per cent at independence, with many rubber estates having converted to oil palm. The returns on rubber had by this time declined, however, making it a seemingly unwise investment—for the federal government, as well.

Growth of Rubber, 1957–1973

Output Growth amid Falling Prices

Increased demand for automobiles after World War II saw the world's consumption of rubber almost doubling between 1957 and 1971 (Barlow et al., 1994). Technological breakthroughs in new synthetics, however, meant that the bulk of the increase in consumption was of synthetic rubber and, in 1962, global production of synthetic rubber overtook that of natural rubber.[29] The slower growth of natural rubber may in part have reflected its lower price elasticity of supply compared to synthetic rubber: the output of natural rubber is dependent on the planted area and maturity of trees, and cannot adjust quickly to changes in demand. By 1970, global production of synthetic rubber was close to double that of natural rubber—about 5.8 million metric tonnes versus 3.1 million metric tonnes—even though it had been less than half that of natural rubber in 1950. The ratio of synthetic rubber to natural rubber consumed in the US tyre sector was now 75:25, compared with 40:60 in 1950 (Sultan Nazrin Shah, 2019).

To safeguard the survival of the natural rubber industry, the federal government sought to ensure that its rubber production matched demand at competitive prices (Rudner, 1976). A federally funded rubber replanting scheme was implemented between 1952 and 1955, but this did not achieve the desired outcomes. This was because a larger proportion of the grants it

---

29 In 1960, the discovery of stereo-regular synthetics, which replicated the regular linkage pattern found in natural rubber polymers, enabled synthetic rubber to enter markets that had previously relied on natural rubber for its greater elasticity and high tensile strength (McHale, 1961).

disbursed went to high-output producers, typically estates, instead of small-holders who could not bear the cost of replanting without the help of grants (Rudner, 1976). In 1955, a revised rubber replanting scheme was implemented to encourage all estates and smallholdings to undertake replanting activities on a fifth of their estates or smallholdings using government grants. These were financed through the cess on rubber exports of M$0.045/lb. For estates, the grants were effectively a rebate of their cess payments (Fong, 1989).

In 1954, the government commissioned a fact-finding mission led by Sir Francis Robert Mudie to investigate the prospects of the rubber industry. The report by the mission emphasized the need to replant (Tate, 1996). A second mission report by the IBRD in 1955 stressed the importance of expanding research activities. Replanting and research were thus made priorities in the First and Second Five-Year Malayan Plans, covering the periods 1955 to 1960 and 1961 to 1965 (Federation of Malaya, 1956 and 1961). At the same time, the downtrend in rubber prices in the 1960s, which shrank both federal government revenue and the current account surplus,[30] also prompted the government to prioritize diversification within agriculture towards other crops, including oil palm. The allocation of public funds for rubber replanting in the midterm review of the Second Malaya Five-Year Plan, although still large, was revised downwards by about 15 per cent from the original target, making the allocation even lower than in the first plan.

Replanting of rubber trees and improvements in yield boosted Perak's rubber production, and stronger growth was recorded in the latter part of the 1960s as new trees began to mature. Although the gains in yield more than offset the decline in mature acreage, the rise in production was held back because Perak had a higher proportion of smallholdings to estates than the national average. So there was only a 2 per cent increase in total rubber production over 1958–1962—far short of Malaysia's 8 per cent. Only after 1962 did Perak's rubber output register any notable increase. Production grew steadily over the period 1957–1971, rising to 181,000 tonnes by 1971, up from 124,500 tonnes in 1957, while Malaysia's doubled to 1.3 million tonnes, accounting for 63 per cent of the increase in world production (Figure 3.5, left panel). Signs that Perak's rubber industry was losing ground against other states were beginning to appear, however, although it still retained its position as Malaysia's second-largest rubber-producing state. Perak's production

---

30 The price boom during the Korean War was short-lived and prices subsequently plunged to below M$1.50 per kg in 1954, from their peak of over M$5 per kg in 1951. Although prices rebounded in the mid-1950s, they fluctuated wildly and for most of the 1960s remained below M$2 per kg.

growth lagged behind that of other states, particularly Johor, Negeri Sembi-lan, Kedah, and Perlis, so that its share in the country's total output, which had peaked at 23.2 per cent in 1956, had by 1971 declined to 13.8 per cent (Figure 3.5, right panel). Still, Perak retained a 6 per cent share of global out-put, down just a little from its 6.3 per cent in 1957.

With natural rubber output growing and in the face of intense competition from synthetic rubber, natural rubber prices declined between 1957 and 1971, except for temporary recoveries between 1958 and 1960 and in 1969. By 1971, at less than M$1.50 per kg, rubber prices had fallen some 50 per cent from a high of M$3.00 per kg in 1960. Rubber's contribution to Malaysia's merchandise export receipts had fallen to 34 per cent, down from 55 per cent in 1960. Price pressures were further exacerbated by releases of US—and, to a much smaller degree, UK—stockpiles. By 1954, when stockpiling ended, the US had around 1.13 million tonnes of natural rubber in stock, which was now less useful in the face of its booming synthetic rubber industry (White, 2004). Although eager to dump their stocks, in 1959 the US and UK agreed to the Malayan government's request to release their stocks more gradually and at an agreed floor price, although they did not always adhere to this. The increase in output between

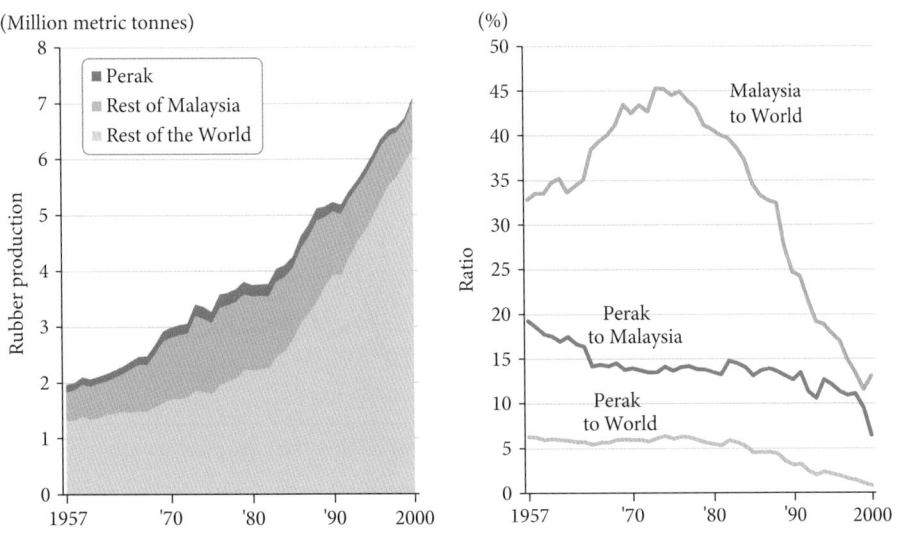

Figure 3.5 **Perak's rubber production plummeted in 1957–1971 as a share of Malaysia's, but was still 6.0 per cent of the global total**

Sources of data: Malaysian data: Department of Statistics–Malaysia, *Rubber Statistics Handbook Malaysia* (various years); Department of Statistics–Malaysia (2015); World data: Food and Agriculture Organization of the United Nations (various years), *Rubber Production.*

1957 and 1971 had kept rubber profitable despite the fall in prices, but with prices significantly affected by the release of stocks below the agreed price, rubber producers found themselves subject to the vagaries of major rubber consumers, notably in the US.

Low rubber prices and shrinking profits encouraged rubber estate owners to allocate more of their land to oil palm cultivation. A shorter gestation period, higher yield per hectare, and lower labour requirements made oil palm production highly profitable. Between 1965 and 1969, United Plantations' rubber contribution margin averaged 27 per cent, around half of its palm oil contribution margin of 53 per cent (Martin, 2003). The acreage under oil palm on estates in the peninsula expanded by around four times between 1960 and 1971, while the annual output of palm oil rose more than five times to reach around 580,000 tonnes. By 1966 Malaysia had become the world's largest exporter of palm oil, with its exports surpassing those of Nigeria, Indonesia, and Zaire (Martin, 2003). Perak was the third-largest palm-oil-producing state, accounting for around 13 per cent of Malaysia's production (Figure 3.6).

Figure 3.6   **Perak's palm oil output began its impressive growth after independence, climbing to more than 10 per cent of the national figure by the early 1970s**

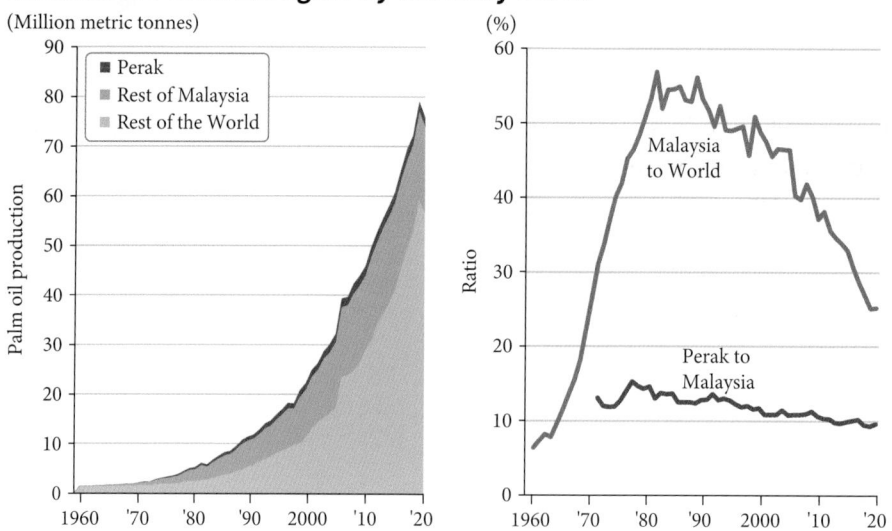

Sources of data: Food and Agriculture Organization of the United Nations (various years), *Oil Palm Production*; Department of Statistics–Malaysia, *Oil Palm, Coconut and Tea Statistics* (various years), Malaysian Palm Oil Board, Oil Palm Statistics (various years).

Note: Data not available for Perak before 1972.

Early Malayanization

At the moment when Malaya's newly independent government turned to focus on the country's socio-economic and rural development, foreign businesses still occupied the commanding heights of the economy, especially in the rubber industry.[31] Over the period 1957 to 1970, economic policies generally remained laissez-faire, and foreign investment, on which much of Malaysia's economic needs depended, was still being encouraged. Some British businesses were becoming more cautious, however, sensing the shift towards increasing economic nationalism amid calls for greater Malayanization of capital and management.[32] The Rubber Growers' Association, for example, did not expect political conditions to be supportive of British investments beyond the first five years following the federal elections in 1959 (White, 2004).

This shift was evident in the establishment of the Malayan Stock Exchange in 1960, and the request to London-registered rubber and tin companies to open branch share-registers locally. Concerned that restrictions might be tightened further if they did not comply, by 1964 around 40 UK companies had made their branch registers available locally. Of the share counters traded on the Malayan Stock Exchange, 60 per cent belonged to rubber and tin companies. British agency houses resisted registering their shares locally, however, and were still mainly owned by London shareholders in 1971. This inertia eventually culminated in the abrupt takeovers of some of the large agency houses in the 1970s.

Malayanization policies also favoured rubber smallholders. At the start of the replanting exercise, government grants were provided to both estates and smallholdings. But by the First Malaysia Plan, 1966–1970, grants to estates had been scaled back, and they were removed from the official replanting scheme (White, 2004). Of the 189,000 hectares of Malaysian rubber land that had been replanted by the end of the First Plan, 65 per cent was on smallholdings and only 35 per cent on estates, although this ratio may be skewed by the fact that a higher share of estates had already been replanted before the plan. In 1970, even with the push to replant on smallholdings, the figure for high-yielding trees on smallholdings, at

---

31 In the 1950s the industry was still dominated by foreign-owned estates, with Europeans, particularly British agency houses, controlling around 70 per cent of total planted rubber acreage (Jones, 2000). The agency houses also controlled shipping lines as well as insurance and foreign exchange services, giving them almost full control of the rubber sector (Fong, 1989).

32 Several early beneficiaries of the Malayanization policy later became very successful. One of these was Lee Loy Seng who acquired the British-owned Kuala Lumpur Kepong Amalgamated in the mid-1960s. He limited the role of the London-based board, relocated its head office to Ipoh, transferred its tax residence to Malaysia, and created senior-level jobs for Malaysians (Salt Media Group, 2021). He thus transformed his family tin-mining business in Kampar into a major multinational publicly listed plantation company, Kuala Lumpur Kepong Berhad, and his philanthropy supported health and education initiatives in Perak.

63 per cent of total smallholdings' acreage, was still lower than the estate sector's 92 per cent (EPU, 1971).[33] Still, roughly halfway through the plan, in 1968, the rubber output of Perak's smallholders overtook that of the estates and remained ahead thereafter: in 1971 the figures were 95,300 metric tonnes versus 86,100 tonnes, a reversal of the position in 1964 of 64,800 tonnes versus 67,100 tonnes (Figure 3.7).[34]

Early Malayanization policies were generally moderate, and before the 1970s foreign firms continued to operate and make business decisions unhindered. At that time, the Federal Land Development Authority (FELDA) lacked production facilities and distribution networks, and the government was focused on strengthening its capacities.[35] The agricultural sector still needed British investment, and so the government left the British rubber estates alone, although it did restrict the sale of land to them (Saruwatari, 1991). British agency houses

Figure 3.7   **Smallholdings came to dominate the rubber industry in Perak after 1971**

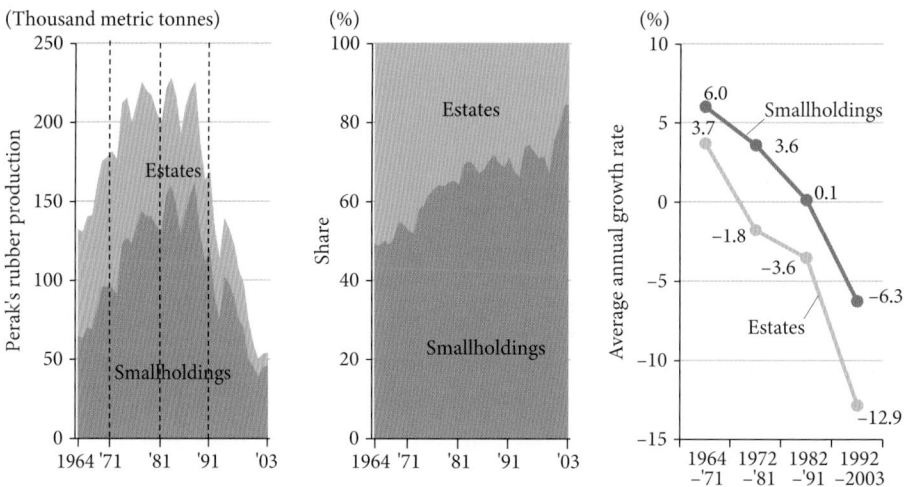

Sources of data: Department of Statistics–Malaysia (various years), *Rubber Statistics Handbook Malaysia*; for 2001–2003: Ministry of Primary Industries–Malaysia (various years), *Statistics on Commodities*.

---

33 The steep decline in rubber prices, which fell in nominal terms by 40 per cent between 1957 and 1970, hit Perak's smallholders and estate workers hard (Azrai Abdullah, 2022, p. 144).

34 In 1971, smallholdings' production nationally was still less than that of estates, and only exceeded the latter in 1974.

35 FELDA was established in July 1956 under the Land Development Ordinance of 1956. Its purpose was to develop land and relocate landless rural poor into the newly developed agricultural areas in order to help eradicate poverty through the cultivation of oil palm and rubber. FELDA implemented several rubber schemes in Perak, but after 1964 its focus shifted to oil palm.

continued to grow, posting rising profits. Barlow & Co., for example, which merged with Boustead's plantation arm in 1966 to become Barbeal, trebled its profits in the first decade of Malaysia's independence, while Guthrie reaped impressive profits from its oil palm planting operations (Purdie, 2018). In 1968, foreigners still controlled almost two-thirds of Malaysia's rubber assets. Only after the NEP began did Malayanization policies take stronger hold.

Rubber's Stagnation, 1974–1987

National Control and Eclipse of British Agency Houses

By end-1970, over half of the acreage of the peninsula's rubber estates was still owned by foreign interests, with almost all of the rest owned by non-Malay Malaysians.[36] For the peninsula's oil palm estates, the ratio of foreign ownership to that of non-Malay Malaysians was 75:25 (EPU, 1971). Malay owners of rubber and oil palm estates were conspicuous by their absence.

The NEP sought to rectify these imbalances by setting a 20-year target of 30 per cent in ownership, management, and employment in all commercial and industrial companies for Malays and other *Bumiputera* (a group comprising aborigines and other natives of Sabah and Sarawak). This marked the beginning of the end of the British agency houses, which had dominated the rubber and oil palm industries for so long.[37] Whereas previously business transactions had led to the transfer of estate ownership from foreign residents to locals—mostly asset-rich Malaysian Chinese in urban areas—the NEP saw a dramatic shift in policy on corporate ownership from foreign residents to Malays and other *Bumiputera* (see 'The New Economic Policy—A Fundamental Shift', below).

This policy change was to be achieved through public agency investment vehicles, such as PERNAS and the National Equity Corporation (Permodalan Nasional Berhad, or PNB). PNB, a government-owned investment company, was established in 1978 to purchase and manage share capital on behalf of Malays and other *Bumiputera*,[38] and to facilitate the divestiture of

---

36 Amid uncertainty surrounding the Malayanization policy, some foreign rubber estate owners, who still held close to 150,000 hectares of planted area, began to relinquish their ownership to local buyers, mainly to Malaysian Chinese (Drabble, 2000).

37 In the 1950s, the largest British agency house was Harrisons & Crosfield, which controlled 63 companies with 91,500 hectares; after which came Boustead's 47 companies with 68,400 hectares; Guthrie's 21 companies with 63,100 hectares; Sime Darby's 32 companies with 44,500 hectares; and Harper Gilfillan's 25 companies with 67,200 hectares (Jones, 2000).

38 This happened through organizations such as Amanah Saham Nasional Berhad (ASN), as well as other trust schemes designed to support Malay and other Bumiputra communities.

shares to particular individual *Bumiputera*—opening the door to the possibility of high-level corruption. Backed by government funding,[39] PERNAS began acquiring control of British-owned tin and rubber conglomerates, and within 10 years had become heavily involved in a wide spectrum of activities ranging from construction, services, and manufacturing to hotels and shipping (Fong, 1989).

British agency houses that failed to comply with the equity ownership targets of the NEP were targeted by the government, which took steps to seize control of their plantations, starting with the accumulation of Sime Darby shares on the London Stock Exchange by PERNAS. In December 1976 the takeover of Sime Darby was complete, and four British board directors were replaced with three Malaysian appointees of PERNAS (Saruwatari, 1991). Tan Siew Sin, who was president of the Malaysian Chinese Association until 1974 and a former finance minister, was appointed as Sime Darby's first non-British chairman.[40]

In 1979, Sime Darby then sought to take over Guthrie by rapidly accumulating 30 per cent of its share capital. The initial takeover bid failed, however, and by the rules of the London Stock Exchange, Sime Darby was forced to sell all of its shares in Guthrie—which it did, to PNB (Purdie, 2018). Another chance came on 7 September 1981 when, in a matter of hours after the opening of trade on the London Stock Exchange, PNB increased its stake in Guthrie from around 25 per cent to more than 50 per cent (Shakila Yacob and White, 2010, p. 1), in what became known as the 'dawn raid'. Although it was hardly a unique action, the UK press dubbed the acquisition 'hostile' and 'Backdoor Nationalization' (HC. 196–i, 1983, p. 53). Within weeks, the London Stock Exchange had amended its rules to restrict the speed at which people could acquire a substantial portion of a company's shares, or rights over them. They would have to wait seven days before buying shares that gave them a controlling interest. It did this both to protect the interests of minority shareholders and to safeguard British interests in other companies.

This change in the London Stock Exchange's rules following the dawn raid caused dismay in Malaysia, especially as the acquisition of Guthrie shares had been legal and in accordance with the rules at the time (HC. 196–i, 1983, p. 54). This rule change worsened already strained relations between the two

---

[39] The growth of the petroleum sector, which benefited PERNAS and PNB in the form of grants and interest-free loans from the government, made acquisitions possible because at this time petroleum was the largest commodity export from Malaysia; payments from the state-owned petroleum company, Petroliam Nasional Berhad (PETRONAS), made up 32 per cent of federal government revenue (Fong, 1989).

[40] After the incorporation of PNB in 1978, PERNAS transferred to it, at cost, its shares in Sime Darby and in the Malaysia Mining Corporation (Gomez and Jomo, 1999).

countries, and in October 1981 the Malaysian Prime Minister Mahathir Mohamad announced a 'buy British last' campaign which continued for several years.[41]

With the takeover of Sime Darby and Guthrie, at a cost much lower than their asset value, by 1981 the ownership and control of 160,000 hectares of rubber and oil palm plantations—18 per cent of total planted acreage—had been transferred into *Bumiputera* hands (Fong, 1989). PNB's 'dawn raid' on Guthrie, vividly remembered as one of the most hostile takeovers during the NEP period, signalled clearly that the government was determined to 'Malayanize' control of the country's resource-based companies. The gloves were off.

Not all British agency houses and foreign plantation companies faced such hostile takeovers, however, and those willing to cooperate with the government experienced more amicable transfers of ownership. In 1976, the Barlow family agreed to sell 30 per cent of their 75 per cent interest in Barbeal to FELDA, the Pilgrimage Fund (Tabung Haji), and the Armed Forces Fund (Tabung Angkatan Tentera) (Purdie, 2018). In 1982, Harrisons & Crosfield, which owned Harrisons' Malaysian Estates—Malaysia's largest plantation company at the time—finally agreed to place the estates under a new Malaysian company, with PNB as a partner holding a controlling stake of more than 50 per cent of the shares (Shakila Yacob and White, 2010).

The 1982 takeover of United Plantations, headquartered in Teluk Intan, by the Food Industries of Malaysia Berhad (FIMA) was more amicable than most. The incoming chairman, Basir Ismail, who was also the chairman of FIMA, retained a strong working relationship with the Danish shareholders and those remaining in management.[42]

In 1983, the headquarters of the Rubber Growers' Association was transferred from London to Kuala Lumpur, and by the early 1990s the remaining stakes of foreign estate owners and British agency houses had largely been sold off. This marked the end of foreign—and particularly British—dominance of Malaysia's rubber industry. In its place a new group of elite Malay capitalists emerged, many with close political links to the ruling party. These new business leaders now headed the country's leading resource-based companies and controlled its illustrious rubber industry—unfortunately, just when it was about to lose that lustre.

---

41 Mahathir was also upset by increased university fees in 1979 for Malaysian (and other non-European Economic Community) students studying in the UK, and a perception of reduced British interest in Malaysia following the UK's entry into the European Economic Community (HC 368–i, 1986).

42 United Plantations' top management were well versed in the local business environment and placed strong emphasis on employees' welfare (Martin, 2003).

The leading British plantation companies—Sime Darby, Kumpulan Guthrie, Harrisons Malaysia, and Boustead Holdings—with their new Malaysian corporate names, had been brought under Malay and other *Bumiputera* control. Later, these same companies diversified into oil palm and other businesses.[43]

No Bounce-back for Rubber

After trailing estates throughout the rubber boom of the first half of the 20th century, rubber smallholdings became more prominent in the first 10 years of the NEP. With the sub-division of some large estates into smaller units, the conversion of others into oil palm estates, and the government's replanting and new planting activities, Perak's rubber output from smallholdings rose from 95,000 tonnes at end-1971 to 128,000 tonnes in 1981, while the output of estates fell from 86,000 tonnes to 71,000 tonnes. In 1976, when rubber production by smallholders was close to 1.5 times that of the estates, Malaysia was the largest producer of natural rubber, accounting for 45 per cent of the world's output.

In 1968, Perak's four main rubber-producing districts—Kuala Kangsar, Batang Padang, Manjung, and Kinta—collectively accounted for two-thirds of the state's rubber output. Production by smallholders in these districts had more than doubled by 1983 (Figure 3.8). Batang Padang accounted for around 20 per cent of this growth, becoming the district with the highest output by rubber smallholders. Much of the expansion in Perak's smallholdings stemmed from the work of the Rubber Industry Smallholders Development Authority (RISDA), which offered subsidies and financing for the purchase of fertilizers.[44]

Nationally, however, between 1972 and 1981 the planted acreage of rubber remained virtually stagnant, even as the oil palm sector saw aggressive expansion, fuelled in particular by FELDA and the Federal Land Consolidation and Rehabilitation Authority (FELCRA).[45] FELDA's focus moved away from rubber and towards oil palm in the 1970s, but this shift was already apparent in the mid-1960s

---

43 For example, Sime Darby, Guthrie, and Golden Hope plantations merged and re-entered the Kuala Lumpur Stock Exchange under the name of Sime Darby in 2007, with the Group's other major business activities ranging from automobiles and manufacturing to property, energy, and utilities.

44 RISDA was established in January 1973 under the Ministry of Rural Development to improve the social and economic well-being of smallholders and turn them into viable, progressive, and independent entrepreneur owners. RISDA in fact took over the functions of the Rubber Industry Replanting Board and the Smallholders' Advisory Service of the Rubber Research Institute. It facilitated rubber replanting on smallholdings through the provision of direct subsidies to smallholders, and provided technical and marketing assistance. RISDA's first rubber project in Perak was in 1968 in Hilir Perak, covering 6,500 acres of land.

45 FELCRA was established in April 1966 to develop idle land and to help landowners of fragmented plots of land to consolidate their holdings and develop them into efficient producing units. In 1995, 15 per cent of all FELCRA projects in Malaysia (by number) were in Perak.

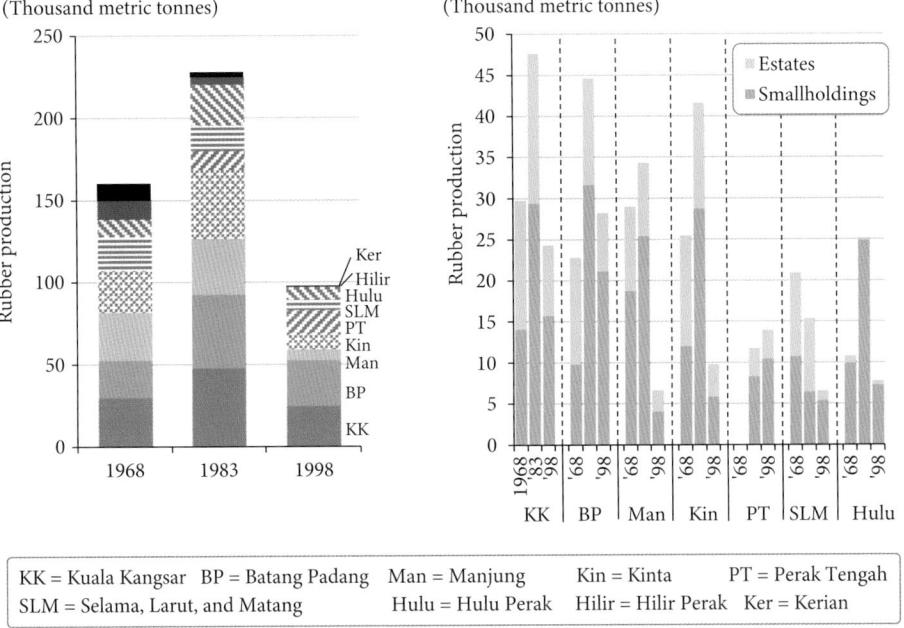

Figure 3.8

Kuala Kangsar and Batang Padang were Perak's main rubber-producing districts in 1968–1998

KK = Kuala Kangsar BP = Batang Padang Man = Manjung   Kin = Kinta   PT = Perak Tengah
SLM = Selama, Larut, and Matang   Hulu = Hulu Perak Hilir = Hilir Perak Ker = Kerian

Sources of data: Malaysia data: Department of Statistics–Malaysia, *Rubber Statistics Handbook Malaysia*
(various years).

in Perak, where, between 1964 and 1970, two schemes were conducted for oil palm but none for rubber (Wikkramatileke, 1995). And although FELCRA continued to run rubber schemes in the 1970s before refocusing on oil palm, its projects were smaller than FELDA's and were no match, by acreage, to FELDA's large oil palm projects.

Although the Rubber Research Institute of Malaya produced high-yielding varieties and discovered better tapping tools and techniques (Tate, 1996), the increase in productivity[46] and the higher output from smallholdings in the latter part of the 1970s was too small to offset the fall in output stemming from the decline in estate hectarage, which fell from 573,100 hectares in 1976 to 493,300 hectares in 1981. As a result, total rubber output declined during this period. In Perak, it fell from 225,000 tonnes in 1977 to 199,000 tonnes in 1981, erasing most of the gains made in the first half of the 1970s. Rubber's contribution to Malaysia's export earnings also fell, from 33.4 per cent in 1970 to 16.4 per

---

46 By 1970, around 85 per cent of rubber acreage had been planted with high-yielding clones, including about 60 per cent of smallholdings' acreage (Fong, 1989). Rubber plantations therefore saw an increase in productivity between 1972 and 1981, from 1.0 to 1.2 metric tonnes per hectare on estates, and from 0.48 to 0.62 metric tonnes per hectare on smallholdings.

cent in 1980, and in 1981 rubber lost its long-held position as the country's top export earner, giving way to both petroleum and manufacturing, with palm oil fast catching up.

Oil Palm Expansion

The expansion of oil palm planting was greatly boosted in the late 1950s by innovative research in crossbreeding, which led to the development of the Tenera variety. Tenera palms yielded a third more than the traditional Dura variety, thus greatly increasing planters' returns. The first Tenera palms in Malaysia were planted on United Plantations' Jendarata and Ulu Bernam estates in Perak. Between 1972 and 1981, the planted hectarage of oil palm increased fourfold and its output fivefold, amounting by 1981 to 56 per cent of rubber's hectarage and almost twice its output. By then, Perak's plantings for oil palm accounted for just under 10 per cent, and its palm oil production for almost 15 per cent, of Malaysia's total.

With Perak's oil palm industry undergoing rapid expansion, ever-increasing amounts of new land were brought under cultivation, notably between 1971 and 1980. This included 55,000 hectares under FELDA, FELCRA, RISDA, and other state agencies for agricultural and natural resource development, with oil palm as the major crop. Yet alienation for plantations and agricultural cultivation, together with the expansion of the timber industry, along with urban and industrial development, came at great cost to Perak's forests (Box 3.5). From 1970 to 1980, the area under oil palm cultivation increased by nearly 58,000 hectares. While some of this would have been converted from areas previously under rubber, felling and burning of forest land to prepare for oil palm cultivation was common. FELDA's land conversion activities also increased from the 1970s, with 34,730 hectares alienated for Perak's FELDA projects (FAO, 1985). During the 1970s, thousands of hectares were also alienated for smallholder agricultural projects, mainly from Perak's lower-lying state forest or reserve forest land.

Perak's forest land was also alienated for other large essential projects, such as in the Hulu Perak district where the Belum Temenggor artificial lake was created to provide Temenggor Dam with water for hydropower, flooding 15,200 hectares of natural forest in the 1970s. Other less essential development projects, as well as illegal logging, have also contributed to deforestation (Box 3.5).

Box 3.5	Perak's deforestation: Towards improved conservation

At independence in 1957, 69.1 per cent of Perak's land area was classified as forest—some 1,389,000 hectares—of which 54 per cent was gazetted as 'forest reserves' (Smith, 1958). According to the World Resources Institute (2021), 52 per cent of the state's land area, or some 1,092,000 hectares, was identified as 'natural forest' in 2020—a slightly higher estimate than that of the Perak government of 1,014,618 hectares (Forestry Department of Peninsular Malaysia, 2021). Although differences in definitions of natural forest complicate comparisons over time, these data suggest a sharp drop in Perak's forest cover since independence (Table 3a). Most of this loss is permanent and is due to human activities.

Table 3a	Forest coverage declined substantially in Perak, but remains higher than the peninsula's average

		Share of forest coverage of total state area (%)			
	Perak	Johor	Selangor	Pahang	Peninsular Malaysia
1957	69.1	62.2	46.7	89.1	72.4
2021	48.6	23.2	31.8	56.9	43.5

Sources of data: Smith (1958); Forestry Department of Peninsular Malaysia (2021).

Post-independence, state development priorities trumped conservation. High rates of rural poverty and landlessness, and rapid population growth, left little room for conservation concerns. Perak's rural development committees placed little value on non-timber forest services and products—for instance, the protection of water catchments, carbon sequestration, natural habitats, the preservation of bio-diversity, and other ecosystem services—instead giving priority to the development opportunities created by alienating forest land for other uses.

The 1960s saw increasing incursions into Perak's forest reserves, many of them illegal. In many areas, including the Bintang Hijau Reserve in Hulu Perak district, Kuala Kangsar, and the Kinta Hills, squatters cleared forest areas to plant lucrative tobacco and cassava crops. And, until 1965, there was no replacement for the thousands of hectares of forest reserves that were excised under FELDA land-settlement schemes, such as in the Terulak Forest Reserve (Kathirithamby-Wells, 2005, p. 275).

In circumstances where there was an acute shortage of trained forestry personnel, illegal and unregulated logging activities proliferated. Perak's log production in 1970 was more than twice that in 1957 (Yusuf Hadi, 1982). During the 1960s,

(Continued)

46,338 hectares were excised from Perak's forest reserves, equivalent to about 6 per cent of the gazetted reserve areas of 1957 (Kathirithamby-Wells, 2005, p. 297). By 1970, the forested area was 10 per cent smaller than it had been at independence.

Accelerated deforestation after 1970

From the 1970s, the NEP created further stresses for Perak's forests as rural development and land settlement took on greater political and economic importance. Additionally, logging was becoming a major source of state revenue, with high export demand from industrialized countries, particularly Japan.

Clearing forests to prepare land for new oil palm plantations provided a ready source of timber for Perak's logging industry. From the Third Malaysia Plan, 1976–1980, to the Fifth Malaysia Plan, 1986–1990, logging took on additional significance as a 'targeted' sector. Malaysian planners saw the expansion of the fast-growing timber industry as an opportunity for economic development, and the industry boomed. Logging activity soared, and the state's forests were mined for wood. Logging licences covering nearly 8 per cent of Perak's total land area were issued from 1971 to 1980, and nearly 28 million cubic feet of timber was harvested. Given the prevalence of illegal activity, the area harvested was larger than the area licensed, while the process of removing logs, typically higher-value older trees, often damaged or destroyed younger trees.

Despite recognition of the need for sustainable forest management, articulated in the national Forestry Policy of 1978 and the Forestry Act of 1984, as well as in national plans from the mid-1980s, deforestation continued largely unchecked. Remote-sensing data suggest that Perak's natural tree cover contracted by 4.2 per cent between 1988 and 2000 (Wan Shafrina et al., 2020). Major areas of deforestation were in the south, northwest, and west of Perak, and typically occurred where there was nearby road access. Plantation agriculture accounted for most of the forest land alienation, although population settlement also contributed.

The Federal Forestry Act of 1984 standardized forestry law and regulations across states (including coupe sizes and minimum tree harvesting diameters), with the aim of making forestry sustainable. The law was gazetted by the Perak State Council at end-1985 (Adzidah Yaakob, 2014). An amendment to the Act was promulgated in 1993 (adopted in Perak in 1994) to recognize the multiple uses of forests and their role in environmental protection. Despite the national policy overlay, authority for the management of Perak's forests remains with the State Forestry Department.

The attrition of Perak's forests has continued since 2000. Wan Shafrina et al. (2020) estimate that, between 2000 and 2018, Perak lost just over 12 per cent of its mangrove and terrestrial forests. Hulu Perak has been the district with the most absolute loss of total tree cover, but the districts of Hilir Perak, Batang Padang, and Kuala Kangsar have also seen significant losses. In 2000, 10.5 per cent of Perak's natural forests were 'intact forest', showing no sign of anthropogenic impacts. Yet, despite being in 'protected areas', 9,450 hectares of these forests were lost between 2002 and 2019. The total area of primary forest gazetted in protected areas of Perak also decreased by 3.5 per cent over this period. The lack of human resources and inadequate law has contributed to illegal logging activities, which often encroach into *Orang Asli* settlements, endangering their livelihoods and traditional culture.

Towards conservation
In Perak, as in all Malaysian states, official gazetted forest reserves (986,862 hectares) comprise two categories: *permanently protected forest (49 per cent)* where no logging or any other commercial activity is allowed, and *productive forest (51 per cent)* where commercial activities, such as quarrying and sustainable logging, are permitted under strict licensing conditions set by the Forestry Department after weighing their potential environmental impact. To further protect endangered species such as elephants and tigers, there is a Central Forest Spine in which multiple vital ecological corridors across Perak and bridges to other state forests have been identified. These are important steps, yet forestry authorities also need to share information about conservation measures and strictly enforce them.

Some important initiatives have been taken in partnership with international organizations to preserve Perak's natural forests and prevent their commercial exploitation. In 2007, the state government gazetted 117,500 hectares as a state park—the Royal Belum State Park—in the Belum Temenggor forest in the Hulu Perak district. The state also has smaller recreational forest and nature reserves, including the Kledang Saiong Forest Eco Park and the Matang Mangrove Forest Reserve.

Other initiatives include the Roundtable on Sustainable Palm Oil—an international multi-stakeholder process that entails voluntary commitments by its members to no deforestation, no new development on peat, and no labour exploitation. This

(Continued)

has helped to advance sustainability standards in the oil palm sector. In 2008, United Plantations became the world's first company to produce and export certified sustainable palm oil. A national scheme is also in operation—the Malaysian Sustainable Palm Oil certification scheme—with similar goals. Corporate investment in green technology is also increasing in Perak, including in two large biomass projects (MIDA, 2021).

As education levels and real incomes have risen, Perak's citizens have come to take more interest in forest conservation and have placed a higher value on the environmental, social, and other benefits provided by forests. These benefits need to be carefully weighed in decisions affecting forest management, so as to preserve the state's forests for future generations and to ensure sustainable development.

Rubber's Decline, 1988 Onwards

The International Natural Rubber Agreements

Natural rubber prices fluctuated wildly in the early 1980s,[47] with the price of Ribbed Smoked Sheet (RSS) No. 1—a benchmark grade of natural rubber—eventually rising to over M$4.00 per kg (Box 3.6). The first five-year INRA (1980–1985, but extended to 1987), an arrangement between the major producers and consumers of natural rubber intended to secure price stability had already been formalized but was yet to become operational. Prices then plunged, prompting the International Natural Rubber Organization to intervene in the market and begin stockpiling in October 1981. This kept prices around the 'may-buy' intervention level of M$1.79 per kg until January 1983, when the global economy began to recover and prices strengthened to reach the upper 'may-sell' intervention level of M$2.42 per kg. Between October 1981 and January 1983, the buffer-stock manager purchased around 6 per cent of the world's annual natural rubber consumption and succeeded in preventing a free-fall in rubber prices (Stubbs, 1988).

---

47 These fluctuations had their roots in the twin oil shocks of the 1970s.

> **Box 3.6** **From the Malaysian Crash Programme to the International Natural Rubber Agreements**

The oil price shock of 1973 reduced demand for automotive parts and new vehicles. An oversupply of rubber spurred discussions—led by Malaysia and Indonesia—about the formation of an international buffer stock to be held by the Association of Natural Rubber Producing Countries (ANRPC), which had been formed in 1970. At the end of November 1974, to mitigate the drastic fall in rubber prices and the simultaneous steep rise in the consumer price index reflecting a shortage in global oil supplies,[a] the government pursued the Malaysian Crash Programme, aimed at influencing prices by reducing output (Barlow et al., 1994).[b] For 18 months, rubber estates were barred from using certain chemical fertilizers and from tapping on Sundays, and the government purchased rubber directly from smallholders and stockpiled it.

In 1975, there was a decline of 12 per cent in production on estates and of 4 per cent in total output (on estates and smallholdings combined) (Barlow et al., 1994). At end-1975 the price of RSS No. 1 had risen to just over M$1.60 per kg from under M$1.00 per kg in November 1974, just before the programme was launched (Stubbs, 1983). Although the Crash Programme achieved early success, the Malaysian government recognized that such unilateral intervention could be sustained only over a short period and would easily be derailed if low price pressures persisted.

Between 1976 and 1979, UNCTAD kickstarted a series of negotiations between rubber producers and consumers, underpinned by the ANPRC Agreement. These negotiations culminated in the INRA in 1980. Under the INRA, a reference price of M$2.10 was set as the basis of all other benchmarks, with respective discretionary and compulsory intervention bands established at beyond 15 per cent and 20 per cent of either side of the reference price. The floor and ceiling prices were set at M$1.50 and M$2.70, and the capacity of the normal buffer stock at 400,000 tonnes, with another 150,000 tonnes as contingency.

The buffer stock was managed by the International Natural Rubber Organization, whose operations were funded by all member countries in proportion to their production or consumption of natural rubber, as well as their voting power (Barlow et al., 1994). It was the first commodity agreement in which buffer stocks were financed by contributions from the governments of importing *and* exporting countries. With a two-thirds majority between producers and consumers required to make any major change, Malaysia—which had 48 per cent of the votes of producers—held veto power (Stubbs, 1983).

---

[a] Oil price shocks in the short run make production of synthetic rubber more expensive because of higher input prices, as seen in the brief upward spikes in natural rubber prices between 1973 and 1974, and 1979 and 1980, as producers switched from synthetic to natural rubber. The boom in natural rubber prices quickly reversed, however, as softer global demand set in.

[b] As the world's largest producer of rubber at that time—with a 44 per cent market share—Malaysia sought to influence the price of rubber on the market and aimed to stabilize prices of RSS No. 1 at M$1.20 to 1.30 per kg.

The first INRA helped to provide some income stability to producers of natural rubber by setting a floor price and maintaining prices within a set range. For rubber consumers, the buffer stock ensured a continuous supply of natural rubber and mitigated any sharp price spikes above its upper limits. Nonetheless, renegotiation of the INRA, which was due to expire in 1985, was challenging. Divergences between the rubber producers and consumers were apparent at the May 1982 review of the reference price. Rubber producers had sought to have the price raised, arguing that production costs had risen since the initial reference price was calculated and that this was causing hardships (Box 3.7). The terms of the agreement, however, called for an automatic 5 per cent cut in the reference price because the daily market indicator price had been below the lower intervention price for six months preceding the May 1982 review. Producers and consumers finally agreed that the reference price would be reduced by 1 per cent.

| Box 3.7 | Poverty rates among rubber smallholders shot up as intervention prices fell |

In 1985, when the first INRA was set to expire, the average cost of Malaysian production for RSS No. 1 had risen to M$1.95 per kg, from M$1.20 to 1.35 per kg when the INRA was first negotiated (Stubbs, 1988). But in 1985 the lower intervention price was reduced by 1 per cent to M$1.77, which could no longer cover the cost of production. Producer countries, especially Malaysia and Indonesia, were concerned that consumer members would not vote to keep the lower intervention price above the cost of production.

This lower intervention price, together with the lower yields of rubber smallholdings and their often inadequately-sized holdings, were the cause of pervasive poverty (EPU, 1976). The proportion of rubber smallholders living below the poverty line rose to 34.5 per cent in 1983, from 26.4 per cent in 1980 (Stubbs, 1988). Among estate workers, the poverty rate had risen to more than 50 per cent from 35 per cent over this period. In 1984, the poverty rate among rubber smallholders in Peninsular Malaysia remained high, at 43.4 per cent, though this had declined from 58.2 per cent in 1976 (EPU, 1986, p. 89).

The situation improved slowly, but not significantly, as indicated by a small-scale survey of rubber smallholders conducted in 2016, more than three decades later, in four states—Perak, Negeri Sembilan, Sabah, and Sarawak. The survey showed that crude hardcore poverty (defined as monthly income below the food poverty line needed to cover the nutritional needs of a family) among rubber smallholders in these states was highest in Perak at 39 per cent, much higher than Perak's official poverty rate (Siti Murni Wee and Singaravelloo, 2018).

Although the first INRA had reduced price volatility, it had led to a transfer of income from lower-income producing countries to higher-income consuming countries (Barlow et al., 1994). Links between commodity production and poverty reduction, however, are complex, highly variable and specific to each situation—and in the case of Malaysia to each state (Sultan Nazrin Shah, 2019).

After many rounds of negotiations, and after concluding that they would still be better off with the INRA, in 1987 the parties eventually agreed to pass the second INRA.[48] This was essentially a renewal of the first INRA, with no change to the reference price and intervention bands, although it did contain revisions to make it more responsive to market conditions. By this time, however, the price range maintained by the INRA had begun to take its toll on Malaysia's rubber industry, where the cost of production was higher than in Indonesia and Thailand, its two major competitors. Between 1987 and 1988 there was a temporary increase in demand due to the AIDS-inspired latex boom (Gilbert, 1995). In 1989, after reaching a high in 1988, Malaysia's natural rubber output began to decline even as natural rubber output in Indonesia and Thailand—and indeed the world in general—was rising. By 1991 Malaysia had lost its position as the world's largest producer of rubber to Thailand, and its share of the world's natural rubber output had fallen to 24 per cent (see Figure 3.5, right panel).

In sum, over the 20 years between 1970–1990, Perak's rubber output declined by 8.3 per cent. This resulted in Perak's production share of Malaysia's total dropping from the second to the sixth highest. Agricultural support during this period, including for rubber production, was mostly concentrated in the poorer states.

Ascendency of Palm Oil

The area cultivated with oil palm in Malaysia doubled in the decade to 1991, to more than 2 million hectares, surpassing rubber which had fallen to 1.8 million hectares, down from 2 million hectares in 1981. Perak's palm oil output had soared to more than 1 million tonnes in 1996 and was on a steep upward trend (Figure 3.9). Perak was Malaysia's fourth-largest contributing state.

---

48 The second INRA was open to signature from May to December 1987. It came into force provisionally in December 1988 and definitively in April 1989, and expired in December 1995.

| Figure 3.9 | As Perak's rubber production declined after 1988, palm oil production soared until 2008 |

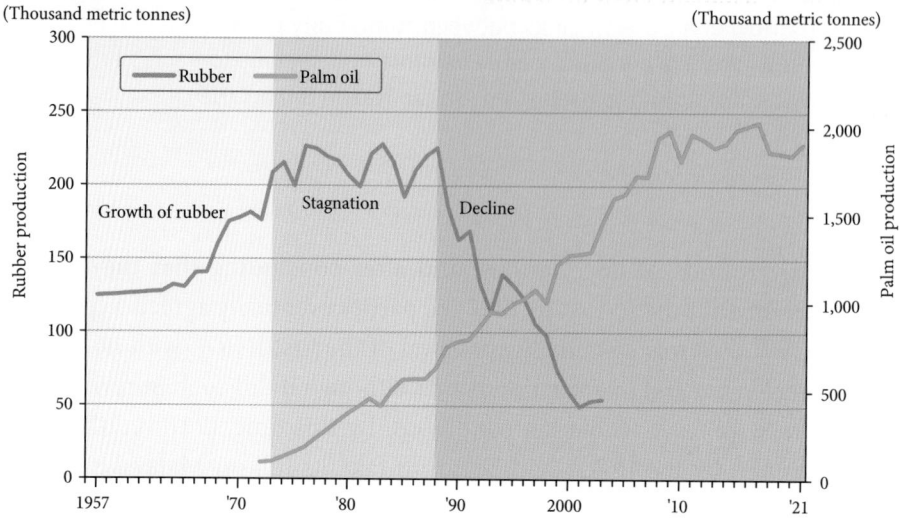

Sources of data: Department of Statistics–Malaysia, *Rubber Statistics Handbook Malaysia* (various years), and *Oil Palm, Coconut and Tea Statistics* (various years); Malaysian Palm Oil Board–Malaysia, *Oil Palm Statistics* (various years); Ministry of Primary Industries–Malaysia, *Statistics on Commodities* (various years).

Multiple factors contributed to the rise of the palm oil sector. As Malaysia industrialized, the Investment Incentives Act of 1968 provided tax incentives to encourage export-oriented and labour-intensive industries. To increase the value added of exports and to break the dominance of Western companies in palm oil refining, the federal government granted tax exemptions on locally processed palm oil exports. It thus became more profitable to export processed and refined palm oil,[49] despite higher import duties on it in Western countries compared to crude palm oil.[50] Unitata—a joint venture between United Plantations and India's Tata Oil Mills Company—was one of the first refineries to take advantage of the Act. It began operating as a palm oil refinery and bulk producer of vegetable fats and soap products in 1974, near the Jendarata estate in Teluk Intan, Perak. Its success in pioneering the Tirtiaux fractionation technique of splitting a fat into its solid and liquid parts—an important breakthrough—triggered a rush to build palm oil refineries across Malaysia, and by

---

49 Palm oil is refined into food-grade oil by removing the degraded fats and free fatty acids through distillation to improve the oil's taste, odour, and colour as well as to increase its shelf life.

50 Malaysia's refining of its own palm oil was strongly opposed by the UK, which sought to retain the value added (Borge Bek-Nielsen of United Plantations in personal correspondence with Claude Fenner of The Rubber Growers' Association on 11 September 1974).

| Figure 3.10 | **Since 1972, Hilir Perak district has had the most hectares planted with oil palm** |

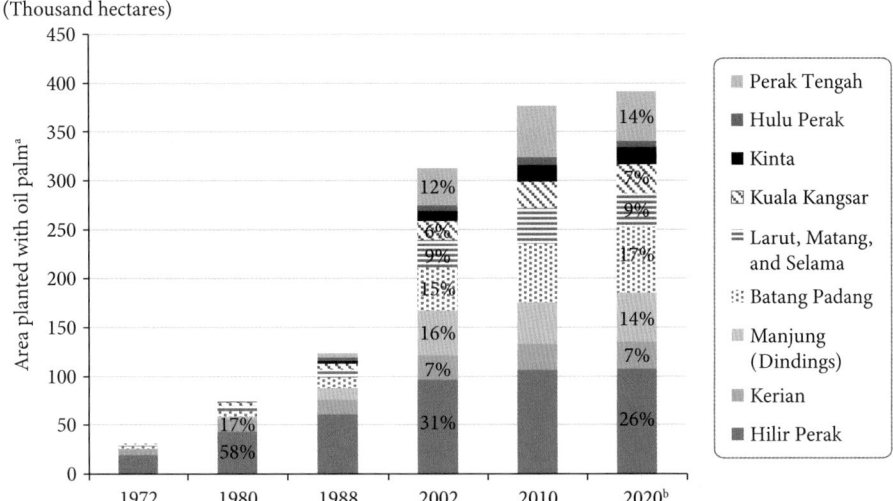

Sources of data: For 1972–1988: Department of Statistics–Malaysia (various years), *Oil Palm, Coconut and Tea Statistics*; for 2002–2020: Direct data request to Department of Statistics–Malaysia, April 2021.

Notes: [a] Data excludes smallholdings.

  [b] Data for Kampar added to Kinta, Muallim added to Batang Padang, and Bagan Datuk added to Hilir Perak.

1980 the peninsula had 44 refineries (Martin, 2003).[51] Perak underwent a phenomenal expansion in area planted with oil palm, with the biggest concentration of estates in the districts of Hilir Perak and Manjung, and more recently in Larut, Matang, and Selama, Batang Padang, and in Perak Tengah (Figure 3.10).

Partly reflecting an increasing recognition of the greater health benefits of vegetable oils, global demand for these oils was growing faster than demand for animal oils and fats, even as demand for all oils has seen a secular increase as incomes have risen around the world. By 1990, palm oil had become the world's second-most important vegetable oil in value terms, second only to soya. One of the key advantages of oil palm over other oil crops is its much higher productivity, yielding up to 10 times as much oil per unit area than any other major oil crop (Corley and Tinker, 2003).[52] An expansion in downstream refining and processing industries in Malaysia from the 1980s onwards, in response to increased demand for refined palm oil in Europe and the US, and then in China in the mid-1980s, also greatly expanded the end-uses of palm oil in the food processing, chemical, pharmaceutical, biofuel, and cosmetic industries, spurred by further technological breakthroughs in fractionalization and other processes.

---

51 In 1968, before the Act, only two refineries operated in Malaysia, one run by Unilever and the other by Lam Soon, a Malaysian-Singaporean company (Martin, 2003).

52 On the demand side, in addition to its wide non-food applications, other advantages of palm oil are that it is free from trans-fat and cholesterol, and does not change its chemical composition when used for deep frying, allowing it to play a major role in food processing.

By 1991, imports of palm oil into Europe from Malaysia had risen to 0.69 million tonnes from 0.31 million tonnes in 1981, while imports into China had jumped to 0.75 million tonnes from just 14,000 tonnes over the same period (FAO, 2021; United Nations Statistics Division, 2022). Correspondingly, Malaysia's total exports of palm oil rose to 5.5 million tonnes from 2.4 million tonnes over the period, with China and the EU its main export markets at that time.

Summary

Perak's rubber industry prospered in the first 15 years after independence, producing more than 200,000 tonnes in 1973, against 124,500 tonnes in 1957. Production then hovered around that mark for the next 15 years, even as total output in Malaysia reached a new high in 1988. By that time, the rubber industry's contribution to the country's export earnings and its share of the world's rubber output were in decline.

The NEP's rural development priorities were targeted towards lower-income states. These priorities played a big part in determining state trends in rubber output. FELDA's large land-development projects in rubber and oil palm were in Pahang and Johor, while rural development was prioritized in the least developed states. The consequences for Perak, designated a middle-income state, was that the growth of smallholdings was slower, and the decline in its estates faster, than in Malaysia as a whole. Perak's share of national rubber production declined relative to that of many other states.

The INRAs also did little to help producers and were unable to do much to sustain the livelihoods of rubber smallholders. Though they did help to curtail unwarranted unloading of stockpiles and prevented a freefall in prices, they did not support prices at a level that responded to the interests of the major rubber producers, particularly Malaysia. Instead, rubber producers were obliged to ensure the continuous availability of rubber supplies for consumers according to the terms of the agreement. Even during periods of low prices, the interests of rubber producers came second to that of rubber consumers, notably the US.

Rubber remained more important for Perak's economy than for neighbouring Penang and Selangor, where manufacturing had overtaken agriculture in its contribution to GDP. Agriculture—notably rubber and palm oil—was still the largest contributor to Perak's growth in 1980. At that time, rubber's planted hectarage was 2.8 times that of oil palm, while palm oil production was 1.8 times that of rubber. The impressive growth in oil palm between 1981 and 1990, when its planted acreage overtook that of rubber and its production doubled, sealed rubber's decline in Perak. In short, the state's dependence on rubber, which outlasted that in Penang, Selangor, and Johor, fed into its lagging socio-economic growth.

Independence but Continued British Economic Dominance, 1957–1970

At independence in 1957, Perak's economy still had a highly dualistic structure. A large subsistence agricultural sector coexisted alongside a modern estate and mining economy, dominated by rubber and tin production. The agricultural hinterland was home to most Malays, who eked out a living by cultivating *padi*, rubber, and coconuts on smallholdings, and from fishing. Although the state was still predominantly rural, urbanization was advancing, with major centres of population in Ipoh, Taiping, and Kuala Kangsar, as well as in the secondary towns that had formed and grown to house tin-mining workers and to service the large number of rubber estates that fringed these townships. The state's economy had industrialized little beyond a scattering of small-scale activities focused on simple fabrication processes and production—largely of foodstuffs—for local consumption.

Under British administration, development policy and planning in Perak, as elsewhere in Malaya, had been highly skewed towards colonial economic interests. Economic management was largely laissez-faire, with the British authorities providing policy and administrative support to a private sector that was largely foreign-owned and was the main driver of growth. After independence, this laissez-faire philosophy was maintained by Tunku Abdul Rahman—the first prime minister of the Federation of Malaya, and later of Malaysia. Gomez (2006, p. xxv) has argued that UMNO, fearing Chinese economic dominance, had a 'tacit agreement' with the colonialists 'to allow British companies to retain their ownership and control over large segments of the economy'.

In 1961, Tunku Abdul Rahman had proposed that a Malaysian federation be established comprising Malaya, Singapore, the sparsely populated and resource-rich British colonies of Sarawak and North Borneo, and the British protectorate of Brunei. The proposal, under consideration by the British and Malayan

Globalization: Perak's Rise, Relative Decline, and Regeneration. Sultan Nazrin Shah, Oxford University Press. © Sultan Nazrin Shah (2024). DOI: 10.1093/oso/9780198897774.003.0020

governments for some years, faced several external challenges.[53] In 1962, the Philippines claimed sovereignty over North Borneo, based on its interpretation of an 1878 agreement between the British North Borneo Company and the Sultan of Sulu. From early 1963 to August 1966, Indonesia waged a campaign of armed obstruction, 'Konfrontasi', over the inclusion of Sabah and Sarawak in the federation. Still, on 16 September 1963, Malaysia was formed—but without Brunei, which had withdrawn from negotiations because of disagreements over the position of its sultan and control over its oil revenue. In 1965, Singapore separated from Malaysia over political and economic differences.

This decade-plus, 1957–1970, was a period during which British business interests continued to play a crucial role in influencing the country's economic direction.[54] The English-speaking leaders of the three communally based political parties—aristocratic Malays, wealthy Chinese business leaders, and Indian professionals—were united in their aversion to any radical economic or political change, and formed an upper-class alliance through a 'marriage of convenience' (Myrdal, 1968, p. 161). They opposed any nationalization of foreign assets,[55] sought to remain attractive to private foreign capital, welcomed the continued presence of British military forces, and strove for internal stability through political compromise. Their economic interests were closely tied to those of British and locally owned mining and rubber-plantation companies, with only limited government ambitions for national economic planning so as to maintain ethnic harmony. In 1969, ethnic riots radically changed the country's political, economic, and social direction.

The evolution of Perak's post-independence economy is thus closely tied to the role of its natural resources, the influence of geography, as well as the state's diminishing sway over centralized federal policies, and over the institutions and choices that affected it.[56] The state's development goals were now being driven by national five-year plans.

---

53 It also faced internal challenges. A few days before Malaysia came into being, the Kelantan state government attempted to void the Malaysia Agreement, arguing that it violated the 1957 Federation of Malaya agreement since the Sultan of Kelantan was not consulted.

54 British multinational companies such as Fraser and Neave, and Unilever started to invest in Malaya's emerging manufacturing sector to produce consumer products (Uqbah Iqbal et al., 2014).

55 At independence, some 70 per cent of company profits remained in foreign, mainly British, hands. These were largely repatriated. British and European-owned agency houses controlled 70 per cent of Malaya's international trade. Independence hardly changed the extent of foreign control over the economy (Curtis, 2003).

56 Although Perak has long been a unified territory, the extent to which it can be treated as an internally integrated economic unit post-independence is less clear. Perak is not a bounded geographical unit that is separated physically, economically, socially, and culturally from its neighbouring states. Indeed, physical infrastructure, flows of migrants, movement of capital and labour resources, and institutions and policies all bind Perak closely to its neighbours and to Malaysia more generally.

Perak's Economy at Independence

Perak's economy was one of the largest of the 11 states in 1957, and its standard of living, as measured by GDP per capita, was among the highest in Asia.[57] It was Malaya's largest producer of tin—accounting for about 61 per cent of national and 20 per cent of global output. Perak was second only to Johor in rubber cultivation. Rubber and tin together formed its two largest economic activities, and were the two principal sources of Malaya's export revenues. Rubber exports still contributed over 50 per cent of Malaya's total export revenue at the end of the 1950s despite growing competition from synthetic substitutes and low prices (Sultan Nazrin Shah, 2019). In 1957, the country was the world's largest exporter of natural rubber, and the revenues from rubber, as well as from tin, largely determined the scale of government spending. Like Malaya's as a whole, Perak's economy was highly vulnerable to the booms and busts of its major trading partners, primarily the US and the UK.

Perak's other major economic activities revolved around agriculture. After Kedah, Perak was the second-largest producer of *padi*. Productivity in *padi* had made advances after heavy investments by the colonial administration in irrigation and drainage, especially in Kerian and Hilir Perak (Drabble, 2000). Although some of Perak's estates had already begun to switch to oil palm, it was still not yet an economically important crop. Smallholders in Perak—mainly Malay, and to a lesser extent Chinese—produced a variety of other agricultural crops, including fruit and vegetables for consumption and sale. Perak's coastal waters, estuaries, and rivers supported a lively fishing industry.

Perak's economy, like those of other states, was still largely pre-industrial (Box 3.8). It did not produce manufactured goods to meet domestic needs, because colonial policy had prioritized imports, mainly from the UK, thereby stunting local industrial development. This practice was common among the colonial powers, which generally acted to limit the growth of local industries based on the processing of indigenous natural resources. For example, while India had been a major exporter of processed cotton textiles before colonization, after it was absorbed into the British Empire Indians were instead encouraged to export their raw cotton to English textile mills for processing there. They were then encouraged to wear imported British factory-made clothes.

---

57 National accounts are available for Malaya dating from the start of the 20th century (Sultan Nazrin Shah, 2017). Disaggregated state-level estimates became available only from 1970, and even then only sporadically and in rudimentary form until around 2000. This constrains a more detailed assessment of Perak's economic performance over the period 1957 to 1970, although its main features can be discerned from the fragmentary data.

Box 3.8   Limited downstream economic activity

Given its bountiful resource endowments, why had Perak, by independence, not been able to leverage its tin and rubber resources through investments in related downstream and value-adding economic activities?

Part of the answer, of course, lies in the priorities of the colonial administration, which had long exploited Perak for its resources, treating it as a centre for tin extraction and rubber cultivation. It also saw Perak as a source of agricultural produce, particularly rice, to meet domestic food needs. The idea of promoting investment in vertically integrated downstream manufacturing activities was inimical to colonial thinking, which was much more concerned with sheltering metropolitan manufactured exports from competition. So the enabling conditions for industrial expansion, such as support for technologies, knowledge, and skills, were not created.

The lack of expansion into downstream activities was also, in part, resource-specific. The physical characteristics of tin restricted opportunities. Tin is found as a mineral, along with other materials, and the smelting and refining of it entails separating the concentrated tin from waste products and other elements. Given the bulk and weight of the unprocessed raw material, and resulting transport costs, the smelting and production of tin ingots generally take place close to tin deposits. In the 1950s, the smelting of tin mined in Perak took place in neighbouring Penang. Tin was used largely for metal coatings, soldering, and food packaging. Although an essential input in these products, the quantities (and value) of tin used in their production were low: even by the 1950s, tin cans were not made of tin but of tinplate steel, that is, lower-cost steel containers just coated with tin to prevent corrosion.

The manufacturing processes that used tin were typically sited close to the centres of demand for the final products—proximity to sources of ore deposits was of little economic import, given the low quantities of tin involved. Only a small amount of Perak's tin found its way into locally produced pewter artefacts, for example. Nevertheless, this demand from the tin-mining industry, initially for repairs and then for fabrication, did help to create the technological conditions and knowledge that eventually spawned Perak's light-engineering and metal industries (Thoburn, 1977). In fact, the steel industry in Ipoh and Kampar was much bigger in terms of capital investment and size, was better organized, made greater profits, and employed more people than those in Penang and Selangor (FIDA, 1969).

As with tin, the main rubber products of the mid-20th century also served to limit the potential for downstream processing and manufacture of rubber locally in Perak. Products such as rubber tyres gain in weight and bulk during the manufacturing process, confining any market opportunities to domestic and nearby areas. Malaya had been producing rubber tyres, rubber shoes, and foam products for some time before independence, but even by 1967 only 2 per cent of the rubber produced locally was used in local manufacturing (Thoburn, 1977).

In terms of broader industrial opportunities, Perak, as elsewhere in Malaya, faced other disadvantages. Its cost base and wages were higher than those in neighbouring countries in Southeast Asia, in part because of the heavy demands on labour and capital created by its rubber and tin industries (IBRD, 1955). High energy costs were also a deterrent. The limited downstream economic activity was clearly a national, and not only a Perakian, problem.

Perak's manufacturing sector was limited to activities and goods that enjoyed a degree of natural protection from external competition, for reasons of bulk, weight, and value. These included iron and steel foundries, basic rubber processing, handicrafts, processing and manufacture of timber and furniture products, local engineering and fabrication activities, and food preparation for local consumption. Industrial units were typically small, and many were Chinese family concerns which lacked the capital, specialized technologies, or organizational capabilities of the larger Western-owned enterprises. There were locally owned commercial, transport, and logistical services, which facilitated shipments of tin and rubber to processing facilities and onwards to major ports for export, and of imports for domestic consumption. There were also other smaller-scale service-sector activities focused on meeting the needs of a population whose incomes were still, by modern standards, relatively meagre.

The Changing Employment Profile—A Continuous Move from Agriculture

At independence, almost one in every five people in Malaya lived in Perak, with non-Malays, predominantly Chinese, accounting for some 60 per cent of the state's population (Sultan Nazrin Shah, 2019).[58] Perak was the largest employer among Malaya's states with around 18 per cent of the country's jobs. The state's economic profile was reflected in its employment structure, with 53.9 per cent

---

58 Despite being the most populous state, Perak's population density measured in persons per square kilometre was far lower than that of Penang to its north and Selangor to the south, as much of its land area was agricultural or covered by native forests.

employed in agricultural activities—working on estates and smallholdings, cultivating *padi* and other crops on family-owned or -leased land, or involved in low-productivity services (Table 3.2).

At independence, the share of employment in agriculture was lower than in 1947 when it stood at 60.9 per cent. However, unlike in the classical 'dual economy' model described by Lewis (1954), these workers did not move off the land and into higher-productivity industrial jobs. Instead, it was the service sector that largely absorbed Perak's 'surplus' agricultural labour. In 1957, services, including public administration, accounted for 28.6 per cent of total employment.[59] The growth of government services as an important employer stemmed from the emerging need of the newly independent state to have a larger human resource base in order to be able to offer a wider and more equitable provision of social services. Manufacturing was a marginal employer, accounting for just 6.2 per cent of all jobs at independence. Perak's output per capita would have been far

Table 3.2	The share of people employed in Perak's agricultural sector continued to fall sharply between 1957 and 1970		
Sector or subsector	Share of employment (%)		
	1947	1957	1970
Agriculture, forestry, hunting, and fishing	60.9	53.9	47.5
Mining and quarrying	7.4	7.4	6.8
Manufacturing	6.8	6.2	8.7
Construction	0.7	3.1	2.0
Electricity, gas, water, and sanitary services [a]	0.4	0.7	0.9
Commerce [a]	8.8	9.5	10.3
Transport, storage, and communication [a]	2.5	2.6	2.7
Community, social, and personal services [a]	12.4	15.8	17.1
Not adequately described	0.2	0.9	3.9
Total (%)	100.0	100.0	100.0
Total (numbers)	369,642	406,159	454,236

Sources of data: Del Tufo (1949); Fell (1960); Chander (1975).

Note: [a] Subsectors in the service sector.

---

59 In all Malaya, in the decade leading up to independence, jobs in public services, including nationals employed in the armed forces and the police, rose from 113,400 in 1947 to 201,000 in 1957 (Del Tufo, 1949; Fell, 1960). Young rural Malays were recruited into the uniformed services and low-level administrative positions as new opportunities were created in response to the Emergency, and by the need to centralize and strengthen public administration and services.

below that in Selangor—Malaya's most affluent state—but above all other Malayan states.

In 1957, Perak's population was still predominantly rural, with just 25 per cent urban. Only the town of Ipoh, about halfway between Kuala Lumpur to the south and George Town in Penang to the north, had a population of over 100,000. Second-tier towns, such as Taiping and Teluk Anson, had populations larger than 30,000. At a third level, Kuala Kangsar, Kampar, Sungai Siput, Pasir Pinji, and Batu Gajah had populations greater than 10,000.

The growth of these towns can be traced to the discovery and exploitation of tin resources. The settlements initially grew as workers, many of them migrants, arrived to work in tin mining. Later, the settlements became service centres for the tin industry and subsequently hubs for distribution and related activities. Over time, road and rail networks were built to connect major urban nodes. The New Villages created during the Emergency and the locational concentration of a previously scattered, largely Chinese population led to the development of satellite hamlets around existing population centres. Likewise, the concentration of public services in first- and second-tier towns solidified the spatial structure that had been largely determined by the physical location of ore deposits. Another emerging type of human settlement involved the new townships created by FELDA for its settlers on land development schemes.

The volatility of prices of both rubber and tin undoubtedly affected Perak's economy. The impact was felt in workers' wages, particularly in labour-intensive rubber activities, as well as in local purchases of equipment, materials, and supplies. Although 'leakages' of dividend income to overseas investors remained significant, estimates by Thoburn (1977) suggest that 75 per cent of total sales from rubber plantations were retained in Malaysia. An even higher proportion of earnings would have been retained by rubber smallholders. The same was true for tin mining. Thoburn (1977) estimates that between 72 per cent (dredging) and 86 per cent (gravel-pump mining) of revenues were kept in Malaysia in 1967, much of which now accrued to the federal government as duties, cess payments, and taxes (over 20 per cent for rubber estates and over 35 per cent for tin dredging).

Nation-Building—Policy and Interventions

The constitution of the newly created federal system of Malaya, based largely on the 1948 Federation of Malaya Agreement, provided very little independence for state governments. It created a strong unitary state, with extensive federal powers over legislation and control of major policies (Colonial Office, 1957). Although Perak did retain control over land use and its allocation, as well as agricultural and forestry resources, the role of state entities was mainly confined to implementing policies, set at national level (IBRD, 1955). Perak had few revenue-raising powers, despite the substantial contribution of its rubber and tin exports to the national treasury. Further, the state government was urged to use its resources—federal and state funds—on programmes reflecting the priorities of national development plans.

During this 'long decade', Perak's planning was aligned with the First and Second Malaya Plans, 1956–1960 and 1961–1965, and with the First Malaysia Plan, 1966–1970 (Federation of Malaya, 1956 and 1961; EPU, 1966). Economic development planning aimed to support the country's modernization and nation-building efforts by raising living standards and promoting economic growth. This approach to development planning reflected a growing recognition of a number of economic challenges that were facing the country, namely: the economy's over-dependence on tin ore, which was depleting, and on rubber, which was suffering from falling world prices; the need to create decent jobs for the rising number of new entrants to the labour force; the skills shortages among the labour force; and the disparities in income distribution, especially between rural and town dwellers (EPU, 1966). Unfortunately, planning and programme implementation for the new nation was held back by internal troubles, political turbulence, and external threats.

While no new major institutions were established between 1957 and 1970 for state-level planning, Perak, like other states in Malaysia, already had a Rural Development Committee and a State Operations Room linked to similar district-level structures. These were controlled by a National Operations Room in Kuala Lumpur.[60] As their names suggest, these arrangements were adapted from the military structures set up by the British administration when battling the communist insurgency.

Government planners recognized that the lagging rural sector—on which the vast majority of Malays in Perak and other states depended for their livelihoods—would require assistance. But they did not yet explicitly prioritize ethnic distributional considerations, or a more balanced pattern of regional development (Drabble, 2000). Investments in infrastructure, agriculture, and rural development at this time were made primarily to sustain national-level economic growth.

---

60 The National Operations Room was close to the office of the Deputy Prime Minister, Tun Abdul Razak, who in the mid-1960s was also the Minister of National and Rural Development and the Minister of Defence. The Operations Room maintained an information base on progress in the development programmes being implemented at state and district levels (EPU, 1966).

Early Moves to Industrialize

Recognizing the need to diversify the economy and create jobs for a burgeoning labour force, the federal Pioneer Industries Ordinance was introduced in 1958. Its strategy aimed primarily at the creation of import-substituting industries. The initial assistance provided by federal and state governments to support industrialization came in the form of infrastructure and, particularly, serviced industrial estates, as these can promote the development of clusters of economic activity and support agglomeration economies.

Perak's first such estate, the Tasek Industrial Park in Ipoh, was established in 1962 at a cost of M$20 million, funded jointly by the federal and state governments. Its earliest operations focused on the production of cement and steel; wooden furniture; newspapers, magazines, and books; and chemicals—all activities largely sheltered from competition outside Malaysia. The Tasek Industrial Park had only limited success, however, and by 1970 just 24 per cent of the industrial lots were occupied by investors (Azrai Abdullah, 2022, p. 234). The state also set aside two smaller areas around Ipoh, intended for small-scale and cottage industries at Menglembu (70 acres) and Falim (7 acres), but these also had limited take-up.

During this 'long decade', the federal government provided targeted support for industrialization in the form of tariff and quota protection, and tax subsidies. These measures were directed at selected import-substituting activities. Investors' initial response was muted, prompting the federal government to further expand support measures under the auspices of the Investment Incentives Act of 1968.[61] This act, in addition to extending incentives, was also intended to encourage the wider spatial dispersal of industry. It delineated 'development areas' within which industrial activities would be eligible for additional incentives. However, in Perak only one geographically confined location was eligible for targeted industrial support: the Kamunting Industrial Estate, close to Taiping. Operational from 1968, it later became a hub for rubber and related products.[62] The act also gazetted free trade zones (FTZs)—one

---

[61] At end-1969, Perak, with 17 pioneer companies, was ranked third of all states, behind Selangor with 89 and Johor with 25 (FIDA, 1971).

[62] The entirety of Melaka, Perlis, Sabah, Sarawak, and Terengganu, as well as vast areas in Kedah and Pahang, in addition to eastern Johor were all designated 'development areas' and were thus eligible for support. This was in stark contrast with Perak. Locational incentives such as these are not always effective, however, as although land costs in the more developed states may be higher, it is still often more costly for firms to produce in lesser developed states when under-developed supply chains and transportation links are also taken into account (Hasnah Ali and Asan Ali Golam Hassan, 2008).

at Sungai Way, Selangor, and one at Bayan Lepas, Penang—both of which turned out to be highly successful (their success was aided by these two states' advantages, as discussed below).

In Perak, the development of the industrial sector was left largely in private hands. However, the technological, material, and organizational preconditions as well as the enabling policies needed to foster the discovery and growth of new industrial activities were generally lacking. While there was a base of entrepreneurs (IBRD, 1955), there was little by way of relevant technologies, knowledge, and skills for new economic activities to latch on to, and to 'recombine' in new related economic activities (Hidalgo et al., 2018).

From an investor's perspective, the neighbouring states of Penang and Selangor—the latter being the location of the federal government and its administration—enjoyed the key advantages of population density and proximity to markets, the presence of a pool of suitable labour, enabling infrastructure, and access to industrial knowledge and know-how. Azrai Abdullah (2022) suggests that there may also have been some hesitancy among political leaders and senior policymakers about the consequences of a swift move towards industrialization in Perak. Their concerns hinged on the fact that what would necessarily have been a private-sector-led approach to industrial development would largely have benefited the urban Chinese community, thereby exacerbating ethnic income inequalities.

Perak's direct development investments focused instead on the social sectors and on rural development. Spending on education and health increased, with far greater provision of public schools and local medical facilities. As was the case throughout the country, federally funded investments in Perak moved ahead in economic infrastructure, including roads, water supply, and electrification, particularly in the first half of the 1960s.

Early Rural Development

Malaysia's political leaders recognized that direct assistance would be needed in the rural sector to raise productivity and alleviate poverty, given the decline in agricultural jobs (Table 3.2, above). New employment opportunities were needed to absorb a rapidly expanding and young rural population (many of whom decided to vote with their feet anyway—see 'Accelerated Outward Migration, 1957–1970—An Early Marker of Perak's Relative Decline', below). In agriculture, planners emphasized land development, drainage and irrigation, and rubber replanting, as well as diversification so as to broaden the production base to other growth-sustaining activities, including timber, oil palm, and other crops.

Initial assistance was extended through federal agencies such as FELDA, FEL-CRA, and RISDA.[63]

The first FELDA scheme in Perak was in 1962 in the Hulu Perak district. In 1967, FELCRA began a scheme in Slim River, and in 1968 RISDA started a programme in Hilir Perak. These land-settlement initiatives were relatively small, however, covering less than 6,500 acres between them (Azrai Abdullah, 2022, p. 137). Still, these investments—along with federal support for the replanting of rubber, investments in drainage and irrigation, and the provision of extension services—all helped to lift rural productivity and support incomes in the state during the 1960s. FELDA also led the agricultural diversification into oil palm. Oil palm cultivation covered only 32,000 acres in 1961, but by 1970 this had increased to over 80,000 acres (Azrai Abdullah, 2022, pp. 152–153) with FELDA programmes accounting for 14,000 acres of the new planting.

Yet these initiatives and investments were insufficient to absorb the growing pool of young workers in rural Perak, or to stem their drift from the countryside to Perak's towns and beyond to other states. Although Perak's agricultural employment in 1970 was largely unchanged from its 1957 level in absolute terms, as a share of the state's total employment it had continued to decline, dropping to 47.5 per cent (Table 3.2).

Perak's Economy in 1970

Despite efforts to diversify, Perak's economy remained dependent on tin mining and rubber cultivation through to 1970. By that year, mining (mainly of tin) still contributed 18.9 per cent of Perak's GDP in nominal terms, compared with just 5.6 per cent in Selangor and 5.7 per cent in Malaysia as a whole (Table 3.3). The agricultural sector, including rubber, accounted for 30.4 per cent of the state's GDP. Between 1957 and 1970, rubber production in Perak expanded at an annual average rate of 9 per cent due to replanting and the planting of higher-yielding trees. Yet despite the large contribution of agriculture to Perak's output, on average the state was no more dependent on agriculture than other states—indeed, the ratio of Perak's sector share to the national share for agriculture in 1970 was 0.95, suggesting a small under-representation of agriculture in Perak's economy. By contrast, the corresponding figure for Selangor was 0.46, reflecting its earlier transition out of agriculture.

---

63 The Perak State Agricultural Development Corporation was not established until 1973.

Table 3.3	In 1970, manufacturing contributed just 8.9 per cent of GDP in Perak against 21.4 per cent in Selangor					
Sector or subsector	**Perak**	**Selangor**	**Malaysia**	**Perak**	**Selangor**	**Malaysia**
	GDP in 1970 (RM millions)			Share (%)		
Agriculture, forestry, and fishing	486.2	399.4	3,432.0	30.4	14.6	32.1
Mining and quarrying	301.7	154.6	613.0	18.9	5.6	5.7
Manufacturing	142.4	586.0	1,307.0	8.9	21.4	12.2
Construction	39.8	172.4	481.0	2.5	6.3	4.5
Electricity, gas, and water	59.0	78.7	245.0	3.7	2.9	2.3
Transport, storage, and communication[a]	66.4	183.1	606.0	4.2	6.7	5.7
Wholesale and retail trade, hotels, and restaurants[a]	187.7	443.1	1,423.0	11.7	16.2	13.3
Finance, insurance, real estate, and business services[a]	114.2	220.6	836.0	7.1	8.1	7.8
Government services[a]	83.0	280.9	794.0	5.2	10.3	7.4
Other services[a]	117.8	217.9	874.0	7.4	8.0	8.2
Gross domestic product	*1,598.2*	*2,736.7*	*10,708.0*	*100.0*	*100.0*	*100.0*

Source of data: EPU (1976).

Note: [a] Subsectors in the service sector.

Embryonic changes in Perak's economic base may be detected towards the end of the 'long decade' after independence. A reasonable conjecture—bearing in mind that rudimentary, disaggregated state-level estimates became available only from 1970—is that the share of industry in the state's aggregate output had risen. In 1970, manufacturing contributed 8.9 per cent to Perak's GDP in nominal terms, but this was a far smaller share than Selangor's 21.4 per cent (Table 3.3).

While economic diversification was a major post-independence policy thrust, Selangor, not Perak, was the fastest to diversify out of tin and rubber. The 1968 manufacturing census did show that there were more manufacturing establishments in Perak than in any other state except Selangor, but this was partly a function of Perak's physical scale (Department of Statistics–Malaysia, 1968). At the same time, Perak's share in manufacturing gross output, relative to its share in employment, suggests that the state's labour productivity in manufacturing trailed that of Selangor and Johor. Services were becoming more important, stimulated by rising real household incomes, expansion of public services, and the growth of Perak's urban settlements. Services accounted for 39.3 per cent of Perak's GDP in 1970, compared with a national figure of 44.7 per cent.

The period 1957 to 1970 saw a moderate expansion of Perak's economy, spurred by investments and gains in agricultural productivity, robust mining activity, and investments in improved infrastructure. In Malaysia as a whole, annual real GDP growth per capita averaged 3.5 per cent in the 1960s (Sultan Nazrin Shah, 2019), although consumption growth was a more modest 1.7 per cent. But while in 1970 Perak retained its rank as the country's second-largest economy, accounting for 15 per cent of GDP in nominal prices and behind only Selangor at 26 per cent, its GDP per capita had fallen to the national average (Figure 3.11, left panel). Output and consumption growth may have lagged behind broader national performance. On GDP per capita, Perak was the third-richest state in 1970 behind Selangor and Sabah, and broadly at par with Penang (Figure 3.11, right panel).[64]

It is likely that Perak's economic weight had retreated somewhat over the 1960s owing to slower industrialization there than in other states, where a larger structural bonus would have been generated as workers moved from lower-productivity agriculture to higher-productivity industry. National efforts to promote import-substituting industries during the 1960s had limited success, and Perak's industrialization had fallen behind even those trends. Upward pressures on local costs created by rubber and mining activity, distance from major population centres, and thin local markets may have been some of the reasons why industrial investment in Perak lagged behind. Political leaders and senior policymakers may also have felt continuing concerns that Malays, who still had limited contact with urban industrial life, would be further disadvantaged by the aggressive promotion of industry.

Competition from more economically attractive nearby states was probably also a factor. Many new manufacturing ventures regarded neighbouring Selangor as a more suitable location. Selangor was the first mover in seeking to attract and nurture industrial activity, and had a deeper pool of skilled labour, greater technical knowledge, and more advanced infrastructure. By 1963 the state had already established a focal organization—the Selangor State Development

---

64 However, it is unclear to what extent GDP figures accurately reflect the real incomes accruing to the residents of each state. GDP measured at the state level includes profits and rents of enterprises located there, but some part of these would have accrued to residents of other states and to non-Malaysian residents.

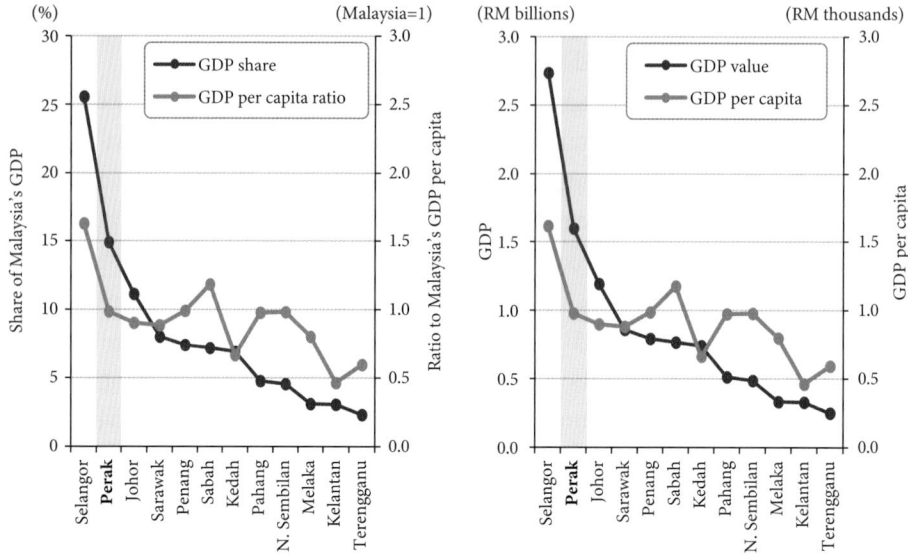

Figure 3.11 By 1970, Perak still made up 15 per cent of Malaysian GDP and its GDP per capita was around Malaysia's average, although both trailed Selangor's

Source of data: Economic Planning Unit–Malaysia (1976).
Note: Selangor includes Kuala Lumpur, and Kedah includes Perlis.

Corporation—to coordinate and promote investment, whereas Perak had no comparable entity until 1971, when it set up the Perak State Development Corporation. In 1970, Selangor was home to 40 per cent of all serviced industrial areas (measured in acres) on the peninsula. By contrast, Perak provided just 6.5 per cent of serviced industrial infrastructure—all of which was located at its Tasek Industrial Park, and much of which was underused. Neighbouring Penang had also vastly expanded its industrial facilities, providing 45 per cent of all Malaysia's serviced industrial land by 1970 (Asan Ali Golam Hassan, 2017).

Owing to its comparatively slow pace of industrialization, the shrinking tin-mining sector, and productivity gains in agriculture, Perak failed to create jobs at the same pace as other states. In 1957, Perak accounted for 19 per cent of Malaya's total employment, but by 1970 this had fallen to only 17 per cent (excluding Sabah and Sarawak, which were not part of the federation in 1957) (Fell, 1960; Chander, 1977). Selangor, by contrast, showed solid employment growth, with its share rising from 16 per cent to 19 per cent over this period (again excluding Sabah and Sarawak). To Perak's north, Penang showed a marginal increase of just 0.2 percentage points on this metric.

From independence through to 1970, Perak created some 40,000 new jobs, almost all in services and manufacturing. These new jobs helped to absorb some of the fast-growing young labour force. Meanwhile, employment in tin stagnated, and by 1970 larger numbers were employed in manufacturing than in mining. In agriculture, the rapid gains being made in productivity blunted potential job creation and the sector's employment share continued to decline (Table 3.2 above).

In 1970, Perak remained predominantly rural, with just 27.5 per cent of its population living in towns. Most town dwellers were Chinese, at nearly seven out of 10 people, with fewer than one in five Malays living in towns. Income distribution was highly skewed in favour of urban areas. Malaysia's economy was still controlled and dominated by foreign plantation companies, agency houses, and local—mainly Chinese—businesses. British companies still owned the largest proportion of firms' share capital, followed at some distance by Chinese organizations; Malays and Indians owned very little.

Accelerated Outward Migration, 1957–1970—An Early Marker of Perak's Relative Decline

Outward migration from Perak—both to other states in Malaysia and abroad—began to accelerate after independence. Perak's inter-state 'lifetime' outward migration— a measure of the persons resident in a state other than their state of birth—far exceeded that of any other state.

From 1957 to 1970, people born in Perak were leaving the state in greater numbers than those born in other states were entering, leading to net outflows. While annual data on inter-state migration flows only became available in 1981 and census information on migration flows is limited, information on the *stock* of lifetime inter-state outward migrants is available. These data show that in 1957 Perak had the highest number of lifetime outward migrants among all states, at 108,000; by 1970 this figure had doubled to 220,000. With lifetime outward migration far exceeding lifetime inward migration, Perak's net lifetime outward migration rose from 31,000 in 1957 to 114,000 in 1970 (Figure 3.12, left panel). This negative outflow was much larger in absolute terms than that from any other state. The overwhelming majority moved to Selangor, with the second largest contingent moving to Pahang to settle on FELDA schemes (Figure 3.12, right panel).

| Figure 3.12 | Perak's lifetime migrants increasing and settling in Selangor and Pahang |

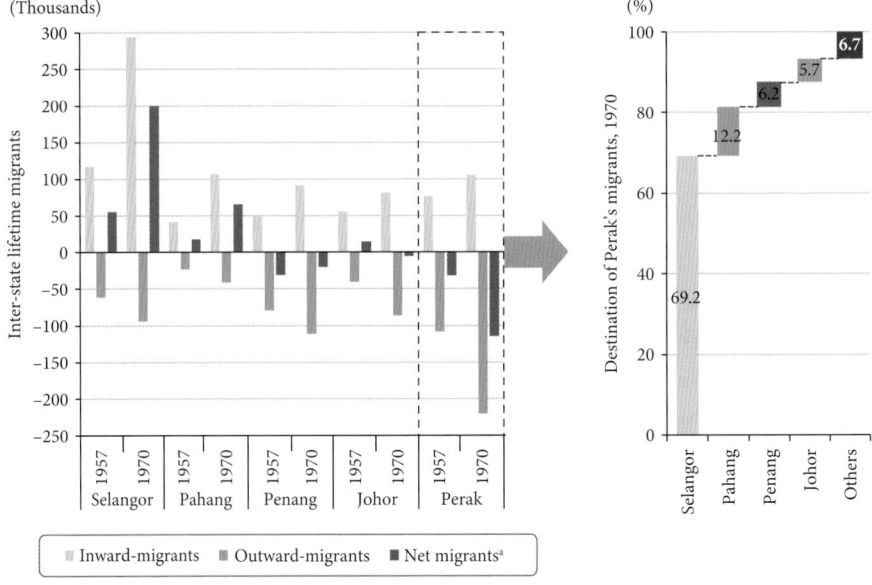

Inward-migrants   Outward-migrants   Net migrants[a]

Sources of data: Fell (1959 and 1960); Chander (1977).

Note: [a] A positive number refers to net inter-state inward-migrants, a negative number to net inter-state outward-migrants.

Why Did So Many People Leave Perak?

A confluence of factors drove Perak's outward migration in the early independence years. Among these, limited employment opportunities was a key factor. Labour force growth outpaced job creation, resulting in high unemployment, particularly among those under 25. Perak's economy recorded slower employment growth and higher unemployment than the country as a whole. This trend was exacerbated by the conversion of many rubber estates to oil palm in the 1960s, which led not only to a decline in rubber estate acreage but also to a reduction in the use of labour per acre of land.

Before independence, primary and secondary schooling provision in Perak was outstanding compared with other states, but, as in other states, there were few opportunities for post-secondary education. The expansion of tertiary education immediately after independence was concentrated in Selangor,[65] and

---

65 Between 1966 and 1970 several new education and training institutes were established, but none in Perak: four vocational institutes were set up by the training division of Majlis Amanah Rakyat (MARA), in Melaka, Alor Setar, Kuala Terengganu, and Petaling Jaya. The National Youth Pioneer Corps was founded in 1966, Tunku Abdul Rahman College in 1969, and University Kebangsaan Malaysia (the National University of Malaysia) in 1970—the latter two in or near Kuala Lumpur. Beyond these, the Industrial Training Institute of the Ministry of Labour and Manpower was expanded as were the College of Agriculture, the Technical College of Kuala Lumpur, and the MARA Institute of Technology.

this became another factor promoting permanent migration out of Perak. With Perak's economy still concentrated in the primary sector, there were limited incentives for Perakians with post-secondary education to return home after graduating, given the shortage of good jobs.

In 1970, absolute poverty rates in Perak remained high, at 48.6 per cent. They were even higher in rural areas, where 58.4 per cent of households, predominantly Malay, lived below the poverty line (EPU, various years). Of Perak's 114,000 net lifetime outward migrants, 40,400 were Malays. Poverty rates were also very high in the New Villages, of which one-third, around 500, were in Perak. With the end of the Emergency in 1960, people living in the New Villages, almost entirely Chinese, had the freedom to move to other states that offered better employment opportunities. Many did so, and by 1970, among Perak's net lifetime outward migrants, 53,700 were Chinese. Faster growth in incomes and employment in some of these states served as 'pull' factors in attracting Perakians, who were already feeling the 'push' factors of high unemployment, slow employment growth, and job losses—all combining to worsen living conditions.

Concurrently, other parts of Malaysia were making huge strides at diversifying within agriculture. Land development schemes were undertaken, including fringe alienation, controlled alienation, and FELDA schemes, to develop land primarily for rubber replanting, oil-palm planting, and timber cultivation. In 1964, the Land Capability Classification Scheme was initiated to facilitate a more concentrated development of land resources on a regional basis.[66] Pahang and Johor were identified as having the most suitable blocks for integrated resources development planning on a regional scale, due to their large contiguous tracts bordered by natural barriers. Although Perak had some of the largest land resources suitable for agricultural development—and the largest among the west-coast states—these lands were not in large contiguous blocks due to geological factors including soil suitability (Lee and Panton, 1971). Pahang and Johor therefore became the loci of large-scale agricultural development, and thus of agricultural employment growth, after the late 1960s.

Where Did They Go?

The destination favoured by Perak's outward migrants between 1957 and 1970 was Selangor (Kuala Lumpur was part of Selangor during this period). The Pioneer Industries Ordinance of 1958, which provided tax relief to firms that had

---

66 Coordinated by the Economic Planning Unit, the Land Capability Classification Programme was initiated by the National Development Planning Committee in 1964, with results compiled for each state in Peninsular Malaysia during the First Malaysia Plan (MP1) (1966–1970).

been granted 'pioneer industry' status, encouraged the location of many new industries in designated industrial estates, where land and utilities were available. The first such estate was developed in Petaling Jaya, Selangor, around 1959. In 1970, Selangor accounted for 69 per cent of the net lifetime outward migrants from Perak, followed by Pahang (Figure 3.12, right panel above), the location of many FELDA resettlement programmes, which mainly involved Malays. Large numbers of Perak's lifetime outward migrants also went to Penang and Johor where, as in Selangor, Chinese formed the majority population group. This pattern of movement suggests that, beyond employment, ethnic networks also influenced the choice of inter-state migration destination—as is often the case for international migration.

Summary

Despite Perak's real progress in building a stronger and more diversified economy during the 1960s, larger socio-economic issues persisted. Unemployment was high, with not enough jobs being created to meet the needs of the growing labour force: in 1970, Perak's unemployment rate was 6.5 per cent, and its overall labour force participation rate of 56.2 per cent was below the national average of 59.8 per cent (Chander, 1977). Poverty remained high, at a level similar to that of the Malay peninsula as a whole—49.3 per cent. Malays experienced the highest poverty rates, reflecting ethnic employment patterns, which saw them largely engaged in traditional agriculture where per capita output was low on average. Many Chinese were involved in urban manufacturing, commerce, construction, and mining where per capita output was much higher. Perak's challenges and tensions mirrored those faced in other states, especially states on the west coast.

The ethnic riots that broke out after the May 1969 general election, largely confined to Kuala Lumpur but with incidents in Perak and elsewhere, radically changed Malaysia's political, economic, and social direction.[67] The root causes of the rioting were multi-dimensional and complex (Leete, 2007). A key factor was the perceived threat to the paramount importance of Malay privileges and rights enshrined in the constitution—in the context of a delicate

---

[67] Slightly over a decade earlier, on 1 May 1959, and reflecting pre-election tensions, a series of serious racial disturbances broke out in the fishing villages on Pangkor Island, off the mouth of the Dindings River in south Perak, where there had been a history of racial violence. These disturbances resulted in death, injury, and destruction of property (Dominions Office [DO], 35/9816, 1959). Some 200 police officers were brought in to quell the disturbances, a curfew was imposed on the Dindings district, and Tunku Abdul Rahman visited the island to calm villagers.

ethnic population balance, a lack of national solidarity, an absence of consensus on policy direction, especially for education, and sharp income inequalities between and within each community (Myrdal, 1968; Sultan Nazrin Shah, 2019). Pluralist and laissez-faire policies gave way to an interventionist developmental state committed to the pursuit of growth with equity. These aims were articulated in the NEP of 1971, which provided a national framework for the ethnically based affirmative action policies of the next two decades and even into the 21st century.

3B

Policy Changes amid Absolute Advance but Relative Decline

Tanjong Malim, manufacturing hub
for Proton cars

Globalization's Impact, 1970–2020—From Basic Commodities to Manufactures and More

The Rise of Malaysia's Export Manufacturing, 1970s–1990s

The 1970s marked the beginning of a fresh wave of globalization, spurred by global institutions that began to formulate new rules for liberalizing international trade, investment, and finance (Stiglitz, 2006).[68] World trade as a proportion of world GDP grew exponentially through to the new millennium, reflecting a confluence of factors: multilateral agreements on tariff reductions; the dismantling of non-tariff trade barriers; dramatically falling transport costs—especially with containerization[69]—and communication costs; the easing of restrictions on foreign direct investment (FDI); digitalization which lowered the cost of knowledge transfers across great distances; and greater policy coherence around monetary and exchange rate management and international capital movements (Baldwin, 2016). These conditions—some of which were later expanded and referred to as the 'Washington Consensus'—also encouraged the geographical fragmentation of industry and company supply chains as it became cheaper to source and ship components from multiple locations.

---

68 These included the World Bank and the IMF, and the General Agreement on Tariffs and Trade (GATT), which subsequently evolved into the World Trade Organization (WTO).

69 Before containerization, ships were loaded manually, and goods in ports were often delayed for weeks. Putting goods into standardized steel containers revolutionized shipping, and the cost of moving goods plunged (Baldwin, 2016).

Globalization: Perak's Rise, Relative Decline, and Regeneration. Sultan Nazrin Shah, Oxford University Press. © Sultan Nazrin Shah (2024). DOI: 10.1093/oso/9780198897774.003.0021

Free Trade Zones—A Success for Malaysia

Malaysia caught on quickly to these new realities, which it was well placed to exploit, especially as its population had the benefit of relatively advanced education and health systems (Sultan Nazrin Shah, 2019). By 1968 it had already started to offer incentives to foreign investors to attract labour-intensive export activities, and these efforts were continued with the passing of the Investment Incentives Act in 1972. The Free Trade Zone Act of 1971[70] paved the way for the establishment of export processing zones (EPZs) and licensed manufacturing warehouses.[71] The EPZs were manufacturing enclaves outside the country's customs area, in which imports and exports could enter and leave free of duties. Initially, three EPZs were built in Penang and two each in Melaka and Selangor.

Free trade zones (FTZs) came to Perak much later. Unlike Perak, Penang had already established the necessary conditions to attract foreign investment with its early vision for industrialization. Its second chief minister, Lim Chong Eu (1969–1990), building on the foundations laid by the first chief minister Wong Pow Nee (1957–1969), was the driving force behind Penang's successful structural transformation, which was enabled by state institutions, in particular the Penang Development Corporation. With strong federal support—despite it being a Chinese-majority state—for infrastructure development and institutional reforms, in 1972 Penang established FTZs in Bayan Lepas, which attracted FDI from several US, German, and Japanese multinational manufacturing corporations. This helped generate agglomeration economies, and the state established itself as a globally prominent manufacturing hub in the electrical and electronics sector.

Malaysia's initiatives were remarkable, and helped the country to attract substantial foreign investment. But the timing of these initiatives was also fortunate. In the early 1970s, the US relaxed its regulations to encourage labour-intensive electronics production facilities to move offshore in order to compete more effectively with Japanese and other lower-cost producers. Intel and National Semiconductor were among the early arrivals to Malaysia's EPZs. They were joined by low-value-added textile and garment manufacturers seeking a cost advantage in fiercely competitive international markets. Export-oriented FDI in Malaysia surged 10-fold between 1970 and 1980.

---

70 The Free Trade Zone Act of 1971 provided a package of incentives for manufacturing companies locating within these zones that were producing or assembling goods for export.

71 These warehouses were for approved manufacturing products with exemption from customs duty on the raw materials and components used in the manufacturing process.

These export-oriented industries were subject to the volatility of external markets, however. Economic recession in the mid-1980s forced the government to address the twin deficits on the balance of payments and in government finances. The package of measures introduced included further encouragement of FDI as well as the privatization of state-owned companies to reduce the size of the public sector and provide more space for private initiatives. A new wave of foreign manufacturing investment followed close on the heels of these reforms.

Industrial growth was fastest in places where successful FTZs had already been established, and where there was a pool of workers with relevant skills. In fast-growing areas such as Penang and Selangor, manufacturing output, export performance, innovation, and productivity all improved in tandem (Lee, 2019). But technology and productivity spillovers from foreign-owned exporting firms to locally owned manufacturing firms were limited. The absence of spillovers meant that there were few trickle-down benefits for localities such as Perak, which lay outside the major manufacturing centres.

The opportunities created for export-oriented manufacturing growth tended to amplify forces that favoured the spatial concentration of economic activity. Foreign firms wanted to be close to each other, to transport hubs, to economic infrastructure, and to locations with dense labour markets. New towns in the Klang Valley, such as Petaling Jaya and Shah Alam in Selangor, began to grow quickly. Disadvantaged by its distance from major transport hubs, by its shallow pool of trainable industrial workers, and by its underdeveloped infrastructure—'physical and human geography'—Perak received an insignificant share of FDI and experienced far slower manufacturing growth. Perak's share in the total population also started to slide as the young and better educated left for jobs in faster-growing neighbouring states and abroad.

The contribution of EPZs to manufacturing exports and to Malaysia's balance of trade was significant. By 1982 EPZs accounted for 53 per cent of manufacturing exports, up from 27 per cent in 1972 (Sivalingam, 1994). Foreign manufacturing firms created jobs, especially benefiting women who made up more than half of all workers in EPZs. Manufacturing exports from the EPZs increased in value terms more than threefold, and by 1990 the EPZs' share of total manufacturing exports had reached 57.5 per cent (Sivalingam, 1994). However, backward linkages into the domestic economy were limited. The bulk of equipment and materials purchased by foreign firms were imported, supplied by their parent companies. Still, in net terms, EPZs contributed positively to Malaysia's trade balance.

Outside EPZs, manufacturing exports in downstream resource-based activities, including palm-oil processing, food processing, wood products, and petrochemicals, were also performing strongly. Even as late as 1990, raw materials and related products—petroleum, natural gas, oil palm, and wood products—remained a much more important source of foreign exchange, contributing three times that of electronics. However, the contribution to exports of rubber products—in which Perak had a comparative advantage—remained marginal, accounting for just 3 per cent of Malaysia's total manufacturing exports in 1990. Exports of electronics goods and even textiles often had very low shares of value added because they relied heavily on imported components or raw materials. In the 1970s, for example, the value added of semiconductors was between 10 and 20 per cent, as the industry consisted of simple components, semiconductor parts assembly, and semi-knocked-down electrical products.[72]

Rapid Industrialization—Speed Differs Spatially

By the 1980s Malaysia was fast industrializing and becoming more deeply integrated with global electrical and electronics products supply chains and with other light manufacturing activities. Its broader industrial strategy, however, steered by government policy, focused on second-round import substitution in heavy industries so as to reduce the import of intermediate and final goods. Substantial investments were made in heavy industries, including automotive manufacturing, during Malaysia's Look East policy phase,[73] but these were then scaled back after these industries failed to be cost-competitive with global rivals (Baldwin, 2016). The geographical locus of Malaysia's trade also pivoted, with the proportions of its markets in the US (17 per cent) and Japan (16 per cent) combined being more than eight times as large as that in Britain (4 per cent) (World Bank, 2020a).

Malaysia's export-led economy continued to grow rapidly into the 1990s as manufacturing—the fastest-growing sector—increased its share of output and employment. However, industrialization proceeded much more quickly in some states than in others. In Perak, the share of industry in the state's GDP was rising, but much more slowly than in Selangor or Penang. Tin and rubber

---

72 By contrast, some 50 years later, in 2020, the valued added was about 80 to 90 per cent as semiconductor operations had progressively upgraded their facilities into integrated manufacturing centres that fuse their manufacturing activities with R&D, such as in wafer fabrication and fabless integrated circuit design.

73 The 'Look East' policy, which started in the early 1980s and continued over two decades, was inspired by and modelled on the successes of similar policies in Japan and the Republic of Korea.

were now contributing far less to the state's output and employment than in previous decades. Tin production had succumbed to the collapse of the ITC in 1985, as well as to rising production costs and the steady physical exhaustion of readily accessible deposits. Meanwhile, much of the land once used for rubber cultivation was being converted to other uses, including the much more lucrative cultivation of oil palm. Production of palm oil grew dramatically, stimulated by investment from international trading companies now largely under local ownership after the adoption of the NEP in 1971 (Jones, 2000).

An array of industrial activities, many of which were not present in 1957, started to take hold in Perak, including the processing of chemicals and of metallurgical products, the production of electrical and electronics equipment, and the assembly of motor vehicles. More traditional processing of primary agricultural products and the manufacture of foodstuffs also figured prominently. Perak's economy was advancing, and its people were becoming considerably better off. Still, compared with other parts of the peninsula, Perak's industrialization came late, penetrated less deeply, and began to taper earlier. Labour productivity in Perak also lagged behind that in the wider economy, partly because its mix of industrial activities was less capital intensive and technologically advanced than that in Penang, Selangor, and Johor.

The country's growing integration with the global economy began to benefit foreign workers as well, as labour shortages prompted a rapid increase in employment of less skilled migrant workers. Growing numbers of them were engaged in agriculture, manufacturing, construction, and services, and much of their income was remitted back home. However, although immigration helped to maintain the momentum in the economy by easing labour shortages and by holding wage growth in check, it also dampened incentives for businesses to invest in skills and technology upgrades or in labour-saving production processes.

Another perverse effect operated through the cross-border movement of labour. Although a net importer of labour overall, by the 1990s Malaysia had become a net exporter of those with high human capital, many from Perak. The country was losing significant numbers of professional and skilled workers who, facing barriers to advancement at home, were migrating in search of improved opportunities abroad (Sultan Nazrin Shah, 2019); and Perak was exporting its human capital to other states with higher per capita incomes, once again through the migration of its better-educated young workers.

Financial Globalization, 1970s–2000s—Upsides and Downsides

In 1968, to boost trade, Malaysia had removed restrictions on international currency transactions (Johnson et al., 2007). When Britain moved from a fixed to a floating exchange rate regime in 1972 and the pound lost value, Bank Negara Malaysia pegged the Malaysian ringgit to the US dollar rather than the pound. When the US Federal Reserve subsequently devalued the dollar, Malaysia—after briefly revaluing the ringgit against the US dollar—also floated its currency. As the economy moved from a fixed to a flexible exchange rate regime, the government acquired greater capacity to absorb and respond to external shocks, and began to ease restrictions on capital-account movements. And although integration with global capital markets had been growing more slowly than trade integration, it started to speed up in the 1990s (Johnson et al., 2007). By this time, however, Malaysia was beginning to face competition from newer manufacturing locations in relatively lower-wage countries, especially China.

In principle, liberalizing cross-border financial flows and integrating with global capital markets—both fundamental aspects of financial globalization—should lower the cost of capital and facilitate investment. In the run-up to the 1997–1999 Asian financial crisis, Malaysia imposed few restrictions on portfolio flows, allowing an offshore market in ringgit to develop. But while globalization had brought immense benefits to the economy through the opportunities it created for trade, this closer integration now left the Malaysian economy vulnerable to swings in global financial market sentiment. Following the crisis, it took until 2002 for real gross national income (GNI) per capita to recover to the level seen in 1996 (Sultan Nazrin Shah, 2019).

A decade later, the 2008–2009 global financial crisis also had economy-wide impact. The collapse in the US of the mortgage-backed securities market and the bankruptcy of Lehman Brothers rattled global financial markets, requiring unprecedented, coordinated intervention by major central banks to stabilize global payment systems and markets. As US dollar liquidity evaporated, demand in major economies contracted sharply. The impacts on Malaysia, which had learned lessons from the Asian financial crisis and made its banking system more robust, were felt through deteriorating terms of trade and contracting exports. FDI in Malaysia plummeted by 79 per cent between 2008 and 2009 (BNM, various years). While some of this sharp contraction was undoubtedly due to the crisis-induced recession, its disproportionate size compared with other countries in the region also suggested that foreign investors were beginning to turn their attention elsewhere.

Deindustrialization and Digitalization, 2000–2020

Deindustrialization—Underlining Malaysia's Need for Broader Diversification

On balance, however, Malaysia's deeper engagement with the global economy had brought huge benefits and had had a transformative impact on the structure of its economy. Industry as a share of GDP climbed steadily through the 1990s, as did the share of industrial employment in total employment. By 2000, manufactured exports—dominated by electrical and electronics parts—dwarfed commodity-based exports, and over half of Malaysia's export trade was with East Asia.

Perak's economy, too, bore little resemblance to that of 1957. It had grown hugely, and the profile of economic activity in the state had been increasingly focused on non-agricultural activities despite the relatively low level of capital investment in manufacturing (UPEN Perak, and MIER, 2009). While Perak's economic growth may not have kept pace with the national average, the state had become more prosperous, productive, and diversified, and its people more urbanized.

However, as Malaysia entered the new millennium, industrialization stalled and even reversed. Worse still, the share of industrial employment in the economy had not attained the peak seen in advanced countries on the cusp of their deindustrialization process (Tengku Mohamed Asyraf et al., 2019). Malaysia's deindustrialization therefore appears to have been premature. It was not associated with rapid manufacturing productivity gains. Two factors, both of which related to globalization and the challenges of operating in a competitive global environment, were responsible for this.

First, Malaysia's dependence on a low-cost, labour-intensive business model and its failure to upgrade to more technologically advanced manufacturing had rendered the economy vulnerable to cheaper sources of international supply. Manufacturing in the newly industrialized economies of the Republic of Korea, Singapore, and Taiwan had advanced much further technologically than in Malaysia, while Thailand—its peer in the Association of Southeast Asian Nations (ASEAN)—had established a niche in car and car parts manufacturing. As international competition intensified—particularly after 2002 when China joined the WTO—Malaysia started to lose out in the race for FDI, and despite its growing trade with China, manufacturing export growth slowed.

Second—and linked more subtly to globalization—by opening up, Malaysia may have imported deindustrialization from advanced economies (Rodrik, 2015). A global fall in the real price of manufactured goods puts a squeeze on manufacturing everywhere. By specializing in the standardized production of parts and components rather than higher-value-added manufactured goods, the squeeze may have accelerated deindustrialization in Malaysia.

Digitalization—Another Double-edged Sword

The digital revolution of the first decades of the 21st century, which in some ways has brought the world even closer together, marks a new phase of globalization that has had a huge impact on economic and social activities. This new phase of the knowledge economy involves growing use of ever-smarter machines powered by artificial intelligence, driven by 'Big Data', along with the growing automation and robotization of factory production processes, which further propels growth in the service sector. This is a blessing for some—especially those in high-skilled information and communications technology jobs—and a curse for others, such as those made jobless by robots.

Malaysia had foreseen this new era when it established Cyberjaya in the late 1990s, but the town has had only limited success so far in generating business, financial, and communication services. If Perak is to prosper in this new phase of globalization, it will also have to achieve two linked turnarounds. The first is to stem the outflow of its young and better-educated people by establishing forward-looking institutions and by introducing policies that support new sources of jobs and productivity gains. The second is to work on narrowing the growing disparities in per capita income with other Malaysian states.

*   *   *

Part 3B analyses in greater detail how Perak responded after ethnic riots broke out in May 1969. Laissez-faire policies gave way to an interventionist developmental state, strongly committed to the pursuit of growth with equity. This policy approach remains largely in place to this day.

The first section describes how these aims were articulated in the NEP of 1971, which provided a national framework for the ethnically based affirmative action policies of the next two decades and well beyond. Perak's state government sought to increase economic growth—also among the core objectives of the NEP—and to address legacy issues of uneven spatial development as well as the economy's over-reliance on exports of tin and rubber. Perak continued to lose ground to other states over these decades, however, giving up the leading economic position it had occupied at independence. And it also lost many of its young and most talented people as outward migration soared.

The second section considers how Perak responded to having fallen behind in economic and income growth by 1990. The economic landscape had changed dramatically since independence. The emerging sources of economic strength lay in modern infrastructure, economic density and diversity, and a readily available pool of workers with the capabilities to adapt to new demands: the location of natural resource endowments was no longer a determining factor. With its dispersed settlement patterns, low economic density, and natural-resource–based economic structure, Perak did not have these advantages.

The state thus redirected its planning strategies in an attempt to modernize and diversify its economy and employment patterns. It built industrial clusters in new industrial estates, opened FTZs to attract foreign and domestic investment, and ventured into heavy industries with automotive manufacturing. It also pursued multiple initiatives to expand private-sector participation in services, especially tourism. Success over most of the period 1970–2020 was mixed, but by 2020 Perak had begun to recapture some of its lost ground—in economic terms, if not in relation to migration.

The New Economic Policy and its Impact on Perak during its Early Relative Decline, 1970–1990

Malaysia's NEP dominated the country's political economy and drove decision-making for two decades from 1970. This was an affirmative action policy zealously adopted at all levels of government, aiming to build national unity among the ethnic communities by restructuring the economy and ending absolute poverty. The NEP also sought to remove the close association of occupation with ethnicity and to redress the weaker socio-economic position of predominantly rural Malays relative to other ethnic groups. Another key element was the restructuring of corporate ownership, as discussed above in relation to the tin and rubber industries (see 'End of British Mining Dominance: Malayanization' and 'Early Malayanization', above).

The state government of Perak was subject to the primacy of federal economic policy, although it was able to contextualize national plans to meet its own needs. It sought to increase economic growth—a core objective of the NEP—and to address legacy issues of uneven spatial development and the economy's over-reliance on tin and rubber exports. The state's dependence on these two primary commodities had made it economically vulnerable in the past, tightly linking Perak's economic fortunes to those of the global economy. This vulnerability gradually diminished with economic diversification. However, Perak still lost ground to other states. At one level, this was due to the emerging global forces that conferred advantages on localities with high levels of economic and population density. At another level, it was also due to the federal government's active promotion of development in poorer states and in Selangor. As a result, Perak lost the position it had held at independence as one of the country's richest and most advanced states. The quality of governance and planning within the state government accentuated these difficulties.

This section traces the intensified planning efforts by federal and state governments to raise Perak's agricultural productivity and to increase the incomes

Globalization: Perak's Rise, Relative Decline, and Regeneration. Sultan Nazrin Shah, Oxford University Press. © Sultan Nazrin Shah (2024).
DOI: 10.1093/oso/9780198897774.003.0022

derived from agriculture, through economic diversification within that sector. It looks at industrialization plans led by both levels of government, and at subsequent moves to privatize heavy industry. It ties all of these government interventions to the overall performance of Perak's economy, including its spatial dimensions, especially relative to the performance of other Malaysian states. The section also reviews structural changes in Perak's economy over the two decades, in particular the changes to the shares of the primary, secondary, and tertiary sectors in the state's GDP, as well as to employment patterns by sector and by ethnic community.

The New Economic Policy—A Fundamental Shift

The planning framework and programmes that evolved for implementing the NEP were articulated in Malaysia's 20-year Outline Perspective Plan, 1971–1990, and in its four economic 'Malaysia Plans', MP2–MP5, covering the period 1971 to 1990 (Sultan Nazrin Shah, 2019). These official planning documents set out goals and quantitative targets, and framed the actions that would support their achievement, with thematic emphasis and expenditure allocations changing over time.

At the start of the 1970s, state governments were being urged to play 'a larger and more dynamic role in the achievement of national objectives' (EPU, 1971, p. 115). Many of the natural resources, such as land, forests, water, and minerals, fall within their jurisdiction rather than under the federal government, and thus national outcomes depended heavily on states' actions. Given the geographical profile of poverty and its association with ethnicity, rural development programmes acquired resonance. MP2, 1971–1975, explicitly asserted that attention to rural development would contribute more widely to 'balanced development in all of its dimensions' (EPU, 1971, p. 46). National planners also recognized, however, that without economic growth and industrialization, redistributive efforts would soon falter.

Spatial concerns were brought to the fore in MP3, 1976–1980, which sought to promote greater economic integration among states and redress structural imbalances between regions (EPU, 1976, p. 199). Its premise was that regional development was a building block for national development. As one of the more economically advanced states at that time, Perak was not a primary focus of these spatial rebalancing efforts, which were concentrated largely on the less developed states of the north and east of the peninsula, and on Sabah and Sarawak.

Still, the NEP's objectives applied to all states, and in Perak they crystallized in several ways. The state government became a much more active agent of economic transformation, endeavouring to galvanize agricultural and industrial development. It created private corporations,[74] notably the Perak State Development Corporation and the Perak State Agricultural Development Corporation, to support NEP activities (Box 3.9). These agencies carried out programmes to diversify the economy away from a dominant primary sector towards the secondary and tertiary sectors, and strongly promoted greater participation of Malays and other *Bumiputera*.

Box 3.9   State implementing agencies in Perak

The Perak State Development Corporation (PSDC) and the Perak State Agricultural Development Corporation (PSADC) are two key state institutions created to carry out NEP programmes to restructure and diversify Perak's economy, promote Malay participation in modern-sector employment (that is, in manufacturing, construction, and services), and reduce rural poverty. The PSDC plays a key role in accelerating industrial and commercial development by opening industrial estates, developing townships, and investing in potential growth areas to support non-agricultural economic diversification. The PSADC plays a similar role in agriculture and agro-industries to support rural development in diversifying within agriculture.

Perak State Development Corporation (Perbadanan Kemajuan Negeri Perak)

Established in 1971, the PSDC led the state's industrialization efforts, notably by providing loans and grants to new manufacturing establishments in industrial estates, and by making direct investments in manufacturing ventures. It also became heavily involved in other economic sectors. For example, during the 1970s and 1980s it invested in 21 logging-related enterprises in joint ventures with private-sector partners. It issued logging licences covering nearly 400,000 acres, or nearly 8 per cent of Perak's total land area (Azrai Abdullah, 2022, p. 158). The PSDC's other activities included mining (with Tronoh Dredging Company), tourism, and infrastructure.

---

74 These were in effect quasi-government agencies that were arms of the government. Although they were established through state or federal legislation, they adopted private-sector principles and modes of operation.

Perak State Agricultural Development Corporation (Perbadanan Pembangunan Pertanian Negeri Perak)

The PSADC, established in 1973, invested along the agricultural supply chain—in estates and nurseries, land clearance, and rehabilitation schemes; in transport and storage facilities; and in downstream agro-processing businesses. One of its pioneering initiatives was the development of agriculture in the districts of Manjung, Hilir Perak, Kuala Kangsar, and Batang Padang, covering 1,182,000 acres (Perak State Government Briefing Notes, 1974). It helped to develop nearly 20,000 acres of land during the 1970s (Azrai Abdullah, 2022, p. 245). As with the PSDC, most of the PSADC's schemes were operated by wholly owned subsidiary companies, although some were also organized as joint ventures with the private sector.

The federal government encouraged Perak, along with other states, to form a State Economic Planning Unit (State EPU) to coordinate and align state and federal plans (Box 3.10). After the State EPU was formed, Perak's economic performance started to become much more closely associated with the state's own bureaucratic capacity, the quality of its governance and regulations, and its relationship with the private sector as well as with federal decision-making.

Box 3.10   The Perak State Economic Planning Unit (Unit Perancang Ekonomi Negeri Perak)

Malaysia's National Action Council, chaired by Prime Minister Tun Abdul Razak, was responsible for coordinating national development plans. In July 1971, the Council directed states to establish state and district action committees to support the NEP's activities. The government felt that there was a pressing need for 'a corps of better trained planners and administrators with a greater awareness of national objectives and an ability to harness the full potential of the state's resources for the implementation of the NEP' (EPU, 1971, p. 115).

At that time, Perak's government had no institutional mechanism for assessing the state's development challenges, formulating medium- and long-term integrated plans, ensuring consistency between state and federal planning, or monitoring implementation. What the state government had initially formed for NEP

(Continued)

implementation, in late 1971, were four priority sector 'task forces', covering agriculture; commerce, industry, and infrastructure; society and culture; and administration. In 1973, the Perak State EPU was established as the secretariat and coordinating mechanism for the four task forces.

The main functions of the Perak State EPU were—and remain—to plan and formulate development policies and strategies; to coordinate intra-state departmental plans and programmes; to implement state and federal government development programmes; to provide advisory services on economic matters; and to monitor the implementation of its economic programmes. The state government could now frame its own comprehensive five-year development plans, aligned with federal development policies and goals. Although the State EPU was initially hampered by a scarcity of human resources, it managed to set out the main objectives of the state's third and fourth development plans (Zaludin Sulong, 1977), which were to:

- Reduce rural poverty by increasing job opportunities through the opening of new land schemes, establishing new growth centres, and increasing opportunities for the poor to acquire land, water, credit, marketing, extension services, and public services.
- Reduce urban poverty by increasing job opportunities in manufacturing and construction, including in small-scale industries, and increasing real incomes through the provision of low-cost housing and other public services.
- Increase access to education, health, family planning, and housing.
- Increase Malay employment in mining, manufacturing, and construction, while increasing the involvement of non-Malays in agriculture and services so that the employment structure would reflect the ethnic composition by 1990.
- Increase Malay ownership of land, fixed assets, and share capital.
- Promote increased private investment inflows from within and outside the state.

Perak's development plans were thus to some extent contextualized to meet its own priority challenges and were intended to ensure 'balanced development' in the state. But as the federal government retained control over the allocation of development funds, it kept a 'strong centripetal influence' over the direction of state programmes (Drabble, 2000, p. 8).

Raising Rural Incomes in Perak

With most of Perak's rural population—primarily, but not exclusively, Malays—engaged in low-income agricultural jobs, rural development promised a pathway out of poverty. From the early 1970s, support for agriculture and measures to improve rural livelihoods stepped up a gear. Rural development now focused on strengthening economic opportunities, diversifying crops, raising agricultural productivity, and expanding access to public goods and modern services, including schools, hospitals, electricity, and safe water and sanitation.

More specifically, efforts focused on land development, double cropping of rice, drainage and irrigation, rubber replanting, and the expansion of oil palm cultivation. In land development, two approaches were adopted: *in situ* improvements for rehabilitating land in settled areas, and the opening of new areas for settlers from other districts facing land pressure, or where land holdings were uneconomic (Drabble, 2000, p. 219). In the 1970s some 300,000 acres of land were alienated for agricultural purposes, mainly for smallholders (this dwarfed the interventions of the 1960s when only about 9,000 acres had been allocated). Of this, 180,000 acres were provided to smallholders for the cultivation of *padi*, rubber, tapioca, oil palm, and on a smaller scale, cocoa and fruit and vegetables.

Diversification within Agriculture—From Rubber to Oil Palm

Perak's agricultural diversification entailed a transition from rubber to oil palm, with huge growth in estate cultivation and palm oil output in the 1970s. Investments in oil palm proved attractive: palm oil prices surged in the 1970s and the return on investment in oil palm far exceeded that on investment in rubber. The area of oil palm under cultivation in 1980 was nearly three times as high as in 1970—90,000 hectares against 33,000 hectares (Table 3.4)—and palm oil production grew commensurately.

In the 1980s, encouraged by the PSADC and federal agencies, many rubber smallholders also converted to oil palm, although a substantial share of the state's agricultural land continued to be used for rubber (UPEN Perak, and MIER, 2009). Apart from the attractive price, oil palm requires shorter maturation—around four years after planting—until the fruit is harvestable; output then increases with age, maintaining a peak between 11 and 30 years after planting (Lim, 1969, p. 141). The area cultivated by oil palm rocketed to reach 248,000 hectares by 1990, of which about two-thirds was in estates. The PSADC

Table 3.4	Oil palm led the diversification of Perak's commercial agriculture between 1970 and 1990		
Crop	1970	1980	1990
	Hectares planted (thousands)		
Rubber	257	254	212
Oil palm	33	90	248
Padi	82	70	83
Coconut	45	55	40
Cocoa	3	25	31

Source of data: Azrai Abdullah (2022, p. 153 and p. 215).

also encouraged diversification into cocoa and coconuts, in keeping with the national policy on crop diversification.

Increasing the Productivity of Rice Cultivation

Efforts were made to increase Perak's productivity in rice cultivation so as to reduce the high levels of poverty among rice farmers. Supported by federal government agencies, the PSADC invested heavily in *padi* irrigation and drainage projects such as the Kerian Extension Scheme and the Trans-Perak Irrigation Scheme, gave subsidies for fertilizer, and provided guaranteed support prices for *padi*. Rural roads with links to main roads were built, and credit and technical inputs were provided to rural farmers. Those in Kerian—Perak's main rice-bowl area—were encouraged to develop a more commercial outlook towards rice farming and to raise productivity (Drabble, 2000). The Kerian–Sungai Manik Integrated Agriculture Development Project (IADP) combined several interventions with the aim of substantially increasing *padi* farmers' monthly income. This scheme was completed in the latter half of the 1980s.

Perak's area under *padi* cultivation shrank dramatically in the early part of the 1970s but then rebounded, and indeed reached a higher level, in the second half of the decade. Even then, however, *padi* output by volume was lower at the end of the 1970s than in 1971 despite continuing assistance to the sector. In the 1980s Perak's area under *padi* expanded by 20 per cent, with output by volume up by 14.5 per cent (Sultan Nazrin Shah, 2017). Yields per hectare *declined*, however. This was partly because Malay reserve land became increasingly fragmented as it was passed down the generations under Malay inheritance rules, rendering cultivation increasingly uneconomic, and partly because marginal lands were brought into production. Rice farmers, especially those with small landholdings, were among the poorest of Perak's rural population.

Perak's Early Industrialization

The NEP envisaged a pivotal role for manufacturing in the country's economic transformation, especially by encouraging Malays into modern-sector jobs. Recognizing that Malaysia's comparatively small market constrained opportunities for firms involved in import-substituting industrialization—which began in the 1960s and which could not create enough jobs to absorb a rapidly-expanding labour force—national planners turned their attention to an export-oriented industrial strategy (Jomo and Wee, 2002).[75] After 1970, Perak's policymakers regarded industrialization in the state as a mechanism for both achieving the NEP's goals and for weaning the economy off its historical dependence on the tin industry.

Tin mining remained important for Perak's economy until the 1980s, supplying state revenues and generating direct as well as indirect employment through the multiplier effects on secondary industries such as foundries, metal fabrication, and engineering, as well as other support services.

Proliferation of Industrial Estates—To Little Effect

At first, most industrial estates were established in the Kinta Valley and other parts of the former tin belt, largely because of the presence of infrastructure, support services, and human resources in these locations. Later, the PSDC began to establish industrial estates in more dispersed areas of the state. By mid-1976—by which time Perak's total area developed for industrial purposes had reached 755 hectares—approved industrial projects had spread beyond Kinta to districts such as Larut, Matang, and Selama; Kuala Kangsar; Manjung; and Kerian. A decade later, more industrial areas had been opened by the state, both in Kinta district and beyond (Perak State Development Office, 1987).

---

75 In addition, early steps taken towards industrialization had been haphazard as 'there was no attempt to plan industrial development' (Drabble, 2000, p. 236). The Industrial Coordination Act of 1975 streamlined existing incentives and was aimed at providing a coordinated approach to industrial development. In 1975, the Malaysian Industrial Development Authority (MIDA)—previously the Federal Industrial Development Authority—was established to promote coordinated industrial development across all states and encourage foreign investment.

As the pace of industrialization quickened, Perak faced strong competition from other states. In the 1970s it attracted just 4.5 per cent of total FDI in Malaysia, losing out to neighbouring Selangor and to Penang, where the new and vibrant FTZs had been created; these competitor states also had the key advantage of being adjacent to major ports and airports. Perak did not build its first FTZ until the late 1980s. As most FDI was concentrated in export industries, Perak did not figure prominently in the manufacturing export boom of the 1970s. Most investors in Perak, with some exceptions such as those in textiles and latex, were producing goods to serve the domestic market, such as construction materials, food, and furniture.

The federal Location Incentive Scheme of the Investment Incentive Act of 1972 provided incentives for both local and foreign investors locating in 'less developed' areas, but this did not include any areas within Perak's state boundaries. The PSDC attracted industry by investing in industrial estates and co-investing in business, as well as offering incentives, including discounts on land rentals.

The Malaysian Industrial Development Authority (MIDA) approved 436 industrial projects in Perak between 1968 and 1980.[76] Just over half of these received incentives, either through pioneer status or tax concessions. Perak's main industries during this period were food manufacturing (21 per cent of MIDA-approved industrial projects); metal products, machinery, and electrical and electronic goods (17 per cent); textiles and leather products (15 per cent); chemical and chemical products (15 per cent); and non-metal products (11 per cent) (Azrai Abdullah, 2022, p. 173). These industries were in general labour intensive and export-oriented. Although state support for infrastructure, loans, and equity investments was important for stimulating industrialization, the response of the local private sector was also significant.

One aspect of industrial development in the 1980s was the markedly higher investment in industrial estates in Perak and other parts of Malaysia.[77] By 1990 Perak had 19 such estates (Asan Ali Golam Hassan, 2017). The PSDC still played the lead role in establishing them, although the private sector had also started to invest.

---

76 Approved MIDA projects were those employing 25 persons or more and with a minimum paid-up capital of RM250,000.

77 There was tough competition among states in the provision of industrial land and, like Perak, Selangor and Johor were also expanding their industrial infrastructure. By 1990 Selangor had 25 industrial estates and Johor had 20. Although Penang had only nine, they were large in area and the state's industrial density was high.

The Perak government's strategy appeared to be driven by that famous yet misguided notion, 'build and they will come'. Although much of the earlier industrial investment in the state had been outside designated industrial estates, and much of the space available in industrial estates remained vacant, new estates continued to be built. A glut of space emerged, and even by the late 1990s more than half of the land in industrial estates remained unsold. Kinta fared better than other districts in Perak in terms of both demand and utilization, selling over 65 per cent of its estate land, compared with an average of only 30 per cent in other districts (Azrai Abdullah, 2022, p. 243). Data on land sales, however, exaggerate the impact that the estates had on industrial growth, simply because much of the land sold remained undeveloped.

The 1980s also saw several other shifts in Perak's approach to industrialization. State planners started to emphasize industries that used local content and pushed to attract foreign investors in high-technology and capital-intensive firms. In 1989, a one-stop Centre of Investment was set up to help facilitate new investment. And there were moves to co-locate related industries that could share common infrastructure, facilities, and capital assets. This began with foundries, which had originated initially to serve the needs of the tin-mining industry. Another initiative was a ceramics park in Kinta.

No Heavy Industries for Perak

Although Malaysia's efforts to attract FDI into export-oriented industries had been successful, senior policymakers were concerned that this investment—mainly in labour-intensive export-processing activities—was not capturing the industrial and technological know-how from abroad required to modernize the economy. The federal government therefore moved to invest in a range of heavy industries with joint-venture partners that could provide this know-how for Malaysia. The argument was that opportunities would flow 'backwards' along supply chains to local small and medium-sized enterprises (SMEs), thereby nurturing a modern entrepreneurial and business community which would draw heavily on Malays and other *Bumiputera*. As these industrial ventures were complex and capital-intensive, and the risks were high, the federal government would have to play a key role in catalysing investment. Although policymakers believed that these new industries would eventually be able to compete internationally, the strategy ended up generating the equivalent of a second round of import-substituting industrialization.

In 1981, another state-invested corporation was created—the Heavy Industries Corporation of Malaysia (HICOM)—to lead heavy industrialization. Khor (1987) estimates that in the early 1980s, HICOM invested well over US$2 billion in multiple ventures, an amount augmented with co-investments from foreign partners.[78] Although HICOM made some of its investments to help develop lagging states, such as Terengganu and Sabah, it did not earmark any investments for Perak. In any case, HICOM's ventures proved largely unsuccessful and costly (Sultan Nazrin Shah, 2019).

Privatization of State Assets and Post-recession Refocus

After the global commodity price shock of 1985–1987, a deep recession in Malaysia, and mounting evidence of the failure of many of the heavy-industry investments, the federal government—burdened by onerous deficits and an over-sized public sector—pushed to privatize state holdings of industrial assets. Federal policymakers, inspired by the global trend of moving state-owned businesses to the private sector, saw privatization as a way of rationalizing public finances. They also hoped it would help to generate a modern business community of Malays and other *Bumiputera*. Perak, along with other states, followed the federal lead in curtailing its commercial interests and activities and transferring them to private ownership. At first, the major privatization projects affecting Perak were federal ones, and cut across state and district boundaries. These involved roads, port and airport services, telecommunications, health facilities, and utilities.

Export-oriented manufacturing, which had been emphasized before 1980, was once again placed front and centre after the recession in the mid-1980s, and the heavy-industry push was scaled back.[79] Perak at the time had no FTZs, and the state was ineligible for most measures intended to encourage the wider national dispersion of industry. Strengthened incentives for less developed areas were targeted at Kelantan, Terengganu, Pahang (excluding Kuantan), and the eastern districts of Johor. Only investments at Perak's Kamunting industrial estate qualified for federal support. At state level, the PSDC offered a reduced assessment for factory sites in the city boundaries of Ipoh and a 30 per cent

---

78 In the 1980s, HICOM invested in a cement plant in Kedah; a steel manufacturing facility in Terengganu; a national car assembly plant, a petrochemicals plant, and an industrial estate in Selangor; a shipbuilding facility in Johor; a pulp and paper venture in Sabah; and factories producing motorcycle engines and motor parts in Penang. According to Chee (1994), by the late 1980s HICOM had invested over RM42 billion in projects that generated fewer than 5,000 jobs directly, and exports from these industries were negligible.

79 The Industrial Incentives Act of 1986 replaced the Investment Incentives Act of 1972 and provided a more extensive and generous array of incentives for export-oriented manufacturing activities. These benefited the FTZs of Johor, Penang, and Selangor, where the bulk of Malaysia's exports were produced (Rasiah, 1993).

discount on the land premium paid to the state land commissioner (Asan Ali Golam Hassan, 2017).[80]

After the mid-1980s, Perak began to pursue a resource-based industrial strategy in line with the 1985 national Industrial Master Plan which emphasized strong backward and forward linkages in manufacturing and between manufacturing and the rest of the economy. Perak's approved investment projects began to attract fast-growing volumes of foreign equity from a low base.[81] The state government refocused industrial development on the Kinta Valley, with the new aim of seeing its development keep pace with that in the Klang Valley. This shift in focus reflected a recognition that, despite the government's earlier attempts to encourage industrial dispersal, investors had not located their plants in Perak's smaller towns, preferring the agglomeration economies that the Kinta Valley offered. Moreover, of the total capital investment of approved manufacturing projects for the country between 1984 and 1989, Perak's share was a mere 3 per cent, compared to 27 per cent for the Klang Valley, 16 per cent for Johor, and 7 per cent for Penang (MIER, 1992). Perak's manufacturing sector continued to suffer from what had now become its locational *disadvantage*.

The PSDC's portfolio was extensively rationalized in 1989 after a rapid review by the state government. By the end of the year it had investments in just 32 businesses, down from 80. Of these only five were wholly owned by the PSDC (Azrai Abdullah, 2022, pp. 247–248). These privatization efforts also extended to smaller investments the corporation had made since the early 1970s. Assets that had been operating profitably and providing valuable state revenues were sold below market price to single Malay owners as part of the NEP's affirmative action programme aimed at widening Malay and other *Bumiputera* asset ownership. The bulk of the PSDC's remaining capital—70 per cent—was concentrated in investments in manufacturing and property as well as in the tin-mining industry, which was still suffering from the fall-out of the mid-1980s' crash.

The PSDC's performance as an investor and catalyst for the state's economic development was mixed. Many of the assets that remained on its books were largely non-performing and did not attract private sector interest (Azrai Abdullah, 2022). In addition to the sale and transfer of state assets to the private sector, the state encouraged and facilitated private Malay ownership of new projects, such as industrial estates and community and housing developments, where previously state entities would have been the lead investor.

---

80 The land premium is paid on any application for a land transaction, such as a request for change in land use, land conversion, sub-division of land, or even amalgamation.

81 Foreign equity in approved industrial projects was RM14.8 million in 1980, RM17.2 million in 1985, RM46.1 million in 1987, RM264 million in 1990, and RM541.6 million in 1991.

Economic Change in Perak, 1970–1990

The two decades after 1970 saw economic growth in Perak that was unimpressive vis-à-vis that of other states. The period also saw changes to its economic structure and to its profiles for sectoral employment, urbanization, and poverty.

Comparative Growth Performance—From a 'Developed State' to a 'Low-income State'

Perak's economic performance during the 1970s and 1980s failed to keep pace with that of the broader national economy. Measured in real terms at 1978 prices, Perak's GDP in 1990 was 2.5 times larger than in 1970. Its GDP growth averaged 4.7 per cent between 1970 and 1990, but this was well below the national average of 7.4 per cent and much lower than in Penang, Johor, and Selangor, which resulted in a widening relative income gap (Table 3.5). Growth rates were much faster in the 1970s than in the 1980s. In per capita terms, annual growth averaged 3.8 per cent over the two decades but slowed dramatically from 5.4 per cent in the 1970s to just 2.1 per cent in the 1980s.

Table 3.5	**Perak's growth in real GDP and GDP per capita lagged behind the national average**					
	GDP average annual growth (%)			**GDP per capita average annual growth (%)**		
	1970–1980	1980–1990	1970–1990	1970–1980	1980–1990	1970–1990
Johor	8.6	5.8	7.2	6.4	3.4	4.9
Penang	9.5	5.0	7.3	7.8	3.6	5.7
Perak	6.4	2.9	4.7	5.4	2.1	3.8
Selangor[a]	10.5	6.3	8.4	6.6	2.9	4.7
Malaysia	9.0	5.7	7.4	6.5	3.2	4.8

Sources of data: EPU (1976, 1986, and 1996).

Notes: Nominal GDP is the value of gross output measured in current prices, whereas real GDP values output at fixed (base year) prices. Comparable state-level GDP data covering the decades 1970 to 1990 do not exist. The Department of Statistics–Malaysia only started to publish state-level nominal and real GDP from 2005. However, GDP data were estimated by the EPU for specific years before 2005. State-level estimates for 1970 are expressed in 1970 prices whereas those for 1980 and 1990 are expressed in 1978 prices. The 1970 national and state-level nominal GDP figures are adjusted using the national-level GDP deflator published in the World Bank's DataBank (World Bank, 2020b) to express them in constant 1978 prices.
[a]*Selangor* includes Kuala Lumpur.

Although, nationally, policymakers had made efforts to promote greater spatial dispersal of economic activity, a pattern of uneven development and *widening* spatial disparities had still taken hold (Mohammad Abdul Mohit, 2009). By 1990 Perak had lost ground to the nation's most economically advanced states. Its share in national GDP had fallen to 9 per cent by 1990, from 12 per cent in 1980 and 15 per cent in 1970 (Figure 3.13). Similarly,

Figure 3.13 **Perak's GDP and GDP per capita failed to keep pace with those in many other states in the 20-year NEP period**

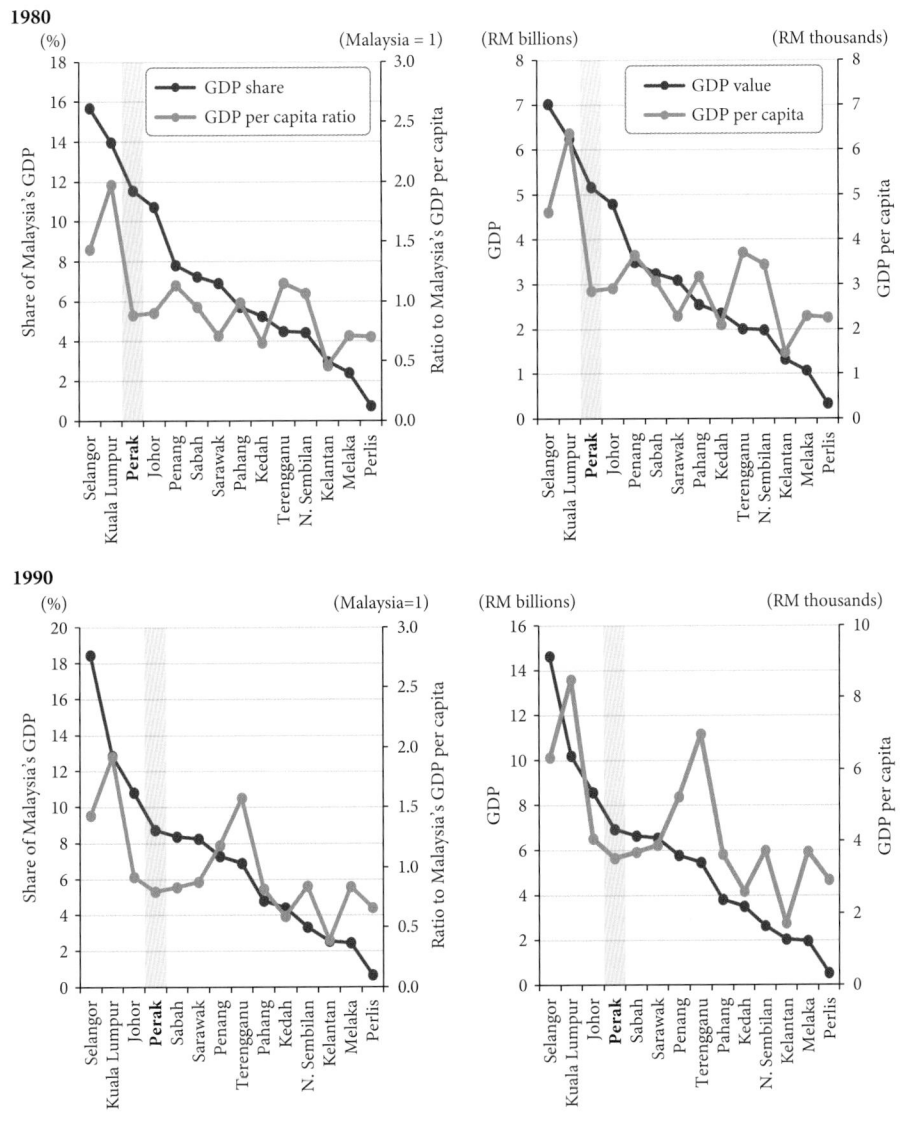

Sources of data: EPU (1976, 1986, and 1996).
Note: GDP data are in 1978 prices.

Perak's GDP per capita was 89 per cent of the national average in 1980 (putting it among the bottom six states), and only 80 per cent in 1990 (among the bottom four), down from 99 per cent in 1970 (when only Selangor's was substantially higher).

By 1990 Perak could no longer be considered one of Malaysia's most advanced states. Selangor, Penang, and Johor had all experienced broader-based economic growth. In official terms, during those two decades Perak had slipped from being a 'developed state' (as stated in MP3) to a 'moderate-income state' (MP4, EPU, 1981), and to a 'low-income state' (MP5, EPU, 1986).

One of the main reasons for Perak's under-performance was the under-representation in its economy of manufacturing, which was booming nationally. In 1980, Perak's manufacturing output share in its GDP divided by the corresponding output share in national GDP—the manufacturing location quotient—was a paltry 0.7. The corresponding quotient for Selangor was 1.8 and for Penang 2.0. Owing to this comparative under-representation, Perak's share in Malaysia's total manufacturing output fell in the 1980s from 8.1 per cent to 6.5 per cent, while its share in manufacturing employment fell even more sharply from 11.4 per cent to 8.8 per cent.

Perak's lagging development in these decades can also be seen in the long-term net emigration of its people to other states and other countries, reflecting their search for better jobs and livelihoods, as well as the paucity of local options for young people seeking a tertiary education. It was only after the mid-1990s that the first university opened in Perak, despite the state having established a reputation as a leader in the provision of education prior to independence. Given the lack of decent jobs in Perak, many young people, having relocated to pursue their studies or training, did not return on completion, draining the local economy of precious human capital and narrowing its skill and entrepreneurial base.

Structural Change—Some Success but Not Enough

Despite lagging behind broader national achievements, Perak did see major changes in its economic structure over the 20-year NEP period. The share of the primary sector in Perak's GDP fell dramatically, from nearly 49 per cent in 1970 to around 34 per cent in 1990, largely reflecting the collapse of mining (Figure 3.14). Agriculture's share of output declined by only 3 percentage points over these two decades, likely reflecting the state's slow economic transformation but also an increase in labour productivity owing to the transition from rubber to oil palm (see 'Structural Transformation, 1970–2020', below).

On the flip side of the decline in the primary sector, the secondary sector's share of GDP climbed from just under 11.4 per cent to around 23 per cent, driven by the growth of manufacturing—albeit from a low base. Also, as noted, measured against national performance, Perak's industrialization was late and slow and the share of manufacturing in total output trailed that in other states.

Labour productivity in Perak's manufacturing sector also trailed the national average. By 1990 manufacturing in Perak was typically more labour intensive and less technologically sophisticated than in the more advanced states of Selangor, Penang, and Johor. And although electrical and electronics products, and textiles, had a growing presence, much of Perak's manufacturing in 1990 was still vertically linked to its upstream natural resources—rubber, timber,

Figure 3.14   **The primary sector's share in Perak's GDP shrank by nearly half as the secondary and tertiary sectors grew in the NEP period**

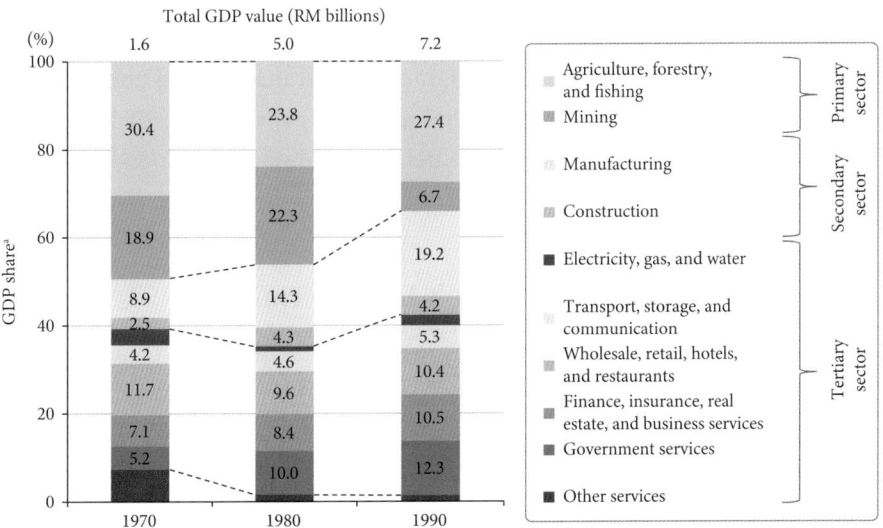

Sources of data: EPU (1976, 1986, 1991a).

Note: 1970 data are in current prices; the 1980 and 1990 data are in 1978 prices as sectoral GDP figures for those years are not available in current prices.
    [a] Excluding imputed bank service charges and import duties in the calculation of GDP share.

and crops—where their potential growth was constrained by the small scale of domestic markets, and where value added in processing these resources was capped.

While still a small share of GDP, the growth of construction between 1970 and 1990 was stimulated by an acceleration of public development expenditure as the state ambitiously pursued implementation of the NEP. The PSDC invested in residential housing, industrial-commercial buildings, and new townships. It also invested in mini-hydro projects for rural electrification, water supply to the rural hinterland, and the construction of hospitals, clinics, and schools. Investments in industrial estates, factories, and warehouses also spurred local construction activity.

The tertiary or service sector also saw its share of GDP rise, from around 39 per cent to 42 per cent between 1970 and 1990, largely stemming from a step-up in the provision of government services and the strong activist role assumed by the public sector as the NEP's implementor. The service sector provided a source of job creation, albeit of low productivity, and was one means through which federal and state governments, including Perak's, promoted the development of a Malay and other *Bumiputera* business community. Falling output and limited job opportunities in Perak's traditional mainstays—notably tin, rubber, and agriculture—virtually demanded an aggressive push for a stronger tertiary sector.

As well as spurring the opening of new townships, the steady growth of manufacturing spawned demand for services, including transport and communications, financial services, other commercial activities, and utilities, while rising incomes more generally contributed to increased demand for social and personal services.

Employment Shares—Agriculture's Falls by Half

These changes in the structure of the economy led to shifts in the size and composition of employment across different sectors (Table 3.6). In 1970, agriculture dominated at 47.5 per cent of the total, but by 1991 its share had shrunk dramatically to just 24.2 per cent. Manufacturing employment had doubled to 17.5 per cent by 1991. By 1980, services employed over three times as many workers as manufacturing, although manufacturing employment was growing faster, albeit from a modest base. Perak's government employment doubled in the 1970s, accounting for much of the service sector's expansion.

Table 3.6	As the share of agriculture in employment shrank in Perak, that of the modern sector surged		

Sector or subsector	Share of employment (%)		
	1970	1980	1991
Agriculture, forestry, hunting, and fishing	47.5	38.3	24.2
Mining and quarrying	6.8	4.6	0.8
Manufacturing	8.7	12.1	17.5
Construction	2.0	4.8	6.1
Electricity, gas, water, and sanitary services[a]	0.9	0.3	0.9
Commerce[a]	10.3	14.2	16.3
Transport, storage, and communication[a]	2.7	3.3	3.7
Community, social, and personal services[a]	17.1	20.0	26.0
Not adequately described	3.9	2.4	2.2
Unknown	0.0	0.0	2.4
Total (%)	100.0	100.0	100.0
Total (numbers)	454,236	562,121	578,617

Sources of data: Chander (1975); Khoo (1983); Khoo (1995a).
Note: [a] Subsectors in the service sector.

Changing Ethnic Composition of Sectoral Employment

Perak's ethnic composition of employment changed in line with the NEP's objective of restructuring this aspect of the economy to reflect the population shares of the country's main communities (Table 3.7). The share of agricultural employment in Perak's total fell sharply, although the share of total agricultural employment among Malays and other *Bumiputera* declined more modestly, from 58.0 per cent in 1970 to 53.2 per cent in 1991 (Figure 3.15). Throughout the period there was a transfer of labour resources out of agriculture and into industry and services.

In manufacturing and services, the number and share of jobs occupied by Malays and other *Bumiputera* surged. The share in total employment of total manufacturing employment for this community rose from just 16.0 per cent in 1970 to 40.7 per cent in 1991 (Figure 3.15). In services, their share jumped from 28.7 per cent to 48.1 per cent. New jobs were created in government administration, in newly established or expanding government-linked entities, and in the uniformed services. Conversely, Chinese continued to dominate employment in the construction and commercial markets between 1970

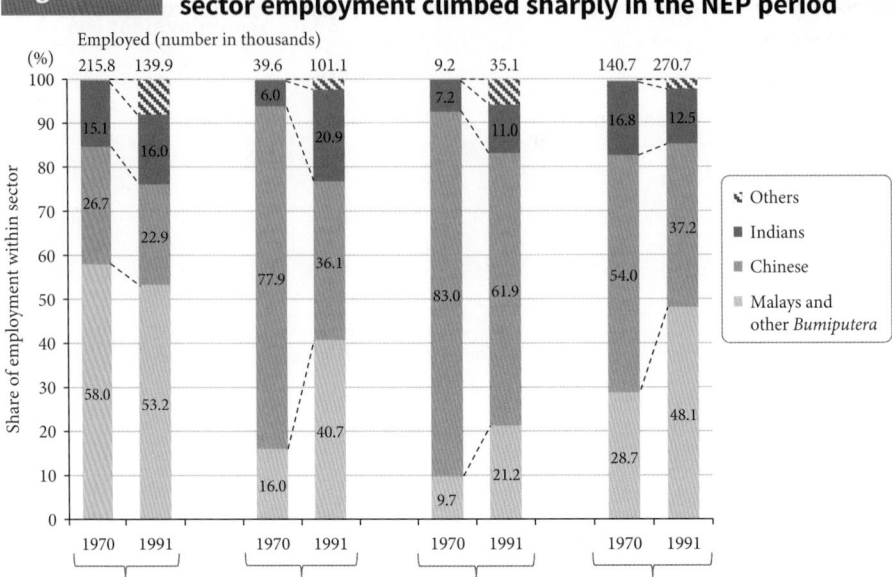

Figure 3.15 **The share of Perak's Malays and other *Bumiputera* in modern-sector employment climbed sharply in the NEP period**

Sources of data: Chander (1975); Khoo (1995a).

and 1991 (although with declining shares), which may reflect their strong kinship networks and supply chain connections in these sectors built over the preceding decades.

Rising Urbanization

Changes in Perak's spatial composition accompanied changes in its economic structure. Several NEP programmes aimed to encourage rural–urban migration, out of the traditionally low-paid and low-productivity agricultural sector, and into higher-paid modern-sector urban jobs. By 1991, for the first time, more people were living in Perak's towns than in the rural hinterlands, and the urbanization rate of 54 per cent was almost double that of 1970. Kinta district—the location of the metropolitan state capital of Ipoh, which had about one-third of Perak's population—was the most urbanized. While Kinta's significance initially stemmed from its historical association with the tin industry, new industries and public administration centres were also locating and rapidly expanding there. Outside Ipoh, other important towns in Kinta were Kampar and Batu Gajah. Beyond Kinta district, the

	By 1991, just 28 per cent of Perak's Malays and other *Bumiputera* were employed in agriculture, and around half had jobs in government and other services					
Table 3.7						

	Share of employment within ethnic group					
Sector or subsector	Malays and other *Bumiputera*		Chinese		Indians	
	1970	1991	1970	1991	1970	1991
Agriculture, forestry, hunting, and fishing	67.1	28.4	28.5	15.3	50.5	26.1
Mining and quarrying	2.6	0.8	11.6	0.9	4.0	1.0
Manufacturing	3.4	15.7	15.3	17.4	3.7	24.7
Construction	0.5	2.8	3.8	10.4	1.0	4.5
Electricity, gas, water, and sanitary services[a]	0.8	1.2	0.5	0.3	2.6	1.3
Commerce[a]	3.6	10.0	16.9	26.7	8.9	11.8
Transport, storage, and communication[a]	1.8	2.6	3.2	4.4	3.8	6.0
Community, social, and personal services[a]	15.4	36.0	17.1	16.7	21.5	20.4
Not adequately described/ unknown	4.7	2.5	3.2	7.8	4.1	4.3
Total employed (%)	100.0	100.0	100.0	100.0	100.0	100.0
Total employed (numbers)	186,391	261,774	202,082	209,130	64,373	85,656

Sources of data: Chander (1975); Khoo (1995a).
Note: [a] Subsectors in the service sector.

second- and third-highest population concentrations and centres of trade and services were in the towns of Taiping and Teluk Intan.

Over the two decades of the NEP, economic growth generated by the expansion of manufacturing, services, and construction, as well as the growth of new townships, had a catalytic impact on urbanization. By 1991, with sustained rural–urban migration, especially of young males, the urban population had become younger and much more cosmopolitan, consisting of 48 per cent Chinese, 36 per cent Malays, and 15 per cent Indians. By now, 40 per cent of Perak's Malay population were living in urban areas, compared with just 10 per cent two decades earlier, and their shares in all modern-sector employment categories had risen.

Falling Poverty Rates

Perak's development efforts were successful in reducing absolute poverty over the NEP period. Rural development programmes, especially those that helped to lift productivity among *padi* farmers and rubber smallholders, coupled with improved access to social services, especially schools and health facilities, helped to raise household incomes and promote economic equity. So, too, did the conspicuous increase in jobs in urban manufacturing and services. Surplus rural labour moved to towns bordering industrial estates and to new townships, which also provided modern-sector jobs. Absolute poverty, which stood at 48.6 per cent in 1970, fell sharply to 30.5 per cent in 1979, and even further to 19.3 per cent by 1989. While this reduction was impressive, Perak's poverty rate at the end of the 1980s was still higher than the peninsula's average and much higher than that in Selangor and Penang (Figure 3.16), where industrialization had penetrated much further.

Figure 3.16 **Perak's poverty rates fell steeply in the NEP period, but less than the peninsula's average**

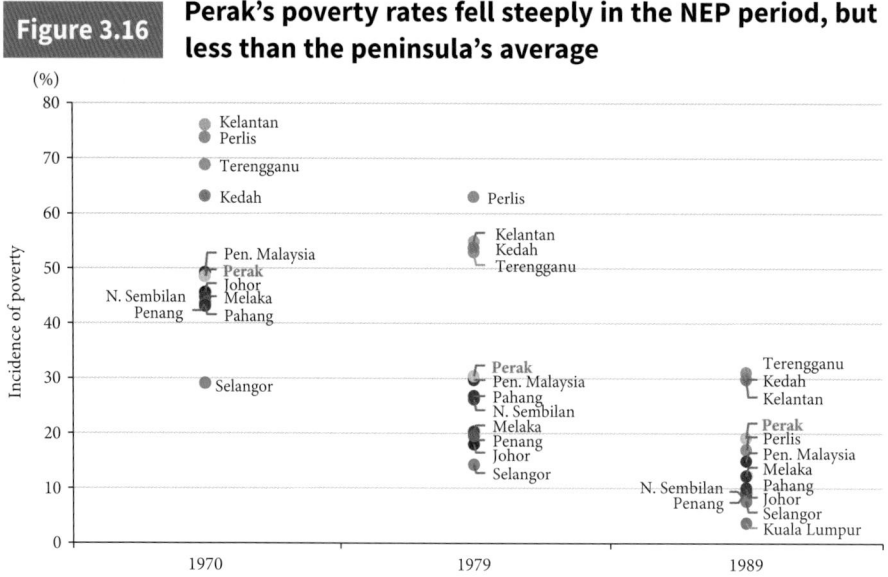

Source of data: Economic Planning Unit–Malaysia (various years), *Incidence of Absolute Poverty*.
Note: Selangor includes the Federal Territory of Kuala Lumpur in 1970 and 1979.

Soaring Outward Migration, 1971–1990

Both inter-state outward migration from Perak, as well as emigration of Perakians abroad, greatly accelerated during the NEP period. Between 1971 and 1990, there was an estimated net outflow of more than 300,000 people to other states, as well as a very large number—though undocumented—leaving for destinations overseas. All ethnic communities were represented among those leaving the state, but outward migration rates were highest among the Chinese. Figure 3.17 shows that the net outflow of inter-state migrants was at a peak in these two decades. This was a period during which Malaysia's economy was fast transforming, leading to rapid employment growth driven by manufacturing and services (EPU, 1976 and 1991a).

While people were leaving Perak, the Klang Valley—the epicentre of Malaysia's economic growth—became a magnet for migrants.[82] It provided expanded

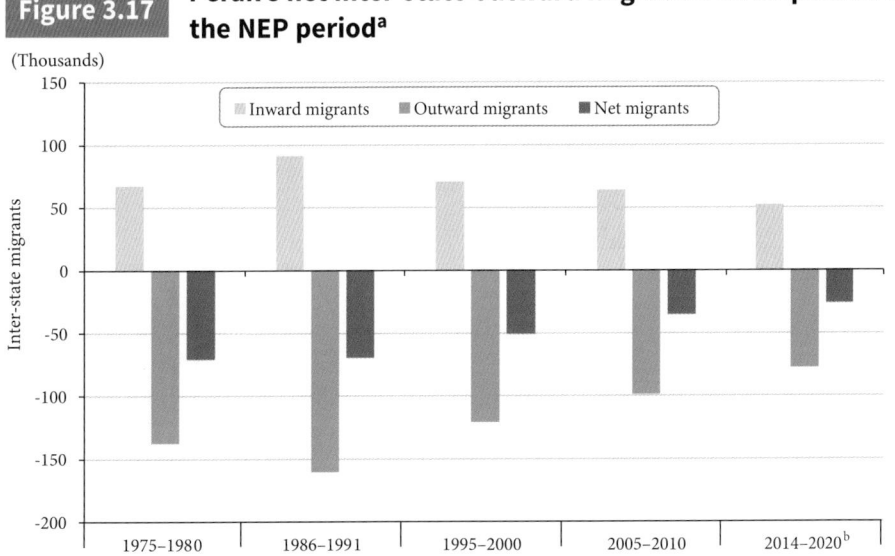

Figure 3.17 **Perak's net inter-state outward migration flows peaked in the NEP period[a]**

Sources of data: For 1975–2010: Khoo (1995d); Shaari Abdul Rahman (2004); Abdul Rahman Hasan (2014); for 2014 to 2020: Department of Statistics–Malaysia (various years), *Migration Survey Reports.*

Notes: [a] A positive number refers to net inter-state inward migrants, a negative number to net inter-state outward migrants.
   [b] The Migration Survey was not conducted in 2017 and 2019.

---

82 In the analysis in this book, the Klang Valley is taken to include the combined area of Kuala Lumpur, Putrajaya, and Selangor to maintain statistical comparability over time. Historically, Kuala Lumpur was part of the state of Selangor until it became Malaysia's first federal territory on 1 February 1974. Similarly, Putrajaya, now the federal government's administrative centre, was also part of Selangor until becoming Malaysia's third federal territory in 2001—the second was Labuan. *(Continued)*

access to the most modern infrastructure, communications, and ancillary services, and had the highest concentration of professional and skilled human resources (Figure 3.18, left panel). The Klang Valley became the country's main industrial hub, accounting for around 41 per cent of total manufacturing output in 1980. Kuala Lumpur was the financial services and administrative hub. Mean household incomes per capita were much higher in the Klang Valley than in other states. In Perak they were about 50 per cent lower than in the Klang Valley, and were even below national levels.

Figure 3.18   **Perak's net outward inter-state migration contrasts with flows into the Klang Valley, the destination of most of Perak's outward migrants[a]**

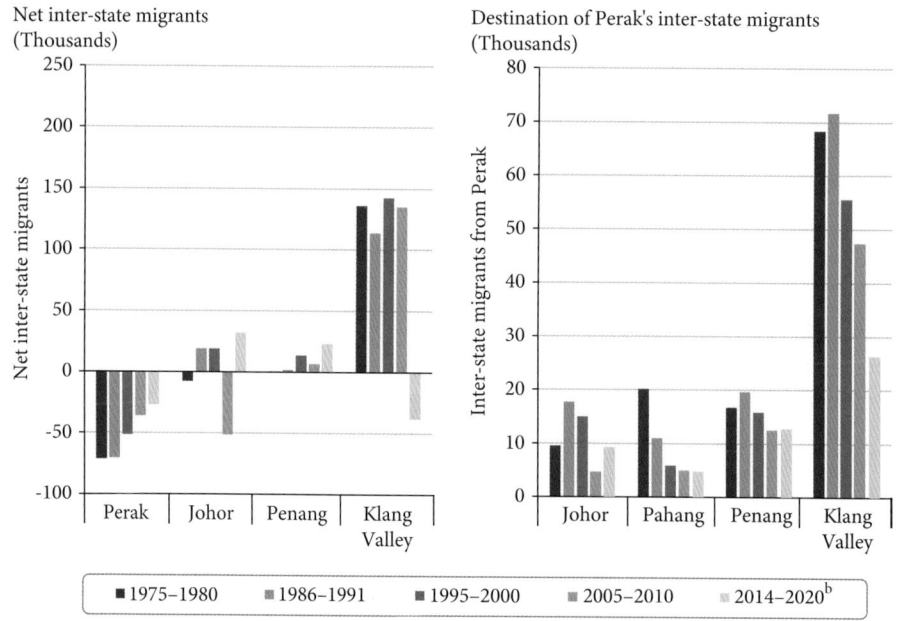

Sources of data: For 1975 to 2010: Khoo (1983), Khoo (1995a, 1995b, 1995c, 1995e, and 1995f); Shaari Abdul Rahman (2004); Abdul Rahman Hasan (2014); for 2014 to 2020: Department of Statistics–Malaysia (various years), *Migration Survey Reports*.

Notes: [a] A positive number refers to net inter-state inward migrants, a negative number to net inter-state outward migrants

[b] The Migration Survey was not conducted in 2017 and 2019.

The Klang Valley has generally been defined as consisting of Kuala Lumpur and its adjacent four districts—Gombak, Hulu Langat, Klang, and Petaling. These are almost entirely urban and have become increasingly tightly linked by an extensive network of transport infrastructure, now comprising the bulk of Selangor's economic activity and population (82 per cent in 2020). Selangor's five lesser populated districts are not formally considered part of the Klang Valley, although as the 21st century has progressed they too have become much more integrated and urbanized.

Industrialization began to gain momentum in other states, too, with the shift towards more labour-intensive, export-oriented industries in the 1970s, and the creation of EPZs throughout the peninsula. Penang, in particular, had a concentration of EPZs with most of the new firms producing electrical and electronics components as well as textiles. As Penang's industrialization accelerated in the 1970s and 1980s, and opportunities for modern-sector employment expanded, it also became an increasingly attractive destination for migrant workers from Perak (Figure 3.18, right panel).

Industrial and commercial activities also expanded in Johor and Pahang, with the establishment of industrial estates as well as the opening of Johor Bahru port in 1977 and Kuantan port in 1978. These developments generated a surge in migration from Perak to Johor and Penang, as well as to Pahang, where the expanding and large-scale FELDA land development schemes also attracted outflows of predominantly rural migrants (Figure 3.18, right panel).

Migration Driven by NEP's Affirmative Action ...

The NEP, as noted above, sought to create modern-sector jobs in the public sector and in industrial and commercial activities for Malays and other *Bumiputera*. It had a powerful impact on migration flows. One of its strategies was to expand the size of the federal administration and build new state institutions with the explicit aim of drawing in rural Malays and other *Bumiputera* from lower-income states such as Perak. The policy worked, and as the ranks of the civil service and state enterprises swelled, the Klang Valley saw a large influx of migrants. Between 1971 and 1980, the number of Malay and other *Bumiputera* inter-state migrants from Perak to the Klang Valley increased by a factor of four compared to the previous 10 years, while the number of Chinese and Indian migrants increased by around 2.5 times.

The NEP also sought to boost the level of human capital of Malays and other *Bumiputera* through expanded post-secondary education. The tertiary education system expanded quickly over this period, with the number of universities rising to five.[83] Tertiary education opportunities in Perak, however, remained

---

83 Universiti Kebangsaan Malaysia (National University of Malaysia) was established in Selangor, and the College of Agriculture was upgraded to Universiti Pertanian Malaysia (University of Agriculture Malaysia, later renamed University Putra Malaysia), also in Selangor. In Johor, Institut Teknologi Kebangsaan was upgraded to become Universiti Teknologi Malaysia (University of Technology Malaysia). Another new university, University Utara Malaysia (Northern University of Malaysia) was founded in Kedah, while branch campuses of Universiti Sains Malaysia (previously University of Penang) were set up in Kelantan and Perak. Five new polytechnics were established, in Kedah, Johor, Kelantan, Negeri Sembilan, and Sarawak.

very limited. Many of the state's students who wanted to continue to higher education went to institutions in the Klang Valley or abroad, with few returning on completion of their studies.

... and by Perak's Lagging Economy

Throughout Malaysia's structural transformation between 1971 and 1990, Perak was industrializing and its manufacturing sector was developing, but the state recorded relatively slow economic growth. Agriculture, which remained the state's largest contributor to GDP, was growing only modestly, with the decline of rubber output compensated by limited gains in agricultural productivity in other subsectors. Although production of palm oil was expanding, the scale of FELDA's land development in Perak for oil palm cultivation fell far short of the large acreages being developed in Pahang, Johor, and Sabah on account of Perak's limited area of large contiguous tracts of land.

Further, the collapse of tin prices in 1985 devastated local communities in Perak's remaining mining towns (see 'Impact of Tin-market Collapse on Perak', above). In the neighbouring townships of Kampar and Tanjong Tualang in the Kinta Valley, for example, not only were mines being closed but many related businesses that depended on the tin industry also folded. The combined population of the two towns fell from 89,000 in 1980 to 74,000 in 1991, as massive unemployment forced many of the youth and young adults to seek employment elsewhere. With the decline in the number of mines and with increased mechanization in surviving mines, mining jobs in the Kinta Valley fell from 17,500 in 1980 to just 5,600 by 1991.

Multiple factors contributed to Perak's inability to retain its better-educated workers, particularly among 20–29-year-olds (Box 3.11). Young and better-educated migrants have a distinct preference for vibrant urban areas and a reluctance to take on rural employment (Tey, 2014). Young migrants formed the largest group leaving Perak for the Klang Valley and Penang, destinations which were the most urbanized and had many more higher-paying job opportunities. This pattern is consistent with migration theories that have found that differentials in real wages and job opportunities have a significant impact on migration (Chitose, 2003; Etzo, 2008).

Box 3.11   Why the young and talented leave Perak

Every year since independence, Perak has suffered huge outflows of its young and most talented, who leave for better opportunities in more prosperous states or abroad.

Big-city dynamism

Many young Perakians, especially college and university graduates, prefer to look for higher-paying jobs in more dynamic cities which offer not only a wider range of job opportunities but also better amenities and leisure facilities. The Klang Valley, in particular, the capital city of Kuala Lumpur, is the top choice for young people who want to leave their birthplace (The Asia Foundation, 2013). Big cities offer broader and more diverse networking opportunities. Many who leave for Malaysian (or international) cities to pursue their tertiary education are reluctant to return after graduation, having discovered new opportunities and established new friendships.

Although life in densely populated cities is not without its challenges—a higher cost of living, especially for accommodation—some migrants would rather undertake part-time work or even do odd jobs, for instance driving for a ride-hailing platform in the city to make ends meet, than return to their hometowns.

Few opportunities in Perak's towns and villages

Life and work in the big cities contrasts starkly with the much simpler life in Perak's slow-paced towns and villages, with their limited career choices, business opportunities, and leisure facilities. The population of former tin-mining towns, such as Batu Gajah, Kampar, Tanjong Tualang, and Teluk Intan, fell sharply as many people left due to the lack of alternative jobs when the tin industry collapsed.

Rural agricultural employment is much less appealing to the young than it was to older generations. As their first migration step, many young people from smaller rural villages relocate to Perak's metropolitan towns—Ipoh and, to a lesser extent, Taiping, which is close to mainland Penang. Still, from a business perspective, Ipoh offers a smaller market than some other Malaysian cities where people have higher earning potential. Perak-born entrepreneurs and business owners appear to be keener to develop and market their products outside the state.

The pursuit of higher education, big city life, better-paid jobs, and wider business opportunities are not the sole reasons for young Perakians to migrate. Marriage and the desire to follow one's spouse or family are other reasons; in a 2018 survey,

(Continued)

some 44.5 per cent of Malaysia's inter-state migrants reported that they had moved for family reasons (Department of Statistics–Malaysia, 2018a).

Appeal of venturing abroad

In today's globalized world, younger generations are more inclined to pursue careers abroad. According to the 2019 Randstad global survey, 90 per cent of young Malaysians would consider emigrating if it meant they could improve their career and work–life balance, especially to countries in the Asia-Pacific, such as Australia, Singapore, and Japan (Randstad, 2019). For Malaysians abroad, the reality of higher incomes and a better quality of life has led many to choose not to return (World Bank, 2011).

Professionals and the highly skilled eye opportunities abroad. The lack of depth and breadth in the national job market, especially in the knowledge and skill-intensive sectors, provides an incentive for such workers to migrate and a disincentive for them to return. Malaysia's job market still caters primarily to 'traditional' jobs, with few opportunities for those who traverse the 'road less travelled' by specializing in niche subjects, whether in the pure sciences or in the arts. Although the appeal of higher wages and job prospects serves to motivate migration abroad, these are not the only factors, especially among ethnic Chinese, some of whom perceive social disincentives for staying put, such as unequal access to scholarships and higher education, and a lack of inclusiveness (World Bank, 2011; Cheong et al., 2018).

Sending students abroad for tertiary studies has been a practice among the well-off since colonial days. Many families encourage their children to study abroad, supported by public or private funding and scholarships. Some are attracted by the lifestyle or achievements of their peers abroad, and the number of Malaysian students going abroad has increased (Cheong et al., 2018). One survey of the Malaysian diaspora showed that nearly half of respondents still visit Malaysia regularly, while 41 per cent are members of a Malaysian diaspora association, indicating their continuing interest in and affiliation to the country (World Bank, 2015).

Towards a more youth-oriented public policy

Perak's continuing 'brain drain' poses a huge challenge to its economic and social development. Creating a wider range of job opportunities—especially for the higher skilled—as well as an attractive lifestyle back home, requires a comprehensive youth-centred development policy that also strives to ensure an inclusive environment based on needs and merit.

Summary—Why Perak Saw Relative Decline in the NEP Period

Between 1970 and 1990, Perak's economic diversification reduced reliance on tin and rubber—the former replaced largely by manufacturing and modern services, the latter by oil palm. Economic output expanded by just 4.7 per cent a year, however, and was far slower in the 1980s than in the 1970s. This placed Perak's growth well below that of Selangor, Johor, Penang, and even the Malaysia-wide average. Why, then, did Perak lose its pre-1970 position as one of Malaysia's leading economies?

First, Perak's economic interests were not well served by its geography. Unlike Penang, and Selangor with Port Klang, it did not develop a deep-water port and its natural resources were no longer the blessing that they had been in the past. New and emerging sources of economic strength now rested primarily on the advantages stemming from modern infrastructure, economic density, and diversity, and a readily available pool of workers able to adapt to new demands. Selangor also had the advantage of providing ready access to federal government agencies and decision-makers. Perak, with its dispersed settlement patterns, low economic density, and its natural-resource-based economic structure, was not well positioned with any of these advantages.

Second, federal policies do not appear to have helped. For decades after independence, national planners and policymakers seem to have persisted in the view that Perak was still the comparatively developed state that it once had been, despite fundamental changes in its underlying circumstances and in global markets. Perak did not directly benefit from the measures introduced in the 1970s and then extended in the 1980s, which vigorously promoted export manufacturing. These appeared to solidify the locational and first-mover advantages enjoyed by Selangor and Penang, and even induced a 'backwash' effect seen in migration outflows and the movement of businesses out of Perak. National decision-makers did not consider Perak as a state which required federal incentives to encourage new activities to locate there. This meant that development allocations to Perak from the federal government in the 1980s were small relative to the size of its population and indeed to its share in national GDP.

Third, state-level policies and governance may also have been a factor in Perak's slow economic growth. In general, there appears to have been a failure to evaluate the effectiveness of state-level development efforts and to recalibrate them when their disappointing results became apparent. One glaring example was the continuing expansion of industrial infrastructure in the presence of a supply glut in the 1980s, and an apparent failure to recognize locational disadvantages. Another was the prevalence of poorly performing PSDC investments. Yet another seems to have been the uninspiring track record of converting approved investments into realized projects. Perak's state government was also slow to appreciate the needs of investors beyond their requirements for serviced industrial land: it was not until 1989 that it established a one-stop Centre for Investors, some two decades after Selangor had done so.

Finally, the spatial dispersal of industries, while important for addressing uneven development within Perak, was likely pursued too fast. Too many industrial parks were built, which were too geographically dispersed to allow for agglomeration benefits. They failed to account for the needs and preferences of investors—'build and they will come' appears to have been the flawed leitmotif—and agglomeration possibilities were not considered. The expanded role of the state government in the development of serviced industrial land likely had the effect of crowding out private investors. Private investors, especially foreign investors, were only encouraged to participate in developing industrial estates by the late 1980s, meaning that private investment in Perak missed out on the early days of the country's industrialization.

Strategic Responses amid New Challenges, 1990–2020

By 1990, Perak, like the rest of Malaysia, had made notable progress in achieving the goals of the NEP. Major advances had been made in employing Malays and other *Bumiputera* in modern urban jobs and in transferring asset ownership to them. Structural economic change was under way, with the shares of output in manufacturing and services increasing, and that of agriculture declining. Perak's historical economic pillars—tin and rubber—had greatly diminished in importance, and oil palm and manufactured goods were starting to take their place, as were tertiary sector services. Although the income levels of Perak's population were less than the national average, they were still growing in real, inflation-adjusted terms; ethnic inequality was narrowing, poverty was decreasing, and the quality of life—in terms of education and health indicators—was improving for the vast majority of people. This, then, was a situation of absolute advance amid relative decline.

This section assesses how Perak responded to falling behind several other Malaysian states in terms of economic and income growth, and how it met new challenges, including the devastating impact of the 1997–1999 Asian financial crisis. It describes how, on the cusp of the 21st century, Perak redirected its planning strategies in order to further modernize and diversify its economy and employment patterns, both within agriculture and into manufacturing and services. With the aim of expanding its manufacturing base, it built industrial clusters in new industrial estates, opened FTZs to attract foreign and domestic investment, and ventured into heavy industries with automotive manufacturing. These policy thrusts were accompanied by multiple initiatives to increase private-sector participation in services, especially in tourism.

At the national level, planning became increasingly focused on promoting balanced regional development through the creation of economic 'growth corridors'—partly funded by federal development allocations. By 2016 Perak had become part of the Northern Corridor Economic Region (NCER). The state

Globalization: Perak's Rise, Relative Decline, and Regeneration. Sultan Nazrin Shah, Oxford University Press. © Sultan Nazrin Shah (2024).
DOI: 10.1093/oso/9780198897774.003.0023

failed to attract substantial foreign and domestic investment, however, in the face of fierce competition from elsewhere in Malaysia—and from Southeast Asia more widely—and its membership of the NCER appeared to yield few early benefits.

Post-1990 Redirection of Federal and State Strategies

As Malaysia entered the 1990s, the federal government articulated its ambitious *Vision 2020*, which envisaged the country becoming an advanced industrialized nation by 2020. In the Sixth Malaysia Plan (MP6), 1991–1995, and MP7, 1996–2000 planners focused on the need to expedite structural transformation. *Vision 2020* placed even greater emphasis on the manufacturing and service sectors as the new drivers of economic growth, with their higher potential for value addition, and also prioritized building human capital through human resource development and skills upgrading.

In 1991, the federal government launched the National Development Policy, which refocused economic goals and targets without de-emphasizing the aims of poverty reduction and social restructuring (EPU, 1991a). It stressed the importance of 'balanced' development—that is, economic growth with equity at national and state levels—and boosted existing efforts to modernize the economy, with the private sector having a much more instrumental role. This represented a sea change from the 1970s and early 1980s, when the public sector had been the major driving force in the economy.

Using the concept of 'Malaysia Incorporated', which encouraged public–private partnerships, policymakers now sought to create a business environment that was conducive to greater private-sector participation. Privatization was expected to 'free' the public sector to focus on infrastructure, human resource development, and social services. Capital- and technology-intensive industrial development was promoted, with an emphasis on product quality in order to gain access to new export markets. The federal authorities also urged states to be more efficient in using their development resources, and to broaden their industrial base, particularly towards resource-based industries.

A federal policy of specialization in industrial estates by location was implemented in order to disperse industries to the less developed states. Well-equipped industrial estates were planned for selected locations and designed to provide both the physical facilities and the other services and amenities necessary to render them attractive to private investors, foreign and domestic. The estates were intended to become new growth centres, and so contribute to regional development. A major new idea that emerged in Malaysia's Second Industrial Master Plan, 1996–2005, was to establish industrial clusters so as to strengthen the growth of manufacturing as well as its supporting industries and services (MITI, 1996a). Two clusters were identified in Perak: the historical tin-mining town of Tanjong Malim for car manufacturing and Lumut for shipbuilding.[84] These clusters were to be run and managed by the private sector, with the state playing a supporting role.

State-level planning aligned with federal policies, and Perak planned for strong manufacturing and service sector growth. During the NEP period, it had suffered more than any other state from the devastating impact of the tin industry's demise, as well as from the decline of the rubber sector. Economic diversification was thus an imperative, as reinforced in the state plans of the late 20th century when Perak pushed towards higher-value-added activities and processes, as well as stronger rural development and improved urban services. Its strategies coming into the 21st century therefore had a sharper focus on balanced development. The social rebalancing objectives of the NEP remained in place, with targeted assistance to help reduce poverty.

Perak's Strategic Plan, 2010–2015, similarly emphasized manufacturing and services, but now with a greater push for services—especially tourism and education—in recognition of the fact that rising household incomes would translate into greater demand for everything from financial services to retailing, restaurants, and entertainment services (UPEN Perak, and MIER, 2009). In 2011, Perak launched its 2020 Development Plan, which embraced the cluster concept and sought to enhance people's socio-economic status through the '3Qs': Quality opportunities, to attain high-level skills; Quality income, achieving a similar income level to the more developed states; and Quality living, through reduced crime and improved environmental management (Institut Darul Ridzuan, 2011; InvestPerak and UKM Pakarunding, 2011).[85]

---

84 Other industrial clusters identified were Kerteh, Terengganu and Gebeng, Pahang for petrochemicals; Muar, Johor, for furniture; Batu Pahat, Johor for textiles and apparel; Subang, Selangor for maintenance, repair, and overhaul services for aerospace; and Penang for electricals and electronics. Tanjong Malim, Gurun in Kedah, and Pekan in Pahang were designated for the automotive industry (MITI, 1996b).

85 In 2014, an ambitious mineral resource blueprint was developed which aimed to re-establish Perak as a premier mining state by exploiting its natural resources, and by building human capacities through industrial training and R&D so as to realize the vision of a 'Tin Valley' (Menteri Besar Incorporated–Perak, 2014, p. xxviii).

From around 2005, federal policy started to place less emphasis on individual states and focused instead on achieving balanced development through regional economic growth corridors, which were a major initiative in MP9, 2006–2010. The main objectives of the corridor approach, which crossed state boundaries, were reducing regional differences; bringing about equitable growth, investment, and job opportunities; and creating new sources of growth (EPU, 2008). MP9 identified five growth corridors nationally, one of which—the NCER, formed in 2007—covered Penang, Kedah, Perlis, and the four districts of northern Perak—Hulu Perak; Kerian; Kuala Kangsar; and Larut, Matang, and Selama.[86] By 2016 the whole of Perak had become part of the NCER, with the designated economic focus areas of agriculture, human capital, infrastructure, manufacturing, and tourism.

Crises Reinforce the Need to Diversify

Despite strong economic growth, which averaged 8.7 per cent in real terms during MP6, 1991–1995, and robust fundamentals during the early years of MP7, 1996–2000, Malaysia's export-led economy was unable to insulate itself against the financial contagion from neighbouring and developed countries (EPU, 1996 and 1999). Malaysia's real GDP per capita contracted by 9.7 per cent at the height of the Asian financial crisis in 1998, the steepest decline since independence. A decade later, in 2008, it shrank by 3.4 per cent during the 2008–2009 global financial crisis (Sultan Nazrin Shah, 2019). The local impacts of these two crises highlight the vulnerability of small open economies to globally driven events, and the resulting sudden outflows of short-term capital.

Perak's economy was not spared from the impacts of these two crises. The human costs were severe, particularly among lower-income groups: job opportunities shrivelled, and unemployment and poverty levels surged. Perak's labour force participation rate, which was catching up with the national average before the Asian financial crisis, tumbled from 62.8 per cent in 1996 to 59.8 per cent in 1999 (Figure 3.19, left panel).[87] The unemployment rate climbed to 4.3 per cent in 1999 from 3.2 per cent in 1996 (Figure 3.19, right panel), and the poverty

---

86 The other four are the East Coast Economic Region; Iskandar Malaysia; the Sabah Development Corridor; and the Sarawak Corridor of Renewable Energy.

87 Perak's labour force participation rate, much lower than the Malaysian average, may be attributed to its lower female participation rate and lower educational attainment.

For 30 years, Perak's labour force participation rates have been persistently lower, and its unemployment rates generally higher, than the national average

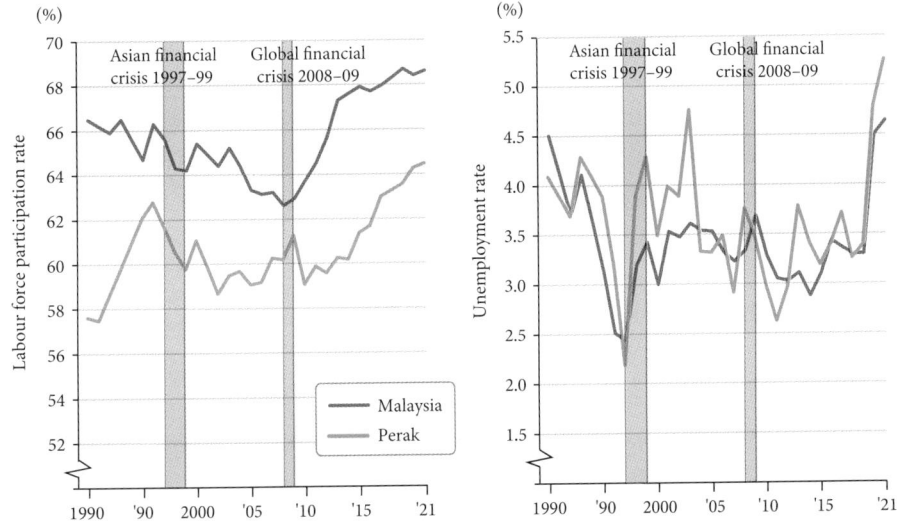

Sources of data: Department of Statistics–Malaysia (various years), *Labour Force Survey Report*; Department of Statistics–Malaysia (various years), *State/District Data Bank*; Khoo (1995a).

rate more than doubled from 4.5 per cent in 1997 to 9.5 per cent in 1999 (EPU, various years). Although the state's economy was somewhat more diversified in the late 1990s than in the 1980s, agriculture, manufacturing, and services were still highly labour intensive. The impact of the global financial crisis on Perak's socio-economic indicators was, by contrast, more muted.

The two financial crises further underscored the imperative for greater economic diversification and structural change in the economy, as national planners had been proposing. Several new economic challenges for Malaysia also emerged at the start of the 21st century. First, increased globalization, with the continued liberalization of trade and investment, was contributing to ever greater market integration and freer but volatile capital flows. Second, the rapid spread of information technology (IT) was revolutionizing manufacturing and business processes. Third, international competition was growing from other emerging Asian countries, especially China and India. Fourth, the labour market in many sectors was getting tighter, with some sectors experiencing labour shortages.

Perak's response to these challenges was to attempt to become more competitive. The state government renewed its push to diversify the economy and modernize its structure, particularly from low-value-added agriculture to higher-value-added manufacturing and services, and into more modern agricultural practices. Given its many forward and backward linkages to other economic sectors, manufacturing was expected to be the leading sector for economic growth. The state government put greater efforts into securing foreign investment, with its development strategy again stressing the importance of balanced development among the state's districts, along with urbanization and further gains in the quality of life. Building up the state's technical and higher-order skill base, primarily in IT, was also recognized as necessary to support the move towards a knowledge-based society.

Broadening Perak's Diversification

Measures introduced before 1990 had laid the foundations for the horizontal diversification of Perak's economy towards manufacturing and services. During the 1990s and subsequently, further rounds of diversification became necessary—along the value chain, and spatially through industrial clusters and activities within economic corridors—given that the resilience of the state's economy hinged on it developing a broader economic base. Other challenges included the need to expand the economy, and the competition for investment from the new 'tiger state economies' of Selangor, Johor, and Penang, with their locational advantages. Perak also needed additional sources of state income to meet its operational and development needs.

Did Perak's efforts to diversify its economy succeed and, if so, what was achieved? Answers to these questions are now proposed by examining the state's three main economic sectors—manufacturing, services, and agriculture—and flows of foreign and domestic investment.

Expanding Perak's Manufacturing Base

By 1990 Perak already had a growing manufacturing sector, which accounted for around 19 per cent of its GDP, somewhat lower than the national level of 26.7 per cent (EPU, 1991a). The sector was quite narrowly based, however, and most of its industries had weak inter-industry linkages as well as poor linkages with other parts of the economy, particularly the SMEs. As was the case nationally, the competitiveness of Perak's export-oriented industries became increasingly dependent on low-cost migrant labour. Other industries, especially domestic-oriented ones, had also developed with the benefit of high protection, rendering them globally uncompetitive.

A broadening and deepening of the industrial base was the principal thrust of Malaysia's industrial strategy from the 1990s. This sought reduced dependence on imported raw materials and components, and focussed on improving the integration between domestic-oriented industries and the export sector, as well as seeking greater expansion of resource-based industries. With the public sector facing financial constraints, the government continued its push for increased private investment—domestic and foreign—while easing access to it. It cut tariffs, lowered corporate tax—from 34 per cent in 1991 to 30 per cent in 1995—and further streamlined the application of rules and procedures.

Industrial Estates and FTZs

A sizeable proportion of federal development allocations to the states (discussed below) went towards industrial estates, being spent particularly on supporting infrastructure and services provision, including roads and drainage, and electricity and water connections. Despite the overhang of capacity from investments made in the 1980s, industrial estates in Perak continued to proliferate. Linkages with SMEs, which accounted for 80 per cent of manufacturing establishments, were enhanced by building the capacity of SME operators to supply products required by larger firms and for exports. Designated industrial estates for SMEs were built in Perak, especially foundries, engineering works, and wood-related industries, which were relocated into Kinta's industrial estates.

In 1990, Perak had 12 industrial estates covering 1,060 hectares, of which five were within 10 km of Ipoh and four within a few kilometres of Taiping (MIER, 1992). Special low-cost industrial estates for SMEs in Ipoh were provided through Malaysian Industrial Estate Ltd. But investment in industrial land saw only partial success, and just 44 per cent of land on Perak's estates was sold by 1998 (Azrai Abdullah, 2022, p. 243). Specialized industrial areas fared little better, as even when industrial land was sold, much of it was left unused. MP6 again called for programmes promoting FTZs, specifically for industries involved in high technology, plastics, foundries, wood, and computing (MIDA, 1985; EPU, 1991b). This was in line with the Medium- and Long-Term Industrial Master Plan Malaysia, 1986–1995, the first such plan established to guide Malaysia's long-term industrial growth strategy. In order to broaden its electronics subsector, Jelapang II and Kinta were designated as FTZs under the Free Zones Act of 1990 (Box 3.12).

Perak was a late mover to FTZs, unlike Penang and Selangor which had established FTZs in the 1970s at a time when US customs regulations provided incentives for US companies to relocate their labour-intensive industries outside the country (Sivalingam, 1994). Several large American multinational corporations and technology companies, including Intel, National Semiconductor, and Western Digital, were thus incentivized to set up manufacturing plants in Penang's Bayan Lepas FTZ. The FTZs in Penang and Selangor also benefited from the exchange-rate realignments following the Plaza Accord in 1985, when firms from Japan and other East Asian countries invested in offshore manufacturing production as their currencies appreciated, with investments by leading companies including Matsushita Electric Industrial (Panasonic) and Hitachi Metals Electronics. Further, in 1989 the Republic of Korea and Singapore graduated from the US Generalized System of Preferences programme which provided non-reciprocal, duty-free tariff treatment to certain products it imported (Congressional Research Service, 2021). This led to a reallocation of investment from these two countries to Malaysia. During this period, Perak was still concentrating primarily on traditional industries, and much of its manufacturing was still vertically linked to its upstream natural resources—rubber, timber, and crops.

Box 3.12   **Jelapang II and Kinta FTZs**

The Jelapang II and Kinta FTZs, both developed by the PSDC and located in Kinta district, were designated 'free industrial zones' under the Free Zones Act of 1990. The 112-acre Jelapang II FTZ, built between 1986 and 1989, was intended for medium-sized resource-based industries. The Kinta FTZ, with 116 acres, was constructed in 1990 for high-tech and more sophisticated industries. Eligibility for FTZ incentives and streamlined regulations under the Act required firms locating within them to export at least 80 per cent of their output.

By 1997, however, Jelapang II had attracted a mere RM14 million in approved project investment, which created just 170 jobs (MIDA, 1997). This investment was mainly in the production and processing of metal and machinery, plastics, and rubber, with products including stainless-steel kitchen utensils, telephone accessories, plastic injection mouldings, and rubber connectors and sheets. By the same year, Kinta FTZ had attracted RM63 million in approved investment, mainly in the electrical and electronics sector and in some mixed industries, creating some 2,200 jobs (MIDA, 1997). Of the two, Kinta FTZ was far more effective in diversifying Perak's manufacturing base, attracting 29 times as much FDI as Jelapang II FTZ by 2016. Together, however, they still accounted for just 4.4 per cent of Malaysia's total capital investment in FTZs (Table 3b).

They received much less investment and had much lower economic performance than Bayan Lepas FTZ in Penang or Port Klang FTZ in Selangor, which were both launched much earlier—1971 and 1972, respectively. These two FTZs have much better sea and air transport links to international markets. And, with time, the industries in Penang's and Selangor's FTZs, particularly in the electrical and electronics sector, have evolved beyond simple manufacturing into higher-value-added activities, such as research and development (R&D), and design and brand development (Yeow and Ooi, 2009). This has further strengthened the pull of these economic clusters.

Table 3b	By 2016, Jelapang II and Kinta had attracted just 4.4 per cent of Malaysia's FDI in FTZs				
Free trade zone	Tenants	Employment	Domestic	Foreign direct	Total capital
			investment (RM millions)		
Jelapang II	17	850	44.2	68.6	112.8
% Malaysia	1.9	0.4	0.7	0.1	0.2
Kinta Industrial Park	29	7,860	23.2	2,001.1	2,024.3
% Malaysia	3.2	4.0	0.4	4.2	3.8
FTZs in Perak	46	8,710	67.4	2,069.7	2,137.1
% Malaysia	5.1	4.4	1.0	4.4	4.0
FTZs in Malaysia	900	197,007	6,618.4	47,115.7	53,734.0

Source of data: ASEAN Secretariat and UNCTAD (2017).

A survey on the willingness of foreign investors to come to FTZs found that, besides the availability of usable land and tax benefits, location and a ready pool of adequately trained labour were critical determinants (Penang Development Corporation, 1972). Yet by the 1990s Perak had a mismatch between the supply and demand for specialized labour due in part to the emigration of its skilled workers. Worldwide today, most finished electronics products and parts—including imports of component parts—and pharmaceutical products are shipped by air because of their time-sensitivity. The small airport in Ipoh offers very few direct flights to other countries, and cannot accept larger planes, discouraging investors from setting up industries in the surrounding area. Perak also has an insufficient critical mass of local contract manufacturers to provide spillover effects in supply chains between FTZs and domestic companies, again making its FTZs less attractive destinations for foreign investors. This is particularly the case for resource-based industries which are likely to source components locally.

Refining Industrial Clusters

Malaysia's manufacturing sector faced multiple obstacles in the early 21st century. Globalization, liberalization, and the information and communications technology revolution had changed the rules and patterns of world trade, capital flows, and competition, undermining one previously accepted basis of competitive advantage—that is, low labour costs. The establishment of the ASEAN Free Trade Zone, under the ASEAN Free Trade Agreement, as well as the WTO, also pushed markets to integrate and increased global competition. Malaysia's industrial strategy therefore continued to focus on improving the quality of infrastructure, and on providing a conducive environment for private investment, including through greater creativity, initiative, and competitiveness. The industrial cluster approach remained the centrepiece of industrial strategy, and although FDI was still important, the federal and state governments also promoted domestic investment, so that a greater portion of the wealth being generated would remain in Malaysia.

National planning continued to stress greater value addition in the manufacturing sector, with a focus on product design, higher-technology-oriented production, and efficient engineering methods.[88] The sector was also gradually moving away from labour-intensive processes, and towards processes that were more capital- and knowledge-intensive. It accorded greater preference to the production of capital goods and of intermediate goods so as to reduce the import content in Malaysian products, with a continuing push towards dynamic industrial clusters that would benefit from agglomeration economies (Box 3.13).

Heavy Industries: Proton's Early 21st-Century Expansion to Tanjong Malim

The federal government continued its push towards heavy industries through HICOM, while also aiming for greater private-sector involvement. It continued to participate even when the capital requirements were too large to attract sufficient investment, and returns were expected to take time to materialize. Several public enterprises began investing in SMEs that provided ancillary products and services to heavy industries. Public enterprises also began to play a bigger role in heavy industries.

---

88 Malaysia's Third Industrial Master Plan (IMP3), 2006–2020, coincided with the MP9, MP10, and MP11 periods, and its primary objective was to achieve global competitiveness through innovation in and transformation of the manufacturing and service sectors (MITI, 2006; EPU, 2006, 2011, and 2016). Key priority areas were upgrading technology, seeking and securing high-quality investment, developing innovative and creative human capital, and integrating Malaysian industries and services into regional and global networks and supply chains.

Box 3.13   **Agglomeration economies**

When firms choose where to locate, many prefer to be geographically close to other firms. This is because their productivity and profitability are likely to be higher when operating in such clusters. Higher productivity then leads to higher wages for employees, attracting migrants into the area. These advantages of location are called 'agglomeration economies of scale'. They are external to the firm and contrast with 'internal economies of scale', which arise when unit costs of production fall as the firm's size increases, regardless of its location. Firms and their employees may also experience agglomeration diseconomies as they cluster in cities, stemming from high land prices and house rents, road congestion, air pollution, and urban crime.

Agglomeration economies take one of two forms: *localization economies* and *urbanization economies.*

Localization economies
Localization economies arise when firms *in the same industry* choose to locate close to other similar firms. There are many examples of such clustering:

- Roughly a decade ago, more than a third of aerospace engines were produced in three US cities: Hartford, Connecticut (18 per cent of total employment), and Cincinnati, Ohio and Phoenix, Arizona with another 18 per cent between them (World Bank, 2009).
- In California, Silicon Valley serves as a global centre for high technology and innovation, while Hollywood, decades ago, became a global centre for movie production.
- In the past, Sheffield in northern England and Scranton, Pennsylvania in the US were centres for steel manufacturing firms, while Detroit, Michigan attracted many US vehicle manufacturers including Ford, General Motors, and Chrysler.

Firms may initially locate to areas with clear geographical advantages for them. For example, Sheffield became a centre for steel manufacture largely because fast-running streams were available to power grinding wheels (Collier, 2018). Steel firms locating there because of this natural advantage soon prospered further through localization economies. Locations in which firms and workers concentrate have advantages over places where they are thinly scattered.

Urbanization economies
Agglomeration is closely identified with processes of urbanization. Urbanization economies arise when firms choose to be located close to firms *in different industries*. The presence of these economies is a key factor in the growth of large metropolises throughout the world. Examples include:

(Continued)

- New York's Wall Street, the City of London, Singapore, and Hong Kong have long attracted financial firms, insurance companies, and banking syndicates that benefited from being close to one another.
- Corporate headquarters of firms often cluster in cities to share business services like marketing, accounting, and legal services provided by third-party firms.

As countries transition from agriculture to industry, agglomeration and economic density take on added significance. The internal economies of scale that drive productivity in many industries are amplified by agglomeration economies external to the firm. As firms cluster together and locate close to a large pool of workers and to their customers, opportunities are created for productivity growth through increased scale and specialization. Public investment in urban infrastructure, and in economic and social services, as well as investment in other assets, intensify the advantages of clustering.

Factors in agglomeration economies
Factors responsible for agglomeration economies can be organized into three groups (Duranton and Puga, 2004):

- *Sharing*: Firms located close to others will be in a better position to share many public goods, production facilities, and marketplaces. A larger number of firms can exploit internal economies of scale in producing their inputs. So, for example, vehicle firms in Detroit lowered their costs by sharing parts suppliers (World Bank, 2009).
- *Matching*: When firms cluster in urban areas, there is likely to be better matching between employers and employees and between buyers and suppliers. For example, the likelihood of filling a vacancy with someone with appropriate skills is enhanced.
- *Learning*: Firms in urban settings are more likely to learn of and adopt new technologies and business practices that they observe in other firms, especially those in the same industry. For example, a firm will profit by hiring a worker with experience in a neighbouring, highly productive firm.

Evidence for agglomeration economies
Firms located closer to other firms are observed to have higher productivity than firms in more isolated locations. This finding is based either on wages earned by employees (reflecting their productivity) or on direct measures of the firm's total factor productivity. The evidence of benefits is stronger when firms are in the same industry, and particularly strong in high-tech industries (Henderson, 2003). According to the World Bank: 'A somewhat-oversimplified (but not altogether incorrect)

generalization would be that market towns facilitate scale economies in market-ing and distributing agricultural produce, medium-size cities provide localization economies for manufacturing industries, and the largest cities provide diverse facilities and foster innovation in business, government, and education services' (World Bank, 2009, p. 128).

Agglomeration economies in Malaysia
In Malaysia, the areas that have benefited from agglomeration economies are Selangor and Penang, which have specialized clusters of electrical and electronics firms concentrated in FTZs. These firms, at first engaged in simple manufacturing, have gradually moved into higher-value-added activities, such as R&D, design, and brand development, and have attracted a pool of highly skilled workers. Perak, by contrast, has so far benefited little from such agglomeration economies.

The company Proton (Perusahaan Otomobil Nasional Bhd), which was incor-porated in 1983 and took up headquarters in Shah Alam, Selangor, launched the Proton Saga car in 1985 as a joint venture between HICOM and Mitsub-ishi, with many of its parts and technology imported from Japan. Mitsubishi contributed 30 per cent of the equity capital, with the balance from HICOM (Athukorala, 2014). Aiming to expand Proton's sales and to enable it to dom-inate the domestic market, the government imposed high tariffs on imported cars, 40 to 60 per cent on 'completely knocked-down' units and 80 to 150 per cent on 'completely built-up' cars, as well as other protectionist measures. The 'infant industry' case for setting these tariffs was that once the industries were established the tariffs would be removed.

The manufacture of Malaysia's first national car, the Proton Saga, was intend-ed to accelerate the country's industrialization. It arose out of Prime Minister Mahathir Mohamad's Look East Policy, which began in the early 1980s, inspired by the post–World War II successes of heavy industries in Japan and the Repub-lic of Korea. State involvement in such industrialization—in line with NEP objectives—was a way of promoting the interests of Malay businesses along the car supply chain, through assembly to distribution and sales networks, which were at the time dominated by foreign and Malaysian Chinese interests.

In 1996, as part of Proton's ambitious expansion plans, a second integrated car manufacturing plant was conceived to complement the main plant in Shah Alam, Selangor, in line with the Second Industrial Master Plan, 1996–2005. The plan was to spur development of the national automotive industry and to expand its linkages with motor assembly, fabrication of component parts, trade information services, and warehousing.

Perak was the main beneficiary. In the late 20th century its industrial development became more systematic, especially with the corridor approach. State-level planning was refocused on four economic corridors, each with its own specialized activities, based on access to resource inputs and markets.[89] Of Perak's specialized industrial clusters within these corridors, the automotive centre, Proton City, was in Tanjong Malim, a predominantly rural Malay heartland bordering Selangor.[90] With a substantial initial federal investment of RM1.52 billion, the Proton City car plant was targeted to produce 150,000 units in 2000 (Fujita, 1999), rising to 250,000 in 2003, and eventually to 500,000 units (Athukorala, 2014). The project, however, did not take off until 2003, being disrupted by the Asian financial crisis (Box 3.14).

Early industrialization activities in Proton City and the growth of car-related workshops led to the upgrading of Tanjong Malim's infrastructure, commercial and residential property, and recreational facilities (Yazid Saleh et al., 2016). However, plans to further accelerate the development of Tanjong Malim, through investments in autonomous vehicles (vehicles with some automatic driving features) and through creating a vibrant city of youth and entrepreneurship, have yet to materialize.

Manufacturing's Modest Performance

In the 1990s Perak's manufacturing sector performed reasonably well relative to its historical performance, growing at an average annual rate of 8.6 per cent. However, it slowed to 5.5 per cent in the first two decades of the 21st century. Manufacturing's share of the state's GDP hovered around 19 per cent over these three decades.

---

89 The four economic corridors as designated by EPU–Perak were: the *Southern Corridor*, covering Tanjong Malim–Slim River and Teluk Intan–Hutan Melintang, focusing on the automotive industry, ceramics, and education; the *Central Corridor*, Ipoh–Lumut, specializing in engineering, pharmaceuticals, marine-related activities, and tourism; the *Northeastern Corridor*, Hulu Perak–Selama, for eco- and agro-tourism, agriculture, and wood-based industries; and the *Northern Corridor*: Parit Buntar–Taiping, focusing on support services for manufacturing (Azrai Abdullah, 2022).

90 Proton City, a 4,000-acre site, is in the district of Muallim (part of Batang Padang until 2016).

| Box 3.14 | **Proton City, Tanjong Malim: Spillover for the national car industry** |

At the end of 2003, the Tanjong Malim plant became the manufacturing hub for Proton's Gen-2 and Savvy cars (Prakash et al., 2017). In 2004, Proton established a short-lived strategic partnership with Volkswagen, allowing it to use the plant to assemble cars for export to the ASEAN market, but the partnership ended in November 2007 without this happening (Athukorala, 2014).

Proton reached a peak in 1990, when it accounted for almost two-thirds of the domestic passenger vehicle market—a share it maintained for several years. This share declined sharply from 2000 onwards, reaching a low of just 17 per cent in 2015 before rebounding somewhat to 24 per cent in 2020 (Table 3c), a year when car sales were disrupted by the Covid-19 pandemic. Strong competition from Perodua, the second, lower-cost, national car, has also cut into Proton's market share.

Table 3c	**Proton's share of national car sales saw a dramatic rise and decline—and uptick**	
	Proton's share of domestic market (%)	**Total cars sold of all makes in Malaysia**
1985	12.0	63,857
1990	64.2	80,420
1995	62.5	224,991
2000	63.4	282,103
2005	40.3	416,692
2010	28.9	543,594
2015	17.3	591,298
2019	18.3	550,179
2020	24.0	457,755

Sources of data: For 1985–2000, Tham (2004); for 2005–2018, Malaysia Automotive Association (2021); for 2019 and 2020, PROTON–Malaysia (2021).

By 2010 the Tanjong Malim plant was producing little more than 70,000 units, and employed just over 2,000 workers (Figure 3a). Faced with problems of capacity under-utilization at its two manufacturing plants, in 2017 Proton announced plans to consolidate them into a single location in Tanjong Malim (Prakash et al., 2017).

(Continued)

This has not yet come to fruition, however, and the town is still waiting to benefit from this boost to its ambitions to evolve into a dynamic industrial hub.

According to Baldwin (2016, p. 252), the earlier offshoring of the stages of production destroyed Malaysia's import substitution strategy at around the time that Proton City was conceived, with Proton's cars thus 'lacking scale-competitiveness'. Yet Proton persisted in keeping its second plant despite the low sales volumes from it. Proton City was planned as an industrial cluster on the basis that a manufacturing supply chain of producers and vendors of automotive parts would be locating around the plant.

Figure 3a   **Production of Proton cars and number of employees at the Tanjong Malim plant showed only modest growth during the first two decades of the 21st century**

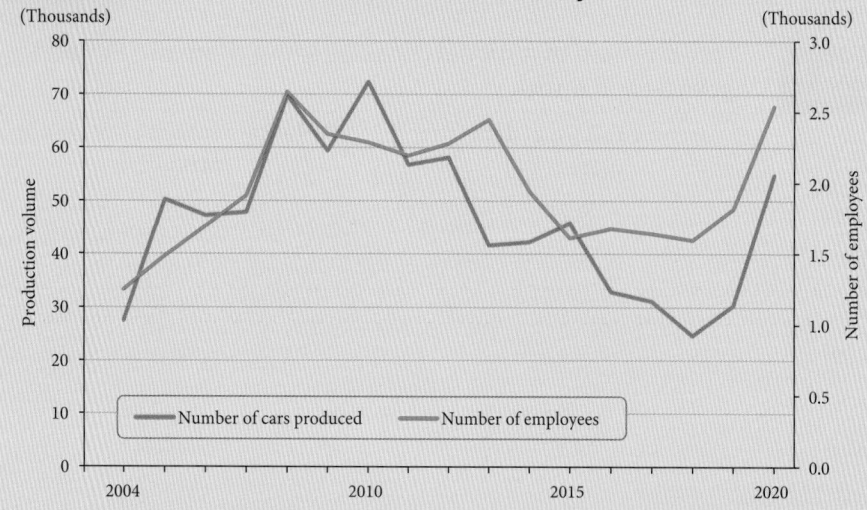

Source: PROTON–Malaysia, unpublished.

By 2020 there were 15 component suppliers and two logistics vendors operating in Proton City. However, even though Proton, along with its network of local vendors, has been shielded to a considerable degree from international competition, it has failed to become a global export-oriented car producer. Its strong political roots, 'packaged as a project of national interest' (Firdausi Suffian, 2020, p. 55), have made opening up the industry a continuing challenge, even though some liberalization in this sector happened elsewhere in ASEAN three decades ago.

Proton City's future

Proton was a bold and aspiring project that has yet to achieve economies of scale. It remains a high-cost producer, unable to gain entry to international markets. At the same time, its share of the domestic market has diminished. In an attempt to revive its fortunes, in 2018 DRB–HICOM formed a new strategic partnership with China's Zhejiang Geely Holding Group, which bought a 49.9 per cent stake in Proton.

The Tanjong Malim plant did see expanded investment by Proton from the fourth quarter of 2019, with a domestic investment of RM2.6 billion. All Proton's new models and engines will be produced in Proton City. Proton plans to create an additional 766 jobs in R&D and manufacturing in several phases from 2019 until 2023 (MIDA, 2020). Shortages of local semi-skilled and skilled human resources, and the difficulty of attracting new talent to work in Tanjong Malim, remain serious obstacles, however. The launch of a National Automotive Cluster and plans for an Automotive High–Technology Valley designed to make Proton City a hub for local and foreign automotive vendors has also been announced. If these initiatives are successful, Proton City should have a brighter future; if they are not, the forces of globalization may leave Tanjong Malim behind.

Jobs in Perak's manufacturing sector grew at 4.2 per cent a year in the 1990s, but then slowed to just 0.8 per cent annual growth in the first decade of the 21st century before picking up very slightly to 0.9 per cent in the second. The share of employment in manufacturing, however, saw a dip, from 22.5 per cent in 2000 to 16.7 per cent in 2020. This may reflect the onset of deindustrialization or alternatively the rising capital intensity of industrial production.

Perak has been moderately successful in the structural transformation of its economy, although the high expectations for manufacturing appear not to have been met, in part because of the excessive supply of industrial estates relative to demand.[91] The maintenance and management of the infrastructure and utilities of these estates was also inadequate (InvestPerak and UKM Pakarunding, 2011). According to observations from Perak's private SME manufacturers, the state's 'public sector development agencies are neither focused nor committed, do not have a sense of priority, and have lost touch with the requirements of the manufacturing sector' (UPEN Perak, and MIER, 2009, p. 68). A lack of policy

---

91 The concentration, or density, of industrial estates is an indicator of agglomeration. In 2020, Perak had 95 industrial estates which were widely dispersed (72 classified as major and 23 as minor), compared with just 18 each in Selangor and Penang (MIDA database, unpublished).

coordination in Perak's investment promotion activities and slow implementation of approved industrial projects have also undermined progress.

In the 1990s, electrical and electronics products had become the country's most important manufacturing activity, accounting for 65.7 per cent of total manufacturing exports, although this share fell to 51.0 per cent in 2010, and then further to 45.5 per cent in 2020 (BNM, various years). The resource-based products in which Perak specialized, in contrast, accounted for 16.7 per cent of total Malaysian exports in 1995, rising to 20.5 per cent in 2010 before falling back to a mere 10.4 per cent in 2020. Electrical and electronics products—mainly lower-end and component parts—had become the second-largest manufacturing subsector in Perak by 1995, contributing 19 per cent of manufacturing output; food-processing industries still accounted for the largest share of output, with rubber and plastic processing activities coming third.

Perak's manufacturing sector remains more narrowly based than that of the country as a whole. In 2005, electrical and electronics products at 27.4 per cent and rubber and plastic processing at 25 per cent together were the largest subsectors of Perak's manufacturing output. Processing of agro-products (including coconut, palm oil, and refined palm) and preserving of fish products contributed 13.8 per cent. This pattern has changed markedly, however. By 2020, Perak's electrical and electronics share of manufacturing output had risen to 33.6 per cent, with two large Malaysian companies operating in the state—Carsem and Unisem—having global outreach.[92] Rubber and plastic processing has since declined a little to 23 per cent, while processing of agro-products and preserving of fish products has risen to 16.7 per cent.

There is also growing evidence of product and spatial clustering in Perak, especially in Kinta (Box 3.15). This district has become the target for manufacturing, given that it has the state's largest industrial areas, and there is still former tin-mining land available for industrial use. In 2017, the state government, in partnership with Gas Malaysia Sdn Bhd, initiated a four-year project to supply clean energy through a 140 km natural gas pipeline running from Ayer Tawar, in Manjung district, to the Kinta Valley. The project was completed in 2021 and is expected to encourage private investment to support the further growth of Kinta's manufacturing sector.

---

92 Carsem manufactures semiconductors and related solid-state devices, and Unisem is a global provider of semiconductor assembly and test services.

Box 3.15	**Product and spatial clustering of approved manufacturing investment in Perak, 2015–2020**

Over the period 2015–2020, cumulative approved domestic investment in Perak's manufacturing was concentrated in transport equipment, followed by rubber, electrical and electronics, and plastic products (Table 3d). The large share of transport equipment stemmed mainly from Proton's expansion in Tanjong Malim (see Box 3.14).

Foreign investment followed a similar pattern, especially in the subsectors of rubber products and electrical and electronics products. While these do still have the potential to develop into a critical mass of manufacturing clusters, there is no robust evidence of this happening as yet, as there is no discernible pattern of investment in these manufacturing subsectors.

Table 3d	**Transport equipment dominated approved domestic investment in Perak's manufacturing, 2015–2020**

Manufacturing subsector	Approved domestic investment		Approved foreign investment[a]	
	(RM thousands)	Share (%)	(RM thousands)	Share (%)
Transport equipment	4,862,120	36.7	343,598	4.0
Rubber products[b]	2,823,104	21.3	1,759,485	20.7
Electrical and electronics products	1,797,667	13.6	2,222,237	26.1
Plastic products	841,904	6.3	503,357	5.9
Others	2,940,555	22.2	3,682,408	43.3
Total	13,265,349	100.0	8,511,084	100.0

Sources of data: Department of Statistics–Malaysia (2018b and 2020c).

Notes: [a] Others includes a large approved foreign investment for basic metal products in Bagan Datuk which did not materialize.

[b] During the peak of the Covid-19 pandemic in 2021, approved domestic investment in rubber products rose to over 80 per cent of the total.

Spatial clustering

With about one-third of Perak's population, its largest metropolitan city of Ipoh, and the best transport connections and facilities, Kinta district was the destination of choice for domestic and foreign investors between 2015 and 2019 (Figure 3b). Apart from the large approved domestic investment in Proton in Tanjong Malim, two other

(Continued)

distinct clusters of economic density—as approximated by the number of manufacturing establishments per 100 square km—are Kinta district and the rest of Perak.

In 2015, over half of all Perak's manufacturing establishments were in Kinta district—at 182 per 100 square km—partly reflecting investment made in industrial estates in earlier decades, as well as agglomeration economies.[a] In the electrical and electronics sector, Kinta is home to multinational firms such as Finisar[b]—Perak's largest private employer, contributing about one-quarter of the state's manufacturing GDP—as well as Yamaha and Murata Electronics; along with Carsem and Unisem. Among resource-based industries, Top Glove, the world's largest rubber glove maker, has three factories in Kinta district. The district of Larut, Matang, and Selama, which includes the town of Taiping, is the second-most economically dense district, with 35 manufacturing establishments per 100 square km.

Figure 3b **Foreign and domestic manufacturing investment is heavily concentrated in Perak's Kinta district**

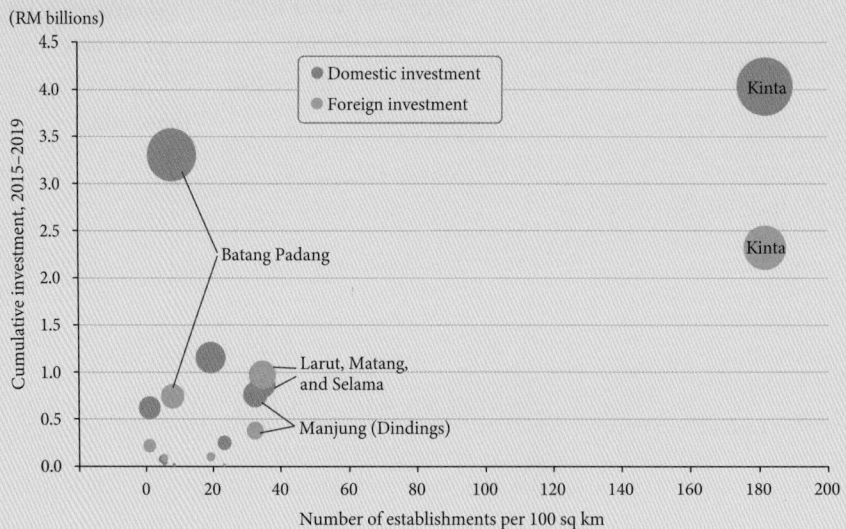

Source of data: Department of Statistics–Malaysia (2018a and 2020c).

Notes: The data plotted are for Perak's 10 districts as in 2015. In 2016, Muallim, which had been part of Batang Padang, and Bagan Datuk, which in 2017 had been part of Hilir Perak, were made separate districts, bringing the total to 12.

The size of the bubbles indicates the share of district investment in total investment.

Achieving sufficient density by harnessing market forces to ensure concentration and promote convergence in living standards between urban and rural areas is the most important local dimension for economic development (World Bank, 2009). The more economically dense a district is in terms of manufacturing establishments, the more foreign investment it can attract. While there may be some foreign interest in lower-density districts, this interest generally picks up sharply when the number of establishments reaches a threshold of about 30 per 100 square km. Approved domestic investment, however, appears to be somewhat less strongly correlated with economic density, perhaps reflecting a greater openness to locating in districts being promoted and incentivized by different government policies. The correlation coefficients of cumulative foreign and domestic investment with density are 0.91 and 0.71, respectively.

With the right planning of manufacturing product clusters, Kinta district can still accommodate further expansion of manufacturing activities. This shift is unlikely to achieve a convergence in living standards across the whole of Perak, however, which may, instead, diverge.

[a] For Perak as a whole, new investment accounted for 48 per cent of total investment over the period 2015–2019, and as disaggregated data are unavailable for districts, it is assumed that this level of new investment applies.

[b] Finisar provides technology for fibre-optic subsystems and components that enable high-speed voice, video, and data communications for telecommunications, networking, storage, wireless, and cable TV applications.

Rising Private-Sector Services Growth amid Deindustrialization

As Perak's manufacturing sector grew and its economy diversified, services began to play an increasingly important role, including transport and communications, financial services, public utilities, wholesale and retail trade, and government services. From the 1990s, the state's service sector GDP and employment growth were led by private services; this was in contrast to the 1970s and 1980s when government services played the leading role. While public services did continue to expand, they did so at a slower rate than Perak's overall economy, as some government functions were increasingly privatized and corporatized and as private-sector participation strengthened.

Greater liberalization under the ASEAN Framework Agreement on Services—which came into force in 1998—along with commitments to freer flows of services under WTO and other free trade arrangements, further boosted competitiveness and efficiency in the service sector. Like other sectors of the economy, Perak's services gradually migrated into more knowledge-intensive and high-value-added activities. There was some shift towards modern and emerging services, including Islamic finance, information and communications technology, digitalization, and creative industries, and efforts to build comparative advantage in these areas. Growing national and state prosperity brought rising incomes, further boosting Perak's service sector. The sector added 64,000 new jobs between 1991 and 2000, a further 136,000 between 2000 and 2010, and a massive 194,000 in the decade to 2020. The bulk of these were in the private sector, and especially in the growing tourism and education subsectors.

Tourism's Growth

Tourism promotion by the federal and state governments helped to boost the growth of Perak's service sector. Increased state and private investment in tourism reflected the industry's growing importance—RM533.3 million and RM287.7 million were allocated under Perak's MP6 and MP7 to upgrade tourism-related infrastructure, products, and services. State tourism benefited from several public–private partnerships to boost the number of tourists and increase their spending: this included tourism promotion, investment in tourism infrastructure such as hotels and tourist sites, and the creation of tourism products and services.

The state's adoption of economic clusters and corridors also provided new avenues for tourism. The state sought to exploit its diversity and the comparative advantages of its rich multicultural heritage sites and historical traditions, as well as to promote ecotourism, especially in the Belum Temenggor tropical rainforest area. Other tourist attractions include Kuala Kangsar royal town, Pangkor Island, archaeological sites such as that at Lenggong, the caves at Gua Tempurung, Kinta Valley's geopark, and the hot springs at Tambun. Domestic tourist arrivals surged over the period 2012 to 2015, rising from 5.7 million to 8 million (Zambry Abdul Kadir, 2016, p. 13), stimulating strong growth in the wholesale and retail trade and hotels and restaurants subsector. The share of employment in this subsector more than doubled between 1991 and 2020, from 14.1 per cent to 29.4 per cent (Table 3.8). As some tourism destinations are located far from urban areas, this growth has helped to reduce regional income disparities in Perak.

Table 3.8	Since 1991, the share of Perak's labour force in agriculture has fallen by more than half, while the share in services has more than doubled

Sector or subsector	Share of employment by sector or subsector (%)			
	1991	2000	2010	2020
Agriculture, forestry, hunting, and fishing	24.2	15.0	13.5	11.8
Mining and quarrying	0.8	0.4	0.2	0.6
Manufacturing	17.5	22.5	18.3	16.7
Construction	6.1	7.6	8.5	7.1
Electricity, gas, water, and sanitary services[a]	0.9	0.7	0.5	1.3
Commerce[a]	16.3	21.8	25.3	31.2
Wholesale and retail trade, and hotels and restaurants	14.1	18.2	23.9	29.4
Financial, insurance, real estate, and business services	2.2	3.6	1.4	1.8
Transport, storage, and communication[a]	3.7	5.2	3.8	4.9
Community, social, and personal services[a]	26.0	23.3	24.3	26.4
Not adequately described[a]	2.2	3.4	5.6	0.0
Unknown	2.4	0.0	0.0	0.0
Total (%)	100.0	100.0	100.0	100.0
Total (thousands)	578.6	655.8	874.5	1043.0

Sources of data: Khoo (1995a); Shaari Abdul Rahman (2003); Wan Ramlah (2013a); Department of Statistics–Malaysia (various years) Labour Force Survey Report.

Note: [a] Subsectors in the service sector.

Expansion of Higher Education

Universities can have a powerful impact in propelling the economic, social, and cultural development of towns and cities. They can help create synergies with industries and spur technological innovation through multidisciplinary research collaborations, as well as contribute to shaping public discourse and policy (Goddard and Vallance, 2013). The early post-independence expansion of national public universities in Malaysia was mainly in the Klang Valley, however, and did not directly benefit Perak.

By the late 1980s pressures were mounting on the education system at all levels. These pressures continued into the 1990s as the labour market experienced chronic shortages of the skilled workers and qualified graduates required to engage in the growing knowledge economy, including R&D.[93] With ever-larger cohorts of students reaching the age of higher education, public expenditure on education was surging, but was insufficient to meet demand. With limited places in public universities for non-Malay and other *Bumiputera* students, many went abroad to study (Sultan Nazrin Shah, 2019). There were also concerns about the quality of teaching at all levels.

Against this backdrop of mounting pressure, the federal government began to liberalize higher education policy. With the enactment of the Private Higher Education Institutions Act in 1996, the private sector was encouraged to enter tertiary education, and private universities became a new phenomenon (Leete, 2007). Some government-linked companies were tasked with setting up education and training institutions, consistent with the aim of increasing the private sector's participation in economic development.

Tertiary education and skills training expanded in line with the federal and state governments' aims of developing human resources as a vehicle for supporting economic growth.[94] Perak had ambitions to become known as an education hub, although efforts to open a branch campus of Universiti Malaya, or a leading international university, were unsuccessful (Perak State Government, 1996). As the government began to liberalize higher education policy, and as colleges and institutes were upgraded to universities, a small number of private and public universities began to form an emerging education hub in a geographical triangle that included Kampar, Ipoh, and Tronoh. Several universities were sited within it, complementing Perak's existing universities such as the branch campus of Universiti Sains Malaysia (USM), and Universiti Pendidikan Sultan Idris (UPSI) (Box 3.16).

The presence of university students, lecturers, and support staff generates multiplier effects by boosting business and commercial activities in towns and cities. For example, UTAR Kampar became an economic lifeline for the former mining town, with the student population stimulating the local property

---

93 Singapore, which also faced the problem of skill shortages, adopted a liberal, outward-looking, but publicly unpopular foreign talent recruitment policy, as well as investing heavily in higher education (Yeo et al., 2020).

94 Even earlier, in 1969, the Ungku Omar Polytechnic opened in Ipoh to provide technical skills training and was supported by UNESCO. Much later in 1986, Olympia College established a campus in Ipoh as a private initiative.

Box 3.16   Perak's first public and private universities

Universiti Sains Malaysia (**USM**) was established in Penang in 1969, with the aim of increasing the supply of engineers and researchers in support of the state's growing interest in the electrical and electronics industries (OECD, 2011). In 1984, USM's School of Applied Science expanded to become the School of Engineering Science and Industrial Technology—with a School of Industrial Technology focusing on polymer and food technologies, a School of Electrical and Electronics Engineering, and a School of Materials and Mineral Resources Engineering. The School of Industrial Technology remained in Penang, but the expansion required an increase in the physical campus space, and in 1986 a USM branch campus was established in Perak for the engineering schools. The campus started off in the former Ipoh Town Council building, moving to a new campus in Seri Iskandar, Perak Tengah, in 1989. In 1997, the Ministry of Education decided to transfer the schools of engineering back to Penang to help meet Penang's growing human resources needs. The campus in Seri Iskandar was taken over by UTP (see below).

Post-independence, the Sultan Idris Training College for Malay teachers was rebranded the Sultan Idris Teachers' Training College. In 1975, the College broke with tradition by accepting female students in its traditionally male-only enrolment. It was upgraded to an institute of higher learning in 1987 in order to help improve the quality of teachers. It continued with this mission, and in May 1997, when training as a teacher had become a degree-level qualification, the institute became a university and was renamed Universiti Pendidikan Sultan Idris, **UPSI**. With an initial intake of 350 students, UPSI began with six administrative staff and 29 academics, across four faculties—languages, art and social sciences, science and technology, and cognitive science and humanities. Additional faculties have been added and, although no longer purely a teacher training facility, UPSI specializes in teaching and education, offering diplomas as well as undergraduate and postgraduate degrees, with some 70 per cent of its growing student body being undergraduates (Table 3e).

Universiti Teknologi Petronas *(UTP)*—originally called the Institute of Technology Petronas—at Bandar Seri Iskandar, Perak Tengah, was founded by Petronas. It was inspired by the need to nurture skilled industrial workers in technology, construction, oil and gas, and civil engineering. Its first academic year was 1995, and it was granted university status in January 1997. It became known as UTP after receiving accreditation to provide undergraduate courses. In keeping with the aim of combining academic knowledge and practical experience, UTP requires its students to undergo a seven-month internship programme with

(Continued)

partner companies to undertake industrial work, and its undergraduates serve as interns, mainly for oil and gas companies. As technical R&D skills are in such high demand, UTP students undertake extensive R&D activities in six areas—self-sustainable building, transport infrastructure, health analytics, hydrocarbon recovery, contaminant management, and autonomous systems. With a rising number of undergraduate and graduate students (Table 3e), UTP has become the northern region's largest academic and research university for civil, mechanical, chemical, and electronics engineering. Only around 1 per cent of those enrolled are international students.

Universiti Tunku Abdul Rahman *(UTAR)*—previously the Tunku Abdul Rahman College—was established as a private university in 2002 with investments from the Malaysian Chinese Association. Initially housed in a temporary campus off Petaling Jaya, UTAR began its first academic year in 2002 with an intake of 411 students before finding a permanent home in the Klang Valley. It then built a second campus in the former tin-mining town of Kampar in 2003, enrolling its first batch of students in May 2007. Its main faculties are arts and social science, business and finance, engineering and green technology, information and communications technology, and science. Industrial training is also compulsory for all its students, to provide them with experiential learning opportunities. UTAR has attained a high international ranking, with student enrolment peaking in 2016 (Table 3e). About 2 per cent of those enrolled are international students.

Universiti Sultan Azlan Shah *(USAS)* was formerly the Kolej University Islam Sultan Azlan Shah, a private higher education institution that was upgraded to full university status in 2016. The college was inaugurated by Sultan Azlan Shah in 1999, and operated from a temporary campus in Ipoh until its new campus in Kuala Kangsar was completed in 2008. The university offers courses in Islamic studies, business administration, and management. Student enrolment has soared over the past decade from just 588 in 2010 to almost 7,000 in 2020.

The Universiti Teknologi MARA *(UiTM)* Perak Campuses were formerly a branch of the Institut Teknologi MARA in Shah Alam, Selangor. The institution was upgraded to university status in 1999 when it moved from Manjung district—where it had been established in 1985—to Bandar Seri Iskandar. In 2010, UiTM expanded its presence in Perak with campuses established for its faculties of computer science and mathematics, accounting, and applied science at Tapah, and a small faculty of medicine at Teluk Intan. UiTM admits *Bumiputera* students only, and in 2020 had some 14,000 students enrolled in more than 30 programmes at its three campuses.

Table 3e	Student enrolment at UPSI far outnumbers that at Perak's other universities					
University	2010	2012	2014	2016	2018	2020
UPSI	14,353	15,773	18,204	19,490	22,177	24,814
UiTM	11,644	13,286	13,407	12,484	14,470	14,063
USAS	588	1,409	3,124	5,149	6,709	6,988
UTP	1,061	1,056	1,761	1,682	1,374	1,735
UTAR Kampar	11,572	13,217	14,413	14,654	12,700	11,107
QIU[a]	—	166	563	570	779	670

Sources of data: Unpublished data provided by the universities.
Notes: [a] The private Quest International University, established in Ipoh in 2011.
— denotes not applicable.

and amenity markets, especially through living off-campus. However, although higher education reforms have helped Perak expand its service sector and have boosted the share of its population with tertiary qualifications, they have been insufficient, as yet, to create the critical mass of local, skilled graduates necessary to attract new industries, or to stem the flow of higher-educated migrants from the state.

Service Sector Dominance

Perak's tertiary sector has played a pivotal supporting role for the primary and secondary sectors in the growth and structural transformation of its economy. It has boosted GDP growth, generated employment, and contributed to social restructuring. Whereas in 1990 services accounted for 42.5 per cent of Perak's GDP, by 2020 the sector's share had jumped to 62.1 per cent (EPU, 1991a). Over the same period, the service sector's share of total employment soared from 47 per cent to 64 per cent, reaching 68 per cent among Malays and other *Bumiputera* in the labour force (Table 3.9).

The rising share of services in Perak's economy, coupled with the relative decline of agriculture, and the levelling off of manufacturing, reflect the state's transition to a service-oriented economy. Given the high rate of urbanization, and income and consumption patterns, distributive trades have the potential to be the largest of the service subsectors in GDP and employment. However, new developments in distribution chains, such as online purchasing of goods and

| Table 3.9 | Perak's Malays and other *Bumiputera* were increasingly employed in manufacturing and services |

Sector or subsector	Share of employment within ethnic group								
	Malays and other *Bumiputera*			Chinese			Indians		
	2000	2010	2020	2000	2010	2020	2000	2010	2020
Agriculture, forestry, hunting, and fishing	16.7	14.1	10.3	11.3	10.7	10.3	13.7	12.0	7.1
Mining and quarrying	0.3	0.2	0.6	0.4	0.1	0.4	0.5	0.3	1.4
Manufacturing	22.2	15.7	15.7	18.5	18.8	16.6	30.4	21.4	26.8
Construction	4.2	7.4	5.6	12.7	10.3	9.4	6.1	8.8	6.6
Electricity, gas, water, and sanitary services[a]	1.0	0.7	1.6	0.4	0.1	0.6	0.9	0.6	2.0
Commerce[a]	14.4	21.7	26.4	36.5	33.3	42.9	17.1	25.0	23.3
Wholesale and retail trade, and hotels and restaurants	11.6	20.4	24.9	31.1	31.6	40.4	13.7	23.7	21.2
Financial, insurance, real estate, and business services	2.8	1.3	1.5	5.3	1.7	2.5	3.4	1.3	2.1
Transport, storage, and communication[a]	4.3	3.3	4.9	5.4	4.1	3.0	9.1	5.7	12.3
Community, social, and personal services[a]	33.2	32.3	34.8	11.9	14.7	17.0	18.3	20.7	20.6
Unknown	3.7	4.5	..	3.0	7.9	..	3.7	5.5	..
Total (%)	100	100	100	100	100	100	100	100	100
Total (thousands)	319.3	450.8	559.1	215.5	269.0	306.6	91.4	105.4	106.1

Sources of data: Shaari Abdul Rahman (2003); Wan Ramlah bt Wan Abd. Raof (2013a); for 2020, Department of Statistics–Malaysia, unpublished data.

Note: [a] Subsectors in the service sector.

services, coupled with the premium for efficiency and competitiveness, may erode the subsector's employment-creation potential. In financial services, for example, with online banking and the consolidation of banks, as well as other changes in work processes, the employment share has been shrinking.

Rising Agricultural Productivity

By the 1990s, and even more so by the 21st century, rubber was no longer the main focus of Perak's agricultural sector. Besides *padi*, the major activities in the sector in terms of their contribution to the economy and employment are now palm oil, cocoa, animal husbandry, aquaculture, the production of commercial vegetables, fruit farming, and floriculture.

Although by historical standards rubber prices were moderately high for most of the 1990s, they were not high enough to arrest the secular decline in rubber production and its share of agricultural output. Malaysia's rubber production fell steeply, as did Perak's, at first in estates as they transitioned to oil palm, and then with a lag among smallholders as well, who by 2000 were producing about 75 per cent of output, but with much of it on uneconomically sized land parcels (Department of Statistics–Malaysia, 2002). In 2004, Perak still maintained its share of the country's total rubber output, but the state's production had fallen by 17 per cent since 1989. The rate of decline in rubber production quickened and Perak's share of the total tumbled in the first two decades of the 21st century. By 2020, Malaysia's rubber output was just 48.3 per cent of what it had been in 2004, and Perak's share of even that diminished output had declined to just 7.1 per cent, down from 13.0 per cent in 2004 (Table 3.10).

The shift into oil palm cultivation from rubber is reflected in the soaring acreage devoted to that crop, which became the single largest use of Perak's agricultural land. In 1999, oil palm accounted for 360,000 hectares of cultivated land, compared with 210,000 hectares for rubber (Perak State Government, 2001). Privately owned estates, smallholders, and agricultural land schemes sponsored by the federal government as well as by the state of Perak, all contributed to the rapid expansion of oil palm cultivation. Oil palm's higher yield and its much higher prices compared to rubber continued to make it more commercially attractive as an export crop. Palm oil production grew threefold between 1990 and 2020, although Perak's share of total palm oil output fell from 12.8 per cent to 9.6 per cent (Table 3.10). A variety of programmes were enacted to expand opportunities and raise living standards among Perak's rural Malays, helping to sustain advances in agricultural productivity, and underwriting successful crop diversification. These productivity gains released workers from the agricultural sector, while supporting higher levels of agricultural output (Sultan Nazrin Shah, 2019).

Table 3.10	By 2000, Perak's output of palm oil had doubled and production of rice had also grown, but rubber production was declining			
	1990	**2000**	**2010**	**2020**
Palm oil production				
Perak's share (%)	12.8	11.4	10.1	9.6
Malaysia (thousand tonnes)	6,094.6	13,976.2	16,993.7	19,140.1
Rubber production[a]				
Perak's share (%)	13.1	13.0	10.5	7.1
Malaysia (thousand tonnes)	1,415.6	1,168.6	857.0	564.2
Rice production				
Perak's share (%)	11.9	11.8	12.1	11.3
Malaysia (thousand tonnes)	1,251.3	1,381.7	1,588.5	1,886.6

Sources of data: For rubber, Department of Statistics–Malaysia (various years); for palm oil, Malaysian Palm Oil Board (various years); for *padi*, Ministry of Agriculture and Food Industries–Malaysia (2020).

Note: [a] Rubber production figures relate to 1989, 2004, 2009, and 2020.

Padi remained Perak's main food crop, with cultivation concentrated in IADPs in Kerian, Sungai Manik, and Seberang Perak in the district of Hilir Perak. The state's rice production grew steadily between 1990 and 2019, and Perak has consistently produced 11 to 12 per cent of the country's rice output (Table 3.10)—only Kedah produces more. Land consolidation, farm restructuring, and the use of modern technology have raised *padi* farming productivity. In 1990, FELCRA initiated an IADP in Seberang Perak, with an estate covering nearly 13,000 hectares. This was Malaysia's first rice plantation to have good bunds and a central irrigation system, and a uniform plot size for settlers. It became the first estate to deploy drone technology on a large scale for spraying *padi* fields. The estate has proven to be a viable commercial enterprise with continuous double cropping (Najim et al., 2007). *Padi* production in marginal areas has been de-emphasized, consistent with national agricultural policies. However, a resurgent role for agriculture is planned, in line with the national objective of increasing food security.

So although Perak's agricultural production, including of palm oil, was still sizeable in 2020, contributing 15.4 per cent of the state's GDP, only slightly more than 1 in 10 workers were employed in agriculture (see Table 3.8). The numbers engaged in agricultural activities have declined sharply, with increased labour productivity freeing workers for modern, urban-sector jobs.

Lagging Foreign and Domestic Investment

Perak's investment demand appeared to accelerate in the 1990s. Investment approved by MIDA in the 1990s was in nominal value terms over five times as high as in the 1980s.[95] Commitments per project also rose steeply, suggesting a trend towards greater capital intensity. Similar trends were present at the national level. While FDI inflows to Perak increased during the 1990s, its share in Malaysia's total FDI remained low, and below that warranted by its economic size. Over the period 1990 to 2000, approved domestic and foreign investments in Perak were of similar orders of magnitude, at RM8.6 billion or 6.8 per cent of Malaysia's RM127.3 billion, and RM9.2 billion or 6 per cent of Malaysia's RM154.1 billion, respectively (Table 3.11). Of Malaysia's total investment, Perak attracted less than neighbouring states at just 6.4 per cent, far below Selangor's 17.7 per cent, and lower even than Penang at 8.6 per cent. Private investment was not proportionate to Perak's population share, and this low share has undoubtedly weakened the state's ambitions to diversify and expand economically (Mohammad Abdul Mohit, 2009).

The reasons for weak investment are unclear, but a high failure rate,[96] with some approved investment not realized, raises questions about the quality of Perak's investment climate. It is probable that policy failures, a lack of responsiveness to investor needs, inadequate bureaucratic capacity, and other failings in the business ecosystem, might help to explain the investment gap.

The pattern continued in the first two decades of the 21st century: while Malaysia's average annual investment increased sharply, Perak attracted a low proportion of domestic and foreign investment, at just 4.4 per cent of the total (Table 3.11). As well as the effects of the 2008–2009 global financial crisis, this may also have reflected the political instability of the state government[97]

---

95 All new investment manufacturing project applications are subject to approval by MIDA. In subsequently measuring realized investment, approved projects may be at different stages of implementation or already completed, with some approved projects also not implemented at all.

96 As of 30 June 1994, nearly 29 per cent of projects approved in Perak between 1980 and 1993 had never taken off, compared with 19.3 per cent in Selangor and 14.6 per cent in Penang (MITI, 1996b). Between 1996 and 2000, 23.5 per cent failed to take off, compared with 18.8 per cent in Selangor, and 23.4 per cent in Penang. Between 2016 and 2020, by contrast, the percentage of projects not implemented was just 7.8 per cent, but this figure still lagged behind Selangor and Penang, at 2.9 per cent and 5.6 per cent, respectively (MIDA database, unpublished).

97 In 2009, less than a year after being elected to office in March 2008, the Pakatan Rakyat-led Perak government collapsed after the defection of three assembly persons to the Barisan Nasional, the opposition party at the time. With majority support in the Perak State Legislative Assembly, Barisan Nasional formed the new government. This triggered a legal dispute over the legitimacy of the state government, and the case was eventually decided in the Federal Court in February 2010.

towards the end of the first decade. During this period, Selangor maintained roughly the same share of national investment as in the 1990s, while Penang increased its share to 12.5 per cent (Table 3.11). In recent years, Perak has not succeeded in attracting substantial FDI, with the exception of investments from Taiwan, China, Japan, and Singapore.

Structural factors are also likely to have had a continued influence on invest-ment rates, including mismatches between investors' requirements and the skills of the local labour force. The attainments of Perak's population, although rising over time, have continued to lag behind the national average, and even further behind those of the populations of Selangor and Penang (Table 3.12), where investors have been putting their money. The main factor driving Perak's human capital deficit remains, of course, the continuing outflow of the state's young and most talented.

Table 3.11	Perak's share of approved domestic and foreign investment has lagged markedly behind that of Selangor and Penang		
	Domestic investment (% shares)	Foreign investment (% shares)	Total investment (% shares)
1990–2000			
Penang	5.9	10.8	8.6
Perak	6.8	6.0	6.4
Selangor	20.5	15.5	17.7
Malaysia	100.0	100.0	100.0
Total (RM billions)	127.3	154.1	281.4
Average per year (RM billions)	11.6	14.0	25.6
2001–2020			
Penang	7.5	16.1	12.5
Perak	5.5	3.5	4.4
Selangor	20.0	16.3	17.8
Malaysia	100.0	100.0	100.0
Total (RM billions)	465.1	591.0	1056.0
Average per year (RM billions)	23.3	29.5	52.8

Source of data: MIDA database unpublished, supplied by MIDA.

Table 3.12	Perak's share of population with tertiary education lags behind the Malaysian average and even further behind Selangor's share			
	Population aged 15+ with tertiary educational attainment (%)[a]			
	1991	2000	2010	2020
Perak	2.9	6.4	10.1	26.4
Penang	4.7	10.7	16.1	33.6
Selangor	10.8	19.2	27.5	41.1
Malaysia	5.1	10.3	15.1	29.6

Sources of data: Khoo (1995a, 1995b, and 1995c); Shaari Abdul Rahman (2002); Wan Ramlah (2013b); for 2020, Department of Statistics–Malaysia unpublished data.
Note: [a] Excludes post-secondary (form 6), pre-university, and technical and vocational training courses.

Shortfalls in Federal Development Allocations, 1991–2010

State Allocations

Allocations for development expenditure from the federal government play a key role in a state's economic performance. Over the long term, Perak appears to have suffered from substantial shortfalls in the allocation of federal development expenditure, both in terms of its population size and per capita. Over the period 1991 to 2010—a period covering four Malaysia development plans—Perak's share of total development allocations (excluding multi-state allocations) was just below 6 per cent of the national total, far short of its population share of around 9 per cent (Figure 3.20, left panel). Per capita, its allocation was consistently at the bottom end of all the country's 13 states and the Federal Territory of Kuala Lumpur (Figure 3.20, right panel).

This may have reflected an over-estimation by the federal authorities of Perak's socio-economic development status, with an outdated perception that it was still a wealthy state dominated by particular interests. Kinta Valley's tin towns did not receive resources or policy support in a coherent manner that reflected the wider geography of tin in Perak, which would have been necessary for the state to diversify its economy. Inadequate bureaucratic diagnostics may well have led to a failure to understand the state's development needs and potential. It may also have been that the state lacked the implementation capacity to

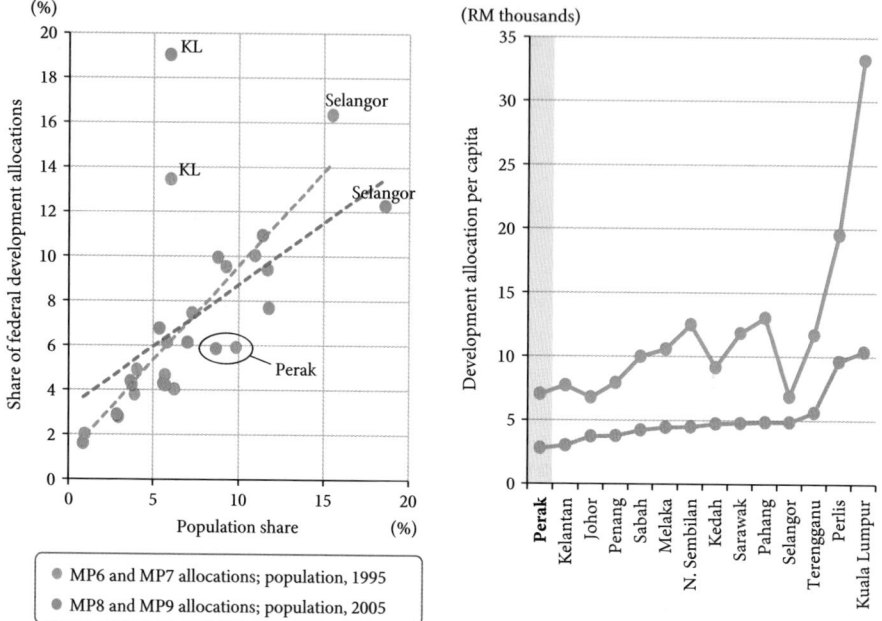

Figure 3.20 **Perak's federal development allocations have been well below its population share, and were the lowest per capita of all states in 1991–2010**

Sources of data: Economic Planning Unit–Malaysia (1991b, 1996, 2001, and 2006).

Note: MP6 and MP7 cover 1991–2000, and MP8 and MP9 cover 2001–2010. Excludes multi-state allocations for projects that benefit several states or Malaysia as a whole.

spend larger allocations. Whatever the reason, Perak was disadvantaged by its lower federal development allocations relative to many other states. This affected the adequacy of its social and economic infrastructure, and contributed to its lagging economic performance.

Multi-state Allocations

A sizeable share of federal development funding, which is several times greater than that of all state development expenditure combined, is apportioned to multi-state infrastructure projects, especially airports, highways, and railways. This approach has allowed Perak, with its limited direct global connections—having only inland ports and a small, largely domestic airport—to leverage Penang's and Selangor's deep seaports and international airports, as well as to derive benefits from their established multinational business ecosystem, strong presence of multinational corporations, and large talent pool (Hutchinson, 2017; Athukorala and Narayanan, 2017). Substantial allocations have been made to achieve spatially connected infrastructure, boost trade and investment, and improve access to social amenities by expanding and upgrading the peninsula's road network, thereby lowering transport and transaction costs. While Perak's economy has certainly been boosted by such projects, it is not possible to ascertain the extent to which it benefited disproportionately or otherwise from federal multi-state allocations.

An early initiative was the 215 km East–West Highway, which opened in 1982, connecting Kedah to Kelantan through Gerik in northern Perak. Far more important economically was the North–South Expressway, a stretch of almost 750 km. Completed in 1994, it connects Kedah to Johor, via Perak and Kuala Lumpur, and also improves access to border crossings into Singapore to the south and Thailand to the north. The expressway dramatically reduces inter-city travelling times—it is now just two hours from Kuala Lumpur to Ipoh, and one and a half hours from Ipoh to Penang—and provides road connections between export-oriented industrial areas, natural resource areas, and ports.

Along with other Malaysian states, Perak has benefited greatly from the North–South Expressway, which allows easy movement of goods through the Ipoh Cargo Terminal—an inland port at the heart of Ipoh city—to and from the Kinta Valley and Port Klang. The Expressway has also facilitated new industrial developments and supporting facilities, including the second Proton car assembly plant in Tanjong Malim. Two new maritime facilities were developed: the Lumut Maritime Terminal and adjacent Lumut Industrial Park, which opened in 1995 to handle both dry and liquid bulk cargoes such as coal, limestone, petroleum products, and raw fabrication materials; and the Lekir Bulk Terminal, which opened in 2002 to handle coal for the Sultan Azlan Shah Power Station.

From around 2015, Perak has also started to benefit from infrastructure built to promote closer economic integration in the NCER (Map 3.1).[98] In 2014, construction began on the 233 km West Coast Expressway, running from Banting in Selangor to Taiping. When complete, it will connect Perak's smaller towns on the west coast, including the historically important secondary town of Teluk Intan. Originally scheduled for completion by 2019, it experienced serious delays due to problems of land acquisition,

---

98 Perak's trade has also benefited from the construction of many new secondary and minor roads connecting industrial and new mining areas to highways and ports.

route realignments, and lack of workers during Covid-19 and its prospective opening was rescheduled to the end of 2024. It provides an alternative to the North–South Expressway—to which it runs parallel—for long-haul heavy vehicles, and connects Lumut to Port Klang. It is expected to provide a major boost to the state's economic growth, especially in manufacturing, real estate construction, and tourism.

First announced in 2019 as part of the NCER's Strategic Development Plan 2021–2025, a 140 km Northern Corridor Highway is also planned to connect the hinterland of the northern region, running from Perlis through Sungai Petani, Kedah, to Kamunting and Changkat Jering in Perak (NCIA, 2021). It aims to bridge the rural–urban divide in these states, and is expected to have a 'high multiplier' effect on the region's economy. It is hoped that these major infrastructure investments will significantly boost Perak's economy.

Balanced Regional Development: A New Approach with the NCER after 2007

As touched on earlier, MP9, 2006–2010, embraced a new strategic planning initiative to promote balanced regional development—the economic corridor approach—with growth centres and growth corridors in designated geographical areas in different parts of Malaysia, and crossing state boundaries (EPU, 2008, p. 65). The concept of economic corridors had been introduced much earlier in MP5, 1986–1990, as the framework for regional planning and to replace the state-level planning of earlier plans. It was thought that the adoption of broader spatial units as a basis for development planning would enable states with resource and growth constraints to benefit from regional gains, thereby reducing spatial inequalities.

Economic corridors aim to reduce spatial economic disparities by increasing modern-sector job opportunities and per capita incomes, taking into account comparative advantages and complementarities. In an economic corridor, infrastructure and other facilities are integrated within a geographical area to support production and supply chains and to stimulate regional development. Corridors are anchored by transport connections between the various economic nodes of cities, industrial zones, and gateways (World Bank, 2009).

Typically, an economic corridor consists of one or more specialized clusters of economic activity which are spatially concentrated to facilitate agglomeration. The aim is to accelerate regional development by focussing on a few high-density clusters in corridors with sectoral and geographical advantages. The general idea is that clustering will enable firms to take advantage of agglomeration, including common resources, labour-market matching, and knowledge sharing. Clustering within corridors should also help to reduce infrastructure costs. The state would work with the private sector and the regional development authorities to build a few priority industrial clusters. These corridors and clusters would be the responsibility of 'anchor' private investors, with the government playing a facilitating role.

Five national economic growth corridors were identified, as mentioned, including the NCER, established in 2007 and covering Kedah, Penang, Perlis, and the four northern and northwestern districts of Perak—Hulu Perak; Kerian; Kuala Kangsar; and Larut, Matang, and Selama (Map 3.1). In 2008, a new federal institution, the Northern Corridor Implementation Authority (NCIA), was established to promote strategies and programmes for the NCER, with the vision of making it a 'world class' economic region by 2025, and of achieving growth with social equity (Sime Darby Berhad, 2017).

Malaysia's regional strategy in MP10 and MP11, 2011–2020, thus now focused on economic clusters located within economic corridors. Perak was divided into four clusters—the northern cluster comprising Kerian district, Larut, Matang, and Selama district, and Kuala Kangsar; the southern cluster comprising Batang Padang, Muallim, Bagan Datuk, and Hilir Perak; the central cluster comprising Kinta district, Perak Tengah, and Manjung; and the northeastern cluster comprising Hulu Perak—each with its own areas of economic specialism based on its respective comparative advantages. Muallim, for example, was to become a leading regional automotive hub, and Tapah the 'EduCity' for technical and vocational training, while within the newly created district of Bagan Datuk, the waterfront and town were to be developed as a 'Water-City'.

Perak's Increasing Absorption into the NCER

The NCER region initially included only northern Perak (Map 3.1). In 2014, the district of Manjung—which includes Pangkor Island and the maritime facility of Lumut—was added, and at the beginning of 2016—the start of MP11—the NCER was extended to cover the rest of Perak.

The NCER envisaged that building on Penang's strengths as an advanced and dynamic manufacturing hub, with global transport connections, would benefit other states through the spatial diffusion of economic growth. Endowed with land and natural resources, these states could help to ease Penang's congestion and enable it to specialize in more advanced and higher-value-added manufacturing activities. This complementary arrangement was expected to attract domestic and foreign investors to a larger, now integrated, region, with a mature business ecosystem and a pool of skilled workers (Athukorala and Narayanan, 2017). A new blueprint was launched in 2016 to provide refreshed strategic directions for the NCER, which 'leverages on the strengths of all four states to create synergy and proposes measures to address the development needs of the region as a whole' (NCIA, 2016, p. 16).

Map 3.1   Perak's progression into the NCER, 2007–2016

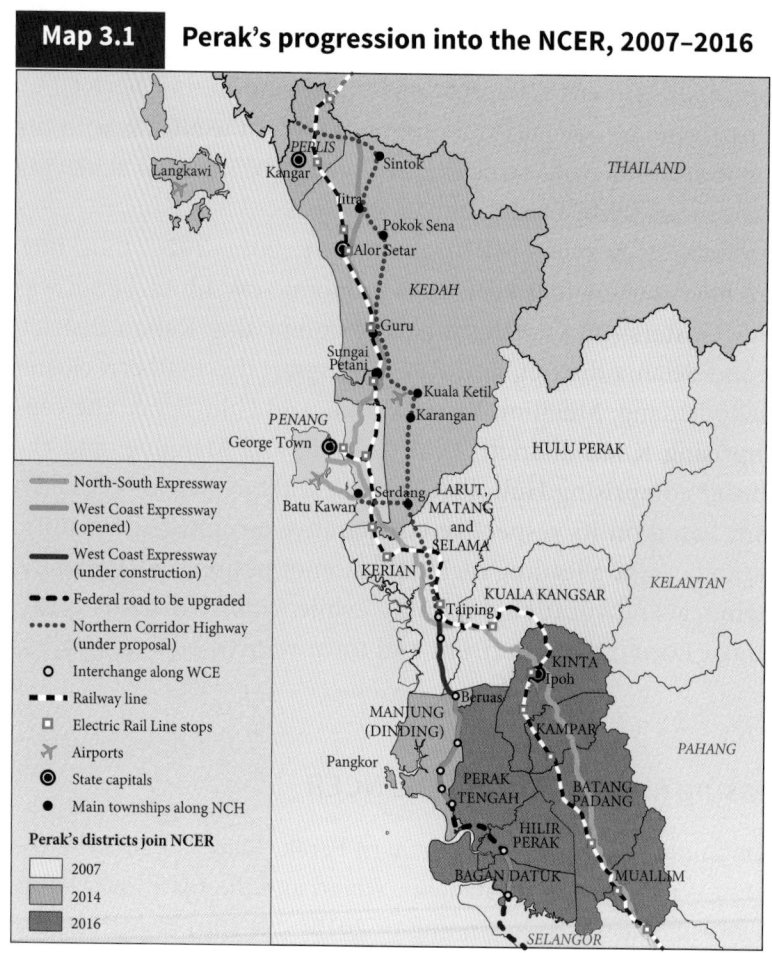

Sources of data: Adapted from NCIA (2016 and 2021).

Reducing Spatial Disparities

The NCER's strategies and programmes are regulated, managed, and funded by the NCIA, whose functions are approved and overseen by the NCIA Council, chaired by the prime minister. Other federal institutions, such as MIDA, FELCRA, and the Federal Agricultural Marketing Authority, play supporting roles. State-level bodies retain control over matters relating to the allocation and use of land within their boundaries, however. Foreign investors are encouraged to set up companies in the NCER through a package of incentives, which includes income tax breaks, investment allowances, and import duty exemptions on machinery, raw materials, and consumables used in production. Soft loans and grants are also offered to encourage companies to undertake promoted activities, such as R&D. In 2006, Perak established a one-stop Investment Management Centre (InvestPerak) to manage and further encourage investment.

Strengthening intercity links inside and outside the NCER was among the early objectives of the corridor. Perak's public transport connections were boosted by the completion of the Ipoh–Padang Besar double-track electrified railway in 2015. Also under way is the expansion of Lumut's maritime facility, with the construction of a new bulk-cargo terminal and upgrades to the facility's infrastructure. While the potential benefits of strengthened internal transport links are obvious, there is also the risk that without complementary measures to increase job opportunities and raise local skill levels, these transport links could pull resources *out* of the hinterland, including Perak, towards Penang, the dominant metropolitan centre of the NCER.

Beyond such infrastructure, the NCIA identified three priority sectors for investment—manufacturing, services (especially tourism, global business services, and logistics and connections), and agriculture, including bio-industries (NCIA, 2016). More than half of total investment in the NCER region up to 2020 has been driven by domestic direct investment. Both domestic and foreign direct investments in the NCER have been highly concentrated in manufacturing, with the bulk going to Penang and Kedah (NCIA, 2021). Since 2016, Perak has attracted only a small share of total NCER investment, the largest being domestic investment in Proton in 2019. The NCIA collaborates with financial institutions to provide support to micro-enterprises and SMEs in several sectors, with Malays and other *Bumiputera* as key targets. Cumulatively, between 2007 and 2020, Perak attracted RM20.7 billion of NCER investment, which created 16,600 jobs—representing a huge per capita investment for each job.

In manufacturing, specialized clusters in Perak that have attracted some investment include the Silver Valley Technology Park in the Kinta Valley; Proton City car hub (as discussed above); and Kamunting Industrial Estate (via upgrading), which hosts several large rubber-glove manufacturing plants. However, Perak has not fared as well as the other NCER states, especially Penang and Kedah, in electrical and electronics investment: from 2016 to 2018, out of RM13.2 billion of investment in the sector in the NCER (44 per cent of Malaysia's total investment in the sector), 75 per cent went to Penang, and only 12 per cent to Perak (Lim, 2019).

In services and agriculture, NCER investment and job creation have been much lower than in manufacturing. In Hulu Perak, Belum Temenggor tropical rainforest and the Lenggong Valley (the latter a UNESCO World Heritage site) were developed into tourism destinations; Pangkor Island was gazetted as a duty-free zone in 2020 to help spur its economic growth; and there is ongoing promotion of heritage tourism in Ipoh. Social inclusion programmes include training in ecotourism for *Orang Asli* in Belum Temenggor to create new sources of income for them. Meanwhile, Perak's agricultural sector saw the continuation of the Estate Management Model programme introduced in 2011 to increase *padi* yields through 'best farming methods' in the Trans-Kerian Development Zone. Under the NCIA, the Hilir Perak National Food Security Zone was designated the national granary area for *padi*.

Investment in the NCER

From the establishment of the NCER in 2007, total approved domestic and foreign investment up to 2020 amounted to RM129 billion—of which 59 per cent was domestic. Almost all foreign and nearly half of domestic investment has been directed towards manufacturing (Figure 3.21, top left panel), with Penang and Kedah receiving most of the approved FDI since 2014 (bottom left panel). In MP11, 2016–2020, Perak attracted just 5.4 per cent of federal investment, in sharp contrast to Kedah (60 per cent), and on a per capita basis Perak received the least (top and bottom right panels).

Attempting to Discern the Impacts of the NCER

Has the NCER been able to close gaps with wider national economic and social achievements? In 2007, the NCER (here including Perak in its entirety) accounted for 16.2 per cent of Malaysia's GDP in nominal prices; by 2015, this had slipped to 15.8 per cent, but it rebounded to 16.2 per cent in 2020 (Table

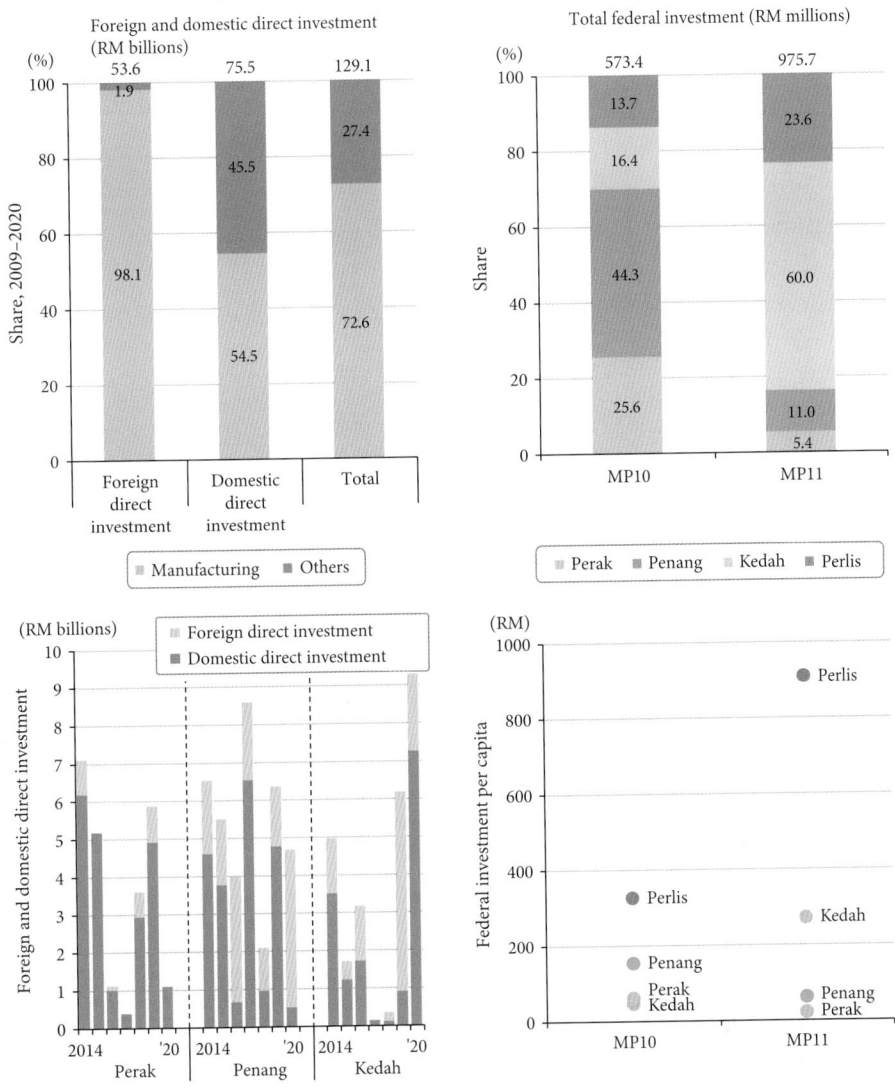

Figure 3.21 Manufacturing dominates NCER investment, with FDI largely bypassing Perak

Source of data: NCIA (private communication).

Note: MP10, 2011–2015; MP11, 2016–2020.

3.13). Penang, the largest economy in the NCER, saw its share in national GDP drop very slightly between 2007 and 2020, as did the share of Perlis, while that of Perak rose slightly.

Similarly in relation to per capita incomes, in 2007 Kedah, Perak, and Perlis all trailed the national average, and by 2020 only Perak had made some incremental progress in closing this gap (Table 3.13). The extent to which these

Table 3.13	Economies of the NCER and the individual states failed to advance significantly on the national average between 2007 and 2020					
	GDP share (% of national)		GDP per capita (RM)		Ratio of GDP per capita	
	2007	2020	2007	2020	2007	2020
Perak	5.1	5.6	14,832	31,626	0.60	0.72
Penang	7.1	6.8	31,381	55,774	1.28	1.28
Kedah	3.4	3.4	12,160	22,693	0.49	0.52
Perlis	0.5	0.4	14,500	21,099	0.59	0.48
NCER	16.2	16.2	18,188	34,630	0.74	0.79
Malaysia	100.0	100.0	24,589	43,702	1.00	1.00
(RM billions)	(665.3)	(1,418.0)				

Sources of data: Calculated from state GDP data in: Department of Statistics–Malaysia (various years), GDP by State National Accounts; Department of Statistics–Malaysia (various years), Laporan Sosioe-konomi Negeri.
Note: GDP is measured in current prices.

aggregate outcomes can be attributed to the NCER and its many initiatives is unclear as the counterfactual is unknown. The small economic gains made by Perak are unlikely to be linked to its membership of the NCER, however. Continuing outward migration, shortfalls in labour productivity, lagging labour force participation, high unemployment, and low levels of educational attainment (Penang aside), all suggest continued structural weaknesses in NCER states (NCIA, 2021).

Reviewing development corridor schemes internationally, the World Bank (2009) concludes that many such initiatives have failed largely because of misguided governance. Decision-makers have frequently failed to realize the extent to which centres of trade and industry evolve in response to market conditions and the cumulative forces of agglomeration that the 'atomistic' decisions of firms and households set in motion. Agglomeration economies tend to emerge organically in places that have natural and historical advantages. Replicating these complex conditions through planning and the use of instruments such as subsidies and tax breaks is not easy.

Locally focused, inclusive financial institutions can help to bring about success, however, as they have a vested interest in promoting the vitality of the local economy, given that their future depends on the success of the small businesses and start-ups that they support. By harvesting and assessing information about business opportunities and extending advice and support to their clients, these financial institutions can help to ensure the success of businesses, and promote the creation of jobs. Once firms start to invest, and workers are attracted to a locale, the forces of agglomeration start to set in. The NCER has yet to produce this effect for Perak, however (see 'Harnessing the Strategic Development Plan, 2021–2025', Part 4).

Where federal- and state-level control has rested with different political parties at variance over their development priorities, the NCIA has been unable to arbitrate between them so as to ensure mutually beneficial outcomes (Athukorala and Narayanan, 2017). Challenges have arisen in relation to governance, as well as to the processes required to resolve land matters, which are the domain of the states, with the NCIA having no control over land decisions. This jurisdictional split has led to serious programme delays, especially for the West Coast Expressway, where land acquisition has been slow. Many ongoing projects also lack adequate monitoring, and projects that have broken ground are behind schedule, especially in the hinterland of Perak and other NCER states (Hill and Menon, 2020).

Summary—Most of the Right Moves but Still Limited Results in Perak

From the 1990s and continuing into the 21st century, Perak's economy underwent a major structural transformation with investment directed at the diversification of rural agriculture, the growth of manufacturing and services, the upgrading of infrastructure, and increasing access to education, health, and other services. Although the state's economy was somewhat more diversified than it had been a decade earlier, agriculture, manufacturing, and services were still highly labour intensive. Economic diversification became a pressing imperative and the state pushed towards higher-value-added activities, expediting rural development and improving the quality of urban services.

By the turn of the 21st century, production of palm oil, commercial vegetables, and fruit farming were the mainstays of Perak's agriculture. Diversifying out of rubber helped to enhance farm incomes and was supported through the cultivation of higher-value crops.

With broader and deeper diversification, Perak's manufacturing sector moved towards higher-value-added production and higher-quality products. However, Perak's corridor efforts have had only very limited success in achieving more spatially balanced industrial development, with at least half of Perak's industrial activity still concentrated in Kinta. The service sector has also broadened well beyond government services, with tourism growth the main catalyst, supported by transport and communications, financial services, public utilities, and wholesale and retail trade. The state is inexorably transitioning to a service-oriented economy.

Perak embraced the new national strategic planning initiative to promote balanced regional development through its membership of the NCER. So far, however, it has failed to benefit significantly from FDI flows into the NCER, which have gone mainly to manufacturing activities in Penang and Kedah. Perak is also yet to benefit from the agglomeration economies of the cluster approach, and the economic gains that have been made by the state over the second decade of the 21st century are unlikely to have resulted from its NCER membership. Clearly, the large investments in the NCER to achieve spatially connected infrastructure did not fully benefit Perak, given that the state still lacks an internationally connected airport or port. The state also appears to have been disadvantaged by relatively small federal development allocations to meet its economic, social, and infrastructure needs.

*   *   *

The focus of Part 3C is threefold: it looks first at the extent to which Perakians have enjoyed higher standards of living over the three decades since 1990; second, at how Perak's economic performance has compared relative to neighbouring states and to Malaysia as a whole; and third, at how far the benefits of economic growth have been shared by Perak's population groups, reviewing the extent to which these have been equitably distributed across the state's districts.

By 2020, Perakians living in the median income household were almost four times as well off in real ('absolute') terms as 30 years earlier. Yet, even into the 21st century, this and other advances were not enough to stem the continuing outward migration, particularly of the most educated and skilled, to places offering better opportunities—undermining Perak's human capital base, sapping the vitality of its townships, weakening traditional family support systems, and changing the state's ethnic composition. Nevertheless, within the state, Perak's population has become more urbanized.

3C

Economic, Income, and Demographic Changes with Relative Decline

Bulk terminal, Lumut Port

Economic Change, 1990–2020

This section discusses the economic changes that have taken place at national and state levels in the three decades since 1990. Not all states fared equally, and Perak continued to lose ground to some of the best performers. Its economy, on some measures, hit a trough in the mid- to late 2000s before starting a slow, sometimes barely perceptible, recovery. With continuing growth of its service and manufacturing sectors, alongside increasing urbanization and advances in agriculture, by 2020 the state's output and income levels had started to recover just a little of that lost ground.

Still Lagging Behind the Rest of the Country, 1990–2000—but with Reasons for Optimism

During the 1990s Perak's real GDP grew at an average annual rate of 4.3 per cent, with per capita growth averaging 3.8 per cent (Table 3.14). These rates lagged behind those of Malaysia as a whole, however. By 2000 Perak's economic base, measured in terms of its contribution to GDP, was built on services and manufacturing industries. Tin and rubber, its former economic powerhouses, had become economically inconsequential.

By 2000 Perak's share of Malaysia's GDP had declined to 7.1 per cent, placing it seventh among Malaysia's 13 states and the Federal Territory of Kuala Lumpur, compared to a GDP share of 9 per cent, and a ranking of fourth, in 1990. Its GDP per capita was 19 per cent below the national average, with only Kedah, Kelantan, Pahang, Perlis, and Sabah having lower per capita incomes (Figure 3.22, top panel).

The structural components of output and employment shifted markedly in this decade. In 2000, agriculture produced 18.1 per cent of the state's GDP, but employed just 15 per cent of its workers, compared with corresponding figures

Globalization: Perak's Rise, Relative Decline, and Regeneration. Sultan Nazrin Shah, Oxford University Press. © Sultan Nazrin Shah (2024). DOI: 10.1093/oso/9780198897774.003.0024

Table 3.14	Perak's economic performance lagged behind Malaysia's in the 1990s, but the gap narrowed over the next two decades			
	GDP (2010 prices)		**GDP per capita (2010 prices)**	
	Perak	**Malaysia**	**Perak**	**Malaysia**
	Value (RM millions)		**Value (RM)**	
1990	18,734	263,459	9,401	14,554
2000	28,737	523,445	13,739	22,279
2010	43,313	821,434	18,206	28,733
2020	68,235	1,215,325	27,338	37,456
	Average annual growth rates[a] (%)			
1990–2000	4.3	6.9	3.8	4.3
2000–2010	4.1	4.5	2.8	2.5
2010–2020	4.5	3.9	4.1	2.7

Sources of data: For 1990, Economic Planning Unit–Malaysia (1996); for 2000, EPU (2001); for 2010 and 2020, Department of Statistics–Malaysia (2017b and 2022).

Note: [a] The growth rate is calculated by using ln function (log to base e).

of 27.4 per cent and 24.2 per cent in 1990. However, compared with broader national patterns, Perak's agricultural sector was outsized, with its share of output twice the national average (Table 3.15). The conditions required for the creation of a 'structural bonus' for GDP—when workers move out of lower-productivity agriculture and into higher-productivity secondary and tertiary activities (Baumol, 1967)—while not eliminated, had diminished by 2000.[99]

This unusual configuration of output and employment may reflect the success of earlier crop substitution and land settlement policies, as well as other initiatives that raised agricultural labour productivity. It may also point to the rather lacklustre productivity performance of Perak's tertiary and industrial sectors. Mohammad Abdul Mohit (2009, p. 38) attributes Perak's lagging performance in overall national job creation to a deficit

---

99 Structural change, as described above, can be an important source of growth and productivity gains. If surplus labour in less productive parts of the economy, such as agriculture, shifts to higher-productivity industrial sectors, it is beneficial for aggregate productivity growth. Even within industry, shifts towards more productive sectors can boost aggregate productivity.

Figure 3.22 Perak's share of Malaysia's GDP and GDP per capita lag behind those of the leading states

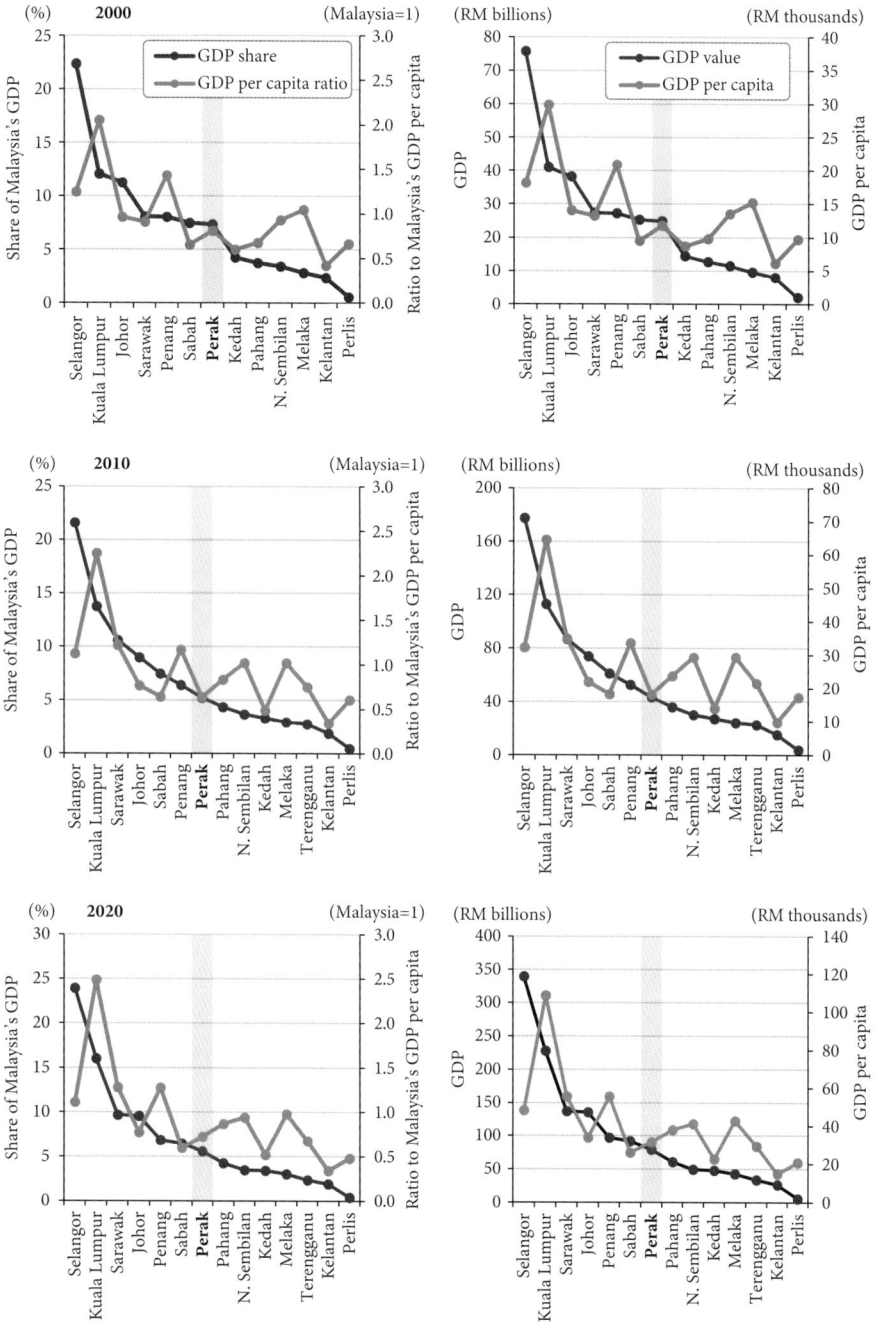

Sources of data: Economic Planning Unit–Malaysia (2003 and 2006); *Department* of Statistics–Malaysia (various years), *Laporan Sosioekonomi Negeri*.

Notes: For 2000, Terengganu is not shown because the data include the petroleum sector, which resulted in an extremely high value of GDP per capita. Supra-state production activities beyond the centre of predominant economic interest for any state was 6.3 per cent of GDP. GDP data are in current prices. Sabah includes Labuan.

Table 3.15	Perak's share of agriculture in GDP was at times roughly twice Malaysia's, while its manufacturing share was still behind the national average in output location quotients[a]			
Sector or subsector	**Perak's output location quotients**			
	1990[b]	**2000**	**2010**	**2020[b]**
Agriculture, forestry, and fishing	1.71	2.17	1.95	2.07
Mining[c]	10.33	2.24	1.20	0.91
Manufacturing	0.80	0.61	0.74	0.82
Construction	0.77	0.59	0.82	0.69
Utilities, transport, storage, and communication	0.84	1.48	1.57	1.54
Wholesale and retail trade, and hotels and restaurants	0.80	0.78	0.92	0.89
Finance, insurance, real estate, and business services	1.31	1.10	0.80	0.66
Government services	1.40	1.88	1.38	1.27
Other services	0.46	1.82	1.40	1.12

Sources of data: Calculated from GDP data in state publications, Department of Statistics–Malaysia (various years), *GDP by State National Accounts*; Department of Statistics–Malaysia (various years), *Annual GDP National Accounts Malaysia*; Economic Planning Unit–Malaysia (1991a).

Notes:[a] The location quotient is defined as the sector's share in Perak's output divided by the same sector's share in Malaysia's output. A value of 1 denotes the same as the national average, a value above 1 denotes higher than the national average, and a value below 1 denotes lower than the national average.
[b] For years in which nominal GDP are unavailable, 1990 and 2020, GDP is measured in 1987 and 2015 prices respectively.
[c] Excludes crude oil and natural gas from the mining sector.

in the 'competitiveness' of its industries relative to the rest of the country. The competitive components of Perak's industries are strongly negative, suggesting that these industries are less competitive than those at the national level.

Manufacturing employed 22.5 per cent of Perak's labour force in 2000 and contributed 18.2 per cent of its GDP. This was 39 per cent lower than the national average—based on a 0.61 output location quotient, as shown in Table 3.15. A feature differentiating Perak from Malaysia's most advanced states was the manufacturing share in their GDP. In the Klang Valley, the share was 44 per cent and in Penang it was 46 per cent. Johor and Melaka also had higher manufacturing shares in GDP, at 41 per cent. Just over half of Perak's labour force was employed in tertiary activities in 2000, which produced 61.1 per cent of its GDP.

Stability and Gradual Growth, 2000–2020

The measures taken to strengthen Perak's economy after the destabilizing effects of the Asian financial crisis seem to have helped its economic performance. Because of its smaller exposure to manufacturing than frontier states, Perak was less affected by the crisis, and its recovery from the effects of the 2008–2009 global financial crisis was stronger than that of the country as a whole. Over the subsequent decade, 2010–2020, annual growth in both aggregate GDP and per capita GDP, of 4.5 per cent and 4.1 per cent respectively, exceeded that of the national average (3.9 per cent and 2.7 per cent) (Table 3.14). Although Perak's annual growth in aggregate real GDP over the period 2000–2010 was lower than that for Malaysia as a whole, its per capita growth was slightly higher, thereby narrowing the gap (Table 3.16).

Perak's share of Malaysia's GDP, after falling to 5.3 per cent in 2010, had risen to 5.6 per cent in 2020. By then, its GDP per capita was 72 per cent of the national average (Figure 3.22, middle and bottom panels), 65 per cent of that of Selangor, and just 57 per cent that of Penang.

The share of manufacturing in Perak's output continued to grow modestly over 2000–2020, rising from 18.2 per cent to 19.1 per cent (Figure 3.23), although its employment share declined from 22.5 per cent to 16.7 per cent (see Table 3.8), suggesting some improvement in manufacturing labour productivity. Perak's share of manufacturing output relative to Malaysia's share—the location quotient—increased from 0.61 to 0.82 over the period 2000–2020, while that in all other sectors declined, except for agriculture: in short, Malaysia was deindustrializing faster than Perak (Table 3.15).

Table 3.16	Over the first two decades of the 21st century, the gap between Perak's GDP per capita and that of Malaysia narrowed, but remains wide					
	GDP (current prices)			GDP per capita (current prices)		
	Perak	Malaysia	Perak: Malaysia	Perak	Malaysia	Perak: Malaysia
	Value (RM millions)		Share (%)	Value (RM)		Share (%)
2000	25,474	356,401	7.1	12,419	15,313	81.1
2010	43,313	821,434	5.3	18,207	28,733	63.4
2020	78,939	1,418,000	5.6	31,626	43,702	72.4

Sources of data: Economic Planning Unit–Malaysia (2001 and 2003); Department of Statistics–Malaysia (2017b and 2022).

The share of the service sector also grew steadily, mainly attributable to the wholesale, retail, hotels, and restaurants subsector, which benefited from strong growth in tourism. Over 2000–2020, this subsector's share of output grew from 10.1 per cent to 17.7 per cent, while its share of employment jumped from 18.2 per cent to 29.4 per cent. This growth in the share of output was, however, still below the national average, as reflected in the location quotient, which nevertheless rose from 0.78 in 2000 to 0.89 in 2020 (Table 3.15). Tourism readily absorbs labour when there are few other more productive job opportunities.

The higher growth in the share of employment than in the share of output of the service sector may partly reflect the fact that Perak was increasingly recruiting lesser-skilled and lower-paid migrant workers in a context of rising labour force participation and low unemployment (Figure 3.19). The 1990s saw a liberalization of Malaysia's foreign labour policy. Documented foreign migrant workers employed in Perak grew from just 6,000 in 1991 to 28,000 in 2000, and then to 47,000 in 2010, before doubling to 94,000 in 2019.[100] At first, these workers came mainly from Indonesia, but after 2000 they were increasingly

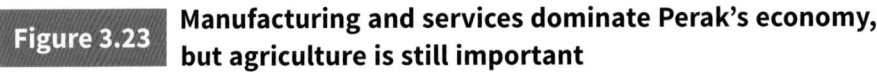

Figure 3.23   **Manufacturing and services dominate Perak's economy, but agriculture is still important**

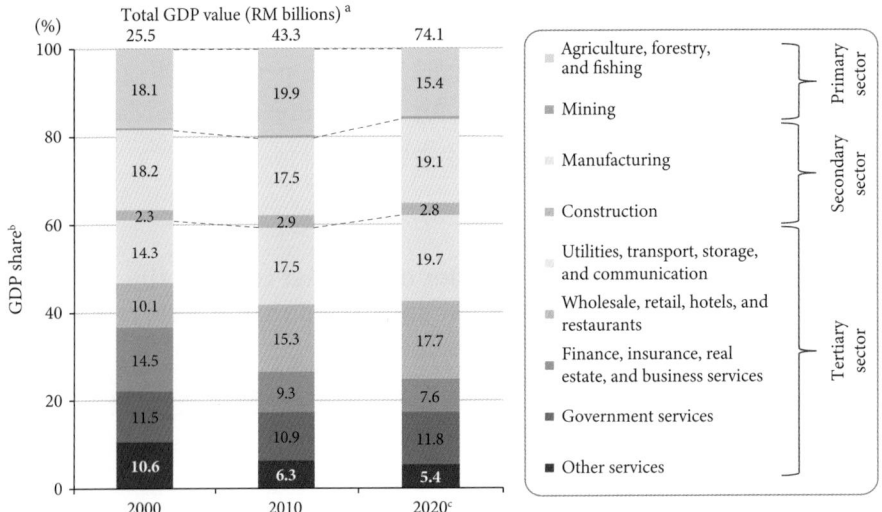

Sources of data: For 2000: Official Portal of Perak State Government (2007); for 2010: Department of Statistics–Malaysia (2017b); for 2020: Department of Statistics–Malaysia (2022).

Notes: [a] GDP data for 2000 and 2010 are in current prices; GDP data for 2020 are in 2015 prices.
[b] Excluding imputed bank service and import duties in the calculation of GDP share.
[c] Data for 2020 are Department of Statistics–Malaysia estimates.

---

100 The number of documented foreign migrant workers in Perak, as elsewhere in Malaysia, fell back sharply during the Covid-19 pandemic, to an estimated 68,000 in 2020 and 62,000 in 2021, before rising to 71,000 in 2022.

drawn from Nepal and Bangladesh, working in services as well as in other sectors. This influx likely exerted downward pressure on overall wage growth, and appears to have displaced local workers, including in many lower-skilled jobs in agriculture, manufacturing, and services. In 2020, GDP per worker was lowest in the service sector.

The agricultural sector, which continues to diversify, grew by an impressive 64 per cent between 2000 and 2020—reflecting an annual average rate of 2.5 per cent. Although the direct contribution of oil palm production to the state's GDP has declined (Figure 3.24), a significant part of oil palm and other tree-crop output now goes into resource-based manufacturing, which translates into agriculture's contribution to manufacturing's value added. There has been vertical diversification from crude palm oil to refined palm oil and its other end products, such as cooking oils. Similarly, cultivated rubber acreage and rubber's share in GDP have both fallen, but value-added gains have been made through the production and export of rubber-based products which were in high demand during the pandemic. Fruit and vegetable farming, which has higher-value-added, has also expanded its share in agriculture.

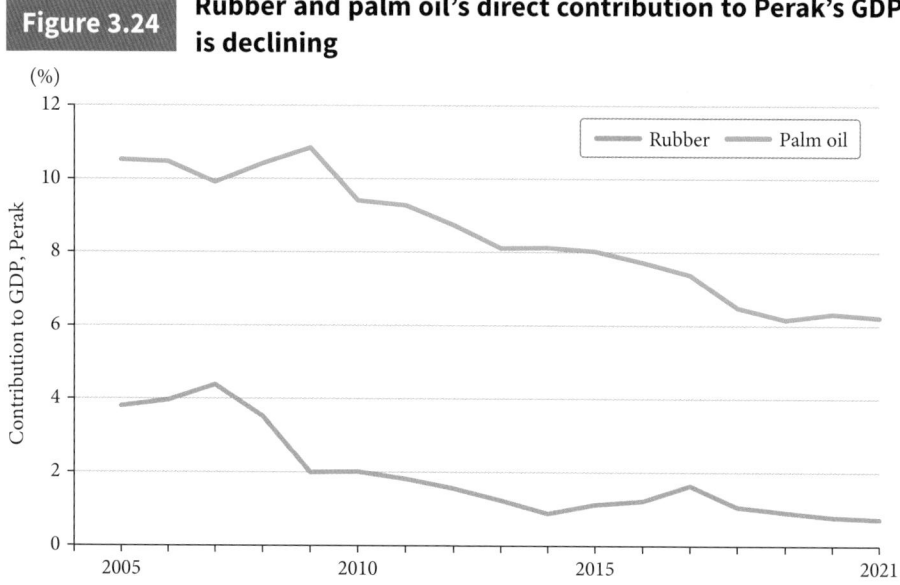

Figure 3.24 **Rubber and palm oil's direct contribution to Perak's GDP is declining**

Source of data: Department of Statistics–Malaysia, unpublished data.

Note: 2010 constant prices.

Structural Transformation, 1970–2020

Agricultural transformation has proceeded in a remarkably similar fashion around the world over the past 150 years (Timmer, 2009 and 2013). In the first phase, less labour is used to produce the same output, reflecting increasing labour productivity. In the second, labour, capital savings, and tax revenues from the agricultural sector are mobilized to help propel the non-agricultural sector forward. In the third phase, the agricultural sector integrates more deeply with the rest of the economy through improved infrastructure and product markets. The fourth and final phase is industrialization and modern employment. These phases are characterized by a declining share of agriculture in GDP and of total employment in agriculture, as well as by GDP per capita increases.

Malaysia, Japan, and Indonesia have all experienced similar long-term structural transformations, with differences in the timing of these agricultural transformations helping to explain differences in progress towards industrialization and in living standards (Sultan Nazrin Shah, 2019). The structural transformation of low-income rural agrarian economies into industrial- and service-based economies located mainly in urban areas is the only sustainable pathway out of poverty.

Over the period 1970–2020, Perak's share of agriculture in GDP and its share of employment in agriculture were both on a downward trend, while per capita GDP continued to increase (Figure 3.25, top panel). By 2020, agriculture's contribution to GDP had fallen by half—to about 15.4 per cent from 30.4 per cent 50 years earlier—and the share of employment in agriculture had declined from 47.5 per cent to 12 per cent over the same period. Intriguingly, in recent years Perak's agricultural labour productivity has overtaken that of the non-agricultural sector, although much of this can be attributed to higher prices of primary commodities, particularly rubber and oil palm (Sultan Nazrin Shah, 2019).[101]

In 1970, Selangor and Penang already had lower shares of agriculture in GDP and of agricultural employment in total employment; by 2020, both measures were negligible in these states. When measured from the same level, the path of their structural transformations has been faster, less volatile, and has gone further than in Perak (Figure 3.25). In Perak, it took about 22 years for the share of employment in agriculture to fall from about 25 per cent to 15 per cent, compared with about 14 years for Selangor and 9 years for Penang. Their faster pace of structural transformation is to be expected given that both Penang and Selangor

---

101 Labour productivity (AgGAPshr) is measured by the difference between the agricultural share in total GDP and the employment share of agriculture in total employment. Positive values denote higher labour productivity in agriculture than non-agriculture, and negative values denote the opposite.

were able to ride the post-independence wave of globalization by attracting large FDI flows to their manufacturing sectors in the 1970s.

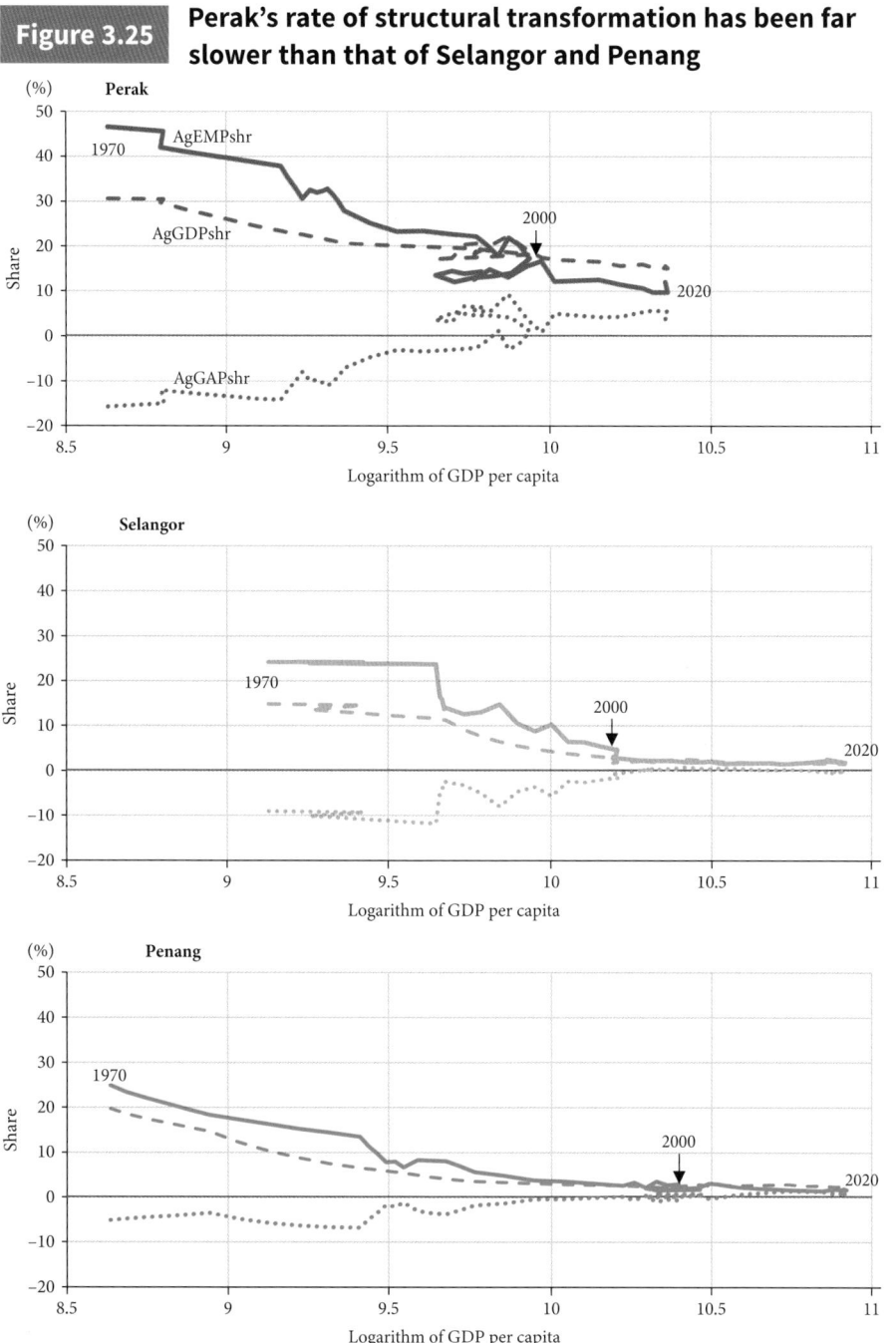

Figure 3.25 Perak's rate of structural transformation has been far slower than that of Selangor and Penang

Sources of data: Economic Planning Unit–Malaysia, Malaysia Plan (various years), and Department of Statistics–Malaysia, GDP by State National Accounts (various years); Employment: Department of Statistics–Malaysia, Labour Force Survey Report (various years).

Perak's slower structural transformation has resulted in much slower GDP per capita growth over the last 50 years. Despite having been at a similar level to Penang's in 1970, by 2020 the state's GDP per capita was around 43 per cent below Penang's and 35 per cent below Selangor's (Figure 3.25). Nevertheless, despite Perak's slower transformation, living standards have been substantially raised, with GDP per capita 5.8 times higher in 2020 than it was in 1970. Absolute poverty rates have fallen sharply. Labour has migrated out of rural agriculture and into urban employment, and there have been multiple welfare-enhancing measures (Sultan Nazrin Shah, 2019). In the agricultural sector itself, a new generation of agripreneurs has benefited from the introduction of higher-value crops and modern sustainable farming, which improved yields and boosted downstream processing activities.

Summary—The Tide May Be Turning for Perak's Economy

With a fast-rising share of the state's population working in modern urban manufacturing and service-sector jobs, especially in tourism and related services, by around 2010 Perak's economic performance had gradually started to strengthen. Although GDP growth continued to lag behind that of Malaysia as a whole, by 2020 growth in aggregate and per capita GDP exceeded the national average. The state's economy was dominated by services, which accounted for about two-thirds of its GDP and employment. Output in manufacturing and services, especially tourism, grew at impressive rates, as did that of agriculture. Despite being disadvantaged by shortfalls in federal development allocations, as discussed above, the state achieved healthy increases in per capita income. Service-led growth was anchored by the wholesale and retail trade, and by the hotels and restaurants subsector, driven by strong growth in tourism.

Diversification within agriculture continued apace and the sector remains an important contributor to the state's GDP, even though its share has diminished. Perak's agricultural sector grew by 64 per cent between 2000 and 2020, at an annual average rate of 2.5 per cent, although palm oil's direct contribution to the state's GDP declined. Manufacturing shifted modestly towards higher-value-added production and higher-quality goods, and its share of GDP continued to grow moderately over the period 2000–2020, although its employment share declined from 22.5 per cent to 16.7 per cent, suggesting that the sector's labour productivity improved.

Although significant, the structural transformation of Perak's economy has been slower than that in leading Malaysian states. Its GDP per capita growth has been slower, and by 2020 the state's GDP per capita was substantially below Penang's and Selangor's. Nevertheless, Perak's economic performance over the period 2000–2020 saw substantial absolute economic growth, with the state's GDP growing threefold in nominal terms, from RM25,474 million in 2000 to RM78,939 million in 2020.

Income Change, 1990–2020

This section examines changes in household income in Perak vis-à-vis those in Malaysia as a whole, and considers the extent to which economic growth has narrowed inequalities between (and within) various groups, categorized according to ethnicity, district, educational attainment, and household size.

Rising Household Incomes, Nationally and in Perak

At the turn of the 20th century, Perak's GDP per capita was 81 per cent that of Malaysia. By 2005 it had fallen sharply to 59 per cent, and only Kelantan, Kedah, and Sabah had lower GDP per capita. Perak's relative position improved over the next decade and a half, however, and by 2020 its GDP per capita was back up to around 72 per cent of Malaysia's, largely a reflection of modestly rising aggregate GDP.

Perakians have enjoyed rising standards of living over the three decades since 1989, as reflected in the multiple indicators for which comparable data are available. In 2019, those living in median income households were nearly four times better off in real terms than they had been 30 years earlier (Table 3.17). Incomes of Chinese in Perak remain above those of Malays and other *Bumiputera*, but the wide gap between these two ethnic communities has narrowed. Conversely, Indians increasingly lag behind both these communities. Income inequalities among Perak's districts have also tended to narrow, though Kinta is still the richest (Map 3.2). But with continuing out-migration of its highest skilled due to a shortage of higher-paid jobs, Perak's average living standards remain below those of the average Malaysian citizen (Table 3.17).

Globalization: Perak's Rise, Relative Decline, and Regeneration. Sultan Nazrin Shah, Oxford University Press. © Sultan Nazrin Shah (2024). DOI: 10.1093/oso/9780198897774.003.0025

Income Growth—Impressive Absolute Gains, but Less Impressive Relative Gains

In determining changes and differentials in average income, a key challenge is to determine how best to define 'average income'. There are two clear possibilities: to use the mean or the median. Because the mean is heavily skewed by the top income earners, the median is used here—in other words, a household halfway along the 'distribution' of households ranked by household income per head.[102]

Perak's lower levels of output per head compared to the national average between 1989 and 2019 imply that household incomes should also be below the national average.[103] Indeed, income per head in Perak's median household was 12 to 21 per cent below that of the median household in Malaysia as a whole (Table 3.17). However, although its average household is poorer in money income terms than the average Malaysian household, the difference is not as wide as the lower output per head would suggest, and the gap has been closing a little in recent years.

Perak's median household income has surged in nominal terms, growing ninefold over the three decades since 1989. As prices of goods and services purchased by households have also risen due to inflation, money incomes need to be far higher in 2019 than in 1989 just to maintain real living standards. When comparing incomes over time, nominal incomes should be 'deflated' by the consumer price index to obtain 'real' income, reflecting changes in the purchasing power of money incomes. A household's *real* income per capita is defined as the household's money income per capita deflated by the national consumer price index.[104]

Over the three decades since 1989, Perak's median real income per household member grew at an annual rate of 4.66 per cent—just a little less than the national rate—and the median household was nearly four times as well off in real terms in 2019 as three decades earlier. In short, sustained economic growth has led to much higher standards of living, nationally and in Perak.

---

102 The median is expected to be below the mean, as income distributions tend to have long 'upper tails', which raise the mean but do not affect the median.

103 The analysis in this section is based on six household income surveys (HISs) conducted by the Department of Statistics–Malaysia over the period 1989–2019. Perak's sample constituted just over 10 per cent of the total HIS coverage in 1989, falling to about 7 per cent in recent surveys, consistent with its declining share of Malaysia's population. Details of households by district are not available in the 1989 HIS, so the analysis here is limited to the two decades after 1999.

104 The base year for Malaysia's consumer price index is 2000.

Table 3.17	Perak's median household income soared over 1989–2019, but still lagged behind Malaysia's		
	Perak	**Malaysia**	**Ratio of Perak to Malaysia**
Median annual nominal income per household member (RM)			
1989	1,996	2,265	88.1
1999	4,280	5,200	82.3
2004	5,637	6,770	83.3
2009	7,425	9,384	79.1
2016	14,808	17,450	84.9
2019	17,300	20,524	84.3
Median annual real income per household member (RM)			
1989	2,916	3,310	
1999	4,345	5,279	
2004	5,323	6,392	
2009	6,070	7,671	
2016	10,332	12,176	
2019	11,446	13,579	
Average annual growth of real incomes (%)			
1989–2019	4.66	4.82	

Source of data: Department of Statistics–Malaysia, Household Income Surveys, 1989–2019, unpublished data.

Income Inequality between Households in Perak and Malaysia as a Whole, and among Perak's Households—A Solid Performance from Perak

The distribution of income can be analysed using three indicators: the Gini coefficient, the P90/P10 ratio, and the relative poverty rate (Box 3.17). Using these indicators, the analysis shows that Perak's incomes over the full income distribution have become more equally distributed than at the national level (using the Gini coefficient and the P90/P10 ratio), but the state has a higher level of 'relative poverty'.

Box 3.17   Measuring income inequality

Income inequality can be measured using three commonly used indicators:

- *The Gini coefficient.* This takes a value between 0 and 1. The closer the Gini is to 0, the more equally incomes are distributed; and the closer it is to 1, the greater the inequality.
- *The P90/P10 ratio.* The numerator of this ratio, P90, is the lowest income earned by the richest 10 per cent of the population; the denominator, P10, is the highest income earned by the poorest 10 per cent of individuals. With no income inequality, the ratio takes the value 1, rising above this as income is more unequally distributed.
- *The relative poverty rate.* This measures the proportion of the population with incomes below 60 per cent of the median income over all Malaysian individuals. It is the poverty definition used in many countries.

Relative inequality measures are preferred to *absolute* measures of income dispersion such as the standard deviation. For example, the *P90/P10* ratio of per capita incomes in Perak in 1989 was 5.79 and its value two decades later was much the same, at 5.76, suggesting hardly any change. Because of income growth over this period, however, the *absolute* real per capita income gap between the 90th percentile and the 10th doubled, from RM5,760 in 1989 to RM11,919 in 2009. In a *growing* economy any absolute measure of inequality will suggest greater inequality, so relative measures will be more revealing (Milanovic, 2016). For similar reasons, as per capita income rises over time, relative poverty measures are preferred to absolute measures.

There are two ways to measure the income of individual household members. The first is household income per household member—*income per capita* (Table 3.17). The second is income per equivalent adult—*equivalized income* (Hagenaars et al., 1994). In the second approach, used below, total household income is divided by the number of 'adult equivalents' in the household using an 'equivalence scale'. A weight is given to each member of the household to reflect his or her needs, and these are summed to arrive at the 'equivalized household size'.

A widely used equivalence scale is that developed by the Organisation for Economic Co-operation and Development (OECD), which attaches a weight of 1.0 to the first adult, 0.5 to the second and to each additional member aged 14 and over, and 0.3 to each child aged under 14 (Eurostat, 2002). For a one-member household, total income, income per capita, and income per equivalent adult are the same. For a household of two adults, total income is divided by 2 to obtain income per capita, but is divided by 1.5 to obtain 'equivalized income'. The use of equivalized income takes into account the different age-dependent needs of household members, and

(Continued)

also recognizes that households can 'share jointly consumed goods'—housing, household durables, and so on.

Gini coefficients published by the Department of Statistics–Malaysia (2020b) are based on the distribution of household income among all households, taking no account of household size. So while a large household with a large income will be placed at the upper end of the household income distribution, its members may well be worse off than members of a smaller household with a lower total income. A Gini coefficient based on equivalized income and income per capita and calculated across individuals, rather than households, gives a more accurate measure of how individual well-being is distributed.

Incomes are more evenly distributed in Perak than in Malaysia as a whole,[105] as shown in an improving—albeit fluctuating—downtrend (improvement) in the Gini coefficient since 1989 (Figure 3.26, left panel).[106] The P90/P10 ratio is also lower in Perak (again suggesting greater equality) (Figure 3.26, centre panel). Yet the proportion of Perak's population living in 'relative poverty' is higher than the all-Malaysia figure in every year (Figure 3.26, right panel). All three indicators, nationally and in Perak, showed a slight reversal in 2019.

Summarizing the distribution of income in a single index such as the Gini coefficient does not reveal precisely where in the distribution it is that incomes are more equally distributed, however. Figure 3.27, which plots real equivalized income growth over the three decades for each percentile in the distribution, provides more insight. For example, the income of the 10th percentile refers to the highest income of the poorest 10 per cent of individuals. In 1989, the real equivalized income of the 10th percentile in Malaysia was RM2,261 per year, rising to RM8,514 three decades later—3.8 times or 276 per cent higher.

---

105 The corresponding results for the distribution of income per capita are very similar to those of equivalized income and are not reported here. Inequality measures using equivalized income are generally lower than those based on per capita income because per capita income is substantially lower in large households, whereas the reduction in equivalized income in large households is more muted.

106 In 2019, the Gini coefficients for Perak and Malaysia were 0.356 and 0.400 respectively, compared with 0.399 and 0.426 in 1989, meaning that equivalized incomes had become more equitably distributed among individuals in both Perak and in the country generally.

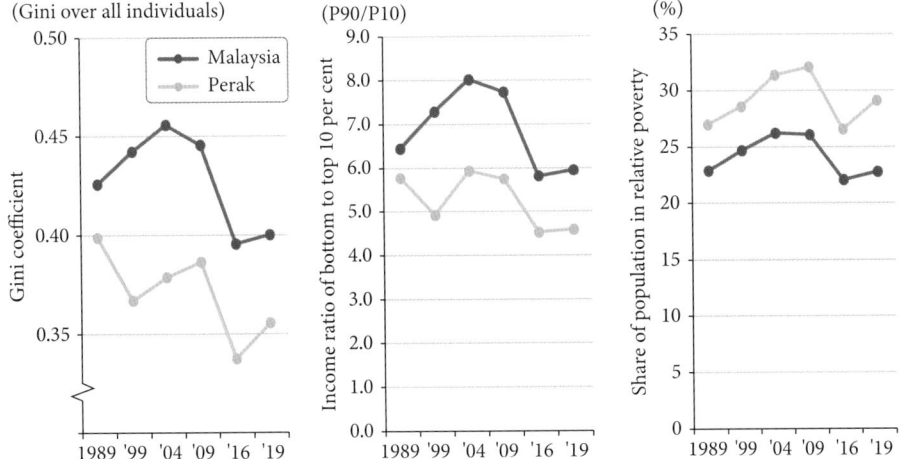

Figure 3.26 | **Perak's improving trend in equivalized income inequality and relative poverty reversed somewhat in 2019**

Source of data: Department of Statistics–Malaysia, Household Income Surveys, 1989–2019, unpublished data.
Note: Income defined as income per equivalent adult.

If incomes among all percentiles grew at the same rate, the solid lines in Figure 3.27 would be horizontal, and the Gini coefficients in 2019 would be equal to their values in 1989. However, as the figure shows, the incomes of the poorest percentiles grew fastest in both Perak and the whole of Malaysia, while those of

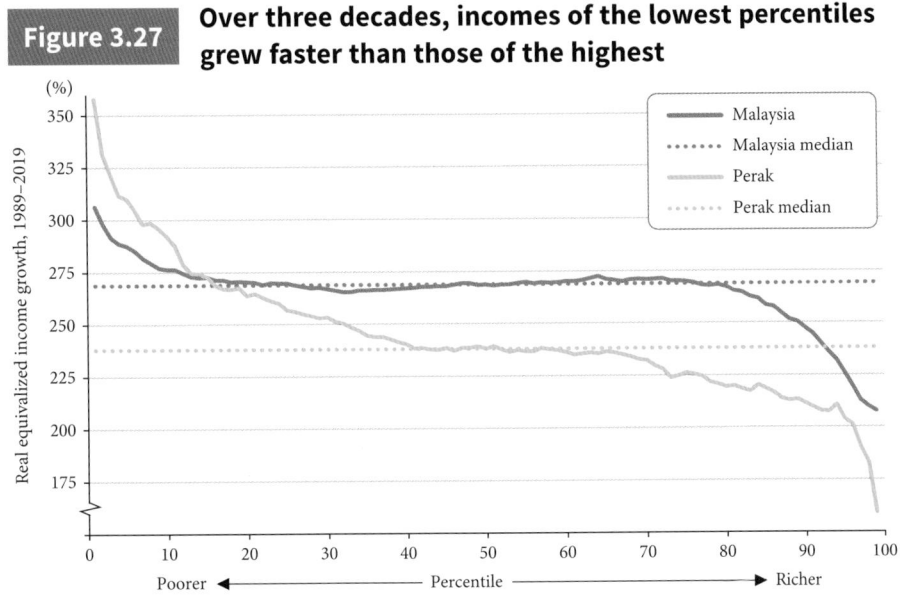

Figure 3.27 | **Over three decades, incomes of the lowest percentiles grew faster than those of the highest**

Source of data: Department of Statistics–Malaysia, Household Income Surveys, 1989 and 2019, unpublished data.

the richest percentiles increased far less than the median. This is contrary to the experience of many countries, notably China and the US (World Bank, 2020b).[107] Yet, despite this pattern of income growth, the state's relative poverty was still higher in 2019 than it had been three decades earlier.

Inequalities by Ethnic Group in Perak—Generally Narrowing

Between 1989 and 1999, the median equivalized income of Malays and other *Bumiputera* grew much faster than that of Chinese and Indians—at an average annual rate of 4.4 per cent, against 3.9 per cent and 3.6 per cent respectively. This led to a narrowing of income differentials among Perak's three main ethnic groups, consistent with the continuation of the NEP's affirmative action measures and the increasing employment of Malays in urban modern-sector jobs. Thus, whereas in 1989 the median equivalized income of Chinese individuals was 59 per cent higher than the median equivalized income of Malays, this gap narrowed to only 9 per cent in 2016 before widening to 17 per cent in 2019

Figure 3.28 **Perak's ethnic income differentials are decreasing, but Indians are lagging behind on equivalized income growth**

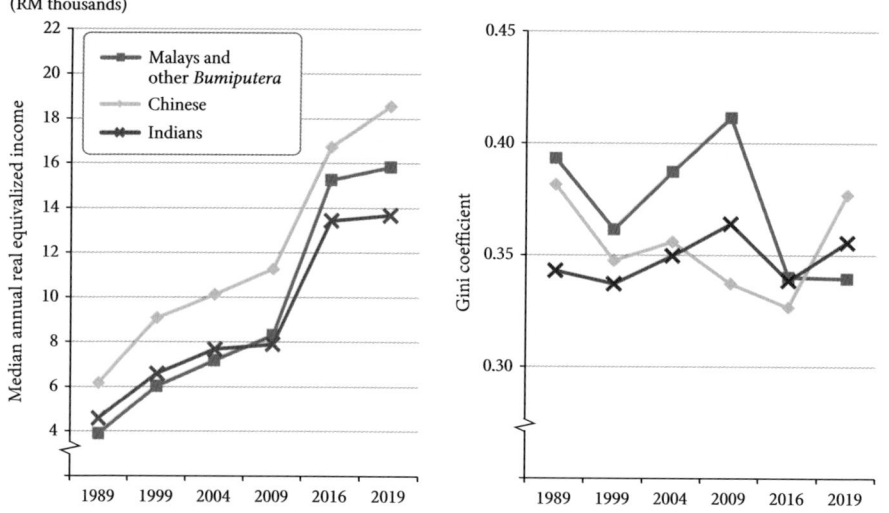

Source of data: Department of Statistics–Malaysia, Household Income Surveys, 1989–2019, unpublished data.

107 This feature is even more prominent in Perak than Malaysia as a whole, where the growth in incomes between the 13th and 82nd percentiles was within 5 percentage points of the median. Incomes for around three-quarters of the population grew at a rate close to that of the median. For Perak, the percentile range with income growth less than five points from the median is far narrower—38th to 68th percentiles, meaning that percentiles 1 to 37 grew faster than the median, and percentiles 69 to 100 grew more slowly.

(Figure 3.28, left panel). The equivalized income of the median Indian has fallen behind that of Malays (and remains behind the Chinese figure).

Intra-ethnic income inequality among Perak's three main communities varied little over the three decades after 1989. Income inequality tended to be highest within the Malay and other *Bumiputera* groups for most of the period, except in 2019 when its Gini coefficient was lowest; the Chinese Gini coefficient was 15 per cent higher in 2019 than it had been in 2016 (Figure 3.28, right panel).

Inequalities among Perak's Districts—Also Generally Narrowing and Lower than National

Map 3.2 shows the 2019 population shares and income levels of Perak's 12 districts,[108] including the new districts of Bagan Datuk, Kampar, and Muallim.[109] Median equivalized annual incomes are highest in the more populous and urban district of Kinta at RM27,600, as well as in Larut, Matang, and Selama at RM25,000, and in Manjung at RM24,900. Meanwhile, median equivalized annual incomes are lowest in Hilir Perak at RM19,900, and Hulu Perak at RM21,000. The median individuals in Kampar and Muallim are a little poorer than those from the districts they were formerly part of, though the differences are small. The median income in Bagan Datuk is above that of Hilir Perak.

In 1999, the median individual in Kinta was far better off than counterparts elsewhere in Perak, while the state's poorest lived in the least populous districts of Hulu Perak and Perak Tengah. Two decades later, the most prosperous individuals still lived in Kinta, but those in the poorer districts were catching up, having seen faster average income growth in a remarkable convergence (Figure 3.29). Over these two decades, median incomes in the districts of Hulu Perak and Perak Tengah grew fastest, though the small samples in these districts may mean their estimates are more prone to sampling error.

---

108 Perak was divided into nine districts until May 2009, when Kampar, formerly part of Kinta district, became the state's 10th district. The new district of Kampar is included in Kinta in analysis of time trends in household incomes to allow for comparisons over time. Time trend analysis is thus made for Perak's nine original districts. Kampar, Muallim, and Bagan Datuk are treated separately only where data are available in 2019; otherwise they are included as part of their original districts.

109 The most populous district, Kinta, accounts for around one-third of Perak's population. By contrast, the least populous districts—Kampar, Hulu Perak, and Perak Tengah—together account for around 12 per cent of the population. Measures of income and inequality are likely to be more prone to sampling error when coverage is thin.

| Map 3.2 | In 2019, Kinta had the largest population and highest median income in Perak |

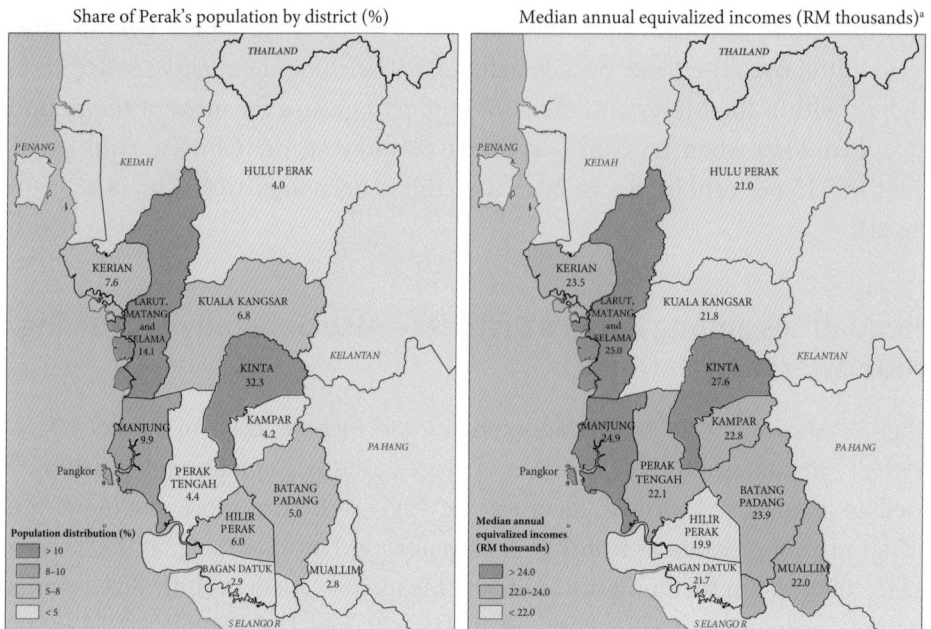

Source of data: Department of Statistics–Malaysia (2020a).
Note: [a] Nominal income.

Perak's districts with the highest incomes are overwhelmingly urban. In the 2019 household income survey (HIS), 98 per cent of individuals in Kinta were living in urban areas and, as seen, the district's median equivalized income was the highest (Figure 3.30). By contrast, the poorer districts were largely rural—in the 2019 HIS there were no urban households in Hulu Perak, and it had the second-lowest median income. Perak has become notably more urban in the last three decades: by 2019 over 80 per cent of individuals covered by the HIS were living in urban areas, a steep jump from the 30 per cent in 1989.

Perak's spatial income inequality can be measured by the Gini coefficient for each of the nine original districts (Figure 3.31).[110] Incomes in Perak's districts are more equally distributed than national incomes. Six districts saw a rise in inequality between 1999 and 2019, but none went above the 2019 national coefficient of 0.4. By contrast, Kerian's Gini coefficient improved to below 0.3 in

---

110 The small sample size for some districts in the HIS could cause their inequality measures to take unexpectedly extreme values. However, all district Gini coefficients were generally in the range of 0.32 to 0.38 in the first two decades of the 21st century.

Figure 3.29 **Districts with lower incomes have recorded faster annual income growth[a]**

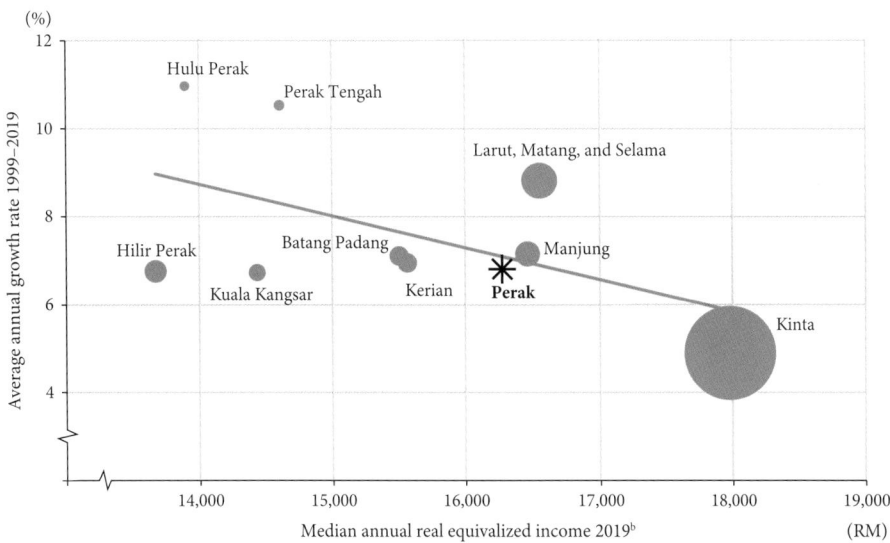

Source of data: Department of Statistics–Malaysia, Household Income Surveys, 1999 and 2019, unpublished data.

Notes: [a] The size of the bubble represents the relative population size.

[b] Nominal income.

Figure 3.30 **Richer districts are predominantly urban[a]**

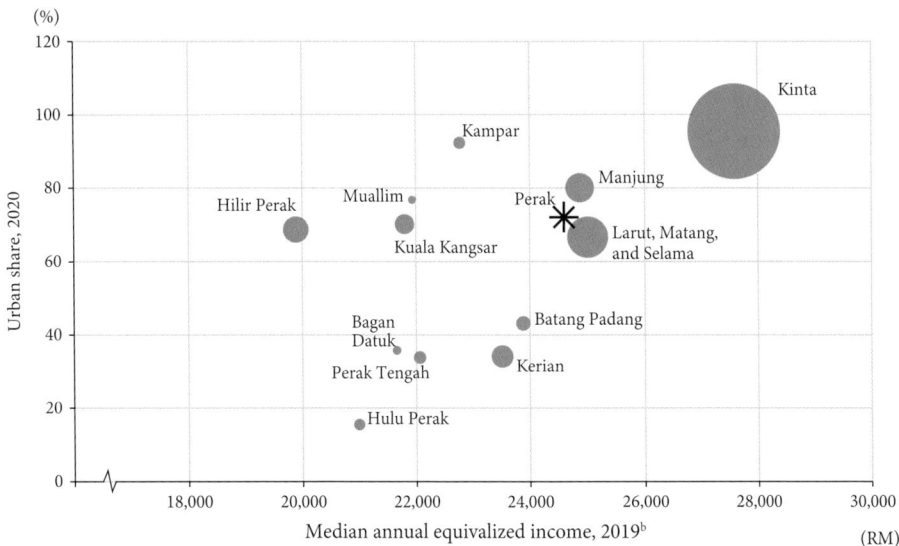

Source of data: Department of Statistics–Malaysia, Household Income Survey, 2019, unpublished data.

Notes: [a] The size of the bubble represents the relative population size.

[b] Nominal income.

| Figure 3.31 | **Gini inequality has risen in six of Perak's districts over the past two decades, but remains below the national rate** |

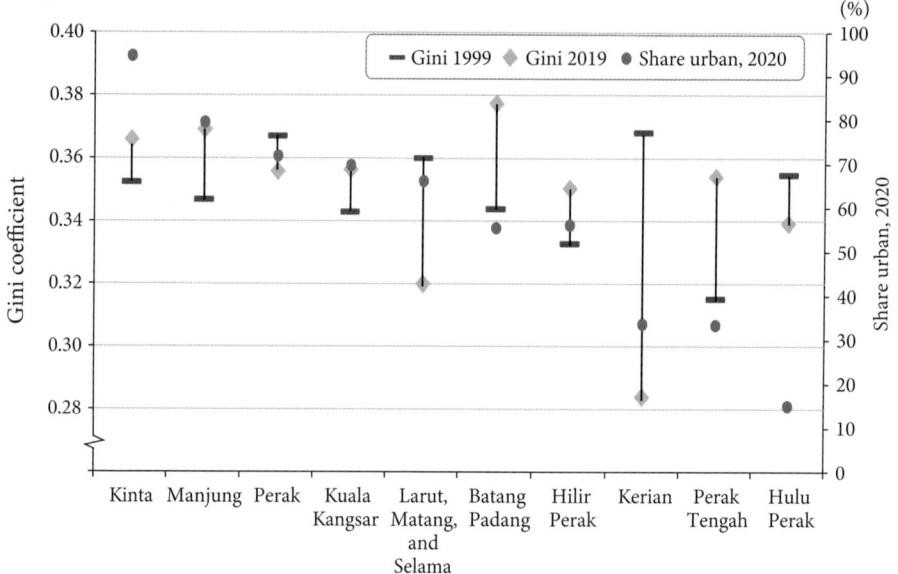

Source of data: Department of Statistics–Malaysia, Household Income Surveys, 1999 and 2019, unpublished data.

2019, though this was based on a sample of only 424 households. Perak's overall Gini coefficient was 5 per cent higher in 2019 (0.356) than in 2016, and Kinta's was 12 per cent higher (0.366).

Income inequality in Perak's districts in 2019, at 0.28–0.38, was lower than in Malaysia as a whole, at 0.400. Perak's inequality indices are at similar levels to those of some OECD countries: the Gini in the UK was 0.366 in 2018, and it was 0.390 in the US in 2017. The Gini in the more egalitarian northern European countries is lower than in Perak, however; for example, 0.261 in Norway (2018) and Denmark (2016), and 0.275 in Sweden (2018).[111]

Perak's Inequalities by Educational Attainment and Household Size

The education of the household head and the size of a household both have a significant bearing on the distribution of income. The head of household is usually the main source of household income and his or her income will be closely related to educational attainment. Education and/or skill level is highly correlated with occupational status, with the most educated in the highest-paid jobs. In large households with more children, equivalized incomes are likely to

---

111 For data on OECD inequality measures, see https://data.oecd.org/inequality/income-inequality.htm.

be lower. Poorer households tend to be those with the lowest level of education and largest number of household members (Sultan Nazrin Shah, 2019).

Perakian households headed by a person with tertiary education have much higher incomes than those headed by a person with little or no schooling. In 1989, median income per 'equivalent adult' (see Box 3.17) in the latter group was just above a quarter of the former. This gap narrowed, however, to just under half in 2019 (Figure 3.32, upper-left panel). With sustained investments in education at all levels, Perak's households are increasingly headed by a person

Figure 3.32 **Perak's larger households and those where the head has little education have lower incomes**

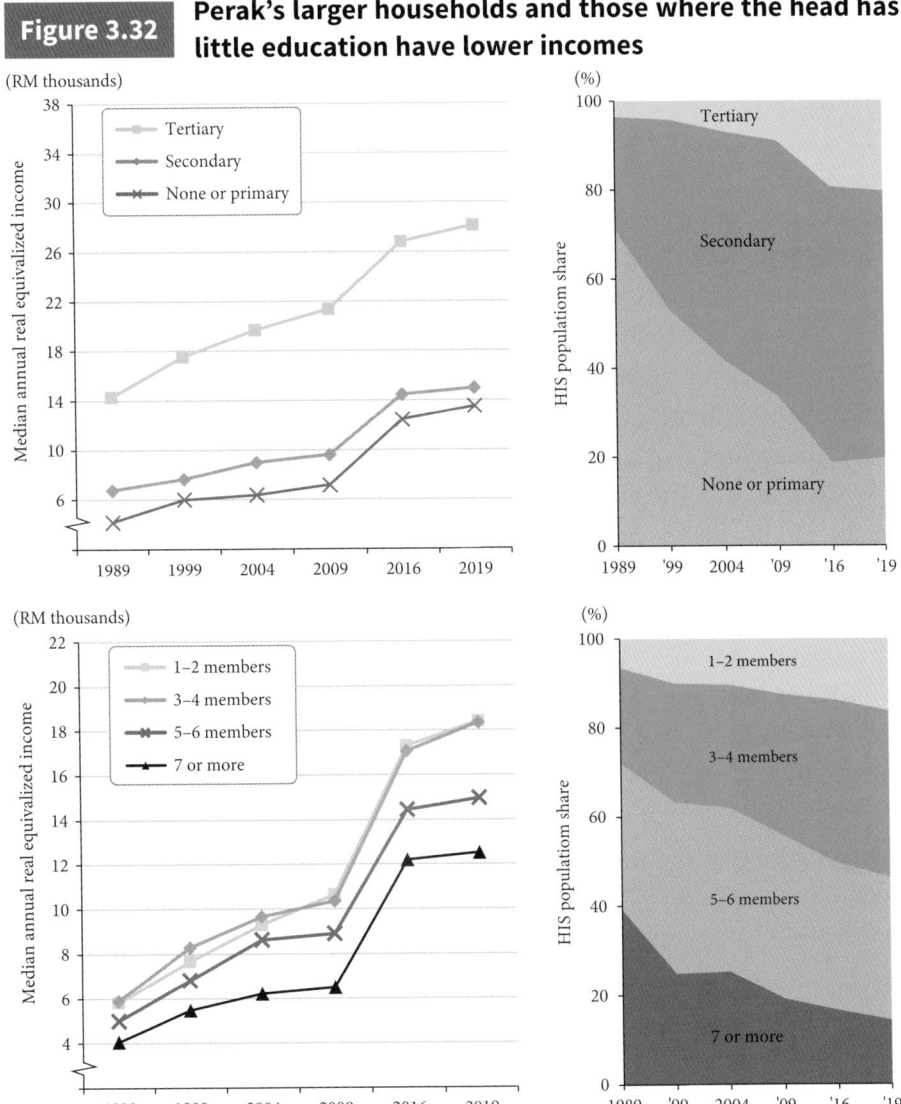

Source of data: Department of Statistics–Malaysia, Household Income Surveys, 1989–2019, unpublished data.

with at least a secondary education; this represents a significant change from 1989, when most household heads had no schooling or primary schooling only (Figure 3.32, upper-right panel).

Perakian households with fewer members have higher incomes. The median equivalized real income in households with seven or more members was around 70 per cent of that in one- or two-member households, averaged over the period 1989–2019 (Figure 3.32, lower-left panel). The share of large households has diminished as fertility has declined, however, and households with four or fewer members have become the majority (Figure 3.32, lower-right panel).

Summary—Solid Social Outcomes but Challenges Remain

Perak's citizens have benefited from rapidly rising incomes, with those in the median income household nearly four times as well off in real terms in 2019 as they had been 30 years earlier. The incomes of all communities have grown, although to a lesser extent for Indians than for Chinese and Malays. Median incomes are lower for households that are large and/or where the head has low educational attainment. Conversely, they are highest for the most educated, and for those living and working in Kinta district. Despite income gains, relative poverty is still higher in Perak than in Malaysia as a whole.

Perak's public policy has therefore been largely successful in helping to achieve a high degree of social equity, with incomes more evenly distributed than in Malaysia as a whole, and with incomes of the poorest percentiles growing fastest, and those of the richest percentiles increasing far less than the median. It has been less successful, however, in stemming the continuing outward migration of its 'best and brightest'. One factor in this outward migration is that in 2022 Perak's median household income was the third lowest of all states—slightly above that of Kedah and Kelantan, but just 45 per cent the level of Selangor which attracts many of Perak's migrants. And Perak has the largest number of households in the bottom 40 income group, comprising some 59 per cent of the state's total households.

Demographic Change, 1957–2020

This section reviews how more than half a century of outward migration has markedly changed Perak's ethnic composition, with Malays becoming an ever-increasing majority. Concurrently, Perak's growing population has become more urbanized. Within the state, the population has become much more concentrated in and around the Kinta Valley—its manufacturing and services hub.

Slowing Outward Migration from Perak, 1991–2020

Perak's net inter-state outward migration continued during the 1990s and the first two decades of the new millennium, although more slowly than in the 1970s and 1980s (Table 3.18). In the most recent period, 2014–2020, the state's net migration rate was just 1.1 per cent, compared with 1.6 per cent between 2005 and 2010, and 2.6 per cent between 1995 and 2000.

Table 3.18	Perak's steep net inter-state outward migration rates have slowed sharply			
Period	Perak	Johor	Penang	Klang Valley
	Net migration rate (% of population)			
1975–1980	−4.1	−0.5	0.1	5.8
1986–1991	−3.8	0.9	0.2	3.3
1995–2000	−2.6	0.7	1.1	2.7
2005–2010	−1.6	−1.6	0.4	2.2
2014–2020	−1.1	0.9	1.3	−0.4

Sources of data: For 1975 to 2010, Khoo (1983); Khoo (1995a, 1995b, 1995c, 1995e, and 1995f); Shaari Abdul Rahman (2004); Abdul Rahman Hasan (2014); for 2014 to 2020, Department of Statistics–Malaysia (various years), *Migration Survey Reports*.

Note: The Migration Survey was not conducted in 2017 and 2019.

Globalization: Perak's Rise, Relative Decline, and Regeneration. Sultan Nazrin Shah, Oxford University Press. © Sultan Nazrin Shah (2024).
DOI: 10.1093/oso/9780198897774.003.0026

In 2020, an estimated 731,500 Perakians were residing elsewhere in Malaysia—down from 881,200 in 2010—and more than half of these inter-state lifetime migrants were Malays and other *Bumiputera* (Figure 3.33). Some 58 per cent of all Perak's inter-state lifetime migrants live in the Klang Valley.

Although the Klang Valley has continued to attract substantial domestic and foreign investment, its GDP per capita and employment growth have slowed in the second decade of the 21st century. These trends, coupled with the higher cost of living, especially for accommodation, have somewhat diminished its previously strong pull factors for potential migrants. In fact, in the period 2014–2020, for the first time there was a small net out-migration from the Klang Valley, especially from Kuala Lumpur (Table 3.18).

Perak's post-independence net migration has been both inter-state and international. Malaysia's diaspora has grown from a negligible number in 1957 to well above 1.6 million at present. The majority are skilled and highly skilled Chinese Malaysians living and working abroad, mainly in Singapore, Australia, the US, and the UK. Although it is not possible to identify diaspora numbers according to their state of birth with complete accuracy, very rough estimates

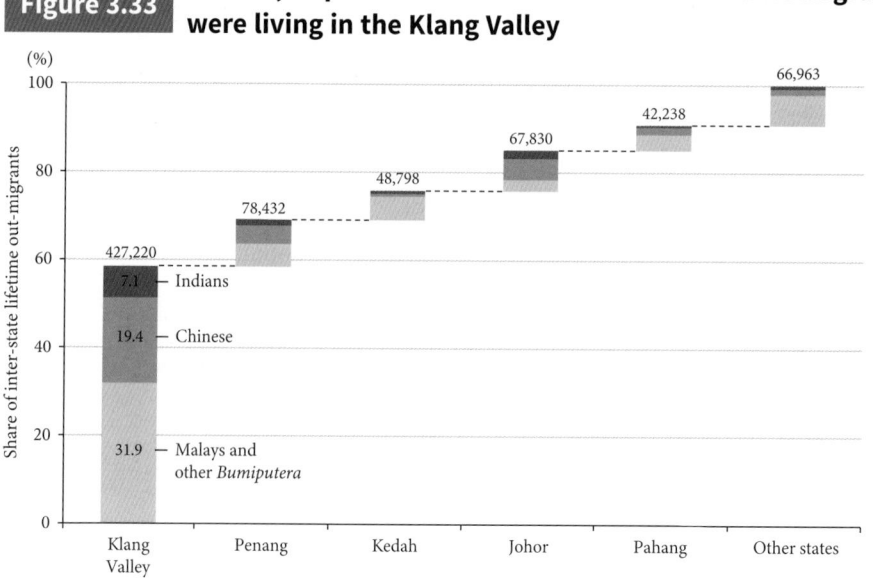

Figure 3.33   **In 2020, 58 per cent of Perak's inter-state lifetime migrants were living in the Klang Valley**

Source of data: Unpublished preliminary data from Malaysia's 2020 population census supplied by the Department of Statistics—Malaysia.

for Perak's Chinese and Indian communities can be made.[112] An estimated half a million Chinese Perakians—about double the number of inter-state lifetime outward migrants from this community—and some 100,000 Indians emigrated abroad after 1970 and were still living abroad in 2010.

The Negative Economic Impacts of Perak's Outward Migration

Perak's population outflows have acted as a break on its development and constitute a key challenge facing its regeneration (Part 4). The cumulative impact of net inter-state and international outward migration over more than six decades has hurt Perak economically and socially. The huge population outflows, including of some of the most educated and skilled—many seeking to pursue their tertiary education in other states or abroad—have undoubtedly weakened the state's human capital base and reservoir of entrepreneurial talent, even as they contribute to economic development in receiving areas.

These outflows have also caused a loss of vitality in townships and weakened traditional family support systems. They have been responsible for Perak's relatively low population growth rate, its lower share in Malaysia's population, its changed ethnic composition, and its rapid population ageing. By 2020, the median age was 31.0 years, up from 25.1 in 2000 and 18.0 in 1957—although increased life expectancy at birth has also been a key factor in this change.

---

112 An estimate of the number of Perak's Chinese-born people who have emigrated and were still living abroad in 2010 was obtained as follows. It was assumed that in a closed population, with no state differences in Chinese fertility and mortality, Perak's 1970 share (0.212) of the total number of Chinese (5,340,000) living in Peninsular Malaysia in 2010 would be the same (this also assumes zero net inter-state lifetime migration). The resulting expected figure of 1,132,000 excludes Chinese among Malaysia's 1,607,000 diaspora. Assuming, on a fairly arbitrary basis, that two-thirds of the Malaysian diaspora are Chinese gives an adjusted total amount of Chinese in 2010 of 6,400,000. Applying Perak's 1970 share to this adjusted figure gives the expected number of Chinese living in Perak in 2010 as 1,357,000. The number in Perak in 2010 was 596,000, and there were 258,000 Perakian lifetime migrants living in other states; subtracting the total observed (854,000) from that expected (1,357,000) gives an estimate of 503,000. This method could not be used for Malays because their population share in Perak in 2010 was greater than in 1970.

Halving of Perak's National Population Share and a Changed Ethnic Composition

Perak's demographic configuration has changed dramatically since independence. Its population more than doubled, from 1.2 million in 1957 to 2.5 million in 2020, despite continuing high levels of net outward migration. However, during this period, the state's share of Malaysia's population fell by more than half, from 16.3 per cent—when it was the country's most populous state—to just 7.7 per cent. In each decade from 1957 to 2020, Perak consistently registered the slowest average annual population growth among all states. Its average growth rate over the 63-year period, at 1.13 per cent, was half the 2.33 per cent registered for Malaysia as a whole, mainly reflecting the legacy of its high levels of outward migration. At independence more people were living in Perak than in the Klang Valley, but by 2020 the state's population had fallen to just 30 per cent of the latter's (Figure 3.34).

Figure 3.34   **Perak's share in Malaysia's population has fallen by half in six decades, reflecting its much slower population growth largely due to outward migration**

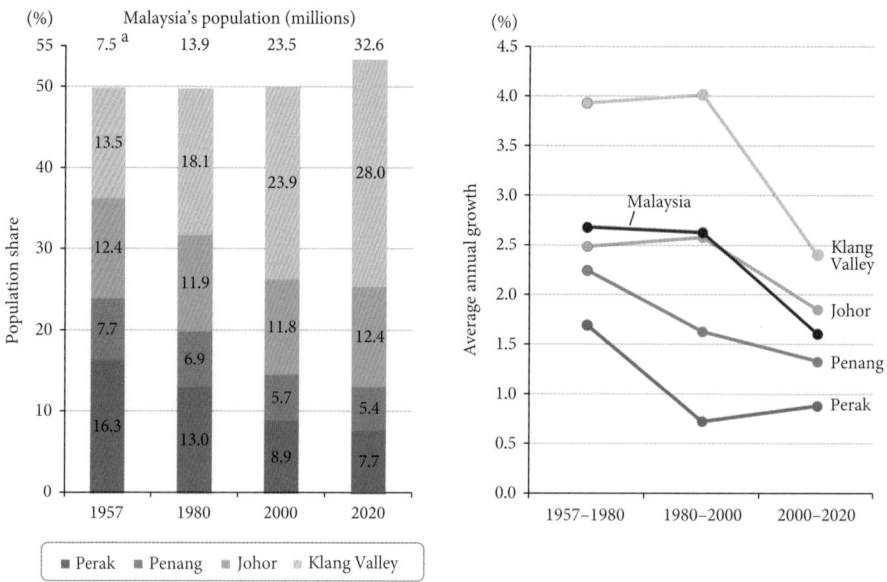

Sources of data: Fell (1960); Chander (1977); Mohd Uzir Mahidin (2022).

Note: [a] Includes 1960 population of Sabah and Sarawak.

In 1957, Chinese were Perak's largest ethnic community, accounting for 44.2 per cent of its population, with Malays and other *Bumiputera* at 39.7 per cent. By 2020 the Chinese share had declined to 25.7 per cent, while that of Malays and other *Bumiputera* had surged to 57.7 per cent (Figure 3.35, upper

Figure 3.35	Perak's population size and composition have changed radically in six decades

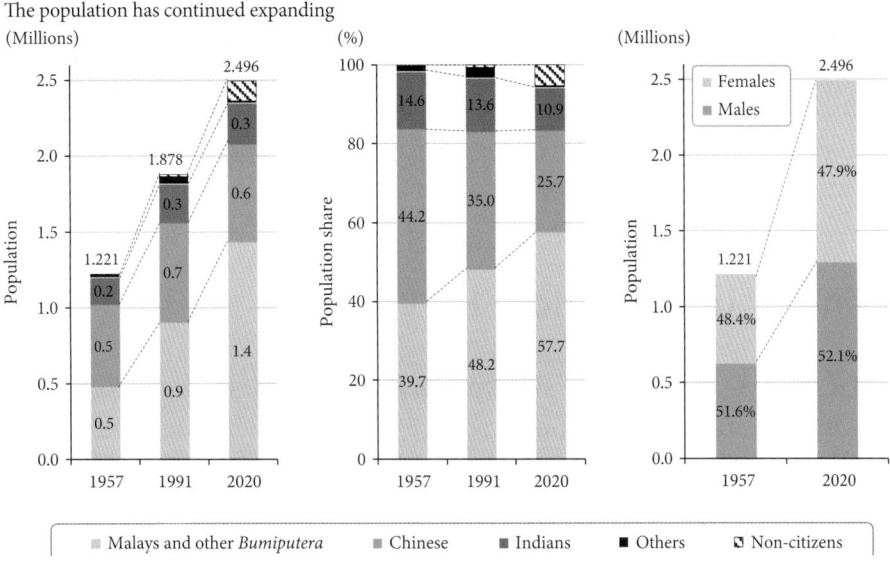

The population has continued expanding

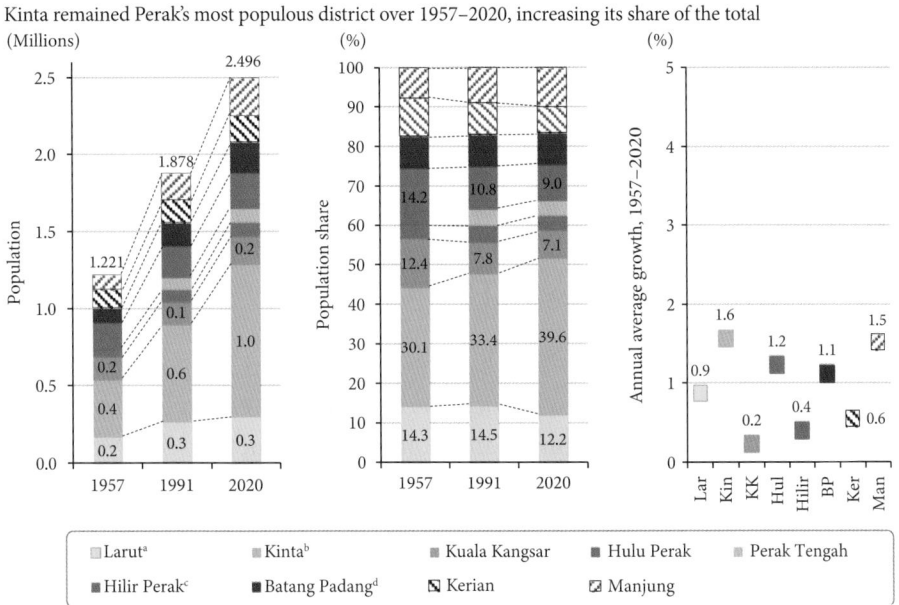

Kinta remained Perak's most populous district over 1957–2020, increasing its share of the total

Sources of data: Fell (1959); Khoo (1995d); Mohd Uzir Mahidin (2022).

Notes: [a] Larut, Matang, and Selama combined.
　　　[b] Kinta includes Kampar.
　　　[c] Hilir Perak includes Bagan Datuk.
　　　[d] Batang Padang includes Muallim.

panel). This sea change in ethnic composition reflects the different rates of outward migration of the various communities and, to a smaller degree, differences in fertility transition by ethnic group.

At the district level, Perak's population has become increasingly concentrated in Kinta, especially in Ipoh city (Figure 3.35, lower panel). By 2020, Kinta's population including Kampar—at 987,500—was 2.7 times what it had been in 1957, and the district's share of the state's population had climbed to 39.6 per cent from 30.1 per cent. Larut, Matang, and Selama district, where Taiping is located, is the state's second-largest. Although its population has grown, its share of Perak's overall population has declined from just over 14 per cent in 1957 to 12.2 per cent in 2020. Manjung is the only other district to have increased its population share, due to the expansion of the maritime and shipping industry in Lumut, and of coastal fishing and tourism in Pangkor.

Continuing Urbanization, 1991 to 2020

With the secular decline in the share of Perak's agricultural labour force, and the rise in the share of jobs in modern services and manufacturing, Perak's population has become largely urbanized.[113] By 2020, some 72 per cent of the state's population were living in urban areas, mainly in Ipoh (a metropolitan city with a mayor) and Taiping, compared with just over half in 1991 (Figure 3.36, left panel). But over the last three decades, some of Perak's urban settlements have at times lost population due to outward migration, precipitated by the demise of tin as well as by their own failure to attract new industries and jobs—Taiping and Kampar both saw depopulation in some years.

All of Perak's communities have become more urbanized, and Malays and other *Bumiputera*—whose share of the urban population at the beginning of the 21st century was lower than that of Chinese—were in 2020 by far the most populous urban group, at 49.9 per cent, compared with 31.8 per cent for Chinese (Figure 3.36, right panel).

The state's urban population has benefited both from broader economic opportunities and from improved services, as reflected, for example, in substantial gains in life expectancy at birth, and continuing reductions in infant and child mortality rates, with gaps between the main ethnic communities also having almost disappeared (Figure 3.37).

---

113 Urbanization also reflected the redefinition of former suburban and built-up areas as urban, where the bulk of the population is engaged in non-agricultural activities.

Figure 3.36

By 2020, 72 per cent of Perak's population were urbanized, and Malays and other *Bumiputera* were the biggest urban population group

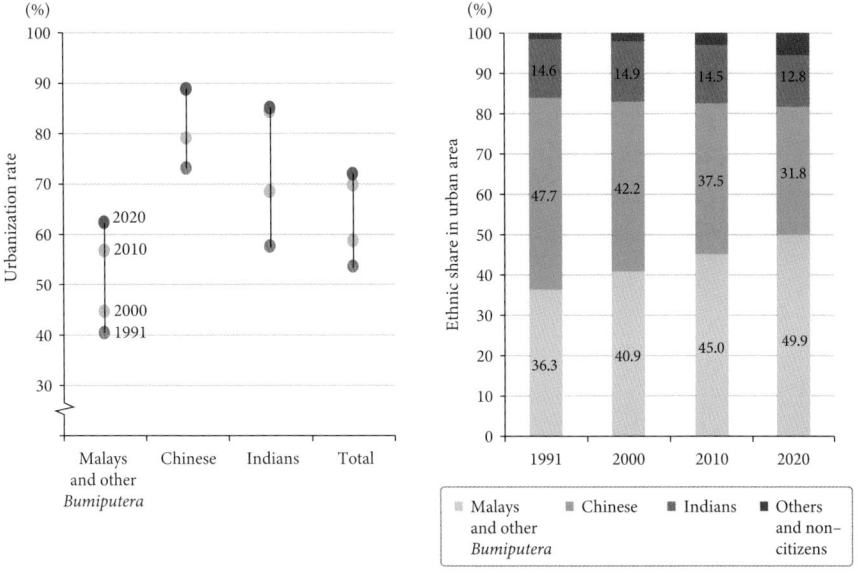

Sources of data: Khoo (1995a); Shaari Abdul Rahman (2001); Wan Ramlah (2011); Mohd Uzir Mahidin (2022).

Figure 3.37

Life expectancy at birth in Perak has climbed as under-5 mortality has plunged, but with annual fluctuations

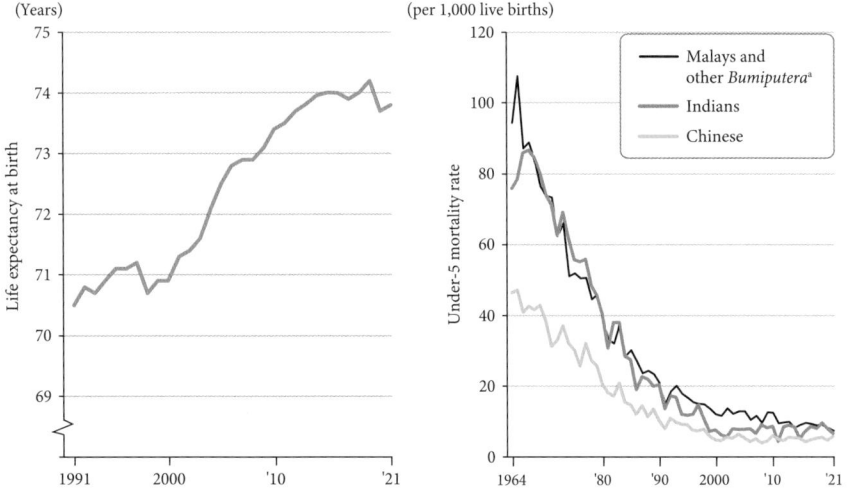

Source of data: Department of Statistics–Malaysia, unpublished data.

Note: [a] 1964 to 1990 refers to Malays only.

Summary—Perak's Major Demographic Changes

Perak's demography has experienced huge changes since independence, with outward migration markedly affecting its population growth, cutting the state's share of Malaysia's population by half to just 7.7 per cent. Outward migration—disproportionately of Chinese—has also changed the state's ethnic composition, with Malays becoming an ever-increasing majority. And as employment patterns have shifted from agriculture, the rural population has fallen steeply, with most Perakians now living in urban areas.

Reflections on Six Decades of Progress

Perak has changed fundamentally in the six decades since 1957, when tin and rubber defined the contours of its economy, its population, and its society. By the early 1990s, these two industries—on whose revenues the modern state was built—were fading into insignificance. The state has had to diversify its economy, first within agriculture to oil palm, and later into manufacturing and services. But as a late mover to manufacturing, Perak was at a disadvantage from which it has been unable to recover.

By the early 21st century, Perak had become further entrenched in the increasingly globalized trading system through its export of agricultural and manufactured goods, its income from tradeable services, such as tourism and education, its dependence on FDI, and its heavy reliance on a growing, lesser-skilled labour force of foreign migrants. These shifts have brought benefits in the form of export earnings, jobs, higher incomes, and the spread of ideas; but there have also been costs, including greater vulnerability to the spillover effects of downturns in international trade, travel, and investment. To mitigate these risks, Perak will have to continue to move up the value chain and broaden and deepen its diversification efforts. It will also need to attract high-quality investment, find new product lines, and build the human capital required for jobs in higher-value-added industries—including by stemming the outward migration of its higher-skilled individuals.

By the start of 2020, Perak's socio-economic profile had been transformed from that at independence. Its economy had become much more prosperous, productive, and diversified. All of its communities were more urbanized, had far higher real incomes, and were living healthier and longer lives than their parents. Although some small remnants of ethnic and economic segmentation persist, incomes within the state are distributed more evenly; absolute poverty, though not yet eradicated, is low; and quality of life indicators have improved markedly. These are considerable accomplishments.

Globalization: Perak's Rise, Relative Decline, and Regeneration. Sultan Nazrin Shah, Oxford University Press. © Sultan Nazrin Shah (2024). DOI: 10.1093/oso/9780198897774.003.0027

Yet despite these undeniable achievements, Perak has continued to lose ground to the neighbouring west-coast states of Selangor and Penang, as well as to Johor and some other states. The forces of agglomeration have exerted a strong influence on investment decisions and firms' location choices, favouring states that moved first, had greater economic density, and possessed better transport links to the outside world. The 'spread effects' from the proximity of these better-performing states to Perak have been comparatively weak, and Perak's economy has yet to benefit perceptibly, even after joining the NCER in 2016. While spatial disparities primarily reflect market forces associated with agglomeration economies and flows of capital, goods, services, and labour, they are also affected by competing political interests. Perak has been out-competed by other states for domestic and foreign investment.

Another major reason for Perak losing ground is the heavy toll of massive net outward migration, both to other Malaysian states and abroad, that has continued—albeit at a gradually slowing pace—over six decades. Perak's Chinese community has accounted for a disproportionately large share of this outward migration. The composition of the population has shifted as the share of Chinese—who had historically contributed much to the state's growth and development—shrank from nearly half to just over a quarter. This brain drain, which includes skilled workers from other communities, has weakened the state's human capital base.

In manufacturing, clusters have emerged in resource-based industries, the electrical and electronics sector, and the automotive industry. However, the growth of these clusters has yet to generate substantial financial returns. There appears to have been a lack of capacity in state economic planning and in its understanding of economic development needs, as well as weak coordination of investment promotion, and shortfalls in federal budget allocations. All these interrelated factors have held back Perak's development. It has, though, become well diversified and remarkably productive within agriculture, including in vegetable and fruit farming, duck farming, and ornamental fishes.

Perak's economy, now much less reliant on the primary sector, has become increasingly dependent on services. By 2020 that sector employed nearly two-thirds of the state's labour force. Many of these jobs were created in the wake of the NEP's affirmative action programmes, which continued into the 21st century. In the private sector, a wide range of largely non-traded activities have emerged to meet demand from a growing and now largely urbanized and higher-income population. Perak has also made significant inroads into more lucrative areas, such as tourism, and has considerable scope for further growth of its business and financial services, as well as expansion of the provision of high-quality higher education and technical and vocational training.

The Covid-19 pandemic, which started in early 2020 and continued into 2023, has had a devastating impact on virtually all national economies, and was a major setback to Perak's economic progress and its aspirations for an even better future. With many economic sectors almost unable to function, especially services linked to travel and tourism, business output and household incomes were battered, and unemployment and poverty levels rocketed. Part 4 assesses just how much the pandemic has hindered Perak's development progress, and sets out an ultimately hopeful vision for the state's future.

PART

4

**Towards a *New Vision*
for Perak**

Royal Belum Park, Lake Temenggor

Globalization: Looking Back, and Forward, in a Post–Covid-19 World

The processes that bind together the economic fortunes of far-flung places have a history that stretches back millennia. The Silk Road—a transcontinental artery for the horse- and camel-drawn movement of goods and people, the communication of ideas, and the spread of cultures and religions, extending from the eastern seaboard of ancient China, through Central Asia, to the Levant and on to Europe—dates back more than two thousand years. As Frankopan (2015, p. 12) observes:

> We think of globalisation as a uniquely modern phenomenon; yet 2,000 years ago too, it was a fact of life, one that presented opportunities, created problems and prompted technological advances.

Entering the Globalized World

In the early 19th century, however, globalization acquired a new-found intensity as the commodity-producing countries of what has come to be called the 'Global South' were drawn into the orbit of the rapidly industrializing economies of Europe and North America. By this time the industrial revolution in the UK was well under way, with steam power increasingly being used around the world, allowing goods to be moved between countries—whether by sea in ships or by land in trains—at lower cost and far greater speed than had previously been possible. International trade boomed in the Malay peninsula's trading entrepôts of Penang and Singapore, and to a lesser extent in Melaka. From the late 18th century, these port cities had progressively come under the authority of the British East India Company, which had eclipsed its Dutch counterpart after the latter's finances were drained by the Anglo-Dutch war of 1780–1784. The Company, with its large global network of trading posts and trading systems, connected the Malay peninsula to the rest of

Globalization: Perak's Rise, Relative Decline, and Regeneration. Sultan Nazrin Shah, Oxford University Press. © Sultan Nazrin Shah (2024). DOI: 10.1093/oso/9780198897774.003.0028

the world, while the bulk of global trade between east and west passed through the Strait of Melaka. Perak in this period was already one of the main suppliers of tin ore for re-export from Penang and Melaka, even before its tin industry reached its famed heights from the 1840s onwards.

The industrial revolution, which was now also advancing rapidly in Europe and North America, spurred demand for raw materials, including tin, and Britain's own tin-plate industry continued to grow. At first, the country's demand for tin was met almost wholly by mines in Cornwall, England, the global centre of the tin industry in the first half of the 19th century, but Cornish tin became more difficult and expensive to mine as deposits started to be depleted. The eventual decline of the Cornish industry was sealed by the discovery of an abundance of easily accessible alluvial tin deposits in the valleys and rivers of Larut in the 1840s, and in the Kinta Valley in the 1880s. Having been drawn into the international tin market by these events, Perak's subsequent economic and social trajectory was moulded by external forces, with the wealth of its towns and people rising and falling with the ebb and flow of global tin prices. Perak's ability to produce tin at lower cost ensured that, by the late 19th century, it had supplanted Cornwall as the global centre of tin. By the turn of the 20th century, Perak was producing 25 per cent of the world's output of tin ore.

Not only was Perak a global producer and exporter of tin, it was also the Malay peninsula's centre for the globalization of ideas, technology, and people, first Chinese and then Europeans—a good number of them Cornish—as well as others from across the Malay archipelago. By the late 19th century, the continued influx of migrant labour—mainly from China—alongside increasing European investments and technical expertise, came together to make Perak's tin industry truly global. By the early 20th century, with its successful adoption of the UK's state-of-the-art bucket dredge, Perak was at the forefront of technological advances in tin mining and production, with positive spillover effects on the Malay peninsula's other tin-producing states.

Deeper Integration in the Global Economy

Perak's other key global export was, of course, rubber. The first Model-T Ford motor car rolled off Detroit's production lines in 1908. Rubber tyres—an essential component for these vehicles—created opportunities for the highly profitable cultivation of natural rubber.[1] The first rubber tree in the Malay peninsula

---

1 Petroleum-based synthetic rubber began to appear only after World War I, and only after World War II did it offer real competition to natural rubber.

had been planted in 1877 in Kuala Kangsar, from seedlings brought from Brazil via Kew Gardens near London. Perak's soil, as well as its hydrological and climatic conditions, proved favourable for rubber, and, in the early 20th century, cultivation soared to meet skyrocketing demand for motor vehicle tyres. Perak's rubber industry experienced a similar boom to that which had earlier propelled its tin industry, this time with the help of migrant labour coming mainly from southern India. At the peak of production in the 1930s, Perak and other states of colonial Malaya were producing more than half of the world's natural rubber.

Beyond trade flows, the mining of tin, and the cultivation of rubber, Perak was linked to the global economy in multiple ways. Major investments in rubber and tin were made by British agency houses and financiers, Europeans—French and later Danish—as well as Chinese merchant families and *chettiers*. These groups, with the support of the Malay aristocratic elite, came to exercise control over much of Perak's primary-commodity production. As one of the largest rubber producers in Malaya, Perak's trade and investment links with the rest of the world were boosted by the role of the British agency houses. They provided financial and management services, securing large amounts of capital and resources from international—mainly British—investors for working the rubber—and, much later, oil palm—estates.

Throughout its late-19th and early-20th century tin and rubber booms, Perak's laissez-faire policies and institutions—transplanted from Britain and from other colonies—were tailored to the needs of these far-off investors. Rubber and tin export earnings from Perak, as well as from other parts of Malaya, added substantially to metropolitan sterling reserves. But Perak's dependence on commodity export production and revenues also exposed its economy to the volatility of global commodity markets. During the 'roaring twenties' the good times rolled, but when in 1930 the US and industrial Europe were hit by the Great Depression, Perak and the rest of Malaya suffered economically and socially as rubber and tin prices collapsed. Only in the latter part of the decade, when the global economy began to recover, did economic conditions in Perak start to improve.

Downturn of Perak's Primary-commodity Exports

Perak's primary-commodity-exporting economy was decimated during the four years of Japanese occupation, and only started to rally in the late 1940s. Post-war reconstruction efforts, coordinated from London but mainly financed locally, focused largely on restoring the contours of the pre-war commodity-exporting economy. By the early 1950s, Perak's tin and rubber industries had regained much of the ground that had been lost in the 1930s and 1940s. However, their rehabilitation, and the resulting return to a reliance on tin and rubber revenues, also meant a return of exposure to volatility in global markets. International price stabilization agreements did little to buffer Perak's economy from the ensuing short-run booms and busts in demand and supply, or to protect it from intensified competition as new sources of supply came on stream.

Longer-term structural challenges also loomed. The inexorable depletion of Perak's ore deposits, and rising extraction costs, eroded profits and foreshadowed the tin industry's eventual demise in the 1980s. The rapid diffusion of synthetic rubber substitutes during World War II and their advancing global market share weighed on exports and thus returns from the cultivation of natural rubber.

After Malaya's independence in 1957, investments in Perak's domestic agricultural sector helped to raise productivity and improve rural livelihoods. Oil palm, a more lucrative export crop, with a growing number of diversified uses, increasingly replaced rubber. The benefits to Perak's economy from oil palm cultivation were limited, however, by the presence of large, state-owned plantation entities that channelled most of their profits to the federal government, and there was limited trickle-down effect. Beyond agriculture, Perak was slow to diversify its production base. The state's geography, its legacy of natural resource-intensive activities, and its high cost base were all impediments to rapid industrialization.

Globalization Accelerates ...

As globalization gathered pace in the 1970s, Perak's economy slipped further behind. Although Perak's industries and services were now growing faster than agriculture, they advanced more slowly than in the broader Malaysian economy, with industrial development lagging that in the leading states. Neither tin nor rubber presented viable opportunities for investment in downstream, vertically integrated manufacturing industries at that time. Federal policies were a further impediment. Support for industrialization bypassed Perak (see 'Federalism and a New In-country "Periphery"?', above) and the state was not eligible for the incentives given to investors in the poorest regions of Malaysia. Federal investments in new export-processing zones, industrial parks, and ports, were largely concentrated in Penang, the Klang Valley, and Johor.

The character of Perak's industrialization was also different from the broader Malaysian economy. Investments were focused more on industries serving the local and domestic Malaysian market, and less on export-led manufacturing. At the start of the 20th century, Perak's relative affluence had attracted workers from other parts of Malaya, but during the second half of that century as incomes fell further behind those in Selangor and Penang, many of its young workers left to seek more attractive opportunities elsewhere. In addition, many of Perak's students left the state to continue their education, and chose not to return upon completion of their studies.

From 1990 into the 21st century, globalization moved at high speed, with the rise of containerization and fast-falling shipping costs; a revolution in digital communications; cuts in tariffs and non-tariff barriers to trade; market reforms in China, India, Russia, Eastern Europe, and Latin America; and deeper international financial integration and interconnectedness spurring burgeoning trade and international capital movements. Manufacturing supply chains increasingly encircled the globe as firms sought lower-cost locations. These trends amplified the advantages of areas with high economic density and good transport and industrial infrastructure (World Bank, 2009).

Globalization played to the advantages of the booming metropolitan areas of Penang, Selangor, and Johor—locations with ports and where agglomeration economies could be most readily leveraged. Perak was largely powerless in the face of these dynamics. The state authorities had limited powers and resources, as well as few levers that they could deploy to invigorate the economy, while federal industrial and investment policies did not work in Perak's favour. Having depended on the tin and rubber industries for longer than most other states, Perak was now losing out, and was falling behind those states that were successfully exploiting the opportunities created by the offshoring revolution in manufacturing industries.

... Only to Stall

Even for those states or countries that were benefiting more from it, globalization was not a one-way bet. With the onset of the 2008–2009 global financial crisis, globalization stalled. Global trade did pick up when economic growth eventually resumed, but global integration on other fronts has been advancing much more slowly than before. For example, intermediate goods imports as a share of global GDP—an indicator of the reach of global supply chains—began to fall as a share of total trade, and FDI flows, which amounted to 3.5 per cent of global GDP in 2007, dropped to just 1.3 per cent in 2018. Likewise, gross cross-border capital flows, which had peaked at 7 per cent of global GDP in 2007, had shrunk to 1.5 per cent a decade later (*The Economist*, 2019a).

A year before the start of the Covid-19 pandemic, *The Economist* (2019b) issued a warning about the 'slowbalization' of the global economy—a slowdown in global trade, FDI, and the profits of multinational companies.[2] A widening trade dispute between the US and China, a continuing structural shift towards services, and pressures in many countries to reshore jobs (returning production processes back to where they originated) and 'buy local', slowed the pace of integration. Some analysts even speculated about a retreat from globalization, suggesting that countries would increasingly attempt to insulate themselves from dependence on external trade and investment.

Many factors contributed to slowing globalization following the global financial crisis: trade tariffs were increased, transport costs for goods were no longer falling, and the continued expansion of automated manufacturing processes was blunting the advantages of relocating to take advantage of cheap labour. Economic returns to FDI fell, from 8.1 per cent in 2012 to 4.8 per cent in 2020 (UNCTAD, 2021). New risks also surfaced as offshore economic activities contended with shifting regulatory regimes. Sharp cuts in corporate taxes in the US encouraged capital to move back home (or, if already in the country, to stay there), and opportunities for cross-border cost arbitrage narrowed as global labour costs per unit of output started to converge, and as tax harmonization efforts gathered pace. In June 2021, the G7 group of the world's largest industrialized economies agreed to harmonize corporate taxation, setting a global minimum tax (GMT) of 15 per cent on large corporations, levied based on where these corporations do business rather than where they choose to report their profits.[3] By October 2021, some 135 countries, including Malaysia, had signed up to implement the GMT, which will reduce the scope for using competitive tax rates as a means to attract FDI.

More generally, capitalism, free markets, and free trade also had to face serious questions of legitimacy, including about fairness and the inequality they bring. Crucially, the benefits of globalization have been unequally distributed between and within countries, with many localities and their people left behind despite dramatic reductions in *absolute* poverty. The Scottish economist Adam Smith, in his seminal late-18th-century work *The Wealth of Nations*, rightly observed that the higher the degree of specialization of labour, the higher the labour productivity, which is what determines a society's potential income, and therefore ultimately its wealth. Whereas specialization through the division of labour was

---

2 The term 'slowbalization' was coined by Bakas (2016) and popularized by *The Economist* (2019b).

3 In Malaysia, corporation tax is levied at 24 per cent for resident and non-resident corporations, above the G7 agreed global minimum rate.

previously limited by the extent of the market, globalization has greatly expanded the extent of these markets, and can therefore raise labour productivity and the average standard of living—for those countries able to exploit it.

Unfortunately, in a relatively free-market capitalist economy, the gains in economic wealth have not been distributed equally within and between societies. And although more than a billion individuals have been lifted out of absolute poverty, especially in China, millions of others have gone on to become millionaires, and thousands even billionaires. The resulting inequality is straining economic, social, and geopolitical ties.

Disparities in the distribution of the gains from globalization have galvanized political constituencies advocating for domestic economic protection. There has also been pushback on trade liberalization efforts. This has been seen in the US withdrawal from the Trans-Pacific Partnership; in the increased use of heightened tariffs to protect domestic jobs—US tariffs on imports from China rising sixfold in 2019, for example; and in the prevention by the US government of Huawei, a Chinese digital technology provider, from building 5G data networks, as this was perceived to pose security risks (Roberts and Lamp, 2021). Multinational firms are increasingly diversifying their investments in new factories and production away from China, with Viet Nam and Indonesia becoming Asia's major beneficiaries.

Trade is also increasingly being used to exert political pressures in geopolitical relations, as seen, for example, in China's banning of certain imports from Australia after the latter called for an investigation into the origins of Covid-19. And with weakening international political support for its free trade mandate, the legitimacy and coordinating functions of the WTO have been damaged, and its authority to adjudicate trade disputes has diminished.

As globalization has slowed—and some commentators would even argue that it is starting to reverse—trading arrangements among regional groups of countries have deepened. North America, Europe, and Asia have all expanded their own regulations and rules governing trade and investment (*The Economist*, 2019b). Alternative and competing regional technology platforms are also emerging. For example, China was developing its own 5G and other technological platforms even before Huawei was banned from acquiring US technology (Fujita and Hamaguchi, 2020). A multipolar and more fractured world thus seems to be emerging, characterized by a collapse, or at least a significant diminishment, of international cooperation. The world may even be heading towards a new 'geopolitical cold war'. There are likely to be no winners in such a scenario. It would make it much more difficult to take the drastic and coordinated actions that are needed for combating climate change, and for achieving net zero by 2050.

Impact of Covid-19 and the Russia–Ukraine War on Globalization

The Covid-19 pandemic added further uncertainties. Population movements have always served as an accelerant of disease transmission, but in today's world, with hundreds of millions living in densely populated cities and criss-crossing the globe, Covid-19 spread extremely quickly, infecting virtually every corner of the world. During its initial spread in 2020, the pandemic devastated the global economy, harming the health and well-being of communities in almost all nations—see Box 4.1 for its impact on Perak. As epicentres of the disease, cities became like ghost towns, shadows of their former vibrant selves. Many national borders were sealed, and countries became focused primarily on ensuring the survival of their own people. The pandemic severely disrupted global manufacturing supply chains, and halted face-to-face service industries, including international travel, hospitality, and tourism. This caused widespread economic damage as containment measures upended the familiar world of work and trade. Governments had to spend huge sums to mitigate the effects of the virus, and the essential need to prioritize health over the economy had manifold consequences. The pandemic also widened the income gap between the rich and poor.

According to the IMF (2023), the world economy contracted by 2.8 per cent in 2020, and global trade volume fell by 7.8 per cent.[4] Although the economic impact of Covid-19 was severe everywhere, it was those nations that invested heavily in vaccination programmes, and those that introduced strong fiscal support for flagging demand, that recovered faster.[5]

---

4 As of 12 September 2022, 605.9 million people had been infected with Covid-19 worldwide with 6.5 million deaths (WHO, 2022).

5 By comparison, the 1918 Spanish influenza infected about one-third of the world's population and possibly caused more than 50 million deaths. There are few estimates of its economic impact, but Barro et al. (2020) estimate that the disease cut real GDP per capita by 6 per cent, and consumption by 8 per cent, in affected countries—an economic shock roughly equivalent to that experienced during the Great Depression. However, the world of 1918 is not a particularly useful guide to the present. Back then, agriculture was still a major economic activity even in industrial economies, and the world was much less interconnected. More recent pandemic threats, including SARS, MERS, and avian flu, left no major impression on the global economy, but their rate of transmission and disease burden were tiny compared to Covid-19.

| Box 4.1 | **Devastating economic and social impact of the Covid-19 pandemic in Perak** |

With the outbreak of the Covid-19 pandemic in early 2020, the Malaysian government—like most others around the world, albeit to varying degrees—imposed measures that prioritized public health and suspended large parts of the market economy. In March 2020 it imposed an unprecedented nationwide full lockdown on the country's population: all businesses, except a few essential services, were temporarily shut. International and interstate travel was banned. Although restrictions were subsequently relaxed, a partial lockdown remained in force, with the reimposition of further controls from end-May 2021 as new virus variants emerged. The lockdowns continued until well into the second half of 2021, by which time the bulk of the population had been vaccinated.

The pandemic restrictions had severe economic and human impacts despite mitigation measures.[a] Many businesses were badly hurt, jobs were permanently lost, and assets were destroyed. Vulnerable groups, such as smaller businesses and lower-income workers, were the worst affected, widening existing socio-economic inequalities. Overall, Malaysia's economy contracted by 5.5 per cent in 2020—much the same as Singapore's 5.8 per cent, but less severe than Thailand's 7.0 per cent. It recovered to grow modestly by 3.1 per cent in 2021 (BNM, 2021).

At the start of the pandemic in 2020, 56.8 per cent of Perak's labour force was engaged in private-sector services. This was the most vulnerable sector, and experienced huge losses of jobs and income. In 2020 and 2021 the state's unemployment rate was the worst in over two decades, eclipsing even that seen in the 1997–1999 Asian financial crisis. The retail sector was badly hit as consumer confidence plummeted and shoppers reined in their spending.

Perak's GDP had been growing steadily in the years immediately preceding the pandemic, but with its tourism sector particulary badly affected by restrictions, GDP declined by 2.4 per cent in 2020, and per capita income by 2.3 per cent (Department of Statistics–Malaysia, 2022). Perak contracted less than the wider Malaysian

[a] The impact on mortality of the Covid-19 pandemic in Perak and in Malaysia as a whole pales in comparison to the highly infectious Spanish influenza of 1918, when healthcare services were rudimentary. Urgent diplomatic telegram dispatches were sent between colonial leaders to prepare for what was described as a malady that 'is infectious in the highest degree and produces extreme prostration with an appalling death rate' (Malaysia Archive Documents, 1918). More than 10,000 people in Perak died during that pandemic and an estimated 40,000 in British Malaya. The death rate was much higher among Indians than other communities because of the crowded and insanitary living conditions on rubber estates (Nathan, 1922).

(Continued)

economy, however, as its manufacturing sector, helped by a robust performance in rubber products, grew at 3.5 per cent and its agricultural sector by 1.0 per cent. Still, by end-2021 the state's economy had made only a modest recovery and average household incomes remained below pre-pandemic levels.

Tourism and related industries

As it has become a popular tourist destination, a large segment of Perak's labour force is involved in tourism and related activities, including hotels, retail, and restaurants, tour guiding, recreation, and arts. Perak received 10.1 million tourists from other states in 2019. While an even higher number was expected in 2020, however, the actual figure more than halved, to just 4.9 million, with even fewer arrivals in 2021 (Department of Statistics–Malaysia, 2020c and 2022). With the national border sealed and most flights cancelled globally, there were virtually no international tourist arrivals. Domestic tourism was also severely limited by the prolonged bans on inter-state travel, as well as by risk aversion among domestic travellers. Some of Perak's established hotels, smaller motels, home stays, and related tourist businesses had to close permanently as their income streams and funds dried up and planned investments were cancelled. Many workers were laid off or put on reduced working hours.

Manufacturing

Perak's manufacturing sector was affected in various ways. First, under the nationwide lockdown from mid-March 2020, the impact of the suspension of non-essential production was felt particularly by SMEs. Second, global manufacturing supply chains were fractured by the closure of national borders, which disrupted the flows of both raw materials and finished goods. Third, the pandemic-induced global recession curtailed demand for Perak's manufactured products. The Silverstone tyre plant in Kamunting, in operation since 1986, permanently ceased activity in 2021. There were some industries that bucked this trend to an extent. For instance, due to higher global demand in response to the pandemic, the rubber glove industry in Ipoh and Kamunting saw an upturn in investment and job creation. Still, the rubber glove factories were not spared production losses due to the occasional Covid-19 outbreak among their workers. Fourth, the national lockdown restricted inflows of migrant workers into Malaysia, leading to labour shortages and project delays in manufacturing and other sectors (Lim, 2020). Like other countries that draw heavily on migrant labour, including neighbouring Singapore, Malaysia has since been re-evaluating its migration policies.

Unemployment

Before the pandemic, official unemployment in Perak was relatively stable, averaging 3.3 per cent from 2010 to 2019 (Table 4a). It then soared to 5.3 per cent in 2021, even exceeding the high levels seen during the Asian financial crisis (4.3 per cent in 1999). Young, casual, and low-skilled workers were disproportionately affected, especially women, including those employed in private-sector services, as well as recent graduates. Youth unemployment rose to 12.6 per cent in 2021, from 11.0 per cent in 2019.

The surge in unemployment exacerbated both absolute poverty and income inequalities, especially among the most vulnerable groups in urban areas—such as single-parent, female-headed households—and in rural areas, in particular the *Orang Asli*. Even those who kept their jobs were affected by myriad cost-cutting measures, including forced unpaid leave, reduced working hours, and the loss of allowances and benefits. Perak's poverty rate shot back up, having fallen substantially in the first two decades of the century, and life expectancy at birth tumbled (Figure 3.37 above).

Table 4a	Perak's unemployment jumped during the pandemic, and was especially high among youth					
	2010	2015	2018	2019	2020	2021
	Unemployment rate (%)					
All ages (15–64)	3.0	3.2	3.3	3.4	4.8	5.3
Youth (15–24)	10.4	10.9	11.0	11.0	12.4	12.6

Source of data: Department of Statistics–Malaysia (various years), *Labour Force Survey Report.*

Supporting recovery

With recovering external demand, Malaysia's economy grew modestly in 2021, but growth was limited by the continued reimposition of partial and full lockdown measures and travel restrictions (World Bank, 2021). The federal government and the central bank introduced several economic stimulus packages to support businesses and protect the welfare of those on low (or no) incomes. In 2020, the Perak state government announced its highest-ever state budget deficit—of RM154 million for 2021, or about 13 per cent of the total budget—to help support economic recovery. This includes an allocation of RM71.3 million—7 per cent of the total budget—for measures to improve the social security of those most affected by Covid-19 (Saarani Mohamad, 2020).

Although there was a sharp rebound in global economic growth to 6.3 per cent in 2021, the IMF (2023) had forecast that it would slow again to 3.4 per cent in 2022, and would be even lower at 2.8 per cent in 2023, due to both the direct impact and the global spillover of the Russia–Ukraine war. Russia's February

2022 invasion of neighbouring Ukraine shattered expectations of a fast recovery of the global economy from the pandemic's damaging impact. Three overlapping crises were thus disrupting global supply chains—the pandemic, the Russia–Ukraine war, and a food crisis. Existing bottlenecks were exacerbated during the Russia–Ukraine war by food and energy supply shocks which caused price inflation to surge. Inflation rates rose to levels not seen for over 40 years.

While the overlapping crises cemented international cooperation in some areas,[6] the world has since become more fragmented geopolitically, with emerging divisions in international financial and technological standards, such as payment systems and reserve currencies. Countries have sought to mitigate their risks and exposure to crises by reducing their supply chain concentration and moving further towards 'friend-shoring' and 'near-shoring'—even at the expense of efficiency—as well as towards vertical integration (Lagarde, 2022).[7] Against this backdrop of geopolitical tensions, the US and some other developed economies are limiting exports of biotechnology software and diversifying their supply chains for advanced semiconductors (*The Economist*, 2022).

Although global supply chains have gradually recovered, albeit with some serious dislocations, the growing focus by individual countries on building national resilience, including through developing their own manufacturing capacity, appears to have quickened existing trends towards shorter and less complex supply chains and reshoring. Through this route, the crises may have accelerated the deindustrialization already under way in some middle-income countries, including Malaysia, while elevating the barriers to continued industrialization elsewhere, for instance in India. Conversely, if companies seek to build resilience through diversification away from single-source supply chains, as well as by bringing points of production closer to points of consumption, this could provide new globally distributed opportunities for manufacturing investment.

The pandemic triggered forces that, while reversing economic integration in some areas, simultaneously expanded opportunities in others. Sachs, in conversation with McElvoy (2020) and Krugman (2020) argued that, rather than

---

6 Strengthened international cooperation can be seen in the provision of emergency financial assistance by the IMF and the World Bank to help low- and middle-income economies, including through debt service relief grants, with debt service payments suspended for eligible countries (IMF, 2021). There was also extensive international collaboration to obtain a vaccine for Covid-19 prevention through the Global Access Facility (Covax).

7 Friend-shoring refers to trade and production among a circle of allies. Near-shoring refers to trade and production with nearby countries.

spelling the end of globalization, the pandemic made the case for it, based on the need for global policy cooperation.[8] While the pandemic was a serious setback to globalization, it did not signal a fundamental collapse of market integration but more a realignment or a reset—a tendency reinforced by the Russia–Ukraine war.

Nevertheless, de-globalization has become a possible economic scenario as powerful countries move towards regionalism. O'Neil (2022) contends that it was regionalism, and not globalization, that fuelled the rise in economic gains over the past 40 years. Arguably, and despite economic interdependence, it is the heightened competition for regional dominance by the world's leading powers that has put global governance under stress.[9] Fiscal support for economic recovery in the world's major economies has concentrated on subsidizing and protecting domestic economic interests. The days when everyone seemed to be working for a world without borders are past; 'suddenly, everyone recognizes that at least some national borders are key to economic development and security' (Stiglitz, 2022, p. 1).

One area where the pandemic greatly spurred activity is in the provision of digitally based services, including e-commerce platforms, especially in retail. It promoted an acceleration in the digital delivery of services as well as in trends in remote working using digital tools, demonstrating its feasibility, productive potential, and efficiency. In the future, it may matter little whether an employee is telecommuting from the suburbs, the next town or county, or from another continent. This suggests the possibility of expanded opportunities for those who can choose or are able to work digitally in distant, lower-cost locations— so-called digital nomads—provided the necessary legal and regulatory infrastructure is in place and there are no significant language barriers.

At the same time, there are also forces promoting greater localization, which stem in part from advanced production techniques—including robotics and 3D printing—that may encourage the reshoring of some labour-intensive manufacturing processes (Stiglitz, 2020). Hence, while the pandemic raised opportunities for higher-skilled workers for whom telecommuting is possible, it has left lower-skilled workers much more vulnerable to job losses. This exacerbates already heightened social and economic inequalities, including among foreign

---

8 According to the Chief Executive Officer of DHL Express, the pandemic saw sizeable growth in cross-border e-commerce, and companies with global outreach were doing much better than those with only national or regional focus (Pearson, 2020).

9 Zakaria (2020, p. 172) argues that multiple de-globalizing factors came together to 'reverse the free flow of goods, services, money and people that has transformed the world in these last four decades'.

migrants. The full and partial lockdowns, physical distancing, and widespread isolation, had profound impacts on social life, and exacerbated mental health issues for people of all ages. These restrictions had a substantial impact on young people's well-being in particular, hugely setting back the education of school and college cohorts (Box 4.2).

There is broad agreement among academics and policymakers that for nations to become more economically resilient and fairer, the way in which institutions support people needs to be rethought, as do the values placed by markets on what really matters, such as public health services and safety nets for the vulnerable. Piketty (2020a), for example, believes that governments and citizens will now be prompted to re-evaluate the importance of a well-re-sourced and efficient welfare state along the lines set out in his *Capital and Ideology* (2020b).[10] Zakaria (2020) argues similarly that the impact of the pandemic will open up a pathway to a 'new world', entailing a transition away from neoliberal free-market capitalism. He maintains that governments must now play a more interventionist role in the economy—something that has already been happening in some countries. He foresees a world in which the provision of public services and social protection are valued as investments rather than as spending, and where income and wealth taxes are structured to promote income redistribution, as occurs in Denmark and other Nordic countries.

Post-crisis Perak

Despite numerous plans and interventions, spatial development in Malaysia remains highly uneven, and Perak, along with some other states, has not partic-ipated fully in the broader national economic advances that have taken place since independence. The country has no comprehensive blueprint for 'levelling up' spatial development. There are examples, however, of how this has been achieved in other places, such as in Sheffield, in south Yorkshire, northern Eng-land, in the 1990s, where the devolution of authority and resources allowed

---

10 Piketty (2020b) highlights the profound impacts on economic organization of major historical turbulence, such as the two World Wars— in particular, the creation of the welfare state after World War II, which led to reduced inequality. In the wake of the Covid-19 pandemic, he foresees an eventual reorganization of the global economy leading to more equitable societies, financed through more progressive tax regimes on income and wealth, equal access to higher education, and a special tax on billionaires.

| Box 4.2 | Impact of Covid-19 on children's well-being in low-income urban Malaysian families |

Lacking adequate social protection, and with little or no savings, many low-income Malaysian households struggled desperately during the series of full and partial lockdowns, despite some minimal government financial relief and other welfare programmes. A series of surveys carried out by UNICEF and UNFPA between May 2020 and March 2021 on families living in 16 public housing estates in Kuala Lumpur revealed that the lockdowns had severe consequences on children's well-being, education, and mental health, especially in low-income, single-parent, female-headed households (UNICEF and UNFPA, 2020a, 2020b, and 2021). And among children who caught Covid-19, some also suffered post-traumatic stress, the symptoms of which included impaired memory, and attentive and dissociative problems (UNDP, 2021).

Limited income affected the ability of parents to provide a nutritionally balanced diet for their children, which includes fresh vegetables, fruit, and milk. Fresh fish and meat were often replaced with canned sardines and eggs, the consumption of which rose by more than 50 per cent. School closures meant that children could also no longer access free school meal programmes.

School closures during lockdowns led to more online teaching. Most children from low-income households, however, had no access to personal computers or tablets for online learning, and had to rely on their parents' mobile phones. In many households, these had to be shared among multiple siblings, with parents unable to supervise their studying. Further, connectivity to the Internet was often slow and unstable, especially for those living in rural areas. When children were allowed to go back to school, during periods of only partial lockdown, parents reported that their children had diminished interest in schooling, and some 7 per cent failed to return when schools reopened.

As in many countries, children in Malaysia were deprived of social interaction and physical exercise. Households reported greater feelings of depression among children and other mental health problems, as well as negative behavioural changes such as tension among family members. The pandemic is likely to have had long-term harmful effects on children. It will no doubt have trapped some in an intergenerational cycle of poverty, given that education is the most effective way to break out of this cycle. It is also likely to have raised dropout rates among those in full-time education, resulting in lower education and skill attainment, and also to have increased mental and physical health issues. Covid-19 thus widened social inequalities.

greater experimentation and learning at the local level; this indeed appears to be a key ingredient of economic regeneration.

In order to reinvigorate Perak's economy, positive and negative experiences in Malaysia—along with those of Sheffield and the city of Scranton in northeastern Pennsylvania—all point to the importance of delegating authority and resources from the federal level to the level of the state, the local community, and local businesses. For this process of regeneration to be sustainable, the state needs to have the freedom to make its own policy choices and the resources to implement them. Businesses themselves need to become more competitive and more productive. This requires strong local financial institutions vested in the local economy to which they lend (Collier, 2018). These financial institutions can collect and disseminate information about the local economy, serving as a vital conduit for sharing the experiences of successful business experiments. The federal government must therefore learn to work better *with* the states, while the states must learn to work better with, and support, local businesses and communities.

It is ironic that, at a time when the federal government has had to expand its remit in order to address the economic and social convulsions of the pandemic and the Russia–Ukraine war, what the post-crisis world requires is far greater decentralization and devolution of resources, decision-making, and regulation away from the federal government to the level of the states and below. Federal resources are, however, still very much necessary to help reinvigorate the less advanced state economies, and get their businesses back on a pre-pandemic footing.

What might a post-crisis Perak look like? Before outlining a roadmap for Perak's journey forward and describing key elements of a longer-term vision, the next section will first briefly assess the experiences of other localities in industrialized countries. These are places where earlier prosperity had similarly been based on natural resource advantages, and which were then left behind by globalization. In what ways did the impact and imprint of tin mining in Perak resemble that of steel in Sheffield, or steel and coal in Scranton, or the decline of natural- resource-based industries in Cornwall and Pittsburgh? What policies were used to support their recovery? And, crucially, what lessons can be learned?

Cities and Towns Blighted by Globalization

Sheffield and Scranton are notable examples of cities that prospered by harnessing natural assets in their area. Sheffield's prosperity was initially due to the ready availability of water power and fuel. Scranton's early prosperity was based on anthracite coal. As growing numbers of firms located in these cities, agglomeration economies were created (see Box 3.13, above). Having been shining examples of late 19th- and early-20th-century industrialization and economic progress, however, their fortunes turned with the advent of technological disruption and new sources of competition. Each of these once-thriving places became an 'emblematic broken city' (Collier, 2018, p. 7) as manufacturing employment fell, unemployment rose, and workers left with their families for other places.

Cities and regions that once thrived through the presence of natural resources face many challenges when those resources are depleted, or when their markets falter due to changes in technology, demand, or competition. Sheffield and Scranton suffered from globalization and the deindustrialization that it prompted: Sheffield lost its steel industry, and Scranton its coal, steel, and railway industries. The decline of their industrial bases had multiple impacts: as skilled workers were more likely to migrate for employment elsewhere, average incomes fell in the communities that remained. With a declining, lesser-skilled, and poorer population, and fewer firms, the local tax base in each city was hugely diminished, hitting local government finances.

The economies of Sheffield and Scranton went into a spiral of decline in the second half of the 20th century. Sheffield's population fell from 577,000 in 1951 to 513,000 in 2001, while Scranton's fell by half. Yet over the first two decades of the 21st century, Sheffield's economy fared far better than Scranton's: its population had recovered to reach 575,424 in 2016, 12 per cent higher than in 2001, but Scranton's remained low at 77,000 in 2019, only fractionally higher than at the turn of the century.

Globalization: Perak's Rise, Relative Decline, and Regeneration. Sultan Nazrin Shah, Oxford University Press. © Sultan Nazrin Shah (2024).
DOI: 10.1093/oso/9780198897774.003.0029

Sheffield's Prosperity and Decline ...

Sheffield's natural advantages of fast-flowing streams for water power, oak woods for charcoal, and iron ore for smelting, attracted a burgeoning steel industry, and even before the industrial revolution the city had become a producer of high-quality knives (Lane et al., 2016). During the industrial revolution, clusters of local steel-making companies took advantage of the shared infrastructure of watermills and skills passed down through generations, and the development of a supply chain of raw materials that linked to nationwide distribution networks. Sheffield developed from a small production centre into a major industrial hub (Jones, 2017). The invention of stainless steel in 1913 produced a cheaper and more durable material that led to the mass production of goods and machinery, furthering Sheffield's global reputation (Lane et al., 2016). Following World War II and right up until the impact of the first oil shock in 1973, there was virtually full employment, wages were high, and Sheffield prospered as the world's pre-eminent steel producer.

However, this prosperity did not last. Sheffield's pre-eminence was eroded by a combination of the 1973 oil shock, increasing competition—at first from US steel makers and later from Asian producers—and the failure of its steel firms to adapt to new market realities. In the late 1970s, Sheffield's iron and steel industries began to lose their competitive advantage and started to shed labour. Sheffield's firms could not compete with the Republic of Korea's *chaebols* (large family-run business conglomerates), which had learned how to manufacture, sell, and ship high-quality steel to global customers at lower cost than Sheffield. As the Asian country's market share grew, it harnessed scale economies and specialization to its advantage. Conversely, as Sheffield's steel industry contracted, the benefits of agglomeration—which had once given the city an unparalleled advantage in steel making—ebbed away, and it lost further ground to more efficient competitors.

The devastation caused by the decline of steel in Sheffield was not confined to jobs and incomes in this industry alone: the wider community was greatly affected. Housing, commercial property, and land prices all declined; businesses came under financial stress; and bankruptcies and unemployment mounted. In 1978, Sheffield's unemployment rate was just 4 per cent, but by 1984 it had soared to 16 per cent (Lane et al., 2016). Although new investment opportunities were created by the falling prices of local assets, these led to largely unskilled and low-paying jobs that were unsuitable for the high-skilled steelworkers who had been made redundant.

… And Recovery

During the 1980s, Sheffield saw increasing antagonism between the City Council—which was striving to create a brighter future for a city abandoned by the private sector—and the central government, which, for its part, was determined that the private sector should play the major role in regenerating cities (Winkler, 2007). Through the 'rate capping' scheme introduced in 1985, the Conservative central government severely limited the scope of local government spending, which tied the hands of Sheffield's local authorities. When the neoliberal Margaret Thatcher was replaced by John Major as UK prime minister, and especially when New Labour replaced the Conservatives in 1997, central and local government became more active in assisting cities like Sheffield (Lane et al., 2016).

Crucially, because the UK was then a member of the EU, it was able to take advantage of EU financial support for poorer regions. Sheffield benefited from 'Objective 1' funding—the highest form of EU regional aid, which accounted for more than a third of the EU's overall budget.[11] As EU funding had to be matched by national and local funds, public-sector assistance to Sheffield at the start of the 21st century was substantial. However, Di Cataldo (2017) argues that, apart from the investments in education and human capital, the benefits of this funding tended to be short-lived.

Sheffield's successful regeneration programmes were public–private partnerships. In 1992, the City Liaison Group was established, not as a committee of the City Council but as an independent agency representing a wider array of interests, including the private sector, development agencies, higher education, and the health services. This new approach to regeneration, in which the City Council worked collaboratively with a network of non-municipal stakeholders to achieve its goals, 'provided a turning-point in Sheffield's recovery trajectory' (Winkler, 2007, p. 20). Organizations like Sheffield One—an urban regeneration company—and Sheffield First for Investment, both set up in 2001, operated at arm's length from the City Council, which had 'within the space of a decade … transformed its stance towards business from hostility to pro-partnership' (Winkler, 2007, p. 20).

Between 2000 and 2007, Sheffield One invested around £1.2 billion of external funding, with 70 per cent of this sum coming from the private sector.

---

11 Objective 1 funding aimed to promote the development of regions with GDP per capita of less than 75 per cent of the EU average. South Yorkshire's GDP per capita hovered around this threshold, and from 2000 South Yorkshire became eligible for Objective 1 support, losing this status in 2006.

Sheffield First for Investment played its part in the sixfold increase in inward investment into Sheffield, using Objective 1 funding to help attract firms (Winkler, 2007, p. 44). Niche products linked to Sheffield's steel heritage were areas for potential growth. The manufacture of surgical steel blades and scalpels for specialist medical use, for example, had survived when other steel manufacturers lost their markets to Asian competition. The Swann-Morton Company, established in Sheffield in 1932, remains a world leader in manufacturing such blades and scalpels.

Other key features supported Sheffield's relative recovery. Infrastructure development—especially improvements to road and rail connections—attracted substantial private investment and played an important regenerative role. An improved rail service to London and a new airport 18 miles from the city (Doncaster Sheffield Airport) helped to attract inward investment. Sheffield Development Corporation demolished most of the Lower Don Valley's abandoned steel mills, constructed a major road through the middle of the valley to improve access, and created a new, low-density landscape of commercial, conference, and music venues. These initiatives, combined with housing and neighbourhood-renewal programmes, transformed Sheffield's image, particularly the city centre. It became a vibrant place for firms to operate and for people to live in, attracting human capital and entrepreneurs.

A chief concern for investors was whether they would find a local workforce with the right skills. A JOBMatch service was set up in 2001 to link employers and jobseekers in the city, partly resourced with Objective 1 funding. JOBMatch liaised with firms already in or coming to Sheffield about their staffing needs, and organized training to provide local jobseekers with the skills that employers required. The proportion of local jobseekers with no educational qualifications fell from 18.7 per cent in 2000 to 15.4 per cent in 2005 (Winkler, 2007, p. 44).[12]

The city has also benefited from having a highly ranked Russell Group research-intensive university: the University of Sheffield is one of the largest in the UK, with over 25,000 students, more than one-quarter of them international students. It also benefits from Sheffield Hallam University, established in the early 1990s, which has around 30,000 students. The universities help to make the city an attractive, vibrant, and cosmopolitan location—especially for hi-tech manufacturing firms and those offering commercial services—while continuing to provide the sources of human capital. Most university

---

12 A JOBMatch project run jointly by the City Council and the private construction firm Kier LLP trained unemployed local residents for work in the construction industry.

students come from other areas of the UK, and many are inclined to stay in the city when offered employment. The ready availability of high-quality graduates has been a major attraction for high-tech and commercial firms. The spending of the students, teaching and research staff, and administrators has helped to support a dynamic local economy with significant multiplier effects.

Scranton's Prosperity and Decline ...

Scranton's natural advantage was the presence of anthracite coal, which has the fewest impurities of any type of coal and is used for heating, energy production, and iron smelting. Supported by economies of agglomeration and strong entrepreneurship, it became a bustling industrial city in the late 19th century, hosting three big industries: mining, manufacturing, and rolling stock for railways.

Following the 'anthracite strike' in 1902 by miners for better wages and conditions, the Lackawanna Iron and Steel Company relocated from Scranton to Buffalo, New York, along with 70 per cent of its workforce. This marked the beginning of Scranton's slow and gradual decline (Brown, 2010). Scranton's eventual fate was sealed by technological change and shifts in demand for its major products. By the time of the Great Depression, gas and oil had begun to replace anthracite coal as fuel sources, and demand for Scranton's railway rolling stock weakened as automobiles and trucks became an increasingly favoured mode of transport.

Scranton's population peaked at 143,433 in 1930, after which the city began to experience demographic decline through emigration. By 2000 its population had fallen to 76,000, just over half its 1930 level (Norcross and Millsap, 2016). Efforts to revive Scranton's economy through strengthening the role of the service sector have seen little success, and Scranton has remained in the backwaters of US economic life as part of the 'Rust Belt'—an area in northeastern and midwestern US that has experienced industrial decline since the 1980s.

... And Stagnation

Scranton offers several lessons on how *not* to go about regeneration, including running large fiscal deficits and spending on 'trophy' projects. Scranton's local government has even struggled to raise enough revenue for its relatively high-cost public services. In 1992, it was classified by the Pennsylvania state government as a 'distressed municipality' under Pennsylvania Act 47 on Financial Distress, which led to the appointment of a coordinator responsible for preparing a plan to assist the city in resolving its fiscal problems.

Nearly three decades later, however, Scranton's fiscal position has not improved. In fact, it has steadily worsened to near insolvency. Despite plans to revitalize the city, inward investment and job creation have been sluggish. As recently as 2017, the Scranton Community Revitalization Plan noted the lack of progress in job creation, and stated that the city government's financial distress 'has created a climate of uncertainty for existing and prospective business owners due to high property, wage, and business taxes' (Scranton Chamber of Commerce, 2017, p. 7).

There has been no rebound in its population, and Scranton remains a distressed city unable to compete for investment with other cities in Pennsylvania and elsewhere in the US (Norcross and Millsap, 2016). It has struggled to retain or attract high-quality human capital, and has failed to attract entrepreneurs. Scranton today is a faint echo of what it was in the early 20th century.

Parallels with and Lessons for Perak

In Perak, Larut and later Kinta rose to great prosperity in the late 19th and early 20th centuries, largely through tin mining. The rise and subsequent decline of Perak's towns stemmed mainly from changes in the global demand for and supply of tin, and the exhaustion of easily accessible deposits.

Are there similarities between Perak's tin towns and these two 'blighted' cities? Sheffield and Scranton benefited from their location, as well as from ready access to coal, water, and good transport links. In Perak, the Larut and Kinta Valleys are situated close to the Main Range (see Part 2, Map 2.1), which was endowed with alluvial cassiterite (tin oxide) deposits, and has the Perak River running alongside it. Proximity to these natural resources provided Perak with an initial natural advantage.

Perak's experience was different from that of Sheffield and Scranton, however, in that the growth of the tin industry took place under colonization and relied on imported labourers. The British administration saw local production opportunities as a way to support global trade and provide tin to the industrial west at a time when there was strong demand. Unlike Sheffield and Scranton, which smelted iron ore and manufactured steel products from it, tin remained a primary commodity for Perak, and most of the smelting—along with its sizeable economic benefits—went elsewhere. However, like those cities, Perak also had an over-dependence on a single commodity. When Sheffield's and Scranton's narrow range of products was undermined by low-cost producers elsewhere, their production declined, and so did the cities themselves. Likewise in Perak, over-dependence on tin mining eventually blighted many of the state's once-booming towns, such as Batu Gajah, Gopeng, and Kampar. As tin deposits were steadily exhausted and tin prices collapsed, the economic life of Perak's towns wilted, leaving the young and skilled with little option but to seek jobs elsewhere.

As Sheffield and Scranton declined, larger cities with a wider economic base—often metropolitan areas such as London and New York—thrived. Individuals and firms in these cities enjoyed 'rents of agglomeration'—that is, earnings in excess of what would be required to secure their services. These rents are reaped partly by owners of land and property benefiting from inflated property prices, 'but mainly by those workers with high skills and low housing demand' (Collier, 2018, p. 195). Conceptually, these rents enjoyed by firms and workers in areas of high economic density are no different from rents earned on mining. When Perak was prospering, taxes on its tin-export rents helped neighbouring states to prosper, as the taxation income was redistributed by the colonial administration and the early post-colonial government. As Perak declined, however, there was no such redistribution of the agglomeration rents enjoyed by states like Selangor, Penang, and Johor. In fact, relative to its population size, Perak has received disproportionately less than it should have from the federal government.

Lessons to be taken from Sheffield's regeneration include the importance of the major stakeholders demonstrating their commitment to common development objectives, as seen in the matching of national and local funds with EU funds; the vital role of the private sector; and the success of investments in niche products linked to Sheffield's steel heritage. By contrast, Scranton's lack of success was due partly to large fiscal deficits, spending on trophy projects, and the city's financial instability.

Perak could also learn lessons from the models used in Cornwall's and Pittsburgh's successful regeneration, especially in relation to attaining the decentralized powers necessary to shape its own development agenda, the importance of strengthening local institutional capacities and partnerships, and the emphasis it must place on human capital development, economic innovation, ethical mining, and high-quality food production (Box 4.3).

| Box 4.3 | **Lessons from Cornwall's and Pittsburgh's economic recoveries** |

Cornwall

Cornwall's last operational tin mine, at South Crofty, closed down in 1998—the culmination of an industry in steady decline for over a century (see 'Tin Mining—From Cornwall to Perak', above). The county had become largely dependent on fishing, agriculture, and food processing, and increasingly also on tourism and allied services (Sharpe, 2005). When the UK was still in the EU, Cornwall obtained the highest level of EU regional funding (lost with 'Brexit'), as its GDP per capita was below 75 per cent of the EU average (Di Cataldo, 2016). Yet, despite support from the EU and the UK government, Cornwall remains one of the UK's poorest counties.

Still, between 1961 and 2011 Cornwall experienced one of the highest levels of migration of any county from elsewhere in the UK: its population increased at an average annual rate of 0.9 per cent, close to three times that of the UK as a whole. Cornwall's lower property prices helped to attract people: these low prices were particularly appealing to those enticed by the 'counter-urbanization' movement— the younger generation moving away from high-cost urban living to a healthier, rural environment—as also seen with the Covid-19 pandemic. Many of these migrants were of working age and had more schooling than locals. Moving to Cornwall, however, did not necessarily benefit them economically as many took up low-paid tourism jobs (Williams, 2003).

Much like Pittsburgh in the US and Sheffield in the UK, Cornwall houses a major university with research strengths in engineering, sciences, and renewable energy, through the University of Exeter's campus in Penryn, west Cornwall, and the Camborne School of Mines near Falmouth on the southern coast. The School of Mines' internationally recognized research has attracted strong industry collaboration, supporting renewed momentum for mining exploration.

Mining companies such as Cornish Metals Inc—which in 2017 bought the rights to operate South Crofty—Cornish Lithium Ltd, and Cornwall Resources have been exploring for tin, lithium, and copper. With the global movement towards environmental, social, and governance (ESG) considerations in consumption and investment, demand for ethically sourced mineral resources will increase. Cornwall's granite rocks are rich in lithium, which is a vital component in fast-growing technologies—including batteries for electric vehicles, robotics, solar power, 5G, and cloud storage. One source of lithium being explored by Cornish Lithium is waste material left behind from many years of mining kaolin, also known as China clay, as used in the production of ceramics. In Breage in the southwest of the county,

Cornish Tin Ltd is working to revive the Great Wheal Vor group of mines—26 former tin mines that operated in the mid- to late-19th century—using new mining processes and green technology.

In 2015, Cornwall became the first non-urban area in the UK to negotiate a measure of devolution. Following these negotiations, the Cornwall Council was established, which had far greater powers than those held by the former county council. Decentralized government is more responsive to local opinion and better informed about local opportunities. It gives greater control of resources and can support a stronger economy with improved people-centred services. While it is too early to determine whether devolution will help to lift Cornwall's economic prosperity, a case can be made that it will (Longlands and Round, 2021). One recent local frontier initiative involving the Council and the private sector has been to establish Cornwall as the centre of innovation in the UK's space and aerospace sector.

Lessons
The high degree of government centralism in Malaysia disadvantages Perak (and other states). Perak needs to find new sources of revenue, and to be granted greater fiscal authority to allow it to set a higher proportion of taxes locally, enabling it to fund locally determined development priorities. Once it has achieved this breakthrough, Perak could consider introducing investment incentives for environmentally safe mineral exploration using advanced technologies, to make abandoned tin mines productive again, and to discover new mineral deposits, similar to Cornwall's approach.

Pittsburgh
Pittsburgh, Pennsylvania, sits on a peninsula at the confluence of the Allegheny River to the north and the Monongahela River to the south. These two rivers form the Ohio River, which connects, via the Mississippi River, to the Gulf of Mexico, from where navigation to the Atlantic Ocean and the rest of the world is possible.

In the late 19th century, Pittsburgh produced steel to build railway tracks and became the leading regional railway hub in the US. Its locational advantages were boosted by the discovery of extensive deposits of bituminous coal (Allen, 2016). With an abundance of cheap coal and steel, Pittsburgh became a major manufacturing centre, specializing in iron and steel products, aluminium, and glass. Supporting these industries were financial and educational institutions, and an increasingly skilled workforce, mostly based on European immigration. The wealth generated by this booming economy helped to create a number of rich foundations, including the Carnegie, Frick, and Mellon Foundations, which played a

(Continued)

crucial role in revitalizing Pittsburgh's economy after the decline in coal mining, steel production, and most of the manufacturing sector by 1980.

Key political, private sector, and non-profit institutions responded aggressively over a number of decades to reverse Pittsburgh's abrupt and steep decline. Pittsburgh is now hailed as a great success in economic revitalization, and has become a university-centred technological hub with both the University of Pittsburgh and Carnegie Mellon University ranking high in R&D funding (Piiparinen, 2021). Carnegie Mellon University, which integrates design, art, and technology in computer science teaching and research, has worked closely with industry and government to help revive the city. Pittsburgh now has a creative urban economy with extensive parks—many reclaimed from former coal strip mines—and attractive artisanal coffee shops and bistros.

Why has Perak not become another Pittsburgh? Perak might have become a world centre of tinplate manufacturing, given that it controlled as much of the world's supply of tin as Pittsburgh did of steel. Perak might also have become a world centre of rubber tyre manufacturing, as it produced a large share of the world's rubber supply. Such industrial emergence in Perak was thwarted, however, by British colonial interests. The colonial authorities sought to protect home industries, using Perak purely as a source of raw materials and as a destination for British manufactures, thereby preventing the state from moving to greater value addition. Independence came too late to put Perak on an industrial path, and post-independence Penang moved much faster to be at the forefront of Malaysia's industrialization.

Lessons

Pittsburgh's 'comeback' experience offers some lessons. First is the need to continuously invest in training and retraining of the workforce as a supply-side labour market policy. A skilled and flexible talent pool will help a region to be more adaptable to changes in technology or sectoral shifts and improve occupational mobility. Additionally, local leaders in business, government, and non-governmental organizations need to be better empowered to make for themselves the decisions that affect their communities. The quality of local leadership is crucial in building the coalitions—both within Perak and with federal and international partners—that mobilize ideas and financial resources for well-articulated strategic goals for the region, and that convert these strategic goals into policies for economic regeneration.

Second is the role of innovation as a foundation for building a modern economy. While Pittsburgh already had a significant advantage because of the strength of its local universities and research centres, it was notable that these institutions took a proactive and visible leadership role in revitalizing the city.

Third, an opportunity also exists to build local support networks for high-quality food production through small family-based producers of fresh fruit, vegetables, and livestock products for local consumers and neighbouring states and countries. Ipoh already has a reputation as a *foodie* town, boasting a number of trendy coffee shops and cafés, and this reputation could be stretched backwards to local supply chains.

Regenerating Perak

Beyond securing greater federal funding and more devolved decision-making powers, if the state government is to turn Perak's economic fortunes around, its first priority should be to create an enabling entrepreneurial environment, both to attract new investment of the kind that brings with it highly productive and well-paid jobs, and to nurture its own SMEs—the state's economic and employment backbone.

Second, it should map out in detail all of its assets, including government, business, and community institutions, industrial zones, natural recreation sites, and historical and heritage city centres (Eyles, 2007). Clearly identifying these current and potential assets will lay the groundwork for towns and cities to leverage these assets in changing global conditions as part of the state's broader pursuit of innovative economic drivers.

Third, Perak needs to ensure that its blighted towns become better at retaining their human capital and at attracting returnees and newcomers. The further development of large-scale, high-quality education and training is an important part of the solution, as it contributes to building a deep pool of local talent.

This penultimate section of the book reviews key regenerative strategies for Perak, and considers some initiatives that could contribute to the success of the state's future development.

Encouraging Investment as a Catalyst of Sustainable Development

To accelerate economic growth and create good, productive jobs, Perak must attract more investment, both domestic and foreign. The state must position itself as an appealing destination for foreign investors in search of a Malaysian platform. It must also create a conducive environment that incubates and promotes the growth of home-grown businesses, including in high-technology areas. Public investment must be directed to address priority development needs, such as skills training, which promise a significant social as well as economic return, and which further encourage and attract complementary and supplementary private investment.

Globalization: Perak's Rise, Relative Decline, and Regeneration. Sultan Nazrin Shah, Oxford University Press. © Sultan Nazrin Shah (2024). DOI: 10.1093/oso/9780198897774.003.0030

Perak has an abundance of development plans at state, district, and city council level. A single state masterplan—such as the Perak Sejahtera Plan 2030—involving stakeholders in public, private, and civil society sectors, and aligned to a *New Vision* for the state and its development goals, would help to attract investment as well as to improve coordination and exploit complementarities. Perak's track record in attracting inward foreign investment has been on a downward trend of late, however, and the current approach that targets specific industries requires review.

An alternative approach would be to identify and incentivize successful global companies that might be drawn to Perak's natural resource assets. The state's rich marine and terrestrial ecology and mineral resources provide potentially lucrative opportunities for firms in the biosciences, the green economy, and in ethical and sustainable mining (Box 4.4). These resources have already attracted a few international companies, such as Imerys from France, Omya from Switzerland, and Lhoist from Belgium. Perak's climate, its fertile soils, and its low-cost land should also be attractive to firms that specialize in producing and exporting high-value-added fruit and vegetables. Beyond that, the state's rivers, wilderness, coastal geography, and heritage hold huge potential for high-end ecotourism. The high levels of amenity, low congestion, good Internet connectivity, and public safety and security, may also attract professional service providers who can deliver their services remotely.

Box 4.4   **Sustainability and sustainable mining**

The mining of minerals—a finite and non-renewable resource—is not necessarily at odds with sustainability, which in the Brundtland Commission's widely accepted definition is conceptualized as the ability of the current generation to meet their own needs 'without compromising the ability of the future generations to meet their own needs' (UNWCED, 1987, p. 43).

To the extent that income accruing from mineral extraction is invested in assets that are economically and socially productive, it contributes to opportunities for and the well-being of future generations. Conversely, if such income is consumed by the current generation, with none set aside and invested for the next generation, the activity can be deemed not sustainable.

(*Continued*)

Historically, Perak's natural resources, including its minerals, have defined the character of the state's economic and social development. The exploitation of Perak's rich tin deposits, and the cultivation of natural rubber, generated incomes and jobs. These economic activities determined the state's settlement patterns, its population trends, and its infrastructure locations. At the same time, Perak's extensive rainforests have provided a ready supply of timber, while its climate and fertile soils have created the conditions for the cultivation of a wide range of crops, from rubber and oil palm to fruit and vegetables.

The richness and diversity of Perak's mineral wealth offer still unexploited opportunities for mining. Perak remains rich in metallic minerals, especially tin ore, as well as in non-metallic minerals, notably limestone, kaolin, clay and earth material, silica and river sand, and granite. Indeed, the 2021–2025 NCER strategy identifies 'sustainable mining' as one of its new targeted economic sectors. Although the strategy is not specific about what sustainable mining actually entails, the conventional framework emphasizes the importance of reducing the environmental impact of any project, including by minimizing land and other natural disturbances; reducing pollution through the adoption of new 'cleaner technology'; and making plans for reclaiming and restoring exhausted mines or for responsible exit strategies. There can, however, be no presumption that the mining of minerals can be safe and intergenerationally beneficial without comprehensive assessments of the economic, social, environmental, and ecological benefits and costs, which then form the basis for the actual planning and implementation of any project.

In addition, local communities in areas affected by mining should be engaged before the start of new mining activities. More broadly, a sound fiscal framework is needed to ensure that mining rents accrue to the state of Perak. This will also require a capital investment strategy to help finance the state's development needs. State revenues collected from mining should be invested in ways that are socially productive, including compensating those directly affected by the mining activities.

All these elements—impact mitigation, community engagement, benefit sharing, and distribution of rents and revenues, together with state regulation and monitoring of compliance—could be articulated in a 'charter for responsible mining'. This would help to promote transparency, discipline investment decisions, and transform natural-resource wealth into expanded opportunities for current and future generations (UNDP and UN Environment, 2018; Revenue Watch Institute, 2010). The Perak Mining Blueprint 2020, which aims to promote sustainable mining and the value of the state's mineral resources, provides a way forward (Menteri Besar Incorporated–Perak, 2014).

To explore investor potential, Perak needs an entity that can identify opportunities within the state and promote them to prospective external investors. InvestPerak could learn from best practices in other countries. Ireland, which rapidly transformed itself from an economic backwater in the 1970s to an advanced economy by the 1980s, is a prime example of what can be achieved by a highly professional investment promotion and facilitation entity. Ireland also benefited from exceptional educational institutions and a deep pool of skilled and educated workers, as well as from large remittances from its diaspora together with a low tax regime for offshore entities and insurance companies.

For Perak, business zones that are well serviced and managed, along with decent industrial infrastructure, will also be crucial. Market analysis and appraisal of needs and demand will be essential to minimize the risks of over-supply and unused facilities. The private sector, working with an effective investment promotion agency and responsive state government, should be encouraged to play a larger role in building, owning, and operating business zones and other industrial infrastructure. This could be facilitated through a small Advisory Council, consisting of senior representatives from the private and public sectors, reporting to the Menteri Besar, and working closely with the Perak State Executive Council and international experts.

A highly skilled and innovative labour force is another prerequisite for attracting investment in high technology, artificial intelligence, the Internet of things, and other areas of digitalization; these kinds of investment are already planned for Ipoh's Silver Valley Technology Park in Kinta Valley. Perak needs to extend and upgrade its technical and vocational education and training programmes to meet international standards (*The Economist*, 2019c). Programmes that help to develop frontier industries should be encouraged, and those with an over-emphasis on general skills or sunset industries should be minimized. Perak could learn from the Republic of Korea's model, in which the government invests in establishing research institutions that have strong links with industry. These entities then formulate policies for workforce development that meet rigorous accreditation standards (EPU, 2014) and that are aligned with development goals. Closer to home, the Penang Skills Development Centre, which has more than three decades of successful experience in meeting the demands for technically skilled workers for Penang's industries, is another model that could be considered.

Public investment will be required in areas where the private sector is unable or unwilling to invest. The state government's role in promoting industrial growth and structural transformation will remain vital (Hausmann and Rodrik, 2003). Public resources will be needed, for instance to expand and upgrade basic physical infrastructure, particularly in rural areas; to preserve environmental assets; and to improve healthcare and education provision. Wherever possible, opportunities for private-sector participation in the building and operation of public investments should be considered with a view to easing the burden on public resources and increasing the efficiency of service delivery. If public assets can be viably owned and operated by private entities, they can be divested at fair market value if there is adequate regulatory protection of the public interest. The Perak State Development Corporation should coordinate effective stakeholder communications and help create best-practice public–private collaboration, covering good governance and rigorous transparency standards to ensure accountability in the use of public funds (Romeo and Ravenscroft, 2018).

Nurturing Perak's SMEs

SMEs are the backbone of Perak's economy.[13] They will remain crucial for generating income and creating jobs throughout the state. SMEs can enhance productivity and employment and, because they are typically more agile than larger firms, they are able to generate more employment opportunities (Rodrik, 2021). Yet, despite their noted contribution, SMEs face a raft of barriers that limit their potential. These include regulatory hurdles that increase the time and money costs of starting a business. SMEs typically also have difficulty in accessing credit, and SMEs can rarely compete for business on a level playing field, as exemplified in the procurement criteria used by public-sector entities and the bigger private companies, which often favour larger 'proven' firms. As barriers to market entry are removed, new sectors will emerge, especially those using digital technologies and artificial intelligence. SMEs' participation must be actively supported by federal and state agencies.

An ecosystem that incubates start-ups and enables SMEs to evolve and expand will be an important element in Perak's future prosperity. SMECorp and SMEBank, which are federal government entities, have representative offices in Perak that administer national programmes, but there is no purely local entity dedicated to supporting SME development within the state. There are also features of federal programmes that constrain the reach and impact of SMEs. For example, businesses that are not majority-owned by *Bumiputera* are ineligible

---

13 In 2016, SMEs accounted for 61 per cent of Perak's GDP and 74 per cent of its jobs (Department of Statistics–Malaysia, 2017a).

for some programmes because of continuing NEP practices. The creation of *inclusive* local financing mechanisms, and financial institutions that have a vested interest in the success of local businesses, can have a powerful transformative impact (Collier, 2018).

Perak's state government and local district councils should more actively support SME development in specific frontier fields, such as Fintech. On the regulatory front, the state should streamline or remove unnecessary regulations required to start or license new businesses. Government procurement regulations could be designed to allow local SMEs to compete on level terms more easily. Technical support for SMEs could also be expanded in several ways. For example, for Perak-based entrepreneurs, the state government could expand access to and facilitate the provision of business services. Financial support could be considered with the aim of catalysing private resources to support SMEs, including encouraging them to forge public–private partnerships. Co-investment with private investors in a dedicated Perak SME venture capital fund is another option, similar to that available to Canada's venture capital industry (Government of Canada, 2021). Partial credit guarantees to encourage commercial bank lending to SMEs have worked well in Europe and elsewhere.

Generating New Sources of Revenue

With the levelling of public expenditure and limited avenues for revenue growth (Box 4.5), Perak needs to seek new sources of revenue. This is challenging, however. Under current federal–state financial arrangements, which are guided by the federal constitution—almost entirely unchanged from the 1948 Federation of Malaya Agreement—there is a clear divide in financial powers between the centre and the states. While the federal government has access to a much wider and more remunerative range of revenue sources, the state government is left with minimal sources under its revenue-raising authority, the majority of which are related to land transactions.

Broadening Perak's revenue base would involve negotiating for a more equitable share of the tax revenues collected by federal authorities, through income, corporation, sales, and service taxes, based on agreed criteria. For instance, state governments could be given a share of the personal and corporate taxes collected in the state but destined for the national coffers. Perak would also benefit from greater fiscal authority to expand the local tax base beyond the terms enumerated in the federal constitution. And although Perak depends significantly on tourism, its yield from tourism taxes has so far been miniscule. More efficient spending and revenue collection must also be explored.

Perak's revenue challenges

Perak's total revenue (comprising tax revenue, non-tax revenue, and non-revenue receipts) has increased modestly since 2010 except for a dip in 2020 and 2021, caused primarily by the Covid-19 pandemic (Figure 4a, left panel). The state's revenue sources are narrow, however, being confined to land taxes, royalties, receipts from goods sold, licences, and receipts from federal government agencies, which together accounted for about 80 per cent of total revenue in 2021. Two issues stand out: the state's narrow revenue base, and its declining non-tax revenue. Of the main revenue categories, non-tax revenue has been sliding both in absolute terms and as a share of total revenue. Licences and permits, and receipts from goods sold—both important for non-tax revenue—fell sharply.

Perak's total expenditure (operating spending 66 per cent, development spending 34 per cent) rose from RM762.8 million in 2010 to RM975.5 million in 2021, but was down from its peak of RM1,064.7 in 2017 (Figure 4a, centre panel). Proportionally, development expenditure saw the greater rise between 2010 and 2021, doubling over the period from a low base. Operating expenditure rose from RM622.4 million in 2010 to RM662.1 million in 2021, though it had peaked in 2017 at RM765.1 million. This rise in operating expenditure was reflected in most expenditure components, especially 'emoluments' (up 58 per cent). Of the components of development expenditure,

Figure 4a **Perak's revenue and expenditure uptrend reversed during the pandemic**

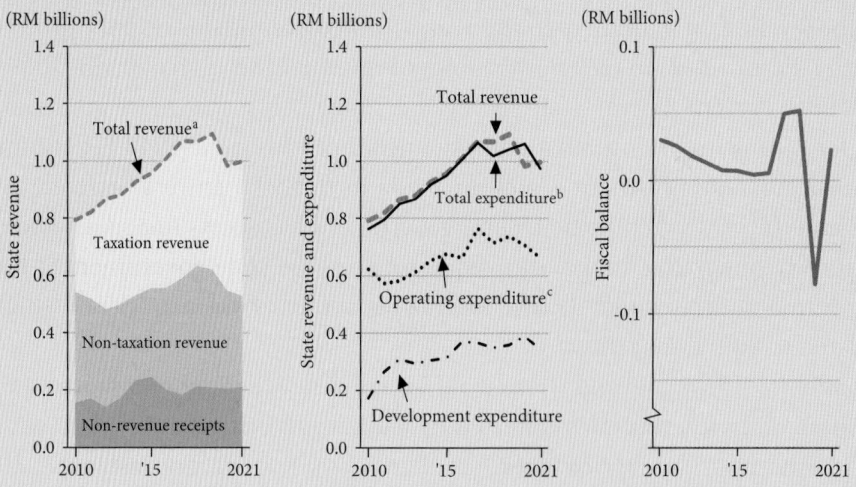

Notes: [a] Perak's main sources of *tax revenue* are: taxes on land, royalties, and taxes on forest products; of *non-tax revenue*: receipts from goods sold, investment income, licences and permits, and service payments; of *non-revenue receipts*: receipts from federal government agencies, returned expenditure, and other receipts/transfers/contributions.
[b] Includes net development fund transfers.
[c] Operating expenditure excludes development fund transfers.

the largest authorized spending was by the State Secretary's Office and the Finance Office, which together account for about two-thirds.

The state's narrow revenue base constrains its potential. Development spending has plateaued since 2016—even declining in years other than 2020—and the state's fiscal balance was sharply negative during the pandemic (Figure 4a, right panel). Perak's revenue as a share of its GDP increasingly limits the ability of the state to fund development programmes (Table 4b).

Table 4b	Perak's government revenue is a declining share of its GDP (%)											
2010	2011	2012	2013	2014	2015	2016	2017	2018	2019	2020	2021
1.8	1.7	1.6	1.6	1.6	1.5	1.5	1.5	1.4	1.4	1.2	1.2

Perak has long suffered from substantial shortfalls in the allocation of federal development expenditure, both in relation to its population size and on a per capita basis, compared to other states. This meagre federal development support is one factor that is likely to have contributed to lacklustre foreign and domestic investment in the state. Increased federal regional aid for Perak would support its development, just as EU funds and matching UK government support helped Sheffield and Cornwall to strengthen their infrastructure and human resource development. To support the recovery of blighted cities, Collier (2018) proposes differential taxation: lower corporate taxes in cities that are struggling and higher taxes in thriving metropolises, thereby effectively taxing agglomeration rents.

Perak should also proactively explore potential opportunities for new and unconventional revenue sources—carbon credits, offsets, and the green bond market—consistent with its objective of conserving and enhancing its spectacular natural environment (Box 4.6).

> **Box 4.6** **Carbon credits, offsets, and the green bond market**
>
> The global agenda for managing climate change and moving towards sustainable green financing offers potential new revenue sources for Perak. The carbon trading market is growing rapidly as individuals and companies seek to reduce their own
>
> *(Continued)*

carbon footprints by leveraging the carbon-reducing efforts of others. The green bond market is also growing rapidly. This is a financial market in which companies or organizations seeking to raise funds for green projects find a match in investors who are green-conscious, and who see the potential for such projects to generate future revenue and profit. These markets present opportunities for conserving and managing the state's natural resources, and can provide the financing needed to pursue green and sustainable development initiatives.

Firms are increasingly participating in the rapidly growing carbon credit and carbon offset markets to reduce their carbon and greenhouse gas emissions. Perak's large forested areas offer the potential for creating carbon offsets through projects that sequestrate emissions—for instance forest restoration, avoidance of deforestation, and mangrove planting—which can then be traded globally. These projects also have the potential to create jobs for local communities, including indigenous people. The UN's COP26 Climate Change Summit, held in Glasgow in 2021, finalized the voluntary international carbon trading mechanism that had been outlined in Article 6 of the Paris Agreement. This paved the way for countries that are under-emitters of CO_2 to sell their surplus carbon credits to countries that exceed their carbon emissions allowance, as part of their compliance with mandatory emission caps. This, as well as the approval for public and private entities to trade carbon offsets under a UN-supervised mechanism, will afford more carbon trading opportunities for Perak, as will the establishment of Malaysia's voluntary carbon market in 2022, announced by Bursa Malaysia.

In the green bond market, where proceeds are solely to be used for projects that have a positive environmental impact, total issuances of green bonds globally had reached USD1 trillion by 2020, up from USD100 billion in 2015 (World Economic Forum, 2021), reflecting strong demand for such bonds. With Malaysia at the forefront of the Islamic green bond market, Perak could tap into the bond markets and issue its own green *sukuk* (sharia-compliant bonds).

Harnessing the Strategic Development Plan, 2021–2025

The NCER's Strategic Development Plan, 2021–2025, formulated under the theme of *Shared Prosperity through Balanced Regional Development*, is intended to provide the development framework for Perak and the other three NCER states (NCIA, 2021). This second five-year strategy broadly attempts to align with Perak's state development plans, and is designed to lift the state's economic growth and development (Box 4.7). Where possible, implementation should also be aligned with the priorities of the Perak Sejahtera Plan 2030, including in relation to food security, the digital economy, and sustainable mining, as well as upgrading workers' skills (Perak State Government, 2022).

Box 4.7   **An economic corridor: Will it work for the NCER?**

Land-based economic corridors are essentially political and administrative planning constructs. They are instruments intended to integrate places, markets, and communities in a defined geographical area. Although corridors focus on initiatives to promote development *inside* an area, they also endeavour to widen and deepen opportunities *outside* their boundaries by strengthening connections through identified external *gateways*.

The logic is that, by leveraging complementarities and economies of scale and scope, by developing and linking physical networks, and by solving coordination problems, regional economic corridors will generate synergies that lead to advances in productivity and better economic and social outcomes. Improved intersectoral coordination among government agencies between and within states, including in planning, sharing expertise, and in R&D, would increase the chances of success for NCER programmes.

Evidence suggests that economic corridors work best where they leverage market potential and the competitive advantages of an area; but governments, too, are crucial. The potential of an economic corridor depends, among other things, on government decisions about land use and zoning; the location of public investments in hard and soft infrastructure; and the government policies and regulatory parameters that shape the investment and business climate.

The Strategic Development Plan, 2021–2025, seeks to assist the NCER in maximizing its economic potential in a way that is sustainable and reduces geographical and socio-economic disparities. It sets out a range of targets for the region, and for the four states, on private investment, job creation, incomes, and other variables, and identifies key economic clusters to be promoted in different places, as well as numerous initiatives. The strategy features 6 clusters, 21 sector drivers, and 30 economic zones or 'hotspots'. Within each zone, the strategy then identifies specific 'catalytic' projects (NCIA, 2021, p. 28). Strategic infrastructure, a business-friendly ecosystem, skilled workers and talent, and advanced technology are all identified as key enablers of the plan.

The 2021–2025 plan embodies a high level of ambition. The severe impact of the pandemic and other crises has somewhat moderated these ambitions, notably by lengthening the timescale of the plan; an addendum to the strategy explains how the region could respond to the effects of the pandemic. Past performance, aspects of the design of the strategy, its implementation model, and its resourcing arrangements all temper the grounds for optimism.[14] 'Ownership' of the plan by its various stakeholders will be crucial to its success. There needs to be selectivity and prioritization among the plethora of initiatives it features, and the plan needs also to acknowledge strategic trade-offs. For example, the 'Sustainable Mining' initiatives to be led by the private sector in the Belum Temenggor state park and the Lenggong UNESCO heritage site hint at underlying tensions in priorities over land use in Perak, and at possible conflicts between the state's interests in securing new sources of revenue and its conservation objectives.

Given the extensive array of initiatives in the strategy, covering many economic sectors and geographical areas, questions of implementation capacity naturally arise. Most of the plan's initiatives are high-level concepts, with few if any details provided about design, implementation, and funding. The role and functions of the federal government and the four states in implementing public projects could be made clearer. While the strategy identifies opportunities for public–private partnerships and for private-sector-led initiatives, formidable institutional capacity (both within the NCER and in the individual states) would still be required to move from 'broad-brush' concepts to implementable projects, and then to monitor and systematically report on them. Indeed, some of the signature projects outlined in the plan are largely aspirational and are far from project blueprints.

For some key initiatives, the NCIA lacks the authority and resources to implement its own strategy.[15] Crucially, decisions about land use—which is vital to the spatial development of the NCER—rest with each state, as does control over natural resources. Conversely, budgetary powers remain largely centralized at the federal level, and control at the pinnacle of the NCIA (in its governing council) rests with the prime minister. These arrangements and rival

---

14 The performance data presented appear to be selective, often inadequately benchmarked, and mask underlying trends (NCIA, 2021). There have been some successes at project and programme level, but not everything that has happened *inside* 'the region' has occurred at the behest of the NCIA, nor should everything be attributed to the creation of the NCER region.

15 The NCIA's functions are limited to policy and planning, investment and trade facilitation, training and human capital development, and advice to federal-level agencies about investment priorities and incentives.

interests at state level complicate not only the plan's design and implementation but ultimately also accountability for NCIA initiatives and outcomes.

These challenges faced by the NCER are by no means unique. Economic corridors and similar initiatives have often failed, and at the root of many of these failures have been ill-designed governance arrangements (World Bank, 2009). Issues of lagging development and inequality in the states of Kedah, Perak, and Perlis could have been addressed in other ways. Hill and Menon (2020, p. 25) observe that the 'assignment principle' suggests that other measures may be more effective than corridors in tackling inequalities, infrastructure and human capital deficits, financial and labour-market failures, and environmental problems. If, for example, lagging incomes are determined to be a priority by policymakers, the most direct instrument to redress this imbalance would be fiscal transfers from the centre.

The NCER is ultimately a political construct, signalling to voters that federal and state governments are working hard to create prosperity and to build unity through the elimination of spatial disparities in economic outcomes. However, abundant global evidence shows that efforts to promote spatial convergence in economic outcomes are both costly and likely to disappoint when up against the powerful forces of agglomeration and concentration (World Bank, 2009).[16]

A strength of the NCER strategy, however, is that it recognizes the vital importance of investing in people, and this is where it could have its most enduring impact. Empowering people, irrespective of ethnicity, through investments in high-quality education and educational infrastructure; a focus on skills training and upgrading; and providing support for local businesses and entrepreneurs, are all important for Perak's development and align with its priorities. It will take substantial investments in education and modern employment opportunities,[17] however, to arrest the long-term migration of Perak's young and most talented.

Promoting Synergies with High-income Selangor

There is also the matter of the geographical structure of the NCER and its constituent states. The state capital of Perak, Ipoh, is roughly equidistant between Penang and the federal territory of Kuala Lumpur. Yet the NCER strategy is

16 According to Rasiah and Krishnan (2020), the NCIA lacks a strategy for effective clustering and agglomeration, such that many science parks have become stagnant due to the lack of coordinated links to knowledge nodes.

17 Modern employment may be defined as jobs that can provide a 'high enough wage to afford a decent living condition, social benefits, an opportunity for career progression' (Rodrik and Stantcheva, 2021, p. 2).

largely silent on initiatives that might help Perak to draw on Selangor's much larger economic mass. The level and scale of economic activity, spending power, and knowledge and skills in Selangor, and its diverse range of facilities and networks, create agglomeration benefits that Perak, located to its north, could potentially tap into. This could be in agri-food production or in other industries located along Perak's border with Selangor. There are some initiatives under way that promote potential synergies between the two states—for instance, the West Coast Highway project which, on completion (now scheduled for 2024), will strengthen connections between Perak and the dynamic Klang Valley. This scheme, however, predates the full absorption of Perak into the NCER. Other than for Perak's northern districts—Kerian, Hulu Perak, and the district of Larut, Matang, and Selama—there would appear to be few immediate synergies with Kedah. Besides, Kedah, and even Penang, have a smaller economic mass than Selangor. All of this indicates that Perak should do more to promote the potential benefits of its geographical proximity to Selangor.

As Perak has long failed to attract significant FDI—an area in which Selangor has been markedly successful—it needs a new approach, refocusing on those enabling factors that attract investors.[18] A pool of labour with skills and talents, world-class IT connectivity, well-serviced infrastructure, and an environment that offers security, amenities, and high-quality living, are among the key attractions for foreign investors and their workers. Developing these attributes, and promoting them effectively, will enhance Perak's appeal in an age when services activity is on the rise and traditional industrial boundaries are being wrenched apart by the 'fourth industrial revolution'.

Technologically advanced manufacturing will remain crucial for growth and well-being, and a sizeable manufacturing sector will contribute to better living standards (Aiginger and Rodrik, 2020). Perak needs to look to a future in which the physical, biological, and digital spheres intersect, and it needs to recognize that market opportunities will traverse administrative boundaries to congregate in areas with the greatest economic mass. Perak's proximity to Selangor is still a largely untapped asset.[19]

---

18 Perak's 'one stop investment centre', InvestPerak, identifies several industries for promotion, including iron and steel, automotive industries, machinery, *halal* products, minerals, and electrical and electronics goods.

19 Sonoma County, in northern California, at the northern end of Silicon Valley, has flourished by tapping into its proximity to San Francisco.

Towards a *New Vision* for Perak

Much like its past, Perak's future will be shaped by global forces that it cannot control but which it can exploit—this time for its own and Malaysia's benefit. Technological upheavals, shifts in geopolitical and economic alignments, climate change, and economic concentration and dispersion within Malaysia's borders will all create huge challenges and opportunities.

The following innovative, inclusive development agenda—a *New Vision* for Perak—is an adjustable outline for revitalizing Perak's economy and creating a prosperous, inclusive, and 'green' outward-looking state. The *New Vision*, which will ultimately comprise a set of interrelated time-bound goals, seeks to ensure the maintenance of inter-ethnic harmony, safety, and security through effective institutions that promote fairness and opportunities for all.

Main Elements of the *New Vision* for Perak

The *New Vision* aims to help put Perak on a path to renewed prosperity and pre-eminence, at least on a par with leading Malaysian states. It bases this strategy on five key 'blocks':

- Ensuring efficient and transparent institutions.
- Rebuilding human capital and increasing employability.
- Investing in global gateways.
- Leveraging and enhancing Perak's spectacular natural and historical assets.
- Decentralizing more revenue-raising and decision-making powers to Perak.

Promoting inclusion must remain a key objective within all of these, including providing all communities with equitable access to opportunities and social protection (Sultan Nazrin Shah, 2019). Policies and programmes must ensure that those in the state's less developed areas are not neglected, while striving to improve their upward mobility and so supporting inclusive development. This more inclusive

Globalization: Perak's Rise, Relative Decline, and Regeneration. Sultan Nazrin Shah, Oxford University Press. © Sultan Nazrin Shah (2024). DOI: 10.1093/oso/9780198897774.003.0031

approach to the state's development must become a central objective, aimed at lifting community participation and curbing opportunities for narrow sectional interests to extract and expropriate benefits (Acemoglu and Robinson, 2012).

The New Vision will outline broad and inclusive macro goals, thus setting a direction that is embraced by all communities and stakeholders, and is embedded within an implementable and well-funded institutional framework. It will anchor the plans and decisions of diverse stakeholders and reset citizens' expectations, as well as providing a powerful tool to help redirect Perak's trajectory. Political and institutional leadership with a global mindset will be vital in championing and pushing for this 'change agenda', especially when it comes to invigorating the private sector and stimulating innovation and creativity. Engaging all members of the community—including owners of businesses both small and large, as well as other stakeholders—and seeking their inputs on aspirations for the state, will help to ensure buy-in and public support for achieving the goals of the *New Vision*.

Ensuring Efficient and Transparent Institutions

An effective state government is one that delivers beneficial outcomes in an efficient, cost-disciplined way. Organizational arrangements that assign functions, and in which core competencies are embedded, are essential to execute and coordinate actions. Responsibility for Perak's development is currently spread across multiple state agencies, and is hampered by deficits in capabilities and by inefficiencies in managing resources.[20] The overlay of federal control further complicates governance and accountability. A review of the relevance of current mandates and the performance of existing entities would be a useful starting point for clarifying and assigning roles. A new state development agency, or an existing agency repurposed, might help to oversee the *New Vision* holistically, and a new funding mechanism could be established to help direct the investment of public funds into private-sector activities that also promote social objectives (Collier, 2018). Increased public–private partnerships to provide public goods and/or advance new sectoral niches can also be considered. Rationalizing and reforming existing state agencies to align them with the aims of the *New Vision* will be essential for inclusive development.

Successful and sustainable development of the state will require the capacity to think ahead, plan, and build understanding and trust; to clearly and

---

20 The Twelfth Malaysia Plan (MP12), 2021–2025, calls for the rationalization of state development agencies and regional economic corridor authorities, with the aim of achieving more effective planning and implementation, improved coordination, and strengthened public service efficiency (EPU, 2021).

strategically communicate on aims and progress through public feedback mechanisms; to fund, with sufficient resources, priority programmes and projects; to follow up and troubleshoot implementation problems with senior policymakers; to monitor and report on outcomes; and to represent the state's interests effectively at federal level. Other functions, too, will be needed, including more effective investment promotion and enterprise support. Different organizational designs could be used to manage and coordinate these functions. Perak's size and population concentrations would favour streamlined arrangements.

A lack of clarity about functions, and the multiple overlapping mandates across government entities, raise expenditure and transaction costs, and exacerbate coordination problems. Clear mandates and tight outcomes-based coordination mechanisms are essential, given that the implementation of Perak's development strategy will require taking actions that fall within the purview of government institutions at different levels and with different jurisdictions, namely the state government, the federal government, and the NCIA.

Transformed governance will be crucial to meet emerging challenges and take advantage of new opportunities. Responsive, effective, and well-functioning public institutions are vital if private enterprise is to flourish, and if the diverse needs of Perak's communities are to be well served through the provision of public services. The social, cultural, and religious values of all communities must be respected to ensure inclusiveness. If decision-makers and those in authority are exposed to greater scrutiny, higher levels of societal trust in the state government and improved probity will follow. The adoption at state level of recruitment and human-resource policies which cultivate merit and reward performance is another essential element of transformation.

Rebuilding Human Capital and Increasing Employability

It is vital to arrest the secular outflow of Perak's people, and to work towards creating decent jobs that can attract young talent. The continuing long-term outflow of Perak's most skilled and talented citizens from all communities has taken a heavy toll on the state's human capital base and its entrepreneurial capacities. In response, Perak must create a greater number of higher-income jobs, including skill-intensive, higher-value-added ones especially given the immense opportunities and threats from new technologies, including artificial intelligence.

Incentives should be provided to encourage Perak's diaspora to return to the state, and to attract other regional and international talent, particularly among those drawn towards a more rural, 'green' lifestyle, using the best elements of the federal government's TalentCorps programme.[21] A key theme in such incentives—in the face of fierce national and international competition—would be to stress the state's affordable housing, lower living costs, attractive landscapes, and quieter pace of life. Attracting entrepreneurs will also help SME growth—the backbone of the state's economy. For Perak to stem its net outward migration flows and retain its young population, and even more so to attract new talent, it needs to step up its provision of higher education to world-class standards while developing and promoting specialized niches in particular subjects and research areas. Workers across all sectors need to be upskilled or reskilled, and higher education must endeavour to equip new students with knowledge aligned to IT and information sciences.

In other countries, universities, and the development of university towns and cities, have played a major part in energizing and revitalizing geographical areas, retaining skilled and creative talent, and bringing economic and social development through increased human capital (Perry and Wiewel, 2005). Universities help build human capital by increasing both the supply of higher-educated persons and, through investments in R&D, the demand for skilled people. There is increasingly intense competition among universities to attract the brightest students and academic staff, as well as to secure research funds, venture capital, and business support (Teo, 2014 and 2020), and Perak must be able to compete.

Foreign university campuses have been established in Malaysian states.[22] The University of Nottingham Malaysia campus, established in 2005, has been a key factor in the growth of Semenyih town in Selangor. The state of Johor has succeeded in attracting several well-established global education providers to its Educity Iskandar development,[23] drawing both students and international skilled labour to the area. Education was the fifth-highest sector in terms of total cumulative investment in the Iskandar region—RM2.11 billion from 2006 to 2020—and the establishment of a city of campuses has created a synergistic platform. These research-based universities are clustered within the same

---

21 TalentCorp is a national agency responsible for repatriating skilled Malaysians through its Returning Expert programme, as well as for attracting skilled foreign talent through its Residence-Pass Talent programme. With the recent establishment of TalentCorp's office in Penang in 2022, aimed at supporting the growth and development of human capital, the state government can work closely with the agency to attract talent to Perak.

22 Five UK universities have set up campuses in Malaysia: the University of Nottingham, the University of Reading, Heriot-Watt University, Newcastle University, and the University of Southampton.

23 Educity Iskandar is Asia's first multi-campus education city, comprising 305 acres of universities, higher education institutions, and R&D centres, as well as student accommodation and recreational and sports facilities. Among the international universities that have established campuses there are Newcastle, Reading, and Southampton from the UK, and the Maritime Institute of Technology from the Netherlands.

economic region as strategic manufacturing and service industries, facilitating collaborations with local and international businesses.

Perak should strive to develop partnerships with top-ranked international research universities. As an example, given Perak's historical association with Cornwall, international collaboration with the UK's University of Exeter, which has a distinguished branch campus in Cornwall, the Camborne School of Mines, could help to revive Perak's international links and establish its place in international education. This highly ranked university has research strengths in the physical sciences, computer science, engineering, environmental science, and renewable energy, among other areas. The Camborne School of Mines' internationally recognized research has attracted strong industry collaboration. Student and academic exchanges would bring international students to Perak to study and conduct research on its mines and minerals, and could potentially place the state at the forefront of research on geology, mining, and mineral and natural resources in Southeast Asia. This would help to promote Perak throughout the entire region as a training centre in environmental sciences and sustainable mining, as well as further incentivizing the state to engage in ethical and sustainable mining and the green economy (Box 4.4).

Investing in Global Gateways

Due to the resulting higher transport costs, a lack of nearby international gateways has been a serious trade barrier for Perak in recent decades. Generally, the greater the distance between the two ports or airports offering access to the source and destination markets, the higher the transport costs. Perak's spatially well-connected network of roads, railways, and rivers needs efficient and high-quality international gateways to help boost its export trade and increase its competitiveness, as recognized in Perak's 2040 structural plan (PLANMalaysia@Perak, 2022).

The lack of such gateways until now has pushed international investments instead towards neighbouring Selangor and Penang, which have the crucial advantage of being adjacent to major ports and airports. Both have reaped the rewards of agglomeration economies as a result, attracting and continuing to attract substantial new manufacturing investment. Ipoh's small airport, in contrast, offers few direct flights to other countries, and cannot accept larger planes, discouraging international investors and tourists.

As Perak's trade grows, a new international airport with cargo handling facilities and the expansion of Lumut's existing maritime facilities into a modern and efficient container seaport—along the lines of Antwerp–Bruges' technologically advanced port—would give the state direct regional links (especially with neighbouring North Sumatra, Indonesia) as well as worldwide connections. Such an expansion is envisaged in the 2022 collaborative agreement between the Perak State Development Corporation and the Port of Antwerp–Bruges International to develop the Lumut Maritime Industrial City; this would make the state more attractive to foreign—and local—investors, especially for time-sensitive cargoes. It would increase trade, generate economic spillovers, and greatly support the continued growth of Perak's niche tourism and ecotourism sector.

Leveraging and Enhancing Perak's Spectacular Natural and Historical Assets

Economic growth, though essential for bringing about prosperity, must not be the only preoccupation of Perak's planners. If growth is pushed too far, beyond the 'ecological ceiling', irreparable human and environmental harm will result (Raworth, 2017).[24] Climate change is already contributing to extreme weather conditions worldwide, threatening development progress, and causing hardship to local communities across Malaysia, especially due to the interaction of climatic and societal drivers (UNDP, 2021). Urbanization and deforestation contribute to rising temperatures and the destruction of natural coastal barriers, with surges in coastal waters leading to coastal flooding. Climate change indicators—greenhouse gas concentrations, sea level rise, ocean temperature, and ocean acidification—continue to set new records (WMO, 2022). Although these are markers of *global* threats and planetary health, the impacts are, of course, affecting Perak and the rest of Malaysia, with devastating impact on lives and livelihoods.

Perak must be bold, therefore, in taking urgent steps to mitigate the risks to the state from climate change, and to adapt to the challenges it presents, so as to ensure intergenerational equity, and to conserve and protect its magnificent

---

24 Raworth (2017) argues that a focus on economic growth alone is misguided, inadvertently bringing about crises, such as the global financial crisis, and contributing to climate change. She offers a new paradigm based on a 'doughnut' visualization of economics. She contends (p. 44) that, instead of pursuing economic growth as an end, 21st century economists should focus on the human and environmental aims embodied in the 17 United Nations Sustainable Development Goals, which provide a 'social foundation' for humanity. Attention to economic efficiency which incorporates environmental costs would ensure long-run sustainability.

biodiversity and natural environment. The state is blessed with a rich portfolio of natural assets. Belum Temenggor is one of the world's most ancient rainforests. Estimated to be 130 million years old, it is a complex forest ecosystem containing certain species of vegetation and wildlife that are unique to the state. Encroachment and illegal logging undermine the ecosystem services that the forest provides, however, and threaten to turn this blessing into a curse. Enhancing Perak's natural environment will, therefore, require innovations in land use, agriculture and food production, and waste management.

Perak's river system—a network of 14 rivers totalling hundreds of kilometres in length—has long been a source of life and livelihoods for its people, providing fresh water, fish, and a means of transport. The state's rivers also provide a habitat for aquatic flora and fauna, and support rich biodiversity. However, these rivers have been degraded by run-off from activities in industry, mining, and agriculture, as well as by expanded human settlements.

Crucially, Perak must help to control carbon emissions and make the transition to clean energy to support structural economic changes, including through the use of electric vehicles. It must also take action to control river pollution from chemical waste and plastics as well as to prevent the further loss of biodiversity through deforestation. With its many rivers, the state should take the lead to incentivize the use of renewable, clean, and sustainable energy sources by exploiting the use of hydropower. In addition, Perak should implement a 'polluter-pays' policy in which all corporates conducting any activity that has a negative impact on the environment must reimburse the state government for the environmental and social costs. This will compel polluters to adopt cleaner technologies and sustainable work practices.

Perak's natural environment is under considerable stress, and, although a sustainable development model has been proposed (Yayasan Hasanah, 2021), a comprehensive, multi-dimensional, and multi-disciplinary assessment has yet to be conducted. Federal and state laws and regulations have systematically discounted the conservation value of environmental assets while undervaluing the services that they provide. Nevertheless, given careful policy choices along with the right economic incentives, and regulatory and administrative guidance from the state government, conserving the natural environment need not entail an extensive trade-off between development and environmental objectives. All development programmes should have thorough expert evaluations of their environmental impact, and the state will need to strengthen its legal and regulatory framework, including monitoring and enforcement, to clamp down on activities that harm the environment.

These moves towards 'economic efficiency' can provide a wealth of opportunities, which include, for example, investments in 'greening' Perak's economy, leveraging its natural environmental assets for educational and research purposes, and promoting ecotourism. Other areas include rehabilitating rivers and mining pools to expand opportunities for food security in aquaculture and fishing, and investing in high-value fruit farming.[25] Exploiting these opportunities requires inclusive state-level policy support. Moreover, a successful transition to an environmentally sustainable development model will require environmental interests to be mainstreamed in both state and regional development strategies, incentives for conservation to be adopted, and regulations to be well designed and tightly enforced.

Conserving and protecting Perak's natural heritage—including its coastline and rivers, mangrove swamps, limestone caves, flora and fauna, wide range of species, and natural rainforests—is vital for preserving its natural capital. The *New Vision* must prioritize environmental conservation and tailor its targets to achieve the relevant United Nations Sustainable Development Goals (SDGs)—primarily SDGs 8, 9, 11, 12, 13, 14, and 15 (UNDESA, 2021).[26] Consideration should be given to a new dedicated high-level state agency for environmental coordination, with devolved powers and working with international organizations.

Perak's unique combination of historical, natural, and geological heritage provides a wealth of short- or longer-term vacation destinations in a relatively small area. Visitors will also be able to sample local cuisine and hospitality. For Perakians, especially young entrepreneurs, avoiding mass-market tourism, innovating, thinking creatively, and developing niche products in tourism would provide substantial numbers of jobs and other economic benefits, while also helping to preserve the very assets that generate income from tourism. Environmental awareness programmes could help Perakians to take more pride in their wonderful natural heritage, and school curricula should, from a young age, inculcate appreciation of the natural environment.

Solidarity among communities over generations is vital for protecting and conserving Perak's natural heritage. It may be that many Perakians do not appreciate just how fortunate they are to live in a state of such incredible natural

---

25 With the Russia–Ukraine war leading to serious shortfalls in food supply, especially wheat and vegetable oils, food security has become a policy priority for many nations seeking to ensure economic and political stability.

26 SDG 8 is decent work and economic growth; SDG 9 is industry, innovations, and infrastructure; SDG 11 is sustainable cities and communities; SDG 12 is responsible consumption and production; SDG 13 is climate action; SDG 14 is life below water; and SDG 15 is life on land.

beauty—and improved environmental stewardship is needed to maintain that good fortune.

Decentralizing More Revenue-raising and Decision-making Powers to Perak

Since independence, a highly centralized system of government has emerged in which the autonomy of state and other local levels of government has been systematically eroded. State-level entities are typically extensions of federal institutions and are guided by federal policies. National development plans are highly centralized and so have helped to further consolidate powers at the centre, specifically within the Prime Minister's Department. Likewise, responsibilities for spatially focused development initiatives, such as the NCER, are federally conceived, funded, and managed.

Stronger devolution of powers from federal to state bodies would allow greater local ownership of Perak's development goals. Decentralized decision-making has many advantages. First, state and local governments are likely to have a better understanding of local community needs, as well as more information about them, than remote central entities ever can; this puts state and local government representatives in a better position to build trust, and engenders more responsiveness and accountability. Second, decentralization enables greater community voice and ownership of programmes, improving programme design and helping to ensure that assistance reaches intended beneficiaries. Third, responses to localized challenges can be faster, avoiding costly delays. Fourth, decentralization enables greater customization of service delivery mechanisms and administrative solutions to local circumstances, and avoids the inefficiencies of a national one-size-fits-all approach.

Making such decentralization work and realizing its benefits requires changes in three main areas: technical and administrative skills, to be reinforced at state and local levels; collaborative interfaces, to be constructed among local, state, and federal layers of government; and financial resources, to be devolved and managed at the state level.

This final point is crucial: Perak and other states have few areas where they can mobilize revenue to support development programmes, and are almost totally dependent on federally controlled funds. Devolving more powers for revenue collection to Perak (and to other state governments) would help it to realize its *New Vision* of renewed prosperity and inclusiveness—for current and future generations.

References

Abdul Azmi Abdul Khalid (1992), 'The Social Organization of the Mining Industry During the Depression, 1929–1933 in Malaya', *Journal of the Malaysian Branch of the Royal Asiatic Society*, 65/2 (263), 85–98.

Abdul Ghani (1989), 'Pengeluaran Timah Malaysia', *Timah Malaysia*, 16/4, 2–15.

Abdul Karim Bagoo (1962), 'The Origin and Development of the Malay States Guides', *Journal of the Malayan Branch of the Royal Asiatic Society*, 35/1 (197), 51–94.

Abdul Rahman Hasan (2014), *Migration and Population Distribution, 2010 Population and Housing Census of Malaysia* (Putrajaya: Department of Statistics–Malaysia).

Abdul Talib Ahmad (1959), *Riwayat Kinta* (Kuala Lumpur: Pustaka Rusna).

Abdullah Firdaus Haji (1985), *Radical Malay Politics: Its Origins and Early Development* (Petaling Jaya: Pelanduk Publications).

Abdur-Razzaq Lubis, and Khoo, S. N. (2003), *Raja Bilah and the Mandailings in Perak: 1875–1911*, Monograph No. 35, Malaysian Branch of the Royal Asiatic Society (Penang: Phoenix Printers).

Abdur-Razzaq Lubis, Wade, M., and Khoo, S. N. (2010), *Perak Postcards 1890s–1940s* (Penang: Areca Books).

Abraham, C. (2006), *'The Finest Hour': The Malaysian-MCP Peace Accord in Perspective* (Petaling Jaya: Strategic Information, Research and Development Centre).

Acemoglu, D., and Robinson, J. A. (2012), *Why Nations Fail: The Origins of Power, Prosperity, and Poverty* (New York: Crown Publishers).

Adzidah Yaakob (2014), 'A Legal Analysis on Law and Policy on Forest Conservation in Peninsular Malaysia', PhD thesis, University of Malaya.

Aiginger, K., and Rodrik, D. (2020), 'Rebirth of Industrial Policy and an Agenda for the Twenty-first Century', *Journal of Industry, Competition and Trade*, 20/2, 189–207.

Ali Liaqat (1966), 'Principle of Buffer Stock and Its Mechanism and Operation in the International Tin Agreement', *Weltwirtschaftliches Archiv*, 96, 141–187.

Allen, D.-W. (2016), *Beyond Rust: Metropolitan Pittsburgh and the Fate of Industrial America* (Philadelphia: University of Pennsylvania Press).

Allen, G. C., and Donnithorne, A. G. (2003), *Western Enterprise in Indonesia and Malaya: A Study in Economic Development* (London: Routledge).

Allen, J. D. V., Stockwell, A. J., and Wright, L. R. (1981), *A Collection of Treaties and Other Documents Affecting the States of Malaysia, 1761–1963*, vol. I (London: Oceana Publications).

Andaya, B. W. (1979), *Perak, the Abode of Grace: A Study of an Eighteenth-Century Malay State* (Kuala Lumpur: Oxford University Press).

Andaya, B. W., and Andaya, L. Y. (2015), *A History of Early Modern Southeast Asia, 1400–1830* (Cambridge: Cambridge University Press).

_____ (2017), *A History of Malaysia* (3rd edn., London, United Kingdom: Palgrave Macmillan).

Andaya, L. Y. (2002), 'Orang Asli and the Melayu in the History of the Malay Peninsula', *Journal of the Malaysian Branch of the Royal Asiatic Society*, 75/1 (282), 23–48.

Anderson, I. (2011), *Ipoh, My Home Town: Reminiscences of Growing Up, in Ipoh, in Pictures and Words* (Ipoh: Media Masters).

Anderson, J. (1856), *Political and Commercial Considerations Relative to the Malaysian Peninsula and the British Settlements in the Straits of Malaya* (Singapore).

ARABIS (2018), *How and Why I Became a Rubber Planter in Malaya*, Agricultural Research & Advisory Bureau, http://www.arabis.org/index.php/articles/articles/plantation-history/how-and-why-i-became-a-rubber-planter-in-malaya, accessed 18 August 2020.

Asan Ali Golam Hassan (2017), *Growth, Structural Change and Regional Inequality in Malaysia* (London: Routledge).

ASEAN Secretariat, and United Nations Conference on Trade and Development [UNCTAD] (2017), *ASEAN Investment Report 2017: Foreign Direct Investment and Economic Zones in ASEAN (ASEAN@50 Special Edition)* (Jakarta: ASEAN Secretariat).

Athukorala, P.-C. (2014), *Industrialisation Through State-MNC Partnership: Lessons from Malaysia's National Car Project*, ACDE Working Paper No. 2014/06, Australian National University, Arndt-Corden Department of Economics, Crawford School of Public Policy, ANU College of Asia & the Pacific.

Athukorala, P.-C., and Narayanan, S. (2017), *Economic Corridors and Regional Development: The Malaysian Experience*, Asian Development Bank, ADB Economics Working Paper Series, No. 520, Manila, Philippines.

Azrai Abdullah (2022), *From Natural Economy to Capitalism: The State and Economic Transformation in Perak, Malaysia c. 1800–2000* (Perak: Universiti Teknologi PETRONAS.)

Badriyah Haji Salleh (1985), 'Malay Rubber Smallholding and British Policy: A Case Study of the Batang Padang District in Perak (1876–1952)', PhD thesis, Columbia University.

Bakas, A. (2016), *Capitalism & Slowbalization: The Market, the State and the Crowd in the 21st Century* (Netherlands: Dexter).

Baldwin, R. (2016), *The Great Convergence: Information Technology and the New Globalization* (Cambridge: Harvard University Press).

Bank Negara Malaysia [BNM] (1972), *Quarterly Economic Bulletin*, September (Kuala Lumpur: Bank Negara Malaysia).

———— (2021), 'Economic and Financial Developments in Malaysia in the 4th Quarter of 2020—Press Release', 11 February, https://www.bnm.gov.my/-/quarterly-developments-q4-2020, accessed 25 April 2021.

———— (various years), *Monthly Statistical Bulletin*, https://www.bnm.gov.my/publications/mhs, accessed 13 December 2021.

Barlow, C., Jayasuriya, S., and Tan, C. S. (1994), *The World Rubber Industry* (London: Routledge).

Barlow, H. S. (2018), 'The Malaysian Plantation Industry: A Brief History to the Mid 1980s', ARABIS (Kuala Lumpur: Southdene Sdn. Bhd.).

Barro, R. J., Ursúa, J. F., and Weng, J. (2020), 'The Coronavirus and the Great Influenza Pandemic: Lessons from the "Spanish Flu" for the Coronavirus's Potential Effects on Mortality and Economic Activity', NBER Working Paper No. 26866, April 2020 (National Bureau of Economic Research), https://www.nber.org/papers/w26866.

Barton, D. B. (1989), *A History of Tin Mining and Smelting in Cornwall* (Exeter: Cornwall Books).

Bauer, P. T. (1944), 'Some Aspects of the Malayan Rubber Slump 1929–1933', *Economica*, New Series, 11/44, 190–198.

———— (1947), 'Malayan Rubber Policies', *Economica*, New Series, 14/54, 81–107.

Baumol, W. J. (1967), 'Macroeconomics of Unbalanced Growth: The Anatomy of Urban Crisis', *The American Economic Review*, 57/3, 415–426.

Beckert, S. (2014), *Empire of Cotton: A Global History* (New York: Alfred A. Knopf).

Belfield, H. C. (1902), *Handbook of the Federated Malay States* (London: Edward Stanford).

Bell, T. (2018), 'The Tin Market Crash of 1985', 11 January, https://www.thebalance.com/the-tin-market-crash-of-1985-2339936, accessed 30 November 2020.

Belogurova, A., (2019), *The Nanyang Revolution: The Comintern and Chinese Networks in Southeast Asia, 1890–1957* (Cambridge: Cambridge University Press).

Birch, E. W. (1896), *Annual Report on the State of Perak for the Year 1895* (Taiping: Government Printing Office).

———— (1907), *Perak Administration Report for the Year 1906* (Kuala Lumpur: Government Printing Office).

———— (1910), 'My Visit to Klian Intan', *Journal of the Straits Branch of the Royal Asiatic Society*, no. 54, 137–146.

Birch, E. W., Berkeley, H., and Luang Raj Bharakii (1910), 'The Taking Over from Siam of Part of Reman or Rahman', *Journal of the Straits Branch of the Royal Asiatic Society*, no. 54, 147–155.

Bird, I. L. (1883), *The Golden Chersonese and the Way Thither* (New York: G. P. Putnam's Sons).

———— (2010), *The Golden Chersonese* (Singapore: Monsoon Books).

Blattman, C., Hwang, J., and Williamson, J. G. (2007), 'Winners and Losers in the Commodity Lottery: The Impact of Terms of Trade Growth and Volatility in the Periphery, 1870–1939', *Journal of Development Economics*, 82/1, 156–179.

Bogaars, G. (1955), 'The Effect of the Opening of the Suez Canal on the Trade and Development of Singapore', *Journal of the Malayan Branch of the Royal Asiatic Society*, 28/1 (169), 99–143.

Bonney, R. (1974), *Kedah 1771–1821: The Search for Security and Independence* (Kuala Lumpur: Oxford University Press).

Brown, P. (2010), *Industrial Pioneers: Scranton, Pennsylvania and the Transformation of America, 1840–1902* (Tribute Books).

Budiman, A. F. S. (2003), 'Recent Developments in Natural Rubber Prices', paper presented at the Consultation on Agricultural Commodity Price Problems Conference, 25–26 March 2002, Rome, Italy.

Burke, G. (1990), 'The Rise and Fall of the International Tin Agreements', in K. S., Jomo (ed.), *Undermining Tin: The Decline of Malaysian Pre-eminence* (Sydney: Transnational Corporations Research Project, University of Sydney).

Burns, P. L. (1965), 'The Constitutional History of Malaya with Special Reference to the Malay States of Perak, Selangor, Negeri Sembilan and Pahang, 1874–1914', PhD thesis, University of London.

_____ (1971), 'Perak State Council Minutes, 3 November 1789', in Wilkinson, R. J. (ed.), *Papers on Malay Subjects* (Kuala Lumpur: Oxford University Press), 208.

_____ (1976) (ed.), *The Journals of J. W. W. Birch. First British Resident to Perak, 1874–1875* (Kuala Lumpur: Oxford University Press).

Burns, P. L., and Cowan, C. D. (1975) (eds.), *Sir Frank Swettenham's Malayan Journals 1874–1876* (Kuala Lumpur: Oxford University Press).

Burt, R., and Kudo, N. (2015), 'Not by Tin Alone: The Polymetallic Content of Primary Tin Production and Cornwall's Role in the International Mining Industry', in Ingulstad, M., Perchard, A. and Storli, E. (eds.), *Tin and Global Capitalism: A History of the Devil's Metal, 1850–2000* (New York: Routledge).

Capie, F. (1978), 'The British Tariff and Industrial Protection in the 1930's', *The Economic History Review*, New Series, 31/3, 399–409.

Census and Economic Information Center [CEIC] database (2020), www.ceicdata.com, accessed 30 November 2020.

Chai, H.-C. (1964), *The Development of British Malaya, 1896–1909* (2nd edn., Kuala Lumpur: Oxford University Press).

Chander, R. (1975), *1970 Population and Housing Census of Malaysia: Basic Population Tables*, pt. IX, Perak (Kuala Lumpur: Department of Statistics–Malaysia).

_____ (1977), *General Report, 1970 Population Census of Malaysia*, vol. I and vol. II (Kuala Lumpur: Department of Statistics–Malaysia).

Chapman, F. S. (1949), *The Jungle is Neutral* (London: Chatto & Windus).

Cheah, B. K. (1981), 'Sino-Malay Conflicts in Malaya, 1945–1946: Communist Vendetta and Islamic Resistance', *Journal of Southeast Asian Studies*, XII/1, 108–117.

_____ (1987), *Red Star Over Malaya: Resistance and Social Conflict During and After the Japanese Occupation of Malaya, 1941–1946* (Singapore: Singapore University Press).

_____ (1991), 'Letters from Exile–Correspondence of Sultan Abdullah of Perak from Seychelles and Mauritius, 1877–1891', *Journal of the Malaysian Branch of the Royal Asiatic Society*, 64/1 (260), 33–74.

_____ (1998), 'Malay Politics and the Murder of J. W. W. Birch, British Resident in Perak, in 1875: The Humiliation and Revenge of the Maharaja Lela', *Journal of the Malaysian Branch of the Royal Asiatic Society*, 71/1 (274), 74–105.

_____ (2002), *Malaysia: The Making of a Nation* (Singapore: Institute of Southeast Asian Studies).

Chee, P. L. (1994), 'Heavy Industrialisation: A Second Round of Import Substitution', in K. S. Jomo (ed.), *Japan and Malaysian Development in the Shadow of the Rising Sun* (London: Routledge), 244–262.

Cheong, K.-C., Goh, K.-L., and Li, R. (2018), 'Brain Drain and Talent Capture in Malaysia: Rethinking Conventional Narratives', in Tyson, A. (ed.), *The Political Economy of Brain Drain and Talent Capture: Evidence from Malaysia and Singapore*, Routledge Malaysian Study Series in association with the Malaysian Social Science Association (MSSA) (London and New York: Routledge).

Cheong, K. C., Lee, K. H., and Lee, P. P. (2013), 'Surviving Financial Crises: The Chinese Overseas in Malaysia and Singapore', *Journal of Contemporary Asia*, 45/1, 26–47.

Chiang, H. D. (1966), 'The Origins of the Malaysian Currency System (1867–1906)', *Journal of the Malaysian Branch of the Royal Asiatic Society*, 39/1 (209), 1–18.

_____ (1978), *A History of Straits Settlements Foreign Trade 1870–1915* (Singapore: National Museum).

Chin Peng (2013), *My Side of History* (Ipoh: Media Masters Publishing).

Chitose, Y. (2003), 'Effects of Government Policy on Internal Migration in Peninsular Malaysia: A Comparison Between Malays and Non-Malays', *The International Migration Review*, 37/4, 1191–1219.

Clifford, H. (1898), *Annual Report of the State of Pahang for the Year 1897* (Kuala Lumpur: Government Printing Office).

Cloake, J. (1985), *Templer: Tiger of Malaya* (London: Harrap Limited).

Coates, J. (1992), *Suppressing Insurgency: An Analysis of the Malayan Emergency, 1948–1954* (Boulder, CO: Westview Press).

Collier, P. (2007), *The Bottom Billion* (New York: Oxford University Press).

_____ (2018), *The Future of Capitalism: Facing the New Anxieties* (United Kingdom: Allen Lane).

Collier, P., and Venables, A. J. (2011) (eds.), *Plundered Nations? Successes and Failures in Natural Resource Extraction* (Hampshire: Palgrave Macmillan).

Colonial Office (1957), *Constitutional Proposals for the Federation of Malaya* (London: Her Majesty's Stationery Office).

Comber, L. (2012), 'The Malayan Emergency: General Templer and the Kinta Valley Home Guard, 1952–1954', *Journal of the Malaysian Branch of the Royal Asiatic Society*, 85/1 (302), 45–62.

Congressional Research Service (2021), *Generalized System of Preferences (GSP): Overview and Issues for Congress*, Updated 7 January 2021, https://sgp.fas.org/crs/misc/RL33663.pdf, accessed 12 June 2022.

Corley, R. H. V., and Tinker, P. B. (2003), *The Oil Palm* (Oxford: Blackwell Science).

Cornwall Heritage Trust (2022), *Industry in Cornwall*, http://www.cornwallheritagetrust.org/discover/industry-in-cornwall/, accessed 19 February 2022.

Cowan, C. D. (1952) (ed.), 'Sir Frank Swettenham's Perak Journals, 1874–1876', *Journal of the Malayan Branch of the Royal Asiatic Society*, 24/4 (157), 1–148.

Curle, R. (1923), *Into the East: Notes on Burma and Malaya* (London: Macmillan and Co).

Curtis, M. (2003), *Web of Deceit: Britain's Real Role in the World* (London: Vintage Books).

_____ (2022), 'Malaya—Britain's forgotten War for Rubber', Economic History of Malaya Project, https://www.ehm.my/publications/articles/malaya%E2%80%94britains-forgotten-war-for-rubber, accessed, 19 August 2022.

Cushman, J. W. (1986), 'The Khaw Group: Chinese Business in Early Twentieth-Century Penang', *Journal of Southeast Asian Studies*, 17/1, 58–79.

D'Almeida, W. B. (1876), 'Geography of Perak and Salangore, and a Brief Sketch of Some of the Adjacent Malay States', *The Journal of the Royal Geographical Society of London*, 46, 357–380.

Daly, D. D. (1882), 'Surveys and Explorations in the Native States of the Malayan Peninsula, 1875–82', *Proceedings of the Royal Geographical Society and Monthly Record of Geography*, IV/7, 393–412.

de la Croix, J. E. (1881), 'Some Account of the Mining Districts of Lower Perak', *Journal of the Straits Branch of the Royal Asiatic Society*, no. 7, 1–10.

De Witt, D. (2007), *History of the Dutch in Malaysia* (Kuala Lumpur: Nutmeg Publishing).

Del Tufo, M. V. (1949), *A Report on the 1947 Census of Population, Malaya (Comprising the Federation of Malaya and the Colony of Singapore)* (London: The Crown Agents for the Colonies).

Department of Information–Federation of Malaya (1950), *Malaya Under the Emergency Report by Sir Harold Briggs, 1950* (Kuala Lumpur: The Standard Engravers & Art Printers).

_____ (1951), *Communist Banditry in Malaya: The Emergency with a Chronology of Important Events, June 1948–June 1951* (Kuala Lumpur: The Standard Engravers & Art Printers).

Department of Statistics–Federation of Malaya (various years), *Malaya Rubber Statistics Handbook* (Kuala Lumpur: Department of Statistics–Federation of Malaya).

Department of Statistics–Malaysia (1968), *Census of Manufacturing Industries West Malaysia* (Kuala Lumpur: Department of Statistics–Malaysia).

Department of Statistics–Malaysia (2002), *Rubber Statistics Handbook Malaysia 2001* (Kuala Lumpur: Department of Statistics–Malaysia).

_____ (2015), *Malaysia Economic Statistics, Time Series 2015* (Putrajaya: Department of Statistics–Malaysia).

_____ (2017a), *Economic Census 2016, Profile of Small and Medium Enterprises* (Putrajaya: Department of Statistics–Malaysia).

_____ (2017b), *GDP by State National Accounts 2010–2016* (Putrajaya: Department of Statistics–Malaysia).

_____ (2018a), *Migration Survey Report, Malaysia 2018* (Putrajaya: Department of Statistics–Malaysia).

_____ (2018b), *My Local Stats, Perak 2017* (Putrajaya: Department of Statistics–Malaysia).

_____ (2020a), *Household Income and Basic Amenities Survey Report 2019* (Putrajaya: Department of Statistics–Malaysia).

_____ (2020b), *Labour Force Survey Report 2019* (Putrajaya: Department of Statistics–Malaysia).

_____ (2020c), *My Local Stats, Perak 2019 (various district reports)* (Putrajaya: Department of Statistics–Malaysia).

_____ (2022), *Laporan Sosioekonomi Negeri Perak, 2021* (Putrajaya: Department of Statistics–Malaysia).

_____ (various years), *Annual GDP National Accounts Malaysia* (Putrajaya: Department of Statistics–Malaysia).

_____ (various years), *GDP by State National Accounts* (Putrajaya: Department of Statistics–Malaysia).

_____ (various years), *Labour Force Survey Report* (Putrajaya: Department of Statistics–Malaysia).

_____ (various years), *Laporan Sosioekonomi Negeri* (Putrajaya: Department of Statistics–Malaysia).

_____ (various years), *Migration Survey Reports* (Putrajaya: Department of Statistics–Malaysia).

_____ (various years), *Oil Palm, Coconut and Tea Statistics* (Kuala Lumpur: Department of Statistics–Malaysia).

_____ (various years), *Rubber Statistics Handbook Malaysia* (Kuala Lumpur: Department of Statistics–Malaysia).

_____ (various years), *State/District Data Bank* (Putrajaya: Department of Statistics–Malaysia).

Di Cataldo, M. (2016), 'Gaining and Losing EU Objective 1 Funds: Regional Development in Britain and the Prospect of Brexit', LEQS Paper No. 120/2016, November 2016, LSE 'Europe in Question' Discussion Paper Series (United Kingdom: London School of Economics and Political Science).

_____ (2017), 'The Impact of EU Objective 1 Funds on Regional Development: Evidence from the U.K. and the Prospect of Brexit', *Journal of Regional Science*, 57/5, 814–839.

Dobby, E. H. G. (1952), 'Resettlement Transforms Malaya: A Case-History of Relocating the Population of an Asian Plural Society', *Economic Development and Cultural Change*, 1/3, 163–189.

Dodge, N. N. (1981), 'The Malay-Aborigine Nexus Under Malay Rule', *Bijdragen tot de Taal-, Land- en Volkenkunde Deel 137*, 1ste Afl., ANTHROPOLOGICA XXIII, 1–16.

Doyle, P. (1879), *Tin Mining in Larut* (London: E. & F. N. Spon).

Drabble, J. H. (1991), *Malayan Rubber: The Interwar Years* (London: Macmillan Academic and Professional Ltd).

_____ (2000), *An Economic History of Malaysia, c. 1800–1990: The Transition to Modern Economic Growth* (London: Macmillan Press Ltd).

Drabble, J. H., and Drake, P. J. (1974), 'More on the Financing of Malayan Rubber, 1905–23', *The Economic History Review*, 27/1, 108–120.

Drake, P. J. (1969), *Financial Development in Malaya and Singapore* (Canberra: Australian National University Press).

_____ (1979), 'The Economic Development of British Malaya to 1914: An Essay in Historiography with Some Questions for Historians', *Journal of Southeast Asian Studies*, 10/2, 262–290.

Duranton, G., and Puga, D. (2004), 'Micro-foundations of Urban Agglomeration Economies', in Henderson, J. V. and Thisse, J. F. (eds.), *Handbook of Regional and Urban Economics*, vol. 4, *Cities and Geography* (Amsterdam: North Holland).

Economic Planning Unit–Malaysia [EPU] (1966), *First Malaysia Plan, 1966–1970* (Kuala Lumpur: Government Printers).

_____ (1971), *Second Malaysia Plan, 1971–1975* (Kuala Lumpur: Government Printers).

_____ (1976), *Third Malaysia Plan, 1976–1980* (Kuala Lumpur: Government Printers).

_____ (1981), *Fourth Malaysia Plan, 1981–1985* (Kuala Lumpur: Government Printers).

_____ (1986), *Fifth Malaysia Plan, 1986–1990* (Kuala Lumpur: Government Printers).

_____ (1991a), *The Second Outline Perspective Plan, 1991–2000* (Kuala Lumpur: Government Printers).

_____ (1991b), *Sixth Malaysia Plan, 1991–1995* (Kuala Lumpur: Government Printers).

_____ (1996), *Seventh Malaysia Plan, 1996–2000* (Kuala Lumpur: Government Printers).

_____ (1999), *Mid-term Review of the Seventh Malaysia Plan, 1996–2000* (Putrajaya: Government Printers).

_____ (2001), *Eighth Malaysia Plan, 2001–2005* (Putrajaya: Government Printers).

_____ (2003), *Mid-term Review of the Eighth Malaysia Plan, 2001–2005* (Putrajaya: Government Printers).

_____ (2006), *Ninth Malaysia Plan, 2006–2010* (Putrajaya: Government Printers).

_____ (2008), *Mid-term Review of the Ninth Malaysia Plan, 2006–2010* (Putrajaya: Government Printers).

_____ (2011), *Tenth Malaysia Plan, 2011–2015* (Putrajaya: Government Printers).

_____ (2014), *Complexity Analysis Study of Malaysia's Manufacturing Industries 2014 – Final Report* (Putrajaya: EPU).

_____ (2016), *Eleventh Malaysia Plan, 2016–2020* (Putrajaya: Government Printers).

_____ (2021), *Twelfth Malaysia Plan, 2021–2025* (Putrajaya: Government Printers).

_____ (various years), 'Incidence of Absolute Poverty, Socio-economic Statistics', https://www.epu.gov.my/en/socio-economic-statistics/household-income-poverty-and-household-expenditure, accessed January 2021.

Eichengreen, B. (2019), *Globalizing Capital: A History of the International Monetary System* (3rd edn., New Jersey: Princeton University Press).

Etzo, I. (2008), 'Internal Migration: A Review of the Literature', MPRA Paper No. 8783 (Italy: University of Cagliari).

European Economic Community [EEC] (1976), 'Fifth International Tin Agreement', *Official Journal of the European Communities*, No. L 222/3–L 222/36, https://op.europa.eu/s/owh8, accessed December 2020.

Eurostat (2002), *European Social Statistics—Income, Poverty and Social Exclusion: 2nd Report* (Luxembourg: Office for Official Publications of the European Communities).

Eyles, J. (2007), 'Urban Assets and Urban Sustainability: Challenges, Design and Management', *WIT Transactions on Ecology and the Environment*, 102, 135–142.

Faulkner, O. T. (1938), *Annual Report of the Department of Agriculture, Malaya for the Year 1937* (Kuala Lumpur: Government Press).

Federal Industrial Development Authority [FIDA] (1969), *Report on a Techno-Economic Survey of Foundries in Perak and Penang*, Annex to the Report on the Techno-Economic Survey of Foundries in Selangor.

_____ (1971), *Annual Report 1970* (Kuala Lumpur: FIDA).

Federated Malay States Railways (1935), *Fifty Years of Railways in Malaya: 1885–1935* (Kuala Lumpur: Kyle, Palmer & Company Limited).

Federation of Malaya (1950), *Draft Development Plan of the Federation of Malaya, 1950–1955* (Kuala Lumpur: Government Printer).

_____ (1953), *Progress Report on the Development Plan of the Federation of Malaya 1950–1952* (Kuala Lumpur: Government Printer).

_____ (1956), *A Plan of Development for Malaya, 1956–1960* (Kuala Lumpur: Government Press).

_____ (1961), *Second Five-year Plan, 1961–1965* (Federation of Malaya: Government Press).

Fell, H. (1959), *Population Census of the Federation of Malaya*, Report No. 8 (Kuala Lumpur: Department of Statistics–Federation of Malaya).

_____ (1960), *1957 Population Census of the Federation of Malaya*, Report No. 14 (Kuala Lumpur: Department of Statistics–Federation of Malaya).

Fels, R. (1949), 'The Long-wave Depression, 1873–97', *The Review of Economics and Statistics*, 31/1, 69–73.

Fernando, J. M. (2003), 'British Attitude Towards the Alliance Party, 1952–1957', *Jurnal Sejarah*, 11/11, 41–56.

Firdausi Suffian (2020), 'The Politics and Institutional Arrangements in Malaysia's Automotive Industry', *Journal of Southeast Asian Economies*, 37/1, 47–64.

Fong, C. O. (1989), *The Malaysian Economic Challenge in the 1990s: Transformation for Growth* (Singapore: Longman).

Food and Agriculture Organization of the United Nations [FAO] (1985), 'Fishermen Relocation Programme in Peninsular Malaysia', http://www.fao.org/3/ac063e/AC063E10.htm, accessed January 2021.

_____ (2021), 'Food and Agriculture Data', http://www.fao.org/faostat/en/#data/TP, accessed 25 March 2021.

_____ (various years), 'Oil Palm Production, Food and Agriculture Data', http://www.fao.org/faostat/en/#data/QD, accessed November 2020.

_____ (various years), 'Rubber Production, Food and Agriculture Data', http://www.fao.org/faostat/en/#data/QC, accessed June 2020.

Foong, C. H. (1997) (ed.), *The Price of Peace: True Accounts of the Japanese Occupation*, Singapore Chinese Chamber of Commerce and Industry (Singapore: Asiapac Books).

Foreign Office–Great Britain (1909), *Treaty Between the United Kingdom and Siam: Signed at Bangkok, March 10, 1909* (London: Her Majesty's Stationery Office).

Forestry Department of Peninsular Malaysia (2021), *Forestry Statistics of Peninsular Malaysia* (Kuala Lumpur: Forestry Department of Peninsular Malaysia).

Frankopan, P. (2015), *The Silk Roads: A New History of the World* (London: Bloomsbury Publishing).

French, L. (2012), 'Titanic: Cornish Tin Mining Decline "Forced" Miners Abroad', https://www.bbc.com/news/uk-england-cornwall-17547490, accessed 19 May 2022.

Fujita, M. (1999), 'Industrial Policies and Trade Liberalization: The Automotive Industry in Thailand and Malaysia', APEC Study Center, Institute of Developing Economies, 149–187.

Fujita, M., and Hamaguchi, N. (2020), 'Globalisation and the COVID-19 Pandemic: A Spatial Economics Perspective', https://voxeu.org/article/globalisation-and-covid-19-pandemic, accessed 10 April 2021.

Gamba, C. (1962), *The Origins of Trade Unionism in Malaya: A Study in Colonial Labour Unrest* (Singapore: Eastern Universities Press Ltd).

Geer, T. (1970), 'The Post-war Tin Agreements: A Case of Success in Price Stabilization of Primary Commodities?', Schweizerische Zeitschriftfiir Volkwirtschaft und Statistik, 106/2, 189–236.

German, R. L. (1937), *Handbook to British Malaya* (London: The Malayan Information Agency).

Giacomin, V. (2018), 'The Emergence of an Export Cluster: Traders and Palm Oil in Early Twentieth-Century Southeast Asia', *Enterprise & Society*, 19/2, 272–308, https://doi.org/10.1017/eso.2017.10, accessed 5 October 2021.

Gilbert, C. L. (1995), 'International Commodity Control: Retrospect and Prospect', Policy Research Working Paper 1545 (Washington, DC: The World Bank).

Glamann, K. (1958), *Dutch—Asiatic Trade, 1620–1740* (The Hague: Danish Science Press).

Goddard, J., and Vallance, P. (2013), *The University and the City* (Oxon: Routledge).

Gomez, E. T. (2006), 'Foreword' in Abraham, C., '*The Finest Hour': The Malaysian-MCP Peace Accord in Perspective* (Petaling Jaya: Strategic Information, Research and Development Centre).

Gomez, E. T., and Jomo, K. S. (1999), *Malaysia's Political Economy: Politics, Patronage and Profits* (2nd edn., Cambridge: Cambridge University Press).

Gordon, M. (2021), *Extreme Violence and the 'British Way': Colonial Warfare in Perak, Sierra Leone and Sudan* (London: Bloomsbury Academic).

Gough, J. (2013), 'Recognising Perak Hydro's Contribution to Perak', *Ipoh Echo*, 1–15 February, Issue 159, 1–2.

Government of Canada (2021), 'Venture Capital Action Plan', SME Research and Statistics, 23 December 2020, https://www.ic.gc.ca/eic/site/061.nsf/eng/h_03033.html, accessed 25 May 2021.

Greig, G. E. (1924), 'Mining in Malaya', in Sunderland, D. (ed.), *British Economic Development in South East Asia, 1880–1939*, vol. 2 (London: Routledge).

Gullick, J. M. (1953), 'Captain Speedy of Larut', *Journal of the Malayan Branch of the Royal Asiatic Society*, 26/3 (163), 1–103.

_____ (1958), *Indigenous Political Systems of Western Malaya*, London School of Economics Monographs on Social Anthropology, vol. 17 (University of London: The Athlone Press).

_____ (1993), *They Came to Malaya: A Travellers' Anthology* (Singapore: Oxford University Press).

_____ (2010), 'The Economy of Perak in the Mid-1870s', *Journal of the Malaysian Branch of the Royal Asiatic Society*, 83/2 (299), 27–46.

Hack, K. (2022), *The Malayan Emergency: Revolution and Counterinsurgency at the End of Empire* (Cambridge: Cambridge University Press).

Hagan, J., and Wells, A. (2005), 'The British and Rubber in Malaya, c. 1890–1940', in Patmore, G., Shields, J. and Balnave, N. (eds.), *The Past is Before Us: Proceedings of the Ninth National Labour History Conference* (Australia: University of Sydney), 143–150.

Hagenaars, A. J. M., de Vos, K., and Asghar Zaidi, M. (1994), *Poverty Statistics in the Late 1980s: Research Based on Micro-data* (Luxembourg: Office for Official Publications of the European Communities).

Hale, A. L. (1885), 'On Mines and Miners in Kinta, Perak', *Journal of the Straits Branch of the Royal Asiatic Society*, vol. 16, 303–320.

Hall, P. (1966), *Von Thunen's Isolated State* (London: Pergamon Press).

Hall, W. T. (1888), *Report on Tin-mining in Perak and in Burma, Rangoon*.

Hamilton Jenkin, A. K. (1927), *The Cornish Minor: An Account of His Life Above and Underground from Early Times* (London: George Allen & Unwin).

Hampton, J. H. (1886), *Tin Deposits of the State of Perak, Straits Settlements*, read at Camborne, on Thursday, 14 October 1886, Mr R. J. Frecheville presiding.

Hare, G. T. (1902), *Census of the Population, Federated Malay States, 1901* (Kuala Lumpur: Government Printer).

Harper, T. N. (1999), *The End of Empire and the Making of Malaya* (Cambridge: Cambridge University Press).

Harrison, B. (1954), 'Malacca in the Eighteenth Century Two Dutch Governors' Reports', *Journal of the Malayan Branch of the Royal Asiatic Society*, September 1953, 27/1 (165), 22–34.

Harrison, C. W. (1923), *Illustrated Guide to the Federated Malay States* (London: General Books).

Harrison, R. J. (1907) (ed.), *Papers on Malay Subjects: History, Part III. Council Minutes, Perak, 1877–1879* (Kuala Lumpur: F. M. S. Government Press).

Hashim Sam. (2002), *The Royal Commoner: The Life and Times of Imam Perang Jabor 1858–1921* (Kuala Lumpur: Perpustakaan Negara Malaysia).

Hasnah Ali, and Asan Ali Golam Hassan (2008), 'Investment Incentives and Regional Differentials in the Malaysian States', *International Review of Business Research Papers*, 4/4, 147–162.

Hausmann, R., and Rodrik, D. (2003), 'Economic Development as Self-discovery', *Journal of Development Economics*, 72/2, 603–633.

Henderson, J. V. (2003), 'Marshall's Scale Economies', *Journal of Urban Economics*, 53/1, 1–28.

Heng, P. K. (1988), *Chinese Politics in Malaysia: A History of the Malayan Chinese Association*, East Asian Historical Monographs (Singapore: Oxford University Press).

Hennart, J-F. (1986), 'Internationalization in Practice: Early Foreign Direct Investments in Malaysian Tin Mining', *Journal of International Business Studies*, 17/2, 131–143.

Hertslet, L. (1856), 'Treaty with Sultan of Perak dated 25 October 1826', in *Hertslet's Commercial Treaties: A Complete Collection of the Treaties and Conventions, and Reciprocal Regulations, at Present Subsisting Between Great Britain and Foreign Powers*, vol. 1–31 (London: Harrisons and Sons), 909–912.

Hicks, E. C. (1958), *History of English Schools in Perak* (Ipoh: The Perak Library).

Hidalgo, C. A., Balland, P-A., Boschma, R., Delgado, M., Feldman, M., Frenken, K., Glaeser, E., He, C., Kogler, D. F., Morrison, A., Neffke, F., Rigby, D., Stern, S., Zheng, S., and Zhu, S. (2018), 'The Principle of Relatedness', Papers in Evolutionary Economic Geography No. 18.30 (Urban & Regional Research Centre Utrecht, Utrecht University), http://econ.geo.uu.nl/peeg/peeg1830.pdf.

Hill, H., and Menon, J. (2020), 'Economic Corridors in Southeast Asia: Success Factors, Impacts and Policy', Economics Working Paper, No. 2020-03, ISEAS–Yusof Ishak Institute.

Hill, R. D. (1973), *Rice in Malaya: A Study in Historical Geography* (Singapore: University of Singapore).

Hillman, J. (1988), 'Malaya and the International Tin Cartel', *Modern Asian Studies*, 22/2, 237–261.

_____ (2010), *The International Tin Cartel* (New York and London: Routledge).

Hinds, A. (1999), 'Sterling and Decolonization in the British Empire, 1945–1958', *Social and Economic Studies*, 48/4, Federation and Caribbean Integration, 97–116.

Ho, H. L. (2006), 'The Rubber and Tin Industries in Malaya During the Emergency, 1948–1960', paper presented at the 19th International Association of Historians of Asia (IAHA) Conference, 22–25 November 2006, Manila, Philippines.

Ho, T. M. (2005), *Generations: The Story of Batu Gajah* (Ipoh: Perak Academy).

_____ (2009), *Ipoh: When Tin was King* (Ipoh: Perak Academy).

Hood Salleh (2006) (ed.), *The Encyclopedia of Malaysia: Peoples and Traditions*, vol. 12 (Singapore: Archipelago Press).

Huff, G. (2023), 'Malayan Independence, Malay Inequality, and the "Bargain"', *Economic History of Malaya Project*, https://www.ehm.my/publications/articles/malayan-independence-malay-inequality-and-the-bargain, accessed 21 May 2023.

Husni Abu Bakar (2015), 'Playing Along the Perak River: Readings of an Eighteenth-Century Malay State', *Southeast Asian Studies*, 4/1, 157–190.

Hutchinson, F. E. (2017), 'Evolving Paradigms in Malaysia's Regional Development Policy', *Journal of Southeast Asian Economies*, 34/3, 462–487, http://www.jstor.org/stable/44685076, accessed 1 February 2021.

Ingulstad, M., Perchard, A., and Storli, E. (2015), '"The Path of Civilization is Paved with Tin Cans": The Political Economy of the Global Tin Industry', in Ingulstad, M., Perchard, A., and Storli, E. (eds.), *Tin and Global Capitalism: A History of the Devil's Metal, 1850–2000* (London: Routledge).

Institut Darul Ridzuan (2011), Unpublished briefing notes (Ipoh, Perak).

International Bank for Reconstruction and Development [IBRD] (1955), *The Economic Development of Malaya: Report of a Mission Organized by the IBRD at the Request of the Federation of Malaya, the Crown Colony of Singapore and the United Kingdom* (Washington, DC: IBRD).

International Monetary Fund [IMF] (2021), *World Economic Outlook: Managing Divergent Recoveries: Update*, April 2021 (Washington, DC: IMF).

_____ (2023), *World Economic Outlook: A Rocky Recovery*, April 2023 (Washington, DC: IMF).

International Tin Council [ITC] (1960), International Organization, 14/2, 371.

International Tin Study Group (1952), *Tin and the Paley Report extracts from Resources for Freedom: The Report of the USA President's Materials Policy Commission, 1952* (Washington, DC: United States Government Printing Office).

InvestPerak, and UKM Pakarunding (2011), *Perak Industrial Development Action Plan, 2011–2020* (Ipoh, Perak).

Ismail Bakar (2004), 'Fiscal Federalism: The Study of Federal-State Fiscal Relations in Malaysia', PhD thesis, University of Hull.

Jackson, N. R. (1963), 'Changing Patterns of Employment in Malayan Tin Mining', *Journal of Southeast Asian History*, 4/2, 141–153.

Jackson, R. N. (1965), *Pickering: Protector of Chinese* (Kuala Lumpur: Oxford University Press).

Jain, R. K. (1993), 'Tamilian Labour and Malayan Plantations, 1840–1938', *Economic and Political Weekly*, 28/43, 2367–2370.

Jaunay, A. (2020), *Jacques de Morgan's Explorations in the Malay Peninsula, 1884* (Singapore: Malaysian Branch of the Royal Asiatic Society).

Johnson, S., Kochhar, K., Mitton, T., and Tamirisa, N. (2007), 'Malaysian Capital Controls: Macroeconomics and Institutions', in Edwards, S. (ed.), *Capital Controls and Capital Flows in Emerging Economies: Policies, Practices and Consequences* (Chicago: University of Chicago Press).

Jomo, K. S. (1986), *A Question of Class: Capital, the State, and Uneven Development in Malaysia* (Singapore: Oxford University Press).

_____ (1990) (ed.), *Undermining Tin: The Decline of Malaysian Pre-eminence*, Transnational Corporations Research Project (Sydney: University of Sydney).

Jomo, K. S., and Todd, P. (1994), *Trade Unions and the State in Peninsular Malaysia* (Kuala Lumpur: Oxford University Press).

Jomo, K. S., and Wee, C. H. (2002), 'The Political Economy of Malaysian Federalism: Economic Development, Public Policy and Conflict Containment', WIDER Discussion Paper No. 2002/113 (Helsinki: United Nations University–World Institute for Development Economics Research/ UNU–WIDER).

Jones, G. (2000), *Merchants to Multinationals: British Trading Companies in the Nineteenth and Twentieth Centuries* (New York: Oxford University Press).

Jones, R. (2017, 14 May), 'How Sheffield Became Steel City: What Local History Can Teach Us About Innovation, Soft Machines', http://www.softmachines.org/wordpress/?p=2057, accessed 15 April 2021.

Kathirithamby-Wells, J. (2005), *Nature and Nation: Forests and Development in Peninsular Malaysia* (Copenhagen: Nordic Institute of Asian Studies (NIAS) Press).

Kaur, A. (1980), 'The Impact of Railroads on the Malayan Economy, 1874–1941', *The Journal of Asian Studies*, 39/4, 693–710.

_____ (2004), *Wage Labour in Southeast Asia Since 1840* (New York: Palgrave Macmillan).

_____ (2012), 'Rubber Plantation Workers, Work Hazards, and Health in Colonial Malaya, 1900–1940', in Sellers, C. and Melling, J. (eds.), *Dangerous Trade: Histories of Industrial Hazard Across a Globalizing World* (Philadelphia: Temple University Press).

Khasnor Johan (1984), *The Emergence of the Modern Malay Administrative Elite* (Oxford: Oxford University Press).

Khoo, K. K. (1966), 'The Origin of British Administration in Malaya', *Journal of the Malaysian Branch of the Royal Asiatic Society*, 39/1 (209), 52–91.

_____ (1972), *The Western Malay States, 1850–1873: The Effects of Commercial Development on Malay Politics* (Kuala Lumpur: Oxford University Press).

_____ (1986), 'The Perak Sultanate: Ancient and Modern', *Journal of the Malaysian Branch of the Royal Asiatic Society*, 59/1 (250), 1–26.

_____ (1991), 'Taiping (Larut): The Early History of a Mining Settlement', *Journal of the Malaysian Branch of the Royal Asiatic Society*, 64/1 (260), 1–32.

_____ (2002), 'Tanjong, Hilir Perak, Larut and Kinta. The Penang–Perak Nexus in History', paper presented at The Penang Story–International Conference 2002, Penang, The Penang Heritage Trust and STAR Publications.

_____ (2017), 'Geography as a Determinant of Settlement Development in Malaysian History', *Journal of the Department of History*, University of Malaya, 10/10, 1–20.

_____ (undated), 'J. W. W. Birch: A Victorian Moralist in Perak's Augean Stable?', unpublished.

Khoo, S. G. (1995a), *Perak State Population Report, 1991 Population and Housing Census of Malaysia* (Kuala Lumpur: Department of Statistics–Malaysia).

_____ (1995b), *Penang State Population Report, 1991 Population and Housing Census of Malaysia* (Kuala Lumpur: Department of Statistics–Malaysia).

_____ (1995c), *Selangor State Population Report, 1991 Population and Housing Census of Malaysia* (Kuala Lumpur: Department of Statistics–Malaysia).

_____ (1995d), *General Report of the Population Census, 1991 Population and Housing Census of Malaysia*, vol. II (Kuala Lumpur: Department of Statistics–Malaysia).

_____ (1995e), *Johor State Population Report, 1991 Population and Housing Census of Malaysia* (Kuala Lumpur: Department of Statistics–Malaysia).

_____ (1995f), *Wilayah Persekutuan KL State Population Report, 1991 Population and Housing Census of Malaysia* (Kuala Lumpur: Department of Statistics–Malaysia).

Khoo, S. N., and Abdur-Razzaq Lubis (2005), *Kinta Valley: Pioneering Malaysia's Modern Development* (Perak Darul Ridzuan: Perak Academy).

Khoo, T. H. (1983), *General Report of the Population Census, 1980 Population and Housing Census of Malaysia* (Kuala Lumpur: Department of Statistics–Malaysia).

Khor, M. K. P. (1987), *Malaysia's Economy in Decline: What Happened? Why? What to Do?* (Penang: Consumers Association).

_____ (2019), *The Malaysian Economy: Structures and Dependence* (Penang: Institut Masyarakat/ Third World Network).

Khor, N., Isa, M., and Kaur, M. (2017), *The Towns of Malaya: An Illustrated Urban History of the Peninsula Up to 1957* (Kuala Lumpur: Didier Millet).

Kiernan, V. G. (1956), 'Britain, Siam, and Malaya: 1875–1885', *The Journal of Modern History*, 28/1, 1–20.

King, A. W. (1939), 'Plantation and Agriculture in Malaya, with Notes on the Trade of Singapore', *The Geographical Journal*, 93/2, 136–148.

Kinloch, R. F. (1966), 'The Growth of Electric Power Production in Malaya', *Annals of the Association of American Geographers*, 56/2, 220–235.

Kinney, W. P. (1975), 'Aspects of Malayan Economic Development, 1900–1940', PhD thesis, University of London.

Koay, S. L. (2018), The Genesis of Higher Education in Colonial Malaya, https://www.ehm.my/publications/articles/the-genesis-of-higher-education-in-colonial-malaya.

Koster, G. L. (2005), 'Of Treaties and Unbelievers: Images of the Dutch in Seventeenth- and Eighteenth-Century Malay Historiography', *Journal of the Malaysian Branch of the Royal Asiatic Society*, 78/1 (288), 59–96.

Kratoska, P. H. (2018), *The Japanese Occupation of Malaya and Singapore, 1941–45: A Social and Economic History* (2nd edn., Singapore: National University of Singapore Press).

Krug, J. A. (1945), *Minerals Yearbook* (Washington, DC: United States Government Printing Office).

Krugman, P. (2020), ADIPEC Session: How COVID-19 Changes World's Long Held Assumptions on Global Growth, Abu Dhabi International Petroleum Exhibition & Conference (ADIPEC) Virtual 2020, 11 November 2020, https://www.oilreviewafrica.com/exploration/industry/paul-krugman-speaks-on-how-covid-19-changes-world-s-long-held-assumptions-on-global-growth, accessed 24 March 2021.

Lagarde, C. (2022, 22 April), 'A New Global Map: European Resilience in a Changing World' [Keynote speech], Peterson Institute for International Economics, Washington, DC.

Lam, N. V. (1978), 'Incidence of Tin Export Taxation in West Malaysia', *The Developing Economies*, 16/4, 434–446.

Lane, L., Grubb, B., and Power, A. (2016), 'Sheffield City Story', CASEreport 103, May 2016, Centre for Analysis of Social Exclusion (CASE) (United Kingdom: London School of Economics and Political Science).

Laplanche, F. (2020), *France and Perak—The Historic Links*, personal communication of unpublished manuscript.

Lee, C. (2019), 'Globalisation and Economic Development: Malaysia's Experience', Economic Research Institute for ASEAN and East Asia, ERIA Discussion Paper Series, No. 307 (Singapore: ISEAS–Yusof Ishak Institute).

Lee, K. H. (1978), 'A Socio-economic History of Perak 1920–1939', in Lee, P. P. and Lee, K. H. (eds.), *Some Socio-economic Aspects of Perak Society, Malaysia*, Joint Research Project, No. 6, Institute of Developing Economies, Japan.

Lee, P. C., and Panton, W. P. (1971), *First Malaysia Plan Land Capability Classification Report, West Malaysia* (Kuala Lumpur: EPU).

Lee, S. Y. (1990), *The Monetary and Banking Development of Malaysia and Singapore* (Singapore: Singapore University Press).

Leech, H. W. C. (1879), 'About Kinta', *Journal of the Straits Branch of the Royal Asiatic Society*, no. 4, 21–33.

—— (1894), 'Some Notes on the Padi Industry of Krian', in Wray, J. L. (ed.), *The Tin Mines and the Mining Industries of Perak and Other Papers*, Perak Museum, Notes No. 111 (Taiping: Government Printing Office).

Leech, J. B. M. (1891), *Perak Government Gazette*, vol. IV, 1048.

Lees, L. H. (2017), *Planting Empire, Cultivating Subjects: British Malaya, 1786–1941* (Cambridge: Cambridge University Press).

Leete, R. (2007), *Malaysia: From Kampung to Twin Towers, Fifty Years of Economic and Social Development* (Kuala Lumpur: Oxford University Press).

Levitt, T. (1983), 'The Globalization of Markets', *Harvard Business Review*, May/June 1983, 92–102.

Lewis, D. (1969), 'The Tin Trade in the Malay Peninsula During the Eighteenth Century', *New Zealand Journal of History*, 3/1, 52–69.

Lewis, W. A. (1954), 'Economic Development with Unlimited Supplies of Labour', *The Manchester School*, 22/2, 139–191.

Liew, K. K. (2010), 'Planters, Estate Health & Malaria in British Malaya (1900–1940)', *Journal of the Malaysian Branch of the Royal Asiatic Society*, 83/1 (298), 91–115.

Lim, C.-Y. (1960), 'A Reappraisal of the 1953 International Tin Agreement', *The Malayan Economic Review*, 5/1, 13–24.

_____ (1967), *Economic Development of Modern Malaya* (Kuala Lumpur: Oxford University Press).

_____ (1969), *Economic Development of Modern Malaya* (Kuala Lumpur: Oxford University Press).

Lim, G. E. (2019, 17 September), Belanjawan 2020 Focus Group Discussion: Moving Up the Value Chain for the Electrical & Electronics Industry [Speech], https://www.treasury.gov.my/index.php/en/gallery-activities/speech/item/5500-speech-by-the-honourable-mr-lim-guan-eng-minister-of-finance,-belanjawan-2020-focus-group-discussion-moving-up-the-value-chain-for-the-electrical-electronics-industry.html, accessed 15 December 2020.

Lim, L. L. (2020), *The Socioeconomic Impacts of COVID-19 in Malaysia: Policy Review and Guidance for Protecting the Most Vulnerable and Supporting Enterprises* (Geneva: International Labour Organization).

Lim, M. H. (1981), *Ownership and Control of the One Hundred Largest Corporations in Malaysia* (Kuala Lumpur: Oxford University Press).

Lim, T. G. (1971), 'Peasant Agriculture in Colonial Malaya: Its Development in Perak, Selangor, Negri Sembilan and Pahang, 1874–1941', PhD thesis, Australian National University.

_____ (1974), 'Malayan Peasant Smallholders and the Stevenson Restriction Scheme, 1922–28', *Journal of the Malaysian Branch of the Royal Asiatic Society*, 47/2 (226), 105–122.

_____ (1977), *Peasants and Their Agricultural Economy in Colonial Malaya, 1874–1941* (Kuala Lumpur: Oxford University Press).

Lines, T. (2007), *Supply Management: Options for Commodity Income Stabilization* (Canada: International Institute for Sustainable Development (IISD)).

Lo Cascio, E., and Malanima, P. (2009), 'GDP in Pre-modern Agrarian Economies (1–1820 AD). A Revision of the Estimates', *Rivista di Storia Economica*, XXV/3, 391–420.

Loadman, J. (2005), *Tears of the Tree: The Story of Rubber—A Modern Marvel* (Oxford: Oxford University Press).

Loh, F. K. W. (1988), *Beyond the Tin Mines: Coolies, Squatters and New Villagers in the Kinta Valley, Malaysia, c. 1880–1980*, East Asian Historical Monographs (Singapore: Oxford University Press).

_____ (1990), 'From Tin Mine Coolies to Agricultural Squatters: Socio-economic Change in the Kinta District During the Inter-war Years', in Rimmer, P. J. and Allen, L. M. (eds.), *The Underside of Malaysian History: Pullers, Prostitutes, Plantation Workers* (Singapore: Singapore University Press).

Loh, P. F.-S. (1972), 'Malay Precedence and the Federal Formula in the Federated Malay States, 1909–1939', *Journal of the Malaysian Branch of the Royal Asiatic Society*, 45/2 (222), 29–50.

Longlands, S., and Round, A. (2021), 'Why Devolution Matters: The Case of Cornwall', Institute for Public Policy Research, https://www.ippr.org/publication/why-devolution-matters-the-case-of-cornwall.

Louis, W. R. (1999), 'Introduction', in Brown, J. M. and Louis, W. R. (eds.), *The Oxford History of the British Empire: Volume IV: The Twentieth Century* (Oxford: Oxford University Press).

Lynn, M. (1999), 'British Policy, Trade, and Informal Empire in the Mid-Nineteenth Century', in Porter, A. (ed.), *The Oxford History of the British Empire: Volume III: The Nineteenth Century* (Oxford: Oxford University Press).

Mahani Musa (1999), 'Malays and the Red and White Flag Societies in Penang, 1830s–1920s', *Journal of the Malaysian Branch of the Royal Asiatic Society*, 72/2 (277), 151–182.

Mahathir Mohamad (2011), *A Doctor in the House: The Memoirs of Tun Dr Mahathir Mohamad* (Kuala Lumpur: MPH Group Publishing).

Mako, Y. (2008), 'Japan's Economic Policy for Occupied Malaya', in Yoji, A. and Mako, Y. (eds.), *New Perspectives on the Japanese Occupation in Malaya and Singapore, 1941–1945* (Singapore: National University of Singapore Press).

Malayan Government (1948), *The Federation of Malaya Agreement, 1948* (Kuala Lumpur: Government Printers).

Malayan Railway Economics Commission (1961), *Report of the Malayan Railway Economics Commission*, vol. I (Kuala Lumpur: Government of the Federation of Malaya).

Malaysia Automotive Association (2021), 'Latest Sales and Productive Data', http://www.maa.org.my, accessed 28 January 2021.

Malaysia Federation (1970), *Report of the Royal Commission of Enquiry to Investigate into the Workings of Local Authorities in West Malaysia* (Kuala Lumpur: Jabatan Chetak Kerajaan).

Malaysian Investment Development Authority [MIDA] (1985), *Medium and Long Term Industrial Master Plan Malaysia, 1986–1995* (Kuala Lumpur: MIDA and United Nations Industrial Development Organization (UNIDO)).

_____ (1997), *Laporan Prestasi Pembangunan Perindustrian Negeri-Negeri Sehingga Julai 1997* (Kuala Lumpur: MIDA).

_____ (2020), *Malaysia Investment Performance Report 2019* (Kuala Lumpur: MIDA).

_____ (2021), *Malaysia Investment Performance Report 2020* (Kuala Lumpur: MIDA).

Malaysian Institute of Economic Research [MIER] (1992), *Final Report: Perak Long-term Development Plan, 1991–2000*, unpublished.

Malaysian Palm Oil Board [MPOB] (various years), *Malaysian Oil Palm Statistics* (Selangor: Malaysian Palm Oil Board).

Mallory, I. A. (1990), 'Conduct Unbecoming: The Collapse of the International Tin Agreement', *American University International Law Review*, 5/3, 835–892.

Manderson, L. (1987), 'Health Services and the Legitimisation of the Colonial State: British Malaya, 1786–1941', *International Journal of Health Services*, 17/1, 91–112.

Maphill (2020), Malaysia, Perak, Detailed Terrain Map, http://www.maphill.com/malaysia/perak/detailed-maps/terrain-map/, accessed 9 May 2020.

Martin, S. M. (2003), *The UP Saga* (Copenhagen: Nordic Institute of Asian Studies (NIAS) Press).

Maxwell, P. B. (1878), *Our Malay Conquests* (Westminster: P. S. King).

Maxwell, W. E. (1879), 'The Aboriginal Tribes of Perak', *Journal of the Straits Branch of the Royal Asiatic Society*, no. 4, 46–50.

_____ (1882a), 'The Dutch in Perak', *Journal of the Malayan Branch of the Royal Asiatic Society*, vol. VI, 246–268.

_____ (1882b), 'A Journey on Foot to the Patani Frontier in 1876. Being a journal kept during an expedition undertaken to capture Datoh Maharaja Lela of Perak', *Journal of the Straits Branch of the Royal Asiatic Society*, vol. 9, 1–67.

_____ (1890), 'The Laws Relating to Slavery Among the Malays', *Journal of the Straits Branch of the Royal Asiatic Society*, no. 22, 247–297.

Maxwell, W. G. (1944), *The Civil Defence of Malaya* (London: Hutchinson & Co).

McElvoy, A. (Host). (2020, June 11), 'Will COVID-19 Reverse Globalisation?' [Audio podcast episode], in *The Economist Asks: Jeffrey Sachs*, *The Economist*, https://www.economist.com/podcasts/2020/06/11/will-covid-19-reverse-globalisation, accessed 25 March 2021.

McFadden, E. J. (1986), 'The Collapse of Tin: Restructuring a Failed Commodity Agreement', *The American Journal of International Law*, 80/4, 811–830.

McHale, T. R. (1961), 'The Malayan Economy and Stereo-Regular Rubbers', *Asian Survey*, 1/4, 25–28.

McNair, F. (1878), *Perak and the Malays: 'Sarong' and 'Kris'* (London: Tinsley Brothers).

Means, G. P. (1969), 'The Role of Islam in the Political Development of Malaysia', *Comparative Politics*, 1/2, 264–284.

Menteri Besar Incorporated–Perak (2014), *The Perak Mining Blueprint for the Development of Mineral Resource in Perak Up to 2020* (Ipoh, Perak).

Merewether, E. M. (1892), *Report on the Census of the Straits Settlements, Taken on the 5th April 1891* (Singapore: Government Printing Office).

Milanovic, B. (2016), *Global Inequality: A New Approach for the Age of Globalization* (Cambridge: Harvard University Press).

Milner, A. C. (1982), *Kerajaan: Malayan Political Culture on the Eve of Colonial Rule* (Tucson: University of Arizona Press).

Ministry of Agriculture and Food Industries–Malaysia [MAFI] (2020), *Agrofood Statistics, 2019* (Kuala Lumpur: MAFI).

Ministry of International Trade and Industry–Malaysia [MITI] (1996a), *Second Industrial Master Plan, 1996–2005* (Kuala Lumpur: MITI).

_____ (1996b), *Malaysia International Trade and Industry Report, 1995* (Kuala Lumpur: MITI).

_____ (2006), *Third Industrial Master Plan, 2006–2020* (Kuala Lumpur: MITI).

Ministry of Primary Industries–Malaysia [MPI] (various years), *Statistics on Commodities* (Kuala Lumpur: MPI).

Mohammad Abdul Mohit (2009), 'Structural Changes of the Malaysian Economy and Its Spatial Incidence on Regional Economic Growth', Planning Malaysia, *Journal of the Malaysian Institute of Planners*, VII, 25–46.

Mohammed Yusoff (1990), 'The Effects of Tin Export Tax on Production, Export, and Prices in Malaysia', *ASEAN Economic Bulletin*, 6/3, 330–338.

Mohd Uzir Mahidin (2022), *Key Findings, Population and Housing Census of Malaysia 2020* (Putrajaya: Department of Statistics–Malaysia).

Mohd Zamberi A. Malek (2001), *Larut Daerah Terkaya* (Bangi: Universiti Kebangsaan Malaysia Press).

_____ (2017), 'Pertikaian Kawasan Perlombongan di Hulu Langat', in Mohamad Rashidi Pakri, and Nik Haslinda Nik Hussain (2017) (eds.), *Klian Intan, Perlombongan Bijih Timah dan Perkembangan Sosioekonomi* (Penang: Universiti Sains Malaysia Press).

Mustapha Hussain (2005), *Malay Nationalism Before UMNO: The Memoirs of Mustapha Hussain* (Kuala Lumpur: Utusan Publications & Distributors).

Myrdal, G. (1968), *Asian Drama: An Inquiry into the Poverty of Nations*, vol. I and vol. II (New York: Twentieth Century Fund).

Nadaraja, K. (2016), 'Malay Reaction to the 1930s Economic Depression in Malaya', *Jebat, Malaysian Journal of History, Politics* & *Strategic Studies*, 43/1, 46–64.

Najim, M. M. M., Lee, T. S., Haque, M. A., and Esham, M. (2007), 'Sustainability of Rice Production: A Malaysian Perspective', *Journal of Agricultural Sciences*, 3/1, 1–12.

Nathan, J. E. (1922), *The Census of British Malaya (The Straits Settlements, Federated Malay States and Protected States of Johore, Kedah, Perlis, Kelantan, Trengganu and Brunei), 1921* (London: Waterlow & Sons Limited).

National Archives of Singapore [NAS] database (2020a), Perak Topographical Map Searches, 1925–1957, https://www.nas.gov.sg/archivesonline/maps_building_plans/, accessed May 2020.

_____ database (2020b), Perak Topographical Map Searches, 1919–1933, https://www.nas.gov.sg/archivesonline/maps_building_plans/, accessed July 2020.

_____ database (2020c), Perak Topographical Map Searches, 1898–1937, https://www.nas.gov.sg/archivesonline/maps_building_plans/, accessed September 2020.

New Straits Times (1930), *T. P. A. Appeal to Chinese Miners*, 14 January, p. 13.

New York Times (1986), *Malaysia Loss in Tin Venture*, 12 November.

Nim, C. S. (1953), 'Labour and Tin Mining in Malaya', Southeast Asia Program, Data Paper No. 7 (Cornell University: Department of Far Eastern Studies).

_____ (1961), 'Labour and Tin Mining in Malaya', in Silcock, T. H. (ed.), *Readings in Malayan Economics* (Singapore: Eastern Universities Press).

Norcross, E., and Millsap, A. A. (2016), 'Can Power Be Restored in the Electric City? A Case Study of Scranton, Pennsylvania', *Mercatus Research*, Mercatus Center (Arlington: George Mason University).

Northern Corridor Implementation Authority [NCIA] (2016), *The Northern Corridor Economic Region (NCER) Development Blueprint 2016–2025 (Blueprint 2.0)* (Penang: NCIA Corporate Communications Unit).

_____ (2021), *Northern Corridor Economic Region Strategic Development Plan (2021–2025)*, vol. 1 and vol. 2 (Penang: NCIA Corporate Communications Unit).

Nyce, R. (1973), *Chinese New Villages in Malaya: A Community Study* (Singapore: Malaysian Sociological Research Institute Ltd).

O'Brien, P. K. (2007), *Philip's Atlas of World History* (London: George Philip).

O'Neil, S. K. (2022), *The Globalization Myth: Why Regions Matter* (New Haven & London: Yale University Press).

O'Rourke, K. H., and Williamson, J. G. (2000a), 'When Did Globalization Begin?', NBER Working Paper 7632, April 2000 (National Bureau of Economic Research).

_____ (2000b), *Globalization and History: The Evolution of a Nineteenth-Century Atlantic Economy* (Cambridge: The MIT Press).

Official Portal of Perak State Government (2007), http://www.perak.gov.my, accessed March 2021.

Ooi, K. G. (2014), 'Between Homeland and *Ummah*: Re-visiting the 1915 Singapore Mutiny of the 5th Light Infantry Regiment of the Indian Army', *Social Scientist*, 42, no. 7/8, 85–94.

Organisation for Economic Co-operation and Development [OECD] (2011), *Higher Education in Regional and City Development: State of Penang, Malaysia 2011* (Paris: OECD Publishing), http://dx.doi.org/10.1787/9789264089457-en.

Osborne, F. D. (1911), 'The Tin Resources of the Empire', *Journal of the Royal Society of Arts*, 59/3039, 325–339.

Ostwald, K. (2017), 'Federalism Without Decentralization: Power Consolidation in Malaysia', *Perspective*, Issue 2019, No. 66, ISEAS–Yusof Ishak Institute, https://papers.ssrn.com/sol3/papers.cfm?abstract_id=3048550.

Palmer, D., and Joll, M. (2011), *Tin Mining in Malaysia, 1800–2000: The Osborne & Chappel Story* (Perak: Muzium Gopeng).

Parkinson, C. N. (1964), *British Intervention in Malaya, 1867–1877* (Kuala Lumpur: University of Malaya Press).

Parmer, J. N. (1990), 'Estate Workers' Health in the Federated Malay States in the 1920s', in Rimmer, P. J. and Allen, L. M. (eds.), *The Underside of Malaysian History: Pullers, Prostitutes, Plantation Workers* (Singapore: Singapore University Press).

Pearson, J. (2020), 'Why COVID-19 Shows the Future Not the End of Globalization', *World Economic Forum*, 3 December, https://www.weforum.org/agenda/2020/12/covid-19-future-of-globalization-trade/, accessed 25 March 2021.

Penang Development Corporation [PDC] (1972), *Annual Report and Financial Statements of the Free Trade Zones in Penang for 1972* (Penang: PDC).

Penrose Jr, R. A. F. (1903), 'The Tin Deposits of the Malay Peninsula with Special Reference to Those of the Kinta District', *The Journal of Geology*, February–March, XI/2, 135–154.

Perak State Development Office (1987), *Unpublished* (Ipoh, Perak).

Perak State Government (1974), *Unpublished Briefing Notes* (Ipoh, Perak).

_____ (1996), *Briefing Notes* (Ipoh, Perak).

_____ (2001), *Briefing Notes* (Ipoh, Perak).

_____ (2022), *Ringkasan Eksekutif 2030 Perak Sejahtera* (Ipoh, Perak).

Perry, D. C., and Wiewel, W. (2005) (eds.), *The University as Urban Developer: Case Studies and Analysis* (Oxon: Routledge).

Perusahaan Otomobil Nasional–Malaysia [Proton] (2021), 'Proton Records Even Higher Sales in 2020—Press Release', https://www.proton.com/en/press-release/2021/january/proton-records-even-higher-sales-in-2020, accessed 28 January 2021.

Piiparinen, R. (2021), 'Pittsburgh v. Cleveland: Winning in Football (Finally), Losing in Economic Development (Still). A Story Told in Graphs', *Urban Publications*, 0 1 2 3 1739, https://engaged scholarship.csuohio.edu/urban_facpub/1739.

Piketty, T. (2020a, 16 May), *The World After Coronavirus: The Future of Inequality* [Video], YouTube, https://youtu.be/220XAnjXcOI, accessed 15 May 2021.

_____ (2020b), *Capital and Ideology* (Cambridge: Harvard University Press).

PLANMalaysia@Perak (2022), *Rancangan Struktur Negeri Perak 2040 (Kajian)*, https://www.mdbg.gov.my/ms/rancangan-struktur-negeri-perak-2040, accessed 3 June 2022.

Pountney, A. M. (1911), *The Census of the Federated Malay States: Review of the Census Operations and Results, 1911* (London: Darling & Son Limited).

Prakash, A., Pin, F., and Siddiq, M. S. B. (2017), 'Proton: Strategizing for Sustainability in Automobile Industry', *ECONSPEAK: A Journal of Advances in Management IT & Social Sciences*, 7/7, 112–119.

Pura, R. (1986), 'Malaysia Plan to Control Tin Led to Disaster', *Asian Wall Street Journal*, 22 September 1986.

Purcell, V. (1955), *Malaya: Communist or Free* (California: Stanford University Press).

_____ (1965), *The Memoirs of a Malayan Official* (London: Cassell).

_____ (1967), *The Chinese in Malaya* (London: Oxford University Press).

Purdie, G. E. (2018), 'The British Agency House in Malaysia and Nigeria: Evolving Strategy in Commodity Trade', PhD thesis, University of Glasgow.

Puthucheary, J. J. (1960), *Ownership and Control in the Malayan Economy* (Singapore: Eastern Universities Press).

Raffaelli, M. (2009), *Rise and Demise of Commodity Agreements: An Investigation into the Breakdown of International Commodity Agreements* (United Kingdom: Woodhead Publishing Limited).

Raja Chulan (2015), *Karya Agung: Hikayat Misa Melayu* (Kuala Lumpur: Yayasan Karyawan).

Raja Nazrin Shah (2006), *Landmarks of Perak*. (Kuala Lumpur: RNS Publications).

Ramachandran, S. (1994), *Indian Plantation Labour in Malaysia* (Kuala Lumpur: S. Abdul Majeed & Co.).

Ramli Ngah Talib (2022), *The Malays: Pathfinders and Trailblazers* (Kuala Lumpur: Malaysian Institute of Translation and Books).

Randstad (2019), *Global Report: Randstad Workmonitor Q3 2019: Working Abroad and Cultural Diversity* (Randstad N. V., The Netherlands.)

Rashid Maidin (2009), *The Memoirs of Rashid Maidin: From Armed Struggle to Peace* (Petaling Jaya: Information and Research Development Centre).

Rasiah, R. (1993), 'Free Trade Zones and Industrial Development in Malaysia', in K. S., Jomo (ed.), *Industrialising Malaysia: Policy, Performance, Prospects* (London: Routledge), 118–146.

Rasiah, R., and Krishnan Gopi (2020), 'Industrialization and industrial hubs in Malaysia', in Oqubay, A. and Lin, J. Y. (eds.), *The Oxford Handbook of Industrial Hubs and Economic Development* (New York: Oxford University Press), 701–722.

Raworth, K. (2017), *Doughnut Economics: Seven Ways to Think Like a 21st Century Economist* (United Kingdom: Random House).

Reid, A. (2006) (ed.), *Verandah of Violence: The Background to the Aceh Problem* (Singapore: National University of Singapore Press).

Reilly, C. (2002), *Metal Contamination of Food: Its Significance for Food Quality and Human Health* (3rd edn., Oxford: Blackwell Science).

Revenue Watch Institute (2010), *Transforming Resource Wealth into Well-being* (New York: Revenue Watch Institute).

Roberts, A., and Lamp, N. (2021), *Six Faces of Globalization: Who Wins, Who Loses, and Why It Matters* (Cambridge: Harvard University Press).

Rodrik, D. (2011), *The Globalization Paradox: Why Global Markets, States, and Democracy Can't Coexist* (Oxford: Oxford University Press).

_____ (2015), 'Premature Deindustrialization', NBER Working Paper 20935, February 2015 (National Bureau of Economic Research).

_____ (2021), 'Prospect for Global Economic Convergence Under New Technologies', paper presented at the Brookings Institute Global Forum on Democracy and Technology, 8 December 2021, http://tinyurl.com/ydenbnrn, accessed 20 May 2022.

Rodrik, D., and Stantcheva, S. (2021), 'A Policy Matrix for Inclusive Prosperity', NBER Working Paper 28736, April 2021 (National Bureau of Economic Research).

Roff, W. R. (1967), *The Origins of Malay Nationalism* (Kuala Lumpur: University of Malaya Press).

Romeo, M. J., and Ravenscroft, J. (2018) (eds.), *History RePPPeated: How Public Private Partnerships are Failing* (Brussels: Eurodad and Heinrich-Böll-Stiftung).

Roslelawati Abdullah (2017), 'Industri Bujih Timah' in Mohamad Rashidi Pakri and Nik Haslinda Nik Hussain (2017) (eds.), *Klian Intan, Perlombongan Bijih Timah dan Perkembangan Sosioekonomi* (Penang: Universiti Sains Malaysia Press).

Ross, C. (2014), 'The Tin Frontier: Mining, Empire, and Environment in Southeast Asia, 1870s–1930s', *Environmental History*, 19/3, 454–479.

Rowe, J. (1953), *Cornwall in the Age of the Industrial Revolution* (Liverpool: Liverpool University Press).

Royal Asiatic Society of Great Britain and Ireland (1898), *A Map of the Malay Peninsula*, compiled and published for the Straits Branch of the Royal Asiatic Society, Singapore (London: Edward Stanford), https://nla.gov.au/nla.obj-231529372/view, accessed 12 May 2020.

Rudner, M. (1968), 'The Organization of the British Military Administration in Malaya, 1946–48', *Journal of Southeast Asian History*, 9/1, 95–106.

_____ (1976), 'Malayan Rubber Policy: Development and Anti-development During the 1950s', *Journal of Southeast Asian Studies*, 7/2, 235–259.

_____ (2018), *The Evolving Political Economy of Malaya's Rubber Development from Colonial Times to Independence*, https://www.ehm.my/publications/articles/the-evolving-political-economy-of-malayas-rubber-development-from-colonial-times-to-independence, accessed 15 August 2020.

Saarani Mohamad (2020), *Perak 2021 Budget Speech* (Ipoh, Perak).

Sachs, J. D. (2020), *The Ages of Globalization: Geography, Technology, and Institutions* (New York: Columbia University Press).

Sachs, J. D., and Warner, A. M. (2001), 'The Curse of Natural Resources', *European Economic Review*, 45/4–6, 827–838.

Sadka, E. (1954) (ed.), 'The Journal of Sir Hugh Low, Perak, 1877', *Journal of the Malayan Branch of the Royal Asiatic Society*, 27/4 (168), 1–108.

_____ (1960), 'The Residential System in the Protected Malay States, 1874–1895', PhD thesis, Australian National University.

_____ (1968), *The Protected Malay States, 1874–1895* (Kuala Lumpur: University of Malaya Press).

_____ (1971), *The Protected Malay States, 1874–1895* (Kuala Lumpur: Oxford University Press).

Salt Media Group (2021), *Lee Loy Seng: The Taiko of Plantations* (Ipoh: Wan Hin Investments).

Sandhu, K. S. (1969), *Indians in Malaya: Immigration and Settlement 1786–1957* (Cambridge: Cambridge University Press).

Saruwatari, K. (1991), 'Malaysia's Localization Policy and Its Impact on British-owned Enterprises', *The Developing Economies*, XXIX/4, 371–386.

Scranton Chamber of Commerce (2017), *Our Transformative Period: Community Revitalization Plan* (Scranton: The Greater Scranton Chamber of Commerce).

Shaari Abdul Rahman (2001), *Population Distribution and Basic Demographics Characteristics, 2000 Population and Housing Census of Malaysia* (Putrajaya: Department of Statistics–Malaysia).

_____ (2002), *Education and Social Characteristics of the Population, 2000 Population and Housing Census of Malaysia* (Putrajaya: Department of Statistics–Malaysia).

_____ (2003), *Economic Characteristics of the Population, 2000 Population and Housing Census of Malaysia* (Putrajaya: Department of Statistics–Malaysia).

_____ (2004), *Migration and Population Distribution, 2000 Population and Housing Census of Malaysia* (Putrajaya: Department of Statistics–Malaysia).

Shakila Yacob, and White, N. J. (2010), 'The "Unfinished Business" of Malaysia's Decolonisation: The Origins of the Guthrie "Dawn Raid"', *Modern Asian Studies*, 44/5, 919–960.

Sharpe, A. (2005), 'The Evolution of the Cornwall and West Devon Landscapes as a Result of Industrialisation from the Mid-Eighteenth Century to the Early Twentieth Century', *Landscape History*, 27/1, 65–70.

Shennan, M. (2014), *Our Man in Malaya* (Singapore: Monsoon Books).

_____ (2015), *Out in the Midday Sun: The British in Malaya 1880–1960* (Singapore: Monsoon Books).

Short, A. (1975), *The Communist Insurrection in Malaya 1948–1960* (London: Frederick Muller Ltd).

Short, D. E., and Jackson, J. C. (1971), 'The Origins of an Irrigation Policy in Malaya: A Review of Developments Prior to the Establishment of the Drainage and Irrigation Department', *Journal of the Malaysian Branch of the Royal Asiatic Society*, 44/1 (219), 78–103.

Sime Darby Berhad (2017), *Northern Corridor Economic Region Socioeconomic Blueprint, 2007–2025* (Kuala Lumpur: Sime Darby).

Singh, B. (1960), *A History of Tin Mining in Perak, 1896–1928* (Singapore: University of Malaya).

Singh Dhillon, K. (2009), *Malaysian Foreign Policy in the Mahathir Era, 1981–2003: Dilemmas of Development* (Singapore: National University of Singapore Press).

Siti Murni Wee Jamil Wee, and Singaravelloo, K. (2018), 'Income Targets and Poverty of Rubber Smallholders in Four States of Malaysia', *Journal of the Malaysian Institute of Planners*, 16/1, 381–396.

Sivalingam, G. (1994), 'The Economic and Social Impact of Export Processing Zones: The Case of Malaysia', Multinational Enterprises Programme Working Paper No. 66 (Geneva: International Labour Organization).

Smith, J. S. (1958), *Report on Forest Administration for the Year 1957, Federation of Malaya* (Kuala Lumpur: Government Printers).

Smith, S. C. (1995), *British Relations with the Malay Rulers from Decentralization to Malayan Independence, 1930–1957* (Kuala Lumpur: Oxford University Press).

Stevens, P., Lahn, G., and Kooroshy, J. (2015), *The Resource Curse Revisited* (London: Chatham House), https://www.chathamhouse.org/sites/default/files/publications/research/20150804ResourceCurseRevisitedStevensLahnKooroshyFinal.pdf, accessed 12 April 2020.

Stiglitz, J. E. (2006), *Making Globalization Work* (New York: W. W. Norton & Company, Inc.).

_____ (2020), 'Conquering the Great Divide', Finance & Development, September 2020, *International Monetary Fund*, 0057/003, 17–19.

_____ (2022), 'Getting Deglobalization Right', Project Syndicate, 31 May 2022, https://www.project-syndicate.org/commentary/deglobalization-and-its-discontents-by-joseph-e-stiglitz-2022-05, accessed 18 May 2023.

Stillson, R. T. (1971), 'The Financing of Malayan Rubber, 1905–1923', *The Economic History Review*, New Series, 24/4, 589–598.

Stockwell, A. J. (1979), *British Policy and Malay Politics During the Malayan Union Experiment 1945–1948*, Monograph No. 8, Malaysian Branch of the Royal Asiatic Society (Kuala Lumpur: Art Printing Works).

_____ (1984), 'British Imperial Policy and Decolonization in Malaya, 1942–52', *The Journal of Imperial and Commonwealth History*, 13/1, 68–87.

_____ (1999a), 'British Expansion and Rule in South-East Asia', in Porter, A. (ed.), *The Oxford History of the British Empire: Volume III: The Nineteenth Century* (Oxford: Oxford University Press).

_____ (1999b), 'Imperialism and Nationalism in South-East Asia', in Brown, J. M. and Louis, Wm. R. (eds.), *The Oxford History of the British Empire: Volume IV: The Twentieth Century* (Oxford: Oxford University Press).

Stopford, M. (2009), *Maritime Economics* (3rd edn., London and New York: Routledge).

Straits Settlements (1882), *Correspondence Respecting the Protected Malay States, August 1881* (London: Her Majesty's Stationary Office).

Straits Settlements Blue Book (1868–1871), Singapore.

Stubbs, R. (1983), 'Malaysia's Rubber Smallholding Industry: Crisis and the Search for Stability', *Pacific Affairs*, 56/1, 84–105.

_____ (1988), 'Renegotiating the International Natural Rubber Agreement', *ASEAN Economic Bulletin*, 5/2, 140–151.

Sultan Nazrin Shah (2017), *Charting the Economy: Early 20th Century Malaya and Contemporary Malaysian Contrasts* (Kuala Lumpur: Oxford University Press).

_____ (2019), *Striving for Inclusive Development: From Pangkor to a Modern Malaysian State* (Kuala Lumpur: Oxford University Press).

_____ (2022), 'Historical GDP Accounts', Economic History of Malaya Project, https://www.ehm.my/data/historical-gdp-accounts.

Swettenham, F. A. (1893), *About Perak* (Singapore: Straits Times Press).

_____ (1903), *Malay Sketches* (3rd edn., London: John Lane).

_____ (1906), *British Malaya: An Account of the Origin and Progress of British Influence in Malaya* (London: John Lane).

_____ (1952), 'Sir Frank Swettenham's Perak Journals, 1874–1876', in Cowan, C. D. (ed.), *Journal of the Malayan Branch of the Royal Asiatic Society*, 24/4 (157), 1–148.

Syed Husin Ali (2019), *A People's History of Malaysia: With Emphasis on the Development of Nationalism* (Selangor: Vinlin Press).

Syed Muhd Khairudin Aljunied (2015), *Radicals: Resistance and Protest in Colonial Malaya* (DeKalb: Northern Illinois University Press).

Tai, W. Y. (2013), *Chinese Capitalism in Colonial Malaya, 1900–1941* (Bangi: Universiti Kebangsaan Malaysia Press).

Tan, T. P. (2020), *Behind Barbed Wire: Chinese New Villages during the Malayan Emergency, 1948–1960* (Selangor: Vinlin Press Sdn. Bhd.).

Tan, T. W. (1982), *Income Distribution and Determination in West Malaysia* (Kuala Lumpur: Oxford University Press).

Tantalum Producers International Study Centre (1983), 'Malaysia Smelting Corporation Sdn. Bhd.', *Quarterly Bulletin*, no. 33, https://tanb.org/images/Bulletin33.pdf, 1–8.

Tate, D. J. M. (1979), *The Making of Modern South-East Asia*, vol. II, The Western Impact: Economic and Social Change (Kuala Lumpur: Oxford University Press).

_____ (1996), *The RGA History of the Plantation Industry in the Malay Peninsula* (Kuala Lumpur: Oxford University Press).

Tempany, H. A. (1935), *Annual Report of the Department of Agriculture, Straits Settlements and Federated Malay States for the Year 1934* (Kuala Lumpur: Government Press).

Tengku Mohamed Asyraf, Nadaraja, D., Afif Shamri, and Sivabalan, R. (2019), 'Is Malaysia Experiencing Premature Deindustrialisation?', *BNM Quarterly Bulletin*, https://www.bnm.gov.my/documents/20124/766189/p3ba.pdf, Economic and Financial Developments in the Malaysian Economy in the First Quarter of 2019, Bank Negara Malaysia.

Teo, A. S. C. (2014) (ed.), *Univer-cities. Strategic View of the Future from Berkeley and Cambridge to Singapore and Rising Asia*, vol. II (Singapore: World Scientific Publishing Co.).

_____ (2020) (ed.), *Univer-cities. Reshaping Strategies to Meet Radical Change, Pandemics, and Inequality: Revisiting the Social Compact?* vol. IV (Singapore: World Scientific Publishing Co.).

Teoh, A. (2004), *Old Taiping*, self-published.

Tey, N.-P. (2014), 'Inter-state Migration and Socio-demographic Changes in Malaysia', *Malaysian Journal of Economic Studies*, 51/1, 121–139.

Tham, S.-Y. (2004), 'Malaysian Policies for the Automobile Sector: Focus on Technology Transfer', in Busser, R. and Sadoi, Y. (eds.), *Production Networks in Asia and Europe: Skill Formation and Technology Transfer in the Automobile Industry* (London: Routledge), 513–570.

Tharoor, S. (2017), 'British Colonial "Divide and Rule" Policy in Malaya: Echoes of India', *Economic History of Malaya Project*, https://www.ehm.my/publications/articles/british-colonial-divide-and-rule-policy-in-malaya-echoes-of-india, accessed 8 August 2022.

The Asia Foundation (2013), 'The Youth Factor: 2012 Survey of Malaysian Youth Opinion', https://asiafoundation.org/2012/12/13/the-asia-foundation-launches-the-youth-factor-2012-survey-of-malaysian-youth-opinion/.

The Daily Telegraph (1875), 'Our War with the Malays', 15 November 1875.

The Economist (2019a), "The Global List: Globalisation Has Faltered', 24 January 2019, https://www.economist.com/brieing/2019/01/24/globalisation-has-faltered.

_____ (2019b), 'Slowbalisation: The Steam Has Gone Out of Globalisation', 24 January 2019, https://www.economist.com/leaders/2019/01/24/the-steam-has-gone-out-of-globalisation.

_____ (2019c), 'Young Malaysians Have Big Economic Worries—and Growing Political Clout', 28 September 2019, https://www.economist.com/asia/2019/09/26/young-malaysians-have-big-economic-worries-and-growing-political-clout.

_____ (2022), 'Reinventing Globalisation', 18–24 June 2022, https://www.economist.com/weeklyedition/2022-06-18.

The Graphic (1875), 'The War in the Malay Peninsula', 20 November 1875.

The Illustrated London News (1876), 'The Expedition Against the Malays', 26 February 1876.

The Times (1875), 'The Malay Outbreak', 21 December 1875.

Thoburn, J. T. (1973), 'Exports and Economic Growth in West Malaysia', *Oxford Economic Papers*, 25/1, 88–111, https://doi.org/10.1093/oxfordjournals.oep.a041249.

_____ (1977), *Primary Commodity Exports and Economic Development: Theory, Evidence and a Study of Malaysia* (London: John Wiley & Sons).

_____ (1994a), 'The Tin Industry Since the Collapse of the International Tin Agreement', *Resources Policy*, 20/2, 125–133.

_____ (1994b), *Tin in the World Economy* (Edinburgh: Edinburgh University Press Ltd.).

Thomas, W. A. (1998), 'An Intra-empire Capital Transfer: The Shanghai Rubber Company Boom 1909–1912', *Modern Asian Studies*, 32/3, 739–760.

Thong, W. H. (2011, 9 December), 'The Collapse of the ITC: Why 10,000 Ipohites Had to "Jump Aeroplane" (Work Illegally) in America', *weehingthong*, https://weehingthong.org/2011/12/09/the-collapse-of-the-itc-why-10000-ipohites-had-to-jump-aeroplane-work-illegally-in-america/, accessed 20 October 2020.

Timmer, C. P. (2009), *A World Without Agriculture: The Structural Transformation in Historical Perspective*, Henry Wendt Lecture Series, American Enterprise Institute (Washington, DC: AEI Press).

_____ (2014), 'Managing Structural Transformation: A Political Economy Approach', 18th WIDER Annual Lecture (Helsinki: UNU-WIDER).

Treacher, W. H. (1892), *Annual Report on the State of Perak for the Year 1891* (Taiping: Government Printing Office).

Tregonning, K. G. (1962), 'Straits Tin: A Brief Account of the First Seventy-five Years of the Straits Trading Company, Limited, 1887–1962', *Journal of the Malayan Branch of the Royal Asiatic Society*, 36/1 (201), 79–153.

_____ (1964), *A History of Modern Malaya*, History of Modern Southeast Asia Series (London: Eastern Universities Press Ltd).

_____ (1965), 'The Origin of the Straits Steamship Company in 1890', *Journal of the Malaysian Branch of the Royal Asiatic Society*, 38/2 (208), 274–289.

Tunku Abdul Rahman Putra (1977), *Looking Back: The Historic Years of Malaya and Malaysia* (Kuala Lumpur: Pustaka Antara).

Turnbull, P. (2000), 'Contesting Globalization on the Waterfront', *Politics & Society*, 28/3, 367–391.

Unit Perancang Ekonomi Negeri [UPEN] Perak, and Malaysian Institute of Economic Research [MIER] (2009), *Pelan Strategik Perak Maju 2015: Final Report*, unpublished.

United Nations [UN] (2015), *Charter of the United Nations and Statute of the International Court of Justice* (New York: UN).

United Nations Children's Fund [UNICEF] Malaysia, and United Nations Population Fund [UNFPA] (2020a), *Families on the Edge: The Immediate Impact of the Movement Control Order Period*, Issue 1, August 2020 (Putrajaya: UNICEF Malaysia and UNFPA).

_____ (2020b), *Families on the Edge: Status of the Households Post-MCO*, Issue 2, October 2020 (Putrajaya: UNICEF Malaysia and UNFPA).

_____ (2021), *Families on the Edge: Two-Steps Forward, One Step Back: The New Normal for Malaysia's Urban Poor?*, Issue 4, May 2021 (Putrajaya: UNICEF Malaysia and UNFPA).

United Nations Conference on Trade and Development [UNCTAD] (1976), *The Integrated Programme for Commodities: Resolution 93*(IV) (Geneva: UNCTAD).

_____ (2021), *World Investment Report 2020* (Geneva: UNCTAD).

United Nations Department of Economic and Social Affairs [DESA] (2021), 'Sustainable Development Goals', https://sdgs.un.org/goals, accessed 8 June 2021.

United Nations Development Programme [UNDP] (2015), *Human Development Report 2015* (New York: UNDP).

_____ (2021), *Human Development Report 2021* (New York: UNDP).

United Nations Development Programme [UNDP], and UN Environment (2018), *Managing Mining for Sustainable Development: A Sourcebook* (Bangkok: UNDP).

United Nations Statistics Division (2020), 'National Accounts—Analysis of Main Aggregates (AMA)', https://unstats.un.org/unsd/snaama/Index, accessed 20 October 2021.

_____ (2022), 'Trade Statistics', UN Comtrade Database, https://comtrade.un.org/data, accessed June 2022.

United Nations World Commission on Environment and Development [UNWCED] (1987), *Our Common Future: The Report of the World Commission on Environment and Development* (Oxford: Oxford University Press).

United States Geological Survey (various years), 'Minerals Yearbook', *National Minerals Information Center*, https://www.usgs.gov/centers/nmic/tin-statistics-and-information, accessed November 2020.

University of Groningen (2018a, 11 January), Maddison Project Database 2018, *Blog: GGDC News*, https://www.rug.nl/ggdc/blog/blog-11-01-2018-maddison-project-database-2018, accessed 8 August 2018.

_____ (2018b), 'Maddison Historical Statistics', Historical Development, https://www.rug.nl/ggdc/historicaldevelopment/maddison/?lang=en, accessed 10 August 2020.

Uqbah Iqbal, Nordin Hussin, and Ahmad Ali Seman (2014), *The Historical Development of Foreign Investment in the Formation of the Malaysian Economy. Colonial Period-Post Independence*, Research paper, November (Germany: GRIN Verlag).

van der Eng, P. (1994), 'Food Supply in Java During War and Decolonisation, 1940–1950', Occasional Paper No. 5 (United Kingdom: Centre for South-East Asian Studies, University of Hull).

Vlieland, C. A. (1932), *A Report on the 1931 Census and on Certain Problems of Vital Statistics, British Malaya (The Colony of The Straits Settlements and the Malay States Under British Protection, namely The Federated Malay States of Perak, Selangor, Negri Sembilan and Pahang and the States of Johore, Kedah, Kelantan, Trengganu, Perlis and Brunei)* (London: The Crown Agents for the Colonies).

Wagstyl, S. (1986), 'Paying the Price of the Market's Collapse', *Financial Times*, 12 March, 16–17.

Walker, R. S. F. (1901), *Perak Administration Report for the Year 1900* (Taiping: Government Printing Office).

Wan Ramlah (2011), *Population Distribution and Basic Demographics Characteristics*, 2010 Population and Housing Census of Malaysia (Putrajaya: Department of Statistics–Malaysia).

_____ (2013a), *Economic Characteristics of the Population*, 2010 Population and Housing Census of Malaysia (Putrajaya: Department of Statistics–Malaysia).

_____ (2013b), *Education and Social Characteristics of the Population*, 2010 Population and Housing Census of Malaysia (Putrajaya: Department of Statistics–Malaysia).

Wan Shafrina, Khairul Nizam Abdul Maulud, Aisyah Marliza Muhmad Kamarulzaman, Asif Raihan, Syarina Md Sah, Azizah Ahmad, Siti Nor Maizah Saad, Ahmad Tarmizi Mohd Azmi, Nur Khairun Ayuni Jusoh Syukri, and Wasseem Razzaq Khan (2020), 'The Influence of Deforestation on Land Surface Temperature—A Case Study of Perak and Kedah, Malaysia', *Forests*, Special Issue, 11/6 (670), https://www.mdpi.com/1999-4907/11/6/670, accessed 12 February 2021.

Wee, C. S. (1952), *Ngah Ibrahim in Larut 1858–1874*, Graduation Exercise (Singapore: University of Malaya).

White, N. J. (1997), 'The Frustrations of Development: British Business and the Late Colonial State in Malaya, 1945–57', *Journal of Southeast Asian Studies*, 28/1, 103–119.

_____ (1998), 'Capitalism and Counter-insurgency? Business and Government in the Malayan Emergency, 1948–57', *Modern Asian Studies*, 32/1, 149–177.

_____ (2004), *British Business in Post-colonial Malaysia, 1957–70: Neo-colonialism or Disengagement?* (London and New York: Routledge Curzon).

_____ (2014), 'The Trouble with Tin: Governments and Businesses in Decolonizing Malaya', in Ingulstad, M., Perchard, A., and Storli, E. (eds.), *Tin and Global Capitalism, 1850–2000: A History of the Devil's Metal* (New York: Routledge).

Whittlesey, C. R. (1931), *Governmental Control of Crude Rubber: The Stevenson Plan* (Princeton: Princeton University Press).

Wikimedia Commons (2021), Media file repository, https://commons.wikimedia.org/wiki/Main_page, accessed October 2021.

Wikkramatileke, R. (1995), 'Federal Land Development in West Malaysia, 1957–1971', in Lim, D. (ed.), *Readings on Malaysian Economic Development* (Kuala Lumpur: Oxford University Press).

Wilkinson, R. J. (1907) (ed.), *Council Minutes, Perak, 1877–1879, Papers on Malay Subjects: History, Pt. III* (Kuala Lumpur: Government Press).

_____ (1909) (ed.), *Council Minutes, Perak, 1880–1882, Papers on Malay Subjects: History, Pt. IV* (Kuala Lumpur: F. M. S. Government Press).

_____ (1923), *A History of the Peninsular Malays* (Singapore: Kelly and Walsh).

_____ (1957), 'Papers on Malay Customs & Beliefs', *Journal of the Malayan Branch of the Royal Asiatic Society*, 30/4 (180), 1–87.

Williams, M. (2003), 'Why is Cornwall Poor? Poverty and In-Migration Since the 1960s', *Contemporary British History*, 17/3, 55–70.

Williamson, F. (2016), 'The "Great Flood" of 1926: Environmental Change and Post-disaster Management in British Malaya', *Ecosystem Health and Sustainability*, 2/11, https://www.e01248.doi:10.1002/ehs2.1248, accessed 3 September 2018.

Williamson, J. G. (2013), *Trade and Poverty: When the Third World Fell Behind* (Cambridge: The MIT Press).

Winkler, A. (2007), 'Sheffield City Report', CASEreport 45, Centre for Analysis of Social Exclusion (CASE) (London: London School of Economics and Political Science).

Winstedt, R. O. (1935), 'A History of Malaya', *Journal of the Malayan Branch of the Royal Asiatic Society*, 13/1 (121), iii–270.

_____ (1948), *Malaya and Its History* (London: Hutchinson's University Library).

Winstedt, R. O., and Wilkinson, R. J. (1934), 'A History of Perak', *Journal of the Malayan Branch of the Royal Asiatic Society*, 12/1 (118), v–180.

Wong, L. K. (1965), *The Malayan Tin Industry to 1914* (Tucson: University of Arizona Press).

World Bank (1981), *Tin Handbook: Commodity Handbook* (Washington, DC: The World Bank), http://documents.worldbank.org/curated/en/519961492626073675/Tin-handbook, accessed 21 October 2020.

_____ (2009), *World Development Report 2009: Reshaping Economic Geography* (Washington, DC: The World Bank).

_____ (2011), *Malaysia Economic Monitor: Brain Drain* (Washington, DC: The World Bank).

_____ (2015), *Improving the Effectiveness of TalentCorp's Initiatives: Assessment of Returning Expert Programme & Residence Pass-Talent* (Washington, DC: The World Bank).

_____ (2020a), 'World Integrated Trade Solutions (WITS)', https://wits.worldbank.org/CountryProfile/en/Country/MYS/Year/1990/Summarytext, accessed 16 December 2020.

_____ (2020b), 'DataBank: World Development Indicators', https://databank.worldbank.org/source/world-development-indicators, accessed March 2020.

_____ (2021), *Aiming High: Navigating the Next Stage of Malaysia's Development* (Kuala Lumpur: The World Bank).

World Economic Forum (2021), 'What are Green Bonds and Why is This Market Growing So Fast?', https://www.weforum.org/agenda/2021/10/what-are-green-bonds-climate-change/, accessed 31 October 2022.

World Health Organization [WHO] (2022), WHO Coronavirus (COVID-19) Dashboard, https://covid19.who.int/, accessed 1 October 2022.

World Meteorological Organization [WMO] (2022), 'Four Key Climate Change Indicators Break Records in 2021', Press Release Number: 18052022, 18 May 2022, https://public.wmo.int/en/media/press-release/four-key-climate-change-indicators-break-records-2021, accessed 1 August 2022.

World Resources Institute [WRI] (2021), 'Global Forest Review: Top 10 Lists', https://research.wri.org/gfr/top-ten-lists, accessed January 2021.

Wray, L. (1893), *Rubber Growing in Perak*, Perak Museum Notes, No. I, 93–100 (Taiping: Perak Government Printing Office).

_____ (1894), *The Tin Mines and the Mining Industries of Perak, and Other Papers* (Taiping: Government Printing Office).

Wynne, M. L. (1941), *Triad and Tabut: A Survey of the Origin and Diffusion of Chinese and Mohamedan Secret Societies in the Malay Peninsula A.D. 1800–1935* (Singapore: Government Printing Office).

Yap, K. M. (2006), 'Gravel Pump Tin Mining in Malaysia', Jurutera, May, 6–11.

Yayasan Hasanah (2021), *Perak Sustainable Development Model: A Report by Yayasan Hasanah* (Kuala Lumpur: Yayasan Hasanah).

Yazid Saleh, Mohmadisa Hashim, Nasir Nayan, Hanifah Mahat, and Mohamad Suhaily Yusri Che Ngah (2016), 'Functional Changes of Malaysia's Small Towns in the Era of Globalization: Evidence from Tanjong Malim, Perak', *Geografia: Malaysian Journal of Society and Space*, 12/6, 24–33.

Yeo, G., Tan. K. G., Tan, K. Y., and Loo, W. (2020), 'An Evidence-based Analysis of Industrial Hubs, in Oqubay, A. and Lin, J. Y. (eds.), *The Oxford Handbook of Industrial Hubs and Economic Development* (New York: Oxford University Press), 673–700.

Yeow, T. C., and Ooi, C. I. (2009), *The Development of Free Industrial Zones: The Malaysian Experience* (Washington, DC: The World Bank).

Yip, Y. H. (1969), *The Development of the Tin Mining Industry of Malaya* (Kuala Lumpur: University of Malaya Press).

Yong, C. F. (1997), *The Origins of Malayan Communism* (Petaling Jaya: Strategic Information and Research Development Centre).

Yong, L. (2007), *The Dutch East India Company's Tea Trade with China, 1757–1781* (Leiden: Brill).

Yusuf Hadi (1982), 'Planning Timber Supply from the Forests of Peninsular Malaysia', PhD thesis, The University of British Columbia.

Zakaria, F. (2020), *Ten Lessons for a Post-pandemic World* (United Kingdom: Penguin Random House).

Zaludin Sulong (1977), 'Pembangunan Negeri Perak', paper presented at a Seminar Desa/JKKK Peringkat Daerah, 27–29 December, Hulu Perak, Gerik, Perak.

Zambry Abdul Kadir (2016), *Perak 2017 Budget Speech* (Ipoh, Perak).

Malaysia Archive Documents

_____ (1918), 'Outbreak of Spanish Influenza in South Africa'. Telegram from the Governor General, South Africa, to the Governor, Straits Settlements, 12 October 1918. Accession Number 1957/0606314.

_____ (1926), 'The Origin of Federation in the Malay States'. Personal letters of Sir F. A. Swettenham. Accession Number 2006/0037588W.

_____ (1942), 'System of Government Perak'. Personal letters of Raja Kamarulzaman bin Raja Mansur, 1892–1962. Accession Number 2003/0008174W.

UK National Archive Documents

Board of Trade (BT)

BT 34/2489/14056, (1880–1932), *Company number: 14056; Redruth Mining Exchange Company Ltd. Incorporated 1880. Liquidator's Accounts on the dissolution of the company at some point between 1880 and 1932.*

Colonial Office (CO)

CO 882/2, (1872–1874), *Correspondence relating to the affairs of certain native states in the Malay Peninsula, in the neighbourhood of the Straits Settlements. Includes reports of disturbances and unrest in Larut, Perak and elsewhere, and piratical acts.*

CO 882/3, (1875), *Correspondence respecting affairs at Perak. Includes despatches reporting murder on Perak River by Malays of J. W. W. Birch, British Resident in Perak. Request and arrangements for troops and reinforcements.*

CO 882/2 (1876), *Further correspondence relating to the affairs of certain native states in the Malay Peninsula, in the neighbourhood of the Straits Settlements.*

CO 574/14, (1915), *Government Gazettes, October–December 1915.*

CO 852/33/11, (1936), *Tin: Export Duties on Tin Ore; Malaya and Nigeria.*

CO 809/1, (1946–1948), *Correspondence about the Monuments, Fine Arts and Archives restitution procedure.*

CO 1022/29, SEA10/72/01, (1951–1953), *Resettlement of squatters into the New Villagers in Malaya.*

CO 1022/54, SEA10/409/01, (1952), *Punishment of the Malayan town of Tanjong Malim for non-co-operation with the administration: reconciliation with the town after the visit of the High Commissioner, General Sir Gerald Templer in August 1952.*

Dominions Office (DO)

DO 35/9816, (1959), Original Correspondence. Malaya Department. 'Racial Disturbances in Perak'.

Foreign Office (FO)

FO 422/8, (1882–1884), *Confidential Print, Siam and South East Asia. Rectification of the Boundary Between Perak and Siam. Correspondence.*

FO 422/107, (1882–1887), *Confidential Print, Siam and South East Asia. Siam (Thailand): Memoranda and Correspondence; Proposed Rectification of the Boundary Between Perak and Siam, 1882–1887.*

Ministry of Aviation (AVIA)

AVIA 55/218, (1947–1948), 'Applications from Tin Companies in Malaya for Rehabilitation Advances'.

Treasury (T)

T 220/134, (1950–1951), 'Rehabilitation of the Tin Industry and Effect of Post-war Prices on Rubber and Tin'.

T 220/186, (1950–1951), 'Export Duties on Tin and Rubber'.

UK Parliamentary Papers

Command Papers (C)

C. 465 (1874), Further correspondence relating to the affairs of certain native states in the Malay Peninsula, in the neighbourhood of the Straits Settlements. In continuation of Command Paper (465) of 1872. Presented to both Houses of Parliament by command of Her Majesty, 31 July, 1874.

C. 1111 (1875), Further correspondence relating to the affairs of certain native states in the Malay Peninsula, in the neighbourhood of the Straits Settlements. In continuation of Command Paper (C.1111) of July 1874. Presented to both Houses of Parliament by command of Her Majesty, 6 August, 1875.

C. 1320 (1875), Further correspondence relating to the affairs of certain native states in the Malay Peninsula, in the neighbourhood of the Straits Settlements. In continuation of Command Paper (C.1111) of July 1874. Presented to both Houses of Parliament by command of Her Majesty, 6 August, 1875.

C. 1505 (1876), Further correspondence relating to the affairs of certain native states in the Malay Peninsula, in the neighbourhood of the Straits Settlements. In continuation of Command Paper (C.1320) of August 1875. Presented to both Houses of Parliament by command of Her Majesty, 1876.

C. 1505–I (1876), Maps and sketches. Referred to in C.1505 of May 1876. Further correspondence relating to the affairs of certain native states in the Malay Peninsula, in the neighbourhood of the Straits Settlements. Presented to both Houses of Parliament by command of Her Majesty, June 1876.

C. 1709 (1877), Further correspondence relating to the affairs of certain native states in the Malay Peninsula, in the neighbourhood of the Straits Settlements. In continuation of Command Paper (C.1512) of 1876. Presented to both Houses of Parliament by command of Her Majesty, June 1877.

C. 3285 (1882), Straits Settlements. Correspondence respecting slavery in the Protected Malay States. In continuation of Command Paper (C.2410) of July 1879. Presented to both Houses of Parliament by command of Her Majesty, July 1882.

C. 3429 (1882), Straits Settlements. Further correspondence respecting slavery in the Protected Malay States. In continuation of Command Paper (C.3285) of July 1882. Presented to both Houses of Parliament by command of Her Majesty, November 1882.

C. 4192 (1884), Straits Settlements. Correspondence respecting the Protected Malay States, including papers relating to the abolition of slavery in Perak. In continuation of Command Papers (C.3428) and (C.3429) of 1882. Presented to both Houses of Parliament by command of Her Majesty, August 1884.

Cmd. 4276 (1933), Report of Brigadier-General Sir Samuel Wilson, G.C.M.G., K.C.B., Permanent Under-Secretary of State for the Colonies on his visit to Malaya 1932. Presented to Parliament by the Secretary of State for the Colonies by command of His Majesty, March 1933.

Cmnd. 451 (1957–1958), Colonial Office. The Colonial Territories (1957–1958). Presented to Parliament by the Secretary of State for the Colonies by command of Her Majesty, June 1958.

House of Commons (HC)

HC. 234 (1877), The Eastern Question—Resolutions (Mr Gladstone) debated on Thursday, 10 May 1877.

HC. (1933–1934), Dindings Agreement [Hansard], Fifth Series, Volume 293, cc. 506–518.

HC. 196-i (1983), Industry and Trade Committee. Session 1982–83. UK trade with ASEAN countries. Minutes of evidence. Wednesday 15 December 1982. Department of Trade. Ordered by the House of Commons to be printed 9 February 1983.

HC. 176-i (1986), Trade and Industry Committee. Session 1985–86. The Tin Crisis. Minutes of evidence. Wednesday 22 January 1986. Geevor Tin Mines Plc. N Holman & Son. Camborne School of Mines. Ordered by the House of Commons to be printed 22 January 1986.

HC. 176-ii (1986), Trade and Industry Committee. Session 1985–86. The Tin Crisis. Minutes of evidence. Wednesday 29 January 1986. The Group of 16 Creditors. The London Metal Exchange. Ordered by the House of Commons to be printed 29 January 1986.

HC. 176-iv (1986), Trade and Industry Committee. Session 1985–86. The Tin Crisis. Minutes of evidence. Wednesday 12 February 1986. L.M.E. Ring Dealing Members. Rio Tinto-Zinc Corporation Plc. Medway Tin Ltd. Ordered by the House of Commons to be printed 12 February 1986.

HC. 305 (1986), Second Report from the Trade and Industry Committee. Session 1985–86. The Tin Crisis. Volumes 1 & 2. Report and proceedings of the Committee. Ordered by the House of Commons to be printed 24 March 1986.

HC. 368-i (1986), Foreign Affairs Select Committee. Foreign Affairs Select Committee The United Kingdom & South East Asia. Minutes of evidence. 30 April 1986. (Received 2 June 1986) (Reprinted in HC 114 1986/87). Ordered by the House of Commons to be printed 30 April 1986.

HC. 457 (1986), Fifth Special Report from the Trade and Industry Committee. Session 1985–86. The Tin Crisis. Observations by the Government on the Second Report of the Trade and Industry Committee in Session 1985–86. Ordered by the House of Commons to be printed 11 June 1986.

HC. 532 (1986), Trade and Industry Committee. Session 1985–86. The Tin Crisis. Minutes of evidence. Tuesday 15 July 1986. Department of Trade and Industry. Foreign and Commonwealth Office. Ordered by the House of Commons to be printed 15 July 1986.

House of Lords (HL)

HL. (1874), Correspondence relating to the affairs of certain native states in the Malay Peninsula in the neighbourhood of the Straits Settlements. In continuation of Command Paper (465) of 1872. Presented to both Houses of Parliament by command of Her Majesty, 31 July, 1874.

Historical Administrative and Annual Reports

Annual Report of Perak
_____ 1874–1905, 1900–1939, 1906, 1907, 1909, 1911, 1913, 1918, 1920, 1929, 1930, 1936, and 1939.

Annual Report of the Protected Malay States, 1892.

Annual Report on the State of Perak
_____ (1889–1897), *Annual Report on the State of Perak for the Year* (Taiping: Government Printing Office).

Department of Mines, Ministry of Primary Industries–Malaysia (various years, 1971–1979), *Bulletin of Statistics Relating to the Mining Industry Malaysia*.
_____ (various years, 1980–1999), *Statistics on the Mining Industry*.

Department of Mines–West Malaysia, Ministry of Primary Industries–Malaysia (various years, 1961–1970), *Bulletin of Statistics Relating to the Mining Industry Malaysia*.

Federated Malay States
_____ (1903–1935), *Report of the Administration of the Mines Department and the Mining Industries, Supplements of the Federated Malay States Government Gazette, 1903–1935*.
_____ (1904–1933), *Perak Administrative Report for the Year* (Kuala Lumpur: Government Printing Office).
_____ (1912), *Report of the Director of Agriculture for the Year 1911, Supplement to the Federated Malay States Government Gazette* (Kuala Lumpur: Government Printing Office).
_____ (1934–1940), *Annual Report on the Social and Economic Progress of the People of Perak for the Year* (Kuala Lumpur: Government Printing Office).

Federated Malay States Annual Report
_____ 1897, 1904, 1908, and 1927.

Federated Malay States Railways Report

_____ 1906, 1909, and 1935.

International Tin Council (various years), *Tin Statistical Year Book.*

Report of the Mines Department

_____ (various years, 1918, 1919, 1922, 1925–1935, and 1949), *Supplements of the Federated Malay States Government Gazette.*

Minerals and Geoscience Department–Malaysia (2000), *Statistics on Mining Industry.*

_____ (various years, 2001–2018), *Malaysian Minerals Yearbook.*

Perak Administration Report

_____ (1998–1904), *Perak Administration Report for the Year* (Taiping: Government Printing Office).

Perak Government Gazette, 30 March 1943.

Acknowledgements

Globalization: Perak's Rise, Relative Decline, and Regeneration chronicles the successes and failures of globalization from the unique perspective of a former colonized—and now federalized—natural resource-rich state. In researching and writing this book, I am indebted to many individuals and institutions for generously sharing their time, information, insights, and ideas without which the book would not have seen the light of day. The list is long—too many to mention everybody here.

Let me begin by thanking the Asia–Europe Institute of the University of Malaya for continuing to host the Economic History of Malaya (EHM) project, which I started on my return to Malaysia from Harvard University more than two decades ago, and which may be viewed at www.ehm.my. Further, it is a pleasure to acknowledge the continued leadership and inspirational support provided by Richard Leete, Director of the EHM project. I extend my appreciation to David Demery, Frank Harrigan, and C. Peter Timmer who have provided valuable input.

For reviewing and providing helpful feedback on earlier drafts of this book, either in its entirety or specific sections, I would like to thank Afifi al-Akiti, Jemilah Mahmood, Mohamad Othman Zainal Azim, Mohamed Shah Redza Hussein, Nicholas Khaw, Carl Bek Nielson, Nungsari Ahmad Radhi, Thillainathan Ramasamy, and Timor Rafiq. My appreciation also to the three anonymous reviewers of Oxford University Press for their considered observations.

Special thanks for sharing data and historical documents go to Mohd Uzir Mahidin, Chief Statistician, Department of Statistics–Malaysia; and Jaafar Sidek Abdul Rahman, Director General, National Archives of Malaysia. I also received valuable institutional support from the staff of the National Archives UK, the UK Parliamentary Archives, the British Library, and the National Archives Singapore.

Many individuals and institutions in Perak provided historical information and data. I would like to thank the Perak State Secretary's Office; the Perak State Finance Office; the Perak State Economic Planning Unit; the Perak State Development Corporation; the Perak State Forestry Department; the District Officers in the state's 12 districts; and the Perak Museum, Taiping. I would also like to thank Galeri Sultan Azlan Shah, Gopeng Heritage Museum, Hakka Tin Mining

Museum (Han Chin Pet Soo), Kinta Tin Mining Museum, and the Sitiawan Settlement Museum.

I have benefited greatly from stimulating discussions with Annuar Zaini, Ayob Hashim, Lee Oi Hian, Anthony Milner, Mohd Azumi, Mohammad Faiz, Mohd Zahidi Zainuddin, Nordin Kardi, Ramli Ngah Talib, Rajah Rasiah, Johan Raslan, Rohana Mahmood, M. Shanmughalingam, the late Visu Sinnadurai, and Zainal Adzam.

Several senior researchers have worked with the EHM project and provided helpful inputs, including Cheng Fan Soon, Koay Su-Lyn, Vincent Lim Choon Seng, Shahriman Haron, Sharon Ng, Sonia Persson, Linda Tham, Sarah Chok, and Rabbi Royan.

Finally, I would like to thank my family for their continued encouragement and forbearance.

I hope that the ideas put forward in this book will provide the basis for realizing a *New Vision* for Perak—regenerating the state, including its environment, and enhancing the well-being of all its people.

Index

Note: Page numbers in **bold** indicate reference to maps, tables, boxes or figures.